Contemporary Transportation

Second Edition

The PennWell Marketing and Management Series

Louis E. Boone, Consulting Editor

Second Edition
Contemporary
Transportation

DONALD F. WOOD
San Francisco State University

JAMES C. JOHNSON
St. Cloud State University

To two teachers who helped us

Alexander Gerschenkron, late of Harvard University
Edmund A. Nightingale, University of Minnesota

Manufactured in the United States of America.

Library of Congress Cataloging in Publication Data

Wood, Donald F., 1935–
   Contemporary transportation.

   (The PennWell marketing and management series)
   Includes index.
   1. Transportation—United States. 2. Trans-
portation. I. Johnson, James C., 1944–
II. Title. III. Series.
HE203.W66 1982   380.5′0973   82-19109
ISBN 0-87814-205-3

1 2 3 4 5—87 86 85 84 83

Preface

Transportation is one of the most pervasive aspects of American society, and it is also one of the most interesting. We have tried to convey to the reader the excitement and challenge of a career in transportation—especially in light of transportation deregulation which began in the late 1970's and continues to take place. A major change in this Second Edition is the inclusion of discussion about (a) why deregulation took place, (b) what specifically is involved in the deregulation statutes, and—most importantly—(c) what have been the *effects* of these massive changes in our transportation environment.

We believe that deregulation will prove to be greatly beneficial to college graduates. In the more competitive marketplace, carriers will emphasize marketing activities, and they will be upgrading their sales and management staff with college graduates. Shippers will find a greater variety of price/service combinations available and they will also seek more college graduates who can carefully analyze the alternatives and choose the "best" trade-off between available rates and services. In addition, both carriers and shippers will seek individuals who have the ability to be effective rate negotiators.

One of this book's co-authors served as a consultant to the staff of the National Transportation Policy Study Commission and must acknowledge that meetings with the commission's staff and some of its other consultants were useful in terms of obtaining a fuller understanding of some of the transportation issues currently facing the nation.

The co-authors also wish to acknowledge that several meetings held for the benefit of college and university teachers of transportation were also useful to them in terms of achieving a better understanding of how our transportation system functions. Specific meetings of this type we attended were hosted by the American Trucking Associations and the Association of American Railroads, at the University of Minnesota; the Association of Oil Pipe Lines, in Houston; the 1907 Foundation Business Logistics Educators' Workshop, at the Harvard University Graduate School of Business Administration; the Yellow Freight System's meetings in Kansas City; and the ATA-Dana Foundation seminars.

Many people helped in the preparation of *Contemporary Transportation*, in either its original or revised form. We would like to acknowledge their help. They are: Benjamin J. Allen, Donald Berger, Kenneth M. Butcher, Oliver Callson, Michael R. Crum, Donald O. Crutchley, James M. Daley, William H. Dodge, the late Laurence P. Dowd, Thomas Faranda, Carl M. Guelzo, James M. Highsmith, James R. Hill, Gary V. Hunter, Sylvester J. Jablonski, George C. Jackson, Henry Karel, Frank J. Lichtanski, Ernie Maitland, Walter McComas, Chinnubbie McIntosh, Joseph F. Moffatt, Eric Mohr, Gerhardt Muller, A. Gerald Peters, Lee Plummer, David S. Provance, Roger C. Schoenfeldt, Paul E. Selig, Joseph J. Stefanec, Walter G. Stringer, Roy D. Voorhees, Peter F. Walstad, and Terry C. Whiteside.

Several individuals helped develop some of our cases. We wish to thank Peter Bowman and Doreen Wood.

Don Karecki, Van Huntley, Gene Boone, Ruth Steyn, and George Alexandres of PennWell's Book Division were of continual assistance. Special thanks are due to them and to Mrs. Diane McClure, who helped prepare the manuscript.

San Francisco, California　　　　　　Donald F. Wood
St. Cloud, Minnesota　　　　　　　　James C. Johnson
November 1982

Preface

Transportation is one of the most pervasive aspects of American society, and it is also one of the most interesting. We have tried to convey to the reader the excitement and challenge of a career in transportation—especially in light of transportation deregulation which began in the late 1970's and continues to take place. A major change in this Second Edition is the inclusion of discussion about (a) why deregulation took place, (b) what specifically is involved in the deregulation statutes, and—most importantly—(c) what have been the *effects* of these massive changes in our transportation environment.

We believe that deregulation will prove to be greatly beneficial to college graduates. In the more competitive marketplace, carriers will emphasize marketing activities, and they will be upgrading their sales and management staff with college graduates. Shippers will find a greater variety of price/service combinations available and they will also seek more college graduates who can carefully analyze the alternatives and choose the "best" trade-off between available rates and services. In addition, both carriers and shippers will seek individuals who have the ability to be effective rate negotiators.

One of this book's co-authors served as a consultant to the staff of the National Transportation Policy Study Commission and must acknowledge that meetings with the commission's staff and some of its other consultants were useful in terms of obtaining a fuller understanding of some of the transportation issues currently facing the nation.

The co-authors also wish to acknowledge that several meetings held for the benefit of college and university teachers of transportation were also useful to them in terms of achieving a better understanding of how our transportation system functions. Specific meetings of this type we attended were hosted by the American Trucking Associations and the Association of American Railroads, at the University of Minnesota; the Association of Oil Pipe Lines, in Houston; the 1907 Foundation Business Logistics Educators' Workshop, at the Harvard University Graduate School of Business Administration; the Yellow Freight System's meetings in Kansas City; and the ATA-Dana Foundation seminars.

Many people helped in the preparation of *Contemporary Transportation*, in either its original or revised form. We would like to acknowledge their help. They are: Benjamin J. Allen, Donald Berger, Kenneth M. Butcher, Oliver Callson, Michael R. Crum, Donald O. Crutchley, James M. Daley, William H. Dodge, the late Laurence P. Dowd, Thomas Faranda, Carl M. Guelzo, James M. Highsmith, James R. Hill, Gary V. Hunter, Sylvester J. Jablonski, George C. Jackson, Henry Karel, Frank J. Lichtanski, Ernie Maitland, Walter McComas, Chinnubbie McIntosh, Joseph F. Moffatt, Eric Mohr, Gerhardt Muller, A. Gerald Peters, Lee Plummer, David S. Provance, Roger C. Schoenfeldt, Paul E. Selig, Joseph J. Stefanec, Walter G. Stringer, Roy D. Voorhees, Peter F. Walstad, and Terry C. Whiteside.

Several individuals helped develop some of our cases. We wish to thank Peter Bowman and Doreen Wood.

Don Karecki, Van Huntley, Gene Boone, Ruth Steyn, and George Alexandres of PennWell's Book Division were of continual assistance. Special thanks are due to them and to Mrs. Diane McClure, who helped prepare the manuscript.

San Francisco, California   Donald F. Wood
St. Cloud, Minnesota   James C. Johnson
November 1982

Contents

List of Figures

List of Tables

Fueling a Junkers F 13 in 1926, a time when aviation fuel was not a major cost item. Plane in background is a Fokker F III.

Photo courtesy Lufthansa German Airlines.

A Boeing 757, shown being rolled off the assembly line, is designed with fuel efficiency in mind. According to a Boeing representative, this short- to mid-range jet will save up to 48 percent of the fuel used on a per-passenger basis compared with the planes it is expected to replace.

Photo courtesy Boeing Commercial Airplane Company.

1 Transportation and the Economy

Probably more than three-quarters of the whole benefit [England] derived from the progress of manufactures during the nineteenth century has been through its indirect influences in lowering the cost of transport of men and goods, of water and light, of electricity and news: for the dominant fact of our own age is the development not of the manufacturing, but of the transport industries. . . . It is they [the transport industries] which have done by far the most toward increasing England's wealth.

> ALFRED MARSHALL
> Principles of Economics
> 1920

What the university is to the scholar, what the church is to the faithful, the freeway is to the Los Angeles motorist. It is not the only place where the activity of driving occurs, but it is a sanctuary for such activity, designed specifically to service its needs.

> DAVID BRODSLY
> "A Culture in Concrete"
> San Francisco Examiner
> November 29, 1981

Two-thirds of American workers drive to work alone every day, and the number of people using public transportation has dropped to one in 16 despite two periods of fuel scarcity since the last census when the figure was one in 12.

> From report on the 1980 Census
> San Francisco Chronicle
> April 20, 1982

Introduction

In the United States, transportation permeates our entire life style, and because it does, it accounts for a substantial segment of our economy. By comparing the way we live in the United States of today with the way people lived at the turn of the century, we can see that most of the changes in life style are due to improvements in our transportation system. We are today a more mobile society. Travel for us—both within the vicinity of our homes or from our homes to any part of the world—is easier, faster, and often less expensive than it was for our parents or grandparents.

1

Products and raw materials also move over short and great distances, more easily, quickly, and less expensively today. No longer must the individual, the family unit, or the small community be virtually self-sufficient. Instead, because of an efficient transportation system, each area can produce what it grows or manufactures best and trade these products with other areas—in the nation or in the world—who likewise have specialized.

The purpose of this book is to discuss the transportation systems within the United States and between it and other nations of the world. The book is written for individuals who want a better understanding of our transportation system, its workings, its problems, and its future. We hope that many of our readers will decide to pursue careers in transportation activities, working for carriers, shippers, or the government.

Transportation: What It Means to the Individual

As transportation grew, so did our nation. Railroads were especially important in the nineteenth century. They facilitated travel and made it possible for agricultural products to reach our growing cities and ports for shipment to overseas markets. Railroads determined the location of many of our cities and influenced the location and growth of much of our industrial activity (and of job opportunities).

In this century the automobile has changed life styles, precipitated suburban development, and hastened the decline of small-town America. In high schools throughout the country, post-puberty rites known as drivers' training classes are conducted. Individuals soon win their driver's license and with it an ability to escape parental supervision as never before. With an auto, one's horizons extend and distance barriers fade. The automobile becomes virtually an extension of the body and assumes functions for which the feet and legs were once intended. The auto also becomes an extension of one's personality. This can be observed by noting detectives on television and comparing their cars with their personalities. When reading a story, you can determine much about a character who arrives by bus, or in an old VW camper, or in a Lear Jet aircraft.

Transportation has also historically represented a means of escape. The whistle of a train or of a ship beckoned many. For people who lived where things were not good, the whistle told them that they could leave if they *really* wanted to. Frederick Jackson Turner, the great U.S. historian of nearly a century ago, had a "safety valve" theory describing the significance of the West. So long as the frontier and nearly free land existed, it would be impossible for the industrialists of the East to fully exploit their workers. Employees could always leave the cities and move west to settle new lands if their situation became intolerable.[1]

U.S. Travel and Freight Statistics

Table 1–1 shows statistics for travel between U.S. cities in selected years since 1940. From 1940 to 1980, passenger-miles of travel quadrupled, while population less than doubled.

- *Passenger-mile* is a transportation measure meaning one person traveling one mile. By this measure, one person traveling fifty miles counts the same as fifty persons, each traveling one mile. Speed is not taken into account.

Figures for 1943, in the middle of World War II, show how the nation traveled when there was little gasoline for automobiles. Post–World War II figures show a return to the auto, a sharp decline in rail, and a very slight use of air. Air travel increased and by 1957 it equaled travel by rail and exceeded that by bus. Jet aircraft were introduced into commercial service in the late 1950's, and passenger travel by air more than tripled between 1960 and 1970.

Effects of fuel shortages and increased price of gasoline are shown in the differences between 1973 and 1974. Auto travel declined for the first time since World War II. Domestic air travel increased significantly in 1978 as a result of increased fare (or price) competition between the airlines. It climbed more in 1979 but, very recently, has declined slightly.

Table 1–2 is similar to Table 1–1 in that it shows the changing market and market shares for intercity freight transportation. The measurement used in ton-miles.

- *Ton-mile* is a transportation measure meaning one ton of freight moving one mile. Ten tons traveling one mile counts the same as one ton moving ten miles. Speed is not taken into account, although for freight carriers it varies widely.

The most significant change in recent years has been the reversal of the long-time decline in the railroads' total market share. Oil pipe-

---

[1] Frederick Jackson Turner, "The Significance of the Frontier in American History," *Annual Report for the American Historical Association, 1893.*

TABLE 1–1 Intercity Travel by Modes (Billions of Passenger-Miles)

Year	Total		Private Carrier						Public Carrier									
			Auto		Air		Total		Air		Bus		Rail		Water		Total	
	Amount	%	Amount	%	Amount	%	Amount	%	Amount	%	Amount	%	Amount	%	Amount	%	Amount	%
1940	330.3	100	292.7	88.6	.1	—	292.8	88.6	1.2	.4	10.2	3.1	24.8	7.5	1.3	.4	37.5	11.4
1943	295.7	100	176.0	59.5	—	—	176.0	59.5	2.0	.7	25.9	8.8	89.9	30.4	1.9	.6	119.7	40.5
1950	504.8	100	438.3	86.8	.8	.2	439.1	87.0	9.3	1.8	22.7	4.5	32.5	6.5	1.2	.2	65.7	13.0
1960	783.7	100	706.1	90.1	2.3	.3	708.4	90.4	31.7	4.0	19.3	2.5	21.6	2.8	2.7	.3	75.3	9.6
1970	1,184.8	100	1,026.0	86.6	9.1	.8	1,035.1	87.4	109.5	9.3	25.3	2.1	10.9	.9	4.0	.3	149.7	12.6
1973	1,348.8	100	1,166.0	86.4	10.7	.8	1,176.7	87.2	132.4	9.8	26.4	2.0	9.3	.7	4.0	.3	172.1	12.8
1974	1,259.4	100	1,071.0	85.0	10.8	.9	1,081.8	85.9	135.4	10.8	27.7	2.2	10.4	.8	4.1	.3	177.6	14.1
1975	1,310.5	100	1,123.0	85.8	11.1	.8	1,134.1	86.6	136.9	10.4	25.4	1.9	10.1	.8	4.0	.3	176.4	13.4
1976	1,390.2	100	1,187.0	85.3	11.6	.8	1,198.6	86.1	152.3	11.0	25.1	1.8	10.2	.7	4.0	.3	191.6	13.9
1977	1,453.2	100	1,240.6	85.4	12.1	.8	1,252.7	86.2	164.2	11.3	25.9	1.8	10.4	.7	not available		200.5	13.8
1978	1,537.4	100	1,297.7	84.4	12.7	.8	1,310.4	85.2	191.6	12.5	25.1	1.6	10.3	.7			227.0	14.8
1979	1,589.4	100	1,322.4	83.2	15.5	1.0	1,331.9	84.2	212.7	13.4	27.2	1.7	11.6	.7			251.5	15.8
1980	1,559.0	100	1,300.4	83.4	15.0	1.0	1,315.4	84.4	204.4	13.1	27.7	1.8	11.5	.7			243.6	15.6
1981	1,559.0	100	1,344.0	84.1	14.7	.9	1,358.7	85.0	201.3	12.6	27.2	1.7	11.8	.7			240.3	15.0

SOURCE: Transportation Association of America.

TABLE 1–2 Intercity Movements of Domestic Freight by Modes (Billions of Ton-Miles)

Year	Rail Amount	Rail %	Truck Amount	Truck %	Oil Pipeline Amount	Oil Pipeline %	Great Lakes Amount	Great Lakes %	Rivers & Canals Amount	Rivers & Canals %	Air Amount	Air %	Total
1940	379	61.3	62	10.0	59	9.5	96	15.5	22	3.6	.02	.00	618
1943	735	71.3	57	5.5	98	9.5	115	11.2	26	2.5	.05	.00	1,031
1947	665	65.3	102	10.0	105	10.3	112	11.0	35	3.4	.11	.01	1,019
1950	597	56.2	173	16.3	129	12.1	112	10.5	52	4.9	.30	.03	1,063
1955	631	49.5	223	17.5	203	15.9	119	9.3	98	7.7	.49	.04	1,274
1960	579	44.1	285	21.8	229	17.4	99	7.5	121	9.2	.89	.07	1,314
1965	709	43.3	359	21.9	306	18.7	110	6.7	152	9.3	1.91	.12	1,638
1970	771	39.7	412	21.3	431	22.3	114	5.9	205	10.6	3.30	.17	1,936
1971	746	38.2	445	22.8	444	22.7	105	5.4	210	10.7	3.50	.18	1,954
1972	784	37.7	470	22.7	476	23.0	109	5.3	229	11.1	3.70	.18	2,072
1973	858	38.5	505	22.6	507	22.7	126	5.6	232	10.4	3.95	.18	2,232
1974	852	38.5	495	22.4	506	22.9	107	4.8	248	11.2	3.91	.18	2,212
1975	759	36.7	454	22.0	507	24.5	99	4.8	243	11.8	3.73	.18	2,066
1976	800	36.3	510	23.2	515	23.4	106	4.8	267	12.1	3.90	.18	2,202
1977	834	36.1	555	24.1	546	23.7	91	3.9	277	12.0	4.18	.18	2,307
1978	868	35.2	599	24.4	586	23.8	119	4.8	290	11.8	4.63	.27	2,466
1979	927	36.1	608	23.7	608	23.7	122	4.7	303	11.8	4.41	.17	2,572
1980	932	37.2	567	22.7	588	23.5	93	3.7	318	12.7	4.53	.20	2,503
1981	926	37.9	565	23.1	547	22.4	94	3.8	309	12.6	4.66	.20	2,446
1984		37.5		24.2		22.7		3.0		12.3		.26	

SOURCE: Transportation Association of America.

line traffic dropped slightly in the last two years, no doubt because of the decline in demand for the product. The overall pattern of Table 1–2, shows that since World War II rail traffic has grown slowly, while truck, pipeline, and river traffic has multiplied many times.

Transportation's Share of Gross National Product

Gross National Product (GNP) is a measurement of the output of goods and services within the U.S. economy. In recent years, transportation's share of GNP grew slightly, to over 21 percent, reflecting the increased prices of fuel which motorists and carriers must pay. Table 1–3 shows for selected years since 1970 the expenditures on passenger transportation. The vast majority goes for owning and operating private automobiles. Indeed, expenditures on private autos account for over 10 percent of our Gross National Product! The major components of expenditures on autos are for "new and used cars" and "gasoline and oil." In Table 1–3, note how the relative importance of each changes from year to year.

Although private automobiles account for the lion's share of expenditures depicted in Table 1–3, notice the many other forms of passenger transportation which also increased their share of GNP. School buses, which we take for granted, are indicative of how transportation has changed our country. At first school buses were used solely in rural areas where they made possible the closing of one-room schools because they could transport rural pupils to larger, "consolidated" schools. However, closing the smaller schools helped to contribute to the decline of the small villages in which they had been located because often the school had been the sole "community" function holding the area together. In the "baby boom" following World War II, school buses were used to help school officials redistribute the pupils to schools in older parts of cities where vacant room still existed. In the past decade, the number of school-age children has dropped in many districts, and schools are being closed. Buses are now used to once again "consolidate" a shrinking number of students into a smaller number of facilities. School buses are also used by districts trying to achieve racial "balance" in their schools (often under court orders); pupils are taken from their own neighborhood to some distant school, where they are "mixed" with children from throughout the community.

TABLE 1–3 Estimated Expenditures for U.S. Passenger Transportation
(In Millions of Dollars)

	1970	1975	1979	1980
PRIVATE TRANSPORTATION				
Auto				
New and Used Cars	32,139	46,024	78,423	74,199
Other Motor Vehicles	2,883	7,061	13,270	8,953
Tires, Tubes, Accessories	7,135	12,386	19,835	22,562
Gasoline and Oil	29,892	53,853	91,161	118,691
Tolls	767	961	1,155	1,113
Insurance Less Claims	4,414	4,544	10,332	11,787
Interest on Debt	4,662	7,309	15,260	18,113
Auto Registration Fees	1,669	2,053	2,796	2,900
Operator's Permit Fees	222	264	332	330
Repair, Greasing, Washing, Parking, Storage, Rental	13,214	22,095	37,866	40,436
	96,997	156,550	270,430	299,104
Air				
Aircraft	354	966	2,085	2,306
Operating Costs	2,275	3,767	4,751	5,313
	2,629	4,733	6,836	7,619
Total Private	99,626	161,283	277,266	306,723
FOR-HIRE TRANSPORTATION				
Local				
Bus and Transit	1,841	4,697	7,536	8,973
Taxi	2,145	3,416	4,460	5,130
Railroad	172	206	257	297
School Bus	1,219	2,174	3,196	3,484
	5,377	10,493	15,449	17,884
Intercity				
Air	6,605	11,242	20,371	25,283
Bus	799	1,016	1,436	1,712
Rail	264	641	1,435	1,791
Water	12	16	20	20
	7,680	12,915	23,262	28,806
International				
Air	1,925	2,469	4,271	5,212
Water	275	278	309	306
	2,200	2,747	4,580	5,518
Total For-Hire	15,257	26,155	43,291	52,208
GRAND TOTAL				
Private and For-Hire	114,883	187,438	320,557	358,931
GROSS NATIONAL PRODUCT				
(Billions of Dollars)	992.7	1,549.2	2,413.9	2,626.1
GRAND TOTAL AS % OF GNP	11.57	12.10	13.28	13.67

Source: Transportation Association of America.

Freight Transportation

Expenditures for freight transportation, measured as a percentage of GNP, remained relatively constant for many years, although they have risen slightly in the past few years. This is shown on Table 1–4.

TABLE 1–4 The Nation's Estimated Freight Bill
(In Millions of Dollars)

	1970	1975	1979	1980
Highway				
Truck-Intercity				
ICC-Regulated	14,585	22,000	41,200	43,000
Non-ICC Regulated	18,968	25,400	48,963	47,384
Truck-Local	28,819	37,287	52,281	58,155
Bus	122	156	219	235
	62,494	84,843	142,663	148,774
Rail				
Railroads	11,869	16,509	24,763	27,858
Water				
International	3,187	4,928	7,892	8,279
Coastal, Intercoastal	834	1,136	2,449	2,963
Inland Waterways	473	950	1,497	1,810
Great Lakes	239	348	593	520
Locks, Channels, etc.	376	526	976	1,144
	5,109	7,888	13,407	14,716
Oil Pipe Line				
Regulated	1,188	1,874	5,585	6,141
Non-Regulated	208	346	621	682
	1,396	2,220	6,206	6,823
Air				
Domestic	720	1,073	1,846	2,048
International	451	765	991	1,326
	1,171	1,838	2,837	3,374
Other Carriers				
Forwarders	358	418	701	721
Other Shipper Costs				
Loading & Unloading				
Freight Cars	1,059	1,279	1,625	1,676
Operation of Traffic				
Departments	374	511	706	756
	1,433	1,790	2,331	2,432
GRAND TOTAL	83,830	115,506	192,908	204,698
GROSS NATIONAL PRODUCT				
(Billions of Dollars)	992.7	1,549.2	2,413.9	2,626.1
GRAND TOTAL % OF GNP	8.44	7.46	7.99	7.79

SOURCE: Transportation Association of America.

Recall from Table 1–2 that the trucking industry carried 22.7 percent of the intercity ton-miles of freight in 1980. However, Table 1–4 shows that trucks earned 73 percent of the money spent for moving intercity freight. Over the years, the trucking industry has been successful in developing freight markets (often taking them from the railroads) where the revenue per ton-mile carried was high.

Post-World War II Economic and Transportation Trends

Figure 1–1 shows and compares growth in three indexes mentioned so far, GNP, intercity passenger-miles, and intercity ton-miles, plus two other figures—population and industrial production. Figures for GNP and industrial production are in constant dollars. Note the especially great growth in intercity passenger miles compared to the growth in population. Improvements in the highway system accompanied increases in use of the auto. The jet aircraft shrunk coast-to-coast travel time from four or five days to four or five hours. Both the auto and the airplane cut deeply into passenger markets served by railroads.

- *Constant dollars* are used to remove the effects of inflation from the data. The purchasing power of a *constant dollar* does not change over time.

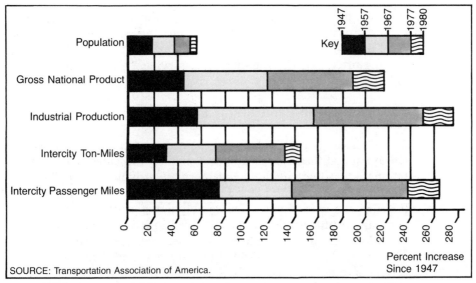

Figure 1–1 Economic and Transportation Trends Since 1947. Source: Transportation Association of America.

Intercity ton-miles of freight grew at a slower rate than passenger travel: highway and air carriers operate under conditions in which the cargo to be transported is limited by the vehicles' weight capacity and dimensions. Hence, road and air carriers developed pricing systems that encouraged shippers to transport products which could be accommodated within the vehicles' limitations. (Also, because trucks and air carriers offered high-quality and faster service, less protective packaging was needed for fragile shipments.) Shippers began dividing their freight business between the transportation modes, shipping the smaller, high-value items by truck or air and using rail for the bulky, low-value products. Truck and air carriers were more responsive to shippers' needs, and shippers began increasing those aspects of their business which utilized truck or air carriers. This was often at the expense of those aspects of their business that utilized railroads, which were often left with the freight no other mode wished to carry. The net effect has been that expenditures on freight transportation have increased by nearly the same amount as GNP has, as shown on Table 1–4. However, much of the growth in expenditures for freight hauling has been paid to air and motor carriers, who specialize in and encourage smaller shipments with relatively high values per unit of weight.

- In most freight hauling transactions, there are three parties: the *shipper*, who sends the goods; the *carrier*, who hauls them; and the *consignee*, who receives them.

- This paragraph has indicated that carriers engage in two forms of competition: *price competition* and *service competition*. Shippers or passengers can usually make choices between varying price and varying quality of service.

Transportation and the Production Process

Alfred Marshall, the great turn-of-the-century British economist who was quoted at the beginning of this chapter, indicated that transportation industries had done the most toward increasing England's wealth. Transportation plays a major role in the production process. It allows the entrepreneur to assemble more easily the raw material and labor inputs needed to make a specific product. The same transportation system moves intermediate products to other producers for subsequent use in their production process, and it moves finished products to consumers.

The transportation system also provides mobility to workers. The automobile is the most widely used transportation mode for getting to work. According to the Federal Highway Administration, in 1977, 80.5 percent of our work force reached their jobs by auto; and 12.5 percent rode in private vans, trucks, or recreational vehicles.[2] Another form of "riding to work" is described in this passage from an article about the Mexican-American community in Los Angeles:

> Mexican men begin lining up on Sawtelle Boulevard, in West Los Angeles, before seven each weekday morning. Two hundred, three hundred of them stand silently, alone or in small clusters, along the six blocks between Santa Monica Boulevard and Olympic Boulevard. Each carries his lunch in a brown bag. For an hour or so, trucks and cars cruise along Sawtelle, stopping in front of a man or a group to negotiate the price of a day's labor. "Three dollars an hour!" Sometimes more. Six men scramble into a dump truck. Two dozen rush to a battered panel truck filled with pipe; only one gets in.[3]

The transportation system also allows workers to relocate to take advantage of better job opportunities. Historically there has been a steady migration from rural areas to urban areas and from the northeastern states to the West and to the South. In the mid-1970's, during a recession, one intercity bus company offered a lower fare to unemployed individuals who were traveling in search of work.

The most important contribution that transportation has made to the production process is that, by widening the market areas a producer can reach, it has encouraged the introduction of more efficient, larger-scale production techniques. Substantial economies of scale were achieved and this resulted in reduced per-unit production costs. This saving in per-unit production costs often more than offset the per-unit transportation costs involved in reaching more distant markets.[4]

- *Economies of scale* result from a producer's increased production. Increasing *economies of scale* means that the average price of the product or service is dropping. Sometimes a firm will

[2] *Motor Vehicle Facts & Figures, '81* (Detroit: Motor Vehicle Manufacturers Association, 1981), p. 39.

[3] Julie Hayden, "Boyle Heights and Beyond," *The New Yorker* (September 14, 1981), p. 141.

[4] Meshing the proper scale of basic production facilities and a nation's transportation network is difficult. A problem common to many "planned" economies (i.e., where the government makes all major capital investment decisions) was that they borrowed Western technology and installed the "largest, most efficient" steel mills only to find that the costs for carrying the finished steel to markets were so high that the cost savings from the mill's large size were lost.

become too large, and *diseconomies of scale* will set in, meaning that as production increases, the average cost of each unit of output or service increases even more.

Development of a transportation system has allowed each locality or region to specialize in producing its most efficient output. As a society we enjoy a richer and more leisurely life than we would if family units or small communities had to be totally self-sufficient. Transportation has also allowed us to trade with countries throughout the world; and this commercial intercourse has helped eliminate many barriers between nations.

However, development of the production processes and of transportation has not been without costs. Natural resources and—sometimes—human resources have been unwisely exploited. The following sections will deal with transportation as a user of resources.

Transportation and Natural Resources

A generation ago, a discussion of this topic would have been brief and would have explained that our transportation system was "good" because it opened areas so their resources could be developed or extracted and shipped off to willing buyers. However, since the early 1960's,[5] the pendulum has swung the other way, and nearly every aspect of economic activity is now scrutinized to determine whether it has an adverse impact on our existing environment. This section will discuss the relationship between transportation and our land, water, air, mineral, and petroleum resources. The discussion of petroleum will indicate how the transportation industry is reacting to increased prices and shortages of petroleum. This particular topic will be touched upon a number of times throughout the book.

Transportation and Land Resources

Transportation provides access to land and allows the land's products to be carried to markets. The price of a product at the farm is the market price, less the costs of transporting the product to the market. "Farm prices of fluid milk in the New York and Boston milksheds decline with distance to market at the same rate as costs of shipping fluid milk increase."[6] Improving the transportation sys-

---

[5] Rachel Carson's *New Yorker* articles and her book *Silent Spring* (Boston: Houghton-Mifflin, 1962) are often cited as being responsible for developing widespread awareness as to how we were rapidly and irreversibly destroying our environment.

[6] A 1937 statement cited in D. Philip Locklin, *Economics of Transportation*, 7th ed. (Homewood, Ill.: Richard D. Irwin, 1972), p. 59.

tem to the market increased prices farmers could receive and, therefore, the value of their land. The same phenomenon was observed for home sites in suburbs: the closer they were to downtown (a source of jobs) the higher the value.[7]

The initial pattern for land development in the United States was influenced, if not controlled, by the survey requirements enacted in 1785 for western (now midwestern) lands. Townships of 36 square miles were laid out and each square mile (or section) was further divided into half and quarter sections. Roads were laid out along sectional lines, and this is what created the checkerboard pattern one sees today when flying over many states. One section of land was set aside for public education, and this became the township's school site and often served as the nucleus of a small community. This pattern of dispersed development worked well for rural areas, although economic and social forces encouraged larger communities to develop (often at transportation interchange points where agricultural products were shifted from one mode of transport to another).

Early railroad and streetcar lines also caused development to follow. Land use still follows transportation development. In the post–World War II construction of freeways, cities grew in the direction of freeways connected with the downtown. Industries relocated from the central city to sites along suburban freeways. Often they had to do this for the benefit of their employees who wanted to drive to work. Motor carrier deliveries were also faster, because of less traffic congestion.

The dependence of many land uses upon transportation is underscored when carriers attempt to cut off service to areas that generate low freight or passenger revenues and are opposed by their remaining users. The users in these areas will protest that if carrier service is withdrawn, the economy of their area will wither and die.

Construction of transportation facilities does, of course, alter the land and many of its natural characteristics. However, today's construction is somewhat more in harmony with nature than was the case a generation or two ago. Civil engineers are no longer taught that they should view the Grand Canyon as being in need of bridges. Many of the high costs of the Alaskan pipeline can be attributed to the public demands that as little damage as possible be done to the natural environment. Indeed, an initially-intended pipeline route was altered when it was discovered that it passed through the only passage used by some form of wildlife. Over the years, local govern-

[7] See: Herbert Mohring and Mitchell Harwitz, *Highway Benefits: An Analytical Framework* (Evanston: Northwestern Univ. Press, 1962).

ments have also been able to reduce the amount of unesthetic development which frequently bordered highways. Many states now control or restrict billboards along the Interstate Highway System.

Noise generated by transportation facilities is also being controlled. In urban areas noise buffers (consisting of high solid fences or plantings) are constructed to shield certain areas from freeway noise. California uses some highway construction funds to "sound proof" school buildings near noisy roads. In the vicinity of airports, land uses are restricted, in part to reduce complaints and lawsuits regarding noise. Aircraft flight paths in the vicinity of airports are channeled so as to minimize the noise in residential areas.[8]

Today, transportation and land use are recognized as being interdependent. In areas of the country where "no-growth" policies are popular the no-growthers will oppose nearly any transportation improvement because of its feared growth-inducing effects. "To those outside the highway agency, the no-build alternative is uncomplicated. It merely means not adding more pavement to the surface of the earth. The advantages include forcing the development of transit, discouraging the purchase of additional automobiles, and preserving environmental values."[9]

Transportation and Water Resources

Water transportation has also caused damage to our environment. For centuries, people have altered shorelines and dredged out harbor and channel bottoms in an effort to accommodate larger ships. Massive series of locks and dams have been constructed along most of our nation's waterways for handling barge traffic. Many of these improvements have been in conjunction with flood control and hydroelectric-generating facilities.

Discharge of human wastes, garbage, and bilge water by vessels in port has been a problem that has slowly been brought under control. Oil spills are a matter of constant concern,[10] and major ports now

[8] See: Donald V. Harper, "The Dilemma of Aircraft Noise at Major Airports", *Transportation Journal* (Spring, 1971), pp. 5–28 and by the same author, "The Airport Location Problem: The Case of Minneapolis-St. Paul," *ICC Practitioners' Journal* (May–June, 1971), pp. 550–582.

[9] G. Robert Adams, "The 'no-build' Alternative: What it is, Why it is Necessary, and How it can be Handled," *Highway Research Board Special Report* 138 (Washington, D.C.,) p. 46.

[10] See: Noël Mostert, *Supership*, (New York: Alfred A. Knopf, 1974) and Noel Grove, "Superspill: Black Day For Brittany," *Natonal Geographic* (July, 1978), pp. 125–134.

have equipment and procedures for preventing spills and keeping spills from spreading.

Transportation and Air Resources

Our vehicles, particularly the automobile, have been unkind to our air resources. The problem is acute in California, especially in the Los Angeles region. Briefly stated, the emissions from autos are trapped by atmospheric conditions so they do not rise over the mountains. The Lake Tahoe basin and the Yosemite National Park site suffer similar unfortunate conditions. At Yosemite, entire strata of plant life have been killed by trapped auto emissions. The air pollution problem in California is more severe than it is in other portions of the United States.[11] Hence, California did adopt more stringent controls on emissions from new automobiles and trucks than the federal government had adopted for new cars sold in other states.

Damage from air pollution is difficult to assess. It can adversely affect human health and certain crops, and it can also have a dismal effect on property values. Another thing to remember is that production of fuel, either the refining of gasoline or using coal to generate electricity (for mass transit), itself causes air pollution.

Most programs for reducing air pollution involve some curtailments on the use of automobiles.[12] This would pose problems for the trucking industry since some of the restrictions might also apply to them. Airlines are curbing their contribution to air pollution by adding cleaner-burning equipment to their engines.

Air pollution, and transportation's role in causing it, was one of the major issues of the 1970's. Solutions are expensive, but the effect has been to shift the costs of pollution closer to those who are causing the problem.

Transportation and Mineral Resources

Most sources of minerals are located in specific, often isolated sites and must rely on transportation to reach markets. Products of mines and petroleum have always been important sources of traffic for rail, barge, and pipeline carriers. In 1980, coal accounted for over 25 percent of the railroad industry's volume, measured in terms of

---

[11] Kenneth A. Small, "Estimating the Air Pollution Costs of Transport Modes," *Journal of Transport Economics and Policy* (May, 1977), pp. 109–132.

[12] Joseph L. Schofer, "Transportation Policy and Air Quality Management: Some Current Perspectives," in *Proceedings of the National Conference on Land Use Planning, Transportation Planning and Air Quality Management* (held at Chapel Hill, N.C., November, 1974).

rail cars loaded.[13] Coal exports are increasing through many of our nation's ports.

There is a two-way relationship between transportation and energy. Fuel is an important cargo for many carriers, and shifts in the markets for fuel have an effect on the revenues of the carriers who move it. Also, all carriers must buy fuel for their own operations. As its price soars, or it becomes difficult to obtain, the carriers' operating costs increase.

Transportation as a User of Fuel

Transportation is a large consumer of fuel. About one-quarter of the energy consumed in the United States is for transportation purposes.[14] Representatives of the various transportation modes disagree as to the relative energy efficiency of a specific vehicle operating under certain conditions. Very little is known about the loads carried by some modes in their day-to-day operations or the load factors at which they operate.

- *Load factor* means the percentage of capacity utilized. An airplane with 100 seats carrying 62 passengers is operating at a load factor of 62. Capacity of a vehicle is sometimes difficult to determine. For example, urban buses contain both seats and straps or poles which standing passengers may grasp.

Two other factors also complicate the process of determining energy efficiency. First, besides counting the energy used to actually move the load, one must add the energy used to construct and maintain both the right-of-way and vehicles. Secondly, domestic carriers' routes between points are often circuitous because they must follow the road, tracks, or waterway. (Even aircraft, when guided by instruments, fly from one ground-based radio navigation marker to another.)

Having made these qualifications, we will present some very general comparisons of the relative fuel efficiencies of carrier modes. Figure 1–2, from Greyhound Lines, shows the number of passenger-miles each of the modes can carry with one gallon of fuel. Studies concerning the relative fuel efficiencies of freight carriers agree that pipelines are the most efficient. Summarizing several studies, we can say that for each gallon of fuel the pipeline consumes, barges

---

[13] *Yearbook of Railroad Facts, 1981* (Washington, D.C.: Association of American Railroads, 1981), p. 26.

[14] Association of American Railroads, *Transportation's Place in the Energy Picture* (Washington, D.C., 1981), p. 3.

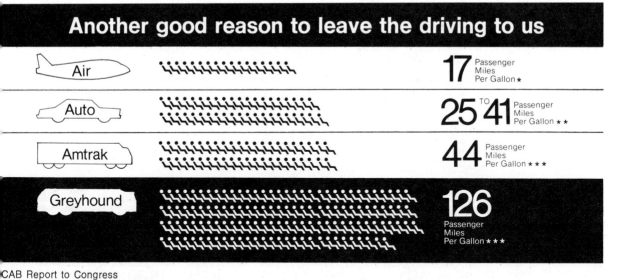

CAB Report to Congress
*1975 Study by The Boeing Commercial Airplane Company
**1976 Annual Report to ICC

Figure 1–2   Relative Efficiencies of Passenger Carriers. Courtesy: Greyhound Lines, Inc.

would require 1.2 to 2.3 gallons to move the same amount of cargo the same distance. Railroads would require 1.5 to 2 gallons; trucks would require 6.2 to 10 gallons; and airplanes would require 43 to 93 gallons to transport the same ton-miles.[15] Note that speed of the vehicles is not taken into account in these measures.

Carriers are adjusting to new fuel prices in a variety of ways. They have been successful in passing much of the costs on to their customers. However, since fuel—as a percentage of costs—has changed, carriers and private shippers have devised systems that attempt to obtain more productivity out of each gallon of fuel. New equipment, such as truck trailers, have been redesigned to lessen wind resistance. Routes are laid out to reduce miles of empty or near-empty travel. Firms owning private fleets are more likely to ask vendors (sellers) to bid on "F.O.B.–origin" basis, which gives the buyers the option to use their empty trucks on the return leg. One of the reasons for deregulating portions of our transportation industry (to be discussed more fully in later chapters) was to reduce or elimi-

[15] Association of American Railroads, *Transportation's Place in the Energy Picture* (Washington, D.C., 1977). See also: Samuel Ewer Eastman, *Fuel Efficiency in Freight Transportation* (Arlington, Va.: The American Waterways Operators, Inc., 1980).

nate certain regulatory rules that contributed to excessive fuel consumption.

- *F.O.B.* originally meant "free on board" the ship moored in port, with the buyer being responsible for subsequent transportation. Today, the term *F.O.B.–origin* generally means that the buyer is responsible for transportation beyond the vendor's loading dock.

Most vehicles consume less fuel on a per-mile basis when they lower their operating speeds. Where the 55 m.p.h. speed limit is enforced, the competitiveness of trucks and buses has been reduced in time-sensitive markets. Some ocean-going containership services have also lowered their operating speeds, which presumably would make them more vulnerable to air competition for products with time-sensitive delivery requirements.

The automobile is a major user of petroleum.[16] Further reduction of gasoline consumption by motorists is desirable. Methods of reaching this goal are difficult to find, especially since the majority of adults both drive and *vote*. The principal obstacle is our suburban-oriented life style.

Shifts in Products Carried

As fuel prices increase, we can expect shippers to become even more sensitive to the higher costs of transportation. There will be incentives to ship products in more highly concentrated forms. As an example, for food or chemical products containing large amounts of water, it will become desirable to remove part or all of the water before shipping and then add water after the product arrives at its destination. Lighter packaging materials will be used to achieve further savings in weight.

Carriers of fuel will also be affected by shifting markets. Railroad managers hope that use of coal will increase since railroads are the primary carriers of coal. Decreases in worldwide movements of petroleum have reduced the need for ocean-going tankers. As this book is being written, a number of large tankers are "laid up" because they have no cargo to carry.

Directions of some cargo movements will also change. In the past decade some pipelines originally built to carry Oklahoma oil to Gulf ports for export have had their pumps reversed so they can now carry imported oil to inland refineries. Because of the much higher

---

[16] See: Charles L. Gray, Jr., and Frank von Hippel, "The Fuel Economy of Light Vehicles," *Scientific American* (May, 1981), pp. 48–59.

price dictated by foreign oil-producing nations, the United States, as a major importer of oil, is suffering from serious trade deficits. A trade deficit weakens the value of the dollar vis-à-vis other currencies, and other nations with stronger currencies have found it advantageous to import more products from the United States. This has reversed product movement patterns.

The nation's transportation system—and, for that matter, the nation itself—has yet to adjust completely to the united power of oil-producing nations from whom we import. Making these changes will continue to be one of the biggest issues in the 1980's.

Transportation and Human Resources

Transportation permeates our economic and social life styles. A complete discussion of the inter-relationships between transportation and human resources would be lengthy. Instead, only two topics will be covered here: (1) transportation and the disadvantaged and (2) transportation as a source of employment.

Transportation and the Disadvantaged

The past decade had witnessed increased concern with the inequalities in opportunities available to racial minorities and to women. While it is known that transportation has contributed to the national wealth and well-being, there is no definitive analysis as to whether transportation has encouraged or discouraged equal opportunity to share in this wealth.

Minorities played important roles in the construction of our transportation network. Figure 1–3 is a letter dated early in this century from a Chicago firm with "twenty years experience in handling all classes of foreigners" in railroad construction work. The letter speaks for itself on the subject of disadvantaged people and how they were exploited to build our transportation system.

In the Southwest, Mexicans were "imported" for use in railroad construction. Chinese helped build western railroads and the phrase "Not a Chinaman's chance" dates from the practice of having Chinese laborers, rather than whites, handle the nitroglycerin needed for blasting. After western railroad construction was finished, the Chinese had no place to go and were virtually "forced" to settle in the ghetto-like Chinatowns of West Coast cities.

The hard and dangerous labor associated with early river navigation in the South was performed by blacks. In *The Adventures of*

E. A. LOOMIS, JR.
CONTRACTING AND INVESTMENT DEPARTMENT

M. R. LABBEE
EMPLOYMENT AND EMIGRATION DEPARTMENT

P. W. BARCLAY
COLONIZATION AND LAND DEPARTMENT

COLONIAL LAND & EMIGRATION COMPANY

SUITE 3, 78 LA SALLE ST., 2ND FLOOR

TEL. 4691 MAIN

INFORMATION BUREAU FOR RAILROAD CONTRACTORS

CHICAGO, May 26th 04

Paulson & Larson

Gents —

After twenty years experience in handling all classes of foreigners, we have established in connection with our land department an EMPLOYMENT BUREAU exclusively to furnish men for railroad construction work, that can be depended upon to do the work, without the annoyance so often attending the securing of competent labor.

We can furnish from 500 to 1000 Austrians, Polish, Italians, Greeks and other nationalities that you may prefer, and can move these men on a days notice. The above men that we have on our books, have had three to five years experience in railroad construction work which we feel would be of advantage to you, by being experienced laborors. It is our desire should you favor us with a small order, to work to your interest by supplying you with laborers that will stay with you until the work is finished. Our agents will place the men upon your work and see that they are installed in their shanties or other accommodations and stay with them until all are satisfied, thus avoiding small misunderstandings, which so often arises when men are first employed. Should you think favorable of our method of handling the men, we trust that you will give us a trial.

You can rest assured that we shall appreciate highly whatever favor you may confer upon us.

We invite you to make our Office your headquarters when in the city, as we have private rooms and telephone at your disposal.

Thanking you in advance for any order you may send us.

We remain yours respectfully,

COLONIAL LAND & EMIGRATION CO.

M. R. Labbee

Figure 1–3 Letter Regarding Railroad Construction Labor.

Huckleberry Finn, the young hero concocts a story to explain to Aunt Sally the reasons for his delay. She asked him if the river boat had gone aground. He

> . . . struck an idea and fetched it out.
> "It warn't the grounding—that didn't keep us back but a little. We blowed out a cylinder head."
> "Good gracious! anybody hurt?"
> "No'm. Killed a nigger."
> "Well, it's lucky because sometimes people do get hurt,"

Aunt Sally nattered on.

In the railroad industry, blacks were able to obtain employment in dining cars and as porters in sleeping cars. For many, this was the best employment available. The late A. Philip Randolph, head of the Sleeping Car Porters' Union, was—for many years—the only black labor leader of national importance.

Even today, racial minorities have difficulty achieving equal employment opportunities in transportation. The jobs they do get are usually less important and lower paying than jobs open to whites. Even when a minority worker's employer and co-workers do not discriminate, the nature of the job—often involving lonely travel and the need to use eating and lodging facilities in strange locations—leaves the minority employee vulnerable to harassment. In the early days of the space program, a black comedian was asked why there were no black astronauts. He replied that blacks were willing to ride a rocket to the moon, but that the bus trip through Georgia to reach Cape Kennedy (then Cape Canaveral) had them worried.

Regrettably, one of the devices used to keep minorities "in their place" has been restrictions on their use of travel accommodations. Carriers, service stations, restaurants, resorts, and hotels either refused service to minorities or else made them sufficiently unwelcome so as to create the same effect. While much progress has been made, this problem has not been solved.

Females, while not a minority, have usually placed "second" in matters involving transportation. Lydia Simmons wrote:

> But one thing did set me apart from my brothers. The car. As far as my father was concerned, women rode in cars and otherwise didn't go near them. Boys? Growing old enough to learn to drive, getting behind the wheel for the first time was a rite of initiation into adult American society. The myth of the automobile, from that point on, engulfed them and swept them along as if their individuality were beside the point. One had to make out in it. One had to roar down narrow, crooked country roads like a "bat outa hell." One had to groom the old Pontiac . . . as a horsetrainer groomed a champion. And before one left home, one had to have had at

least one tremendous wreck driving while drunk or flaunting one's life as a daredevil, and survive it. Otherwise one was not a man.

I watched each of my brothers demolish a car and walk, grinning like one of God's Chosen, away from it.[17]

The federal government is forcing employers, both in and outside of transportation, to increase their employment of racial minorities and of women. This has increased employment opportunities in transportation for these groups, especially for college-trained individuals. The reason for this is that "integration" is believed to be easier to achieve at professional levels.

One of the specific provisions of the *Motor Carrier Act of 1980* is to "promote competitive and efficient transportation services in order to . . . promote greater participation by minorities in the motor carrier system."[18]

Physically-handicapped people also constitute a large minority within our society. Some handicapped people cannot use conventional means of transportation. Current federal mass transit policies require communities using federal mass transit subsidies to make their equipment accessible to all. At this writing, these requirements are encountering opposition from mass transit operators. While separate, specially-equipped buses can be provided, many handicapped individuals scorn this form of segregation and are insisting that all vehicles have special equipment for handling wheelchairs, etc.

Issues involving employment and treatment of minorities and females cause consternation for many transportation executives. Coping with these situations is—and will be—a challenge for which anybody aspiring for management levels in transportation must be prepared.

Employment in Transportation

Employment directly in and related to transportation in the United States is shown on Table 1–5. Employment by carriers is not increasing except in the air and motor carrier fields. However, long-term trends show that employment in transportation equipment manufacturing is increasing while employment by carriers is not. This means that carrier management is becoming capital-intensive, that is, it is substituting equipment for labor whenever possible. Between 1978 and 1981, employment in transportation equipment

---

[17] Lydia Simmons, "Not From the Back Seat," *The Automobile and American Culture*, a special issue of *Michigan Quarterly Review* (Fall, 1980, published by the University of Michigan, Ann Arbor), p. 549. The entire issue is informative and delightful reading.

[18] Section 10101 U.S. Code Annotated, Title 49, Transportation, Revised Interstate Commerce Act.

TABLE 1–5 U.S. Employment in Transportation and Related Industries
(Number of Persons Employed in Thousands)

	1950	1965	1978	1981	*1985*
Transportation Service					
Air	86	229	396	453	
Bus—Intercity & Rural	47	42	38	38	
Local Transport	157	83	72	83	
Railroads	1,391	735	535	503	*276*
Oil Pipeline	29	20	19	22	
Taxi	121	110	68	52	
Trucking & Trucking Terminals	557	882	1,181	1,149	
Water	237	230	207	202	
Totals	2,625	2,331	2,516	2,502	
Transportation Equipment Manufacturing					
Aircraft & Parts	283	624	529	657	
Motor Vehicles & Equipment	926	945	1,103	841	
Railroad Equipment	60	56	57	52	
Ship & Boat Building & Repair	85	160	218	223	
Other Transportation Equipment	25	57	157	160	
Totals	1,379	1,840	2,064	1,933	
Transportation Related Industries					
Automotive & Accessory Retail Dealers	652	902	1,134	1,023	
Automotive Wholesalers	176	255	419	415	
Automotive Services & Garages	161	324	518	578	
Gasoline Service Stations	343	522	644	563	
Highway & Street Construction	210	324	279	211	
Petroleum	282	292	448	587	
Other Industries:					
Truck Drivers & Deliverymen	1,131	1,387	1,307	1,217	
Shipping & Receiving Clerks	260	300	455	490	
Totals	3,215	4,306	5,204	5,084	
Government Transportation Employees					
U.S. Department of Transportation	18	45	74	73	
Highway Employees—State & Local	380	571	592	607	
Post Office	75	83	91	93	
Other	18	16	13	13	
Totals	491	715	770	786	
TOTAL TRANSPORTATION EMPLOYMENT	7,710	9,192	10,554	10,305	
TOTAL EMPLOYED CIVILIAN LABOR FORCE	58,920	71,088	94,373	99,271	
PERCENT TRANSPORTATION OF TOTAL	13.1%	12.9%	11.2%	10.4%	

SOURCE: Transportation Association of America.

manufacturing dipped more than did employment by carriers. This reflects a sluggish economy and delays in the purchase of autos, trucks, and airline aircraft.

Table 1–5 should be of some interest to readers trying to determine whether—and where—job opportunities in the transportation industry exist. A related field, physical distribution and logistics management (PD/L) is not shown in the table. It involves working for firms that ship or receive freight and involves managing the inbound and outbound shipments, determining warehouse and inventory locations, etc. Physical distribution/logistics is considered a "growth" area in transportation, especially for individuals with college or university training. It will be discussed in chapter 10.

Transportation Professional Organizations

Professional organizations exist for individuals who are pursuing careers in transportation. The rationale for these organizations is that transportation and physical distribution/logistics are changing so quickly that it is necessary for professionals to continually update their knowledge. Several of the more general organizations are listed:

▲ AMERICAN SOCIETY OF TRAFFIC AND TRANSPORTATION (AST&T)

AST&T helps its members achieve "high standards of education and technical training, requisite to the proper performance of the various functions of traffic, transportation and physical distribution management." To become a certified member of AST&T, one must pass four comprehensive tests which cover various aspects of traffic, transportation, and PD/L and write an original research paper. For further information, write: AST&T, 1816 Norris Place, No. 4, P.O. Box 33095, Louisville, Kentucky 40232.

▲ ASSOCIATION OF ICC PRACTITIONERS (AICCP)

This group is dedicated "to promote the proper administration of the Interstate Commerce Act and related Acts, to uphold the honor of practice before the Interstate Commerce Commission; to cooperate in fostering increased educational opportunities and maintaining high standards of professional conduct, and to encourage cordial communication among the practitioners." To belong to this organization, one must be an ICC practitioner, which is accomplished by passing a comprehensive test administered by the ICC. For further information write: Association of ICC Practitioners, 1112 ICC Building, Washington, D.C. 20423.

▲ DELTA NU ALPHA (DNA)

DNA is a transportation fraternity dedicated to the education of its members. DNA chapters are very active at the local level and stress the learning process by small educationally-oriented discussion groups. For further information, write: DNA, 1040 Woodcock Rd., Orlando, Florida 32803.

▲ NATIONAL COUNCIL OF PHYSICAL DISTRIBUTION MANAGEMENT (NCPDM)

This organization is dedicated "to develop the theory and understanding of the physical distribution process, to promote the art and science of managing physical distribution systems, and to foster professional dialogue in the field." Further information can be obtained by writing to: NCPDM, 2803 Butterfield Road, Suite 380, Oak Brook, Illinois, 60521.

▲ TRANSPORTATION ASSOCIATION OF AMERICA (TAA)

TAA is a group which has three primary objectives. The first is to resist government ownership or operation of any form of transportation. The second is to develop a favorable climate assuring the best possible transportation service at reasonable cost. The final objective is "promoting and nurturing public understanding of the importance of sound transportation, and public awareness of transport problems." For further information, write: Transportation Association of America, 1101 17th St., N.W., Washington, D.C. 20036.

▲ TRANSPORTATION RESEARCH FORUM (TRF)

TRF is a "joint endeavor of interested persons in academic life, government service, business logistics, and the various modes of transportation. The Forum's purpose is to provide a common meeting ground or forum for the discussion of ideas and research techniques applicable to economic, management, and public policy problems involving transportation." Additional information can be obtained from: TRF, P.O. Box AA, Northfield, New Jersey 08225.

Outline for the Remainder of the Book

The remainder of this book is divided into parts coinciding with various career fields. Chapters 2 and 3 deal with government's involvement in the transportation sector of our economy. Chapter 2 covers government's role as a provider of new transportation facilities and its more recent role as foster parent to certain carriers. Government as a regulator of carriers is covered in chapter 3. In some instances, government must regulate the monopolistic practices of a carrier; in other instances, government must regulate too much competition among carriers. In the past few years, many of these regulations have been either eliminated or reduced.

Chapters 4 through 8 discuss the various transportation modes. Chapter 4 covers highway users and chapter 5 covers the railroads. Pipelines and airlines are the subject of chapters 6 and 7, respectively. Domestic water carriers are examined in chapter 8 and international water carriers are discussed in chapter 9. Also in chapter 9 is a discussion of international airlines.

Chapters 10, 11, and 12 look at shippers and their use of transportation. Physical distribution and logistics management—the management of a firm's transportation, warehousing, and inventories in a manner that supports both sales and production—is examined in chapter 10. The more detailed aspects of managing a firm's traffic activities are covered in chapters 11 and 12.

Carrier management is the subject of the next two chapters. Chapter 13 looks at issues involving management of private carriers, and chapter 14 looks at the management of public enterprise carriers.

Chapter 15 attempts to look at the future, especially the next decade.

Summary

Transportation is very much a part of life in the United States. Individual attachment to the automobile is great and is a hindrance to proposals for reducing use of autos in order to save fuel or to reduce air pollution. About 20 percent of U.S. Gross National Product is accounted for by transportation. Expenditures for passenger transportation are somewhat greater than those for freight transportation. Nearly all travel expenditures are automobile related; and almost 80 percent of expenditures for shipments of products are paid to highway carriers. Clearly, highways are the dominant form of transportation in the United States.

Transportation plays two roles in the production process. First, it allows the entrepreneur to assemble components and labor from a wide geographic area. Second, transportation allows a firm to market its product over a wider area, thereby increasing sales and reducing per-unit costs because of economies of scale. The transportation system has allowed each region to specialize and manufacture or grow whatever it can best produce.

Transportation's relationship to natural resources was once believed to mean only that it allowed one to find markets for products of mines, forests, or land. More recently, transportation has been more critically examined and found to have a damaging effect on some natural resources. The chief problem is auto-caused air pollution. The increased price of fuel has affected transportation simply because vehicles are major fuel users.

Transportation employment is growing, although at a rate lower than that of the entire labor force. Employment by some carriers is declining (except for air and trucks). During the past 30 years, employment has increased in transportation equipment manufacture, transport-related industries, and in government assignments related to transportation.

Questions for Discussion and Review

1. According to Table 1–3, we—as a nation—spend about 11 percent of GNP for automobiles. What percent of your annual income is spent for automobiles?

2. Is our transportation system compatible with an "unspoiled" natural environment?

3. Describe the initial pattern of land development in rural areas of the United States.

4. What is the relationship between an efficient transportation system and the concept of economies of scale?

5. Discuss changes in patterns of transportation employment.

6. Discuss the noise problem created by transportation. Which transport modes do you think are the worst offenders? Why?

7. What are "no-growth" policies? Do you agree with them? Why?

8. Discuss the relationship between transportation and air quality.

9. Assume the price of gasoline increases to two dollars a gallon. How do you think it would affect distribution of personal trips and of freight transportation?

10. How do you think a price increase of gasoline to two dollars a gallon would affect our environmental quality?

11. What modes of transport appear to be fuel inefficient?

12. Why have minorities and females experienced difficulty in finding equal employment opportunities in the transportation industry?

13. Until 1970, relatively few women possessed managerial jobs in the transportation industry. Why was this true? What factors are changing this trend in the 1980's? Discuss.

14. What forms of competition do carriers use when competing with each other?

15. Do you think transportation systems lead or follow development? Why?

16. In the post-World War II period, why did passenger-miles of travel increase much more than did ton-miles of freight movements?

17. Assume you wanted to join a professional transportation organization. Which one would you pick? Why?

18. Examine the quotations at the beginning of the chapter. Which do you find most thought provoking? Why?

19. Total freight and passenger revenues in the United States account for 21.5 percent of Gross National Product. However, the transportation sector (freight and passenger) of the economy accounts for only 10.4 percent of the civilian labor force. Explain why this relationship is true.

20. What concept or idea presented in this chapter was the most interesting to you? Why?

Additional Chapter References

American Public Works Association, *History of Public Works in the United States—1776–1976* (Chicago, 1976).

Batts, Lana R., "Truck/Rail Relative Energy Efficiency-Revisited," *Annual Proceedings of the TRF* (1981), pp. 149–155.

Coyle, John J., Edward Bardi, and Joseph Cavinato, *Transportation* (St. Paul: West Publishing Co., 1982).

Everett, Carol T., *Transportation Policy Plan, An Issue Paper, Economic Role of the State in Transportation* (Madison: Office of the Secretary, Wisconsin Department of Transportation, 1978).

Fair, Marvin L., and Ernest W. Williams, *Economics of Transportation and Logistics* rev. ed. (Dallas: Business Publications, Inc., 1981).

Hazard, John L., "Transitional Administration of National Transportation Policy," *Transportation Journal* (Spring, 1981), pp. 5–22.

Heads, John, "Transport Statistics: Sources and Limitations," *Transportation Journal* (Fall, 1980), pp. 33–46.

Herron, David P., "The Educational Needs Of Physical Distribution Managers," *Annual Proceedings of the National Council of Physical Distribution Management* (1980), pp. 45–52.

Hollander, Stanley C., *Passenger Transportation: Readings Selected from a Marketing Point of View* (East Lansing, Mich.: MSU Business Studies, 1968).

Hyman, William A., "The Environmental and Energy Impacts of Transportation Deregulation," *Annual Proceedings of the Transportation Research Forum* (1979), pp. 354–358.

La Londe, Bernard J., and Martha Cooper, "Career Patterns in Distribution: Profile 1981," *Annual Proceedings of the National Council of Physical Distribution Management* (1981), pp. 15–48.

Lieb, Robert C., *Transportation: The Domestic System*, 2nd ed. (Reston, Virginia: Reston Publishing Co., Inc. 1981).

Locklin, D. Philip, *Economics of Transportation*, 7th ed. (Homewood, Ill.: Richard D. Irwin, 1972).

Mealey, Robert S. and Milan Krukar, "Impact of Energy Constraints on Outdoor Recreation Demands," *Annual Proceedings of the Transportation Research Forum* (1981), pp. 311–319.

Metcalf, Kenneth N., *Transportation: Information Sources* (Detroit: Gale Research Co., 1965).

Meyer, John R., Merton J. Peck, John Stenason, and Charles Zwick, *The Economics of Competition in the Transportation Industries* (Cambridge: Harvard University Press, 1959).

Mostert, Noël, *Supership* (New York: Alfred A. Knopf, 1974).

Owen, Wilfred, "The World Without Automobiles: A Fable," *Transportation Journal* (Spring, 1971), pp. 60–63.

Norton, Hugh S., *National Transportation Policy: Formation and Implementation* (Berkeley, Cal.: McCutchan Publishing Corporation, 1966).

Pegrum, Dudley F., *Transportation: Economics and Public Policy*, 3d ed. (Homewood, Ill.: Richard D. Irwin, Inc., 1973).

Ruppenthal, Karl M., and Kent Schillerstrom, "The Uneconomic Consumption of Automobile Fuel—One Example," *The Logistics and Transportation Review*, Vol. 17, No. 2 (1981), pp. 213–220.

Schueftan, Oliver, and Doris Groff Velona, "Transportation Energy Contingency Planning: An Assessment of Federal, State and Local Responses to the 1979 Fuel Shortages," *Annual Proceedings of the Transportation Research Forum* (1981), pp. 320–331.

Schutt, Jeffrey H., "The Effect of Fuel Price on Logistics System Design," *Journal of Business Logistics*, Vol. 3, No. 1 (1982), pp. 17–44.

Sheskin, Ira M., and Peter R. Stopher, "Transportation and Energy—Some Urban Perceptions," *Annual Proceedings of the Transportation Research Forum* (1981), pp. 332–342.

Smerk, George M., *Urban Mass Transportation, A Dozen Years of Federal Policy* (Bloomington: Indiana University Press, 1974).

Sorenson, L. O., "Agricultural Transportation: Policies and Prospects," *Annual Proceedings of the Transportation Research Forum* (1981), pp. 353–354.

Walker, Michael, *Transportation Impacts on the Environment* (Madison: Office of The Secretary of The Wisconsin Department of Transportation, 1978).

Weseman, Sidney E., and David A. Zavattero, "The Impact of Gasoline Price on Automobile Travel in the Chicago Region," *Annual Proceedings of the Transportation Research Forum* (1980), pp. 264–273.

Wolfgram, Mark J., and Donald J. Harmatuck, "An Evaluation of Econometric Models for Forecasting Gasoline Consumption Using Time Series Techniques," *Annual Proceedings of the Transportation Research Forum* (1981), pp. 343–352.

Case 1–1 Tanzoland Island Cloverleaf Case

Kenneth Harding was an outstanding civil engineering student at Purdue and received a scholarship to continue his studies at M.I.T. His special field of study was freeway construction, and his master's thesis was based on computer simulation of auto-truck traffic flows between 60 and 80 miles per hour on six-lane cloverleafs leading off of and onto hypothetical 12-lane highways. Upon completion of his work at M.I.T. he was immediately hired by California and assigned to the freeway planning section responsible for Los Angeles and Anaheim. Unfortunately for Harding, a year after he was hired he was laid off because of a general cutback in that state's highway program. He checked around and found that the demand for individuals with his specialized talents had vanished. He wished that he had taken some courses in mass transit planning since that was suddenly where the federal money was. He was disgusted with himself and with life in general since there seemed to be little future for one with his particular specialization.

With only a few weeks of unemployment compensation benefits remaining, Harding finally received one promising response to the 125 personalized letters, accompanied by résumés, he had sent out two months earlier. It was from an agency, funded by the United Nations, that performed economic development and transportation planning services for developing nations. The letter said that they had been impressed by Harding's high grade-point averages at both Purdue and M.I.T. He was told to phone them collect, at their New York City office, if he was interested in accepting an overseas assignment.

With no other alternatives in sight, Harding phoned the New York number, apparently said the right things, and was off to New York City for a job interview. The assignment was to become the transportation adviser in the Ministry of Economic Development for the new republic of Tanzoland Island, off the east coast of Africa, near the Malagasy Republic. Tanzoland Island had been granted its independence reluctantly by a western European nation after years of internal warfare and strife. Just before withdrawing its troops, the European nation had systematically stripped the local economy of every movable item of value, including just about every motor vehicle, airplane, and ship. According to a magazine article written at the time of the independence ceremonies, about six months earlier, the Europeans had left the following stock of transport equipment:

> A Douglas DC-3 with only one engine operating; three woodburning steam locomotives—only two of which can hold a head of steam; between 35 and 40 rail cars including six that had fallen into the Sassoon Gorge when the trestle washed away in 1972 and had yet to be recovered; 15 to 20 trucks, the newest of which had been abandoned by Mussolini's army when it had been routed from Ethiopia; five small vessels whose owners had wisely kept them at sea; and no private automobiles.

Harding grinned when he read the clipping and handed it back to Emo Swahli, who had been interviewing him. Harding said: "It will be a while before they have enough autos to need my specialty of designing cloverleaf turnoffs."

Emo Swahli frowned and said: "I'm so sorry, I thought we had explained to you that there will be no autos permitted in the Tanzoland Island Republic. They want to avoid the problems of western societies, such as yours, which devote too much GNP [Gross National Product] toward supporting the private auto and find that they can't cut back on petroleum imports because of their great dependence on the private auto."

"No autos at all?" asked Harding. "None?"

"Well, actually, they have imported some small vans for use as jitney buses. Also a few for ambulances and paddy wagons. They will let in trucks and buses. They just don't want their population to become dependent on individual autos. They have one of the advantages of later developing economies: they can benefit from the western world's experience and can pick and choose which comforts and life styles they desire."

Question One: Do you think that a developing nation, such as the hypothetical Tanzoland Island Republic, would benefit from avoiding the private ownership of automobiles? Why?

Question Two: Should restrictions also be placed on the private ownership of trucks? Why?

Question Three: If the nation avoids private ownership of automobiles, what types of vehicles do you think most people would use? Discuss.

Question Four: In what geographic patterns would new housing develop in a nation without private autos? How, if at all, would these patterns differ from those in a nation that allowed private autos?

Question Five: If private ownership of autos were allowed in Tanzoland Island, what other economic activities do you think would also develop?

Question Six: Do you think Harding should accept the job? Why?

Case 1–2   J. F. Kennedy Boulevard Streetcar Case

"I guess that's what they mean by the expression 'sea of black faces,'" thought Joaquin Neto to himself, as he sat on the stage of the auditorium in the Booker T. Washington Junior High School (an old building, originally named after General Casimir Pulaski of Revolutionary War fame). Neto, recently appointed to the planning commission of a large midwestern city, was presiding over a public hearing concerning a proposal by the city's mass transit authority to raise the level of the two streetcar tracks running along John F. Kennedy Boulevard. At present the tracks ran at street level down the street's center. Streetcars had to stop whenever autos happened to block the tracks, which happened when drivers wanted to turn left at cross streets. Jaywalking pedestrians slowed streetcar traffic as did autos which had to go on to the tracks in order to pass double-parked autos or trucks. This last problem was acute in the mornings when trucks were double-parked to make deliveries to the small stores spread along both sides of the boulevard near the Booker T. Washington school.

Christopher Cartwright, representing the city's mass transit authority, was speaking. He explained that the track rehabilitation program was being funded by a federal grant from the Urban Mass Transit Administration. The transit authority was proposing to (1) elevate the new track several inches above the pavement; (2) build an 8-inch-high curb between the streetcar tracks and the auto/truck lanes to keep cars off the tracks; (3) close every other cross street intersection so that traffic at these "closed" intersections coming along J. F. Kennedy Boulevard could only go straight, or turn right; while traffic from the cross streets could only turn right on to the boulevard; and (4) build a wire mesh fence, four feet high, between the two street car tracks to prevent jaywalking.

Cartwright was now explaining what construction materials would be used and how they would upgrade the appearance of the street and of the buildings on either side. "You people should be pleased with what we have planned for you!" he said in a condescending tone that could belong only to a long-time civil service employee.

Neto grimaced and there was muttering and murmuring in the crowd.

"That ain't so," a voice yelled out. "You ain't telling it like it is, Whitey! You ain't doin' nuthin for us in the Booker T. Washington neighborhood. You're just turning our street into a race track for streetcars so those fancy-assed whites who live in *eggsclusive* lily-white suburbs can ride streetcars to and from their air-conditioned offices a bit faster!"

There was a burst of applause and warm shouts of "Right on!"

Neto banged his gavel and said: "Let Mr. Cartwright continue."

Cartwright, both angry and shaken, said, "What we're trying to do is get people out of their autos for their to-and-from-work trips. Streetcar patronage will increase only if we reduce travel time between the suburbs and downtown. Competent engineers tell us that by removing all these impediments to the flow of streetcar traffic we will reduce the peak-hour travel time between the suburbs and downtown by 15 to 25 percent. This will attract commuters out of their autos and as many as 20 percent of the autos will be taken off of J. F. Kennedy Boulevard. Think, for a moment, of the reduction in carbon monoxide and other pollutants!"

Cartwright sat down, and Neto, looking up, asked the audience: "Are there any questions of Mr. Cartwright? If so, please raise your hand. I'll point to you. I ask that you identify yourself and your organization, if you're appearing for one. Or, if you have no questions of Mr. Cartwright, have you any comments?"

Several hands shot up. Neto recognized a middle-aged woman, smartly dressed, sitting in the front row. She was one of the few whites in the room. She stood.

"My name is Mrs. Amy Withers, co-chairlady of the Mayor's Committee on Promoting Mass Transit. I just want to tell you that our committee is 100 percent behind all these wonderful proposals which Mr. Cartwright so ably described. Further, we believe that our entire metropolitan area will benefit. Thank you for letting me speak." She sat.

A voice shouted out: "She ain't from 'round here. Tell us your address, lady."

Neto banged his gavel and said, sternly, "The speaker has identified herself and her organization. She does not need to give her address."

The audience hissed and booed.

Mrs. Withers, looking a bit pale, stood and said, firmly, "My husband and I live in Foxborough Glen Heights, where we have resided for 15 years." Neto knew that Foxborough Glen Heights was one of the area's wealthiest suburbs containing large estates with homes barely visible through the grilled iron gates. The audience hissed again, then gave a few boos, and was silent.

"How many Ne-gras live in Foxboro Glen Heights, lady?" yelled someone.

"When's the last time you rode a streetcar?" yelled another.

"I'll bet the fancy white lady wants better streetcar service to her suburb so black cleaning help can come out there cheap!" shouted still another.

"Right on!" was being murmured throughout the crowd and it took Neto a few minutes to restore enough order so that he could call on another speaker.

"My name is Larry Dunne," said the earnest young man, "and I am a planner/architect. I'm here tonight speaking for over forty neighborhood businesspeople on both sides of Kennedy Boulevard here, near to Booker Washington High." The room became quiet and some of the crowd started nodding affirmatively as Dunne spoke.

"In planner's jargon," continued Dunne, "we have passed through the 'neighborhood in transition' phase. The Polish-Americans have left and the Blacks have moved in. We believe that we have the makings of a stable neighborhood of which we and our city will be proud. Unfortunately, from our standpoint, the J. F. Kennedy Boulevard streetcar track 'improvements' will work against our community interests. The reason is that in this area the Boulevard is the focus of the neighborhood. This school is on one side, and our two churches on the other. All the stores and small businesses we patronize are on both sides of the boulevard. Your streetcar improvement scheme, while it will help some areas, will cut our neighborhood in two. Because of your concentration-camp-like fence stretching along for four blocks . . ."

"Mr. Chairman!" yelled Christopher Cartwright, jumping up. "I object to Dunne's choice of terms. 'Concentration-camp-like' fence, indeed! It will be only four feet high and of most attractive mesh. Mr. Dunne is playing to his audience, trying to inflame them to . . ."

"I say it's concentration-camp-like," reasserted Dunne, and there was a scattering of applause. Cartwright was silent but beet-red and angry. He sat.

Dunne continued, "It is a widely-known fact that during the 1960's highway engineers located and built urban freeways to bisect and lobotomize black ghettos. They also used urban freeways to build barriers on the edges of black neighborhoods to keep them from spreading into white areas. That was one reason for all the riots. You damned retreaded highway engineers have learned nothing! Now wearing the masks of transit experts you're using Uncle Sugar's money for carrying out your long-term goals of perpetually harassing those poor souls who, through unlucky choice of skin color, are destined to live in our nation's ghettos."

The audience was nodding in agreement with Dunne, whose voice was growing more powerful. "I say the mayor doesn't like our neighborhood. He doesn't like 'our kind' of people. He doesn't like our spirit and he's afraid we'll succeed. He and his lily-white country-club cronies are using the streetcar tracks and fence proposal to cut us in two, as one would cut a fishing worm with a shovel!"

By now the audience, with the exception of Mrs. Withers, Mr. Cartwright, and two reporters, were standing and shouting. Neto let them shout and thought to himself that he was glad he was there only to listen and not to make a statement. This was the first time in four hearings that he had heard any opposition to the proposal. Things finally were quiet, and he recognized a young lady.

"My name is Redbird Stanley," said the speaker, "and I own the store building at 1131 J. F. Kennedy where I also operate the Redbird Record Store, which has been in business 15 months. As one of 40 store owners or operators along this section of the boulevard, let me say that I'm sick and I'm upset over these proposals to raise the streetcar tracks, build a barrier fence, and close off cross street traffic. In addition to splitting the neighborhood and its spirit, which Mr. Dunne already mentioned, the fence will make it difficult for shoppers to cross the street. I realize they're jaywalking but—since autos and streetcars move so slowly here now anyway—it's safe for pedestrians to cross at midblock. I haven't heard of any pedestrians getting hit or hurt since I've been in business here."

She paused and then continued: "For the past two weeks I watched those customers who made a purchase in my store after they left. Of the 83 I watched who left my store, 35 stayed on my side of the street and, of these, 13 went into another store, 11 got into parked autos (on my side of the boulevard), and 11 walked to the end of the block in either direction and disappeared around the corner. Of the 83 customers, 16 walked to the streetcar stop at either end of the block and 8 boarded a streetcar headed downtown and 8 boarded streetcars headed for the suburbs. Of the 83 customers, the remaining 32 crossed the street completely, all but six jaywalking. Of the 32, 14 went into stores across the street, 13 got into autos parked on the other side, and 5 walked in either direction until I lost sight of them."

She paused again and started speaking more slowly for emphasis.

"The point I am trying to make is that our shopping area is on *both* sides of JFK Boulevard. In fact, when I first started making signs to place in my window I made the lettering large enough so it could be read by people standing on the sidewalk across the street. I even have customers come in who've read my signs as they rode by in cars or in streetcars. Any changes on JFK Boulevard, like we're hearing about tonight, will hurt my business and all the others as well. Most of us are barely making it now, and we cannot survive if the streets and tracks are torn up for construction or the barriers make it hard for people to cross the street at midblock."

The crowd was murmuring in approval.

"And, finally, Mr. Chairman," said Ms. Stanley, "I have here a petition addressed to our mayor and to you, signed by 41 JFK Boulevard businesspeople, right here in the neighborhood, respectfully asking that the city not proceed with the boulevard streetcar line improvements as are being proposed by the transit authority." With this, she marched to the stage and handed to Mr. Neto the petition, typewritten at the top and containing many signatures below.

Neto glanced at the document and placed it carefully in his folder. He looked out at the crowd and saw only one raised hand. He pointed to the young man.

"I am David Sanchez-Soissons and I represent the 'Bootstraps Coalition' which is a neighborhood group representing the interests of those who live in the Booker T. Washington area," said the speaker. "The area is trying to help itself succeed, and we fear that the streetcar track improvements will, indeed, cut our blossoming shopping area and neighborhood into two. By way of statistics, the petition you just received was signed by 41 merchants on both sides of Kennedy Boulevard. Along these blocks are 47 storefronts, so we now have 41 of the 47 filled, and only 6 are empty. One year ago, 19 were empty. This shows we're trying to turn the area around, and, until now, we've been succeeding. There are also neighborhoods behind the stores, on both sides of the street. In them, houses are being fixed up, vacant lots have been cleared of trash and junked autos, new trees and shrubs have been planted, and so on. I want you to check with the third precinct police station where they will tell you that the incidence of crime in the area has been reduced. We've pushed out the pimps, the hookers, and the pushers who used to parade on the boulevard at night. Check with the fire department, the health department, and the school board, and they'll all tell you that things are better here than they were one, two, or five years ago."

Sanchez-Soissons continued: "Things have been improving until now. But if you 'improve' the tracks, it will kill our neighborhood, and you will be guilty of destroying the dreams of all those battered souls who thought that finally, for once in their lives, the system would treat them fairly and they would succeed. Once again we're being screwed to help Whitey.''

There was a scattering of applause, but no further hands were raised. Neto adjourned the meeting. As he was packing his briefcase, Christopher Cartwright walked up to him, looking exasperated, and said: "These people just don't understand the needs of our metropolitan area! How are we going to get motorists out of their autos if we can't speed up mass transit?''

Neto shrugged his shoulders, said nothing, and walked out to his parked car.

Question One: Given the facts presented, what do you think Neto should recommend? Why?

Question Two: What additional information, if any, would have been useful to Neto?

Question Three: Are compromises possible that would speed streetcar flow and yet not hurt the J. F. Kennedy Boulevard shopping area? If so, list them.

Question Four: Assume you were the Mayor and wanted, in addition to Neto's recommendation, an analysis of the costs and benefits of the streetcar system improvements. List and quantify—to the extent possible—the benefits that were mentioned.

Question Five: Reread Question Four and then list and quantify—to the extent possible—the project's costs.

Question Six: You are the Mayor. Taking into account the answers to previous questions, what would you decide? Why? (Note—your decision need not be the same as Neto's recommendation).

A shipyard worker dwarfed by the propeller of a supertanker. Today's ocean-going vessels are very large, as are the costs to governments for dredging channels and ports to handle such vessels. Currently the federal government is trying to get other parties to share in the dredging costs.

Photo courtesy Exxon Corporation.

Governments also support transportation research. In this test tank, a radio-controlled model of a tanker is undergoing handling experiments.

Photo courtesy National Maritime Institute, United Kingdom (Crown copyright).

2 Government as a Provider of Transportation Services and Facilities

He introduced himself as "I'm Robert Moses, representing the State of New York. We're going to put a parkway through this section of Long Island." He was very polite, very diplomatic, at first. But when he saw my father wasn't going to sell, he stood up in our kitchen and he said, "You know, Mr. Rasweiler, the state is all-supreme when it comes to a condemnation proceeding. If we want your land, we can take it."

"THE POWER BROKER"
The New Yorker
July 29, 1974

By using the excellent road and rail network, which had been rapidly improved to meet just such a contingency, the German army pulled itself out of the trap. . . .

ALEXANDER SOLZHENITSYN
August, 1914

The atmosphere of euphoria that surrounds the anticipated boom in U.S. coal exports during the 80s has given rise to the prevailing notion that we have to expand the number and the capacity of virtually all our public ports. This is a dangerous concept because, in the euphoria, it is too easy to lose sight of the important principle of costs and benefits.

LEO DONOVAN
World Wide Shipping/World Ports
January, 1982

Introduction

Government's role within the transportation sector of our economy varies with respect to several things: the form or mode of transportation; where a transportation system is geographically located; and the level of government (federal, state, regional, or local) involved in transportation. Both domestic and international carriers operate in markets where many of the operators are government owned or subsidized.

- *Domestic* transportation is that carried on within the 50 states and territories. *International* transportation is between two or more nations.

- *Government-owned* carriers often are operated as a branch or department of government and provide a service to the public. *Government-subsidized carriers* are usually privately owned but have a portion of their total costs paid for by the government.

There are two reasons why we cannot rely completely upon the market forces of "supply and demand" to provide the desired amounts of transportation service. One reason deals with the nature of the demands for many transportation services; the other deals with the nature of transportation technology used to meet the shippers' or passengers' needs. The flows of many commodities, and movements of passengers, are not uniform throughout the year or even throughout the day. Carriers who are willing to serve on a regular basis, when traffic flows are both heavy and light, need protection from more footloose carriers who would enter the market only when demand and prices for carrying the goods were high and then abandon transporting in this market when demand dropped off and more lucrative markets attracted them elsewhere.

- *Skimming the cream* is the term applied to the practice of carriers who serve markets only when prices are high and then abandon them when the prices drop.

The second reason is that transport technology has developed to the point where vehicle capacity is so large that only one or two carriers are needed to serve the entire needs of many markets. One or two carriers are not enough to be considered "competitive." In this situation and in the one described in the previous paragraph, some form of government regulation is needed. The goal of the regulation would be to provide adequate service to the shipping and traveling public at a cost which is high enough to attract entrepreneurs to provide the transportation service but not so high as to include monopolistic profits.

- *Monopolistic profits* result from a single seller's ability to charge higher prices (monopolistic prices) since there is little or no direct competition.

Here in chapter 2 we will deal with situations where neither competition nor regulated private enterprise are relied upon to provide transportation service. We will deal strictly with transportation services provided by government. The federal government provides transportation to fulfill two basic responsibilities. One is national defense. The other is to foster communications within and throughout a country such as by a postal system.[1]

Governments promote economic development because it contributes to the wealth of both individual citizens and to the nation as a whole. The average standard of living is also improved.

> Farmers of north-central Illinois, who could find no profitable way of disposing of the bountiful crops they were producing, were almost unanimous in demanding that the state build a canal that would give them access to a market. They knew that Illinois did not have the money with which to undertake such a costly improvement, but that did not silence them. Borrow it, they argued; a canal would pay for itself in ten years.[2]

This quote describes public attitudes in 1820. Canals were built both by governments (mostly state) or by private firms (which often received either governmental subsidies or assurances that competitive canal routes would not be allowed). In the financial Panic of 1837 a number of states defaulted on bonds they had issued to build canals. This helps to explain why governments did not become involved in the complete ownership and operation of railroads, which started to develop rapidly in the late 1830's. Early railroads enjoyed some subsidies, however, because railroad promoters were adept at playing local communities against each other. The communities along a proposed route which would subscribe to the most railroad stock would be rewarded with the railroad being routed through them.[3]

Today, nearly one and a half centuries later, government has found it necessary to subsidize much of our existing railroad system. Within the past decade the federal government has taken over what remained of the intercity rail passenger service and formed Amtrak, which is being kept alive with large doses of public subsidy. (See Figure 2–1.) Since the early 1960's many cities, with federal assistance, have taken over both ownership and operation of local mass transit systems. Most serious of all has been the federal government's deepening involvement in the Northeast railroad crisis (discussed more fully in chapter 5). A coalition of three groups—the bankrupt railroads' creditors, railroad labor, and communities which do not

---

[1] The U.S. Constitution says that Congress shall have the power to establish post offices and post roads. Little is said about the postal service in this book because readers are familiar with its services.

[2] Harry Sinclair Drago, *Canal Days in America* (New York: Bramall House, 1972), p. 257. No canals, with the possible exception of the main line of the Erie Canal (Albany to Buffalo), paid for themselves in a strict financial sense.

[3] Technology made it easier for railroads to exercise monopolistic pricing policies than was the case for canals. Anyone could launch a small boat or raft and use it in stretches of canal systems between toll collection points.

Figure 2–1 Ad Complaining About Amtrak's Costs. Courtesy: American Bus Association.

want to lose railroad service—have banded together to prevent the government from paring down its railroad (known as Conrail) operations to a scale which would be more economically viable. The Reagan administration would like to sell Conrail as soon as possible because of its losses and because of the administration's dislike of governmental involvement in business enterprise. This is a complicated situation and demonstrates that we cannot easily separate politics from economics.

The inseparability of politics and economics may well be the theme which ties this chapter together. Where a rationale for government involvement is discussed, there is always at least one group which directly benefits. More importantly, these various groups continue to demand assistance; it is unlikely they will be weaned.

Government Involvement by Mode of Transportation

Government involvement in each mode of transportation will be discussed in this section. For each mode, the type and degree of government participation differ. Chapters 4 through 9 will contain more detailed discussions of each mode and its relationship to government.

Railroads

Traditionally, U.S. railroads were privately owned. Most railroads developed in an era when government involvement in economic activities was much less than it is today. There were a few exceptions, such as the U.S. government ownership of the Alaskan Railway and small railroads on military bases. Since World War II, as railroads have attempted to abandon trackage, communities have sometimes purchased small stretches of track (and occasionally operated their own locomotives) so that they could continue to have connections with major railroads. In the early 1960's, the State of New York purchased railroads leading into New York City in order to keep the commuter passenger service alive.

In 1970, the federal government offered to take over the remaining intercity passenger train service; railroads were allowed to "buy out" of their longtime common carrier obligation. Today, Amtrak, which is heavily subsidized, operates its equipment on rights-of-way belonging to other railways, and it owns some of its own track in the Northeast. Several states fund intrastate Amtrak train operations, supplementing the federal subsidies with payments of their own.

- *Common carrier obligations* (discussed more fully in chapter 3) are requirements to provide service, which are placed upon a carrier by a transportation regulatory body. In turn, the regulatory body attempts to protect the carrier from some outside competition. In the case of railroad passenger service, the federal regulatory body, the Interstate Commerce Commission (ICC), could not protect the railroads from outside competition since it came mainly from private automobiles, and from airlines, which were not subject to ICC jurisdiction.

Following the bankruptcy of most railroads in the Northeast, the federal government took over their properties—including 17,000 miles of rail routes—and is operating a subsidized railroad, Conrail. Some states are taking over abandoned rail lines.

"Street railroad" systems were initially privately owned. Streetcars provided service within cities and *interurbans* provided what one would call suburban or commuter service today.[4] Only a handful of cities have streetcar service remaining today, and these operations are owned and operated by the municipality or some other public body.[5] With the help of federal subsidies three new rail transit systems (with major portions underground) have been completed recently in San Francisco, Washington, D.C., and Atlanta. San Diego, using state and local funds, recently completed a 14-mile-long rail passenger system leading to the Mexican border.

Highways

The term "turn-pike" had its origin in the early days of the U.S. when poles—or pikes—barred entrances to a road. When the user paid a coin to the operator the operator turned the pike, permitting the user to enter the road. Only a few toll roads were built, one reason being that it was difficult to exclude nonpayers from entering at other points. Toll bridges were more successful, and many were built through the mid-1950's.

In communities, streets were surfaced (often to keep down dust) and paid for with local tax funds. In rural areas, citizens were often required to put in one or more days of work per year maintaining

---

[4] More recent terminology, adopted by APTA (the American Public Transit Association), refers to streetcar-like operations as "light" rail. "Heavy" rail systems consist of "subway-type transit vehicle railway constructed on exclusive private right-of-way with high-level platform stations. . . ."

[5] Cable cars, representing an earlier technology than electric streetcars still operate in San Francisco as part of that city's municipal transit system. A few city transit systems still operate inclined plane lifts up steep hills. Seattle operates a monorail, originally built to connect the downtown with the site of the 1962 World's Fair.

township roads. Able-bodied welfare recipients were often kept busy trimming brush along the roads' edges and performing other maintenance.

Before World War II Pennsylvania completed a toll turnpike; after the war, a number of midwest and eastern states also built toll roads. In the mid-1950's the federal government started work on the Interstate Highway System, and most of the toll roads were incorporated into its routes, although they were allowed to continue to collect tolls in order to pay off their bonds. Once their bonds are retired they will become portions of the conventional highway systems of their respective states (although some state highway agencies are reluctant to accept them because of the expensive maintenance responsibilities).

- Planning for the *Interstate Highway System* began after World War II, and construction began in the 1950's. The 42,500-mile system is now nearly complete, and it links 90 percent of the cities in the U.S. with populations of 50,000 or more.

The vast majority of streets and highways in the United States are provided by government, with varying combinations of financial participation by federal, state, and local governments. Roads, once built, must be maintained, and this is generally a state and local responsibility. President Reagan, in his attempts to shift programs from the federal to state and local governments, proposed shifting control of all highways to states, except for the *Interstate Highway System.*[6]

Private roads are built on private property. Sometimes very exclusive suburbs retain ownership of their roads and can exclude non-residents from using them. This is contrary to the usual practice of donating the roads to the public.

Parking lots are provided by either local governments or private enterprise. Central cities were often forced into providing public parking lots for use of customers of downtown stores. This was necessary to keep downtown shopping areas competitive with suburban shopping centers.

Most of the traffic on the highway system—passenger autos, freight trucks, and commuter buses—comprises privately-owned vehicles. As one can well imagine, practically all of the automobiles on the highway system are privately owned; even the fleets of the large auto rental and leasing companies are actually privately-owned vehicles. In very recent years, the federal government has become

[6] *Transport Topics* (Feb. 1, 1982).

involved in measures to "save" the domestic auto industry. The Chrysler "bailout" is an example of this.

The freight that is transported on the highway system is carried either by privately-owned motor carrier firms that are in the business of carrying freight for others or by producers who carry their own products in their own motor trucks.

The bus service carrying passengers between cities is almost entirely owned by private companies. (Most of the intracity and suburban bus service is owned and operated by public agencies; in 1976, publicly-owned transit systems carried 91 percent of the intracity and suburban revenue passengers.)[7]

- *Revenue passengers* are the number of users who paid a fare. *Revenue-passenger miles* would be the same figure multiplied by the lengths of each fare-paying passenger's trip.

Most motor vehicles pay forms of "user taxes" on their fuel and tires. The money collected by the state and federal governments from these taxes is generally allocated back to highway construction and maintenance.

Pipelines

Petroleum, petroleum products, natural gas, and industrial chemicals are transported in pipelines that are frequently owned by companies that either produce or consume the product transported through the pipelines. In recent years, some railroads have spawned pipeline subsidiaries along their own rights-of-way.

In urban areas, pipe systems, which are owned by either local governments or regulated private utility companies, are used to deliver water, collect sewage, and—in a few cities—deliver steam. Some cities must transport water several hundred miles from its source. The water runs through pipes or through open aqueducts. In the 1960's California completed a water project which carried water from northern California 600 miles south to the Los Angeles area.

Aviation

U.S. airline companies are privately owned, as are most smaller aircraft used for general aviation purposes. The federal government provides limited subsidies to some airlines for serving specific

---

[7]Some of these operations were on vehicles other than buses. The comparable figure for ten years earlier was 58 percent. See *Transit Fact Book '76–'77* (Washington, D.C.: American Public Transit Association, 1977), p. 19.

points. Local communities, or groups of businessmen in these communities, also may subsidize air carriers.

Some time ago, most airports in the U.S. were privately owned. But today any airport that is paved and lighted is most likely to be owned by a public agency. Airports today are improved with a combination of federal, state, and local funds. A large number of relatively unimproved airstrips remain in private hands.

Air navigation aids—the airport control towers, radar, and radio signals which help guide aircraft—are provided by the federal government. U.S. military aircraft use the same navigation aids. A portion of the costs of the air navigation system is paid for by users of airline and other aircraft through a series of *user fees*, collected by the federal government.

- *User fees* or *user charges* are collected by government agencies from individuals or firms using governmentally-provided facilities. Examples from transportation are the motor fuel tax, landing fees charged at some airports, or bridge tolls. They also are called *user taxes*.

Waterways

Early vessels were small and could pass through most natural waterways. But as the shipping industry developed and ships became larger, the barges and ships encountered difficulty with reefs, shoals, and rapids. It became necessary to dredge the bottoms of waterways so that larger vessels could pass. The federal government made these improvements and developed an extensive waterway system throughout much of the United States. Until recently users were not charged,[8] but in 1978 Congress enacted a tax on fuel used by barge operators. At the present time there are proposals for charging ports or port users for the dredging provided by the federal government.

- A *waterway* is a route within one or more bodies of water used for commercial navigation.

Barges, Great Lakes carriers, and ocean ships are almost always operated by private firms. Certain forms of ocean ship operations are subsidized, which will be discussed in chapter 9. Some railroads own and operate ferry boats for connecting their tracks on either side of a body of water. At one time railroads also operated passenger

[8] An exception was the St. Lawrence Seaway, built in conjunction with Canada, which has assessed tolls on users since its completion in 1958.

ferries, but most remaining passenger ferries are now operated by local public agencies, with some subsidies from the federal government.[9]

Ocean port cargo terminals, which were used to transfer cargo between ships and shore, were at one time completely privately-owned, often by railroads. In recent years these terminals have been provided by municipal or public port agencies competing with public port agencies in other areas for cargo and cargo-handling jobs. A few public port terminals have received federal subsidies through employment-assistance programs. Also, for public port authorities that issue bonds, the bond interest payments are exempt from federal income taxes, thus giving public port authorities an advantage over private enterprise when it comes to borrowing.

Government Transportation Agencies

In this section we will show where transportation fits within the organizational structure of government; we will, of course, also discuss those government agencies that deal with transportation. First we will deal with transportation within the traditional executive-legislative-judicial system. With that background we will then explain the "special purpose" agencies, organized outside the traditional government framework, to deal with transportation problems.

The Executive-Legislative-Judicial System of Government

The federal government, state governments, and most local governments consist of three branches—the executive, the legislative, and the judicial. The three are somewhat separate from each other and—in theory—equal. Most government transportation programs involving the construction or maintenance of transport facilities or the operation of government vehicles are controlled by the executive branch. The legislative body enacts the laws that outline the responsibilities of the agencies and controls their budgets. Courts are not significantly involved in government programs that provide transport facilities. Regulatory bodies (discussed in greater detail in the following chapters) combine portions of the legislative, judicial, and executive functions.

---

[9]Public ferry systems operate in the areas near New Orleans, New York City, San Francisco, and Seattle. Private ferries also exist and mainly serve to connect small islands with mainland points.

Federal Transportation Agencies

Two federal transportation agencies operate within the executive branch and are under the control of the President. The principal agency is the U.S. Department of Transportation (DOT), headed by a cabinet officer, the Secretary of Transportation. The department was formed in 1966 and, with one major exception, combines all of the federal agencies that promote transportation. The one exception is the U.S. Army Corps of Engineers, in the Department of Defense, which provides waterway improvements for commercial navigation. Transportation regulatory bodies were not incorporated into the Department of Transportation. Figure 2–2 shows the department's organization chart.

The Coast Guard

The U.S. Coast Guard (once part of the Treasury Department where it was concerned with smuggling) is now also involved with the safety of navigation in ocean and certain inland waters. The Coast Guard provides much of the communication and signaling system which vessels rely upon for safe navigation. The Coast Guard inspects vessels and licenses certain seagoing professions. In recent years it also assumed responsibility for enforcing some anti-water pollution statutes.

Federal Aviation Administration

Usually referred to as the "FAA," the Federal Aviation Administration provides all of the various navigation aids used by airline and general aviation pilots and is also responsible for licensing pilots and airworthy aircraft. It administers the federal programs for construction of airports.

- *General aviation* covers all aviation except airlines and military. An analogous term is "private flying."

The FAA received considerable publicity recently because it is the agency responsible for air traffic control. After many of the air controllers went on strike in 1981, they were discharged from their jobs. In 1982, the FAA announced plans for upgrading its air traffic control system and making it more dependent upon computers and less dependent upon humans.

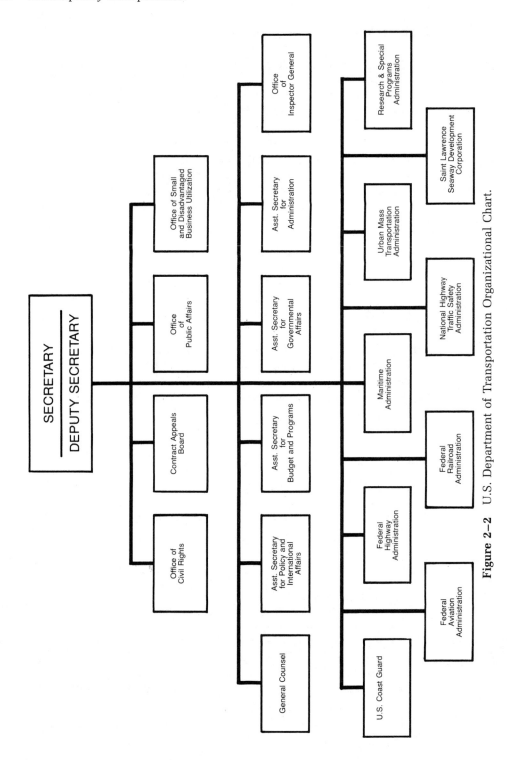

Figure 2–2   U.S. Department of Transportation Organizational Chart.

Federal Highway Administration

Measured by size of budget, the Federal Highway Administration represents the most important activity in the DOT. While individual states are responsible for highway construction, much of the work is paid for with federal funds administered by this agency. Within this agency is the Bureau of Motor Carrier Safety, which enforces the various safety regulations that apply to interstate truckers.

National Highway Traffic Safety Administration

This agency of the U.S. Department of Transportation is responsible for programs devoted to reducing the number of traffic deaths on highways, a figure which in the early 1970's totaled over 55,000 per year. After the fuel crisis and shortage and adoption of the 55 m.p.h. speed limit, the number of deaths dropped about 10 percent to 46,000 in 1976,[10] although the number has since increased.

This agency is the one responsible for the "product recall" campaigns which motor vehicle manufacturers must undertake when safety defects in autos or tires are discovered.

Federal Railroad Administration

The Federal Railroad Administration runs the Alaska Railroad, conducts and monitors research regarding high-speed rail passenger operations, and enforces federal programs for railroad safety. It conducts research into problems of railroad efficiency. It is also concerned with problems of railroads in the Northeast.

Urban Mass Transportation Administration

This agency was formed in 1964 originally as part of the Department of Housing and Urban Development and became part of the new Department of Transportation in 1966. Known as "UMTA," its main objective is to reverse the decline in usage of mass transit facilities. It funded numerous demonstration projects to determine which types of equipment, service, or price offerings were most attractive to users. It also provided capital grants which allowed local public bodies to purchase floundering private transit systems, and new rolling stock. In the mid-1970's, UMTA also received authority

---

[10] *Motor Vehicle Facts and Figures '81* (Detroit: Motor Vehicle Manufacturers Association, 1981), p. 50. In 1980, deaths totalled 53,300, which was lower than in any of the years 1968–1973, inclusive.

and appropriations to subsidize a portion of the operating expenses incurred by local public transit systems, an obligation that grew until it totalled 13 percent of the DOT's overall budget.[11]

- *Mass transit* generally applies to carrying people in urban areas on buses, streetcars, ferryboats, etc. It may even include carpools. One does not hear it used to describe trips in rural areas or between cities that are some distance apart.

- *Rolling stock* is a phrase used in the transit and the railroad industries to describe vehicles that carry passengers or freight.

Maritime Administration

Recently transferred from the Department of Commerce, the Maritime Administration promotes our international shipping industry. Its principal programs subsidize ship construction and some vessel operations.

The Saint Lawrence Seaway Development Corporation

This agency was formed by the United States in the mid-1950's to cooperate with a similar Canadian agency (and hydro-electric power generating agencies of New York State and the Province of Ontario) to construct and operate the St. Lawrence Seaway. It presently operates the two locks it constructed as the United States portion of the Seaway. The Seaway will be discussed in chapter 8.

National Transportation Safety Board

The National Transportation Safety Board is connected to, but somewhat autonomous from, the DOT. It investigates aviation accidents and serious accidents involving other modes of transport. For administrative purposes the Safety Board is connected to the DOT, but when investigating accidents, the Safety Board can issue its findings independent of departmental control. There is a reason for this independence: there may be instances where the accident was, in fact, caused by policies or employees of other agencies within the Department of Transportation.

---

[11]"DOT Secretary Visits Penn," *University of Pennsylvania Transportation* (May–June, 1981), pp. 1–2.

Other Federal Executive Agencies

To this point we have concentrated on those agencies within the DOT. Other agencies also have a somewhat limited interest in the development of transportation; and their functions will be listed here.

In the Department of Defense, in addition to the navigation projects of the U.S. Army Corps of Engineers, there are several significant transportation activities. Within the three branches of military service, army, navy, and air force, are commands reponsible for the movement on land, water, and in the air, respectively, of materials needed by military forces. The military owns and operates its own vehicles, cargo ships, and planes, and also relies on contracts with commercial firms.

Figure 2–3 is an advertisement by a U.S. shipbuilding firm pointing out the military and commercial importance of naval and merchant fleets. One argument given for subsidizing shipbuilding is that it is necessary to keep shipbuilding firms and labor "alive" in peace time, since they are so necessary in times of war.

There are many technological "trade-offs" between military and commercial transportation. A recent example is the U.S. Navy's space satellites, intended for use by Polaris submarines but also used by commercial ship operators for purposes of navigation.[12]

The State Department is involved in international aviation and maritime shipping to the extent that it is the only agency allowed to negotiate with foreign governments. A new, small agency, the U.S. Travel Service, encourages foreigners to travel to and vacation in the United States.

The Customs Service, within the Treasury Department, the Food and Drug Administration, and the Department of Agriculture, all have an interest in monitoring the flow of imported products.

The Postal Service carries mail and small packages between virtually all points in the United States and, linked with postal services of other nations, provides worldwide service. While easy to take for granted, the Postal Service provides service where many other carriers do not. Many commercial carriers have contracts with the Postal Service to carry mail, and these contracts provide an important proportion of their total revenues.

The National Weather Service, part of the Department of Commerce, provides weather forecasting and reporting functions that are especially important to aviation and merchant shipping.

---

[12] *The Wall Street Journal* (July 9, 1981).

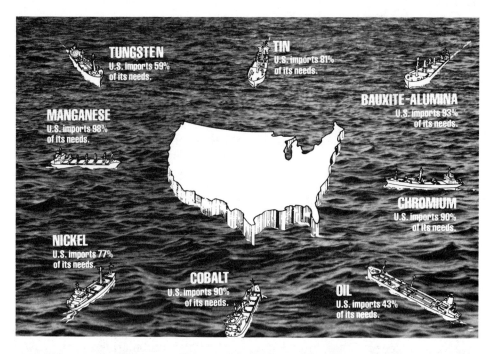

Figure 2–3 Ad About Importance of Maritime Strength. Courtesy: Todd Shipyards Corporation.

The National Transportation Policy Study Commission

In 1976, the National Transportation Policy Study Commission (NTPSC) was formed, and its activities were funded by a $5 million appropriation. It was not an executive agency; it consisted of 19 members, including six U.S. Senators and six members of the House of Representatives. The commission, and its staff, pursued three objectives:

1. Identification of current issues in transportation policy.
2. Projection of transportation trends and needs until the year 2000.
3. Development of recommendations to resolve policy conflicts and to have the nation's transportation system be able to meet the needs placed on it from now until the year 2000.

The commission finished its work in June of 1979 with the issuance of its major report *National Transportation Policies Through the Year 2000.*[13] The report, the recommendations, and the statistics it contains will stand for some time as the major federal government effort at studying our total transportation system and its needs.

When projecting future transportation activity, the NTPSC used several sets of assumptions concerning the rates of economic growth. Their projections for domestic passenger travel, expressed in passenger-miles, were that passenger travel in the year 2000 would be 1.6 to 2 times as much as it was in 1975. Domestic freight movements, measured in ton-miles, in the year 2000 would be 1.7 to 3.2 times as much as they were in 1975. International air travel to and from the United States, measured in terms of *passengers*, would increase, by the year 2000, to anywhere from 2 to 5 times the level of 1975 activity. International trade, measured in *tons* of cargo handled, would reach levels in 2000 that range from 1.6 to 2.9 times the tonnage handled in 1975. Even taking the lowest of the projections would indicate that considerable growth can be expected in all types of transportation activity. Much of the NTPSC's work dealt with projecting costs—both private and public—of vehicles and facilities that will be needed to handle this increase in passengers and freight.

As a common thread running throughout the Commission's report, and evident in many of its recommendations, were six themes. The themes, upon which specific recommendations were based, follow:

---

[13] Available from the Superintendent of Documents, U.S. Government Printing Office, Washington, D.C. 20402.

1. *National transportation policy should be uniform.* The NTPSC felt that many federal policies had been "patchwork" attempts to deal with single problems and the result was very uneven treatment of transportation modes.
2. *There should be an overall reduction in federal involvement in transportation.* The NTPSC felt there were "many instances" where "federal involvement can be reduced, so that private enterprise can function effectively, supplemented with limited state and local government participation."[14]
3. *Economic analysis of intended federal actions should be used.* More use should be made of benefit-cost analysis in order to focus federal involvement on programs where it will be most beneficial.
4. *When the transportation system is used to pursue non-transportation goals, this should be done in a cost-effective manner.* This means that when government involvement is justified on some basis such as national defense, we must be certain that this involvement minimizes distortions of what otherwise would be a "free" market for transportation.
5. *Federal involvement, including financial assistance, is required to deal with problems of transportation safety.* This is one area of concern where the NTPSC felt continued federal financial participation is needed.
6. *Users of publicly-provided transportation facilities, and those who benefit from them, should pay.* According to the NTPSC: "Free markets operate on the principle that those who benefit must pay for the costs. When government provides costly facilities, benefits, or services, it too should assess charges that recover costs. . . ."[15]

Another broad area addressed by the Commission was government involvement in the financing of many transportation activities. Major recommendations on these issues included:

1. Private transportation companies should be allowed to divest themselves of facilities that are unprofitable if neither public nor other private bodies are willing to provide subsidies.
2. Specific modal "trust funds" paid for by users of highways, and of airports, and of waterways, should be retained. The funds should not be merged into one "pot."

[14] *National Transportation Policies Through the Year 2000* (Washington, D.C.: The National Transportation Policy Study Commission, 1979), p. 248.
[15] *Ibid.*, p. 249.

3. Subsidies to the U.S. merchant marine should be continued, but only to the extent these subsidies clearly are of benefit to our national defense.

In addition to the recommendations listed here, the NTPSC also dealt with transportation planning issues, transportation information collection (needed by government agencies to carry out their assignments), and energy issues. The Commission addressed nearly all current issues of our national transportation policy, including regulatory reform. The principal thrust of all their recommendations was that government involvement within transportation be reduced, and that we, as a nation, rely more on "free market" forces to provide and regulate our transportation facilities and services.

State Transportation Agencies

Most states have their own transportation agencies, and they are more or less the same as the ones at the federal level. Ten years after the U.S. Department of Transportation was formed, at least 30 states had formed similar transportation agencies. One reason states follow the federal lead in organizational matters is that federal aid programs often encourage states to create agencies that are the counterparts to the federal agency giving out the funds.[16]

One area where there are some state agencies but no federal counterpart is in the field of port development. Some states, especially those with only one or two major ports, have a state port agency which constructs and operates the port facilities.

States also have transportation regulatory agencies which control the rates and services of intrastate carriers.

Local Transportation Agencies

Some cities and some counties have their own department of public works which is responsible for street construction and maintenance. The department of public works may also be responsible for the local airport as well as the local public transit system. Some cities also operate ports. In larger cities, each of these activities is typically run by a separate department of the local government. The workers are employed either directly by the city or by contractors who have agreed to perform the transportation services for the local agencies.

[16]Relationships among the various levels of government—federal, state, and local—are discussed in the National Transportation Policy Study Commission's report, *State and Local Transportation Policies* (Washington, D.C., 1979).

City and county governments regulate two types of local transportation. They regulate taxicabs by limiting the number of cabs permitted to operate (known as entry control) and by setting the rates that taxicabs may charge. Also, many cities provide local public scales which trucks use for "official" weights before and after loading. This is a necessary form of "consumer protection."

- *Entry control* is one facet of transportation regulation. Limitation on the number of competing carriers is believed necessary to prevent "destructive" competition, i.e., competition so severe that the entire industry is permanently crippled.

Local parking and street use regulations are also enacted by city and county governments. Parking restrictions can discourage motorists from using their autos and, among other things, can restrict truck deliveries to certain hours.

Many state governments have enacted legislation to create regional agencies for dealing with transportation needs or programs involving several adjacent communities. This made it easier for adjoining communities to cooperate with each other in solving transportation programs involving all of them. A typical example would be a large "central" city working with surrounding suburbs to solve problems faced by commuters who lived in the suburbs but travel daily to and from jobs in the central city.

Special Purpose Districts

In many states it is possible to form a special purpose district (sometimes called a public authority) for the purpose of building and operating a transportation facility such as a bridge, port, or airport. These special purpose districts are usually established to be somewhat independent of existing local governments. Because of their wide use in transportation, they deserve additional discussion.

Special purpose districts came into being because the time required to plan and construct a transportation facility was much longer than any single political party might hope to stay in power at the local or state level of government. Projects would become political "pawns," and work under way might not be completed because of a change in control of local government.

Milwaukee, in the pre-Civil War era, provides a useful example. In order to compete with Chicago, which was building a canal to link the Great Lakes with the Mississippi River, Milwaukee felt it had to do likewise. The logical route was to Janesville, about 90 miles to the southwest, where a connection could be made with the Rock River, which flows into the Mississippi. Using city funds, Milwaukee started digging a canal in the direction of Janesville. It did not progress far—however—since the political party in power was ousted by another which felt that railroads were the wave of the future and that a railroad rather than canal should be constructed to Janesville. Work on the canal stopped, work on the railroad began and continued until the parties changed power again, and so on. The railroad was eventually completed.[17]

Corruption was also an issue in many governmental transportation construction projects. Large sums of money were spent for construction, and potential profits from construction contracts were often so high that bribery of public officials was commonplace. Landowners who stood to benefit from completed projects also found reasons and ways to bribe in order to influence the location of routes.

Another problem of large transportation improvement projects was who benefits from them. A canal might benefit a strip of land, only five or ten miles on each side of the canal. An airport built in a rural setting does not serve adjacent farmland; instead, it serves residents in the nearby community. In instances such as these, it was difficult to rely on existing units of government to support the transportation improvement because their boundaries did not coincide with the boundaries of the area benefiting from the improvement.

Special purpose districts are governmental units created by state legislatures to overcome these problems through carrying out only a single purpose of government: for example, construction and operation of an airport. This single purpose distinguishes them from "general purpose" governmental agencies. Also, the geographic boundaries of special purpose districts are drawn up specifically to cover the area to be served by (and, presumably, be willing to pay for) the facility in question. Furthermore, special purpose districts also possess certain other powers of government, such as being able to exercise the right of eminent domain.

- *Eminent domain* is a government power to take land, after fairly compensating its owner, in order to use the land for some public purpose. For example, a state highway agency uses eminent domain to acquire the strip of land (right-of-way) needed for a new highway. States sometimes allow railroads, pipelines, electric utilities, etc., to exercise the right of eminent domain.

Some special purpose districts can assess taxes; most can collect fees from users; and most can issue revenue bonds (pledging their ability to raise funds). Organizationally, these special purpose dis-

---

[17]One portion of Milwaukee's inner harbor today is the original canal route.

tricts are not the same as the conventional executive-legislative-judicial type of government. Usually they are independent of local government, except that local governments sometimes appoint the directors, who sit on the special purpose district's governing board. Sometimes the directors are elected in non-partisan public elections. While the process differs in each state, special purpose districts are somewhat isolated from the conventional political process. In theory, they combine the best of both the public and private enterprise ways of doing things.

However, their advantages were often carried to extremes. Since they dealt only with a single function, they tended to develop "tunnel vision," and they could not see outside their own, single area of concern. They would not cooperate with other agencies. Also, they often became too independent of the political process, and eventually neither knew (nor cared) what the public was thinking. Lastly, they were aided by inflation and able to pay off many debts early. This gave them surplus funds to play with, often to expand further their influence and authority.

High priest of the public authority concept was Robert Moses, a long-time power in New York City and New York State. At one time he controlled four separate New York area authorities, including the Triborough Bridge and Tunnel authority, Jones Beach, Bethpage, the State Power Authority (which constructed and operated the U.S. power facilities of the St. Lawrence Seaway and Power project), plus the New York City Parks Department, the Long Island State Park Commission, and the State Council of Parks.

> With his power, Robert Moses not only shaped New York City but built himself an empire. The capital of this empire was out of public sight—a squat gray building crouching so unobtrusively below the Randall's Island toll plaza of the Triborough Bridge that most of the motorists who drove past the toll booths never knew that the building existed. And most of them were also ignorant of the existence of the empire. But men who were interested in the geography of power were very aware of its existence. They realized that although theoretically it was only a creature of the state, it had in fact become an autonomous sovereign entity.[18]

Moses' power spanned approximately 40 years—1925 to 1965. In this same period, the state's governorship and the city's post of mayor both changed about six times. Moses was a powerful man, and the basis of his financial power was the ability of his various enterprises to generate revenues which could be used as the basis for

---

[18] Robert A. Caro, "The Power Broker," *The New Yorker* (August 19, 1974), p. 42. This is one in a series of four articles appearing in *The New Yorker*, which were later incorporated into a book.

borrowing even more. He realized that since

> . . . each dollar of tolls could capitalize roughly eighteen dollars in bonds, there was an additional built-in multiplier factor at work: the more public works he built, the more money he would have with which to build still more public works. And this factor would work indefinitely—possibly forever.[19]

Because the financial well-being of his empires depended upon toll collections from automobiles, Moses "fought to its death any proposal that city money be spent on mass transit instead of on his highways."[20] This attitude was reflected throughout the country and is one reason why mass transit facilities were allowed to deteriorate. Moses died in 1981.

> Even before his fall [from power], a new generation of urban-affairs experts pilloried him as a power-obsessed elitist who rode roughshod over the niceties of democratic government and wreaked havoc on the neighborhood cohesion of vast areas of the city. But Moses regarded his critics, Caro included, with utter contempt. "Those who can, build," he once said. "Those who can't, criticize."[21]

Special purpose districts and public authorities continue to be used to provide transportation facilities. Ports, airports, and mass transit are the typical examples. Finding the proper balance between insulation and isolation from politics remains difficult.

Public Taxation and Expenditures

Governments raise revenues through a variety of taxes. Most common are taxes on income, sales, property, imports, or on the sale of specific goods such as liquor and cigarettes. Most governments put these receipts into a fund called "general revenue"; at the same time the governing body enacts an annual budget with expenditures totaling about the same amount as receipts. Collecting taxes and allocating the revenue is really a form of "income redistribution." The taxes are collected from one group—those who pay the taxes—and the revenues are spent on programs benefiting other groups. Sometimes the individual paying the taxes receives the benefits, sometimes he or she does not. Some receive more in benefits than they pay in taxes, hence the term *income redistribution*.

Every government program requires revenues and generates benefits and is a form of income redistribution. In order to "sell" a pro-

---

[19]Caro, in *The New Yorker* (August 12, 1974), p. 43.
[20]Caro, in *The New Yorker* (August 19, 1974), p. 62.
[21]*Newsweek* (August 10, 1981), p. 27.

gram politically, it is necessary to design it so that a fairly large segment of society (usually meaning voters) benefits. Thus, some public transportation projects are designed to serve areas that do not need the service. The reality is that the project needs the political support of the people in those areas. This fact is helpful in understanding why some public transportation projects do not seem to follow the same efficiency criteria that would be used by private firms.

- *Efficiency criteria,* as used by private firms, assume that an efficient firm maximizes profits, i.e., the difference between revenues and costs.

Some government receipts are earmarked for special purposes. These receipts are referred to as "dedicated" revenues. As soon as they are collected, these dedicated revenues are placed in a special fund, referred to as a "revolving" fund, which can only be used for specified purposes. The most common transportation example of dedicated revenues is the taxes on gasoline which in many states can be used only for highway purposes. Usually the users do not object to this sort of arrangement because they realize that they are the beneficiaries of the program. The relatively steady flow of funds is necessary to carrying out many construction projects of long duration. Also, projects under way will not be interrupted by the hazards of surviving the annual budget-making process. However, sometimes these funds become too far removed from the political process, and bureaucrats, who proclaim their independence from politicians, have little way of knowing what the public wants. In some large cities in the late 1960's a "freeway revolt" occurred—local citizens successfully fought freeway projects which had been planned for their neighborhoods. Some freeway projects were stopped in their tracks—or in mid-air, if they happened to be elevated. In spite of the opposition from the highway construction and automobile industry it was finally possible for the voters to "crack" the federal Highway Trust Fund and several similar state highway trust funds in the early 1970's. Part of the gasoline tax money collected from motorists is now used to subsidize the construction and operation of mass transit projects.

Funds from federal and state levels of government are usually needed to supplement local funds in order to meet many transportation needs. "Mixing" of funds is common. For example, in 1977, the nation's mass transit industry covered 54 percent of its costs out of farebox receipts. Fourteen percent of its costs were covered by grants from federal programs, 11 percent from state programs, and 20 percent from appropriations made by local units of government.[22] Often federal and state funds have "strings," or requirements, attached. In mass transit aid programs, as an example, the federal program requires local public transit facilities to serve handicapped individuals. The State of California insists that local transit operations receiving state aid cover at least one-third of their costs from farebox receipts. The federal and state requirements conflict with each other to a degree, since serving the handicapped raises a transit operation's costs and may even cut into revenue if handling handicapped passengers increases the time required for buses to complete certain runs to the extent that other passengers are discouraged from using mass transit. Some small California cities have found it cheaper to avoid both the federal and state requirements, pay the subsidies themselves, and run the buses as they choose.

Where governmental revenues are insufficient to cover costs, borrowing is required. A public transportation agency can issue two types of debt obligations. One is called a "full faith and credit" bond: the government or governmental agency pledges its full taxing ability to pay off the bond's interest and principal. The other type of debt obligation, which usually must pay a higher rate of interest, is called a "revenue" bond. Receipts from the project financed by the bond are dedicated to paying off the bond. The most common example of revenue bonds were those issued by toll road authorities in midwestern and eastern states during the 1950's. These bonds were paid off with money collected at the toll booths along these highways.

Interest payments on the debt obligations issued by local and state governments are exempt from federal income taxation. Hence, these securities (often called "municipal" bonds) sell in a market that values them more highly than it does either federal government or private bonds. Therefore, these municipal bonds pay a lower effective rate of interest than do bonds issued by others. Private firms wishing to develop facilities, such as at a port or airport, realize that their total cost will be lower if they can enter into a long-term lease with the unit of government to occupy and operate the facilities and then rely on the governmental unit to count this lease as an asset when borrowing money on the municipal bond market, where interest rates are lower. This money is then used to construct the facility which the private party has already agreed to use. The total cost to the private user is less than if he or she had borrowed in the private (or non-municipal) bond market. The public port or airport authority

---

[22] *Transit Fact Book '78* (Washington, D.C.: American Public Transit Association, 1978), p. 19. One percent of the revenues came from other sources.

can boast of finding a new tenant who would have located else-where, if the authority had not gone along with the proposal. Note that this hastens the spread of public enterprise in those transportation fields where private enterprise might otherwise flourish.

Planning for Public Transportation Facilities

Public transportation agencies use various planning processes in their attempts to meet future public needs. A "chicken or the egg" situation often exists, and it is not clear whether transportation improvements precede or follow growth. Studies of the impact of the San Francisco Bay Area Rapid Transit (BART) system were unable to determine whether this massive undertaking followed or led growth in the area it serves.[23]

Transportation Planning

Public planners initially use population forecasts and estimate that these future populations will "live" in certain areas and work in others. Given these hypothetical passenger "trip-ends" or journey-to-work and return trips, computers are used to assign these projected trips over a number of existing and contemplated passenger transport routes. It is then determined which modal mixes (percentages of people who use auto, bus, and rail) over various routes will provide the best service for a given cost.

Future freight transportation is projected in a similar manner. It is easy to see that consumer goods distribution will follow the location of future populations. Manufacturing firms and wholesalers will be interviewed to determine the present and anticipated flows of materials into and out of their facilities and anticipated changes in resource supplies, such as the depletion of ore or timber. Planners use their best estimates of future freight movements and attempt to design a system of facilities that will best facilitate the anticipated flow.

Costs of contemplated improvements can be estimated and compared with their probable use. Savings in time or in vehicle operating costs to future users can also be estimated, and these are considered as benefits. When the two are compared, the procedure is known as benefit-cost analysis.

[23] Melvin Webber, "The BART Experience—What Have We Learned?" (Berkeley: Institute of Urban and Regional Development Monograph no. 26, 1976).

- *Benefit-cost* analysis is used to compare alternative investment proposals. Potential savings that a proposed project will yield to users are projected into the future, usually over the project's expected life. A rate of interest (often the rate that the public agency must pay to borrow money) is called a *discount rate*; it is used to discount future benefits back to present values (i.e., the value today). Discounting is necessary because future values are worth less today since we must wait to enjoy them. (For the same reason, that is why we collect interest when we loan money we want to be rewarded for postponing our enjoyment from spending it.) The project's present construction costs are taken into account. Future costs, such as maintenance, are also taken into account and discounted back to the present. Comparing the present value of benefits to the present value of costs yields a project's benefit to cost (B/C) ratio. When several projects are compared, the one with the highest B/C ratio should receive the highest priority.[24]

A test of whether the benefits are real would be to institute a system of *user charges* which would collect payments for the benefits each user enjoyed. The money collected in this way should be sufficient to pay for the project. When government fails to institute a system of user charges, it is in effect engaging in a form of *income redistribution*, taking money from whatever sources provided the construction funds. The beneficiaries are those landowners whose properties are close enough to the facilities so that they or their tenants enjoy the time-savings or vehicle operating cost savings that the new transportation facility provides. Landowners will raise the rents charged to tenants to offset whatever values their tenants received from having access to the improved facility. Or if the property owner is a business that ships or receives freight, its own vehicles will benefit from the improvement.

Depending upon the amount of money the public transportation agency has to spend, it programs projects for construction in order of declining B/C ratio. As some projects are completed, they may affect future needs in ways not initially anticipated; hence the evaluation, planning, and programming process is continuous in nature.[25]

---

[24] See: Robert H. Havemen, *The Economics of the Public Sector* (New York: John Wiley and Sons, Inc., 1970), Chapters 5 and 8. Hopefully the B/C ratio is also greater than one. If not, the project's benefits are less than its costs.

[25] As airports are built, their completion and use affects the projected needs for other airports. See: Donald F. Wood, "General Aviation Airport System Planning," *Papers, Transportation Research Forum, 1970* (Oxford, Indiana: Richard B. Cross, 1970), pp. 125–142.

Comprehensive Planning

Public resources devoted to planning transportation are not spent evenly. There is little relationship between the amounts of money spent for planning for the various modes, and the relative importance of each mode to either the total transportation system or to society.

Comprehensive planning is an attempt to overcome these problems. The idea of comprehensive planning is to coordinate planning for all future expenditures on programs for which government is responsible. The goal is to achieve close coordination among different agencies, different levels of government, and the private sector. Through comprehensive planning, proposed transportation projects are evaluated in terms of how well they fit into long-term programs for accomplishing various developmental goals.

Transportation and Land Use Planning

Most usable land in the United States is privately owned. Through *zoning* ordinances, governments are able to control how privately-owned land can be used. For example, zoning can control the height of private structures built outside the end of airport runways; zoning can limit the types of buildings and commercial developments near highway interchanges which could interfere with the safe and smooth flow of traffic using the interchange. The federal Interstate Highway program provided financial incentives to states limiting billboard construction along the Interstate System.[26]

To achieve compatability between a transportation project and its adjoining land, the transportation project can be used to encourage development of the adjoining sites. The single most significant example of transportation's ability to generate land development dates from the nineteenth century when land grants totaling over 223 million acres were given by the federal government to railroads to encourage them to lay track. The grants were in alternate sections (of 36 square miles each) on either side of the tracks.[27] The incentive to the railroad companies was that the value of the land would increase once the track was completed. Conversely, today where it is desira-

---

[26] An alternative to zoning is for government to purchase the land outright to control its use or to purchase an easement, which is the purchase of a portion of the rights associated with the land. Near an airport, for example, an easement might be for everything above 25 feet. The landowner could build no structures or even operate farm implements in the area if they exceeded that height.

[27] Gerald D. Nash, ed., *Issues in American Economic History* (Boston: D.C. Heath & Co., 1964), pp. 322–329. An equal number of sections (the alternates to these given to the railroads) were sold by the government to homesteaders.

ble to retard growth, we can do so by cutting off, or at least not expanding, the capacity of the existing transport facilities. In Yosemite National Park where the large number of visitors and autos is damaging the natural habitat, visitors are encouraged to park their private autos and rely on park-provided buses for traveling within the park. This reduces auto emissions and may even discourage some individuals from visiting the park.

Transportation facilities can also be used as barriers. In the mid-1960's some urban freeways were located to serve as a wall between ghettos and neighborhoods into which the ghettos were expanding. Many housing units were lost to the construction project; these usually came out of the ghetto with the net result being to further increase the pressures on housing existing in the ghetto.

Transportation and Surface Water Planning

There has usually been a gap between planning for land uses and planning for the uses of adjacent surface waters. Planners interested in one were not interested in the other.[28]

Surface water is significant to transportation planners for at least three reasons. First, for rail and highway routes, surface water presents a barrier which is expensive to cross. Surface water crossings, whether bridges, ferries, or tunnels, have great influence on the patterns of traffic leading up to and discharging from the crossing point. Second, surface water is itself a traffic artery, mainly for large vessels (although in Chicago fast boats provide commuter service along the river between Union Station and the North Michigan Avenue area). Third, ports are located at points where it is necessary to change the mode of carriage from water to land. Port facility sites influence both land and water traffic.

Transportation and Human Resource Planning

Government planners were initially concerned only with building public structures. As part of President Lyndon Johnson's "Great Society," government became more involved in a wide range of programs that affected people. Few of these programs dealt directly with transportation, although some programs recognized that there were large groups who were unable to use automobiles and were therefore cut off from the mainstream of a society that assumed everyone either had an auto or had access to one.

[28]Donald F. Wood, "Urban and Basin Planning," *Water Resources Research* (1967), pp. 279–281.

Minority leaders charged that mass transit systems had been laid out in a manner that generally served the community's privileged classes better than it did the needy. (Some claimed that the only job opportunities to which bus routes from the ghettos led were daytime cleaning jobs in white suburbs.) Efforts were made to restructure some bus routes so as to connect the ghettos with additional, more rewarding job opportunities.

In the mid-1970's, considerable interest was shown in the transportation needs of the elderly, the handicapped, and the rural poor.[29] In 1977, the U.S. Department of Transportation went so far as to issue a brochure entitled "The Federal Role in Aiding Pedestrian Traffic," belatedly acknowledging another form of transport.[30] (In some communities, joggers are a political force, demanding paths for their own use and protection from automobiles.)

Encouragement of Research and Development

In a private enterprise system, research and development are encouraged through the motivation for profit. An idea can be patented and the patent holder can sell the rights to use his or her invention. However, as the public role in transportation increases, government also provides more funds for transportation research experimentation.

In the United States, most publicly-funded transportation research is by the U.S. Department of Transportation. In addition, the National Aeronautics and Space Administration (NASA) conducts some research with useful transportation applications, especially aircraft navigation. The military services also experiment with cargo and personnel-handling procedures and equipment. The military services were one of the first major users of the intermodal container system.

- *Intermodal* transportation involves transfer of passengers or cargo between two or more different transport modes in order to make a complete trip. Examples are the combination of airline aircraft and airport limousines used by passengers; another is

[29]Several papers in the 1976 *Proceedings of the Transportation Research Forum* (Oxford, Indiana: Richard B. Cross, 1976) dealt with these topics. For example, see: Alice E. Kidder and others, "Cost of Alternative Systems to Serve Elderly and Handicapped in Small Urban Areas," pp. 131–135; Douglas McKelvey, "Demonstration and the Transportation Disadvantaged," pp. 351–356; and Arthur Saltzman, "Rural Transit Needs and Feasibility Techniques," pp. 491–497.

[30]The brochure was issued by the Federal Highway Administration. Traditionally, many highway improvements have been at the expense of the pedestrian (or bicyclist).

containers, which can be carried by rail car, motor trucks, or ocean vessels.

The supersonic aircraft was first developed for military purposes. In the 1960's federal funds subsidized the design of a proposed U.S. commercial supersonic aircraft (SST). In 1970, the U.S. program was stopped, because of its lackluster prospects for profitability in the future and because of objections of environmental protection interests. The British and French SST, the Concorde, was heavily subsidized by the two respective governments. One reason why these governments continued to subsidize the commercial SST was to help their own aircraft building industry obtain orders from airlines in other countries, although—as it turned out—no other nations bought Concordes.

Research Programs of the U.S. DOT

At present the U.S. Department of Transportation has five sections conducting research into transportation problems. Most of the Department's research activities are centered in the Cambridge, Massachusetts, area, although much of the work is performed by contractors throughout the country.

The Office of Systems Research and Analysis is concerned primarily with data collection and analysis. With the data, this group provides forecasts which are used by government agencies, carriers, and equipment manufacturers. This group also attempts to analyze the impact that contemplated changes in transportation policies will have on shippers and the public.

The *Office of Air and Marine Systems* studies ways of aiding air navigation and improving air travel safety. It is also attempting to develop traffic control procedures for use by vessels in large ports.

The *Office of Ground Systems* has a large testing ground at Pueblo, Colorado, where they test various types of equipment used by mass transit operators. This group is also concerned with problems of rail track and right-of-way construction procedures and the safety of rail operations.

The *Office of Advanced Systems* claims a multi-modal perspective and looks at future solutions to transport problems. This group attempts to point out promising areas for research and development.

The *Office of Energy and Environment* experiments with methods of improving fuel efficiency in vehicles and reducing the adverse environmental impacts of vehicle operations. For example, this group monitored the noise levels of the Concorde SST when it began operating at U.S. airports.

The Taxi Project

An example of how public agencies can attract private efforts to design new vehicles was the Taxi Project of the Museum of Modern Art in New York City.[31] The Museum staff, working with others, drew up specifications for an "urban" vehicle which could also be used as a taxi. Exterior dimensions of the proposed vehicle were not large, although it was to seat two or three passengers comfortably and four, if necessary. Numerous additional specifications covered equipment unique to taxicabs as would be used in New York City, such as meters, exterior lighting, and so on.[32] After the vehicles were displayed, they were to be tested in actual taxi use in New York City.

> The Museum sought the widest American participation for the Taxi Project. Ford, General Motors, Chrysler and American Motors were approached first; other American manufacturers later approached included Mack Trucks and Checker Motors, companies engaged directly in vehicle production; the rest were major American corporations in various ways concerned with engine and/or agricultural and construction vehicle design. . . . All declined to participate. Consequently, the U.S. Department of Transportation, through its Urban Mass Transportation Administration, made funds available—through open-bid competition for two American companies that would create a low-pollution taxi vehicle.[33]

Figure 2–4 shows a vehicle produced by one of the two U.S. firms that received a DOT contract to build the Museum's desired taxi. The Museum also then opened its competition to foreign manufacturers who would "commit themselves to mass-produce such a taxi in the United States if the market proved satisfactory."[34] Volvo and Volkswagen responded to the invitation and displayed vehicles. Alfa-Romeo, an Italian manufacturer, also displayed a vehicle that met the project's specifications, although it indicated that the vehicle was intended for the European taxi market only.

Long-term results of the project are still not apparent. One can only speculate as to the reasons why U.S. manufacturers were reluc-

---

[31] Assisting in the project were the U.S. Urban Mass Transportation Administration, Mobil Oil Corporation, The Taxi and Limousine Commission of New York City, the New York City Taxi Drivers' Union (Local 3036, AFL-CIO), and the International Taxicab Association. The actual Museum display was from June 17, 1976, to September 6, 1976.

[32] *The Taxi Project: Realistic Solutions for Today* (New York: The Museum of Modern Art, 1976), pp. 93–104.

[33] Ibid., p. 16.

[34] Ibid., p. 16.

Figure 2–4 Drawing of Paratransit Vehicle Designed by American Machine and Foundry for TAXI Exhibit. Courtesy: ASL Engineering, Inc.

tant to participate. We did learn what types of vehicles would be forthcoming if the Museum's specifications were to be met.

Summary

This chapter has discussed the government as a provider of transportation programs and facilities. The government does this because private enterprise cannot be relied upon to provide the necessary transportation functions. Historically, the capital investment requirements of some projects were so high that private investors could not raise the needed funds. Landowners often clamored for public transportation improvements which would enhance the value of their land holdings.

Government involvement in transportation differs according to the mode of transportation. Pipelines for carrying petroleum and petroleum products are at the private enterprise side of the spectrum. Their rates and services are regulated, however. At the other end of the spectrum, Amtrak is entirely governmentally owned and operated. Most other modes of transport fall somewhere in between. In the case of highways, government provides the rights-of-way over which private vehicles operate. These vehicles, however, pay for a portion of the highway costs through payment of gasoline taxes and other user charges.

The principal government transportation agency at the federal level is the U.S. Department of Transportation.

Special purpose districts, also called public authorities, are established to provide a specific type of transportation facility. They are somewhat insulated from the routine political processes. In some instances they were too insulated, and became almost completely independent of public control. For example, Robert Moses of New York used public authorities as the basis of his longtime influence and power.

Benefit-cost analysis is used to rate the relative desirability of alternative transportation improvements. Transportation planning must be related to other forms of planning and to the private sector.

Efforts of the New York Museum of Modern Art to find a "new" taxi design showed that U.S. auto manufacturers were uninterested. The U.S. DOT had to fund development of prototype taxis and foreign manufacturers had to be asked to supply vehicles for the display and evaluation.

Questions for Discussion and Review

1. Did you find that governmental involvement in the transportation sector was more, less, or about what you expected it to be before you read the chapter? Why?

2. Why has the federal government historically been actively involved in the transportation sector of the economy?

3. Discuss some examples of "the inseparability of politics and economics" which are mentioned in this chapter.

4. The federal government has been involved to some extent with each of the five basic modes of transportation. With which mode has it been the most extensively involved? With which has it had the least involvement? Discuss.

5. Do you believe the federal government has unfairly assisted some modes of transportation relative to others? Defend your answer.

6. Discuss each of the major operating agencies of the U.S. Department of Transportation.

7. Discuss the work of the National Highway Traffic Safety Administration.

8. What functions does the National Transportation Safety Board perform? Why is it autonomous from the DOT?

9. Discuss the major findings of the National Transportation Policy Study Commission. Which recommendation do you believe is the most important and which the least important? Defend your answer.

10. Discuss the future transportation activity projected by the National Transportation Policy Study Commission. What are the implications of these projections on job opportunities in the transportation sector of the economy?

11. What are special purpose districts? What are their strengths? What are their weaknesses?

12. Robert Moses strongly opposed improvements in the mass transit system for New York City. Why?

13. Benefit-cost analysis is commonly utilized by government units. What is it? What are its pros and cons?

14. Discuss the relationship between transportation system planning and comprehensive planning.

15. How does zoning affect land-use planning?

16. The federal government is actively involved in sponsoring research and development activities. Discuss two areas of federally-sponsored transportation research.

17. Do you believe the federal government should actively sponsor transportation research projects? Defend your answer.

18. Why do you think that U.S. auto manufacturers were not interested in participating in the "taxi project"?

19. What conflicts result if we attempt to both (1) achieve a more equitable distribution of income and (2) have a more efficient economy? Give some examples from transportation.

20. Assume you are a transportation consultant. A client of yours is interested in projecting the role of the federal government as a provider of transportation services and facilities during 1986 to 1990. Based on the current political situation and your understanding of this issue, write a brief memo to your client outlining your position on this question. Be sure to defend your position.

Additional Chapter References

A Survey of Railroads in Selected Industrial Countries (New York: The Union Pacific Railroad Co., 1977).

Armstrong, Ellis L., ed., *History of Public Works in the United States* (Chicago: American Public Works Association, 1976).

Bauer, C. S., and others, *Manpower Analysis in Transportation Safety* (Orlando, Florida: Transportation Systems Institute of the Florida Technological University, May, 1977).

California Transportation Plan Task Force, *Recommended Statewide Transportation Goals, Policies and Objectives* (Sacramento, 1977).

Caro, Robert A., "The Power Broker," a series of four articles appearing in *The New Yorker* (July and August, 1974).

Davis, F. W., and K. Oen, *Solving Public Passenger Transportation Problems: A Need for Policy Reorientation* (Knoxville: University of Tennessee Transportation Center, 1977).

Dorfman, Robert, ed., *Measuring Benefits of Government Investments* (Washington, D.C.: The Brookings Institution, 1965).

Due, John F., "Government Versus Private Financing of the Railroad Industry," *Transportation Journal* (Spring, 1982), pp. 16–21.

Gallamore, Robert E., "Implications of Federal Railroad Assistance," *Annual Proceedings of the American Society of Traffic and Transportation* (1980), pp. 85–89.

Johnson, James C., "Lessons From Amtrak and Conrail," *ICC Practitioners' Journal* (March–April, 1982), pp. 247–256.

Johnson, Marc A., "Planning Rural Freight Transport Systems," *Annual Proceedings of the Transportation Research Forum* (1981), p. 356.

Linehand, Ronald C., Michael Walton, and Richard Dodge, *Variables in Rural Plant Location: A Case Study of Sealy, Texas* (Austin: University of Texas Council for Advance Transportation Studies, research memo 21, 1975).

"Majority of U.S. Communities Dependent on Trucking Industry," *The Kansas Transporter* (September, 1976), pp. 38–39.

Miller, James C., III, ed., *Perspectives on Federal Transportation Policy* (Washington, D.C.: American Enterprise Institute for Public Policy Research, 1975).

National Transportation Policy Study Commission, *National Transportation Policies Through the Year 2000* (Washington, D.C., 1979, available from the Superintendent of Documents, Washington, D.C., 20402).

Rao, Kant, and Thomas D. Larson, "Capital Investment, Performance, and Pricing in Highways," *Transportation Journal* (Spring, 1982), pp. 22–33.

Rayner, Nigel, "Rural Roads and Economic Development in Ethiopia," *The Logistics and Transportation Review*, Vol. 16, No. 4 (1980), pp. 313–324.

United Nations Industrial Development Organization, *The Motor Vehicle Industry* (New York: United Nations, 1972).

U.S. Department of Transportation, *Energy Primer* (Cambridge, Mass.: Transportation Systems Center, 1975).

———, *Mobility of People and Goods in the Urban Environment—Mobility of the Handicapped and Elderly* (Washington, D.C.: Office of the Secretary, Office of University Research, September, 1976).

———, *Rural Passenger Transportation*, a state-of-the-art-review (Cambridge, Mass.: Transportation Systems Center, 1976).

———, *Solving Public Passenger Transportation Problems: A Need for Policy Reorientation*, Vol. 11, Final Report (Washington, D.C.: Office of the Secretary, Office of University Research, January, 1977).

———, *Tourist Traffic In Small Historic Cities: Analysis, Strategies, and Recommendations*, Final Report (Washington, D.C.: Office of the Secretary, Office of University Research, September, 1976).

U.S. Energy Resources Council, The *Report by the Federal Task Force on Motor Vehicle Goals Beyond 1980*, Vol. 1 (Washington, D.C.: The Energy Resources Council, September 2, 1976).

Whitehurst, Clinton H., *The Defense Transportation System, Competitor or Complement of the Private Sector?"* (Washington, D.C.: American Enterprise Institute for Public Policy Research, October, 1976).

Williams, Ernest W., Jr., "The National Transportation Policy Study Commission and its Final Report: A Review," *Transportation Journal* (Spring, 1980), pp. 5–19.

Wood, Donald F., "State-Level Transportation Planning Considerations," *Traffic Quarterly*, Vol. XXII, No. 2, pp. 191–202.

Case 2–1   Electrifying Amtrak Case

In response to increased Congressional criticism concerning the costs of subsidizing Amtrak, one of the railroad's staff was told to estimate the costs and benefits of electrification of a stretch of Amtrak's busy route in the Northeast Corridor. The capital outlay would be extremely high, but afterwards the annual costs would be much lower than if diesel engines continued in use. It was hoped that this electrification would be paid for with a one-time grant from Congress which would be justified as helping Amtrak "get on its feet" and be a viable competitor with other modes of passenger transport. While Congressmen were tiring about hearing just how much more would be needed by Amtrak (or Conrail) in order for them to be healthy, a key member of the Congressional Surface Transportation Committee had confided to Amtrak's managers that the next appropriation would probably be their last chance for any large capital improvements. After that, the Committee's membership was expected to change, and the Northeast would lose two votes.

The planner was told to calculate benefit-cost ratios for two alternatives: electrifying the track (and buying electric locomotives) or upgrading the service by replacing existing diesel engines in the early 1980's. The year 1980 was to be the base-line for the calculations. Costs and benefits in that year were to be taken at the full value. Costs and benefits programmed or projected for future years were to be discounted back to 1980. Inflation could be ignored, and one of the planner's friends, who worked in the Office of Management and Budget, suggested that a 5 percent discount rate be used. (If inflation were to be taken into account, all future costs and benefits would first be increased by the anticipated rate of inflation, and then a higher discount rate, 5 percent plus the rate of inflation, would be used.) The commitment to either electric or diesel power would hold for 20 years, and the benefit-cost calculations were an effort to make the best decision in 1980.

The electrification project would require a $100-million outlay in 1980 for electrifying the right-of-way and purchasing new electric locomotives. Service under the new system would start on January 1, 1981. Electricity for operating the trains was estimated to cost $5 million per year, and maintenance of the overhead wire system and the engines was estimated to cost $10 million per year. At the end of the year 2000 there would be no salvage value remaining in the system.

The diesel-upgrading alternative would require that $5 million a year be spent in four years, 1980, 1981, 1982, and 1983 (total cost $20 million), to purchase new diesel locomotives. Existing locomotives would be phased out and, in each of the four years, could be sold for $1 million (total receipts—$4 million). Diesel fuel would cost $15 million per year and maintenance would be $10 million per year. At the end of the year 2000, the diesels would have a total salvage value of $5 million.

Benefits, measured as ticket sales less expenses of serving passengers, would be $25 million per year for the diesel system and $30 million for the electric system (which was expected to attract more patrons). No other costs or benefits needed to be considered at this time.

Case Table 2–1–1 shows the present value of $1,000 some years in the future discounted back at a rate of 5 percent. That is, if somebody promised to pay you $1,000 in seven years, and you thought that 5 percent was the rate of interest—or discount—to use, that obligation to pay $1,000 seven years from now is worth $711 today.

CASE TABLE 2–1–1   Present Value of $1,000 at 5% Discount Rate

Year	Value	Year	Value
1	$952	11	$585
2	907	12	557
3	864	13	530
4	823	14	505
5	784	15	481
6	746	16	458
7	711	17	436
8	677	18	416
9	645	19	396
10	614	20	377

Question One: Using Case Table 2–1–1, calculate the ratio of benefits to costs for the diesel alternative.

Question Two: Using Case Table 2–1–1, calculate the ratio of benefits to costs for the electrification alternative.

Question Three: Based on data given in the case, which of the two alternatives—electrification or diesel upgrading—would you recommend? Why?

Question Four: Which one of the alternatives is less dependent upon foreign control of oil supplies and prices? Does the analysis to this point give proper weight to this factor? If not, what changes in the analysis are needed?

Question Five: What is the impact of high interest rates on benefit-cost analysis of projects such as these? Discuss.

Question Six: What other factors, not given in the case, should probably be taken into account?

Case 2–2   City of Progress International Airport Case

It was a gloomy post–Proposition 13* meeting in the office of Charles Atkinson, airport director for the City of Progress in southern California. Atkinson was just finishing telling the group what the mayor had told him: "There are no more local funds to support the airport; charge everyone who uses it his or her 'fair' share; and if some won't pay, 'kick their ass out'." Atkinson was a City of Progress

*Proposition 13, adopted by California's voters in 1978, reduced local property taxes.

employee; all of the other people in the room represented the airport's various users. They were Grant Young, the fixed base operator who leased a hangar and another small building and serviced most of the airport's general aviation users; Jaime Trigo, representing Tijuana International Airways, a Mexican airline offering the only direct service between Tijuana and City of Progress, making it an international airport; Catherine Clausen, who operated a newsstand in the airport terminal building and was representing similar tenants; Donald Morrison, station agent for one of the domestic airlines, who was representing all of the airlines using the airport (except Tijuana International); Michael Piscatello, who operated the airport's parking concessions; and Barry Wood, manager of a nearby hotel, who was representing the several hotels and motels near the airport. This group was seated around the table in Atkinson's conference room.

Also present, but sitting on chairs along the wall, were Corrine Hall, a nearby resident who continually campaigned against airport noise and airport expansion, and Mark Connolly, who had spearheaded the pro–Proposition 13 campaign in the City of Progress. Both looked happy when Eddie Yeung, reporter for the *Progress Herald,* walked in and sat along the opposite wall. Atkinson would have preferred that no reporters be present; however, either Mrs. Hall or Connolly probably told Yeung of the meeting, since both of them enjoyed seeing their names in the paper.

Morrison spoke: "What the hell does the mayor mean by 'fair share'? Our industry is going through deregulation, with its horrors, and let me tell you, folks, there's going to be no blood to be found in this turnip!"

"Oh, Morrison, you've been poor-mouthing it ever since they built this airport," scolded Ms. Clausen. "Personally, I'm glad to see you cut fares. It brings more business walking through the airport. I think that is good."

"Listen, Catherine," responded Morrison, "you've got more of a monopoly with your newsstand in the airport than we have. How would you like it if there were three newsstands here? You couldn't get two dollars for a *New York Times* then, could you?"

Ms. Clausen glared at him, started to speak, and decided not to.

Trigo spoke up and said: "I can feel for the U.S. airlines, but we're only a small carrier, barely out of the red. If we have to pay more here, we'll pull out and you'll lose your international status. Also . . ."

"Stuff it," said Morrison. "Pretty soon laetrile will be legalized here, and you'll lose most of your business."

"I resent that slur," said Trigo. "Why are you so uptight when the subject we're discussing is paying one's 'fair' share? Does the idea bother you?"

Atkinson intervened. "Before we get into more arguments, we should have some idea as to what costs we're talking about—past, present, and future. We mustn't forget our plans for expansion."

"Why not?" yelled Corrine Hall. "I don't want you to expand, and I think public airports are one sort of wasteful public operation that Proposition 13 was aimed at. We're through being taxed for your follies! Nobody around here benefits from the airport. We—the airport's 'neighbors'—would be just as happy if you closed down."

"That's not so," interjected Wood. "There are numerous motels and restaurants, off of airport property, who pay property taxes and support large payrolls. We need the airport." There was a silence.

Atkinson said: "The mayor is insisting that every user pay enough to cover his or her share of the costs. I don't know how we will allocate costs since many of them are for features that several types of users or groups share. But I've got some statistics for starters. First of all, the airport is built on 200 acres of land, which we purchased in 1952 at $500 per acre. The terminal occupies only two acres; ten acres are devoted to parking; five acres are devoted to the general aviation hangar and the fixed base operation; five acres are devoted to the ramps outside the terminal where airline aircraft park and 75 acres are devoted to runways and taxiways."

"That doesn't add up to 200," said Piscatello. "Remember, if you're going to divide the cost of the land and assess users, use 200 acres as your total. All that empty area out there between the runways should be assigned to them. Also, you said that ten acres is devoted to parking, my lease says only nine. I use eight acres for long-term parking and one acre for one-hour parking. That's all."

"The other acre of parking is used by the car rental agencies," said Atkinson.

"Well, be sure to charge them for it, not me, in your cost allocation schemes," said Piscatello.

"Wait a minute!" shouted Ms. Clausen. "Piscatello doesn't pay rent for the inside of the terminal while the poor car rental agencies pay small fortunes for their little cubby holes. For what they pay to be inside the terminal they should have that acre outside as a 'freebie'."

"Let them move their business outside, too," argued Piscatello. "In some airports, car rental agencies are outside the terminal building."

"That's right," yelled Wood. "We'd be glad to rent them space in our lobbies. Not only that, we pay *taxes* on our property. The airport doesn't!"

"You tell 'em, son," said Connolly to Wood. "Our leader would be proud of you. He said all these bureaucrats needed a red-hot poker shoved up their you-know-what. Ha-ha."

Atkinson flushed. "Let me continue, I've got a lot more figures. Actually, I didn't quite finish talking about acres. We have ten acres devoted to roads, and they can be allocated this way: airline passenger dropoff and pickup, 25%; air freight, 10%; taxi and airline limousine, 10%; airport hotel/motel pickup and dropoff, 10%; car rentals, 5%; general aviation, 15%; and the rest I can't allocate."

Piscatello spoke up: "You forgot that some of your roads are used solely by airport vehicles, mainly to maintain the runways. Why don't you assign something to them?"

"Don't forget the airport fire station," said Wood. "They're here to protect the planes and have a whole batch of roads set out for themselves."

Atkinson retorted: "Let me go off the record for a minute, if I may, Eddie," and he waited for Yeung to put down his pencil. "Let's keep the fire station and equipment out of this discussion. Right now, they are in the city's fire department budget, and I want to keep it that way. OK, now, we're back on the record."

Eddie Yeung picked up his pencil in anticipation of further discussion, which did not come.

Atkinson continued. "Let's talk about the terminal. It has 10,000 square feet. Half of it was built in 1954 at a cost of $600,000 and the other half was done in 1971 at a cost of $1.1 million."

"Why did the new half cost twice as much?" asked Trigo. "It looks like a carbon copy of the old half."

"Oh, mainly inflation," responded Atkinson. "My dollar figures are for dollars of whatever year I mention. Right now, to replace the entire structure would take $3 million."

"What would it cost to buy the land today?" asked Ms. Hall. "Just think, this could have been a fine residential area and all we have is noise and fumes." While talking, she noticed that Yeung was not writing, so she stopped.

"Frankly, I don't know what the land is or would be worth today," stated Atkinson. "We could sell it for several million, I am sure. Although we could probably buy another 200 acres, a few miles out for two or three hundred dollars per acre. What I want to do now is tell how the terminal building is used. Of the 10,000 square feet, 1,000 are used for restaurants; 200 for car rental agencies; 500 for airport offices; 500 for the newsstand; 200 for the airline limo booth; 2,500 for airline ticket counters; 1,500 for handling airline passenger baggage; 500 for airline air freight; 500 for U.S. customs; 500 for the duty-free shop and currency exchange used by our international passengers; and the remainder is hallways, restrooms, lobbies, etc. This remainder could be allocated to all the others."

"Why?" asked Ms. Clausen. "They're all used by airline passengers. Why not allocate the lobbies, restrooms, etc., directly to the airline tenants?"

"I disagree," said Morrison. "You forget that some locations in the building are more desirable than others. Catherine's shop is closest to the main entrance where everyone walks by. I think choice locations should pay more. That's the way the real estate market works."

"You bet!" added Connolly. "Make 'em pay."

"Tell us about the runways," chimed in Ms. Hall. "Tell us what they cost and who is going to pay for them."

"The initial runway project in 1954 cost $1.4 million. Since then, there have been several additions to the runways, the ramps, and the taxiways. As best as I can tell, we've spent a total of $2.2 million, including the initial $1.4 million. I'd guess the replacement cost of all that pavement and lighting would be $3.5 to $4 million." Atkinson noticed that Connolly had raised his hand. "Mr. Connolly?"

"Let's see your budget, young man," cackled Connolly. "We're not interested in how you wasted money before, or how much it would cost to rebuild this monument to public enterprise which—if my memory serves me correctly—drove a taxpaying, God-fearing private airport operator out of business. We want to see your budget today, and we'll show you how to cut out some expenditures. We'll tell you what Proposition 13 means. Frankly, I wish this meeting would hurry up. I've got to carry the people's message to our local school board as well. They'll be meeting in half an hour."

There was a slight twinkle in Atkinson's eye when he addressed Connolly. "Gee whiz, it's going to take me a half hour to get the budget figures together. Not only that, before the meeting I promised to gather some data on our revenues and our activities. The best I can do," added Atkinson, "is to adjourn this meeting until after lunch." He stood. "How about 2 P.M.?"

"You nurd!" shrieked Ms. Hall. "You're doing this so there will be nothing for the *Progress Herald* to report. They go to press at noon. You've done *this* before! I'm going to call both TV stations and tell them to cover the afternoon meeting. I hope their lights heat up this room real hot!"

"Damned goldbrickers," muttered Connolly. "I'm off to the school board, carrying the Word." The room emptied.

*   *   *

It was 2 P.M. The same group had gathered around the table, although Connolly, Hall, and Yeung were absent from the sidelines. "Where's the TV?" asked Young.

Atkinson replied. "WCOW called at 1:30 but didn't seem that interested in our agenda. They said Ms. Hall had tipped them."

"Where's Ms. Hall?" inquired Morrison. "Dare we start without her?"

"Sure we can start," said Wood. "She's over in my coffee shop, sitting near the window, waiting for the TV truck to roll up. If it comes, she'll show."

"Why doesn't she get her coffee at the airport restaurant?" asked Ms. Clausen.

"She can't afford your prices," retorted Wood. "We don't have the monopoly that the airport concessionaires do."

"Maybe she just wanted some more action than can be found here," retorted Ms. Clausen.

"Enough of that," said Atkinson. "Now, here are the budget figures we wanted. They're from the city budget. They show up two places. Under debt retirement, the 1952 bonds for the land and the 1954 bonds for the first part of the terminal are paid off. The city is still paying off the 1954 runway bonds; they're for 30 years and the annual payment is $108,000. The 1971 bonds for terminal expansion are for 20 years and the annual payment is $134,000. There were some other runway expansion and lighting projects for which the city used some of its general obligation bonds. Our share of the repayment of those is $58,000, annually."

"Who pays those bonds off?" asked Trigo. "I never heard of them before when you've told us about your budget."

Atkinson answered: "The city does. To date, we've only been expected to cover operating costs out of our revenues. Right now, our operating budget runs at one million a year. For the terminal building we're spending $165,000, which includes $100,000 for personnel; $50,000 for supplies; and $15,000 for renovation to the building—in case we have to do something for a new tenant. The rest of the money is spent on the airport outside the terminal building. It runs $575,000 for personnel, $225,000 for supplies and services provided by outsiders, and $35,000 for capital equipment—anything with a life over two years."

"That's a million dollars," said Morrison. "That's about what you get here from your users, isn't it?"

"Right," answered Atkinson. "Last year we earned $525,000 from space rentals in the terminal. We rent on a square foot basis; our highest revenues on that basis come from the insurance vending machines, and our lowest rentals come from the U.S. customs. We get 10 percent of the parking lot's gross, which last year gave us $35,000. We get one percent of the general aviation fixed base operator's gross, which gave us $90,000, plus a penny a gallon on his fuel sales, giving us another $10,000. We get $15,000 from the airport limo operator, who pays us 25 cents for every passenger carried. Lastly, we get landing fees from the airlines by charging $50 for each scheduled flight. That gave us $340,000."

"Wait," said Trigo. "You're over one million."

"Yeah, by a bit," answered Akinson. "Remember, we have to estimate revenues."

Morrison asked: "Does the mayor want you to start covering payments on the bonds?"

"That's right," responded Atkinson. "I should add that he's mad at business and right-wingers for passing Prop. 13, and he said I should be especially sure to see that general aviation gets to pay its 'fair' share."

"We already do," protested Young.

"Like hell you do," answered Morrison. "Those fat-cat customers of yours with dough enough for a plane and a gimmick to write it off as a 'business expense' have been sucking at the public tit for years."

"Cool it," said Atkinson. "Now, here's some measures of airport activity. We board about 175,000 airline passengers a year and 100,000 pounds of air freight. Young estimated his operation boards about 400,000 people a year, but most of that is for training, sightseeing, and the like. Only a couple of corporate planes and some charter jobs provided point-to-point transportation. Also, at his terminal about 5,000 pounds of air freight are loaded."

Morrison said, "I think you ought to be charging him for all the 'touch and go' operations his student pilots make. Sometimes it's several hundred a day."

"You're right in terms of numbers," answered Atkinson. "If you count each one of those as a flight operation, they give us over half of our annual operations. On some weekends they account for 90 percent."

"Yeah," said Young, "but don't try to stick us with the cost of 7,000 feet of pavement or the terminal. We don't use the terminal, and we could do with 2,500 feet of runway thinner and narrower than what we have. It was designed for airline aircraft and I think they should pay for it. We could still get by with that private strip Connolly said our airport drove out of business."

"Is Young right about needing only 2,500 feet?" asked Morrison. "I've seen him handle some 4-engined prop jobs at his operation."

"I hear you," answered Atkinson, "but what he said is close to correct. We have no actual counts, but I'm sure that 99 percent of Young's business needs only 2,500 feet of runway. Just about every airline flight needs over 5,000. On the other hand, airlines accounted for 6,800 operations, and general aviation, somewhere between 300,000 and 400,000."

Piscatello said: "There's no single way to catch all the airport users except at the airport extrance. There's a single road coming in, and you could build a toll booth, with different charges for autos, limos, and those buses . . ."

"But that won't catch all those general aviation pilots practicing their 'touch and gos'," interjected Morrison.

"I think it's important to get the money out of our general aviation users," said Ms. Clausen. "They never use the terminal so the airport doesn't get anything out of them."

"That's not so!" said Young. "The city gets a percent of my gross and also a penny a gallon on fuel. Airlines don't even buy fuel here. Besides, who would use the terminal anyhow except some captive passenger who can't escape your prices. In fact, Wood's motel limo takes some passengers over to his spot for lunch and back just so they can avoid airport restaurant food and prices."

"I didn't know that," said Atkinson. "Wood, you're cutting into our revenues. We get a percent of our restaurants' gross."

"Can't we charge the general aviation students for their 'touch and gos'?" asked Trigo.

"It would be costly to administer," answered Atkinson. "They're hard to count and may use either end of the runway."

"Why should we pay?" asked Young. "The airport wasn't built for us. Why not a tax on each airline passenger? That would be easy to administer and collect. Besides, the airlines could pass the cost on in the ticket price and it would be painless."

"I don't think you should use Proposition 13 as a way of burdening international commerce between California and your neighbor to the south," said Trigo.

"Hell," said Morrison, "you're carrying more Americans south than Mexicans north. You're not helping our balance of payments at all."

"Could we just put higher charges on the parking lot and also charge for parking near the general aviation facility?" asked Ms. Clausen.

"No," said Atkinson. "We'd miss those who show up by limo or cab, hotel bus passengers, and those who are dropped off or picked up by family."

Young said, "I'd like to go back to my earlier point, a head tax on airline passengers. Most of them are paying high fares, anyhow, so they won't notice the addition to the fare. A few dollars isn't much for somebody who's going across the country."

"That's not fair at all," responded Morrison. "Most of your customers just fly for recreation. Why don't they pay more? They'd have to if they played golf or tennis on Sundays."

Question One: Under present procedures, which investment—in the terminal or in the remainder of the airport—appears to be paying more than it should?

Question Two: Taking into consideration your answer to Question One, if the City of Progress were contemplating an additional investment at the airport, which would appear to have the higher rate of return, an investment in expanding the terminal, or an investment in expanding the remainder of the airport? Could this result in an inefficient allocation of resources? If so, how?

Question Three: How equitably do you think the airport's present costs are shared by those who use it?

Question Four: How equitably are they shared in terms of those who benefit from the airport?

Question Five: If you could reallocate costs, how would you do it? (Disregard any problems in collecting fees or administering the allocation scheme.)

Question Six: What benefits does the City of Progress enjoy or receive from having its airport?

Question Seven: Do you think that the benefits listed in the answer to Question Six justify a public subsidy for the airport? Why?

Deregulation and a slumping economy have caused many stresses and strains on our transportation system. This is one of several Eastern Airlines' advertisements featuring Frank Borman speaking on airline issues.

Courtesy Eastern Airlines.

3 Regulating and Deregulating Transportation

Long before it became a pattern of our political economy, the ICC and the transport industries forged a corporate state that utilized public power for private pursuits. . . . All of the now-familiar trappings of such a condition appeared early in the ICC—routine movement of personnel into the industry, absence of rigorous Congressional scrutiny, heavy political overtones to agency decisions, rigid barriers to citizen-consumer access to and participation in ICC proceedings, wholly unjustified secrecy, poor analytic and fact gathering performances, failure to base decisions on reasoned explanations, and a gross dereliction in helping to shape a far-sighted transportation policy.

THE RALPH NADER STUDY GROUP
The Interstate Commerce Ommission
1970

The position of the shipping public was ambivalent and dichotomous. Both the deregulators and those who were against change claimed to have shipper (or receiver) support. If forced to generalize, it could be said that large shippers were in favor of deregulation while small shippers and small consignees were opposed. Rural areas and small communities were apparently against any substantial changes in regulation.

JAMES P. RAWKOWSKI
Traffic Quarterly
October, 1981

We are currently considering the various possibilities in an effort to determine what, if anything, now remains of the common carrier obligation in terms of the commission's ability to enforce such obligation when called upon to do so.

REESE H. TAYLOR, JR.
Chairman, Interstate Commerce Commission
November 4, 1981

It was the pugnacious chairman of World Airways, Edward J. Daly, who unleashed the transcontinental air fare wars in 1979. Today it appears that Daly is scrambling to avoid becoming the first fatality of the ticket discounts. . . .

World Airways executives considered the airline's problems severe enough to seek government help, and on Tuesday [March 23, 1982] it asked the Civil Aeronautics Board . . . to halt what it called "irrational" price-cutting.

Chicago Tribune
March 25, 1982

Introduction

Transportation has been regulated for many years. Even English common law placed certain responsibilities on those who carried passengers or freight for hire. Here in the United States, the federal government began regulating interstate railroads in 1887. Every other form of transportation, in its turn, came under our government's economic regulation.

In very recent years, this has been reversed. Major segments of our air, motor, and rail industries have been freed from governmental regulatory restraints. Many carrier firms have portions of their operations subject to economic regulation while other portions of their operations are not. Regulatory bodies and courts, carriers, and shippers are still attempting to determine what the new laws mean.

Theory of Regulation

Why Governments Regulate Transportation

The transportation industry is a public utility in the sense that it is an industry which is vital to the overall public interest. Almost every business firm and every individual is directly affected by the transportation industry. Therefore, because of the way transportation pervades the health and vitality of our national economy, it became a governmental responsibility to insure that the transportation sector operated fairly and without unfair discrimination against its users. To achieve this objective, government controlled the number of transport competitors, along with their rates and the services they were allowed to offer. Since the full force of competition was suppressed by entry control (which limited the number of new competitors in the transportation industry), it was necessary for the government to insure that the positive attributes of a competitive market—innovative services, competitive prices, new technology—were achieved. A leading scholar in government-business relationships, Professor Clair Wilcox, observed, "Government was, therefore, compelled to intervene to safeguard the public interest. Regulation was thus a substitution for competition. Where competition was impossible, its [regulation's] purpose was to bring the benefits that competition would have brought."[1]

---

[1] Clair Wilcox, *Public Policies Toward Business*, 3rd ed. (Homewood, Ill.: Richard D. Irwin, Inc., 1966), p. 286.

To further appreciate the rationale of regulation of the transportation industry, it is helpful to examine the railroad industry. U.S. transport regulation started with the railroad mode, and subsequent transport regulation was based on the railroad precedent.

Railroads are often described as natural monopolies. It is believed that competition between firms in a "natural monopoly" situ-

- A *natural monopoly* exists when the needs of a market can be supplied most efficiently (i.e., at the lowest cost) by a single producer.

ation wastes resources. Geography, and the known technology of railroad construction, often dictated that a single railroad was the best method of serving many areas of our country. Railroads enjoy increasing economies of scale as their volume of business increases. This is because of their cost structure. About half of a railroad's costs are considered as fixed, or constant, costs; they include property

- *Fixed costs* do not vary with a firm's output and must be covered even if the firm is closed down, such as by a strike or for a holiday. As a railroad's volume of business increases, these fixed costs are spread over a larger volume of shipments, reducing the *average* cost of carrying each. Thus they contribute toward becoming an economy of scale.

taxes, roadbed and track, tunnels, bridges, car classification yards, and similar cost items which do not vary with the amount of traffic the railroad carries.

Railroad's variable costs are also about 50 percent of the total cost structure and consist of the following items: crew wages, fuel, depreciation of equipment based on usage, lubricants, repairs and maintenance, and other items whose cost is not incurred unless the transportation service is produced.

- *Variable costs* change directly with the amount of business. They can only be avoided by not operating; hence a rational businessperson will not operate unless the revenues from a specific operation exceed its variable costs.

An example will indicate the cost advantage to a railroad of achieving a high volume of traffic. Assume that one railroad operates with fixed costs of $5,000 per day and variable costs of $1.00 per ton shipped between origin and destination. If 5,000 tons are shipped per day, the railroad's full costs are $2.00 per ton ($5,000 ÷ 5,000 tons = $1.00 fixed costs per ton + $1.00 variable costs per ton). If the

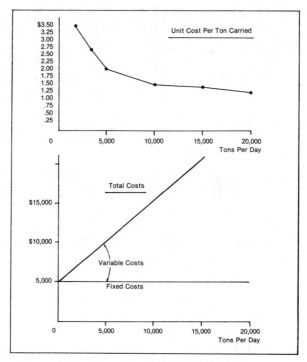

Figure 3–1 Example of Railroad Cost Structure.

railroad can ship 10,000 tons per day its full costs per ton become $1.50 ($5,000 ÷ 10,000 tons = 50¢ fixed costs per ton + $1.00 variable costs per ton). If the carrier can again double its traffic to 20,000 tons per day, the cost per ton becomes $1.25 ($5,000 ÷ 20,000 tons = 25¢ fixed costs per ton + $1.00 variable costs per ton). This is shown in Figure 3–1. With this example in mind, notice the advantage to the shipping public of one large railroad in terms of tons transported as opposed to four smaller carriers. Assuming 20,000 tons of freight are shipped daily, one carrier can perform the service at $1.25 per ton. However, if four carriers compete equally for this traffic, each will transport 5,000 tons at a cost of $2.00 per ton. Therefore, it would appear preferable for society to have one or a limited number of railroads with each operating at a high level of capacity and with each carrier passing its efficiency savings onto the public via reduced freight rates. A. C. Pigou, the renowned English economist, observed:

> In a few peculiar industries, among those concerned with staple goods and services, it may also well be that the prospect of internal economies will

lead to the evolution of single establishments large enough to control a predominant part of the whole output of the industry. One of the most notable instances of this is afforded by the industry of railway transportation along any assigned route. In view of the great engineering cost of preparing a suitable way, it will, obviously, be much less expensive to have one or, at most, a few railways providing the whole of the transport service between any two assigned points than to have this service undertaken by a great number of railways, each performing an insignificant proportion of the whole service.[2]

However, the nagging problem with the above situation is that if there is no competition between railroads, the rail carrier with a monopoly would be able to "gouge" the public and charge very high freight rates regardless of its relatively low per-unit cost of production. To correct this potential problem, the government authorized public utility-type firms to be monopolies, but in return for this favorable "competitive" environment, the firms' rates and services are controlled, or regulated, by an appropriate public authority. The public regulatory body is charged with authorizing the railroad to earn a reasonable profit margin which would be fair and equitable to both the shipper and carrier.

The precedent of controlled competition in the railroad industry has been followed in varying degrees in most other transportation industries. This is ironic, because the cost structures of some other modes of transport—motor carrier, inland water carriers, and air carriers—are dissimilar from the railroads in that their variable costs range between 70 and 95 percent of total costs.[3]

Types of Government Regulation

So far, we have discussed *economic regulation*. Economic regulation involves establishing rates that are fair and equitable to both the shipper and the carrier. There are two other types of regulation.

Service regulation is another form of government interaction in transportation. Service regulation involves insuring that regulated carriers provide service that is consistent with their operating rights. This kind of regulation will be discussed later in this chapter when the types of carriers are examined along with their legal obligations.

One more type of control is *safety regulation*. Safety regulation is designed to protect both the general public and employees of carriers from accidents as well as unhealthy environments. The Department

---

[2] A. C. Pigou, *The Economics of Welfare*, 4th ed. (London: MacMillan and Co., 1962), p. 251. His phrase "internal economies" means savings.

[3] These carriers do not have to provide their own rights-of-way, therefore avoiding many of the railroads' fixed cost obligations.

of Transportation and the Occupational Safety and Health Administration (OSHA) are the two government agencies most directly involved in transportation safety.

History of U.S. Transportation Regulation

The initial state and federal regulation of the railroad industry was not based on niceties of theory—it was a pragmatic reaction to numerous grievances against railroad management in the 1860's and 1870's. Professor Jordan Jay Hillman said:

> In a broad sense any form of economic regulation involves the substitution of public policy objectives for unfettered entrepreneurial motives as a guiding principle in the conduct of the regulated function. Underlying our system of economic organization, however, is the common presumption that more often than not entrepreneurial freedom in the pursuit of profit is at least consistent with the public interest. In general, therefore, the assertion of public regulatory power is preceded by the growth of a significantly held conviction that *experience* has rebutted the presumption. (Emphasis added.)[4]

Railroad Abuses of Economic Power

Railroad management, aware that they had a near virtual monopoly on land transportation after the Civil War, took full advantage of their economic muscle. Six major grievances against the railroads finally resulted in government regulation. Without doubt the most noxious problem dealt with discriminatory rates. Railroad management set their rates according to the concept of "charging what the

- *Discriminatory pricing* involves charging different prices for essentially the same service. It is not necessarily unfair.

market will bear." The railroads charged "special" rates to favored customers and higher rates to those customers from whom they could be extracted. Privileged merchants, paying the lower rates, were able to undersell their rivals and often force them into bankruptcy. Discounts and rebates of 50 to 80 percent to selected shipping customers were not unusual. The effect according to Professor Kirkland was that ". . . the railroad became the irresponsible arbiter of the success and failure of individual businessmen."[5]

---

[4]Jordan Jay Hillman, *Competition and Railroad Price Discrimination* (Evanston, Ill.: Transportation Center at Northwestern University, 1968), p. xi.

[5]Edmund C. Kirkland, *A History of American Economic Life*, 3rd ed. (New York: Appleton-Century-Crofts, Inc., 1951), p. 350.

Location discrimination was also a common rate-making practice. If an origin and destination were served by two or more competing rail carriers, the result was that competition kept the rates low, close to the carriers' cost of production. Occasionally, there were rate wars started by an over-zealous rail carrier which wished to increase its market share. The result would be rates that were far below the railroads' costs of operating in the competitive market. Railroads offset these losses by very high rates in markets where competition did not exist.

Bribery was another grievance against the railroads. In addition, key government employees (congressmen, senators, governors, mayors, and judges) and others in power often received free lifetime travel passes for themselves and their families.

A further complaint dealt with the rude and condescending attitude of railroad personnel to customers and the general public. A writer in 1875 observed, "Taken as a class, the manner of the employees of the Western railroad system are probably the worst and most offensive to be found in the civilized world. It is difficult to see why the official should regard the traveler or the person having dealings with the railroad as his natural enemy; but it is apparent that he does."[6] This attitude can best be summarized by the famous utterance of Commodore Vanderbilt's son, William. When asked in 1877 if his railroad—the New York Central—was run for the public benefit, the younger Vanderbilt retorted, "The public be damned!"[7]

Another problem was that railroad management manipulated the prices of their companies' stocks and bonds. Management issued large quantities of stocks and bonds which were frequently purchased by financially unsophisticated investors. Solicitors promised these naive investors unbelievable appreciation of their investments in railroad securities. More often than not, these securities *decreased* significantly in value because the stocks and bonds were "watered." The railroads capitalized their assets (issued stocks and bonds) at much greater dollar values than the assets actually cost.

A related problem involved fraud which was often responsible for the "watered" condition of railroad securities. The *construction company* was a favorite of certain railroad manipulators. The "construction company" was in fact a financial arrangement instead of a building company. It worked this way: Assume a new railroad were to be built. The railroad's organizers *also* would form and *own* a

[6]C. F. Adams, "The Granger Movement," *North American Review* (April, 1875), p. 402.

[7]Steward H. Holbrook, *The Story of American Railroads* (New York: Crown Publishers, 1947), p. 92.

construction company to build the track. The actual cost of construction might be $10,000 per mile, but the construction company "estimated" that it would cost $35,000 per mile. Therefore, the new railroad would issue stocks and bonds equal to $35,000 per mile of track. Once the securities were sold (to unsophisticated buyers) and the money collected, the funds were transferred to the construction company for actual building of the track. However, the so-called construction company then subcontracted to legitimate construction firms who would build the railroad for about $10,000 per mile. The fictitious construction company belonging to railroad management then "pocketed" the difference between their inflated estimate and the actual costs of construction. Since the organizers of the new railroad made enormous profits during the construction phase of the railroad, they were indifferent if the railroad subsequently went bankrupt because of its watered capital structure. (The organizers, of course, did not own much stock or bonds in the railroad itself.)

The most infamous of the construction companies was the Credit Mobilier. It was formed in the 1860's to build the Union Pacific Railroad. It is estimated that stockholders of the Credit Mobilier achieved a net profit of $47 million. Much of this money came directly from the federal government, which was subsidizing the Union Pacific in order to have rail service to the West Coast. To insure that the federal government did not become suspicious about financial aspects of the Credit Mobilier, Oakes Ames, a United States congressman from Massachusetts and a senior officer of the Credit Mobilier, was given 343 shares of the construction company to distribute among congressmen where it would "do the most good." The stock was sold below its actual value to a number of congressmen to influence their votes, and the trail of bribery was eventually followed all the way to a Vice-President of the United States.[8]

The final grievance involved high local and state taxes assessed against taxpayers. The tax revenues were needed to pay off bonded indebtedness which was originally incurred by residents as special incentives to have the railroad built through their state, county, or town. By 1871, Massachusetts had 171 towns and cities that had issued bonds to pay for railroad aid. "Communities taxed heavily for their (the railroad's) benefit, and municipalities and individuals vied with each other in donating money, rights-of-way, and station buildings."[9]

[8] Harold Underwood Faulkner, *American Economic History*, 7th ed. (New York: Harper and Brothers, 1954), p. 484.

[9] William Larrabee, *The Railroad Question* (Chicago: The Schulte Publishing Co., 1893), p. 125.

Landmark Regulatory Cases

Two landmark Supreme Court cases set the stage for federal regulation of railroads. The first grew out of the agricultural depression of the early 1870's and the farmers' early attempts at regulating railroad abuses.

The organization that spearheaded the drive to regulate the railroads was the National Grange of the Patrons of Husbandry, commonly known as the Grange. Founded in 1867 by Oliver Hudson Kelly, this agricultural order had more than one million members by 1870. With their obsession against railroad management (see Figure 3–2), the state Grange organizations soon found they could exert great political pressure to pass legislation favorable to their cause. This was especially true in Illinois, Iowa, Wisconsin, and Minnesota. In 1870, the Illinois Grange succeeded in inserting a provision in their new state constitution which declared, "The General Assembly shall, from time to time, pass laws establishing reasonable maximum rates of charges for the transportation of passengers and

Figure 3–2 Anti-Railroad Cartoon of the 1870's.
Courtesy: The Culver Service.

freight," and "shall pass laws to correct abuses and to prevent unjust discrimination and extortion in the rates of freight and passenger tariffs." In 1871, Illinois enacted the *Act to Regulate Public Warehouses and the Warehousing and Inspection of Grain.* The same year Minnesota followed the lead of Illinois and passed a stringent railroad control law. Iowa followed suit in 1874, as did Wisconsin.

While each Granger law was somewhat unique, they typically contained the following provisions: (a) maximum rates were prescribed in the statute, (b) longer distance shipments over the same track had to have higher rates than shipments for shorter distances, (c) free passes to public officials were outlawed, and (d) railroad mergers were prohibited in order to encourage railroad competition.[10]

Munn v. Illinois (1877). In 1862, Ira Y. Munn and George L. Scott leased a warehouse and elevator in Chicago for the public storage of grain.[11] In 1871, Illinois enacted its *Warehouse Law,* which prescribed the maximum rates that warehouse operations could charge for the storage and handling of grain. Munn and Scott defied the state and continued to charge higher rates than those allowed by the statute. They were tried in a state court, found guilty, and fined $100. They appealed, but the Illinois Supreme Court upheld the lower court decision. Munn and Scott then appealed to the United States Supreme Court.

Munn and Scott argued that the Illinois *Warehouse Law* violated the 14th Amendment to the United States Constitution, which prohibits a person from being deprived of life, liberty, or property without due process of law. (While property can be condemned and used for the public good, for the condemnation proceeding to be legal, the owner must be fairly compensated for the property taken.) Munn and Scott argued that their warehouse was being taken from them without any form of compensation, and, therefore, due process of law was being denied them. (Their logic was that the value of an asset is its ability to earn revenue. If the State of Illinois decreased the grain warehouse's ability to earn income, then the value of their property is lowered, without any compensation by the state.) The Supreme Court, in 1877, accepted the logic of this argument—but said that there are exceptions to its universal application. Relying on

---

[10] See: Solon J. Buck, *The Granger Movement* (Cambridge, Mass.: Harvard University Press, 1913).

[11] This section relies heavily on James C. Johnson and James M. Highsmith, "Munn v. Illinois (1877): A Centennial Evaluation," *ICC Practitioners' Journal* (July–August, 1977), pp. 618–640.

a sixteenth-century treatise by Lord Chief Justice Hale of England, the Supreme Court found that when private property becomes "clothed with a public interest" so as to "affect the community at large," the property's owner has granted "to the public an interest in that use, and must submit to be controlled by the public for the common good."[12] The Court therefore recognized a special category of private property—property "affected with a public interest"—and declared that "when private property is devoted to a public use, it is subject to public regulation."[13] Since public grain warehouses and elevators were essential to an agricultural society, the State of Illinois could regulate the maximum rates the owners charged.

Several Granger cases had been appealed to the Supreme Court. Each case was reported on March 1, 1877, with the Munn decision being issued first so it could be used as precedent for the remaining five cases. In *Chicago, Burlington, and Quincy Railroad v. Iowa*, the Court stated: "Railroad companies are carriers for hire. They are incorporated as such, and given extraordinary powers, in order that they may better serve the public in that capacity. They are, therefore, engaged in a public employment affecting the public interest and under the decision in *Munn v. Illinois*, just announced, subject to legislative control as to their rates of fare and freight, unless protected by their charters."[14]

Therefore, using *Munn* as a precedent, states had a legal right to regulate railroads since they were clearly an industry "affected with a public interest." Most other states seized upon their new-found power and enacted legislation controlling railroad rates and operations.

Wabash Case (1886). The Wabash, St. Louis and Pacific Railroad charged Elder and McKinney 15 cents per hundred pounds for a carload shipment of products from Peoria, Illinois, to New York City. That same day the Wabash Railroad accepted a similar shipment from Bailey and Swannell and charged them 25 cents per hundred pounds. This shipment was accepted at Gilman, Illinois, bound for New York City. Gilman was on the same rail right-of-way between Peoria to New York City, but it was 86 miles *closer* to New York City. Bailey and Swannell felt discriminated against and took the railroad to court. The Illinois Supreme Court upheld Bailey and Swannell. The railroad then appealed to the United States Supreme Court.

---

[12] 94 U.S. 113, 126.
[13] *Ibid.*, p. 130.
[14] 94 U.S. 155, 161 (1877).

The Wabash Railroad argued that the United States Constitution clearly stated that regulation of commerce between states was a federal function. Therefore, the State of Illinois did not have jurisdiction over *interstate* commerce. Furthermore, the Illinois law was burdensome to the free flow of continuous transportation from one region of the country to another. The Supreme Court accepted this logic and reversed the Illinois Supreme Court. The highest court also declared that states did not have the right to regulate the *intrastate* (totally within one state) portion of an *interstate* shipment. Since about three of every four shipments were interstate in nature, state railroad regulation was dealt a crippling blow. This decision clearly indicated that federal action was needed to fill the regulatory void just created.

The Act to Regulate Commerce, 1887

Congress responded to the *Wabash* decision quickly because federal transportation regulation had been under consideration for a number of years. The 1872 Windom Report and 1886 Cullom Report, both done by Congressional study groups, had detailed railroad abuses of public trust and had recommended either partial nationalization of the railroads (Windom) or federal railroad regulation (Cullom). The year after the *Wabash* decision, Congress enacted monumental legislation—*The Act To Regulate Commerce.*

This law was signed by President Cleveland on February 4, 1887. All railroad common carrier service in interstate or foreign commerce came under federal regulation (see Figure 3–3). The 1887 Act also created the Interstate Commerce Commission (ICC) to administer the law. Congress gave the ICC broad overall guidance, and the Commission was expected to interpret and implement these mandates.

The first six sections of the Act are of prime importance. The section numbers are worth knowing because expressions like "Section 1 discrimination," or "Fourth Section relief," or "Waiving of Section 6 requirements" are commonly used by transportation practitioners. (However, the interstate commerce statutes were renumbered recently. Table 3–1 is a conversion chart showing the new numbers of statute sections referred to in this chapter. The text itself will continue to refer to them by their "traditional" numbers.)

Section 1. All rates must be *"just and reasonable."* The term *just* implies that the rate must be fair to shippers in relationship to what other shippers pay for moving similar commodities under approxi-

Federal and state laws that regulate carriers often place on the carriers a responsibility known as the *common carrier obligation*. Based on English common law and spelled out in our statutes, the obligation on the carrier has four parts:

Service Obligation. Common carriers have a legal obligation to serve *all* customers who request their service. This assumes the requested service is one the carrier has the authority and equipment to serve. For example, a motor common carrier of general commodities may refuse to accept a 10,000-gallon bulk shipment of sulfuric acid if he does not have the proper equipment to handle this type of commodity.

Delivery Obligation. The common carrier has a strict obligation to deliver the products entrusted to it to the consignee (receiver). This delivery must be accomplished with reasonable dispatch, and the products must be in the same condition as the carrier received them. It is this obligation under which the *law of loss and damage* (L&D) is founded. It is generally believed that this duty is the oldest common carrier obligation. Writing in 1703, Lord Holt stated:

> The law charges this person thus intrusted to carry goods, against all events, but Acts of God, and the enemies of the King. For though the force be ever so great, as if an irresistible multitude of people should rob him, nevertheless, he is chargeable. And this is a political establishment, contrived by the policy of the law, for the safety of all persons, the necessity of whose affairs oblige them to trust these sorts of persons, that they may be safe in their ways of dealing: for else these carriers might have an opportunity to undoing all persons that had any dealings with them, by combining with thieves, etc., and yet doing it in such clandestine manner as would not be possible to be discovered. And this is the reason the law is founded upon that point.*

Today, all a shipper or consignee has to prove to have a valid claim against a common carrier is that: (a) the goods were tendered to the carrier in good condition, and (b) when received by the consignee the product was damaged, or (c) the product was lost. When this occurs, the carrier is liable for a loss and damage claim.

Reasonable Rates. Because the number of competitors is limited, it is only logical that the rates of existing carriers be kept at a reasonable level.

Avoidance of Discrimination. The final common carrier obligation is to treat all customers, products, and geographic locations the same when similar circumstances are present.

*Richard R. Sigmon, *Miller's Law of Freight Loss and Damage Claims*, 4th ed. (Dubuque, Iowa: Wm. C. Brown, 1974), p. 3.

Figure 3–3 The Common Carrier Obligation.

TABLE 3–1 Old and New Section Numbers for Certain ICC Statutes

In the late 1970's Congress decided to "codify" (reorganize and renumber) those portions of the United States laws pertaining to the *Interstate Commerce Act*. This activity was completed in late 1980—after both the *Motor Carrier Act of 1980* and the *Staggers Railroad Act* had become law. What follows is an abbreviated "conversion chart" indicating how the numbers of sections referred to in this chapter of the book have been changed. All new section numbers can be found in Title 49 of the United States Code.

O L D	N E W
Section 1	Sections 10102, 10501, 10701, 10702, 10703, 10709, 10901, 10902, 10903, 11101*
Section 2	Sections 10741
Section 3	Sections 10701, 10741, 10742, 10743, 10744, 11103
Section 4	Section 10726
Section 5	Sections 11321, 11342, 11343, 11344, 11345, 11346, 11347, 11348, 11350, 11701, 11702*
Section 6	Sections 10503, 10761, 10762, 10764, 10765*
Section 15a	Section 10704
Section 22	Sections 10103, 10721, 10722, 10723, 10724

* Only a partial listing of new section numbers is indicated here. For complete list see: *United States Code Annotated, Title 49, Transportation, Revised Interstate Commerce Act* (St. Paul: West Publishing Co., 1981).

mately the same conditions. *Reasonable* means that the carrier shall be allowed to earn a fair return on invested capital.[15]

Section 2. *Personal discrimination* is prohibited. All shippers are to receive similar rates and services when the transportation is performed under similar circumstances. This section also rendered illegal the use of free railroad passes which had incensed midwestern farmers.

Section 3. The third section is a *broad anti-discrimination clause.* It prohibits "undue preference or prejudice" to any person, locality, or product. Thus rebates and kickbacks became unlawful.

Section 4. The *long- and short-haul* clause states that, in most instances, a carrier cannot charge *more* for a short haul over the same route than for a long haul. (This was aimed at correcting the railroad practice of charging high rates in markets where there were no competing railroads and low rates in markets where they were competing with other carriers.) The 1887 Act does allow some exceptions to

[15] See: John Guandolo, *Transportation Law* (Dubuque, Iowa: Wm. C. Brown Co., 1973), chapter 24.

this rule, which are known as *"Fourth Section relief."* Figure 3–4 shows an example of "water-compelled Fourth Section relief." Ordinarily, Section Four would require that the railroad's rate between Cities A and C would have to be more than the rates between A and B or between B and C. However, because a water carrier operates between Cities A and C, the railroad would ask the ICC for "Fourth Section relief" to establish a lower rate to meet this water competition. This rate, if permitted by the ICC, could be lower than either the AB or BC rates.

Section 5. This section *prohibits* railroads from *pooling* or *sharing traffic* in markets where they chose not to compete. In the 1887 Act, this was felt to be necessary to ensure competition between railroads in all markets.

Section 6. All rates and fares *must be published*. This requirement reduced the opportunity for discrimination because all rates had to be published and available for public inspection.

Amendments Strengthening the 1887 Act

There were three major amendments to the 1887 Act. In 1903 Congress enacted the *Elkins Act*, also known as the "anti-rebate" act. Railroads were under constant pressure to provide rebates to large shippers, even though this practice had been illegal since 1887. The ICC, in its *Annual Report—1899*, noted the severity of the problem: "It is scarcely too much to say that, on competitive traffic moving between the great centers of trade, the published tariff was little more than a basis from which to calculate concessions and discrimi-

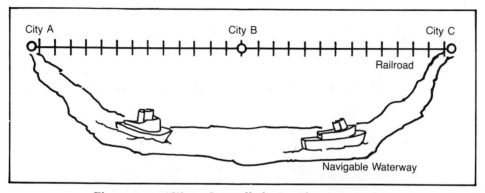

Figure 3–4   "Water-Compelled" Fourth Section Relief.

nations, with the result that shippers who failed to secure these un-lawful favors were in many cases forced to do business at a loss and in some instances driven out of business."[16] Large shippers worked diligently to secure these rebates—even though they knew that they were illegal—because if the federal government became aware of the situation, only the *carrier* would be penalized. The *Elkins Act* specifically made *both the carrier and shipper* equally guilty for all violations of the *Act to Regulate Commerce.*

The *Hepburn Act*, enacted in 1906, allowed the ICC to prescribe *maximum* rates if they found the existing rates were not just and reasonable. The Interstate Commerce Commission was therefore given the power to remedy rate problems; previously the ICC could identify violations, but corrective action had been beyond its jurisdiction.

The second change effected by the *Hepburn Act* involved the inclusion of oil pipelines under the 1887 Act. Oil pipelines became subject to Sections 1 through 6 of the *Act to Regulate Commerce.* The rationale for this was that the old Standard Oil Company appeared to control railroad transportation of all oil products. The rail rates for oil were kept relatively high, and Standard Oil illegally negotiated to receive rebates both on the oil they tendered to the railroads and *also on the oil tendered by competing oil companies.* When this fraud became known, the public was outraged, and Congress decided to "punish" Standard Oil, which then owned virtually all oil pipelines. Congress, in the *Hepburn Act,* declared that all oil pipelines are common carriers and hence had to accept all oil shipments tendered to them. (In 1977 regulation of oil pipelines was transferred from the ICC to the newly-formed Department of Energy.)

In 1910 Congress passed the *Mann-Elkins Act.* The *Hepburn Act* allowed the ICC to change an *existing* rate if it was found to violate the 1887 Act. However, the ICC had no power to determine the reasonableness of a *proposed* rate. The logic of preventing unlawful rates from going into effect was recognized by both the ICC and consumer groups. The *Mann-Elkins Act* gave the ICC the power to suspend proposed rate changes so the Commission would have time to study the changes. The current time period for suspension and investigation is seven months.

Shipping Act of 1916

Congress recognized the need for stabilizing the ocean transportation industry for the benefit of U.S. flag ocean carriers and to pro-

---

[16] *Thirteenth Annual Report of the ICC—1899*, p. 8.

tect the ocean ship users from potential monopoly. The *Shipping Act of 1916* created the United States Shipping Board, the predecessor to the present-day Federal Maritime Commission. This Act dealt mainly with international ocean transportation. Maritime legislation will be discussed in chapter 9.

Transportation Act of 1920

Because of congestion caused by World War I and the inability of railroads (and ports) to coordinate their operations, it was necessary for the U.S. government to operate the U.S. railroad system from 1917 to 1920.[17]

The *Transportation Act of 1920* brought the railroad industry back to private control and operation. The 1920 Act did more than refine the 1887 Act; it attempted to restructure the railroad industry. Congress saw the need for massive railroad consolidation in order to produce a limited number of financially viable carriers who would be able to produce a uniformly high level of service. The ICC was ordered by Congress to prepare a general plan to consolidate all railroads in the United States.

In 1920 the ICC retained Professor William Z. Ripley of Harvard University to prepare a recommendation for the master consolidation plan. In 1921 Ripley submitted his recommendation of 21 major railroads. The ICC reduced this number to 19. The ICC was not enamored with the "master-plan" concept and asked Congress to amend Section 5 (now covering mergers and pooling) to eliminate it in favor of authorizing any rail mergers that were found to be in the public interest. Congress did not respond to this suggestion until 1940.[18]

A second change resulting from the *Transportation Act of 1920* also involved Section 5. Congress recognized that the absolute prohibition against pooling in the 1887 Act was excessive. The 1920 Act allowed railroad pooling arrangements if the ICC found them to be not unduly restrictive of competition and if they allowed the carriers to achieve a more economical operation.

Three other major changes of the 1920 Act dealt with railroad pricing practices. Section 15a—the Rule of Rate-Making—of the *Interstate Commerce Act* (the *Act to Regulate Commerce* was changed

---

[17] For a brief discussion of this period, see: James C. Johnson, "Government Control of the Railroads in World War I: Was It Really Disastrous?" *Traffic World* (April 9, 1973), pp. 68–69.

[18] See: James C. Johnson and Terry C. Whiteside, "Professor Ripley Revisited: A Current Analysis of Railroad Mergers," *ICC Practitioners' Journal* (May–June, 1975), pp. 419–452.

to this name by the 1920 Act) was enacted. It dealt with ensuring that the ICC allowed railroads to earn a fair return on their invested capital if rail management conducted their operations in an honest and efficient manner. In another rate provision, the Commission was allowed to establish *minimum* rates for railroads, in order to prevent rail rate wars. Finally, if the ICC determined that an existing rate was not just and reasonable, it would prescribe the *actual* rate to be used in lieu of the unlawful rate.

Hoch-Smith Resolution of 1925

Because of depressed conditions in agriculture, Congress asked the ICC to establish for agricultural products the "lowest rates compatible with the maintenance of adequate transportation service."[19] This resulted in the *Hoch-Smith Resolution*. The importance of this is in what is *not* said, namely, that other shippers are—by inference—expected to pay more to sustain these low rates for farm products. (Congress recognized that rate structures can be used to redistribute income and wealth.)

Motor Carrier Act of 1935

Motor carrier regulation was patterned after the precedent established in the 1887 Act for railroads. Motor carriers were subjected to the *Interstate Commerce Act*, being designated as Part II carriers. (Part I carriers are railroads and oil pipelines.) The *1935 Motor Carrier Act* recognized three types of motor carriers: common, contract,

- *Contract carriers* agree to provide specific transportation services for a limited number of shippers, often on a regular basis.

- *Private carriers* use their own vehicles to carry their own goods.

and private. Motor common carriers are subject to laws similar to Sections 1, 2, 3, 5, and 6 of the Interstate Commerce Act. Section 4 was eliminated because long and short haul problems seldom develop in the trucking industry.

The essence of the 1935 Act was entry control, which is designed to control the number of motor common carriers by requiring that each carrier possess a certificate issued by the ICC. Motor common carriers existing when federal trucking regulation was enacted in 1935 were allowed to continue in operation on the routes they had

[19] P. Philip Locklin, *Economics of Transportation*, 7th ed. (Homewood, Ill.: Irwin, 1972), p. 256.

served. Thus, all motor common carriers who were in operation on June 1, 1935, were automatically issued "grandfather" certificates so the truckers could serve the same routes they had done prior to federal regulation. All other persons wishing to enter the motor common carrier business in interstate commerce had to apply to the ICC for a new certificate, known as *operating rights*. (Unlike rail regulation, where the problem was too *few* competitors, motor carrier regulation attempted to deal with the opposite problem, i.e., too *many* competitors.)

The 1935 Act contained a number of exemptions from economic regulation. By far the most important exemption is for carrying *agricultural products*. Any type of trucker—common, contract, or private—may transport *unprocessed* agricultural products. Farmers argued that their need for trucking service differed from that of the rest of the business community. Relatively small amounts of farm products were transported most of the year, but at harvest times, the need for trucking capacity was great. The farmers argued that if agricultural products could only be transported by carriers with certificates, it would be impossible to get the products out of the fields during harvest periods. Congress accepted this argument and created the agricultural exemption. This provision states that agricultural commodities, including ordinary livestock and fish, are exempt from economic regulation.

- *Exempt carriers* is the phrase often applied to interstate truckers who carry unprocessed agricultural products since they are not subject to the ICC's economic controls. (It could also apply to the railroads' carriage of perishable farm products, a movement which is now exempt from rate regulation.)

Civil Aeronautics Act of 1938

The first direct involvement between commercial aviation and the United States Government occurred in 1916, when the Post Office Department negotiated its first air mail contracts with private operators. In 1925 *The Kelly Act* stimulated the aviation industry by providing for federal government mail routes to be awarded to private companies on the basis of competitive bids. Additional legislation dealing with air mail compensation involved the 1930 *Watres Act* and the 1934 *Air Mail Act*. The latter law called for three things: the Interstate Commerce Commission to regulate air mail compensation, the Postmaster General to control air mail routes and to award air mail contracts, and the Bureau of Air Commerce to administer safety regulations.

During the period from 1927 to 1938 the airline industry experienced substantial growth. The established carriers sought additional federal aid and, specifically, protection from "excessive competition." The carriers established the Air Transport Association in 1936. This trade group worked with governmental agencies in drafting a comprehensive federal regulatory airline bill. The Air Transport Association sought a law unifying air regulation and promotion into one federal agency. In addition, the new law would provide a welcomed "stabilizing force" for this rapidly growing industry. The 1938 *Civil Aeronautics Act* was the result of the Air Transport Association's lobbying efforts. Professor Watson notes, "The Act of 1938 was passed because of the demands of the airline companies; they shaped the legislation and they lobbied it through to passage. . . . No wonder then that the scheduled airlines are so fond of the *Civil Aeronautics Act*—it is their set of rules."[20]

Under the 1938 Act, the Civil Aeronautics Board both controlled and promoted commercial aviation. Rates, routes, and new entry were tightly controlled. (Nearly all of this law was repealed in the late 1970's.)

Transportation Act of 1940

The *Transportation Act of 1940* contained a number of regulatory changes. First, the railroad "master plan" merger concept—outlined in the *Transportation Act of 1920*—was abandoned, as the ICC had repeatedly requested.

Second, the 1940 Act placed domestic water carriers (those operating *between* U.S. ports) under ICC regulation. They were designated as Part III carriers under the *Interstate Commerce Act*. Those domestic water carriers that are regulated are subject to Sections 1 through 6 of the Act. However, there are two very significant exemptions of carriers from the ICC regulation. First, whenever three or less different dry bulk commodities are carried on a barge (or group of barges lashed together into a single "tow"), the movement is exempt from regulation. Second, movements of liquid bulk products are also exempt. The effect of these two exemptions is that about 90 percent of all domestic water transportation is exempt from economic regulation by the ICC. Why? Because by the late 1930's all five basic modes of transportation (railroad, oil pipeline, motor carrier, air carrier, and international water carrier) were federally regulated and domestic water carriers were not. Therefore, it was obvious that the issue was not *if* domestic water carriers would be federally regu-

[20]Donald S. Watson, *Economic Policy: Business and Government* (Boston: Houghton Mifflin Co., 1960), p. 411.

lated, but *when*. With the railroad industry actively lobbying for domestic water carrier regulation, the trade groups for domestic water transportation decided *not* to oppose regulation. Instead, they opted to control the *coverage* of the proposed regulatory act. They succeeded: domestic water carriers are regulated in name only, for the dry and liquid bulk exemptions render regulation of domestic water transportation impotent. Railroad lobbying achieved, at best, a feeble victory.

The 1940 Act also contained a declaration of the National Transportation Policy which said, in part:

> It is hereby declared to be the national transportation policy of the Congress to provide for fair and impartial regulation of all modes of transportation subject to the provisions of this Act, so administered as to recognize and preserve the inherent advantages of each; to promote safe, adequate, economical, and efficient service and foster sound economic conditions in transportation and among the several carriers; to encourage the establishment and maintenance of reasonable charges for transportation services, without unjust discriminations, undue preferences or advantages, or unfair or destructive competitive practices; to cooperate with the several States and the duly authorized officials thereof; and to encourage fair wages and equitable working conditions;—all to the end of developing, coordinating, and preserving a national transportation system by water, highway, and rail, as well as other means, adequate to meet the needs of the commerce of the United States, of the Postal Service, and of the national defense. All of the provisions of this Act shall be administered and enforced with a view to carrying out the above declaration of policy.

This statement was intended to be a broad policy for the ICC to use in regulating the railroads, oil pipelines, motor carriers, and domestic water carriers. It is a relatively brief statement telling the Commission to provide fair and impartial regulation of all modes and to recognize and preserve the inherent advantages of each. The ICC has generally interpreted this to mean that—in cases involving competition between modes—they (the ICC) should not allow a mode to be driven out of a market. The result has been the development and preservation of our multi-modal transportation system. The statement was revised in the *Transportation Act of 1958*, the *Motor Carrier Act of 1980*, and the *Staggers Rail Act of 1980*. It is now sections 10101 and 10101a U.S. Code Annotated, Title 49, Transportation, Revised Interstate Commerce Act.

Freight Forwarder Act of 1942

In 1942, Congress declared that freight forwarders were subject to the *Interstate Commerce Act*; they were designated as Part IV carriers. The freight forwarders were subject to most of the regulatory

- *Freight forwarders* usually operate in large cities. They pick up many small shipments, sort through them, and consolidate them into large shipments destined for other major cities. These large consolidated shipments are then given to a line-haul (highway or rail) carrier and carried to the destination city. The load is then turned over to the forwarder's office in the destination city, which performs the local delivery function for all of the shipments.

pattern that applies to the railroads, including entry control, rate regulation, and service regulation. A unique feature of this legislation is that freight forwarders cannot own or control any railroad, oil pipeline, motor carrier, or water carrier, but these carriers can own and control forwarders (which some do). Also, since freight forwarders cannot do any intercity transportation themselves, this portion of the haul must be performed by common carriers.

Reed-Bulwinkle Act of 1948

This act created Section 5a of the *Interstate Commerce Act,* which authorized the use of rate bureaus (conferences) for all land common carriers. Rate bureaus establish rates, but each carrier is

- *Rate bureaus* are committees established by common carriers of a single mode serving a specific area. They establish and publish rates to which all their members usually adhere.

guaranteed the right to establish its own rates, which may differ from those set by the bureau. This is known as taking "independent action" or "flagging-out." Finally, the *Reed-Bulwinkle Act* states that rate bureaus which fully conform to the ICC's rules and procedures will be exempt from the antitrust laws. Supposedly, they were to deal only with rates; but sometimes (and, possibly, illegally) they discussed other items of common interest.

Transportation Act of 1958

This law attempted to modify the statement of national transportation policy in the 1940 Act by adding the sentence, "Rates of a carrier shall not be held up to a particular level to protect the traffic of any other mode of transportation, giving due consideration to the objectives of the National Transportation Policy." This was aimed at the problem of "umbrella" rate-making.[21]

[21] The U.S. Supreme Court, in The Ingot Molds Case (decided in the late 1960's) all but eliminated the thrust of the previous sentence.

- *Umbrella rate-making* was a regulatory concept employed by the ICC in situations where different modes were competing for the same traffic. The ICC would not allow the low cost carrier to set his rates so low as to eliminate the competing modes. Hence the rate was kept higher than it otherwise would be and other, higher cost, carriers were sheltered under this rate "umbrella."

The 1958 Act also clarified the definition of the agricultural trucking exemption, removing frozen food from the "exempt" category. In addition, the Act made it easier for railroads to give up or "abandon" rail passenger service in both interstate and intrastate markets.[22]

- *Service abandonment* occurs when a common carrier successfully petitions the regulatory body to be relieved from the obligation for providing certain service.

Department of Transportation Act of 1966

This legislation established the U.S. Department of Transportation (DOT), which was created by President Lyndon B. Johnson to consolidate 38 separate governmental agencies all of which dealt with various aspects of transportation.[23] DOT representatives participate in hearings before administrative law judges of the various transportation regulatory commissions. They represent the executive branch's position in these matters.

Rail Passenger Service Act of 1970

Passenger traffic between cities on railroads had been steadily decreasing since World War II. In 1947 there were 39,921 million intercity passenger-miles, but by 1970, this figure had shrunk to 10,900 million passenger-miles. The ICC estimated that—by 1969—U.S. railroads had suffered $200 million in deficits solely related to passenger business.

Congress had a dual concern over the rapidly escalating rail passenger deficits. First, the deficits certainly were reducing the railroads' ability to provide common carrier freight service. Second, Congress noted that railroads were abandoning passenger business (with ICC approval) so rapidly that the intercity passenger system

[22] For a complete discussion of the 1958 Act, see: George W. Hilton, *The Transportation Act of 1958* (Bloomington: Indiana University Press, 1969).

[23] For a discussion of the DOT and its formation, see: Grant M. Davis, *The Department of Transportation* (Lexington, Mass.: D. C. Heath & Co., 1970).

would soon be defunct. Believing that intercity rail service was in the national interest and that one contributing factor to the deficits was rail management's lack of interest, Congress enacted a bold approach to preserve intercity rail passenger service. The *Rail Passenger Service Act of 1970* in effect nationalized intercity rail passenger business. It created Amtrak (American's travel by track), which would be the intercity rail passenger company. All railroads, with very few exceptions, turned their rail passenger service operations over to Amtrak. Amtrak owns the equipment but uses mainly the rights-of-way of private rail carriers. The 1970 Act originally called for a two-year experiment, but Congress has extended Amtrak's operation to the present. Railroads that discontinued passenger service had to pay Amtrak to take over their service—Amtrak collected about $200 million by this means, and the railroads were able to "buy out" of their common carrier obligation to the passengers.

Northeast Regional Rail Reorganization Act of 1973

This law was designed to address the serious railroad problem that was caused by the bankruptcy of the Penn Central and six other railroads in the northeastern United States. A federal court had appointed trustees to manage the Penn Central during its financial reorganization. During reorganization, the bankrupt railroad's debt payments were reduced or suspended. The purpose of this was to enable the railroad to continue operating during reorganization and at least be able to cover its operating expenses with its operating revenue. However, the Penn Central was not even able to do this, and by 1973 the trustees had announced they were going to cease all operations. Since the Penn Central was large (it accounted for about one-fifth of all U.S. railroad ton-miles), Congress decided that some action was necessary. Although then Secretary of Transportation Coleman argued that the viable assets and rights-of-way of the Penn Central should be sold to the remaining profitable railroads in the East, Congress rejected this approach.

President Nixon signed the *Northeast Regional Rail Reorganization Act of 1973* into law on January 2, 1974. It authorized approximately $2.1 billion of federal expenditures and loan guarantees. The law created two new organizations: the USRA (United States Railway Association) was in charge of planning and financing for a new operating railroad; and Conrail (Consolidated Rail Corporation) was to be a semi-public, *for-profit* operating railroad. USRA was to determine which routes of the Penn Central and other bankrupt carriers in the Northeast were viable—the rest of the rights-of-way would be abandoned. The assets of the bankrupt railroads would be purchased for Conrail for cash and primarily by issuing securities in Conrail.[24]

Rail Revitalization and Regulatory Reform Act of 1976

The 4-R Act, as it is commonly called, contained many provisions in its 132 pages. We will discuss only the most significant ones. The first dealt with government financial assistance to railroads. The $2.1 billion for Conrail mentioned in the 1973 Rail Reorganization Act was funded. In addition, all railroads were eligible for $600 million of government loans for improvement of plant and equipment, and $1 billion of loan guarantees were made available for the same purpose. The other financial aspect involved $1.75 billion to be spent over five years for Amtrak to provide faster passenger service between Washington, D.C., and Boston (known as the "Northeastern Corridor").

The second two significant changes in the 1976 Act involved reform of rate regulations. First, Section 15a—The Rule of Rate-Making—was amended to provide new definitions for the ICC to use when determining whether rates are just and reasonable. Rates that are equal to or greater than variable cost cannot be found to be unjust or unreasonable on the grounds that they are too low. Conversely no rate can be declared to be too high unless the ICC determines that the carrier possesses *market dominance* over the traffic. The 4-R Act states that market dominance is the *absence of effective competition* by other rail carriers and other modes. The ICC, however, must specifically define market dominance, especially regarding what constitutes absence of effective competition.

A substantial controversy developed in formulating this definition. Railroads thought the proposed definition made excessive quantities of their traffic "market dominated," while the Federal Trade Commission and others felt that the ICC's definition was too "liberal" and few situations would be considered as "market dominated." A compromise definition was reached in October, 1976. The presumption is that market dominance exists if at least one of these three conditions is shown to exist: (1) the carrier proposing the rate change has a market share of 70 percent or more of the market in question; (2) the proposed rate is equal to 160 percent of the carrier's variable cost of operation; and (3) shippers or consignees (receivers) have made a significant investment in rail-related facilities or equipment and the effect is that they are "locked-into" rail transportation

[24] See: Jordan Jay Hillman, "The Making of Conrail," *ICC Practitioners' Journal* (November–December, 1977), pp. 18–26.

because it is not economically feasible for them to switch to another carrier or mode.

The second feature of the 1976 Act dealing with rates was the so-called "Yo-Yo Provision." It stated that for a period of two years starting February 5, 1976, the ICC could not suspend a rail rate proposal that was less than a 7-percent increase or decrease over the existing rate, unless one of three situations was present: (1) "market dominance" was determined by the ICC; (2) the rate appears to violate Sections 2, 3, or 4 of the *Interstate Commerce Act;* or (3) the rate would cause unfair, destructive, or predatory competition.

Deregulation of Transportation

Note that the 1976 Act had, as part of its title, the phrase "regulatory reform." The word "reform" has several meanings, one of which means to rebuild or restructure. Other meanings have a somewhat moralistic tone; in urban politics, for example, the "reform" party often consists of outsiders trying to unseat corrupt incumbents. In any event, by the mid-1970's something new was afoot in the relations between government and the transport industry. A movement had gained momentum that would, within a few short years, lead to repeal of many long-standing rules which had guided the conduct of our nation's carriers.

Problems With Regulation

The principal reason for deregulation was that considerable evidence showed regulation was not working. Recall from earlier in this chapter that economic regulations were not applied to significant groups of carriers in several modes of transport. Each year, the share of the total traffic carried by these exempt groups increased, indicating that they were "better tuned" to meeting the needs of shippers and travelers than were regulated carriers. Furthermore, their growth was often at the expense of regulated carriers, robbing the latter of their profitable traffic and leaving them with their obligation "to serve" declining markets. This is related to the issue of "cross-subsidies." For years the regulatory system—for political reasons—permitted and even encouraged carriers to make excess profits in some markets in order to offset losses in other markets they were also required to serve. Eventually those travelers and shippers who had to pay more than their share of costs began to complain, and many switched to unregulated carriers.

Others also were taking a hard look at the regulatory agencies. Ralph Nader, his associates, and other consumer advocates convinced many that transportation regulatory bodies did little more than protect the carriers.[25] The Penn Central bankruptcy debacle raised considerable doubts about the ability of transportation regulatory bodies to protect even the carriers, or anybody else, for that matter. Hence, it was difficult to develop a convincing case that transport regulatory bodies were functioning either as intended or as needed.

Our government's efforts to rescue rail passenger service and the bankrupt northeastern railroads were becoming a frightfully large, and never-ending expense. There was real concern that government would soon be forced to take over other bankrupt railroads in order to preserve a nationwide railroad system.

The several fuel crises of the 1970's focussed attention on several regulatory policies that caused excess fuel consumption. The public wondered why truckers had to return empty, why they often weren't permitted to travel along the shortest routes, and why large airplanes were forced to serve small communities.

The public, increasingly concerned with inflation, watched at first with awe, and then with anger, as Jimmy Hoffa and the Teamsters obtained large pay increases. Hoffa's success was due in part to the regulatory system since the trucking firms would merely increase their rates to cover the new wage costs, and the regulatory commissions would approve the new rates. The increased costs, thus, were passed on to the shippers, who had no part in the union negotiations.

Academics also were partly responsible for deregulation. For years they had argued that regulation was neither achieving the initial purposes of the regulatory statutes nor contributing to a wise use of our nation's resources. College teachers could demonstrate to their classes on a chalkboard that, under competitive pricing, competition drives price down to costs while under regulation, competition drives costs up to meet the established price. Wayne M. Hoffman, of Flying Tiger, said: "The push for deregulation started not in the business community, but in the universities. The movement spread from academia to the executive and legislative branches of the government and finally found acceptance among the public at large."[26]

[25] See: Robert C. Fellmuth, *The Interstate Commerce Omission* (New York: Grossman, 1970).

[26] Cited in Lucile Sheppard Keyes, *Regulatory Reform in Air Cargo Transportation* (Washington, D.C.: American Enterprise for Public Policy Research, 1980), p. 23.

Initial Steps Toward Deregulation

Eventually the government's leaders, as well as its bureaucracy, also favored deregulation. Professor James Rakowski, in describing the formation of battle lines prior to passage of the *Motor Carrier Act of 1980*, said:

> The two major protagonists were the federal government and the trucking industry. . . . The U.S. Department of Transportation, the administration's research and think-tank arm, was strongly in favor of truck deregulation. An independent commission, the National Transportation Policy Study Commission, in its recommendations put regulatory reform as a priority item. The Department of Justice, through its anti-trust division, was in favor of deregulation, especially in respect to collective rate-making. Congress was also in favor of regulatory change in trucking.[27]

Finally, the regulatory bodies themselves—sensing change— took steps toward deregulation, *prior to* Congressional action.

The Civil Aeronautics Board, starting in about 1976, loosened many of the regulatory restraints previously placed on the airlines. This was accelerated in 1977 when Alfred E. Kahn became CAB chairman. Under Kahn's leadership, the CAB allowed discount fares, "stressed fare reductions as an important factor in the selection of applicants for new routes," and "no longer . . . attempted to force cross-subsidization by awarding long-haul routes to subsidized short-haul carriers."[28] Starting in 1978, the Interstate Commerce Commission made a number of decisions that deregulated portions of railroad and motor carrier operations. These actions included:

1. Increasing the boundaries of "commercial zones" around cities, which has the effect of enlarging the areas encompassed by rates to or from the city in question. It also means that a carrier with authority to serve the city in question can now go out into a wider area to pick up freight or to make deliveries.
2. Increasing the "zones" around airports so that airline trucks could serve a wider area with cargo pick up and delivery.
3. Authorizing railroads to enter into contracts with shippers.
4. Deregulating the rail carriage of perishable farm produce.
5. Granting almost all (98 percent) of the requests for new motor carrier operating authorities.
6. Announcing that private truckers could apply for authority to serve as common or contract carriers on their backhauls and

---

[27] James P. Rakowski, "The Trucking Industry in the U.S.: A Study of Transportation Policy in Transition," *Traffic Quarterly* (October, 1981), p. 624.

[28] John R. Meyer and others, *Airline Deregulation: The Early Experience* (Boston: Auburn House, 1981), p. 8.

pick up traffic from any shipper. (The ICC, in a 5 to 1 vote in favor of this change, declared, "The new policy will provide for increased efficiency in the transportation system by filling up otherwise empty backhauls. We are convinced that the high cost of energy, now and into the foreseeable future, requires us to pay close attention to the need for greater operating efficiency."[29]

Hence, one of the purposes of the deregulatory statutes was to write into law (and make somewhat more permanent) policies already adopted by the regulatory commissions. It is interesting to note that the regulatory bodies themselves, with a long-time record of moving at the pace of a dying snail, suddenly sprinted to the front and, in a sense, "led" Congress on the issue of deregulation. One can only speculate as to "what might have been" if—at other times over their long histories—the regulatory bodies had been able to act with the same sense of leadership, flexibility, and speed.

Airline Deregulation Acts, 1977 and 1978

In a move toward less regulation of transportation, Congress deregulated much of the air cargo industry in late 1977. In 1978 it deregulated the remainder of the air cargo industry and the air passenger industry. In these instances, "deregulation" meant repeal of nearly all of the statutes that had controlled airline fares, routes, and competitive practices. The CAB's controls will be eliminated over the next few years, and the CAB itself is scheduled to "self-destruct" in 1985. This act, and its impacts, will be discussed in more detail in chapter 7.

Motor Carrier Act of 1980

Enacted over the bitter opposition of the motor carrier industry, the *Motor Carrier Act of 1980* removed a number of regulations. Entry into new markets was made easier, and the situations in which rate bureaus could be used were reduced. All controls on the use of trucks by airlines to pick up and deliver air cargo were removed, and the agricultural exemption was increased to include some products farmers *buy* in order to give the exempt truckers a backhaul (to the farm). A separate law was passed later in 1980 to change the regulations governing household goods movers. Chapter 4 discusses motor carrier deregulation in more detail.

[29] "ICC Abolishes Rule Limiting Usage of Trucks," *San Francisco Chronicle* (November 21, 1978).

Staggers Rail Act of 1980

This law's major impacts were upon rail industry rate-making practices. In situations or markets where railroads were *not* the dominant carrier, there are no ICC controls on maximum rates. In situations or markets where railroads are the dominant carrier, the ICC's jurisdiction now covers only those rates that are approximately 1.6 times the railroad's variable costs. There was a zone of rate flexibility that allows railroads to keep up with inflation.

The role and importance of railroad rate bureaus was reduced. They no longer could set rates charged by only a single railroad, and only railroads that participate in carrying traffic could vote with respect to changing its rate. Railroad contracts with shippers were authorized, and the definition of unjust discrimination was narrowed.

Northeast Rail Service Act of 1981

Enacted as a portion of the overall federal "budget" bill, the *Northeast Rail Service Act of 1981* reduced some of Conrail's obligations for carrying commuter passengers and speeded up procedures for abandoning unprofitable Conrail freight operations. The act also authorized the Secretary of Transportation to begin negotiations for the sale of Conrail to the private sector.

Bus Regulatory Reform Act of 1982

Signed by President Reagan on September 20, 1982, this law reduced the amount of regulations controlling the nation's interstate bus operations. Bus companies were given more freedom to enter or leave markets, and to set fares. Another law passed in 1982 changed the size of the Interstate Commerce Commission to five members.

Carrier Deregulation: How Is It Working?

The remainder of this chapter will contain more generalized observations about the initial effects of deregulation. An important point to note is that the U.S. economy was in a recession in the early 1980's; this economic situation would have caused financial difficulties for many carriers under any regulatory system. W. E. Greenwood, of Burlington Northern, remarked: "Just as Congress let railroads enter the marketplace, the railroads' marketplace took a leave of absence."[30]

[30] W. E. Greenwood, comments at Conference on Transportation Deregulation, Golden Gate University (March 24, 1982).

- *Intermodal shipments* rely on at least two different, connecting modes of transportation, such as rail to water, or truck to air to truck, in order to travel the entire distance between the shipper and the consignee.

There has been distinct improvement in the ability of carriers to offer to shippers intermodal service for their shipments. The ICC, in early 1981, deregulated all piggyback (trailer or container on flatcar) traffic. ICC chairman Reese H. Taylor explained: "Because trailers and containers can be easily moved from numerous origins and destinations, once they are off the rail car, TOFC/COFC service is very competitive and is not locked to an originating or terminating railroad."[31] The provisions of the *Motor Carrier Act of 1980* removing geographic restrictions on the use of trucks by airlines to pick up and deliver air cargo has been of great benefit to some airlines, and especially to Federal Express, which carries small parcels overnight by air between many cities.[32]

Federal Express was also the specific beneficiary of a provision in the 1977 airline deregulation law which removed size restrictions on the planes they flew. Their fleet presently contains 33 large planes, which they now may fly, 29 727s and four DC-10s, which took the place of a much larger number of smaller Dassault Falcons (which they still use to serve smaller markets).[33] Emery Air Freight, a large forwarder, relied on the 1977 Act's freedoms, and began acquiring its own fleet of planes. It now has a fleet of 66 planes, and John C. Emery, Jr., the firm's chairman, said: "Deregulation has fostered a new ball game. In a few short years we have reached the point where we offer shippers total transportation service."[34] Other carriers, including U.P.S. and the Postal Service, have also improved their air service for small parcels. This is one facet of transportation where service to the shipper has improved markedly since deregulation.

Small communities had long opposed deregulation because they felt that they would lose service. Preliminary evidence indicates that this loss has yet to occur. Airline service to and from small communities dropped slightly and is now more likely to be performed by unknown "upstart" airlines which have taken the place of air carriers with well-known names. The actual service offered by the up-

---

[31] Reese H. Taylor, Jr., remarks before the annual meeting of the Transportation Research Forum, San Francisco (November 4, 1981).

[32] Robert May, of Federal Express, comments at Conference on Transportation Deregulation, Golden Gate University (March 24, 1982).

[33] *Ibid.*

[34] John C. Emery, Jr., "A 'Cause for Optimism' in Air Cargo," *Via Port* (August, 1981), p. 23.

start airlines is often an improvement since they fly direct routes between the small communities and major city airports; before deregulation a small community was likely to be but one stop on a "circuitous multistop" flight.[35] An ICC study, looking at the impact of trucking deregulation, indicated "that the quality and availability of trucking service to small rural communities has remained virtually unchanged during deregulation."[36]

Deregulation has slowed down the wage demands made by unionized carrier employees. Established airlines, whose unionized pilots sometimes earn $100,000 per year, are being undersold by the new non-union "upstart" airlines, which pay pilots $30,000 per year. United Airlines, the nation's largest air carrier, entered into a new contract with its pilots. United received a number of concessions from the pilots in return for an agreement not to establish a separate non-union flying subsidiary. The Teamsters' new contract, effective in mid-1982, is essentially non-inflationary. This was necessary in order to allow the unionized trucking firms to compete with non-unionized owner-operators.

- *Owner-operators* are individuals who own (usually in conjunction with creditors) and drive their own trucks.

Although owner-operators tend to be an abused lot, one of the provisions of the *Motor Carrier Act of 1980*, enacted to protect them, apparently will not be implemented. The provision called for a standard written contract form, to be developed by the ICC in conjunction with the Department of Agriculture, for use by shippers and haulers of agricultural products. Such a standard contract form has not yet been developed, mainly because of agricultural shippers' opposition. They do not want to limit "their ability to adjust carrier compensation at the time of delivery."[37]

A troublesome aspect of the deregulation laws has been that they have undermined the traditional common carrier concept, i.e., the duty for the common carrier "to serve." Often this duty was exchanged for "limited monopoly or oligopoly rights" in certain mar-

- *Monopoly* is one seller and *oligopoly* is a few sellers. *Limited rights* meant that the regulatory body limited the number of carriers in a specific market. This protection from outside competi-

---

[35] Clinton V. Oster, Jr., in John R. Meyers and others, *Airline Deregulation: The Early Experience*, pp. 119–157.

[36] *The Wall Street Journal* (March 8, 1982).

[37] *Transport Topics* (April 5, 1982), p. 22. Readers may speculate as to the trucker's bargaining power at the time the goods are delivered.

tion allowed them to charge somewhat higher rates, and this surplus was to be used to offset losses they incurred in meeting their common carrier obligation elsewhere. These limited rights were also referred to as *operating rights.*

kets. One result of the *1980 Motor Carrier Act* was to sharply reduce whatever market value these rights had.[38] (Before deregulation they could be bought and sold, subject to regulatory body approval.) Some carriers have equated the loss in value of their operating rights with a loss of their common carrier obligation "to serve." No doubt there will be court cases dealing with this issue.

In both the air and motor carrier industry there has been virtually unregulated entry of new carriers and/or expansion of existing carriers into new markets. Considerable rate competition has developed and often it has driven rates far below costs, to the point where the long-term health of some airlines and some motor carriers is seriously threatened. Rail rates, however, have not uniformly dropped. Some have increased, although this was not unexpected since (and unlike the airline and motor carrier situations) rail rate regulation had often been keeping rates too low.

All of these changes have created confusion and made it difficult for travelers and shippers to keep abreast of happenings. One result has been an increase in the status of the shipper's traffic manager since he or she is now confronted with "a new ballgame." A *Wall Street Journal* article (December 31, 1981) describing the new role of the traffic manager, focused on the General Electric plant in Louisville and its traffic manager there, Charles S. Davis.

> Depending on which carrier GE uses, for example, the cost of shipping a truckload of washing machines from Louisville to Chicago could be as little as $359, or as much as $780. With sluggish business conditions depressing their volume, most carriers are eager to discount from posted rates. Dickering with these freight haulers comes naturally to GE's Mr. Davis, a former appliance-truck driver who earned a marketing degree in night school. His gravelly Georgia drawl and down-home demeanor mask shrewd bargaining skills.

In May, 1981, Harbridge House, a Boston-based research firm, surveyed over 200 large shippers (with an annual transportation bill averaging over $32 million each) about savings they had experienced because of deregulation. "Respondents reported average savings of approximately $2.4 million because of actions taken as a direct re-

---

[38] For an idea of how the value of operating rights has dropped, in 1976 Wilson Freight Co. bought "Cincinnati to Atlanta" motor carrier authority for $2.45 million. In 1982, Wilson went bankrupt, and at its bankruptcy auction, these same rights were sold for $6,000. *Transport Topics* (May 24, 1982), p. 1.

sult of deregulation: $1.8 million in trucking; $430,000 in rail; $110,000 in air freight; and $70,000 in air express."[39]

A vexing area of deregulation has dealt with rate bureaus. Recall that rate bureaus were originally given immunity from anti-trust statutes by the *Reed-Bulwinkle Act of 1948*. Because of deregulation, airlines no longer use them for domestic markets, and shortly after the airline deregulation laws were enacted, the U.S. Department of Justice forced U.S. airlines to drop out of international rate-making bodies. Minor chaos in international air rates resulted, and foreign governments asked the U.S. government to change its policy, which it did. As of this writing, U.S. airlines can now again participate in international rate-making bodies.

Both the *Staggers Rail Act* and the *Motor Carrier Act of 1980* sharply reduced the number of situations in which carriers could meet together, through rate bureaus, to establish domestic rates. The motor carrier industry has been especially upset by this change, and is campaigning vigorously to have the rate bureaus saved, in one form or another. Actually, a somewhat convincing case can be argued that rate bureaus are necessary, despite the fact that they stifle competition. Professor Donald Dewey suggests that in many industries, moderate collusion among sellers is desirable. Price stability allows providers of service to plan better and "any price stability achieved through collusion is demand enhancing for sellers when it reduces uncertainty for buyers,"[40] i.e., buyers may spend more at a stable price than at a changing price. The motor carrier industry's great interest in maintaining rate bureaus also suggests that the bureaus may, in fact, be performing more market-regulating functions than merely setting and publishing rates.

Obviously, deregulation is placing many stresses and strains on carrier management. Figure 3–5 is a letter to the authors from transportation consultant Enrico DiGiammarino, Jr., outlining his beliefs as to what motor carrier management must do to meet these challenges.

The last subject to be mentioned deals with deregulation of carriers at the state level. State regulation of railroads was mentioned early in the chapter. In the 1930's, most states followed the federal lead and enacted motor carrier regulation statutes. A few states, California, Pennsylvania, and Texas, even regulated intrastate operations of airlines. The federal airline deregulation laws removed all state

[39] *Transport Topics* (September 28, 1981), p. 7.

[40] Donald Dewey, "Welfare and Collusion: Reply," *American Economic Review* (March, 1982), pp. 276–277. See also pp. 256–275 in the same issue, and Dewey's initial article in the September, 1979 issue, pp. 587–594.

September 1, 1982

ELD
Associates

Dear Professors Wood and Johnson,

Management in the for-hire trucking industry is facing significant challenges.

The regulatory security blanket had virtually eliminated the competitive forces that encourage businesses to employ sophisticated marketing and control techniques. From 1935 until 1980 the barriers to entry, and the collective ratemaking process virtually eliminated new competitors and price competition from the market place. Most management improvements were aimed at increasing efficiency, and improving service to the shipper. Most carriers did not seek managers with industrial engineering skills. Instead they were concerned with carrot/boot managerial skills in people motivation. Marketing consisted only of SALES and relied on the extent of geographical areas served, the service ability and the personal touch of the sales people.

The onslaught of deregulation and the recessionary declines in available traffic have caused changes in these attitudes. With the ICC's permissive position on independently filed tariff actions, easing of barriers to expanding or starting operations and the July 1984 end to antitrust immunity for collectively setting single-line rates (approximately 85% of traffic), new management stances are emerging.

After the regulatory interruption, the industry has restarted movement along its life cycle curve. As it moves through the turbulent shake-out period, the best positioned survivors will be characterized by:
- well defined, clearly stated corporate goals;
- realistic, analytically developed, congruent strategies;
- marketing plans that coordinate the SALES, TRAFFIC and OPERATIONS efforts;
- effective management tools, including market research to target the most appropriate markets, shipment costing to gauge competitive pricing decisions and performance studies to fine-tune operations; and,
- aggressive, creative management attitudes that pull these elements together into a workable, cohesive package.

Clients with whom I am dealing seem most interested in these particular tools:
- systems to determine individual shipment costs at the variable level, fully allocated level and the level necessary to recoup the cost of capital;
- performance studies to underpin the costing system and operating improvements;
- systems to group costed shipment data (e.g. by commodity, lane, shipper, consignee, etc.) so that analysis can detect trends in carrier performance consumed by these shipments and estimate costs on similar types of new traffic; and,
- analysis and research upon which to base strategic and market plans concerning penetration/abandonment, response to competitor originated rate cuts and self initiated rate actions.

Application of such tools is the hallmark of an industry coming of age in professional management techniques. Those who fail to adopt similar measures will find themselves impotent victims, left in the backwaters of this new era of truck transportation.

Sincerely,

Enrico L. (Sam) DiGiammarino, Jr.
Management Consultant - Transportation

P.O. BOX 7647   •   ATLANTA, GEORGIA 30309   •   (404) 971-2529

Figure 3–5 Management Response to Motor Carrier Deregulation.

regulation of airlines. The *Staggers Rail Act*, while not exactly removing state regulation of railroads, required that the new federal rail regulatory rules be applied to intrastate railroad movements. (See Section 11501 of the revised *Interstate Commerce Act*.) Several states have reduced or eliminated their regulation of motor carriers.

Arizona, Maine, and Florida have ended almost all of their regulation; in West Virginia, the state Public Service Commission placed a two-year ban on rate-bureau rate-making by the state's intrastate motor carriers.[41]

Summary

To understand the transportation industry in the United States it is necessary to be familiar with transportation regulation. We started this chapter by examining why governments have regulated transportation. The two primary factors were: (1) to protect the public interest (because all citizens are dependent upon the transportation industry); and (2) to regulate certain industries—natural monopolies, such as the railroads—that are more efficient when only one or a few are allowed to exist. Because each firm is shielded from competition, natural monopolies must be regulated by the public to prevent them from abusing their economic power.

There are three types of transportation regulation: economic, service, and safety. The original effort by states to regulate the railroad industry was a reaction to numerous grievances committed by the railroads during the 1860's and 1870's, such as (a) discriminatory rates, (b) free passes, (c) condescending attitude of rail management, (d) stock and bond manipulation, (e) fraudulent construction companies, and (f) high property tax needed to pay off obligations to railroads. These grievances precipitated the state Granger laws, which resulted in the landmark case of *Munn v. Illinois* (1877). The Wabash Case (1886) necessitated federal transportation regulation, which was enacted in the 1887 *Act to Regulate Commerce*.

Many transportation regulation laws have been subsequently enacted. The *Act To Regulate Commerce* was amended by the 1903 *Elkins Act*, 1906 *Hepburn Act*, and 1910 *Mann-Elkins Act*. The 1906 Act brought oil pipelines under the *Act To Regulate Commerce*.

The *1920 Transportation Act* changed the name of the 1887 Act to the *Interstate Commerce Act*. Interstate trucking regulation was provided by the 1935 *Motor Carrier Act*. The 1938 *Civil Aeronautics Act* brought federal regulation to the airline industry.

Congress issued the National Transportation Policy in the *1940 Transportation Act*. The 1940 Act also placed domestic water carriers under the Interstate Commerce Act. The *Freight Forwarder Act of 1942* brought this industry under federal regulation.

[41] *Transport Topics* (November 2, 1981), p. 26.

Rate bureaus were granted an antitrust exemption by the 1948 *Reed-Bulwinkle Act*. The Rule of Rate-Making was strengthened by the *1958 Transportation Act*. The Department of Transportation was created in 1966. In 1970 the *Rail Passenger Service Act* allowed the federal government to take over intercity rail passenger transportation. The problems of bankrupt railroads in the Northeast were addressed by the 1973 *Northeast Regional Rail Reorganization Act*. The "4-R" Act of 1976 provided some assistance to the U.S. railroad system, especially in regard to rate-setting flexibility.

Because of building criticism that the regulatory system was not functioning well, a number of laws were passed which removed a substantial portion of our regulatory framework. Specific laws dealt with air cargo (1977), all other airlines (1978), motor carriers, and railroads (1980) and intercity buses (1982). The chapter ended with a discussion of the initial impacts of the new statutes.

Questions for Discussion and Review

1. Federal regulation of transportation has existed since 1887. Do you believe it has worked well? Discuss.

2. Why have governments traditionally regulated the transportation industry?

3. What is a natural monopoly? Why are natural monopolies regulated?

4. What are the three types of governmental transport regulation? Which do you believe is the most important? Why?

5. Why did rate wars occasionally break out between railroads? What did competing railroads often do to correct the situation?

6. Of all the railroad abuses that lead to rail regulation, which do you think was: (a) the most serious problem? and (b) the least serious problem? Why?

7. What were the Granger laws? Do you believe they should have been enacted? Why?

8. Discuss the *Munn v. Illinois* (1877) case and its significance.

9. Discuss the *Wabash* (1886) case and its significance.

10. Define and discuss the legal obligations of a common carrier.

11. Discuss each of the first six sections of the *Act To Regulate Commerce.*

12. Why was the *Elkins Act* enacted in 1903?

13. Why were oil pipelines brought under federal regulation in 1906?

14. Discuss two major changes in transportation regulation brought about by the *Transportation Act of 1920.*

15. What was the major problem that lead to interstate regulation of the trucking industry in 1935?

16. What is the motor carrier "agricultural exemption"? Why was it enacted?

17. Why was the airline industry regulated in 1938? Which group actively sought this regulation?

18. What is National Transportation Policy? Why was it enacted? What does it say?

19. What are freight forwarders?

20. What did the 1948 *Reed-Bulwinkle Act* accomplish?

21. What is Amtrak? Why was it created? What is its current status?

22. Discuss the rate provisions of the 4-R Act.

23. The transportation industry was substantially deregulated at the federal level from 1977 to 1980. Do you believe this deregulation was a good idea? Why?

24. Do you believe the transportation industry today is overly regulated? Why? What changes would you recommend to Congress at this time? Defend your answer.

25. Why was the transportation industry deregulated from 1977 to 1980?

26. How has deregulation affected carrier management? Is management's job easier or harder now as compared to before deregulation? Why?

27. How has deregulation affected the shippers? Is their job easier or harder now as compared to before deregulation? Defend your answer.

Additional Chapter References

Allen, Benjamin J., and Dennis A. Breen, "The Nature of Motor Common Carrier Service Obligations," *ICC Practitioners' Journal* (May–June, 1979), pp. 526–549.

Allen, W. Bruce, "The ICC's Extension of the Commercial Zone," *Academics Talk To Motor Carriers* (Washington, D.C.: American Trucking Associations, 1978), pp. 4–40.

Boske, Leigh B., "An Analysis of Recent Developments in Railroad Maximum Rate Regulation," *ICC Practitioners' Journal,* Vol. 48, No. 3 (1981), pp. 294–311.

Chow, Garland, "Studies of Intrastate Trucking Regulation—A Critique," *Transportation Journal* (Summer, 1980), pp. 23–32.

Davis, Grant M., ed., *Transportation Regulation: A Pragmatic Assessment* (Danville, Ill.: Interstate Printers and Publishers, 1976).

Fravel, Frederic Dean, "Returns to Scale in the U.S. Intercity Bus Industry," *Annual Proceedings of the Transportation Research Forum* (1978), pp. 551–561.

Heaver, Trevor D., "Collective Ratemaking by Canadian Railways: An Appraisal," *The Logistics and Transportation Review,* Vol. 17, No. 1 (1981), pp. 3–22.

Horn, Kevin H., "Deregulation of Produce Traffic: Will the Railways Be Able to Produce?," *Transportation Journal* (Fall, 1979), pp. 5–18.

Interstate Commerce Commission, *A Cost and Benefit Evaluation of Surface Transport Regulation* (Washington, D.C.: The ICC's Bureau of Economics, 1976).

Lieb, Robert C., "Regulatory Reform in Transportation: Some Interim Observations," *ICC Practitioners' Journal,* Vol. 49, No. 3 (1982), pp. 273–279.

Mentzer, John T., and Robert Krapfel, "Reactions of Shippers to Deregulation of the Motor Carrier Industry," *Journal of Business Logistics,* Vol. 2, No. 2 (1981), pp. 32–47.

Meyer, John R., and others, *Airline Deregulation—The Early Experience* (Boston: Auburn House, 1981).

Miklius, W., K. L. Casavant, and W. Huang, "Entry, Exit, and Survival of Exempt Motor Carriers," *Transportation Journal* (Fall, 1976), pp. 16–25.

Miller, George H., *Railroads and the Granger Laws* (Madison: The University of Wisconsin Press, 1971).

Miller, James C., ed., *Perspectives on Federal Transportation Policy* (Washington, D.C.: American Enterprise Institute for Public Policy Research, 1975).

Tye, William B., A. Lawrence Kolbe, and Miriam Alexander Baker, "The Economics of Revenue Need Standards in Motor Carrier General Increase Proceedings," *Transportation Journal* (Summer, 1981), pp. 5–28.

Williams, Ernest W., Jr., "A Critique of the Staggers Rail Act of 1980," *Transportation Journal* (Spring, 1982), pp. 5–15.

Wilner, Frank N., "State Commission Practice: A Primer on Financial Ratios," *ICC Practitioners' Journal,* Vol. 47, No. 2 (1980), pp. 162–173.

Case 3–1   Piranha River Barge Company Case

In the 1850's, in a state whose name we've forgotten, flowed the Piranha River, named for the vicious fish that made crossing the river hazardous. "Toeless Joe" Jackson, one of the few settlers to survive a piranha attack, decided to form a barge company which would ferry people and goods across the river. He was assured that the state legislature would grant him "monopoly" rights for 25 years, meaning they would permit no other barges to operate within 20 miles on either side of his crossing. Jackson claimed he needed such protection to insure his investment.

The barge would move along a cable moored to each shore, and a steam engine mounted on the barge would pull the cable around a drum. Jackson and his financial backers realized that they would need to have receipts of at least $500 per year to make their investment worthwhile. They had heard that railroads charged different prices for each type of product carried and decided that the Piranha River Barge Company could do the same. They decided the best way to finance their project was to bargain for as high a rate as they could from each potential user and then to get the individual to sign a long-term commitment to use the barge service, contingent upon the Barge Company's being able to find enough commitments to make the entire venture worthwhile.

After several months of cajoling, begging, arm-twisting, and bribing, Jackson and his associates were able to get long-term commitments from 14 potential users. All commitments were subject to the condition that Jackson and his associates could find enough commitments to produce receipts of at least $500 per year. (Only dollar amounts of the commitments are given here; the actual contracts specified tonnages as well, but the capacity of the barge far exceeded the total expected tonnage.) Commitments are listed here in alphabetical order, and each is the amount a potential user would pay on an annual basis:

▲ Aachen Watch Works (a German firm)—$100 to ship watches and band instruments.
▲ Aardvark Coal Company—$50 to ship coal.
▲ Aaron's Lumber Company—$40 to ship firewood.
▲ Abalone Shell Company—$10 to ship shell chips (used in cement).
▲ Abandon Tools, Inc.—$80 to haul carpenters' tools.
▲ Abattoir Packers—$30 to ship hides.
▲ Abbott Enterprises—$90 for the carriage of books.

▲ Abigail's Grocery—$70 for handling of fresh produce.
▲ Able Flour Mills—$60 for shipping grain.
▲ Abner & Sons—$10 for carrying sand.
▲ Abraham Bros.—$30 for carrying hay.
▲ Mike's Gravel—$15 for the hauling of gravel.
▲ Penelope's Stables—$20 for the carriage of straw.
▲ Zouave Bros. Inc.—$15 for the shipment of cinders.

Question One: Can Jackson and his friends pay for the barge operation?

Question Two: If so, can they rely on average cost pricing? Why or why not?

Question Three: Assume they are concerned that other shippers of similar products may come along and, in fairness to existing customers, Jackson will want to charge the same rate for similar commodities. He therefore constructs a "commodities" tariff, listing each product and its rate. What is the minimum number of different prices he can charge? What would his commodity tariff look like?

Question Four: Are there any products that the Piranha Barge Company should refuse to handle? If so, what are they?

Question Five: What is the minimum rate Piranha should charge for handling any other new business which may develop?

Question Six: Assume that at the end of the 25-year "monopoly" period, an operator of a small, fast boat wants to take away some of the barge company's business. Which customers do you think he would go after first? Why?

Case 3–2   Coup d'Etat Rat Trap Company Case

Employed as the third assistant chef in a dormitory kitchen at a "Big 10" university, Phil Gallagher found that his principal duty was keeping the rat population under control. Utilizing his knowledge of advanced electrical engineering, he designed a simple rat trap equipped with an electronic beam, which the rat would interrupt when it placed its head inside the trap. This in turn would release a trigger and coiled spring, delivering a neat, fatal blow to the rat's head. For bait, Gallagher used the dorm kitchen's Sunday night leftovers, which had a unique odor.

The trap was very successful, and soon he was selling millions of

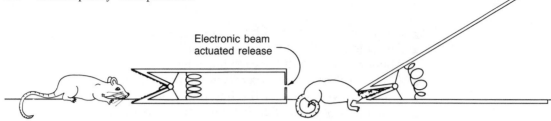

Case Figure 3-2-1   The Coup d'Etat Rat Trap (patent pending). Drawing on the left shows an unsuspecting rat approaching the trap, allured by special bait near the hinge. As the rat sticks its head inside the trap, an electronic beam, not shown, is broken which activates the release on the rear, freeing the coiled spring.

traps per year. Each trap was shipped in an individual carton with the trigger unsnapped and the spring uncoiled (as shown in the right drawing in Case Figure 3–2–2 but without the dead rat). Each trap weighed one pound; each carton weighed one ounce and occupied .5 cubic foot. Gallagher determined that if the traps could be shipped in a "cocked" position with the spring coiled, a carton occupying only .1 cubic foot could be used. There were some real limitations to sending traps in a "cocked" position, not the least of which would be the potential for suits from buyers who injured their fingers while unpacking the "loaded" trap. These limitations will be discussed shortly. Nonetheless, Gallagher was running out of warehouse space and he knew that one possible solution was to compress the trap's spring so that each trap could be packed into a smaller carton.

Gallagher retained Elena Kolenko, a packaging consultant, to help with his calculations. She determined that there were five alternatives. Alternative A was to change nothing and continue packing each trap into a carton occupying .5 cubic foot. Alternative B compressed the spring slightly so that a smaller carton, occupying .4 cubic foot, could be used. Alternative C compressed the spring more so that a package occupying .3 cubic foot could be used, and alternative D compressed the spring even more so that the package need be only .2 cubic foot. For alternatives A, B, C, and D, the trap was not "cocked," or loaded, so there was no danger to buyers' fingers. In alternative E, however, in order for the trap to fit inside a carton occupying .1 cubic foot, the trap had to be compressed so far that it would "cock" itself and pose a danger to individuals during unpacking.

Cartons for alternatives A and B weighed one ounce each; for alternative C, two ounces; and for D and E, three ounces. (The weight increased despite the smaller package size because a much sturdier package was needed to enclose the partially-coiled spring.) Packages

A, B, and C cost three cents each, while packages D and E cost six cents each. In addition, warning stickers, costing one cent each, had to be placed on alternative E's package.

Labor costs for packing traps into cartons were least for alternatives A and E since the traps could be delivered from the assembly line in either the cocked or uncocked position. The packing labor cost for alternatives A and E was seven cents per trap; for alternatives B, C, and D, it was nine cents each; and for alternative E, the total labor cost was eight cents each (including the cost of adding the warning sticker).

Emma Mahrholz, who handled the firm's insurance, said that if alternative E was used, the firm's product liability insurance premium would increase by $9,000 per million units shipped.

All packaged traps had to move through the firm's warehouse once. Rudy Martinez, the warehouse foreman, estimated that it cost $6.00 to move a palletload (approximately 120 cubic feet) in and out of the warehouse once. And Jaime Zaragosa, Gallagher's traffic manager, supplied costs of transportation. The carriers the firm used had incentive rates to encourage denser loading. For packaged rat traps with a density of three to fifteen pounds per cubic foot, the average rate was $1.20 per pound. Traps with a density of under three pounds per cubic foot paid an average rate of $2.00 per pound. (In both instances this included the weight of both the trap and its packaging.)

Question One: What is the cost of packaging materials for each of the five alternatives?

Question Two: What is the cost of labor for packing traps into cartons for each of the five alternatives?

Question Three: Calculate the average costs of warehousing (both in and out) for the five alternatives.

Question Four: Calculate the average transportation costs per packaged trap for each of the alternatives.

Question Five: Which packaging alternative has the lowest total costs? Would you recommend it? Why?

Question Six: Assume for a moment that there was no shortage of warehouse space and, on the average, each rat trap stayed in the factory's warehouse for a month. List and discuss the advantages and disadvantages of storing them unpackaged (for about a month—on the average) and then packaging them just before they were shipped.

In 1925 a designer at Mack Trucks drew this "cruiser" bus, as he envisioned it would appear in 1950.

The furthest such an idea evolved in practice was the "sleeper" bus, built in the late 1920's by Pickwick Stages. The body, custom-built on a Pierce-Arrow chassis, contained 13 two-person sleeping compartments with folding berths and running water. The bus also had lavatories and a galley. It carried a crew of three.

In 1944 Mack designers updated their earlier dream, calling it the Mack "Rocket Bus."

Top and bottom drawings courtesy Mack Trucks, Inc. Middle photo courtesy Railway Negative Exchange of Moraga, California.

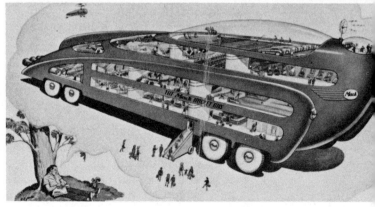

4 Highway Carriers

The use of Highway Trust Fund revenues for non-highway related purposes is diversion of highway taxes. It is a clear violation of the Highway Trust Fund principle. . . . Mass transit should have its own separate funding and not be dependent on "raids" on the highway fund.

BENNETT C. WHITLOCK, JR., PRESIDENT
American Trucking Associations
Traffic World, February 6, 1978

An executive of McLean Trucking Company commented on the effect of deregulation on the trucking industry: "It's a new age for trucks. The good old days are gone forever."

Traffic World
April 27, 1981

Roadway Express Inc., the trucking industry's leader, shattered its historic low profile by cutting rates 12% on much of its bread-and-butter small shipments traffic. The move is already sending competitors in the less-than-truckload (LTL) sector of the industry scurrying to reexamine rates and will probably trigger more price-cutting, putting a further squeeze on profits and hastening the industry's consolidation.

Business Week
February 8, 1982

Introduction

In chapter 1 we mentioned that motor carriers dominate the nation's estimated freight expenditures. While they carry only 23 percent of freight ton-miles, they collect nearly 80 percent of freight dollars. The main purpose of this chapter is to examine freight service produced by the motor carrier industry. Bus passenger service will also be examined briefly.

In 1896, the first self-propelled trucks appeared in the U.S. In 1898, a limited amount of competition was present among the several manufacturers of "motor delivery wagons." By 1912 the "horse versus truck" controversy was in full swing. General Motors Truck Company advertised, "During the next three months it will be no unusual sight to see horses dropping dead on the streets, having succumbed to the heat. . . . The beauty of the motor truck is that it is not affected by the heat."[1] To illustrate this point, G.M.C. issued

[1] Robert F. Karolevitz, *This Was Trucking* (Seattle: Superior Publishing Co., 1966), p. 30.

full-page advertisements showing 10 different pictures of horses dying in the streets, attended by their anguished owners. A later advertisement for trucks stressed their economy over "Old Dobbin." The lead sentence read: "1 GMC; 1 Driver, Displace 16 Horses; 4 Drivers; 4 Wagons."[2] By 1911 there were about 25,000 trucks in operation.

Both the pursuit of Pancho Villa into Mexico in 1916, and World War I provided great stimuli to the motor truck industry. Production soared, and trucks were given an opportunity to demonstrate their strength, speed, dependability, and overall effectiveness. Men were trained to be truck drivers. General John J. Pershing wired to the Army Chief of Staff in 1918:

> At the present time our ability to supply and maneuver our forces depends largely on motor transportation. The shortage in motor transportation is particularly embarrassing now due to shortages of horses for our horse-drawn transport. . . . The need for motor transportation is urgent. It is not understood why greater advantage has not been taken of deck space to ship motor trucks. Trucks do not overburden dock accommodations or require railroad transportation. Can you not impress this upon shipping authorities?[3]

As an indication of the general acceptance of trucks after World War I, 335,000 trucks were produced in the U.S. in 1920.

After the war, the truck manufacturers put new emphasis on research to increase vehicle operating efficiency. Perhaps the most significant improvement was the replacement of the wooden wheels and solid rubber tires with steel wheels and pneumatic tires. The latter development ". . . not only enormously increased their carrying and pulling power, the speed of operation, and the road ease (the last of which permitted the transportation of such breakable goods as eggs and glassware), but the increased traction permitted dozens of adaptations for the motor truck hitherto impossible."[4]

Due to these technical advancements, the numbers of trucks and their acceptance multiplied rapidly. By 1925, about 2½ million trucks were in operation. Of this number, only about 155,000 were operated as motor common carriers.[5] The 1920's are usually thought of as the decade when our modern trucking industry was born.

[2] *Ibid.*

[3] *Ibid.*, p. 63. World War II was to have an analogous impact on aviation.

[4] Howard William Trayer, *The Four Wheel Drive Story* (New York: McGraw-Hill Book Co., 1954), p. 100.

[5] Helen M. Muller, *Federal Regulation of Motor Transport* (New York: H. W. Wilson Co., 1933), pp. 11, 44–45.

Motor Carrier Operating Characteristics

Chapter 3 discussed the four legal forms of carriers: common, contract, exempt, and private. Each of these forms exists in the trucking

- *For-hire carriers* is a phrase sometimes applied to mean both common and contract carriers. The two, when operating in interstate commerce, are also often referred to as *ICC-regulated*, even though the contract carriers' operations are subject to many fewer regulations than are the common carriers. *Non–ICC-regulated* trucks generally applies to exempt and private carriers.

industry. The Transportation Association of America estimates that of the $90.4 billion spent on intercity truck transportation in 1980, less than half, or only 48 percent, was paid to ICC-regulated carriers. Non–ICC-regulated carriers earned the rest.[6]

Number and Size of ICC-Regulated Motor Carrier Firms

In 1980, there were approximately 17,700 ICC-regulated motor carrier firms,[7] although the number of firms has been declining. In 1940, the comparable number was over 26,000. How could there be such an increase in trucking accompanied by a decrease in the number of trucking firms? The answer is that a small number of firms grew even larger by acquiring smaller firms' equipment, terminals, and operating rights. Of the 17,721 for-hire carriers in 1980, 947 were class I carriers, 2,164 were class II, and 14,610 were class III.

- *Operating rights* are granted by regulatory bodies to motor common carriers giving them the right to provide specific services to specific areas. Before deregulation these rights had a value since the regulatory body would limit the number of competitors. The rights could be sold, with the ICC's permission, to another common carrier which was attempting to expand its service area.

- The ICC classifies regulated carriers according to their annual gross operating income. Currently, truckers with revenues in

[6] *Transportation Facts & Trends, 1980* (Washington, D.C.: Transportation Association of America, 1980).

[7] The exact number of unregulated trucking firms is unknown. The Motor Vehicle Manufacturers Association estimates that there are approximately 60,000 firms in the U.S. with fleets of 10 or more motor vehicles. The largest single category is "for-hire" trucking, but it accounts for only 13,600 of the firms with fleets of 10 or more. See: *MVMA Motor Vehicle Facts & Figures '79* (Detroit, Michigan, 1979), p. 48.

excess of $5 million are *Class I carriers;* while carriers with revenues between $1 million and $5 million are *Class II. Class III* are the remainder.

The average Class I ICC-regulated trucking company in 1979 had 1,119 employees, although the largest firms in the industry had many more employees. Consolidated Freightways had 24,400 employees, Roadway Express had 23,000 employees, and Yellow Freight had 15,550 employees. In terms of revenues, the average Class I and Class II ICC-regulated company collected $14,346,567 in 1979. The largest firms in 1981 had these gross revenues: Consolidated Freightways—$1,750 million; Roadway Express—$1,400 million; and Yellow Freight—$860 million.

The great majority of ICC-regulated truckers are common carriers. However, the contract carrier industry is growing; in recent years the ICC has authorized approximately 200 *new* contract carriers per year. Professor Taff's analysis of the 287 largest contract carriers indicates that they were actively involved in petitioning and receiving additional grants of authority from the ICC, and Taff believes that: "contract carriage will continue to expand."[8] In 1979, the ICC further increased the contract carriers' market potential by increasing the number of contracts each individual carrier could enter into,[9] and the *Motor Carrier Act of 1980* removed the restrictions entirely.

Non-Regulated Trucking

The segments of the trucking industry that are not subject to ICC regulation are much larger than those segments that are. No precise statistics exist accurately describing the extent of the unregulated fleet of trucks. In the United States in 1981, there were 35.5 million registered trucks and 520,000 registered buses.[10] However, the vast majority of trucks are small pickups or vans used by a family or individuals for personal transportation. There are only about 1.4 million truck-tractors registered in the U.S. These truck-tractors pulling trailers or semi-trailers are familiar sights on our highways.

- *Truck-tractors* have two or three axles, and pull either a semi-trailer (which has axles and tires only at the rear) or a full trailer

---

[8]Charles A. Taff, "Grants of Motor Contract Carrier Operating Authority—1970–75," *Transportation Journal* (Winter, 1976), pp. 102–103.

[9]*Traffic World* (January 15, 1979) pp. 84–86. Up until this time, contract carriers had usually been limited to eight contracts apiece.

[10]*Motor Vehicle Facts & Figures, '81* (Detroit: Motor Vehicle Manufacturers Association, 1981), pp. 17, 19.

(which has axles and tires at both the front and rear). Many states allow a truck-tractor to pull two or three trailers.

For-hire trucking companies operate about 650,000 trucks. Other categories of firms that own large numbers of truck-tractors are leasing firms (which lease trucks to both regulated and unregulated truckers); food processors; manufacturing firms; retail chains; the construction industry; and petroleum distribution.[11] ICC-regulated carriers also operate some two-axle trucks (known as bobtails), to pick up and deliver shipments within urban areas. Hence, we see that in terms of numbers of trucks, ICC-regulated carriers account for only a small percentage of all truck registrations.

Another category of motor carrier not regulated by the ICC is the trucker who operates solely within a single state. Nearly every state regulates the operations of intrastate common and contract carriers.[12]

Over three million trucks are considered "farm" trucks. Some of these carry unprocessed agricultural commodities on highways and are exempt from ICC regulation. Other farm trucks are seldom on a highway; they are used mainly for work on the farm.

In June, 1979, the phrase "independent trucker" became more widely known as this small band of individualists grouped together long enough to mount a protest that brought trucking to a stop for a few days. Independent truckers are also known as "owner-operators," since they (often in conjunction with one or more creditors) own the truck they drive. This category of trucker moves inside and outside the realm of ICC jurisdiction. *The New York Times* described one independent trucker's activities this way:

> On that trip he was paid $1,400 to haul a load of candy to California, a fee that would have been much higher if he were a regulated carrier with authority for such hauls from the Interstate Commerce Commission. Since he must use trip authority granted him by one of the carriers, he must accept the smaller payment.
>
> For the return trip, hauling produce, an "exempt" commodity not regulated by the ICC, he was paid $1,700.[13]

Because there are so many types of trucking activities, one must be fairly precise when discussing the industry. The number of trucks

---

[11] *Ibid.*, p. 42.

[12] Interstate motor carriers are also subject to state regulation for any traffic they pick up and deliver within a single state.

[13] *The New York Times* (June 29, 1979). With reference to the candy shipment, the regulated carrier collected the full charges from the shipper, but was able to negotiate a lower rate with the independent trucker and pocket the difference.

we see on the road is large, but only a small percentage of these have their activities regulated by the Interstate Commerce Commission.

Products Carried and Service Characteristics

The motor truck is capable of carrying almost any type of product, and it generally does. This capability is one reason why the trucking industry has grown. Table 4–1, taken from the 1977 Census of Transportation, shows how trucks and railroads "share" the markets for carrying various types of commodities.

The trend of truck shipments by Class I intercity common carriers is towards longer shipping distances. In 1945, the average length of haul was 177 miles; by 1979 it was 411 miles. The average shipment tendered to a Class I and Class II motor common carrier is relatively

TABLE 4–1   Market Share of Trucks and Rails in Transporting Manufactured Goods

Percent of Tons Transported and Lengths of Haul
(manufactured goods, 1977)

Commodity (descending order)	Percent of Total*	Transported by		Average Length of Haul (miles)	
		Trucks	Rails	Trucks	Rails
Petroleum & Coal	30.12%	25.01%	6.76%	94	280
Stone, Clay, Glass & Concrete	19.73	91.33	6.60	53	364
Food & Kindred Products	12.88	73.45	22.77	202	596
Lumber & Wood (exc. furn.)	10.78	61.10	19.52	117	445
Chemicals & Allied Prods.	9.76	47.20	33.28	235	528
Primary Metal Products	5.55	63.13	33.74	213	373
Pulp, Paper & Allied Prods.	3.25	51.55	43.14	238	631
Fabricated Metal Products	1.84	80.15	17.76	283	474
Transportation Equipment	1.79	46.73	46.00	299	724
Machinery (exc. electrical)	0.78	80.84	13.42	431	786
Printed Matter	0.75	85.97	3.37	154	791
Rubber & Misc. Plastics	0.57	82.67	16.08	456	730
Electrical Machinery	0.49	74.58	16.12	477	859
Textile Mill Products	0.41	90.93	5.84	321	679
Furniture & Fixtures	0.25	84.05	12.78	439	822
Apparel, Other Finished Textiles	0.17	83.64	4.94	394	656
Misc. Manufactured Goods	0.14	85.32	6.42	545	1,055
Tobacco Products	0.07	67.86	31.21	299	747
Instru., Photo & Med., Watches, etc.	0.07	82.52	9.13	626	1,185
Leather & Leather Prods.	0.05	91.02	1.13	478	1,000
Totals	**100.00%**	**51.11%**	**16.55%**	**148**	**494**

*—Will not add to 100.00% due to rounding.

Source: 1977 Census of Transportation, conducted by the U.S. Bureau of the Census, and reproduced by the Research and Economics Division of the American Trucking Associations, 1981.

small. In 1980, Overnite Transportation Company, a large Class I motor common carrier, received 3.5 million shipments of less than 10,000 pounds. The average shipment weighed 794 pounds. By way of comparison, Overnite received only 107,000 truckload shipments (over 10,000 pounds), with an average weight per shipment of 30,841 pounds.[14] The typical small shipment is almost always finished merchandise having a relatively high value.

A U.S. Department of Transportation survey found that 67 percent of shippers rated motor carrier service as either "excellent" or "good." By way of comparison, only 22 percent of the shippers rated rail carriers as excellent or good.[15] Regarding speed, a truck is gener-

- *Customer service standards* in freight transportation are methods shippers and consignees use to measure the performance of carriers. *Speed-of-delivery* is lapsed time between when the carrier picks up the shipment and when it is delivered. *On-time delivery* means delivering the product when it is expected, no sooner and no later. *Accessibility* means the ability to reach numerous sites to either pick up or deliver a shipment. There are also other service standards.

ally superior to railroad service, especially if the total origin-to-destination distance is less than 500 miles. In addition, when compared to a railroad car, a truck is a fairly small operating unit. Shippers find truckload quantities of goods more convenient to handle. That is, if the shipper is a small manufacturer with a continuous flow of output, he may be able to ship one truckload of product every day. But if he uses rail, he would have to accumulate two or three days' output in order to fill a railroad car.

On-time delivery ignores speed of delivery and concentrates on a carrier ability to deliver a product *when* promised. Time after time, when shippers are asked, "What's more important: Speed of delivery or on-time (promised) delivery?," the latter is chosen.[16] Motor carriers consistently outperform railroads on this aspect of service.

The final service advantage of trucks is their accessibility. Motor carrier service is generally available between almost all origins and destinations within the United States. By this measure, the truck can

---

[14] "Overnite Transportation Company Annual Report," 1980, p. 8.

[15] J. Richard Jones, *Industrial Shipper Survey: Plant Level* (Washington, D.C.: Office of Transportation Planning Analysis, Department of Transportation, 1975), p. 28.

[16] See, for example: Bernard J. LaLonde, John Grabner, and James Robeson, "The Motor Carrier Selection Decision," in *Annual Proceedings of the National Council of Physical Distribution Management* (1971), Section XIII; and James R. Stock, "How Shippers Judge Carriers," *Distribution Worldwide* (August, 1976).

reach many more places than can a railroad. There are 3.8 million miles of public roads in the U.S., nearly 20 times the total mileage of rail track. (In addition, trucks can operate off highways in many locations.) An American Trucking Association study found that the 61,465 communities (places with a counted population) in the United States, only 20,340 had railroad service.[17]

Carriers' Rights-of-Way

Public streets and roads in the United States provide trucks and autos access to virtually every parcel of land in the nation. Complementing and connecting to the 3.8 million miles of public roads are private roads, driveways, logging roads, farmer's lanes, and parking lots. This is what makes our auto, truck, and bus system available everywhere. However, the trucks must share this highway and road system with autos and buses. Sometimes the interests of these three groups are not the same. Tractor-driving farmers, motorcyclists, bicyclists, joggers, pedestrians, and, occasionally, horses also claim rights to use the same pavement. While this chapter deals mainly with trucks and buses, one must remember that they share this ubiquitous road network with many others, and while user fees pretty well cover the costs of building and maintaining our road system, there are continual disagreements as to who is or is not paying his or her "fair" share.

While trucks pay for a share of this vast system's costs, they do so indirectly, through taxes on fuel or tires, and for license and permit fees. To the trucker, the user fees and taxes are variable costs of doing business, rather than a long-term investment or commitment.[18]

The Highway Network

From 1921 to 1976, the federal government spent $104 billion on highways, while state and local governments expended $354 billion.[19] In 1980 alone, federal, state, and local governments spent $36.8 billion to build and maintain the nation's road system. But

---

[17] *Motor Vehicle Facts & Figures, '81* (Detroit: Motor Vehicle Manufacturers Association, 1981), p. 64.

[18] See: Enrico DiGiammarino and Donald F. Wood, "Motor Carrier Section 22 Tenders: Do They Cover Variable Costs?" *The Transportation Law Journal* (July, 1975), especially p. 167.

[19] "Government and Private Expenditures For Highway, Waterway, Railroad and Air Rights-of-Ways," (Washington, D.C.: Association of American Railroads, September, 1976), Table 5.

before we get into the costs of building, maintaining, and further developing this vast highway system, let's first take a look at how it all got started.

The first roads in the U.S. were animal trails. Because animals were a source of food and clothing, hunters followed these trails, and to some degree they probably developed them. At some point in time, the hunters and early settlers widened paths so that horses and oxen-drawn loads could pass through. Although the early roads often followed valleys, they were high enough to avoid flooding and hence became known as *highways*.[20]

Government participation in the construction of roads dates to the time of the American Revolution. In 1779 the legislature of Virginia enacted a law calling for the Wilderness Road to be broadened for wagon transportation from Virginia to Kentucky. The federal government became actively involved in highway construction, starting with the Cumberland Road in 1806. The rationale for early federal participation in this highway was noted by Professor Young: "Military necessity, private initiative and small appropriations by states immediately concerned were not sufficient for the construction of a good road over the mountains through a sparsely settled intervening country. As no single state was financially able or willing to undertake such a work, attention was turned to the Treasury of the United States."[21] Toll-houses were erected every fifteen miles to help pay for the road.

By 1891, the federal government had spent $17 million on highways. The public's desire for "good roads" greatly multiplied after 1900, when bicycles, autos, and trucks all appeared. The 1916 *Federal-Aid Road Act* required each state to establish a highway department to plan the state's road network. This act established the concept—still utilized today—that states retain the initiative in constructing highways and that the federal government will pay a percentage of the construction costs. Maintenance of existing roads was to be exclusively a state function. Local streets and roads are often paid for by local governments relying on local revenue sources, such as the property tax.

Initially proposed in the 1944 *Federal-Aid Highway Act* was an *Interstate System* to consist of the most important routes in the United States and not to exceed 40,000 miles. In 1956 *Federal-Aid*

---

[20]Caroline E. MacGill, *History of Transportation In The United States Before 1860* (Washington, D.C.: Carnegie Institution, 1917), p. 6.

[21]Jeremiah S. Young, *A Political and Constitutional Study of the Cumberland Road* (Chicago: 1907), pp. 12–13. See also: Albert C. Rose, *Historic American Roads* (New York: Crown Publishers, 1976).

Highway Act specifically funded and provided for the Interstate System proposed in 1944. The system was to be formally designated "The National System of Interstate and Defense Highways." It was to be 41,000 miles and its total cost was estimated to be $27 billion.[22] The Interstate System has subsequently been expanded to 42,500 miles, and in 1978 the Federal Highway Administration estimated that the system will cost $104.3 billion.[23] Figure 4–1 shows the Interstate System, which was 95 percent completed as of June, 1981. Drew Lewis, Secretary of Transportation for the Reagan Administration, has stated that completion of the Interstate System by 1990 is one of the administration's top transportation goals.[24]

In terms of user preference, the Interstate System has been highly successful. The system accounts for slightly more than 1 percent of the nation's highway network, yet it carries about 20 percent of all passengers and freight using the road system. Its effects have been far-reaching. Juan Cameron notes:

> The system has played major roles in the redrawing of labor markets, the shifting of population out of cities, and the dispersing of retail stores, warehouses, and factories into suburbs. Because of the Interstate Highway System, businesses have thrived or shriveled, and whole industries have been transformed. The demise of the meatpacking industry in Chicago, Kansas City, and Omaha, for instance, can be attributed in large part to the highway network: smalltown packing-houses, linked by fast highways to major markets have done in the big-city slaughterhouses.[25]

The Highway Trust Fund

The 1956 *Federal-Aid Highway Act* created the Highway Trust Fund, which was to receive its revenues exclusively for highway use taxes. It was designed to be on a "pay-as-you-go" basis so there would be uninterrupted planning and construction of the Interstate System. The fund was to be autonomous from "political forces" because it collected taxes exclusively from highway users and then paid out exclusively to states for highway construction.

The Highway Trust Fund has been a great temptation—almost the "forbidden fruit"—for many politicians. Why? Because it con-

---

[22] William J. Hudson and James A. Constantin, *Motor Transportation: Principles and Practices* (New York: Ronald Press Co., 1958), p. 81.

[23] *Transport Topics* (January 9, 1978), p. 25.

[24] Don Waters, "Interstate System Nears Completion, Dubious Future," *Minneapolis Tribune* (June 29, 1981), p. 8C.

[25] Juan Cameron, "How the Interstate Changed the Face of the Nation," *Fortune* (July, 1971) in Stanley J. Hille and Richard F. Poist, Jr., eds., *Transportation: Principles and Perspectives* (Danville, Ill.: Interstate Printers and Publishers, 1974), p. 66.

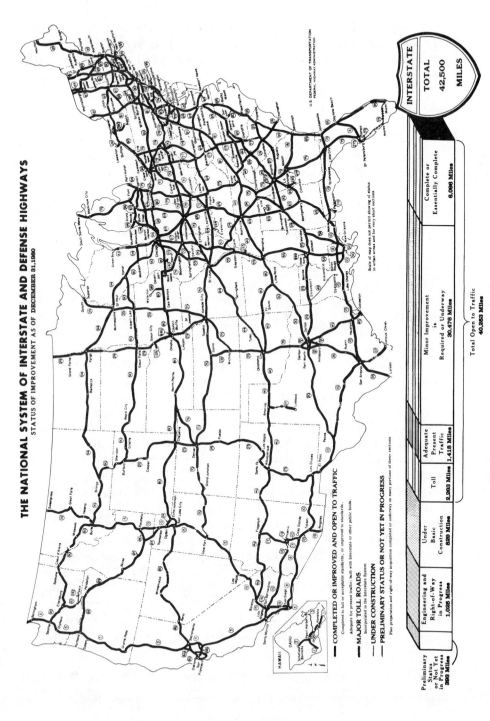

Figure 4-1 The Interstate Highway System. Courtesy: Federal Highway Administration.

sistently generates a surplus. This has been especially true as the system nears completion. In 1980 the fund had $12 billion in idle reserves which generated about $900 million in interest! A vocal, but apparently weak, Congressional bloc suggested that the Highway Trust Fund surpluses be turned over to the general revenue account of the federal budget for funding more "socially" desirable programs.

While these suggestions have not been considered serious challenges to the Highway Trust Fund, its original solidarity of purpose has been cracked twice.

The first time was the 1973 *Federal-Aid Highway Act* which provided that the Highway Trust Fund could provide limited funding to urban mass transportation. Professor George M. Smerk, a proponent of "tapping" the trust fund for mass transit, observed: "The important factor is not the money involved, but the redesign of the highway trust fund as a mechanism that once assured highway construction whether or not it was the most desirable approach. . . . The idea of an inviolate trust fund has withered; the idea of publicly-owned, subsidized mass transit is generally accepted."[26] In 1981 the Highway Trust Fund collected about $8.1 billion and paid out $20 million to mass transit.

The highway carriers have been crying "foul!" because the fund was established as a true *user charge*, defined by the Department of Commerce as a "charge made to beneficiaries or users of services and facilities directly related to transportation. . . . Such charges must be paid for use of such service or facility."[27] Therefore, since the money was collected from highway users, it could be argued that it is only fair, just, and equitable that these funds be expended on highway projects.

The second non-traditional use of the Highway Trust Fund was authorized by Congress in 1976. It authorized $350 million to be spent over two years for maintenance and rehabilitation of the Interstate System. Traditionally, states were responsible for maintenance, but they are trying to shift these costs to the federal government for several reasons. First, state gas tax revenues are down because less fuel is being sold due to the national 55-miles-per-hour speed limit and the sale of smaller new cars. Second, maintenance labor costs and materials have been rapidly increasing in cost. Third, the roads themselves are wearing out faster than originally projected. A

---

[26] George M. Smerk, "How Now, Highway Trust Fund?" *Business Horizons* (April, 1974), p. 38.

[27] *The Doyle Report*, U.S. Senate Report No. 445 (1961), pp. 184–185.

Wall Street Journal reporter noted, "One big reason why roads are wearing out is that trucks are heavier and more numerous than anyone foresaw. . . . Many roads were designed to handle trucks at about 5 percent of their total traffic, but trucks now account for 15 percent to 20 percent."[28] Finally, state highway bureaucracies, thwarted in their attempts to build new roads by the advocates of "no growth," reluctantly decided that using the federal funds for maintenance would be less controversial.

The Interstate System is rapidly deteriorating. In 1975, federal highway officials reported that approximately 4 percent of Interstate mileage had "severe cracks." By 1980, the comparable figure was 10 percent. To help alleviate this situation, funding for maintenance from the Highway Trust Fund has been authorized to substantially increase in the future. The funding level for fiscal year 1982 is $275 million; for 1983, $1.3 billion; and increases to $2.7 billion in 1987.[29]

Because the Federal Highway Trust Fund is collecting less money than in the past, and its payouts are increasing, it is currently operating at a deficit. The deficit is paid by drawing down its reserve. In 1981, the Highway Trust fund collected $8.1 billion and paid out $8.2 billion for new construction and maintenance of the Interstate System. It is projected this income-spending gap will widen in the future.[30]

Trucking Firms' Cost Structure

The preceding section described how the highway system is provided by the public with funds collected from various users, including the general taxpayer. This section will now examine the cost structure of the trucking firms which operate on the highways. The cost structure of the motor carrier industry can be examined by looking at the two basic components of the total costs of operation: fixed costs and variable costs. Fixed costs (also known as constant costs) are expenses which do *not* vary with the quantity or volume of business a firm produces. They are needed to establish the business and can only be avoided by totally discontinuing the operation.

[28] Albert R. Karr, "U.S. Faces Huge Road Repair Bill," *The Wall Street Journal* (January 13, 1978), p. 14.

[29] Ray Hebert, "Cracks Taint Super Dream of Interstates," *Los Angeles Times* (October 2, 1980), p. 27.

[30] "Why The Highway Fund May Run Out of Money," *Business Week* (February 18, 1980), p. 65.

Variable costs change *directly* with the volume of output produced by a company. They are often referred to as "out-of-pocket" costs.

Major fixed costs for a motor common carrier include license fees,[31] property taxes, salaries of supervisory and senior management, and terminals. Major variable costs include wages of hourly employees, depreciation of vehicles based on usage, repairs and maintenance costs, fuel, lubricants, and some marketing costs.

In 1954, the ICC conducted a substantial analysis of the relative percentages of trucking companies' fixed and variable costs and concluded that fixed costs in the regulated trucking industry were about 10 percent of total costs.[32] This finding was reconfirmed by the ICC in a 1968 study.[33] Professor Robert E. Shirley analyzed this issue and concluded that because terminals are becoming more sophisticated and require more capital investment, fixed costs are 25 percent of total costs.[34] Notice that this analysis was conducted *before* fuel price increases of 1973 and 1979.

Economies of Scale

Another characteristic of trucking deals with the question, Are there increasing economies of scale in this industry? In other words, as production increases, does the cost per unit of production decrease? If an industry is subject to significant economies of scale, there will be a "shakeout" of the smaller and less efficient firms, resulting in an industry dominated by a few large firms that can operate at very low costs per unit of service. Alternatively, if an industry is such that there are no significant economies of scale, then small firms can compete equally well with large ones. Therefore, an environment of less governmental regulation will not see industry concentration, since large firms are no more efficient than smaller ones.

[31] License and registration fees can be variable costs if the owner chooses not to renew the license on an idle piece of equipment until he needs it. See: Di Giammarino and Wood, *loc. cit.*

[32] ICC, Statement No. 1-54, *Explanation of the Development of Motor Carrier Costs with Statements as to their Meaning and Significance* (April, 1954), pp. 71–99.

[33] ICC, Statement No. 5-68, *Cost of Transporting Freight by Class I and Class II Motor Common Carriers of General Commodities* (June, 1968), p. 5.

[34] Robert E. Shirley, "Analysis of Motor Carrier Cost Formula Developed by the Interstate Commerce Commission," *Transportation Journal* (Spring, 1969), pp. 22–24. On this same subject, see also: David L. Shrock, "Motor Carrier Analysis—The Next Step," *ICC Practitioners' Journal* (July–August, 1975), pp. 572–587; Dwight Stuessy, "Cost Structure of Private and For Hire Motor Carriage," *Transportation Journal* (Spring, 1976), pp. 40–48; and Garland Chow, *The Economics of the Motor Freight Industries* (Bloomington: Indiana University School of Business, 1978).

There has been no lack of research in this area![35] While arguments over methodology and interpretation of data are rampant,[36] Professor James C. Nelson has presented a summary of the majority opinion in this quandary. He said:

> Past studies of the economies of scale in size of trucking firm have resulted in pessimistic conclusions. And the logic of the economic characteristics of trucking, considering public ownership of the highways and variable cost payments for highway services, points clearly to the conclusion that economies of scale, if any, are not significant and provide no basis for organizing the industry into a few large firms or one firm on each route and in each class of service in the interest of lowering the costs of essential truck transport.[37]

Trucking Industry Problem Areas

This section will discuss briefly problem areas in the trucking industry. Each problem is serious; no attempt has been made to rank them.

Fuel Costs

The trucking industry is highly dependent on fuel availability. The American Trucking Associations noted: "If armies travel only on their stomachs, trucks go nowhere without fuel. The economic viability and sheer operation of no other major segment of U.S. industry is as dependent upon fuel supply and price as highway transportation."[38] Part of the 1979 strike of the independent truckers was aimed at the escalating price of fuel.

Since the trucking industry is a large user of fuel, there has been an unrelenting effort to make the motor carrier industry more fuel-

[35] For a discussion of the major studies dealing with economies of scale in the trucking industry up to 1973, see: James C. Johnson, *Trucking Mergers* (Lexington, Mass: D. C. Heath, 1973), pp. 19–22. For more recent studies, see: Jay A. Smith, Jr., "Concentration in the Common and Contract Motor Carrier Industry—A Regulatory Dilemma," *Transportation Journal* (Summer, 1973), pp. 30–48; and James P. Rakowski, "Motor Carrier Size and Profitability," *Transportation Journal* (Summer, 1977), pp. 36–45.

[36] See: Edwin P. Patton, "Implications of Motor Carrier Growth and Size," *Transportation Journal* (Fall, 1970), pp. 34–52; Gary N. Dicer, "Economies-of-Scale and Motor Carrier Optimum Size," *Quarterly Review of Economics and Business* (Spring, 1971), pp. 31–37; and D. Daryl Wyckoff, "Factors Promoting Concentration of Motor Carriers Under Deregulation," *Transportation Research Forum Annual Proceedings* (Oxford, Indiana: Richard B. Cross, 1974), pp. 1–6.

[37] James C. Nelson, "Coming Organizational Changes in Transportation," in Jack R. Davidson and Howard W. Ottoson, eds., *Transportation Problems and Policies in the Trans-Missouri West* (Lincoln: University of Nebraska Press, 1967), p. 323.

[38] *American Trucking Associations' Annual Report* (1976), p. 5.

efficient. Pacific Intermountain Express is generally considered a leader in the "battle" against fuel wastage.[39] From 1973 to 1976, this large motor common carrier firm achieved a 20-percent fuel reduction per vehicle-mile. This dramatic savings was achieved by using a number of techniques. First, observing the 55-miles-per-hour speed limit saved fuel. Second, "air drag" was reduced by placing an air deflector shield on top of every long-haul tractor. Third, radial tires were used; although more expensive, their stiffness reduces tire-tread/road friction, requiring less fuel to overcome the "drag" of the tires. Fourth, a significant fuel savings was accomplished by a radiator fan "cut-out." The fan normally runs directly off the engine at any time the engine is on. However, the fan is actually only needed about 5 percent of the time to help keep the engine from overheating. A fan "clutch" turns off the fan when it is not needed, and this measure alone can reduce fuel consumption by 5 to 11 percent.[40] Figure 4–2 shows the importance of different fuel-saving measures used by the trucking industry in 1979.

Another issue regarding fuel is the relative efficiency of each mode. In terms of moving ton-miles of freight, a truck is relatively

[39]"Truck Lines Mobilize to Conserve Fuel," *Traffic World* (June 21, 1976).
[40]*Traffic Quarterly* (April, 1976), p. 212.

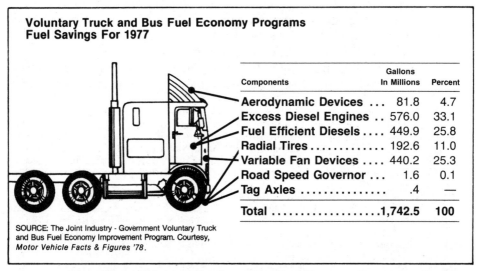

Voluntary Truck and Bus Fuel Economy Programs
Fuel Savings For 1977

Components	Gallons In Millions	Percent
Aerodynamic Devices ...	81.8	4.7
Excess Diesel Engines ..	576.0	33.1
Fuel Efficient Diesels	449.9	25.8
Radial Tires	192.6	11.0
Variable Fan Devices	440.2	25.3
Road Speed Governor ...	1.6	0.1
Tag Axles	.4	—
Total	1,742.5	100

SOURCE: The Joint Industry - Government Voluntary Truck and Bus Fuel Economy Improvement Program. Courtesy, *Motor Vehicle Facts & Figures '78.*

Figure 4–2   Voluntary Truck and Bus Fuel Economy Programs—Fuel Savings for 1979. Source: Adapted from *American Trucking Trends, 1979–1980* (American Trucking Associations), p. 68.

fuel-inefficient compared to rail, and some natural resource-oriented economists have suggested the United States should have a national policy of taking long distance freight off of trucks and putting it onto the railroad system.[41]

Safety on the Highways

United States' highways are the safest in the world. In 1978, the U.S. experienced an average of 3.4 traffic fatalities per 100 million vehicle-miles. Comparable figures for other countries were: United Kingdom—4.2, Australia—5.6, Canada—4.5, Norway—4.3, Italy—5.4, Germany—7.9, Japan—5.2, France—7.2, and Belgium—11.9.[42] Even though U.S. highways are relatively safe, there is continued animosity between motorists and truckers because it is believed truckers are responsible for a disproportionate share of highway accidents and deaths. For example, in the late 1960's, a New Jersey Turnpike Authority spokesperson stated that trucks accounted for 12 percent of vehicles using the turnpike, but they were involved in 31.1 percent of all accidents and 61.8 percent of all fatal accidents. Trucks are more apt to precipitate accidents than autos because of their inability to stop as quickly. At 50 miles per hour, it takes a fully loaded tractor-trailer unit 240 to 280 feet to stop, compared with 140 feet for a passenger car. When cars and large trucks do collide, fatalities are 10 times more likely than when a car hits another car,[43] and this problem will become worse as the average size of passenger cars becomes smaller. (See Figure 4–3.)

Safety figures for heavy trucks have *not* been improving. In 1978, the U.S. Department of Transportation's Bureau of Motor Carrier Safety inspected 26,000 trucks and 42 percent of the vehicles were impounded until repairs could be made.[44] For the year 1978, approximately 50,000 people were killed in highway vehicle accidents. Heavy trucks, although they account for less than one percent

---

[41] Professors Harris and Hille disagree. They say: "This forecasting does show conclusively that energy conservation efforts should stress conversion to smaller autos rather than future modal switches from truck to rail. A policy calling for the latter may disrupt industry and have inconsequential impact on energy conservation." See: Curtis C. Harris, Jr., and Stanley J. Hille, "Rail, Truck, or Small Car—Which is the Energy Saver?" *Business Horizons* (December, 1974), pp. 57–64.

[42] *Motor Vehicle Facts & Figures, '81* (Detroit: Motor Vehicle Manufacturers Association, 1981), p. 52.

[43] Albert R. Karr, "Road Danger Is Rising," *The Wall Street Journal* (December 31, 1976), p. 5.

[44] Thomas Moore, "Truck Safety Legislation," *Transport Topics* (July 23, 1979), p. 8.

"There's that
crunching sound
again."

Reproduced by permission of the artist and Masters Agency.

Figure 4–3   Truck-Auto Accidents Often Result in Serious Injuries. Reproduced by permission of the artist and the Masters Agency.

of total vehicles on the roads, were involved in nearly 35 percent of these fatalities.[45]

Two solutions have been suggested to improve the highway safety of trucks. The first is more vigorous enforcement of the present state and federal motor carrier safety regulations. A second solution—in theory at least—involves requiring larger trucks to have safer brakes. In 1976 the FMVSS (Federal Motor Vehicle Safety Standard) 121 required a new antilock air brake system. It is controlled by an electronic computer which is supposed to "pump" air brakes so they will not "lock." However, it appears the electronic system may be ahead of its time. In October, 1977, the California Highway Patrol randomly checked 3,600 trucks and found 22 percent of trucks with "121" antilock systems so out of adjustment that they rendered them "unfit" to operate on California highways. Prior to the "121"

[45] Ibid.

requirement, a similar inspection found that only 9 percent of trucks had unsafe brakes.[46] In late 1978, the trucking industry prevailed against the "121" standard when the Ninth U.S. Circuit Court of Appeals invalidated the antilock device. The U.S. Supreme Court affirmed this decision by choosing not to review the lower court's decision.[47]

The Declining Role of the Motor Common Carrier

Much of the transportation system of the United States was built on the "common carrier" concept. Motor common carriers are often the sole remaining carrier upon which small businesses and isolated communities can rely for service. Traditionally, the common carrier practiced discriminatory pricing and used high profits from some aspects of his business to offset losses in others. This practice is

- *Cross-subsidization* (or *internal subsidization*) is a widely-used business practice. Excess earnings from more profitable operations are used to offset losses from unprofitable operations. Transportation regulatory bodies encouraged common carriers to practice this, since it meant the carriers (and our transportation system) could serve a larger total number of customers (including some who do not cover their full share of the carriers' costs).

known as "cross-subsidization." A problem faced by common carriers (both rail and motor) is that private carriers, or contract carriers, move in to capture any business where the common carrier's rates are much higher than costs. This deprives the common carrier of revenues and excess earnings needed to internally subsidize losses from handling the business of other shippers which he, as a common carrier, is obligated to haul.

Common carrier business erodes because of several other factors. One has been gray-area motor carriage; another is the rulings that

- *Gray-area motor carriage* is somewhere between being precisely legal and precisely illegal. Often it violates the spirit, if not the letter, of the law. Examples are when owner-operators pretend to "buy" the load of freight they are carrying, so they can claim to be "private" truckers, rather than contract carriers, for which they would need ICC permits.

[46] *Transport Topics* (November 7, 1977), p. 53.
[47] See: Thomas Moore, "NHTSA Chief Vows New Drive on Truck Standards," *Transport Topics* (February 4, 1980), pp. 1, 4.

make it easier for private carriers to obtain loads. A recent example of the latter was the ICC's 1978 decision that private carriers could apply for ICC rights to become a common or contract carrier and then solicit business from other shippers in order to reduce their problem of empty backhaul (and thereby be more fuel-efficient).

Motor common carriers were incensed by this ICC action. (This decision is known as the "Toto" case, because the Toto Purchasing and Supply Company was the company that had asked the ICC for for-hire motor carrier operating rights.) Common carriers sued the ICC in the U.S. Circuit Court of Appeals, asking the court to reverse the above decision. In July, 1981, the court upheld the ICC's decision. The court declared:

> The Commission's sensitivity to the imperativeness of energy conservation is apparent from its consideration of increasing and wasteful empty backhauls experienced by private carriers. We cannot fault its conclusion that "the increasing need for energy-efficient operations has caused the Commission to place added emphasis on coordination between the various forms of transportation, public and private."[48]

A recent survey by Professors Mentzer and Krapfel asked operators of private truck fleets if they would take advantage of their new-found right to apply to the ICC for common and/or contract operating rights. This study concluded by noting:

> The national representatives of the sample indicates that a large number of private motor carrier fleet corporations will, to some degree, take advantage of Toto . . . rights. Given the competitive cost advantage these carriers will have over regular common and contract carriers, the effect upon common and contract carriers will be substantial. A large amount of tonnage lost to the common and contract carriers should be expected. However, considerable efficiency in fuel savings and private carriage-rolling stock usage will result.[49]

The *Motor Carrier Act of 1980* cannot be said to be "helpful" to motor common carriers. This is because the Act made it easier for other individuals and firms to enter into the trucking business, with one result being that they would "whittle away" at certain common carrier markets.

Increased Highway User Charges

As mentioned earlier, the trucking industry pays substantial user charges for the right to use the highway system. At the federal level,

---

[48]"Court Affirms ICC's Toto Policy, Backs Private Trucks In For-Hire Moves," *Traffic World* (July 6, 1981), p. 130.

[49]John T. Mentzer and Robert E. Krapfel, "Reactions of Private Motor Carriers to Toto and Compensated Intercorporate Hauling Rights," *Transportation Journal* (Spring, 1981), p. 71.

there is a 4 cents per gallon tax on motor fuel, and additional excise taxes on lubricating oil, tires, and tubes, and on vehicles with gross vehicle weight in excess of 10,000 pounds. The primary state taxes involve a tax on motor fuel ranging currently from 15.3 cents per gallon (Michigan) to 5 cents per gallon (Texas) and an annual registration tax. In 1979, the above taxes collected $8.1 billion at the federal level and $7.1 billion for state governments. In terms of percentages, trucks paid 38 percent of total highway taxes collected by the states, and 48 percent of those collected by the federal government.

Because highway maintenance and rehabilitation costs are rapidly escalating, it is necessary for both the states and the federal government to increase highway user charges. In 1981, forty states proposed to increase their highway taxes[50] and the federal government was studying a 10 cents per gallon increase in the motor fuel tax.[51]

It is generally conceded that highway user taxes must increase. The controversial issue is which highway users should pay the higher rates? The railroad industry has launched a $2 million publicity campaign designed to show that the trucking industry—not the automobile user—has caused excessive damage to the road system and therefore should pay the higher user charges required.[52] Figure 4–4 is from a brochure, issued by the Association of American Railroads (AAR), entitled *Highway Crisis: How Did It Happen? Who Should Pay?* In this brochure, a study by the State of Oregon on highway deterioration is quoted. It states that weather causes 19 percent of deterioration, cars and light trucks are responsible for 1 percent, and the remaining 80 percent of road breakdown is caused by heavy trucks. The pamphlet also notes a recent U.S. General Accounting Office study that found that one heavy truck—over 50,000 pounds gross vehicle weight—causes the same damage to the highway system as 9,600 automobiles. Finally, the AAR brochure states that while all trucks pay a high percentage of state and federal highway user charges—41 percent in 1978—heavy trucks do not pay their fair share. This is because the vast majority of trucks are pickups and other trucks that have a gross vehicle weight of under 10,000 pounds. Heavy trucks paid only 12 percent of total state and federal highway user charges.

---

[50]"40 States Want To 'Up' Fuel Taxes," *Traffic World* (February 2, 1981), pp. 19–20.

[51]"Carter Sends Congress FY1982 Budget With $25.5 Billion Marked for Transport," *Traffic World* (January 19, 1981), p. 7.

[52]"A Collision Over Subsidies," *Business Week* (July 28, 1981), p. 64.

Figure 4–4   Railroad Publicity to Increase Highway Taxes for the Trucking Industry. Courtesy: *Highway Crisis* (The Association of American Railroads, 1981).

Federal Trucking Deregulation

Motor Carrier Act of 1980

The *Motor Carrier Act of 1980* was signed into law by President Jimmy Carter on July 1, 1980. Present at the signing ceremony was Massachusetts Senator Edward Kennedy, who was one of the principal congressional supporters of transport deregulation. The law is long and complex, and it touches upon many details of motor carrier regulation and operating practices that have not been discussed in this text. In very general terms, the major provisions of the new law are to accomplish the following:

1. Introduce a "zone of reasonableness" into motor common carrier rates, meaning that a carrier may change its rates within a range of plus or minus 10 percent per year without requiring regulatory body approval. Starting in 1982 the zone was adjusted to account for changes in the Producer Price Index.
2. Reduce the power of common carrier rate bureaus by gradually eliminating situations where they can be used to establish rates.
3. Remove all controls on the use of trucks by domestic airlines to pick up or deliver freight that is also carried on that airline's planes.
4. Increase the agricultural exemption to include some additional products such as processed poultry feed, agricultural seeds, and plants. (The purpose of this provision is to provide a "backhaul" for the carrier whose primary business is carrying products of farms to markets.)
5. Remove the restrictions on the number of customers with whom each contract motor carrier can contract.
6. Require all carriers to maintain at least $750,000 insurance. Requirements are much higher for those who carry hazardous materials.
7. Encourage entry to more motor carriers into markets by placing the "burden of proof" on existing carriers to convince the ICC that an additional carrier is not needed. (Previously, the burden had been on the applicant to show the ICC that an additional carrier was needed to serve in that specific market.)
8. Remove many operating restrictions handicapping the present operations of existing carriers. (This is related to the explanation of point 7. Historically, to overcome opposition of existing carriers, new applicants would agree *not* to carry certain goods, *not* to use certain routes or connections, *not* to carry backhauls, etc. Many of these restrictions on their operating authorities were, of course, inefficient; and the ICC is directed by the new law to remove them.)
9. Allow sellers of food and grocery products to use a uniform zone-delivered pricing system and to compensate customers who pick up products (rather than have them delivered).

However, this compensation cannot be more than what would be the actual cost to the seller of making the delivery.

10. Legalize private carriage for different wholly-owned subsidiaries of the same corporation. This is known as intercorporate hauling. (Previously, private carriage operated by one subsidiary could not transport products of another subsidiary of the same corporation.) For many firms, this provision will greatly enhance the feasibility of operating a private truck fleet, because there is greater opportunity to operate the trucks fully loaded in all directions.

11. Permit quotation of released value rates—lower carrier rates for lowered carrier liability for loss and damage claims—in tariffs without ICC prior approval. (Previously, the ICC allowed relatively few released value rates because they are contrary to the traditional surface common carrier responsibility of providing for "full actual loss" in loss and damage situations.)

Responsibility for interpreting the new law rests primarily with the ICC, which held many hearings in 1980 and 1981 to determine how various aspects of the new law should be implemented.[53]

The Effects of the 1980 Motor Carrier Act

The *1980 Motor Carrier Act* has significantly and permanently altered the trucking industry. The 1980 Overnite Trucking Company Annual Report contained this sage statement by Harwood Cochraine, chairman of the board: "The Motor Carrier Act of 1980 has certainly ushered in an entirely new era for our industry both philosophically and legislatively. The die is cast! Old attitudes and decisions must be reconsidered—discarded where no longer applicable to the present."

This section will examine a number of changes that have been precipitated by the new regulatory environment in the for-hire trucking industry.

Rate changes.   For-hire trucking rates, with few exceptions, have decreased significantly since deregulation took place. Complicating the situation, however, has been the fact that the U.S. economy has

---

[53] For a detailed examination of this law, see: Donald V. Harper, "The Federal Motor Carrier Act of 1980: Review and Analysis," *Transportation Journal* (Winter, 1980), pp. 5–34.

been in a recession during the entire time since the new law became effective. Therefore, it is arguable that trucking rates would have decreased without regulatory changes as a natural result of a softening in demand for trucking service. For whatever reason, for-hire trucking rates have been declining. A June, 1981, survey by Harbridge House, Inc., a Boston management consulting firm, asked 2,200 of the nation's largest manufacturers what has happened to their trucking rates during the previous year. Sixty-five percent of the responding firms indicated their trucking rates had decreased.[54] *Forbes* magazine surveyed the common carrier trucking industry and found that about half of the largest 500 trucking companies had cut their rates 10 to 20 percent, despite the fact that their operating costs had increased substantially.[55]

Another indication of the increased level of rate competition in the motor common carrier industry is that the number of carriers filing independent actions is increasing. The Central and Southern

- *Independent action,* allowed by laws which authorize carrier rate bureaus, means that the rate set by a bureau *cannot* be made binding on all member carriers. A carrier who sets or maintains a rate different from that set by the bureau is said to be taking independent action of *flagging out* (meaning a "flag" or footnote symbol appears in the bureau's tariff, indicating that a particular carrier is not charging the bureau's rate).

Motor Freight Bureau reported that in 1980, the number of independently published rates increased over 180 percent from 1979.[56]

Why did many common carrier trucking companies believe they were compelled to become actively involved in price discounting in 1980? Overnite Trucking Company, in its annual report, stated:

> The environment of a declining economy in 1980 produced some unusual discount pricing in the motor carrier industry. As a result, we experienced an erosion in revenue from some of our customers who were offered frivolous and disparate rate proposals such as coupon discounts, contests, aggregate tender and all sorts of gimmicks usually designed to help only large LTL shippers. To compete, Overnite took bold and innovative independent rate action through the various bureaus and published a ten percent across the board rate reduction on all less than truckload class related traffic. This non-discriminatory rate reduction was apparently exactly what the shipping and receiving pub-

[54] John D. Williams, "Truck Deregulation Has Cut Rising Costs, Improved Service in a Year, Shippers Say," *The Wall Street Journal* (June 30, 1981), p. 13.

[55] Lisa Gross, "Down But Not Out in Lima," *Forbes* (November 10, 1980), p. 200.

[56] "Highlights of Recent Activity in the Motor Carrier Industry," ICC Staff Report, Office of Policy and Analysis, mimeographed (December 4, 1980), p. 3.

lic wanted. Since the effective dates in September and October, we have experienced a gratifying increase in shipments and revenue. Our excellent fourth quarter in 1980 can be attributed in large part to our 10 percent rate reduction.[57]

Shippers, of course, have been extremely pleased with the new price competitiveness found in the for-hire trucking industry. Richard G. Velten, general traffic manager for Johnson and Johnson, noted, "We've been able to reduce costs due to the enormous competition."[58] Velten reports that his 1981 trucking rates now equal the same level they were in 1978. This is a significant fact when one remembers the annual "double-digit" inflation that took place during most of this three-year period.

In closing this section, it should be noted that many established members of the motor common carrier industry are somewhat "bitter" over the *1980 Motor Carrier Act*. Overnite hinted at their displeasure in a previous quote. Fred C. Bauer, executive vice-president of McClean Trucking Company, is more blunt:

> Freer entry has brought in a plethora of small, poorly financed "seat of the pants" operators who have skimmed off the cream of heavy LTL and truckload traffic. Many are operating on a shoestring with poor equipment and untrained, undisciplined drivers who lack the capital to use preventive or regular maintenance procedures. They're literally coming out of the woodwork, and we can't afford to let them dry up our volume market.[59]

In 1982, a newsletter for underwriters who insure motor carriers' *cargo* discussed the *1980 Motor Carrier Act* and warned underwriters that:

> One of the basics of the Motor Carrier Act is to increase competition. . . . A very direct result of increased competition may be reduced income, which in turn can affect many facets of a trucker's operation. Underwriting consideration must be given to such things as the following:
>
> Reduced funds or cash flow could cause the trucker to delay paying customer claims. . . . If the financial condition of the trucker gets to the extreme, resulting in bankruptcy, all of these unpaid claims then become the obligation of the motor truck cargo insurance carrier. . . .
>
> Reduced income can adversely affect driver training, terminal and vehicle security, and many other loss control measures.[60]

---

[57] "Overnite Transportation Company Annual Report," 1980, p. 2.

[58] Joan Feldman, "Deregulation Changes Truckers' Tune," *Handling and Shipping Management* (May, 1981), p. 76.

[59] Fred C. Bauer, "Marketing Ramifications of the Motor Carrier Act of 1980," *Annual Proceedings of the NCPDM* (1980), pp. 361–362.

[60] Elroy J. Dyksen, "Underwriting Consequences of 'Deregulation'," *Babco Alarm System News* (Winter, 1982), pp. 1–2.

Service changes.   Service levels in the trucking industry are improving because of the increased number of competitors. In the first year since the *1980 Motor Carrier Act* became law, approximately 2,900 totally *new* common and contract carriers entered the for-hire trucking industry. In addition, in the first six months of 1981, the ICC processed 14,000 applications from existing common carriers who were desirous of expanding (a) the variety of products they can transport, and/or (b) the geographical area they can serve. Approximately 97 percent of the above requests for expanded product or service authority have been approved by the Commission.[61]

The expanded number of competitors has prompted many carriers, such as Roadway Express, to offer service guarantees.[62] In addition, shippers generally prefer to do business with a trucker that can offer one carrier service from origin to destination. This advantage is especially true in regard to tracing and to loss and damage claim settlements.[63]

- *Tracing* involves a carrier procedure to "find" a shipment that has become unusually late.

What has been the effect of deregulation on service levels in small, rural towns? The Texas Railroad Commission stated that a number of "long-haul" common carrier truckers had curtailed or eliminated service to smaller communities. However, other local or regional carriers quickly started to offer trucking services to the cities that had lost service. In general, the Texas regulatory commission stated that small communities were *not* suffering as a result of the *1980 Motor Carrier Act.*[64]

Effects on contract carriage.   Contract carriers were significant beneficiaries of the *1980 Motor Carrier Act.* The law affirmed three changes that the ICC had previously initiated: (a) it eliminated the *rule of eight*; (b) common carriers were no longer allowed to protest

- The *rule of eight* was an ICC doctrine stating that contract carriers could not serve more than eight separate customers. The effect of this rule was to limit the growth potential of contract carriers.

[61] "Gresham Tells How New Laws Have Affected ICC Work," *Traffic World* (June 15, 1981), p. 9.

[62] Feldman, *loc. cit.,* p. 72.

[63] Robert C. Heiden, "1981 Trucking Outlook," *Handling and Shipping Management* (January, 1981), p. 50.

[64] "Highlights of Recent Activity in the Motor Industry," ICC Staff Report (December 4, 1980), p. 9.

to the ICC when a new contract carrier application for operating rights was being sought; and (c) contract carriers were allowed, for the first time, to serve freight forwarders' and shippers' associations.[65]

Many contract carrier salespeople are suggesting to firms operating extensive private trucking fleets that they switch their transportation service to contract carriage. The advantage to the shipper is that they would be able to "free up" all the capital involved in owning highway tractors and trailers. The contract carrier argues that they can "tailor" a service contract that is as competitive as private carriage at a lower overall cost. Illustrative is the arrangement between McClean Trucking and the K Mart Corporation. McClean, a common carrier, created a new contract carrier subsidary, Salem Contract Carriers. Salem is, at this time, providing long-haul service almost exclusively for the K Mart Corporation.[66]

Additional Effects of Trucking Deregulation

The national Teamsters' contract was renegotiated in early 1982. Because of the economic recession and motor carrier deregulation (which allowed an increased role for small, non-union trucking firms), the Teamsters found themselves in a weaker bargaining position than had been the usual case. Specifically, 20 percent of the 300,000 Teamsters were unemployed! In March, 1982, the Teamster membership ratified a new, 37-month contract and, in so doing, made a number of concessions which helped unionized trucking firms keep their costs down. There was no increase in wage rates, aside from cost-of-living increases which will be calculated annually, rather than every six months. An important change in work rules now allows long-distance drivers to make stops in a city to deliver freight. Previously, the long-distance (or "line-haul") driver had to turn the load over to a "city" driver for final delivery to its destination. Teamster President Roy Williams said this about the new contract:

> Considering the economic problems facing the industry as well as the nation, I think we have done very well. One hope is that this agreement will get Teamsters back to work who have been laid off their jobs.[67]

[65] See: Jean V. Strickland, "Contract Carriage by Many Other Names Is Just as Sweet," *Distribution* (November, 1980), pp. 53–56.

[66] "Highlights of Recent Activity in the Motor Industry," ICC Staff Report (December 4, 1980), p. 6. See also: Denis Davis, "New Directions for Trucking," *Distribution* (November, 1979).

[67] *The Wall Street Journal* (March 2, 1982), p. 2.

The Teamsters union is also showing additional flexibility in changing work rules so unionized firms can remain competitive with non-unionized trucking companies. Yellow Freightways, Inc. recently negotiated a work-rule change with its Teamster local. Known as "flexible workweeks," each employee works five consecutive days, but the starting day may be a Saturday or a Sunday. The contract provides for no overtime pay for weekend work.[68]

Most trucking companies see both benefits and problems from deregulation. Benefits include being able to change rates more expeditiously and being able to transport a larger variety of products to an increased geographical area.

Problem areas are also present. Many truckers, because of rate competition, have found their profit margins shrinking. In addition, almost all for-hire trucking companies have "written off" the value of their *operating rights*. Previous to deregulation, for-hire truckers had a semi-monopoly to serve a specific geographic region. This government-granted privilege, known as operating rights, was valuable because the federal government only issued a restricted number of them. Therefore, for-hire carriers typically assigned a value to their operating rights as an intangible asset on their balance sheets. After deregulation, the ICC started to allow an almost unlimited number of new operating rights to be issued. Therefore, the value of *existing* operating rights plunged in value. Illustrative is Roadway Express, which in October, 1980, wrote off $26.8 million of operating rights as an extraordinary one-time expense item.[69]

Deregulation of the Household Moving Industry

President Carter signed into law the *Household Goods Transportation Act of 1980* on October 15, 1980. This act was designed to reduce governmental regulatory "red tape" for the household movers while at the same time offering the shipper—the consumer—more protection than previously available. In the former category, household movers will no longer have to file the following quarterly reports with the ICC: (a) over and under charges, (b) prescribed estimating forms, (c) driver weight certificates, and (d) performance data on commercial and government shipments. Shippers benefit from the new law in several ways: (a) they can request a specific binding written estimate for the total transportation charges involved,

[68]John D. Williams, *loc. cit.*
[69]Accounting rules for writing off intangible assets are complex. See: Thomas Baker, "Reality Takes the Wheel," *Forbes* (October 27, 1980), pp. 133–134.

(b) they can ask for a reweighing of a shipment if its accuracy appears in doubt, (c) they can pay with a credit card, and (d) they can purchase additional insurance directly from the moving company. In addition, moving companies have become much more customer service oriented because of the increased competition resulting from deregulation. The ICC has allowed new firms into the industry and let existing firms expand their areas of service.

Trucking Industry Outlook

The future for the trucking industry is one of guarded optimism. In 1977 Frost and Sullivan, a well-known marketing research firm, published an extensive report entitled, *U.S. Transportation Market to 1995*. They predicted that railroads would increase their share of intercity ton-miles from the present 36 percent to 52 percent by 1995. Truckers, on the other hand, will see a decrease in market share, from 24 percent to 16.5 percent. This decrease was predicted because of a number of factors, the primary one being the switching of freight to more energy-efficient modes of transportation.[70]

In the decade of the 1980's, there will probably be a *decrease* in the number of for-hire trucking companies. Large firms, with highly efficient management—such as Roadway Express[71]—will continue to grow and prosper in the deregulated environment. Many other trucking companies will fail because the government no longer limits the number of competitors. At least initially in the 1980's, there will be many new trucking companies entering the industry and there also will be many new and established firms that will go bankrupt. By the end of the present decade, only the highly efficient for-hire trucking companies will still be in existence. Andros Petery, a trucking analyst with Morgan Stanley and Company in New York, noted, "A dramatic shakeout is under way in trucking, just like the one that started in the securities industry in 1975 [when they were deregulated].[72]

Intercity Bus Passenger Service

Intercity bus service is widely available, connecting over 15,000 cities and communities, over 14,000 of which are not served by any

[70] *Traffic World* (July 25, 1977), p. 17.
[71] Jean A. Briggs, "Roadway Express: Easing into High Gear," *Forbes* (August 31, 1981), pp. 91–95.
[72] John D. Williams, *loc. cit.*

other form of passenger common carrier. By way of comparison, rail passenger service connects 500 cities, and airline service is available at about 700 airports. There are nearly 1,000 firms providing intercity bus service. (Most bus companies also carry parcels on their scheduled bus runs.)[73] Several large firms dominate the industry, but, similar to the trucking industry, many smaller firms, whose operations are intrastate in nature, operate only one or two vehicles. Bus fares are regulated by the ICC and state regulatory commissions.

From 1970 to 1980 the number of intercity travelers using buses has remained about the same. However, the low point in ridership was in 1977 and it has been growing since that date. The American Bus Association reports that intercity bus companies received 17 percent higher total revenues in 1979 compared to 1978.

Intercity bus companies, of which there are 44 Class I firms—carriers with annual revenues of greater than $1 million—have not experienced a rapid increase in net profit, until recently. In 1966, Class I firms earned $54 million with an operating ratio of 85.4. By 1977, the comparable figures were $41 million and 95.3. Notice the improvement in the 1979 figures—$57 million and 95.2.[74]

- *Operating ratio* is an accounting performance measure obtained by dividing a firm's operating costs by its operating revenues and then multiplying by 100. Regulated motor carriers are comfortable with operating ratios in the low 90's.

Unlike any other form of domestic transportation, the intercity bus industry is dominated by one firm, Greyhound. In 1980 this single firm carried 30 percent of all intercity passengers. In 1980 the firm employed 17,600, operated 4,600 buses, and provided service to 14,000 different locations.[75]

In May, 1981, Congress started hearings on the *Bus Regulatory Modernization Act of 1981*. It would essentially adopt the rate and entry provisions of the *1980 Motor Carrier Act* and apply them to the intercity bus industry. Carrier pricing freedom would be expanded and entry controls would be relaxed. Greyhound and Continental Trailways, who together account for 62 percent of intercity bus revenues, both favor deregulating the industry.

Opponents of deregulation believe that small, rural communities

---

[73] Carrying small packages accounted for 15 percent of the Class I bus companies' revenues in 1976. In 1950, this activity represented only 2 percent of their revenues. See: *The Intercity Bus Industry, a preliminary study* (Washington, D.C.: Interstate Commerce Commission, May, 1978).

[74] *ICC Annual Report* (1980), p. 127.

[75] Greyhound Lines, Inc., Fact Sheet (May, 1981).

will lose bus service. Proponents counter by noting that Florida deregulated its intercity bus industry on July 1, 1980. One study of this market declared, "There has been a surge of new ridership on some bus lines where fares were cut and routes added. Overall, carriers are offering increased scheduled service, new charter companies are forming, and charter fares are being reduced."[76] Similar findings are reported from England, which deregulated its intercity bus industry in October, 1980.[77]

Another industry issue is an attempt by the operators to have all states allow the operation of wider buses. Transit buses in many cities are 102 inches wide, and Greyhound Lines, especially, would like to be able to operate intercity buses that wide throughout the country. Forty-four states now allow the 102-inch width; six holdouts allow only 96-inch widths.[78]

Other Highway Users

Tables 1–2 and 1–3 indicated that 84 percent of all intercity transportation expenditures are for various forms of transport which use the highway system. This chapter has dealt primarily with highway common carriers of freight and of passengers, although some mention was made of private trucking.

However, there are many other highway users. By many measures they outnumber the common carriers which have been discussed so far. They deserve mention because they are important to our nation's transportation system.

Local Haulers

There are a number of freight haulers who specialize in short distance markets and are sometimes regulated as intrastate carriers. *Local drayage* firms perform pick-up and delivery service, usually within the same city. *Parcel delivery* firms handle the retail deliveries for various stores. Even local taxicabs can be used for small package delivery.

Several short haul truck operations connect with other forms of common carriage. Airlines may operate their own trucks to pick up and deliver air freight shipments within specified distances from the

[76] "Need for Deregulation of Intercity Bus Lines Seen in Analytical Report," *Traffic World* (March 2, 1981), p. 21.
[77] "Friction Over Freeing Bus Lines," *Business Week* (February 2, 1981), p. 78.
[78] *Wider Means Better*, Greyhound Lines brochure (1981).

airport. Railroads, and some specialized truck firms, move trailers or intermodal containers between the railroad yards and the shipper's

- *Intermodal shipments* rely on at least two different, connecting modes of transportation, such as rail to water, or truck to air to truck, in order to travel the entire distance between the shipper and the consignee.

or the consignees' receiving dock. Freight forwarders—who consolidate intercity shipments which they then tender to railroads, intercity motor carriers, airlines, or vessels—also use trucks for the local pick-up and delivery segment of their operation. Lastly, some large parcel services also use special trucks for local operations. Some of these carriers may be subjected to forms of economic regulation, often by the Interstate Commerce Commission, if the complete haul is interstate in nature.

Local Buses and Cabs

There are 312,000 school buses in the United States operated by either school districts or firms contracting with them. They are not subject to rate regulation, but they are subject to even more stringent safety regulations than conventional buses. Traffic laws and regulations also give them protection not afforded to other carriers.

By way of comparison there are only about 53,000 buses operated by local bus companies.[79] About 80 percent of these belong to publicly-owned transit operators; the others are owned by private firms. Usually, the privately-owned bus companies are subjected to economic regulation of a state regulatory agency. Public transit operators usually are not, although both are subject to safety regulations.

Airport limousines, which deliver passengers to and from airports, are often subject to state economic regulation because they operate in several different local jurisdictions. At large airports, limousine services use buses for major hauls and vans or stretched autos for their lighter loads. Limousine services are also regulated by the airports they serve, and many airports collect revenue from the limousine service operators.

Taxicabs are regulated by the cities in which they operate. If they cross city boundaries, then they are regulated by counties or the state, depending upon the applicable state law.

Airport limousines and taxicabs are significant to intercity transportation because they must provide the first link of each trip—to

[79] *Transit Fact Book '76–77 Edition* (Washington, D.C.: American Public Transit Association, 1977), pp. 16–19.

the airport or rail or bus station—and the last link of the return trip. Local bus services also provide connections to airports.

In recent years several groups who do not and—sometimes—cannot use automobiles have alleged that they have "mobility" rights. In rural areas, this is sometimes interpreted as the "right" to have public bus service in areas that are isolated and generate few passengers. In urban areas, handicapped individuals and the elderly have been insisting upon specialized equipment on regular buses to accommodate their special needs. While not commenting upon the merits of the "mobility rights" concept, it would be accurate to state that these demands have been directed mainly at bus operations. At a demonstration in San Francisco in mid-1978 several hundred handicapped individuals managed to block departing commuter buses of several public transit systems. Forty demonstrators were arrested. A newspaper reported: "Those arrested had to be lifted, chairs and all, into paddy wagons backed into the terminal. 'The thing is, we just don't have wheelchair ramps on paddy wagons,' an officer apologized."[80]

Private Autos

Last, but not least, in the list of highway users is the private auto. There are over 120 million autos in the United States, nearly all of which are for personal use. (Many small trucks also are for personal use.) Worldwide, there are about 14 individuals for each auto. In the U.S. there are less than 2 persons for each auto.[81]

When looking at our nation's entire transportation system, the auto can be viewed from several perspectives. For many individuals, it is the only form of transportation used. For others, it serves as a link to intercity airlines, to Amtrak, or to a commuter train or bus. The automobile allows personal access to land where we live, work, and play. Rental autos can be found at airports and at business and resort areas to allow one to complete a trip that was taken on another mode.

Automobile owners have contributed much of the construction and maintenance costs of our highway system, which they share with motor carriers and buses. Were it not for the auto, the road network of the United States would be much less developed than it is today. Autos made deep inroads into the passenger traffic once carried by railroads, intercity buses, and suburban and local transit operations.

[80] *San Francisco Chronicle* (July 13, 1978).
[81] *MVMA Motor Vehicle Facts and Figures '81*, p. 29.

" I'M SORRY, SIR, BUT YOU HAD YOUR CHANCE. "

Reproduced by permission of the artist and the Masters Agency.

Figure 4–5   Fuel Availability Is Essential to Highway Users. Reproduced by permission of the artist and the Masters Agency.

Automobiles are large users of petroleum, and motorists have been subjected to a tripling of retail prices of gasoline in less than a decade. Our "love affair" with the auto may be ending, and we may have to travel less or use alternate modes of transportation. Cartoons about "running out of gas" (see Figure 4–5) are less humorous than they once were.

Summary

Trucks first appeared at the turn of the century, but it was not until World War I that they had an opportunity to demonstrate their advantages. Their use in the United States has grown to the point where they collect 80 percent of all the money spent on intercity freight transportation.

The highway network in the United States is very extensive—equaling 3.8 million miles of road. The federal government has helped construct roads since the late 1700's. Today, the Federal Highway Trust Fund collects funds for highway construction. There is a trend to also use the Highway Trust Fund for mass transit projects and rehabilitation of the existing Interstate System.

Since government makes the initial investment in highways, the motor carrier contributes to the highways' cost only if he chooses to use them. As a result, the cost structure of a motor carrier consists of mostly variable costs, i.e., those he can avoid paying if he does not operate.

From a regulatory standpoint there are several categories of truckers. They are common carriers, contract carriers, private carriers (who carry their own products), and exempt carriers (who can carry unprocessed agricultural products, free of ICC regulation).

Highway carriers are actively fighting both state and federal proposals to increase highway user charges paid by the trucking industry. The *1980 Motor Carrier Act* profoundly changed the for-hire trucking industry by allowing more pricing freedom and easier entry. The industry is severely threatened by increases in the price of diesel fuel. The ICC and Congress have also reduced railroad regulation, and this is making the railroads more competitive with trucks for certain business.

Other highway users are intercity and local buses, school buses, airport limousines, and taxicabs. Last, but certainly not least, is the private automobile, whose future is also threatened by increased prices and shortages of petroleum.

Questions for Discussion and Review

1. Why was World War I important for the development of the motor truck?

2. Define each of the following terms: (a) for-hire carrier; (b) ICC-regulated carrier, and (c) independent trucker.

3. Discuss briefly the typical motor common carrier, the type of products it transports, and the quality of the service it performs.

4. Do you believe the Interstate Highway System has had a significant effect on the life style and economy of the U.S.? Why?

5. Discuss the Highway Trust Fund. Should the Highway Trust Fund be used for mass transit? Discuss.

6. Discuss the cost structure of the motor carrier industry.

7. Discuss economies of scale in the trucking industry.

8. Several significant problems were discussed concerning the motor carrier industry. What do you believe is the most serious? Why?

9. Some people consider the trucking industry a menace to safety on the highways. Discuss the validity of this position.

10. One section of this chapter is entitled, "The Declining Role of the Motor Common Carrier." Why is this taking place?

11. What was the major issue involved in the *Toto Case?* Why were common carrier truckers not pleased by this ICC decision?

12. Do you believe the trucking industry pays adequate highway user charges? Write a brief essay supporting your position.

13. The *1980 Motor Carrier Act* contained many changes. Discuss the four new provisions that you believe are the most important.

14. What has been the effect of deregulation on rates in the trucking industry? Is this what was expected to happen? Why?

15. Have service levels in the trucking industry increased or decreased as a result of deregulation? Discuss.

16. What has been the effect of deregulation on the viability of contract motor carriers? Why?

17. How has deregulation affected the Teamsters Union? Discuss.

18. What do you believe is the long-term outlook for the trucking industry? Defend your answer.

19. Discuss, in general terms, the current status of the intercity bus passenger industry.

20. How do you think increased prices and shortages of petroleum will affect transportation in the U.S. during the next decade? Discuss.

Additional Chapter References

Allen, Benjamin J., and David B. Vellenga, "Developing National Transportation Policy State-by-State: An Analysis of the Midwest Twin-Trailer Court Decisions," *Annual Proceedings of the Transportation Research Forum* (1980), pp. 230–237.

Boisjoly, Russell P., and Thomas M. Corsi, "An Identification of the Distinguishing Characteristics of Acquired Trucking Firms," *ICC Practitioners' Journal* (July–August, 1981), pp. 560–577.

Breen, Denis A., "The Changing Motor Carrier Share of Intercity Manufactures Traffic: Alternative Explanations," *Transportation Journal* (Fall, 1978), pp. 19–27.

Corsi, Thomas M., and Russell P. Boisjoly, "The Long-Run Effects of Merger in the Motor Carrier Industry: The Implications of Deregulation," *ICC Practitioners' Journal*, Vol. 49, No. 3 (1982), pp. 280–293.

Davis, Grant M., John E. Dillard, Jr., and William G. Middleton, "Growth and Structural Changes in Class One Motor Carriers: An Empirical Analysis," *ICC Practitioners' Journal* (July–August, 1981), pp. 543–559.

Harper, Donald V., "The Federal Motor Carrier Act of 1980: Review and Analysis," *Transportation Journal* (Winter, 1980), pp. 5–33.

Hynes, Cecil V., "A Study of How Deregulation of the Regulated Motor Common Carriers May Affect Movement of Freight In and Out of the Center City Areas: Baltimore, A Case Study," *ICC Practitioners' Journal*, Vol. 48, No. 3 (1981), pp. 312–318.

Jennings, Kenneth M., Jay A. Smith, Jr., and Earl C. Traynham, Jr., "The Participation of Self-Employed Minorities in the Trucking Industry: A Preliminary Analysis," *Annual Proceedings of the Transportation Research Forum* (1981), pp. 41–46.

Krapfel, Robert E., and John T. Mentzer, "Reactions of Private Motor Carriers to *Toto* and Compensated Intercorporate Hauling Rights," *Transportation Journal* (Spring, 1981), pp. 66–72.

Kratochvil, John, "A Case for Uniform State Truck Gross Weights and Sizes," *Transportation Journal* (Fall, 1977), pp. 84–91.

Maister, David H., "Motor Carrier Use of Owner Operators: Efficiency or Exploitation?," *Annual Proceedings of the Transportation Research Forum* (1979), pp. 447–455.

Mentzer, John T., "Shippers' Managerial Reactions to the Reregulated Motor Carrier Study," *Annual Proceedings of the National Council of Physical Distribution Management* (1981), pp. 442–450.

Morash, Edward A., Ed Bruning, and David L. McQuin, "Motor Carrier Capital Costs and Deregulation: A Tentative Assessment," *Annual Proceedings of the Transportation Research Forum* (1981), pp. 221–229.

Mossman, Frank H., and Gregory S. Maiers, "Creative Adjustment to Motor Carrier Deregulation," *MSU Business Topics* (Autumn, 1980), pp. 51–58.

Reimer, Gerald, "The Fuel Outlook and the Trucking Industry," *The Logistics and Transportation Review*, Vol. 17, No. 2 (1981), pp. 153–162.

Roberts, Merrill J., "Agricultural Cooperative Trucking and Transport Efficiency," *ICC Practitioners' Journal* (January–February, 1978), pp. 157–174.

Sen, Lalita, Julian Benjamin, and Richard S. Watt, "Impacts of Regulations on the Use of Taxicabs for Paratransit Services," *Annual Proceedings of the Transportation Research Forum* (1981), pp. 257–264.

Shrock, David L., "Economies of Scale and Motor Carrier Operations: Review, Evaluation, and Perspective," *ICC Practitioners' Journal* (September–October, 1978), pp. 721–745.

Wyckoff, D. Daryl, and David H. Maister, *The U.S. Motor-Carrier Industry* (Lexington, Mass.: Lexington Books, 1977).

Case 4–1 Fernando's Feed Lot Case

Located 21 miles from Soda Springs, Idaho, Emmanuel Fernando's feedlot operated during winter months. Fernando bought cattle from ranchers in central Idaho during the fall and fed them hay he had grown or purchased. Late in the spring, depending on market prices, Fernando would have his cattle transported to a cattle auction yard at Casper, Wyoming, where they would be sold.

There were two ways the cattle could be shipped to Casper. Fernando owned a short-bed truck which he used to carry cattle or feed. When shipping to Casper by rail, he used his own truck to carry the cattle to a holding yard at the Soda Springs rail station.

An alternate method of shipping the cattle was to contract with owner-operators of truck-tractors pulling semi-trailers. These shipments were not subject to ICC rate regulation, and the rate varied each year, depending upon market conditions.

Fernando had kept close records since 1966 and noticed that since 1974 truck rates had been increasing more quickly than rail rates. Case Table 4–1–1 shows the rates or charges in cents per hundred pounds.

For several years, Fernando had contemplated moving his feedlot to a site that was quite far from any rail service. He would use trucks to reach Casper. However, since 1973, costs of all-truck shipments were higher, and Fernando was reluctant to move to a site that was

CASE TABLE 4–1–1 Fernando's Historic Costs

Year	Truck/Rail Shipment		All-Truck Shipment
	Truck to Soda Springs	Rail—Soda Springs to Casper	Soda Springs-Casper
1966	$ 50	$100	$135
1967	55	100	145
1968	53	120	165
1969	58	130	190
1970	45	130	190
1971	62	130	180
1972	66	140	200
1973	58	150	225
1974	69	150	240
1975	70	160	250
1976	72	170	256
1977	74	180	270
1978	85	220	310
1979	92	220	325
1980	106	230	340

farther from rail service. He wanted projections through the year 1990.

(Note to instructor: assign only a few students each to Questions 1, 2, 3, or 4.)

Question One: Using graph paper and a ruler, estimate the costs of shipping cattle from Fernando's present site to Casper, using both routes, in 1990.

Question Two: Using statistical methods (least squares or simple regression), answer the same question as posed in Question One.

Question Three: Using a hand-held calculator that performs statistical functions, answer the same question as posed in Question One.

Question Four: If you have access to your school's computer facilities, use them to calculate the answer to Question One.

Question Five: Are there advantages for Fernando in being able to use two modes of transportation? If so, what are they?

Question Six: What additional information should Fernando have before deciding whether to relocate to another site?

Case 4–2   Melrose Coffee Company Case

Katy Bannister was the operations analyst for Melrose Coffee Company, located in a suburb of Boston, and specializing in the sale of ground, roasted decaffeinated coffee. The firm buys decaffeinated beans, i.e., beans that already have had the caffeine removed. Each year, the Melrose Coffee Company purchases and processes about 10,000 tons of decaffeinated beans.

Melrose buys from two sources. The first source, the Zimmerman Coffee Company in Manchester, New Hampshire, is currently selling beans at $3,500 per ton (2,000 lbs.). If a contract motor carrier is used, transportation costs from Manchester to Melrose are $20.00 per ton and delivery is within the same day (or overnight). Selling terms are F.O.B. source, and the Zimmerman firm collects payment as soon as the outbound truck is fully loaded at its Manchester plant. If railroad is used, the same selling terms apply. Rail charges for the coffee beans are $15.80 per ton from Manchester to Melrose. Service by rail is much poorer than by contract truck. It takes the shipment anywhere from three to six days to reach the Melrose siding.

The second source of beans is from various firms located in Hamburg, Germany. The German sources offer the decaffeinated beans at a lower price because they use the extracted caffeine for other purposes (which the Zimmerman operation does not do). Melrose utilized the services of David Zigal, a Hamburg commodity broker. Selling terms provide that the seller deliver the beans, loaded in ocean-going containers, to the vessel terminal in Hamburg, where Melrose would take possession and, acting through Zigal, pay for the beans. Ocean transportation costs to Melrose Coffee Company beyond that point were $45.00 per ton from Hamburg to New York, including transfer of the loaded containers to rail cars. The rail rate for the loaded containers from New York to Melrose's plant siding was $19.40 per ton. (Billing procedures were such that the water and rail charges were paid when the containers arrived.) There was considerable variation in total shipping time from Hamburg to Melrose, ranging from 16 to 24 days. This variation in transit time made it difficult to schedule an arrival date for the beans that would coincide with when they were needed in the production process. Also, since the average transit time from Germany was 20 days, Melrose had money tied up for a longer period than it would for beans bought from Zimmerman. With interest rates at 18 percent per year, this was a definite cost item.

Question One: What are the costs to Melrose Coffee Company of buying the decaffeinated beans from Zimmerman and using a contract motor carrier to ship them to its plant?

Question Two: If buying from Zimmerman, would it be cheaper for Melrose to use rail? (Don't forget the interest on money tied up in inventory.)

Question Three: The price of decaffeinated beans in Hamburg fluctuates, and now is dropping. Ms. Bannister must determine at what point it becomes advantageous for Melrose to buy. At what price should she tell Zigal to buy?

Question Four: Assume that the decaffeinated beans deteriorate (lose flavor) at the rate of .4 percent per day during the summer. Hence, if there is a 10-day delay between the source and Melrose, an additional eight pounds for each ton of coffee purchased are needed to offset the loss in flavor (.004 times 2,000). Now, answer Question Three incorporating the deterioration figure introduced here.

Question Five: Ignore completely the situation outlined in Questions Three and Four and consider the following. Zigal sends a Telex message that beans in Hamburg have dropped to $1.72 per pound and that their price is expected to rise. Katy thinks the price is too high, but can't make any calculations without knowing the current interest rate. She asks Tony McMahon, Melrose Coffee's owner, and gets a puzzling response. Tony says that he had been secretly saving money for an airplane but his wife (a part owner of the firm) had caught on. Tony had told his wife that the money was for purchasing decaffeinated beans from Hamburg and his wife said she'd "check the books" the next time she was in the office. So Tony said to Katy: "You figure out the highest rate of interest you can pay me which makes the beans in Hamburg the 'best' buy. If it's not unreasonably low, I'll loan the firm the money for 30 days or so, which should get me off the hook with my wife." What is the highest rate of interest the firm could pay to McMahon which would be low enough to justify purchase of coffee beans in Hamburg at $1.72 per pound?

Question Six: Since Melrose Coffee annually buys several thousand tons of beans from Zimmerman in Manchester, Katy has been thinking of entering into a "contract" rate with the railroad (permitted since an ICC ruling in 1978 and also by the *Staggers Act*). From contracts she's heard about, Katy knows that shippers try to obtain more dependable service by negotiating contracts with a provision that the railroads will pay a late penalty for each day beyond a specified number of days that delivery takes. Assume Katy believes that it should take the railroad no more than four days to move the cars from Manchester to Melrose. How much of a penalty, per car per day, should Katy reasonably expect the railroad to pay for cars that take over four days to deliver from Manchester?

Laying sections of track in 1866.

Laying welded track today.

5 Railroads

The worsening condition of the track hampered good operating procedures by increasing derailments, crew costs, and damage claims. It also impaired the railroad's ability to provide reliable, expeditious delivery of goods. In March 1975, the Rock Island entered its third bankruptcy. It continued operating under chapter 11 bankruptcy laws for the next four years. Finally, the Brotherhood of Railway and Airline Clerks and the United Transportation Union strike of August 1979, coupled with the deferral of maintenance, the light traffic density, and the intermodal competition, became the coup de grace.

Roy Dale Voorhees and Richard D. Reed
"The Rock Island Divorce Case"
Journal of Business Logistics
Spring, 1982

The Staggers Rail Act of 1980, which sneaked through Congress at the height of last fall's election campaign and thus contains some very political provisions, is perhaps the most important railroad legislation since 1887.

Tom Shedd
Traffic Management
April, 1981

A marketing executive for an Eastern railroad adds: "We're going to raise our furniture rates double-digit. If this means we lose furniture business to trucks, so be it. If they stay with us despite the higher rates, we'll finally make a profit on furniture."

The Wall Street Journal
October 14, 1980

Introduction

In 1929, railroads transported 74.9 percent of the total ton-miles of freight transported from one city to another. By 1980, the railroads transported only 37 percent of the intercity ton-miles. This chapter will examine the factors that contributed to this decline, although it is necessary to point out that nationwide statistics hide the fact that railroads' prosperity (or lack thereof) differs by the geographic area of the nation they serve. Using the statistic of revenue ton-miles, nationwide the industry moved 932,000 million revenue ton-miles of freight in 1980, which was 108 percent higher than the 447,322 carried in 1929. However, this increase was not spread out evenly in geographic terms. Eastern railroads (serving the area east of Chicago) suffered an actual decline in revenue ton-miles, from 231,420 in

- *Revenue ton-miles* are ton-miles of freight on which revenues are earned. They include most traffic carried. An example of *non-revenue traffic* would be a carload of railroad ties for the railroad's own use.

1929 to 202,036 in 1980. Railroads serving the remainder of the country (the South and the West) tripled their revenue ton-miles in the 1929–1978 period.[1]

This chapter will look at the industry's strengths, weaknesses, and potential. It will look at railroads as freight transporters because freight provides about 95 percent of the industry's operating revenues. Nevertheless, we will also take a brief look at passenger transportation on railroads at the end of this chapter.

Development of Railroads

The first railroad in the United States was the Baltimore and Ohio (B&O), now part of the Chessie System. It was incorporated in 1827, and the next year construction was started, using the standard English track gauge—which is still used today—of four feet eight and a half inches between rails. In 1830 the first steam engine operated over a 13-mile stretch of B&O track.

The strength, speed, durability, and year-round availability of the railroad (waterways often freeze during the winter) rapidly made it the dominant form of surface transportation. Its growth was spectacular. In 1830 there were 40 miles of railroad in the United States. By 1840, this figure had grown to 2,818 miles of track. In 1850 it was 9,022, and by 1860 it had expanded to 31,246.[2]

During the Civil War, the North's superior railroad system was an important factor in supplying the Union soldiers with supplies. General Ulysses S. Grant recognized the importance of railroad transportation to the mobility of his soldiers. General Grenville M. Dodge was Grant's chief railroad engineer and builder. His work often involved repairing railroads that had been sabotaged by the retreating Confederate soldiers.[3]

[1] *Yearbook of Railroad Facts, 1981 Edition* (Washington, D.C.: Association of American Railroads, 1981), p. 29.

[2] Edward C. Kirkland, *A History of American Economic Life*, 3rd ed. (New York: Appleton-Century-Crafts, Inc., 1951), p. 245.

[3] *Personal Memoirs of Ulysses S. Grant* (1886), reprinted by Bonanza Books, New York, Volume II, p. 48.

Land Grants

By 1850, the railroad system was concentrated almost exclusively east of the Mississippi River. It was not by accident that the location of the railroad network closely paralleled the location of the great majority of Americans. Railroads were built where there was a known market for their services.

The federal government was anxious to stimulate population migration to the western region of the United States. To encourage development of railroads in the West *before* there was sufficient population there to support it, Congress enacted the land grant program. The first federal land grant direct to railroads was in 1862 with the passage of the *Federal Aid to the Pacific Railroad Act*. It was designed to aid the first transcontinental railroad, which was completed by driving the famous "Golden Spike" at Promontory, Utah, on May 10, 1869. In the decade between 1862 and 1872, Congress enacted numerous additional railroad land grant programs. The typical land grant to a developing railroad comprised alternating sections, each section one mile square, or 640 acres, in a checkerboard pattern for six miles on each side of the track. The Northern Pacific—running across the northern boundary of the United States from Minnesota to Washington—received every other section for 40 miles on each side of the track. This land grant—by far the largest received by any one railroad—amounted to 39.8 million acres or 31 percent of the total 130.4 million acres received by all railroads under the land grant program. The federal government believed this extensive land grant to the Northern Pacific was necessary because of the difficulty involved in crossing the Rocky Mountains.

It is commonly believed the only beneficiary of the land grant program was the railroads. This is not true. An immediate benefit to the federal government was that the land retained after the land grants was doubled in price when sold to the public. Prior to 1850, federal land was available for $1.25 per acre, and there were few buyers at this low price. With the commencement of the railroad land grant program, federal land prices doubled to $2.50 per acre, and sales were brisk because transportation would soon be available.

Railroads receiving land grants agreed to charge lower rates to the federal government for carrying freight and passengers. These *land grant rates* were approximately half of the normal rate, although mail was carried at only a 20-percent discount. In 1940, Congress voted to eliminate land grant rates—except for military traffic and personnel—because in the 60 to 70 years since the land grants, the railroads had more than fairly compensated the federal government for the free land. The continuation of land grant rates for military transportation proved beneficial to the federal government, and it is estimated the federal government saved in excess of $1 billion from land grant rates from 1940 to the completion of World War II in 1945. Therefore, on October 1, 1946, Congress eliminated land grant rates completely. (However, government traffic can move on individually-negotiated rates.)

A controversy regarding railroad land grants surfaced in 1981. Many western railroads had the foresight to retain large portions of their original land grants. The Burlington Northern Corporation, successor to the previously-mentioned Northern Pacific, owns 1.5 million acres of forest land; controls oil and natural gas rights on 7.5 million acres; has proven coal reserves of 14.7 billion tons; and leases over 1.2 million acres of grazing land. President Richard M. Bressler of the BN noted, "You couldn't put such an array of assets together at any price."[4]

The issue involves whether the federal government should include the present income produced from land grant real estate as part of the revenues allocated to the railroad's operations. At present, all western railroad's are organized into holding companies, with a railroad division, a coal division, a timber division, etc. Each division operates as a profit center. For example, if income from coal

- The *profit center* approach to managing a large enterprise involves having each branch of the business operate somewhat like an independent business. It "buys" supplies and services from other branches of the same business and "sells" to them whatever it can. These intra-firm transactions, plus *real* transactions with outside customers and suppliers, determine the profit center's "profitability."

were assigned to the railroad division, it would be difficult for the railroad to justify future rate increases. The primary advocate of this position is the Water Transport Association, whose members compete with the railroad industry.[5]

Railroad Technological Advances

Three basic advances, which revolutionized the railroad industry, were automatic couplers, air brakes, and diesel-powered locomotives.

[4] Paul Gibson, "Burlington Northern: A Railroad For The Long Haul," *Forbes* (April 27, 1981), p. 126.
[5] See: "Rail 'Subsidy' Showdown Emerging From Century-Old U.S. Land Grants," *Traffic World* (June 8, 1981), pp. 18–19.

Eli Hamilton Janney invented the automatic coupler, and his U.S. patent of 1873 is still the basic design used. When two rail cars come together at a slow speed, they automatically join together with the Janney coupler. Prior to his design, rail cars were held together by the "link and pin" system. This crude system required an employee to stand between the two cars being connected—his job was to guide the link into a socket and then drop a steel pin into place. Stewart H. Holbrook said, "This link and pin coupling was the dread of all men who ever had to couple cars; and there are old railroaders living today [1947] whose memories are filled with the remembered incidents when a comrade lost a finger, or a hand, or his life in that instant when two cars came together."[6]

Stopping a train was originally accomplished by brakemen who rode on top of the rail cars. When a signal was given, each brakeman turned a crank that tightened a brake drag on the rolling wheels. This drag eventually caused enough friction on the wheels to stop the train. Brakemen had dangerous jobs because after they "set" the brake on one car (Figure 5–1), they had to run on top of the cars, from car to car, setting the brakes of each car. Brakemen would frequently fall off the moving train. George Westinghouse, a noted inventor, decided to remedy this hazardous situation. In the famous 1887 Burlington Trials (near Burlington, Iowa) for air brakes, Westinghouse's brakes, using compressed air, stopped a large freight train traveling 40 miles per hour in just 500 feet. In 1893, Congress enacted the *Railroad Safety Appliance Act*, which mandated the use of air brakes on all trains.[7]

The third innovation involved the basic driving power of trains. Steam had been used to power locomotives since the early 1800's. In 1896 Rudolf Diesel invented an internal combustion engine that compressed petroleum vapors to a point where the vapors ignited due to high pressure. In 1936, General Motors Corporation developed successful diesel-electric locomotives (a diesel engine produces power to run a portable electric generating plant—the electricity then powers electric motors, which drive the axles) on the Santa Fe and Baltimore and Ohio railroads. Diesel-electrics became widely accepted from that date for numerous reasons. For one thing, their operating costs were approximately 50 percent less than those of steam locomotives. Second, and more important, the diesel locomotive is relatively simple mechanically compared to a steam locomotive. Diesels

[6] Stewart H. Holbrook, *The Story of American Railroads* (New York: Crown Publishers, 1947), p. 290.
[7] See: H. G. Prout, "Safety In Railroad Travel," in *The American Railway* (1888), pp. 187–202.

Figure 5–1   The Brakeman's Dangerous Job. Source: *The American Railway* (1888), p. 389.

in 1944 had an availability ratio of 95 percent, compared to 60 percent for the most modern steam locomotives.[8] For pulling long trains, or operating in mountains, several diesel engines could also be linked together without requiring additional crew. By the late 1950's, steam locomotives had all but disappeared from the American railroad scene.

- *Availability ratio* is the percentage of time equipment is ready to be used as opposed to either being repaired or receiving routine maintenance.

[8] S. Kip Farrington, Jr., *Railroads At War* (New York: Samuel Curl, Inc., 1944), p. 84.

Railroads Today

A current railroad system route map is shown in Figure 5–2. It shows 184,500 route miles of railroad line. By way of comparison, in 1916 the mileage of railroad line was at its greatest—equalling 254,047. Note the heavy density of railroads in the Northeast.

Railroad Operating Characteristics

In 1980, there were 42 Class I railroads, with average annual freight revenues of $630 million and an average employment of 10,928 persons. Railroads are especially suited to transport large bulky shipments over long distances. In 1980, the average distance of a rail

- According to ICC criteria, a *Class I railroad* has annual operating revenues in excess of $50 million.

shipment was 590 miles, and the railroads collected an average of 2.9 cents per ton-mile transported. By way of comparison, truckers average about 17 cents of revenue per ton-mile.

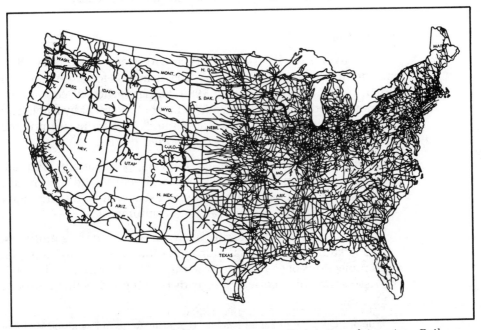

Figure 5–2   Railroad Route Map. Courtesy: Association of American Railroads.

Railroads are very efficient transporters of raw material and other bulk commodities in CL (carload) quantity shipments. In 1980, less than 1/100 of one percent of all railcar loadings were LCL (less-than-carload) traffic.

- Railroad *carload (CL)* traffic fills an entire car; the shipper must load the car, and the receiver (consignee) must unload it. *Less-than-carload (LCL)* traffic must be delivered to the railroad's freight terminal in the origin city by the shipper and picked up by the consignee at the railroad's terminal in the destination city. Railroad personnel consolidate the LCL traffic of various shippers and load it and unload it. Railroads charge much higher rates for LCL traffic. In some states, they have refused to handle any LCL shipments.

Coal is by far the single most important commodity shipped by rail. It accounted for one out of four carloadings in 1980. Nearly 5.7 million rail cars were loaded with coal! Second largest category of product shipped was grain (1.6 million carloads).[9] Other commodity categories accounting for over one million carloads each were: chemicals, grain, lumber products, food products, paper and pulp products, primary forest products, and motor vehicles.

Coal Traffic

For three railroads—the Norfolk and Western, the Chessie System, and the Burlington Northern—coal accounts for more than half of their ton-mile production. In 1980, 66 percent of all coal mined was transported by rail, 11 percent by barge, 12 percent by truck, and 11 percent was consumed near the mine.[10] Unit-trains are utilized for about 65 percent of all coal transported by rail.

- *Unit-trains* consist of identical rail cars, permanently coupled, which carry a single product in one direction, and then return empty for a repeat haul. They are used mainly to carry bulk materials, although some carry new automobiles.

The projected growth of coal as an energy source is significant. Table 5–1 shows the National Transportation Policy Study Commission's projections of coal traffic to be carried by the railroads in 2000. The Association of American Railroads (AAR) projects that railroads

---

[9] *Yearbook of Railroad Facts, 1981 Edition*, p. 26.

[10] *Moving U.S. Coal to Export Markets*, U.S. Army Corps of Engineers, Maritime Administration, Department of Energy, and Department of Transportation (June 10, 1980), p. S-1.

TABLE 5–1 Forecast of Coal Carried by Rail, 1976 and 2000
(In Millions of Short Tons)

Rail Carrier	1976 Originating	1976 Other	2000 Originating	2000 Other
Atchison, Topeka & Santa Fe	1.7	3.3	44.5	57.5
Baltimore & Ohio	23.2	19.2	38.3	53.7
Burlington Northern	42.9	2.9	374.1	7.8
Chesapeake & Ohio	48.2	10.4	80.5	39.3
Chicago, Milw., St. Paul & Pac.	5.0	4.0	15.9	54.9
Chicago & North Western	3.4	12.3	62.3	46.1
Chicago Rock Island & Pac.	1.4	0.9	—	17.8
Clinchfield	7.5	5.9	6.2	23.9
Colorado Southern	—	3.8	—	93.8
Conrail	41.3	40.1	83.4	80.5
Denver & Rio Grande Western	12.3	2.0	81.7	—
Fort Worth & Denver	—	1.0	—	71.2
Illinois Central Gulf	21.2	2.6	64.7	14.0
Kansas City & Southern	0.1	0.5	—	12.8
Louisville & Nashville	56.7	2.7	98.1	7.5
Missouri-Kansas-Texas	0.9	—	1.3	18.3
Missouri Pacific	11.2	3.4	3.3	48.6
Norfolk & Western	67.0	8.4	115.4	13.5
Seaboard Coastline	—	16.4	1.1	44.6
Southern	26.5	8.8	38.9	28.7
Southern Pacific	—	0.5	—	30.4
St. Louis San Francisco	3.9	1.5	—	28.4
Union Pacific	14.1	3.2	54.0	95.5
Western Maryland	6.2	4.5	—	23.2
Total	394.7	158.3	1163.7	912.0

SOURCE: National Transportation Policy Study Commission, 1979.

Note: "Originating" means the movement starts on the railroad mentioned; "other" means that the railroad receives the traffic from the originating railroad.

will have to invest up to $5.9 billion in facilities and equipment to meet this increase in demand. The railroads will have to purchase 485 new locomotives to pull coal trains and 9,700 new coal cars by 1985.

The Department of Transportation (DOT) believes the present rail system will have to be supplemented with only 300 miles of new rail line to meet the 1985 coal requirements. However, the DOT believes the rail investment required to meet coal demands of 1985 will be greater than $10 billion—$5 to $7 billion for new cars and locomotives and $4 to $5 billion for upgrading of existing rights-of-way.[11]

[11] *Railway Age* (November 28, 1977), p. 36. See also: "Coal: Questions Begging for Answers," Railway Age (April 30, 1979), pp. 24–26.

(There is an alternative method of shipping coal, known as slurry pipelines. They will be discussed in chapter 6.)

Railroad Equipment

The railroad industry has a significant variety of equipment available. In 1980 there were 28,663 locomotives in active service; 28,483, or 99.4 percent, were the diesel-electric variety. Twelve were steam engines, and 168 units were electric locomotives. Louis Menk, of the Burlington Northern System, predicted that in the future, it will be feasible to use electric locomotives on heavily traveled mainline tracks.[12] The limiting factor to electrification of American railroads is the high cost of the overhead electric power lines which supply power to the locomotives.

The total number of freight cars is slowly declining. In 1929 there were 2.6 million cars; in 1950—2.0 million; in 1965—1.8 million; and in 1980—1.7 million. In 1980, the three most common types of cars were: boxcars, used for general merchandise—431,000; hopper cars, used for coal, sand, gravel, ores and similar raw materials—348,000; and covered hoppers, used for grain, fertilizers, and related agricultural products—300,000. The newer cars are capable of hauling heavier loads than their predecessors. Most new cars can haul between 100 to 125 tons of freight, over double the capacity of a typical car in the 1929 rail-car fleet.

During certain times of the year, shippers complain that railroads do not possess an adequate number of cars. This was true during the Spring, 1978, as agriculture prices were increasing and farmers opted to ship their stored grain to market. Railroads argue that their number of covered hopper cars is adequate most of the time to meet shipper requirements and that it is unreasonable to expect them to maintain enough cars to meet the peak demands. To do so would result in a significant excess of cars at all times except during the relatively short harvest periods. By late-1981 the U.S. economy was in a recession and shipments of agricultural products were in the doldrums. It was estimated that 20 percent of covered hopper cars were not being utilized because of lack of demand.[13]

Until 1979, railroads were plagued with the problem of inflexible rates which could not change up and down during the course of a year—despite the fact that their shippers' demands did fluctuate.

---

[12] Louis W. Menk, *A Railroad Man Looks at America* (St. Paul: Burlington Northern, Inc., 1976), p. 40. See also: Perry M. Shoemaker, "Coal vs. Electrification," *Railway Age* (July 27, 1981), pp. 90–92.

[13] See: "Santa Fe and the OT-5 Controversy," *Railway Age* (June 29, 1981), p. 29.

Traditionally, half of the time there was a shortage of rail cars, the other half of the time, a surplus. Railroads gained some pricing flexibility in late-1978, when the ICC allowed them to enter into contract (rather than common) carrier relationships with customers, and in 1979, when the ICC exempted railroad carriage of perishable agricultural products from rate regulation. In mid-1979, the Southern Pacific Railroad, a major hauler of California produce to the Midwest, announced that it carried 300 percent more lettuce in the first half of 1979 than in the first half of 1978. The railroad's shipments of other produce had doubled over the same period of comparison.[14] The *Staggers Rail Act of 1980* increased further the railroads' pricing flexibility.

Rail-Car Ownership

Railroads own 80 percent of their car fleet. The other 20 percent of the rail cars are owned by either car leasing companies or shippers.

Railroads use each others' cars, and when a railroad is using a car belonging to another railroad, it must pay the owning railroad for use of its car. This payment used to be known as a *per diem*, or per-day payment. Starting in 1979 the name was changed to *car-hire*, because it is now calculated on an hourly basis. The rate is determined by the value of the car when it was new and also by its current age. The average per hour payment is about $.45, with a range from $.09 to $1.54. A railroad using another railroad's car also pays the owning railroad a mileage payment that ranges from $.04 to $.16 per mile. This payment is in addition to the car-hire payment.

The Association of American Railroads keeps track of the intricate accounting required for car-hire payments. After a railroad uses a car belonging to another railroad, it "routes" the car in the direction of the owning railroad. This requirement is not necessary for *Railbox* owned cars, which are in a nationwide fleet of 50-foot general service boxcars.

- *Railbox* is a rail car-owning pool to which most Class I railroads belong. It owns 13,000 boxcars which can be used by any railroad and do not need to be routed back toward an "owning" railroad, thus increasing their freight-carrying utilization. Such cars are called *free-runners*.

[14]"Fruit, Vegetable Exemption for Rails Assessed," *Transport Topics* (July 16, 1979), p. 17. A rail spokesman acknowledged that their traffic increase was also caused by fuel shortages facing truckers and by the independent truckers' protest.

Coal unit-trains, which carry coal to electric generating plants, often consist of cars owned by the electric utility being served. Electric utilities own coal unit-train cars because financially pressed railroads have difficulty raising the capital required to purchase the unit-train cars. Since the utilities can borrow money at a lower interest rate than the railroads, it is to their advantage to supply the cars to the railroads. In 1976, almost 21,000 coal cars were owned by public utilities.[15]

Roadbed Condition

With few exceptions, the railroads of the United States own their rights-of-way including tracks, tunnels, and bridges. Because of many years of "lean" earnings, some railroads found it expedient to cut back maintenance of their tracks. This is commonly known as *deferred maintenance*. The results of this action are often devastating. From 1966 to 1974, the number of train accidents—such as derailments—increased 58 percent. In 1977, there were about 8,000 derailments—40 percent of them caused by defective track or improper maintenance. Other causes were: 22 percent equipment-related, 24 percent human error, 3 percent grade-crossing accidents, and 11 percent miscellaneous.

The railroad industry is well aware of the problem of deferred maintenance, and improvements are being made. Both the number of ties being replaced and the quantity of new rail being laid is increasing. In 1979 about 27 million new ties were laid, compared with 21 million in 1975. Over 1,064,827 tons of new steel rail were laid compared with only 537,537 in 1975.[16]

Two other solutions are currently helping to alleviate the deferred maintenance problem. One is to abandon trackage that is generating insignificant quantities of traffic. In recent years, the railroads have received ICC authorization to abandon about 3,000 miles of track per year. The Federal Railroad Administration estimates there are currently about 21,000 miles of track that originate or terminate fewer than 25 carloads per mile per year.[17] This track is a good candidate for abandonment, although shippers located on it will protest any steps to do so. Some states, such as Iowa and Minnesota,

---

[15] Gus Welty, "Utility-Owned Coal Cars: A Boom That Rebuts the Skeptics," *Railway Age* (September 26, 1977), pp. 28–29.

[16] *Yearbook of Railroad Facts, 1980 Edition* (Washington, D.C.: Association of American Railroads, 1980), p. 54.

[17] See: *Improving Railroad Productivity*, The National Commission on Productivity and the Council of Economic Advisors (November, 1973), p. 161.

have enacted legislation to help subsidize a rail carrier for keeping marginal rail routes in operation, and the *Staggers Act* makes it easier for "other" parties to take over lines the railroad wanted to abandon.

Roadbed and Track Improvements

Railroad roadbeds (the raised foundation under the ties) must be upgraded periodically because of the heavier loads being transported. Railroads today use rail that weighs from 120 to 140 pounds per yard. In the 1930's and 1940's, standard rail was 70 to 80 pounds per yard of rail. In addition, instead of being laid in 30-foot sections, the rail is welded into continuous rail sections, often miles in length. Over 60,000 miles of mainline track is now jointless welded rail. This eliminates the "clickety-clack" of wheel and rail; more important, jointless rail reduces the wear that took place at each joint.

Railroad ties hold the rail in place. Wooden ties, soaked in creosote, are still the mainstay of American railroads. Some railroads are experimenting with concrete ties. Although they cost more initially, they require less maintenance and they last longer.

Railroad Service Characteristics

Quality of Rail Service

Railroads have historically been known for offering an indifferent level of customer service. Perhaps it is a carryover from the 1830 to 1920 era, when railroads' possessed an almost complete monopoly on surface transportation, and, therefore, their surly attitude toward passengers and freight (See Figure 5–3) would be tolerated because there was no acceptable alternative.

Shippers today who are tied to rail transportation because of the nature of their products believe railroad service would become even more uninspired if it were not for competition within the rail industry. One shipper on the Boston and Maine Railroad regularly uses this carrier, even though its service is "slightly substandard" compared to another competitive railroad, in order to help the B&M from ceasing to operate for lack of business.[18]

Even today, many shippers report lapses in rail service quality.

---

[18] Harry B. Anderson, "Ailing Boston and Maine Still Going It Alone," *The Wall Street Journal* (January 4, 1977), p. 1.

THE BAGGAGE SMASHER.

Figure 5–3 1874 Cartoon Depicting Poor Customer Service by Railroads. Source: Benny H. Taylor, *The World of Wheels* (Chicago: S.C. Griggs & Co., 1874), p. 63.

John French, physical distribution manager for Paul Masson Vineyards declared, "Rail service is deteriorating from the standpoint of transit time. Sometimes it takes 30 to 35 days to New Orleans [from California]. And it's been as high as 40 days to New England."[19]

A 1975 Department of Transportation study dealt with the quality of service offered by the various transport modes. Six percent of shipper respondents said rail service was "excellent," 16 percent rated it "good," 44 percent checked "adequate," 25 percent "minimally acceptable," and 9 percent found rail service "unsatisfactory." Of the four transport modes covered by the DOT study—truck, rail,

[19]Joe Barks, "We Will Ship No Wine After Its Time," *Distribution* (February, 1981), p. 75.

air, barge—the railroads had by far the highest percentage of dissatisfaction with their quality of service.[20]

To combat service deficiencies, railroads are taking many corrective actions. To concentrate their efforts on what they do best, railroads have been withdrawing from the LCL (less-than-car-load) shipments in favor of CL (carload) quantities. To fill this service void, the *freight forwarder* and *shipper association* came into prominence. The freight forwarder is a for-profit company that accepts shipments of LCL size (usually meaning less than 30,000 pounds). The freight forwarder charges a rate to their customer that is less than the LCL rate involved, but more than the applicable CL rate. To understand the freight forwarders' rates, assume the rail LCL rate from City A to City B is $10 per cwt (century weight or 100 pounds) and the CL rate is $5 per cwt. The freight forwarder charges, say, $7.50 per cwt, consolidates the LCL shipments of many shippers, tenders them to the line-haul carrier—typically a railroad or motor carrier—in CL quantities and thereby qualifies for the lower CL rates, $5 in this example. Thus, freight forwarders make a profit by charging their customers more than CL rates but paying only CL rates themselves.[21] Shipper associations are similar in operation to freight forwarders, but they are "non-profit" and serve only their members.

In 1980, freight forwarders and shipper associations accounted for over 2 percent of all rail carloadings; they are important users of trailer-on-flat car (TOFC or "piggyback") services.

Railroad Customer Service Improvements

The railroad industry is highly aware of its reputation for lack of excellence in the area of customer service. Therefore, the industry is working diligently to improve both the *speed* and *consistency* of service. Both ICC policies and the *Staggers Act* have allowed railroads to enter into contracts with shippers, and often shippers insist on performance standards being written into the contracts. The Union Pacific Railroad has contracts to serve both the U.S. Postal Service and United Parcel Service, and both require a monthly 90 percent "on-time" performance. The UP consistently meets these

[20]J. Richard Jones, *Industrial Shipper Survey: Plant Level,* U.S. Department of Transportation (September, 1975), p. 28.

[21]Forwarders also pick up and deliver the shipment at each end. For regular railroad LCL service the shipper must deliver the goods to the rail terminal, and the consignee must arrange for delivery from the rail terminal in the destination city. See also: Leslie Drahos, "Forwarders Favor Unregulated Future," *Handling and Shipping Management* (April, 1981), pp. 43–48.

It was, Jim Wright says, a prime example of what a railroad and a shipper can do if they work openly and honestly with each other.

Late last year, Santa Fe began talking traffic with a major pharmaceutical company—one which did no rail shipping, giving all its traffic to private and contract motor carriage instead. But, the company was becoming increasingly concerned about the fuel situation, price and availability, as it might affect the economics of over-the-road transportation.

The shipper opened its records to Santa Fe, laying out commodity flows, tonnages, costs. Santa Fe, in turn, developed a series of piggyback-based alternatives for each movement corridor, costing-out each alternative and demonstrating the savings that would be possible.

Result: In roughly the first six months after the pharmaceutical company decided to convert to piggyback, Santa Fe got 461 trailers of brand new business, with traffic expected to total about 1,000 trailers over a year's time—and it's all traffic taken from private and contract highway operations.

Figure 5–4   Winning New Business: A Railroad Case History. Source: *Railway Age* (June 29, 1981), p. 30.

minimum requirements and often posts a 99 percent "on-time" service level.[22]

The Santa Fe Railroad established a service-reliability group that consists of both traffic—this is, what many railroads refer to as marketing—and operating officers. If this group detects service problems, senior management has delegated to it the power to take corrective actions. Service failures are detected by monitoring fifty-nine important city-pairs between which large quantities of freight flow on a daily basis. These city-pairs include Chicago to Los Angeles, and Chicago to Richmond. The monitoring process is accomplished by a sophisticated computer program. When the computer model detects a service problem, both traffic and operations people analyze the problem and corrective action is taken quickly.[23] Besides insuring that existing customer service standards are consistently met, the Santa Fe is also searching for innovative service-price packages to win new customers for the railroad. Figure 5–4 examines how the

[22]Gus Welty, "UP's Marketing Philosophy: 'Let's Try It'," *Railway Age* (June 27, 1981), pp. 30–34.

[23]Gus Welty, "Santa Fe: Making (and Meeting) Marketing Goals," *Railway Age* (June 29, 1981), pp. 26–30.

Santa Fe designed a transportation program for a large pharmaceutical company that converted about 1,000 trailer-loads from the highway system to railroad piggyback.

Piggyback Traffic

Piggyback traffic is a commonly used term to describe two types of rail service. TOFC (Trailer On Flat Car) involves loading two or three highway trailers on an 85-foot or longer railroad flatcar. COFC (Container On Flat Car) is the transporting of containers on a rail flatcar. Both services involve the line-haul between cities on railroad. Pick-up and delivery service is performed by motor carriers. Piggyback is a growing segment of railroad business. In 1957 there were about 250,000 piggyback car loadings. By 1965 there were one million loadings, and in 1980 there were 1.66 million piggyback loadings, accounting for 7.4 percent of all 1980 car loadings.[24]

Piggyback service has been growing for several reasons. First, railroads have been stressing "on-time" delivery service for their piggyback traffic, which has made this service more competitive against truckers. Also, schedules have been set to allow for early evening departures with early morning arrivals at key destinations. Rail management understands that if piggyback service is sporadic, no rate reduction will make up for poor service. Martin A. Brieschke, manager of intermodal sales and service for the Santa Fe Railroad, summed up rail management's attitude, "The big thing to sell is dependability."[25]

Illustrative of the railroads' commitment to high-quality TOFC service is the Illinois Central Gulf's "Slingshot" service between Chicago and St. Louis. Each day eight special piggyback trains operate between these two cities—four in each direction. Robert W. O'Brien, director of Corporate Relations for the ICG, is obviously proud of the "Slingshot" concept. In a letter to the authors of August 17, 1981, he declared:

> It is inspiring to be driving along in the Chicago-St. Louis corridor and to see one of our "Slingshot" trains whiz past. One locomotive and a maximum of 15 TTX flatcars, each carrying two trailers, really gallop along the rails. The no-caboose concept used to bother some railfan purists (and union diehards) but "Slingshot's" all-business, service-first operation has been a formidable competitor to over-the-road trucks between the involved cities.

[24] *Yearbook of Railroad Facts, 1980 Edition*, p. 27.
[25] Frank Malone, "Piggyback: The Competitive Pressures Mount," *Railway Age* (October 27, 1980), p. 26.

"Slingshot" almost was killed by the management several times during 1975, 1976 and 1977 when it operated at a loss. No less than the then-chairman, Stanley E. G. Hillman, agreed to continue the experiment. His far-sighted willingness to keep the train has paid off in increased intermodal tonnage for ICG, reduced heavy vehicle traffic for motorists, and results in fuel savings for everybody.

Another key factor that has helped piggyback's growth is its labor efficiency. In the above "Slingshot" operation, the two-person rail crew (when operating with 15 rail cars) performs the same transportation service as thirty truck drivers.

A third factor is fuel economy and ecological considerations. A 100-car train with two trailers per car uses less fuel than 200 tractors each pulling a 40-foot trailer. In addition, the 100-car piggyback train also takes 200 trucks off the highway system, reducing highway congestion by that amount.

A final factor contributing to the growth of piggyback traffic has been the widespread acceptance of "land-bridge" traffic, which involves the substitution of railroads for ships to carry containers for part of their journey. Several forms of land-bridge traffic (including "micro" which does not involve substitution of rail for vessel) are shown on Figure 5–5.

Most piggyback traffic is transported by a fleet of 40,000 intermodal flatcars owned by Trailer Train Company (TTX)—which in turn is owned by twenty-nine railroads.These cars are "free-running," meaning that since they do not belong to a specific carrier they can be routed anywhere as needed.

There are many piggyback "plans" available to shippers. Figure 5–6 illustrates six plans offered by the Missouri Pacific Railroad to its customers.

Plan II½ is by far the most popular and accounted for 49 percent of all trailer-containers the railroads transported in 1979. Plan III was second with 15 percent, and Plans I and IV each had about 11 percent.[26]

In March, 1981, the ICC deregulated rail piggyback service from economic (price) regulation. Under the 1976 4-R Act (*Railroad Revitalization and Regulatory Reform Act*) the ICC can, on its own initiative, exempt from regulation rail service for which it believes regulation is not necessary. It had previously taken this action in deregulating fresh produce products for transportation by railroads.

[26] *Railway Age* (October 27, 1980), p. 26.

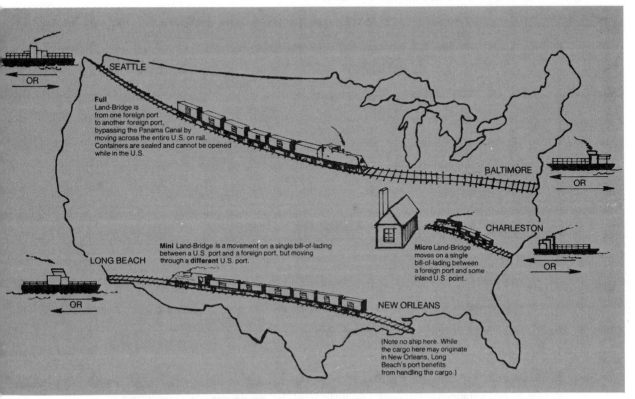

Figure 5-5 Examples of Land-Bridge Rail Traffic in the United States.

When announcing the piggyback price deregulation program, ICC Commissioner Reginald E. Gilliam, Jr., declared:

> I believe the decision to exempt TOFC/COFC services offers the potential for tremendous growth in intermodalism which is, in my opinion, an answer to our transportation needs of the future. I urge all concerned to use this exemption and make this second major experiment in deregulation a successful prototype for the future.[27]

The railroad industry is highly optimistic that piggyback traffic represents one of the real "growth" areas for the railroads in the 1980's and beyond. Hays T. Watkins, president of CSX Corporation,

[27] "ICC Adopts Rules Exempting Railroad Piggyback Service From Regulation," *Traffic World* (March 2, 1981), p. 50.

PIGGYBACK PLANS

Illustrated here are the Standard Piggyback plans. Each provides coordinated transportation services . . . utilizing trucking and Mo-Pac rail line haul in a variety of efficient combinations.

█ **MO-PAC**

☐ **MOTOR COMMON CARRIER**

▥ **SHIPPER/CONSIGNEE**

PLAN I: Motor common carrier handles door-to-door service . . . using Mo-Pac Piggyback Rail Service as the long distance carrier.

PLAN II: Mo-Pac picks up trailers at your door, delivers them to the ramp, handles rail transport and delivers trailers to final destination. Door-to-door service.

PLAN II½: Mo-Pac provides trailers, flat cars and rail transportation; shipper and consignee arrange motor pick-up and delivery from ramps. (*)

49%

PLAN III: Mo-Pac provides ramp-to-ramp rail transport . . . shipper/consignee handles motor delivery of trailers to and from ramps.

15%

PLAN IV: Mo-Pac provides ramp-to-ramp rail haul . . . shipper provides motor delivery to and from ramps.

11%

PLAN V: Mo-Pac or common carrier provides trailers, pick-up or delivery. Mo-Pac provides ramping and de-ramping.

NOTE: All plans also apply to container shipments.
* PLAN II ¼: Mo-Pac provides trailers, rail service and EITHER door-to-ramp or ramp-to-door motor carriage.

Figure 5–6 Various Piggyback Alternatives Offered by Missouri Pacific Railroad. Courtesy: Missouri Pacific Railroad.

a large railroad holding company, is an enthusiastic proponent of the piggyback concept:

> We hope to get a good part of our growth by taking traffic off the highways. The way to do it is through some sort of cooperative activity between the railroads and the truckers. The economics are such that there are bound to be advantages for both modes in using piggyback. I am very optimistic that we can attract more intermodal traffic. If we learn how to do innovative pricing, we ought to be able to get a greater share of the intercity market. There's a tremendous market for intermodal service, and I think that's the next big area where railroads have to make a breakthrough.[28]

Unit-Trains

Unit-trains specialize in transporting only one product or commodity from origin to destination. There are unit-trains transporting U.S. mail, fruits, vegetables, and new automobiles. However, their major usage is in two areas: mainly coal but also grain.[29]

A typical coal unit-train is operated by the Burlington Northern from Colstrip, Montana, to Becker, Minnesota—some 700 miles. At Becker, Northern States Power Company (NSP) operates a large coal-burning electric generating plant. In 1972, NSP signed a 20-year contract with Montana Power to supply coal for its Becker plant. Nine coal unit-trains presently transport the required coal. Each train is 100 cars in length and each car holds 100 tons. It takes about 36 hours for the run, with an average speed of 20 miles per hour (mph) and a top speed of 40 mph. The train stops eight times to change its four-man crew. After unloading—the cars are hydraulically rotated to dump out the coal, which is possible since each coupling device also possesses swivels—the train returns empty at 50 mph to Colstrip to repeat the process.

Railroad Cost Structure

Railroads are an industry with a high proportion of fixed costs, which do not vary with volume of business. These include: the rights-of-way (including tunnels and bridges), classification yards, general management expense, and maintenance expenses caused by weathering and age but not based on usage. These expenses are constant and they are the same no matter how great or how little the volume of traffic the railroad carries.

[28] Frank Malone, loc. cit., p. 30.
[29] See: "BN's Unit Grain Trains Get Shippers' Approval," Traffic World (August 24, 1981), p. 23.

Railroads also have variable costs of operation. These are costs that vary directly with volume—they go up with higher volume and down with lower volume. Examples of railroad variable costs would be maintenance of equipment and rights-of-way based on usage, labor costs, fuel, and lubrication oil.

Prior to the 1940's, many transportation experts believed railroad fixed costs were as much as two-thirds of the total cost structure.[30] Today, it is generally believed that fixed costs are 40 to 50 percent of the total cost structure. The primary reason is that many railroads have greatly expanded their ton-mile production, using the same basic rights-of-way and physical plant. When volume increases over time, the percentage of fixed costs compared to total costs *decreases*.

Because of the still relatively high fixed-cost structure of railroads, they are subject to significant increasing *economies of scale*—as volume increases, the total cost of production decreases on a *per-unit* basis.[31] Why? Because as volume increases, fixed costs stay constant and hence become *less* per unit of output. James C. Nelson, a noted railroad scholar, said: "Railroads, having a substantial investment in plant and equipment and relatively large fixed costs, cannot operate efficiently with low and irregular volumes of traffic. Either adequate traffic flows must be stimulated, or unprofitable operations and high rates will result."[32]

Rail Industry Issues

Seven current railroad issues will now be examined. They are: (a) the merger trend, (b) poor rail-car utilization, (c) labor relations, (d) Conrail, (e) Amtrak, (f) coal slurry pipelines, and (g) deregulation of the railroad industry by the *Staggers Rail Act of 1980*.

The Rail Merger Trend

There is much more rail track than is needed. The present railroad system was built before there was any significant intermodal competition. Rail mergers help to eliminate redundant trackage.

---

[30] See: W. F. Ripley, *Railroads: Rates and Regulation* (New York: Macmillan, 1924), pp. 77–79; and I. Leo Sharfman, *The American Railroad Problem* (New York: The Century Co., 1921), p. 224.

[31] See: George H. Borts, "Increasing Returns in the Railway Industry," *The Journal of Political Economy* (August, 1954), pp. 316–333.

[32] James C. Nelson, *Railroad Transportation and Public Policy* (Washington, D.C.: The Brookings Institution, 1959), p. 148.

Why, then, haven't there been more rail mergers? Observers believe one reason was Willard's Law—named after the late Dan Willard, president of the Baltimore and Ohio Railroad. He said that few railroad presidents will be in favor of a merger when they would undoubtedly merge themselves out of their jobs.

By the early 1980's, for reasons to be examined shortly, Willard's Law seems to be suspended, for railroads, are presently involved in a very active merger movement. Louis Menk of the Burlington Northern declared, "If we're going to have a viable rail system, there will have to be fewer railroads."[33] The Presidential Task Force on Railroad Productivity was more specific: "The industry should be restructured into four, five, or so continental railroad systems that operate and compete with one another nationwide. This would give managements of individual railroads the opportunity to manage independently of other railroads and would create effective intramodal competition in all the major regions of the country."[34]

Two major types of rail mergers are possible. (See Figure 5–7.) First, there are *side-by-side* or parallel mergers. This involves two or more carriers whose route systems are parallel and overlapping. This type of merger has—until the 1970's—been the predominant type of rail merger. A benefit of this type of merger is that redundant trackage can be eliminated. However, where two or more competitive rail carriers once existed, only one remains after the merger. Regarding the loss of competition, the Commission noted: "Railroads have the basic economic characteristics of public utilities and are subject to regulation in the public interest at both the federal and state levels, therefore, it is not realistic to insist that intramodal rail competition must be preserved at all places, at all times and under all circumstances."[35] Shippers, however, may not agree.[36]

The other type of rail merger is the *end-to-end*. This involves two or more carriers joining together when each serves different regions of the country; they typically serve only a few of the same cities

---

[33] *Minneapolis Tribune* (January 8, 1978), p. 11C. For an opposite point of view, see: William J. McDonald, "Are We Expecting Too Much From Mergers?" *Railway Age* (October 9, 1978), pp. 48–51.

[34] *Improving Railroad Productivity*, p. 231.

[35] 320 ICC 122, 207 (1963).

[36] Even though rates are the same, individual railroads do compete in service terms. Traffic managers in Wisconsin, surveyed for their reaction to a parallel line merger proposal, said that service competition between carriers was important. Examples were the railroad's "finding" cars for the shipper to use during rail-car shortages and providing switching service which was coordinated with the shipper's production scheduling. See: Jon P. Nelson, "The Proposed Milwaukee Road—Chicago and Northwestern Merger" in *State Transportation Planning* (Madison: Wisconsin Department of Resource Development, 1966), pp. 29–84.

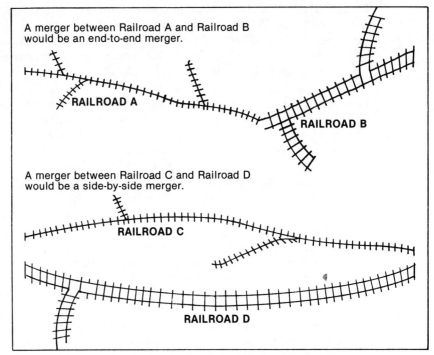

Figure 5–7   "End-to-End" and "Side-by-Side" Rail Mergers.

where each system interfaces or comes together. This is the predominant type of merger being considered in the early 1980's. Competition is *not* reduced by this type of merger because each city or region has as many rail competitors after the merger as they had prior to the merger. The only post-merger difference is that each railroad is now part of a larger rail system.

Traditionally, no railroad has stretched between the east and west coasts, despite the fact that competing modes do. Coast-to-coast railroad lines are probably necessary for the rail industry to survive.

Benefits of Rail Mergers

Two general benefits can be noted for an end-to-end merger. First is improved service to the shipping public. Customers are offered single carrier service and *responsibility* from origin to destination. This allows one railroad to maximize its traffic-handling efficiency by routing over its system without interlining (exchanging traffic) with another rail carrier. Interlining is a constant source of service breakdowns, because each railroad can always blame the other rail-road if something goes wrong. In addition, it is frustrating to a highly service-oriented railroad to have to interline with a partner that does not—or cannot—provide a high level of customer service.[37]

A second advantage of end-to-end mergers would be reduced costs of operation. The Task Force on Railroad Productivity noted that the present system of rail interchange is expensive—in addition to reducing speed and reliability of delivery. Both operational costs (car switching) and clerical costs (record keeping) are involved in the process of switching cars from one carrier to another. A typical interchange involves "breaking up" the train at the terminus of a railroad. Each carrier must hire its own yard crew to "break up" the arriving train and then to assemble cars on the outgoing train. Waybills (operating papers for each car, listing its contents, destination, etc.) are exchanged between interlining carriers. The interchange produces additional paperwork that would not be necessary if one railroad had complete responsibility for the shipment. "Operating and clerical staffs must collect, compile, transmit, and preserve information on cars delivered and received, time of delivery (receipt), and condition of cars and its lading. Other clerical operations arising from interchange include paying or collecting per diems and 'divisions' (shares of freight revenues on interline shipments)."[38]

Current Rail Merger Activity

In 1980, two major rail mergers were approved by the ICC. First, the Burlington Northern Railroad merged the 4,507-mile main-line Frisco railroad into the BN.[39] Secondly, the CSX Corporation was formed on November 1, 1980.[40] It brought together two large railroads, each of which was the product of recent rail mergers. The Chessie System (composed of the Chesapeake and Ohio Railroad and the Baltimore and Ohio Railroad) merged as a co-equal with The Family Lines (composed of the Louisville and Nashville, the Seaboard Coast Line Railroad, the Clinchfield Railroad, and the Georgia and West Point Route).

In 1982, two additional mergers received ICC approval. One involved the merger of the Union Pacific, the Missouri Pacific, and the

[37] See: "Mergers Are Sign That Renaissance Is Taking Place In Rail Industry," *Traffic World* (May 25, 1981), pp. 40–41.

[38] *Improving Railroad Productivity*, p. 239.

[39] See: Gus Welty, "The Era of the Giants: BN/Frisco," *Railway Age* (February 23, 1981), pp. 18–23.

[40] See: Tom Kizzia, "The Era of the Giants: Chessie/SCL Industries," *Railway Age* (March 30, 1981), pp. 26–30.

Western Pacific.[41] The second brought together the Southern Railway and the Norfolk and Western Railroad.[42]

The current merger movement of the 1980's is changing the railroad industry. John T. Collinson, chief executive officer of The Chessie System, recently reflected on the current rail merger trend. His observations deserve quoting at length:

> There is another basic force at work making tremendous changes in railroading. That force is the urge to merger. It is literally restructuring my industry, not only the way we look, but the way we work. Its energies are not yet spent and, indeed, you can expect to see it continue for quite a while.
>
> I have just gone through another merger myself. The parent company of the Chessie Railroads—Chessie System, Inc.—has been merged with the parent company of the Family Lines Rail System—Seaboard Coast Line Industries. The resulting company's name is CSX Corporation, headquartered in Richmond, VA. Besides its railroad members, it includes in its big family enterprises engaged in newspaper publishing, hotel operations, corporate aircraft management, oil and gas exploration, and development of coal lands, forest resources and real estate. . . .
>
> . . . [O]n the whole, the (railroad) amalgamations have prospered, except in the northeastern sector where mergers proved no remedy for the very serious and long-standing railroad problem in that region.
>
> The merger movement is still rolling. The Burlington and Frisco have just been united, and the planned marriages of the Southern and N & W and of UP, Mopac and Western Pacific are now before the ICC.
>
> The result of these mergers . . . has been a radical alteration of our industry. When I began railroading in 1946, one could count over 40 major railroad companies. Today, the number is less than half of that, but the smaller number, for the most part, constitutes a stronger industry, one which has truly benefited from the urge to merge. So has the entire nation, I might add, if the erosion of railroad transportation has been halted, and the industry given the means for rapid, far-reaching self-improvement.
>
> I am sure we will see a continuation of the merger movement through the '80s and the ultimate emergence of a truly rationalized national network of private enterprise railroad systems.[43]

Governmental Policy Toward Rail Mergers

The ICC is authorized, under Section 5 of the *Interstate Commerce Act*, to approve rail mergers on an individual basis when the Commission finds them to be in the "public interest." The ICC's

---

[41] See: "Long Hauls: A Powerful New Rail System," *Fortune* (October 18, 1982), p. 16.

[42] "NW, Southern: All Set For A Big June Wedding," *Railway Age* (April 12, 1982), pp. 12–13.

[43] "Industry Leaders Speak on Transport Law Change Challenges," *Traffic World* (April 13, 1981), pp. 36–37.

attitude towards rail mergers has been favorable. Johnson and Whiteside analyzed rail mergers from 1940 to 1975 and concluded: "We believe that a careful reading of the Commissions' rail merger proceedings, especially over the last 20 years, exhibits both a remarkable consistency of interpretation and an overall positive attitude towards rail unifications."[44] There was one problem, however. The ICC allows all "interested" parties in a rail merger to participate in the hearings, and the result was that the ICC decisions often took an unreasonable length of time. The Great Northern, Northern Pacific, and Chicago, Burlington, and Quincy—now the Burlington Northern—applied to the ICC for merger in 1961. In 1966—five years later—the ICC denied the merger. In early 1967 the Commission decided to reconsider this application, and in November, 1967, the ICC voted to authorize this merger. More recently, the Rock Island Railroad and the Union Pacific requested a merger before the ICC, but it took the Commission more than twelve years to render a decision! In the interim, the Rock Island went bankrupt, and the Union Pacific then decided that it did not want to "marry" the Rock Island.[45]

Congress desired to both encourage rail mergers and reduce the "regulatory lag" in Commission decision making. The 1976 *4-R Act (Railroad Revitalization and Regulatory Reform Act)* addressed these issues.[46] Specifically, three governmental organizations were ordered to help expedite "voluntary" rail mergers. First, the Department of Transportation, through its Federal Railroad Administration (FRA) was to develop plans for rail mergers and coordination projects that would result in a more efficient railroad system that could better serve the public. The FRA could "encourage" rail carriers to go to the ICC for merger approval, but it could not mandate this action. The FRA uses the "carrot" approach by making certain federal funds available to railroads that follow their guidelines.[47]

The Rail Services Planning Office (RSPO), part of the ICC, is the other government agency involved in the study of rail mergers. The *4-R Act* ordered the RSPO to prepare a "comprehensive study" of rail mergers and to present a series of recommendations to the ICC for encouraging and expediting rail mergers. In January, 1978, the

[44] James C. Johnson and Terry C. Whiteside, "Professor Ripley Revisited: A Current Analysis of Railroad Mergers," *ICC Practitioners' Journal* (May–June, 1975), p. 450.

[45] "End of Game for the Rock Island?" *Business Week* (March 20, 1978), p. 145.

[46] T. P. Ellsworth, Jr., "The Merger Merry-Go-Round: Rail Consolidations Under the 4-R Act," *ICC Practitioners' Journal* (May–June, 1977), pp. 446–476.

[47] Tom Ichniowski, "FRA's Merger Man," *Railway Age* (April 10, 1978), pp. 30–31.

final rail merger report of the RSPO was published. The report contained numerous recommendations, including the observation that end-to-end mergers offered more long-term advantages to the public than side-by-side (parallel) mergers.

Finally, the 4-R Act states that the ICC will still decide merger cases, but a statutory time limit is established for it to reach a decision. From the time two or more railroads request ICC approval of a merger, the Commission must render a decision within thirty-one months.

The ICC in February, 1981, stated that all rail merger cases will be "carefully" examined and only authorized if the transaction appears to be in the "public interest." The public interest includes considering the effect of the merger on: (a) the rail carriers involved, (b) the competitor railroads, (c) the shipping public, and (d) the affected carrier employees.[48]

Disadvantages of Rail Mergers—the Penn Central Example

Not all mergers work miracles—the most obvious non-miracle is the Penn Central. What happened? The Pennsylvania Railroad Company and the New York Central Railroad Company applied to the ICC for a merger on March 9, 1962. The Commission authorized the merger on April 6,1966, and it became effective on February 1, 1968. This generally side-by-side merger was designed to eliminate duplicate trackage. The expected result was that two financially anemic railroads would be able to cut operating costs while giving the shipping public an improved level of customer service, using the best facilities of each railroad.

> Despite the essentially negative impetus for this merger, however, it was widely hailed as a forward step. Optimistic press agentry, confident assertions by merger architects, and financial analyses that concentrated only on the benefits expected from the merger resulted in the general belief that the Penn Central would not only be the Nation's largest railroad, but also a newly strengthened pillar of the Nation's economy. Stuart Saunders, generally given most of the credit for bringing the merger to pass, was named businessman of the year for 1968. The Penn Central's stock price shot up shortly after the merger to unrealistic heights. It appeared to many observers that the problems of the Northeast's major railroads had been solved.[49]

[48] "ICC Adopts 'Careful' Policy Governing Consideration of Rail Consolidations," *Traffic World* (February 9, 1981), pp. 40–41. See also: Gus Welty, "Mergers: A Grand Design—But Will Washington Buy It?" *Railway Age* (July 14, 1980), pp. 26–27.

[49] *The Penn Central and Other Railroads*, U.S. Senate, 92nd Congress, 2nd Session (December, 1972), p. xviii in James C. Johnson and Donald V. Harper, "The Shipper Views Proposed Solutions to the Northeast Railroad Problems," *Transportation Journal* (Summer, 1974), p. 6.

The actual results were less impressive. By June 21, 1970, barely two years later, the Board of Directors of the Penn Central stated the firm was "virtually without cash," and, therefore, they filed for bankruptcy and were granted a reorganization petition under Section 77 of the Bankruptcy Act.

What caused the collapse? In the book *The Wreck of the Penn Central* it is noted that there were three major problems: operational, financial, and "people." Operational problems resulted because the two railroads did not properly plan for the merger prior to its consummation. When the combined railroad commenced operation, the terminal freight classification system often became total confusion. Thousands of employees did not understand the new car sorting system, and, therefore, cars piled up in freight classification yards. Cars and their waybills (which tell the railroad the contents and destination of each rail car) became separated from each other for weeks at a time. Harassed freight classification yard supervisors would frequently send out whole trains of cars—without waybills, so the destination was unknown—in order to relieve congestion, or they would reduce congestion in "their" yard by attaching lost cars to any outgoing train. Illustrative of the chaos is that an entire 100-car coal train was "lost" for 10 days outside Syracuse. Even the computer systems of the two railroads did not "mesh."[50]

Financial problems came from three factors. First, each railroad was financially "sick" going into the merger. In 1959, the New York Central and the Pennsylvania railroads achieved returns on invested capital that were among the lowest in the United States. Secondly, the ICC ordered—as a condition to the approval of the Penn Central merger—that the new railroad must also accept the habitually bankrupt New Haven Railroad into the new system. This "albatross" around the neck of the Penn Central constantly drained funds that were needed to revitalize the rights-of-way and to purchase badly needed new equipment.

The third financial problem was caused by the poor customer service that happened after the merger. Consequently, shippers, whenever possible, routed their shipments on competitor railroads or trucks and the result was less revenue for the Penn Central.

The third and undoubtedly the worst problem of the Penn Central was "people" oriented. The Pennsylvania and Central had been bitter rivals for over 100 years prior to the merger. After the merger, this feud did not stop between the "red" team (Pennsylvania) and

[50]Joseph R. Daughen and Peter Binzen, *The Wreck of the Penn Central* (Boston: Little, Brown & Co., 1971), pp. 111–18.

the "green" team (New York Central)—so named for the the colors of their respective boxcars.

The Pennsylvania Railroad was more profitable, giving its employees a feeling of superiority. There were different "personalities" for each railroad. The Pennsylvania was stoic, steady, and traditional. The Central was smaller, more innovative, and had a more centralized management. To get a flavor for the clash between the "red" and "green" teams, read this exchange between Senator Hartke and Alfred E. Perlman, former president of the New York Central:

SEN. HARTKE   As I gather it, you would have instituted, if you had had the authority to have done so, the same basic marketing concept that you used for the Central.

PERLMAN   Yes, sir.

SEN. HARTKE   But you could not get that done; why not?

PERLMAN   If you notice the people at the heads of the departments of the merged company, everyone was from the Pennsylvania Railroad except me. To me it was not a merger, it was a takeover, frankly.[51]

Far from "solving" the northeast railroad problem, the Penn-Central merger actually worsened it. Hopefully, managers of subsequent rail mergers, have learned some lessons from the Penn-Central's errors.[52]

Railroad Car Utilization

Railroads do not utilize their equipment, especially rail cars, as much as they could. Rail-car utilization is the percentage of time a

- Transportation *equipment utilization* measures are relative and usually indicate the percentage or proportion of time that a piece of equipment is being used to transport passengers or freight. The phrase *revenue service* means that the piece of equipment is earning money for its owner. *Non-revenue service* means the equipment is in use but not earning anything; an example is a vehicle traveling to a repair shop for a maintenance check.

car is moving to or from a destination, compared to the rest of the time when it is being loaded, unloaded, moving within railroad sort-

---

[51] *Ibid.*, p. 112.

[52] For a thoughtful examination of the Penn Central collapse, primarily from the viewpoint of David Bevan, the railroad's chief financial officer, see: Stephen Salsbury, *No Way to Run a Railroad: The Untold Story of the Penn-Central Crisis* (New York: McGraw-Hill Book Company, 1982).

ing yards, or standing idle. In 1980, the average rail-car utilization was three hours and eighteen minutes per day. An average rail car in 1980 traveled only 60.2 miles, moving at an average speed—including stops—of under 20 miles per hour. This means a car is in use only about 14 percent of the time, which would appear easy to improve upon. If the car-utilization ratio could be further significantly improved, the net effect is the same as a large increase in the size of the car fleet—because each car would perform more work.

Better car utilization will also help to arrest the loss of rail revenue and the shifting of traffic from railroads to motor carriers. A traffic manager for a major Northeast paper mill said that rail boxcars were the preferred method of transportation for their heaviest, industrial-grade products but sized up the problem for both shippers and the railroads:

> Unfortunately, the railroad just can't seem to give us nearly enough usable boxcars, so we are being forced to use more and more trucks. I don't know what the problem is with boxcars, but it really is a shame we have this shortage. With boxcars we can load to the roof and never have to worry about too much weight, and we get a very attractive rate. With motor carriage it is just the opposite. We can only get a few rolls in a trailer before it weighs out, and the rate is pretty steep. But at least with trucks, we can always count on enough clean trailers.[53]

- *Weighing out* is an operating term and means that a rail car (or truck or cargo plane) is being loaded with a very dense cargo and reaches its weight-carrying capacity even though there is empty space (cubic capacity) remaining. The opposite phenomenon is to load a bulky material—say, inflated basketballs—which fill all the vehicle's cargo-carrying space without reaching its weight-carrying capacity. This is known as *cubing out*.

Increased car utilization is being achieved on progressive railroads by two methods. First, classification yards are being modernized so that railroads can quickly and efficiently sort cars. Classification yard delay is generally conceded to be the most serious "culprit" which must be improved if railroads are to improve car utilization.

The second solution to improved car utilization is to run shorter, more frequent trains. The Florida East Coast (FEC) Railway has effectively used this solution. In 1978, while the railroad industry was averaging 59.5 miles per day per car, the FEC averaged 88. FEC President Winfred L. Thornton notes: "If the industry got that kind of equipment utilization, think how many less billions of dollars of

---

[53] "Keep Those Boxcars Rolling," *Distribution Worldwide* (April, 1977), p. 49.

debt it would have; how much less it would be paying out in interest; how much greater availability of equipment it would have for shippers—who sometimes can't ship on the railroad at all because they can't get the equipment."[54]

The FEC is able to utilize shorter and more frequent trains because it has more favorable labor work rules which do not apply to most other railroads. This work-rule change was achieved after a strike that lasted over 10 years!

- *Work rules* are part of the labor-management agreement and specify how many people are needed for specific tasks (manning formulas), what work is required of them, etc.

Labor Relations

From rail management's viewpoint, labor relations represents one of the most essential—and frustrating—aspects of running a railroad. Most observers believe that major changes *must* be achieved in updating railroad work rules if railroads are to survive. A federal task force studying railroad productivity declared, "Work rules are a serious impediment to the efficient deployment of labor in the railroad industry."[55] Shippers also have their views. Harold H. Plaut, general traffic manager of International Minerals & Chemical Corporation stated, "No private business enterprise in this country is capable of operating profitably when labor costs eat up from fifty-three percent to fifty-seven percent of its revenues. The refusal of the unions to recognize technological advances, labor-saving methods and devices, and areas of productivity gains—in short, their insistence upon more men to do less and less work for greater and greater wages—is a one-way ticket to financial disaster."[56]

Total railroad employment has decreased consistently since the 1920's. In 1929, Class I railroads employed 1.66 million people. In 1960, employment was 781,000, and by 1980 it was 480,000. This decrease in employment parallels the railroads' declining market share of traffic among all modes.

Railroad employees receive about 30 percent higher wages than the average of all production workers in the private sector.[57] In 1980,

---

[54] Luther S. Miller, "FEC: Florida's Productivity Showcase," *Railway Age* (May 8, 1978), p. 40.

[55] *Improving Railroad Productivity,* p. 210.

[56] "Shippers' Message to Rail Bargainers: Compromise," *Railway Age* (April 25, 1977), p. 60.

[57] *Improving Railroad Productivity,* p. 211.

an average rail employee received $24,659. The actual train crew operators are paid higher wages—in 1980, engineers averaged $35,000, conductors $32,000, and brakemen $26,000.[58] A typical train crew consists of four employees—one engineer, one conductor, and two brakemen.

Railroad union representation is different than that in the trucking industry, where almost all types of employees are members of the Teamsters Union. Railroad employees, on the other hand, are represented by thirteen separate unions. Two operating unions, the United Transportation Union and the Brotherhood of Locomotive Engineers, represent the train crew employees. The other eleven are non-operating unions. Examples are the Brotherhood of Railway and Airline Clerks and the International Association of Machinists.

Labor work rules. No aspect of rail labor relations is more controversial than the work rules for the operating unions. In general, *three* major changes are proposed by management. The first and most important is a reduction in a standard train crew. Management says that instead of two brakemen, one, or possibly both, should be eliminated. Assuming one brakeman is not used, the United Transportation Union estimates that 36,000 employees would lose their jobs. Management's position is supported by the Federal Task Force on Railroad Productivity, which estimates that trains can be safely operated with one brakeman in 75 to 95 percent of all situations. Further, it estimates that 20 to 40 percent of all trains do not require any brakemen to operate safely. Finally, 15 to 30 percent of all trains would not require a conductor—the engineer alone can safely operate the train.[59] Management is gaining some ground in this issue. In September, 1978, the United Transportation Union and Conrail signed an agreement that reduced the typical crew size to three per train, by reducing the number of brakemen.[60] This pattern has subsequently been negotiated by other railroads, including the Missouri Pacific[61] and the Burlington Northern.[62] The typical settlement allows three-person crews on trains with fewer than 70 cars. While obviously helpful, this arrangement is of little benefit for unit-train operations, which typically have approximately 100 cars per train.

---

[58] Based on telephone conversation on August 27, 1981 with representatives of the United Transportation Union.

[59] *Improving Railroad Productivity*, p. 219.

[60] *Traffic World* (September 25, 1978), pp. 81–82.

[61] See: Gus Welty, "Crew Consist: The New Pacts Are Paying Off," *Railway Age* (March 31, 1980), pp. 48–50.

[62] See: *1980 Burlington Northern Annual Report*, p. 1.

The second issue deals with a work rule that was originally established in the late 1800's. It involved paying train crews for a day's work when either eight hours had elapsed or 100 miles had been traveled. During the 1880's and 1890's, trains averaged 15 miles per hour, so the time-mileage formula was equitable then. Today it often results in excessive pay, because in eight hours a freight train can travel 400 miles, and the crew is then paid for four days' wages! Management proposes to eliminate the dual formula system in favor of a straight time compensation program. Eight hours would be a "regular" tour of duty, and work over eight hours would be paid time and a half.

The third proposed change would involve the removal of what management refers to as "artificial barriers" to labor flexibility. At present, two issues are involved. First, cross-country trains must switch crews each time a new union-designated "seniority district" is entered. Thus a train may have traveled only 50 miles, but a new crew is required because the train is in a new "district." The train must, therefore, stop, switch crews, and often other rules require the initial crew to be compensated for a day's wages. The coal unit-trains from Montana to Minnesota have *eight* separate train crews for a 700-mile trip. Second, at present, "road" crews are responsible for intercity train operation, and they cannot operate a train within a classification yard; therefore, a separate "yard" crew must be used. Management proposes to use one crew for both road and yard work.[63]

Conrail

Chapter 3 discussed how Conrail originated. It is a government sponsored railroad that was created to operate over the tracks of the Penn Central and six other bankrupt northeastern railroads. It has been called the "first step" towards nationalized railroads in the United States. What has happened to Conrail since its start-up in April, 1976? Doubters of the concept predicted "chaos," and believers predicted a "showcase" of railroad efficiency. In truth, Conrail has achieved the middle ground between these predictions. Conrail worked vigorously to provide the best customer service it was capable of—and shippers have been favorably impressed. J. Robert Morton, Vice-President of Corporate Transportation and Distribution of Combustion Engineering, has stated that of all the railroads in the

---

[63] See: David Kruschwitz, "Railroad Work Rules—The 1970's," and William W. DeLaney, "The Impact of Mainline Rehabilitation on Road Crew Costs," both in *Annual Proceedings of the Transportation Research Forum* (Oxford, Indiana: Richard B. Cross, 1977), pp. 68–74 and 246–54.

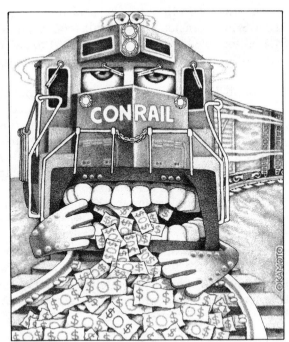

From its start in 1976, Conrail's expenses have been higher—and its revenues lower—than the forecasts.

Figure 5–8 Conrail's Cost. Source: *Business Week* (April 24, 1978), p. 29. Reproduced by permission of the publisher and Michael Okamoto.

country, "Conrail's management is the most communicable and co-operative."[64]

Conrail has cost taxpayers over $6 billion since its inception.[65] Part of these funds were utilized to purchase the assets of the bankrupt railroads, about $3 billion has been spent to refurbish track and equipment, and the remainder has been utilized to make up operation losses.[66] Leaving out capital costs, Conrail lost $220 million on operations in 1979 and $244 million in 1980. In 1976, the U.S. Railway Association (USRA) estimated Conrail would experience a net operating loss of $200 million from 1976 to 1980. In fact, it has been $1.4 billion, or seven times larger than the forecast.[67] (See Figure 5–8.)

[64]Harry B. Anderson, "Long Haul Ahead," *The Wall Street Journal* (December 13, 1977), p. 19.
[65]"Road To Reality," an editorial in *The Wall Street Journal* (March 17, 1981), p. 28.
[66]"Clear the Tracks," an editorial in *The Wall Street Journal* (April 2, 1981), p. 24.
[67]*Federal Funding of Conrail: Rail Service Objectives and Economic Realities*, U.S. Railway Association (December, 1980), p. 12.

The financial future for Conrail can best be described as dismal. The USRA estimates Conrail will require an additional subsidy of $1.5 billion to $2.1 billion between 1981 to 1985. Conrail's own estimate for this time period—in its worst-case scenario—is $3.7 billion.[68]

Conrail has two significant problems that were forseen but are worse than had been expected. First, the Eastern region of the United States is in a slow long-term trend towards less construction and manufacturing. Industry has been leaving this region to go to the "sun-belt" states. A former president of the Penn Central, Jervis Langdon, discerned, "No positive sign that the industrial base in the Northeast, which has been deteriorating for some years, will stabilize, let alone support important increases in rail volume."[69] Second, the rail properties that Conrail took over turned out to be in much worse shape than had been anticipated.

The Reagan Administration advocated a "planned transfer" of Conrail to privately-owned railroads. Congress, in its 1982 fiscal year budget, enacted a program to return Conrail to private ownership. A complicated procedure is established for selling parts of Conrail, beginning in late 1983.[70]

Amtrak

The *Rail Passenger Service Act of 1970*, which was discussed in chapter 3, created Amtrak. It is a nationalized railroad responsible for providing intercity rail passenger service. Amtrak has constantly been plagued with financial problems. One reason is that Amtrak management laid out a route structure to pass through districts represented by influential senators and congressmen. (One of the cross-Montana trains was referred to in Washington as the "Mike Mansfield Special.") The objective of Amtrak to be a "for-profit" railroad, after its initial subsidy from the federal government, has been forgotten.

Amtrak commenced operations on May 1, 1971, after it had received a $200 million subsidy. These funds were rapidly expended and Amtrak has received more than $10.2 billion in additional federal funds.[71] These dollars have been expended to cover Amtrak's

[68] *Ibid.*, pp. 1, 7.

[69] Louis W. Menk, *op. cit.*, p. 20. See also: Stan Kalp, "Conrail's Future," *Barron's* (June 22, 1981), p. 9; and James C. Johnson, "Lessons from Amtrak and Conrail," *ICC Practitioners Journal* (forthcoming).

[70] "For Conrail, Time; For Amtrak, Money," *Railway Age* (August 10, 1981), p. 8.

[71] *Report to the President and the Congress, Effectiveness of the Act-Amtrak,* Interstate Commerce Commission (March 14, 1980), appendix F.

"...Y'KNOW, JESSE....IT'S JUST NOT THE SAME SINCE REAGAN CUT THE AMTRAK BUDGET...."

Bill Schorr, Los Angeles Herald Examiner

Figure 5–9   Amtrak Subsidies Are Being Reduced. Reproduced by permission of the artist, William Schorr.

cumulative losses from operations ($4.6 billion estimated up until FY 1981), to pay for new terminals and equipment, and to fund Amtrak's purchase and rejuvenation of the Northeast Corridor trackage.

In 1980, a federal study found the average ticket subsidy on many routes was $60 to $70 per person. "Subsidy reaches as much as $192 per ticket on the Sunset Limited (New Orleans to Los Angeles) in 1980. It would be cheaper for the government to give someone a *round* trip airline ticket from Washington, D.C., to Cincinnati than to subsidize a one-way ticket on the Shenandoah."[72]

The Reagan Administration has been lessening federal subsidies for Amtrak. (See Figure 5–9.) In August, 1981, Amtrak management cut its route system by about 10 percent, because of reduced appropriations.

---

[72]*Program for Economic Recovery, FY 1982 Budget Proposal* (Washington, D.C.: U.S. Government Printing Office, 1981), p. 259.

Coal Slurry Pipelines

As previously noted, coal is by far the most important single commodity transported by rail. It represented about one out of every four rail carloadings in 1980. At present, the only economically feasible methods of long distance coal transportation are by rail or inland water carrier. The latter mode, however, is constrained in many situations because the inland waterway system is not located near coal fields.

The railroad industry, however, has a serious potential competitor for long-distance coal transportation—the coal slurry pipeline. The technology involves grinding coal into a powder, mixing it with water in a one-to-one ratio (by weight) of coal to water, and transporting this fluid through the pipeline. At destination the coal is dewatered and it is ready for use, typically as fuel for an electric generating plant. Coal slurry pipelines represent a *proven* technology. Two coal slurry pipelines have been built and operated in the United States, and one—the Black Mesa pipeline in Arizona—is still operating. Chapter 6 examines coal slurry pipelines in more detail.

At this point, it should be noted that the railroad industry is prepared to do everything within its legal power to thwart the large-scale development of coal slurry pipelines. The railroad industry sees coal slurry pipelines as capable of undermining their new-found financial renaissance, much of which is based on coal revenues.

The Staggers Rail Act of 1980

The *Staggers Rail Act of 1980,* named after Representative Harley O. Staggers of West Virginia, is a long and complicated law. It contains 61 sections and 71 pages of print. President Jimmy Carter, at the signing of the law on October 14, 1980, declared:

> To move the government out of the free enterprise system when regulations are onerous or costly and at the same time have additional protection for consumers, to stimulate an industry that has been ailing in some way, and to let the free enterprise system actually work with intense competition is an achievement that brings credit to all those assembled here.[73]

This section will examine the major features of the *Staggers Act* and then discuss the effects of this legislation on the railroad industry.

---

[73]"President Signs Staggers Rail Act As 'Capstone' of Decontrol Effort," *Traffic World* (October 20, 1980), p. 22.

Rate flexibility. In markets where railroads do not possess *market dominance* their maximum rates are not subject to ICC controls. In

- *Market dominance,* a term that has crept into transportation regulatory parlance, is believed to exist when one carrier or mode carries a minimum of approximately 60 percent of the traffic within a specified market.

situations where railroads do possess market dominance the ICC may regulate maximum rates only in instances where they appear to exceed 160 percent of variable costs. (This 160-percent limit moves upward to 175 percent in 1984, at which time the ICC will set the figure at somewhere between 170 and 180 percent of variable costs.)

Two other features of the *Staggers Act* allow additional rate flexibility. First, rail carriers can increase or decrease any rate in a "zone of reasonableness"—that is, as much as 6 percent per year for each of the next four years. However, the total increase or decrease over the four year period can not exceed 18 percent. Secondly, *in addition* to the above zone of reasonableness, the ICC will authorize all rail rates to increase quarterly based on the inflation rate of economy. Thus, if the inflation rate were 10 percent in 1982, a rail carrier could—without fear of challenge by either shipper or the ICC—raise its rates in 1982 a maximum of 16 percent (the 10 percent inflation rate plus the 6 percent zone of reasonableness increase).

Rate bureaus. Rail rate bureau activities have been significantly diminished by the *Staggers Act.* Rail carriers can no longer discuss a rail rate that applies to a shipment moving exclusively on one railroad from origin to destination. Rates involving two or more carriers can only be discussed by the carriers actually participating in the transportation service. In general, the scope of rate bureau activity will continue to diminish until 1984, unless the ICC determines that the lessened role for rate bureaus is not feasible.

After 1984 the rail rate bureaus lose their exemption from the antitrust laws. The practical effect of this will be the complete demise of rail rate bureaus. This is more significant than might appear on casual reading. The reason is that rate bureaus often are (or were) the "glue" that holds the industry together, at least on a regional basis. Rate bureaus were a meeting place where railroads could meet and work out problems, such as car supply. For example, within a rail rate bureau, two carriers could discuss the relation of a proposed rate from A to B *and* a proposed rate on another product, but using the same equipment, from B to A, with their intent being to increase utilization of rail cars between A and B.

Contract rates. Since late 1978, the ICC has authorized rail contract rates. However, there were some pending court challenges, and their status was somewhat clouded. The *Staggers Act* clearly legalized rail contracts, although there are some restrictions. First, to protect smaller agricultural and forestry shippers, railroads are limited to signing contracts for a maximum of 40 percent of a carrier's capacity by car type. In addition, large agricultural shippers can only contract for 40 percent of their total rail shipments.

All contracts must be summarized and filed with the ICC. Shippers and ports can protest contract terms under limited circumstances. It should be noted that the *Staggers Act* specifically declared that most contract terms—such as price—between the railroad and the carrier are *confidential.* The only requirement is that non-confidential information be filed with the ICC. Protests by shippers are generally limited to the allegation that the contract would impair the railroads' service ability to other shippers, especially in regard to car availability.

Rate changes after the Staggers Act. As would be expected whenever a complex act is enacted into law, some people are less than enamored with it. Rail management generally favors the *Staggers Act,* with the notable exception of John P. Fishwick, chairman of the Norfolk and Western Railway. He objects to the rate bureau restrictions and new rate flexibility provisions. He observed, "We probably would have been better off letting the ICC set rates."[74] Shippers, on the other hand, are almost unanimous in their dislike of their inability to protest rate increases to the ICC. William H. Dempsey, president of the Association of American Railroads, acknowledged that about two-thirds of all rail rates are *not* subject to market dominance and therefore can be increased without the ICC blocking the increase.[75] Many shippers find their inability to protest most rail rate increases as highly unfair. The National Industrial Traffic League, the nation's largest group of shippers, is planning a major legal battle with the ICC. It hopes to make it easier to prove that a specific rail rate cannot be automatically increased because the railroad possesses market dominance.[76]

Since the *Staggers Act* was enacted into law, rail rates have generally been trending *upward.* This is the opposite of what happened

[74] William Baldwin, "This Is Deregulation?" *Forbes* (October 27, 1980), p. 35.
[75] "Staggers Act Gets Little Praise," *Traffic World* (May 11, 1981), p. 45.
[76] "Shippers Fight To Save Ability To Contest Rail Rate Boosts Before ICC," *Traffic World* (July 27, 1981), p. 65.

after trucking deregulation. One well-known transportation magazine, *Handling and Shipping Management,* noted:

> All the railroads are using their new freedom to quickly adjust specific rates upward—sometimes with little concern for whether or not they keep the traffic. "If it doesn't pay, we don't want it," is easy to say now.
>
> In theory, shippers are protected in extraordinary cases by their retained right to protest increases that exceed the limit of 160 percent of out-of-pocket costs. The catch is that the burden of proof is on the shipper.[77]

As an example of how rail rates, and earnings climbed, ICC chairman Reese H. Taylor, Jr., indicated that in the first nine months following passage of the *Staggers Act,* the income of railroads climbed 38 percent while their traffic increased by only one-half of one percent.[78]

Contract Rates and Service

Contracts between railroads and shippers are growing in popularity.[79] It is generally expected that rail contracts will grow in popularity as both parties become more familiar with the concept. Most rail contracts require specific service minimums that the railroad must maintain. Two examples will be noted. The first involves a one-year contract between Conrail and Union Carbide. The shipper guaranteed minimum tonnages to selected destinations in the Northeast. Conrail is subject to a specific delivery schedule, and receives a bonus for early arrivals and penalties for late deliveries. This agreement has helped Conrail win large quantities of new business that had previously been transported by truck.[80]

A second illustration involves the Seaboard Coast Line and the

---

[77] Patrick Gallagher, "Railroads 1981 Outlook," *Handling and Shipping Management* (January, 1981), p. 36.

[78] *Rail News Update* (November 18, 1981), p. 1.

[79] Many articles have examined the concept of rail contract rates. See: C. J. Miller, "Railroad Contract Rates: A License To Innovate," *ICC Practitioners' Journal* (September–October, 1980), pp. 646–660. Two additional articles in the same journal issue are: Aden C. Adams and Carl W. Hoeberling, "Future of Contract Rates in Rail Transportation," pp. 661–664 and Judith M. Bielenberg and Terrell J. Harris, "Exploitation of Rail Contract Opportunities," pp. 665–673. See also: Robert C. Dart, "Rail-Shipper Contract Marketing Idea: Still on Launching Pad After 3 Years," *Traffic World* (March 2, 1981), pp. 12–14 and a two-part article by Lewis M. Schneider, Peter F. Rousselot, Paul L. Joffe, and George W. Mayo, Jr., "Rail Service Contracts—The New Frontier," *Traffic World* (August 3, 1981), pp. 94–98 and (August 10, 1981), pp. 98–104.

[80] "Staggers Act Gets Little Praise," *Traffic World* (May 11, 1981), p. 43.

Chesapeake and Ohio railroads and International Minerals and Chemical Corporation. This five-year contract involves transporting two million tons of phosphate rock from Bone Valley, Florida, to Detroit. The shipper must provide certain tonnages at specific times. Each round trip from Florida to Detroit and back must be completed in 192 hours. Penalties and bonuses are specified for slower or faster transportation times.[81]

Railroad Financial Condition

As mentioned earlier, the railroad industry has not been able to generate either a reasonable or adequate return on invested capital (ROI). In 1929, the ROI for all United States railroads was 5.3 percent and the industry earned $1.25 billion. In 1965, ROI was 3.69 percent and earnings were $962 million. In 1980 the ROI had increased to 4.25 percent and net income was $1.34 billion. Even the Burlington Northern, generally acknowledged as one of the best-managed railroads in the world, had an ROI in 1980 of only 6.7 percent on its railroad assets.

What had precipitated this inadequate ROI?[82] Many factors are involved and there is little agreement as to which is the most important. However, each of the following has contributed to the problem:

First, and perhaps most important, had been restrictive government regulation. Railroads, as previously noted, did not have adequate pricing freedom. Their merger applications—in some cases—took a decade or more to be approved. Isabel H. Benham, senior vice-president of a large brokerage firm, Shearson Hayden Stone, Inc., summed up this situation when she noted that investors shied away from the railroads because there was a growing concern about the power of government in the day-to-day business of railroads. It was a concern with the bureaucrat's increasing appetite for regulation. . . . The accumulation over the decades of restrictive regulatory processes had created for the railroads an image of being mired in a bog of regulatory restraint on profitability.[83] These problems have been substantially corrected by the 1980 *Staggers Act*. In addition,

[81] "Rails Enter Into Contract With IMC," *Traffic World* (January 19, 1981), p. 58.

[82] Railroads' "ROI" figures cannot be compared with those of other industries since railroads are not permitted to use conventional depreciation accounting. This keeps their investment figures unrealistically large. Starting in 1981, railroads will start to use more conventional depreciation accounting methods.

[83] Isabel H. Benham, "Why Rails Lack Investor Confidence—And What Can Be Done About It," *Railway Age* (April 25, 1977), p. 64.

new tax laws enacted in 1981 were also beneficial to railroads in terms of allowing them more credit for depreciation and allowing them to sell to others tax "advantages" from which they—the railroads—cannot benefit because of low, or non-existent, taxable income.

A second factor affecting the industry's financial performance has been that government has been more generous with railroads' competitors than with railroads when it came to providing facilities. Elsewhere in this book are discussed federal aids which benefit highway and waterway users, and airlines.

The third factor is railroad management itself. For years it was overly concerned about keeping operating costs as low as possible, which in some cases meant ignoring the quality of service that was provided to the shipper public. Shippers reacted in many cases by switching to motor carriers who stressed a high quality, dependable service, even though their rates were higher than those of the railroads. This situation has clearly been recognized by rail management.

Railroad Industry Outlook

Despite some of the historic gloom, two comprehensive studies have concluded that the railroad industry will increase its market share of intercity ton-mileage. The Department of Transportation estimates that in 1990, railroads will account for 42 percent of intercity ton-miles, compared to 37 percent in 1980.[84] The research firm of Frost & Sullivan, Inc, is even more optimistic. They predict that in 1995 railroads will transport 52 percent of intercity ton-miles.[85]

Four factors appear to best explain the projected rail renaissance. First, and most importantly, railroads are an efficient user of energy. Because of the national goal to conserve petroleum products and reduce the quantity of imported fuel, railroads with their inherent fuel efficiency may become transportation's "golden mode." Federal regulators and planners are trying to create an environment in which the railroads can significantly increase their traffic.

A related aspect to the energy efficiency of railroads is that they are the only mode, along with pipelines, that can be operated using electricity as their main source of energy. At present-day usage rates,

---

[84] *National Transportation Trends and Choices to the Year 2000*, U.S. Department of Transportation (January, 1977), p. 69.
[85] *Traffic World* (July 25, 1977), p. 17.

the United States has coal reserves that should last in excess of 300 years. Since coal can be easily converted to electricity—via electric power plants—any transport mode capable of using electricity may have a competitive advantage. The federal government projections indicate that, by 1990, high-density rail routes will have begun installing the necessary overhead equipment for electrified railroads.[86]

The United States is firmly committed to expanding coal production in order to reduce petroleum requirements. Coal production is expected to increase, and railroads are expected to transport about two-thirds of the increased coal production, mostly via unit-trains.

A third benefit for the railroad industry is the improving relationship between the federal government and the railroad industry. The 1976 *4-R Act* has been helpful and beneficial to the long-term growth of the railroads. The 1980 *Staggers Act* is further evidence of this trend toward better relations between the government and the railroads.

The final factor arguing for the long-run improved viability of the railroad industry is railroad management's understanding of the importance of providing an improved level of customer service.

Summary

The railroad industry, which once handled nearly all of the nation's intercity freight and passenger business, is in difficulty. Railroads in the Northeast have been particularly hard hit; the Penn Central and others went bankrupt, and the federal government established Conrail, a subsidized railroad, in the place of the bankrupt carriers.

Likewise, the federal government found it necessary to establish Amtrak, to handle the nation's rail passengers. Amtrak requires huge subsidies and is heavily used in only one market, the "Northeast Corridor" between Boston, New York, and Washington, D.C.

Railroads have historically provided an indifferent level of customer service. To reverse this trend, railroads are now working diligently to improve both the *consistency* and *speed* of their service. Piggyback freight service is expected to continue growing because it is both fuel and labor efficient.

Rail mergers, especially of the end-to-end variety, are becoming very prevalent in the early 1980's. Rail management is actively trying to increase the utilization of their car fleet. A primary objective in railroad labor relations is to decrease the train crew size from four

---

[86] *National Transportation: Trends and Choices to the Year 2000*, p. 207.

people to three and in limited situations to two people. Coal slurry pipelines represent a serious threat to the rail domination of long-distance coal transportation.

The *Staggers Rail Act of 1980* was designed to allow the railroad industry to prosper by removing significant quantities of federal governmental regulation. The *Staggers Act* (a) allows greatly increased rate flexibility, (b) restricts the future activities of rate bureaus, and (c) encourages the utilization of rail/shipper contracts. Although rail profitability is still not robust, the future of the railroad industry appears to be highly favorable.

Questions for Discussion and Review

1. Railroads have generally had a declining percentage of intercity ton-mileage since 1929. Why?

2. What were the railroad land grants? Did the railroads receiving them incur any obligations? Discuss.

3. Do you believe the railroad land grant program was a good or bad idea? Defend your answer.

4. What types of products are typically shipped via railroads? Why?

5. Discuss the importance of coal to the railroad industry.

6. What is deferred maintenance?

7. One section of this chapter is entitled, "Railroad Customer Service Improvements." Discuss two examples of how the railroad industry is attempting to improve customer service.

8. What do you believe will happen to the growth of piggyback service in the 1980's? Defend your answer.

9. What is a landbridge? Compare it to a minibridge.

10. Discuss the cost structure of railroads and then explain why railroads are subject to economies of scale.

11. Seven rail issues were examined in this chapter. Which one do you believe is: (a) the most important to shippers and (b) the least important to shippers? Why?

12. Discuss the two general types of railroad mergers.

13. Discuss the benefits both to the shipper and railroads of a rail merger.

14. Discuss why the Penn-Central merger resulted in bankruptcy.

15. Discuss, in general terms, the labor relations problems in the railroad industry.

16. Note specific problems dealing with railroad labor work rules.

17. What is Conrail? Discuss its current situation.

18. What is Amtrak? Has it been financially successful?

19. Coal slurry pipelines are potential competitors of the railroads in terms of coal transportation. Discuss this issue.

20. Discuss *why* the *Staggers Rail Act of 1980* was enacted into law.

21. What are two major changes in rail regulation brought about by the *Staggers Rail Act?*

22. What has happened to the level of rail rates as a result of deregulation? Was this expected? Discuss.

23. Discuss why "Contracts between railroads and shippers are growing in popularity," as was stated in this chapter.

24. Has the *Staggers Act* brightened the financial outlook for the railroad industry? Why?

Additional Chapter References

Allen, Benjamin J., "The Economic Effects of Rail Abandonment on Communities: A Case Study," *Transportation Journal* (Fall, 1975), pp. 52–61.

Altrogge, Phyllis D., "Railroad Contracts and Competitive Conditions," *Transportation Journal* (Winter, 1981), pp. 37–43.

Anderson, David L., "Measuring the Impacts of Rail Traffic Deregulation: A Case Study of TOFC/COFC Potentials in the 1980s," *Annual Proceedings of the Transportation Research Forum* (1981), pp. 213–220.

Babcock, Michael W., "National and Regional Forecast of Rail Demand to 1985," *Annual Proceedings of the Transportation Research Forum* (1981), pp. 394–402.

Barber, Richard J., "The Market Dominance Test: The 1976 Act's New Approach to Railroad Rate Regulation," *Transportation Journal* (Summer, 1976), pp. 5–14.

Beier, Frederick J., "Costs of Locating On-Rail: Perceptions of Shippers and Practices of Carriers," *Transportation Journal*, (Fall, 1977), pp. 22–32.

Berglund, Mary F., "Freight Car Utilization and Owners' Equity: Unresolved

Economic Issues," *Annual Proceedings of the Transportation Research Forum* (1978), pp. 130–135.

Boske, Leigh B., "An Analysis of the Economic Regulation of Western Coal Unit-Train Operations," *ICC Practitioners' Journal* (January–February, 1981), pp. 156–197.

Conant, Michael, "Structural Reorganization of the Northeast Railroads," *ICC Practitioners' Journal* (January–February, 1976), pp. 207–223.

Cucek, E. M., and E. J. Wasp, "Energy Efficiency of Alternative Modes of Moving Large Volumes of Coal," *Annual Proceedings of the Transportation Research Forum* (1978), pp. 93–96.

Davis, Frank W., Jr., Edwin P. Patton, and Robert E. Tuttle, Jr., "Local Participation: The Key to Preserving Adequate Railroad Services," *MSU Business Topics* (Winter, 1976), pp. 40–46.

Godfrey, Michael B., and Glenn J. Warnebold, "A Procedure for Forecasting MoPac's Freight Car Utilization and Car Hire Expense," *Annual Proceedings of the Transportation Research Forum* (1981), pp. 370–378.

Graham, Kenneth R., "Rail-Based Holding Companies: A View of Some Indicators of Strategy, Management Change, and Financial Performance," *Transportation Journal* (Summer, 1980), pp. 73–77.

Harris, R. G., "Economies of Traffic Density in the Rail Freight Industry," *The Bell Journal of Economics* (Autumn, 1977), pp. 556–564.

Hillman, Jordan Jay, "The Making of Conrail," *ICC Practitioners' Journal* (November–December, 1977), pp. 18–26.

Hirschey, Mark John, and Charles O. Kroncke, "Determining Railroad Rates of Return," *ICC Practitioners' Journal* (November–December, 1978), pp. 64–76.

Johnson, James C., "Railroad Managements' Myopia," *Journal of Business Logistics*, Vol. 3, No. 1 (1982), pp. 114–118.

Lehnert, W. G., "Forecasting Railcar Equipment Needs," *Annual Proceedings of the National Council of Physical Distribution Management* (1981), pp. 255–269.

Lieb, Robert C., *Freight Transportation: A Study of Federal Intermodal Ownership Policy* (New York: Praeger Publishers, 1972).

Martland, Carl D., "Workload Measurement and Train Crew Consist Adjustments: The Boston & Maine Experience," *Transportation Journal* (Spring, 1982), pp. 34–57.

Morgenbesser, Martin J., "The Relationship Between Railroad Work Rules and Operating Plans," *Annual Proceedings of the Transportation Research Forum* (1978), pp. 121–129.

Pike, C. R., "Fuel Realities and Canada's Railways," *The Logistics and Transportation Review*, Vol. 17, No. 2 (1981), pp. 163–168.

Sattler, Edward L., "Diversified Holding Companies and Their Impact on the Railroad Industry," *Transportation Journal* (Fall, 1980), pp. 65–74.

Spraggins, H. Barry, "Rationalization of Rail Line Abandonment Policy in the Midwest Under the Railroad Revitalization and Regulatory Reform Act of 1976," *Transportation Journal* (Fall, 1978), pp. 5–18.

Stenger, Alan J., and Wayne H. J. Cunningham, "Additional Insights Concerning Rail-Truck Freight Competition," *Transportation Journal* (Summer, 1978), pp. 14–24.

Sussman, Joseph M., Carl D. Martland, Jo Ann Kruger, Richard D. Juster, and Richard Gray, "Some Alternatives for Improving the U.S. Railroad System" *Annual Proceedings of the Transportation Research Forum* (1978), pp. 192–200.

Uggen, Michael W., "Railroad Contract Rates: A Working Analysis of Section 10713," *ICC Practitioners' Journal* (July—August, 1981), pp. 526–542.

Voorhees, Roy Dale, and Richard D. Reed, "The Rock Island Divorce Case," *Journal of Business Logistics*, Vol. 3, No. 1 (1982), pp. 102–113.

Williams, John H., "A Revised Public Policy Toward a Restructured Railroad Industry," *Annual Proceedings of the Transportation Research Forum* (1978), pp. 112–118.

Wycoff, D. Daryl, *Railroad Management* (Lexington, Mass.: Lexington Books, 1976).

Case 5–1   Bayonne Ball Company Case

Located in Bayonne, New Jersey, the Bayonne Ball Company was a sporting goods distributor. Over half of their business was export shipments, usually moving through the container facilities in the nearby port. A customer in Iraq was ordering vast quantities (10,000 each) of bowling balls, soccer balls, and basketballs, and it would take several months before the entire order could be assembled and shipped. Bayonne Ball wanted to ship in container lots, where the rate per pound was the same for any type of sports equipment they happened to ship. Checking their inventories they found they had large supplies of bowling balls and basketballs and decided they would assemble one containerload of these two items combined. That first shipment might also keep the buyer satisfied until the remainder of the order could be assembled and shipped.

Each bowling ball was shipped in a package measuring 12" × 12" × 12" and weighing 20 pounds. Each deflated basketball was in a carton 12" × 12" × 3" and weighed two pounds. The container they were going to use had interior dimensions of 2.44 meters wide, 2.44 meters high, 10.675 meters long, and could be loaded to a maximum weight limit of 18,160 kilograms.

Bayonne Ball personnel wanted to load the container to achieve maximum utilization of the container's weight and volume capacity. The bowling balls would be loaded on the bottom.

Question One: How many bowling balls and how many deflated basketballs should be placed in the container to maximize the use of its volume and weight capacity? Show your work.

Question Two: Iraq now seeks to discourage the importation of basketballs by allowing only "inflated" balls through customs. Each fully inflated basketball is in a carton measuring $12'' \times 12'' \times 12''$ and weighs two pounds. Maximize the weight and space usage of the container. Show your work.

Question Three: What is the cost to your firm of the new regulation mentioned in Question Two?

Question Four: Joe Foster, in your export department, checks the new regulation from Iraq and concludes that "inflated" does not necessarily mean *fully inflated*. He suggests packing the basketballs loose and partially inflated in the top part of the container, above the packaged bowling balls. Foster believes a large number of partially inflated basketballs can be jammed into that space. Once in Iraq, they will be removed one-by-one and "pop" back into their regular shape. Discuss this idea and its potential costs and savings.

Question Five: The vessel operator also has a smaller container available. It is 2.44 meters wide, 2.29 meters high, 5.34 meters long, and could carry 12,000 kilograms. Answer the question posed in Question One in terms of this smaller container.

Question Six: Answer the question posed in Question Two in terms of the smaller container.

Case 5–2   Nebraska State Railroad Abandonment Study Case

Anticipating federal legislation that would make it easier for railroads to abandon unprofitable branch railroad lines, the Nebraska State Transportation Planning Office wanted to determine which of two rail lines, the A and B Railroad or the X, Y, and Z Railroad, was of greater value to the state's shippers. Both were owned by a larger railroad conglomerate which had, by all accounting methods, been losing money on both lines. The state's transportation planners wanted to know which of the two lines was more valuable since, in an abandonment proceeding, they might bargain to a position where they would not oppose abandonment of one line if the other were kept in operation. It could be that if one line were abandoned, the other would pick up a portion of its traffic and, possibly, become profitable.

The area served by the two rail lines is shown in Case Figure 5–2–1. All grain produced in the area is shipped to Junction City, which is 24 miles northeast of the northeast corner of the map. Each square on the map is a 36-square-mile township, each of which pro-

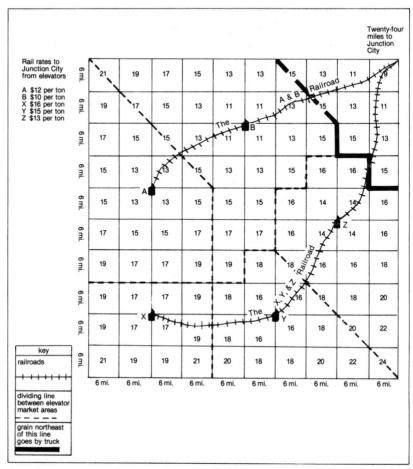

Case Figure 5-2-1   Costs of Shipping Wheat. Each square represents a 36-square-mile township. Figures within the squares are the costs in dollars of shipping wheat to Junction City by the least expensive combination of truck and rail.

duces an equal amount of wheat. Costs of trucking the wheat are shown in Case Figure 5–2–2. It costs $1.00 per ton to take the wheat from anywhere inside the township to one of the main north-south or east-west roads, while along these roads it costs $.333 per ton-mile (or $2 for a ton every six miles) to move the wheat. Wheat from the northeast sector on the map is trucked directly to Junction City, 24 miles from the top right-hand corner of the map.

It is believed that all wheat grown in the area would continue to be shipped to Junction City. However, the state's farmers would have

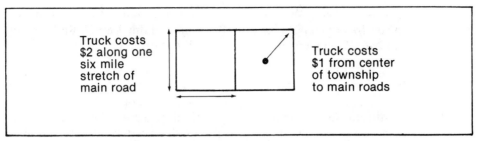

Case Figure 5-2-2   Costs of Trucking Wheat.

to pay more for having their wheat shipped if the rail lines were abandoned. In Case Figure 5–2–1 the number inside each square represents the cost of shipping the wheat from that township to Junction City. For most areas on the map it is the truck costs to the elevator plus the rail costs from the elevator to Junction City. At present, grain from the northeast corner moves directly by truck. The costs saved from not having to use a local elevator are offset by the costs of operating trucks in congested streets near the Junction City flour mills where—at harvest time—trucks sometimes must wait a day to unload. For that area on the map outside the northeast corner, costs of using the elevators are included in the rail rate.

Question One: What would be the additional costs to shippers in the entire area if the A and B Railroad is abandoned?

Question Two: What would be the additional costs to shippers in the entire area if the X, Y, and Z Railroad is abandoned?

Question Three: What would be the additional costs to shippers in the entire area if only the A-to-B segment of the A and B Railroad is abandoned?

Question Four: What would be the additional costs to shippers in the entire area if only the X-to-Y segment of the X, Y, and Z railroad is abandoned?

Question Five: What would be the additional costs to shippers in the entire area if only the X-to-Z segment of the X, Y, and Z Railroad is abandoned?

Question Six: What would be the additional costs to shippers in the entire area if both the A-to-B segment of the A and B Railroad and the X-to-Y segment of the X, Y, and Z Railroad are abandoned?

Question Seven: What would be the additional costs to shippers in the entire area if both the A-to-B segment of the A and B Railroad and the X-to-Z segment of the X, Y, and Z Railroad are abandoned?

Question Eight: The criterion used so far to assess the effect of rail-line abandonment has been an economic one, i.e., additional costs for the entire area. Assume instead a more "political" approach that would minimize the *number* of townships (the six-mile by six-mile squares) adversely affected. If the choice were only between abandoning the A and B Railroad or abandoning the X, Y, and Z Railroad, which choice would have an adverse impact on the smaller number of townships?

More than half of the 800-mile
Alaskan pipeline is built above
ground, sitting on vertical supports.
Heat fins on top of these supports help
dissipate heat from the ground,
keeping the permafrost from thawing.

Photo courtesy Alyeska Pipeline
Service Company.

6 Pipelines

If you've tried to borrow money lately, you'll have a vague idea of what John McMillian is up against these days. Vague, that is, because Mr. McMillian isn't seeking any ordinary loan. He's after more money than has ever been loaned for one project—$22 billion (yes, billion) to build the Alaska natural-gas pipeline.

RICHARD D. JAMES
The Wall Street Journal
July 2, 1981

Coal slurry proponents feel that they have a better chance for passage now than they have had in recent previous congresses because of the deregulation of the railroads last year—on paper at least they can compete better now—and because the bill spells out strict protection of state's water rights. The bill, in one form or another, has been in Congress since 1962, having been proposed by the late President John F. Kennedy.

Traffic World
August 3, 1981

Introduction

Pipelines have been appropriately referred to as the "hidden giant" of American transportation. In 1980, oil pipelines accounted for 23 percent of all intercity ton-mileage. In addition, virtually all intercity natural gas is transported by pipeline. Some pipelines, known as "slurry" pipelines, are capable of transporting solids; and they appear to be a significant growth area for the transportation industry.

History of Pipelines

Colonel Edwin Drake discovered oil in August, 1859, when he drilled a well close to Oil Creek near Titusville, Pennsylvania. At that time there were three methods of transporting the crude, or unrefined, oil. It could be transported by vessel, wagon, or rail. Since Oil Creek emptied into the Allegheny River, water transportation was initially used to ship petroleum to Pittsburgh. However, problems developed. During certain times of the year, Oil Creek dried up, making water transportation impossible. Ice blockages were a constant problem during the winter. Nevertheless, by 1864, over 1,000 boats were transporting oil from Titusville to Pittsburgh.[1]

---

[1] Arthur M. Johnson, *The Development of American Petroleum Pipelines* (Ithaca, N.Y.: Cornell University Press, 1956), p. 3.

Oil could be carried by wagons, an alternative mode that was not subject to the seasonal climatic problems that plagued the water carriers. Wagons were used to deliver oil to relatively nearby destinations and to carry oil from the producing well to collection points where it was tendered to railroads. By 1863, over 6,000 two-horse (or mule) teams were being used to transport oil, although roads were often a problem—because of mud. Teamsters charged extra for each mud hole which caused the oil wagon to get stuck and the transportation charge was doubled if the wheels sunk to the axle.

Obviously, both water and wagon transportation had limitations, and therefore a better source of delivery service was needed to reach the railroad collection points. In 1863 James L. Hutchings built a 2½-mile long pipeline using a two-inch diameter cast-iron pipe and steam-driven rotary pump. Unfortunately, both the pump and pipe were inadequate for the task.

The first successful pipeline was built by Samuel Van Syckel. In 1865, Van Syckel borrowed $30,000 to construct a five-mile pipeline from Pithole to the Oil Creek Railroad. The 32,000 feet of pipe came in 15-foot sections which had to be screwed together. It was laid on the ground, although in some areas it was laid below the level of plow shares. There were three steam pumps which were able to produce an oil flow of 80 barrels (42 gallons per barrel) per hour. This pipeline was an immediate financial success, and Van Syckel soon was building others.

Teamsters, however, were less than enamored with the new transportation competitor because the initial Van Syckel pipeline transported as much oil per day as 300 teamsters could. Sabotage to the pipeline was common. Nevertheless, the pipeline had proven its economic superiority over the wagon. Economic historian Arthur M. Johnson noted, "Here at last was the answer to the mud sloughs and exorbitant charges which had hampered transportation of oil from the wells, and investment in pipelines offered the profits that typically accompany technological innovation."[2]

The First Major Pipeline

The success of the Van Syckel pipeline lead to many similar projects. By 1874 there were several hundred miles of oil pipeline. Most of these pipelines were relatively short—less than 10 miles—and therefore, railroads did not object because they were used primarily to bring oil to the railroad collection points. In 1879 the first trunk

[2] *Ibid.,* p. 8.

- *Trunk line,* a term used in transportation when referring to pipelines, railroads, or airlines, means a major and direct route between two points. *Feeder lines* or *branch lines* connect with the trunk line at various locations. They are of smaller capacity and are used to feed traffic into or out of the trunk route.

pipeline was built. Railroads actively sought to deter its construction because they wanted to maintain a monopoly on long-distance oil transportation. This first trunk line, from Bear Creek, Pennsylvania, to Pittsburgh, was 108 miles long, six inches in diameter, and it transported 10,000 barrels of oil per day. This pipeline dramatically proved the feasibility of long-distance pipelines. By the mid 1880's, almost all large refineries were connected to oil fields by trunk pipelines. Fred F. Steingraber, president of the Colonial Pipeline Company, said, "Notwithstanding intense opposition, economics had sided with the pipeline, and much of the crude oil transportation business was taken away from the railroads. A more economical and efficient method had proven successful, and the transportation of petroleum in the United States entered a new era twenty years after the discovery of the Drake well."[3]

Control by Standard Oil

In 1862 John D. Rockefeller entered the oil refining business in Cleveland, Ohio, and in 1870 he formed the Standard Oil Company. Standard Oil's corporate objective appeared to be the elimination of all competitors. This objective was achieved—to a great extent—by controlling the transportation of crude oil. If producers could not transport their crude oil at reasonable rates to refineries, they would be forced out of business. In addition, competing refineries would also cease operations for lack of crude oil to process. This strategy was the keystone of Standard Oil's plan to monopolize the oil industry.

To successfully dominate crude oil transportation, Standard Oil had to control both railroad and pipeline service. Railroads were forced (some readily participated) to grant Standard Oil substantial rebates on the crude it shipped. In addition, Standard Oil even received rebates on oil shipped by other competing, oil companies! (That is, the railroads paid Standard Oil a portion of the freight charges the railroads collected from Standard's competitors!)

[3] Fred F. Steingraber, "Pipeline Transportation of Petroleum and Its Products," in Stanley J. Hille and Richard F. Poist, Jr., editors, *Transportation: Principles and Perspectives* (Danville, Ill.: Interstate Printers and Publishers, 1974), p. 145.

Standard Oil and its controlled pipelines began to purchase all independent pipeline firms. By the 1890's, Standard possessed a virtual monopoly on pipeline transportation. The ICC declared, "The possession of these pipelines enables the Standard to absolutely control the price of crude petroleum and to determine, therefore, the price which its competitors in a given locality should pay. . . . More than anything else the pipeline has contributed to the monopoly of the Standard Oil Company, and the supremacy of that company must continue until its rivals enjoy the same facilities of transportation of this means."[4]

These competitive restraints slowly became public knowledge, but they were not widely known by the general public until the turn of the century when a small group of crusading journalists made Standard Oil's abusive practices widely known. In 1904 Ida M. Tarbell published *The History of the Standard Oil Company*, and this bold denunciation generated widespread public outcry regarding Standard Oil and its practices. Tarbell charged in her 1904 book, "So long as the Standard Oil Company can control transportation as it does today, it will remain master of the oil industry, and the people of the United States will pay for their indifference and folly in regard to transportation a good sound tax on oil, and they will yearly see an increasing concentration of natural resources and transportation systems in the Standard Oil crowd."[5]

The outcome of this public outrage was the *Hepburn Act* of 1906. Among other provisions in this act, all pipelines were declared to be common carriers and subject to the Interstate Commerce Act and the ICC. Thereafter, pipelines controlled by the Standard Oil had to accept shipments from other producers and charge them just and reasonable rates.

Contemporary Governmental Relations

The pipeline industry is the only mode of transportation that has never received any direct subsidies from the federal government, although two minor forms of assistance should be noted. During World War II, the federal government built a number of petroleum pipelines because intercoastal oil tanker shipments were being attacked by German submarines. In addition, pipeline transportation

---

[4] As quoted in Arthur M. Johnson, *op. cit.*, p. 235.
[5] As quoted in *The Annals of America*, Vol 12 (Chicago: Encyclopedia Britannica, 1968), p. 537.

of oil freed maritime and railroad equipment for carriage of other war-related material. The best known of the wartime pipelines were the "Big Inch" from Texas to Pennsylvania, 1,340 miles long; and the "Little Inch," from Texas to New York, 1,475 miles long. Other World War II pipelines were the 154-mile Southwest Emergency Pipeline, the 200-mile Florida Emergency Pipeline, the 179-mile Plantation Extension Pipeline, and the 82-mile Ohio Emergency Pipeline. All of these pipelines were sold—by competitive bid—to private operators at the war's end. Texas Eastern Transmission Company purchased both the "Inch" pipelines and converted them to carry natural gas.

A second type of assistance—offered at both the federal and state level—is the granting to oil and natural gas pipelines the *right of eminent domain*. This indicates that once construction has been approved by either the federal or state governments, pipeline companies can use the right-of-way selected even if the owners of the land object. The theory of eminent domain is that the public good—in this case a new pipeline—outweighs an individual property owner's right to hamper construction. If the landowner refuses to voluntarily let the pipeline cross his property, then a court will order the landowner to make the needed property available to the pipeline company and the same court will establish the amount of compensation to be paid.

Federal Regulation

From 1906 to 1977 the ICC regulated oil pipelines. Then, the new Department of Energy (DOE) created the Federal Energy Regulatory Commission (FERC), which now regulates the oil pipeline industry. The ICC retained regulatory jurisdiction over slurry pipelines. This form of pipeline transportation regulation was not transferred because Congress believed that railroad unit-trains and slurry pipelines would compete for the same traffic—namely coal.

While the ICC regulates slurry pipelines as common carriers, it regulates them less restrictively than it regulates the railroad and motor carrier industries. For example, pipelines do *not* need a *certificate* from the ICC to commence operation. Thus, there is no entry control. In addition, the ICC does not control the securities issued by pipeline companies; nor does it have to approve their mergers.

The Federal Energy Regulatory Commission commenced regulation of petroleum and natural gas pipelines on September 13, 1977. The FERC was created as part of the new DOE, which in its first year had 20,000 employees and a first-year budget of $10.4 billion. The five-member FERC comes under DOE administratively, but it is independent of the department's policy makers. It should be noted that the FERC is *not* an independent regulatory commission—such as the ICC, CAB, and FMC—which reports directly to Congress. The FERC can best be described as a semi-autonomous agency of the DOE.

Petroleum pipelines are still subject to the Interstate Commerce Act as common carriers, but they are regulated by the FERC. Petroleum pipeline regulation was transferred to the FERC because Congress believed that since petroleum products and natural gas often were competitive sources of energy, they should be regulated by the same federal agency.

Since many common carrier pipelines are controlled by major oil companies, the ICC always claimed that it was keeping oil pipeline rates low, limiting the pipeline companies to a rate of return on invested capital of approximately 7 percent. This low rate of return was felt necessary since the large oil companies would otherwise set very high transportation rates for using common carrier pipelines which they wouldn't mind paying on the oil they shipped themselves since they would merely be transferring the money from one pocket to another. Other pipeline users would be less lucky. They would have to pay exhorbitant rates for using the pipeline, and—in their situation—the money would flow from their pockets to those of the major oil interests.

Because of the close relationship between the major oil companies and the pipelines, it has always been difficult to judge the effectiveness of ICC (now FERC) controls. In 1979, the U.S. General Accounting Office (an agency of Congress) charged that the levels of profits allowed under pipeline regulations "were not enforced" and that 41 of the country's 110 regulated oil pipelines in 1976 "had rates of return higher than what was allowed" under ICC regulation. The report continued that the pipeline's current regulator, the Federal Energy Regulatory Commission, "has not addressed many questionable pipeline practices and presently has no plans to do so."[6]

Natural Gas Pipeline Regulation

Natural gas pipelines have been regulated in interstate commerce since 1938 by the FPC (Federal Power Commission). The ICC was not given regulation of these pipelines because Congress thought that natural gas and electricity were competitive sources of energy, and, therefore, both should be regulated by the same agency. In 1977

---

[6] *San Francisco Chronicle* (May 21, 1979).

the FERC assumed the duties of the FPC, which was disbanded, although all former FPC employees became employed by the FERC.

FPC, originally, and now FERC regulations for natural gas pipelines are more comprehensive than for oil pipelines. A certificate is required to establish a new pipeline, and FERC authorization is required to expand or contract the service area. Pipelines are also subject to federal safety regulations.

Operating Characteristics

The oil pipeline industry is an important part of our transportation system, yet the average person is hardly aware of its existence. This is because it is primarily a "hidden" industry, hidden under the surface of the ground. Pipelines are very capital intensive. Table 6–1 indicates that at *original* cost, $21 billion has been invested in the pipeline industry. The Department of Transportation estimates that it would cost about $70 billion today to replace the U.S. pipeline system.

Pipes, Pumps, and Maintenance

There are over 440,000 miles of intercity pipelines. In the 1930's, 8-inch pipe was commonly used. Today, pipe size is often in the 30- to 40-inch-diameter range. The size of pipe continues to increase in diameter, for reasons that will be discussed later in this chapter. The Alyeska or TAPS (Trans-Alaska Pipeline System) is the largest diameter pipeline in the United States—48 inches. The pipe itself is constructed of special steel alloys designed to last 50 or more years. Specific pipe standards for strength and durability are established by the American Petroleum Institute and the American Standards Association.

TABLE 6–1   Pipeline Investment (in Billions of Dollars)

Pipeline	Cost
Natural Gas	$13.5
Petroleum	7.0
Other	0.5
Total	$21.0

SOURCE: *National Transportation Trends and Choices,* DOT (January, 1977), p. 291. These figures are "historic costs," i.e. based on the value of the dollar at the time the investment was made.

Compressors force natural gas through pipelines, and pumps force liquids through pipelines. Pumps for large-diameter oil pipelines are often in the 3,000- to 6,000-horsepower range, and they increase the pressure of the fluid in the line to a range between 500 to 1,500 pounds per square inch. Pump stations are positioned along the route of an intercity pipeline every 30 to 100 miles, depending upon the terrain.

Maintenance of the pipe is a key factor in insuring that it will be used safely and won't harm the environment. Before being placed in the ground, the pipe is coated with a number of layers of protective resins and paints.

Sophisticated techniques are used to counteract the forces that cause pipe corrosion once the pipe is in the ground. Metal in the ground "rusts" because of a natural flow of mild electric current from the soil to the exterior of the pipe. This natural flow of electric current can be neutralized by creating a similar flow of direct electric current in the opposite direction, i.e., from the pipeline to the surrounding soil. Hence, pipeline rust is inhibited.

Corrosion within the pipe is limited by using chemical agents. From time to time, the pipeline's interior is scoured with what looks like a giant kitchen scouring pad, the size of the pipeline's diameter, which is passed through the line from pumping station to pumping station.

The flow of products within the pipeline is controlled and monitored by computers attached to gauges which measure the flow of product and the pressure within the system. Leaks or breakages between gauges can be easily detected, although a visual search is sometimes necessary to find their exact location.

Service Standards

Pipelines provide an extremely high level of service dependability—which is defined as a transportation mode's ability to deliver the product when promised. Pipelines have no equal regarding dependability. This is because weather has virtually no effect on them and because they require such a small labor force that if a strike takes place, supervisory management can continue to operate the pipeline system.

The high degree of dependability is achieved by careful monitoring of shipments by the dispatcher. The dispatcher is assisted by computers and communications with the entire system and is in charge of scheduling the commodities for the pipeline. Petroleum pipelines require the most sophisticated scheduling because a number of different grades of petroleum products can all be in the pipe-line at the same time. There are 15 separate grades of crude oil; in pipelines transporting refined products, there are: jet fuel (kerosene), regular gasoline, leaded regular gasoline, premium gasoline, premium unleaded gasoline, diesel fuel, aviation high octane gasoline, heating oil, and other refined products. When two or more different grades of product are in the pipeline at the same time, it is referred to as a "batch" movement. Generally, two different types of petroleum products can be run in sequence with relatively little mixing because each product has a different specific gravity and, therefore, the two barely mix.[7] If products of similar specific gravities are to be shipped together, a batching "pig" or rubber ball is placed in the pipeline to physically separate them.

Types of Pipelines

This section will examine each of the four major types of pipelines, classified by the commodities they transport. They are: oil (both crude and refined products), natural gas, slurry, and "other." Table 6–2 presents the total mileage of intercity pipelines (natural gas pipelines account for 60 percent of the total).

Oil Pipelines

There are three types of oil pipelines: gathering oil pipelines, crude oil pipelines, and refined products pipelines. Figure 6–1 shows how the three types stretch from producing fields to markets.

[7] The mixing is so slight that the quality of either product is unaffected. In those rare situations where mixing is a problem, the "mixture" is loaded aboard rail tank cars and returned to the refinery for re-refining.

TABLE 6–2   Miles of Intercity Pipeline

Pipeline	Miles
Natural gas	265,409
Crude Oil	103,127
Petroleum Products	67,764
Slurry	273
Chemicals	4,050
Total	440,623

SOURCE: *National Transportation Trends and Choices*, Department of Transportation (January, 1977), p. 291.

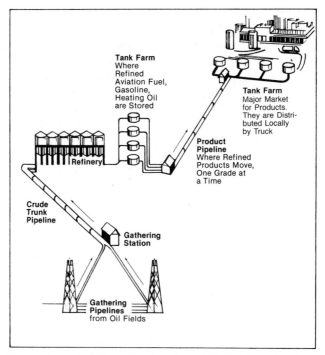

Figure 6–1   Pipelines Stretch from Oil Fields to Markets.

- *Gathering oil pipelines* are small in diameter (2 to 8 inches) and connect individual producing wells to gathering stations. They are laid on the surface of the ground so that they can be relocated when the well they are serving runs dry. *Crude trunk pipelines* are larger, often 16 to 42 inches in diameter, and lead from gathering stations to refineries. *Refined products lines* lead from refineries to major markets throughout the U.S. Their diameters range from 20 inches to 35 inches.

The refinery produces several grades of petroleum products, and they are stored in individual tanks, in tank farms, near the refinery. Competing oil firms are likely to have refineries in the same area and also store refined products in their own nearby tank farms. Major petroleum companies also own distribution tank farms near major markets from which the finished products are distributed locally, usually by truck. Competing oil firms may also have distribution tank farms on the outskirts of the same city.

The competing oil companies may join together to own the product pipeline which connects the area near their refineries and major markets. Each month the pipeline's dispatcher will learn of every shipper's needs and will schedule all shipments of kerosene first, then all shipments of high-grade gasoline, then all shipments of medium-grade gasoline, and so on, all the way through heating oil. (If the pipeline is a common carrier, it will also have to accommodate the needs of independent shippers, scheduling their products along with the shipments being made by the pipeline's owning companies.) At the end of the cycle, after the lowest grade of product has been shipped, the pipeline will be scoured, and the batches of kerosene will start moving again.

Figure 6–2 shows the general location of the nation's major crude oil trunk pipeline system. Major product pipelines are shown on Figure 6–3.

Ownership and common carrier status of oil pipelines. In 1980 there were about 100 pipeline common carriers and 10 "joint interest" pipelines which serve as private carriers. The latter belong to individual oil companies, and they neither solicit nor accept oil

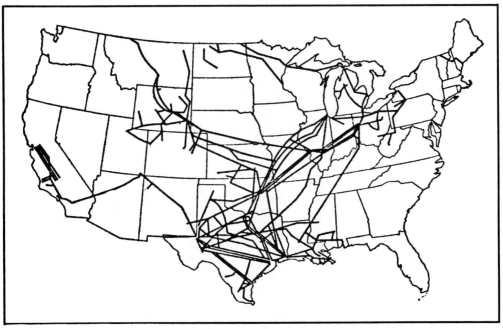

Figure 6–2   Major Crude Oil Trunk Pipelines. Courtesy: Amoco Oil Company.

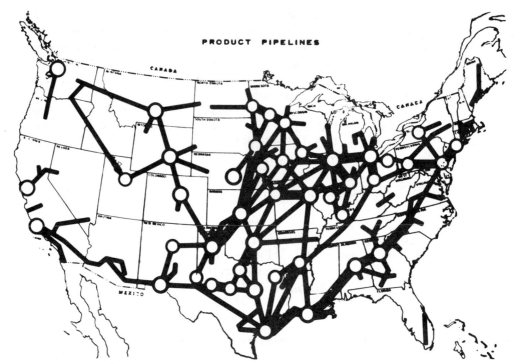

Figure 6–3 Major Product Pipelines. Courtesy: Amoco Oil Company.

- A *jointly-owned* or *joint-interest pipeline* is owned by several competing oil firms. They find it advantageous to join together to build one large pipeline rather than several small pipelines. Pipelines enjoy increasing economies of scale as the pipeline diameter increases.

from shippers outside their company. These pipelines, since they are private carriers, do not appear in many reports of total nationwide transportation activity. The Transportation Association of America estimated that in 1980 regulated oil pipeline common carriers accounted for 40 percent of all oil pipeline intercity ton-mileage.

In terms of total revenues for oil pipeline common carriers, 46 percent are owned by individual vertically-integrated oil companies,

- A *vertically-integrated* firm is one that controls all activities, stretching from the extraction of raw materials, through the production and refining processes, to and including retail distribution.

27 percent are jointly owned by oil firms, 9 percent are owned by railroads, 7 percent by independent pipeline companies, and the other 11 percent are owned by other industrial firms.[8]

The Trans-Alaska Pipeline System (TAPS)

In the mid-1960's, geologists had determined that northern Alaska had 9.6 billion barrels of proven oil reserves. There was a real need for this oil in the "lower 48" states because oil production there was decreasing as the older oil fields became depleted. The problem was how to transport the "black gold" safely and economically to the lower 48 states. Many potential solutions were analyzed, including the following: Arctic Ocean tankers (one ship, the *Manhattan*, actually made the trip north of Hudson Bay once); all-truck routes through Canada; all-rail routes through Canada; jet aircraft tankers; and submarine tankers. The two plans that appeared most economical and ecologically safe were (1) an all-pipeline route from Alaska to the United States via Canada and (2) a pipeline from the oil fields in northern Alaska near Prudhoe Bay to the port at Valdez, Alaska, 800 miles to the south. Valdez is a year-round port, where large ocean tankers would load the oil to be transported to the "lower 48" states.

The all-pipeline route idea was eliminated because since much of the pipeline would be in Canada, expenditures for construction and operation would flow to a foreign country. Therefore, it was decided to build a pipeline to Valdez. Planning for the TAPS pipeline started in 1968, but construction could not begin because of numerous objections raised by environmental protection groups. Construction finally commenced in April, 1974.

The original owners of TAPS were Atlantic Richfield Company, Humble Oil and Refining Company (now Exxon, USA), and BP (British Petroleum) Oil Corporation. Subsequently, other firms joined in this massive project. Today the owners are Amerada Hess Corporation, ARCO Pipe Line Company, SOHIO Pipe Line Company, Exxon Pipeline Company, Mobil Alaska Pipeline Company, Phillips Petroleum Company, Union Alaska Pipeline Company, and BP Pipelines, Inc. The eight companies formed the Alyeska Pipeline Service Company to design, construct, operate, and maintain the TAPS or Alyeska pipeline.

Figure 6–4 illustrates the route of the 798-mile TAPS pipeline. It starts at the Arctic plains near Prudhoe Bay and climbs 4,800 feet

[8] *1974 National Transportation Report*, U.S. Department of Transportation (July, 1975), p. 340.

Figure 6–4 Trans-Alaska Pipeline System. Courtesy: Alyeska Pipeline Service Company.

over Dietrich Pass in the Brooks Range. It then crosses the Yukon River and then rises another 3,300 feet over Thompson Pass in the Chugach Mountains before descending to the port of Valdez, on the Gulf of Alaska.

Expenditures on TAPS. The Alyeska pipeline experienced large cost overruns based on its original 1968 estimate of total expenditures. The initial cost of TAPS was expected to be nearly $1 billion. In 1974 *The Oil and Gas Journal* estimated production costs to be $4.5 billion.[9] In the 1977 *ICC Annual Report*, the actual cost of TAPS was officially reported to be $9.2 billion.[10] Two factors—among many—best explain these cost miscalculations. First, the original

[9]Howard M. Wilson, "Alyeska Gears Up For Awesome Job On Trans-Alaska Line," *The Oil and Gas Journal* (March 18, 1974), p. 52.
[10]*91st ICC Annual Report* (1977), p. 67.

estimates did not start to take into consideration the costs of the environmental safeguards that the U.S. Congress and the State of Alaska mandated for TAPS in order to receive its construction permits. Second, the high rate of inflation had not been originally anticipated.

TAPS pipe and equipment. In the early 1970's Alyeska purchased from Japanese steel firms the 48-inch pipe required for the 800-mile pipeline. United States steel mills—at that time—did not have the production capabilities of manufacturing 48-inch steel pipe. The pipe was supplied in two thicknesses (.452 and .562 inches) and in three grades, depending on pressure and stress requirements of each location. All grades of pipe can safely accept inside pressure of 1,450 pounds per square inch. However, the maximum actual operating pressure of the pipeline, when it is operating at maximum daily throughput of two million barrels per day, is 1,180 pounds per square inch.

To transport the crude oil at about 7½ miles per hour at the two million barrels per day flow rate required 12 pump stations, each having four 13,500-horsepower gas turbine powered pumps. Of the four pumps at each location, three pumps are always operating, and one is on "standby" to replace a pump that malfunctions or requires routine maintenance.

Environmental safeguards. The TAPS pipeline was engineered to be the most environmentally safe pipeline ever constructed. Much of the land along the pipeline's route is permanently frozen (and called permafrost). A feared environmental hazard was that heat from oil in the pipeline (it's necessary to heat the oil to 135 degrees Fahrenheit so it can be pumped) would melt the permafrost. The melted permafrost would weaken, causing the support under the pipeline to give way.

To overcome this problem, two solutions were used, both illustrated in Figure 6–5. First, about half of the 800-mile pipeline is not buried, but is *elevated* above the level of the ground. Second, in a few situations it became ecologically desirable to bury the pipeline, even though melting permafrost was also a danger. (This generally occurred in areas where an elevated pipeline would interrupt an important migration route used by wildlife.) The bottom drawing in Figure 6–5 shows refrigerant lines used to keep the permafrost from melting. The anodes indicated on the drawing are to offset the electric current flow between the soil and the pipe, which was discussed earlier in this chapter.

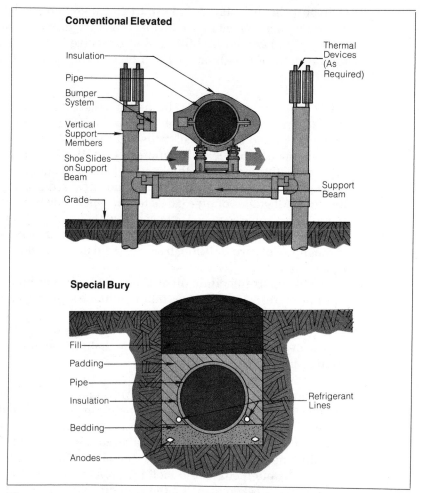

Figure 6–5   Environmental Protection Measures on the Alaskan Pipeline. Cross-sectional views of elevated and buried pipe are shown. Courtesy: Alyeska Pipeline Service Company.

The Alaska Pipeline was one of the major engineering accomplishments of the 1970's. It is indicative of the compromises that had to be made with interests who are concerned with protecting our environment.

Natural Gas Pipelines

Of all types of intercity pipelines, those transporting natural gas account for the largest total investment and the greatest number of intercity pipeline miles. Natural gas is most efficiently transported by pipeline. Although it is possible to liquify natural gas, it is an expensive procedure.

Figure 6–6 is a map of the 265,000-mile intercity natural gas pipeline system. It is more extensive than both crude and petroleum pipeline mileage combined. But what you see on this map is a small percentage of the total natural gas pipeline system. The total natural gas distribution system is composed of 1.4 million miles of pipeline, including 660,000 miles of urban distribution pipe and 440,000 miles of pipeline to individual houses and business users.

Ownership of natural gas pipelines.   The natural gas industry can be thought of as composed of three segments—production, transporta-

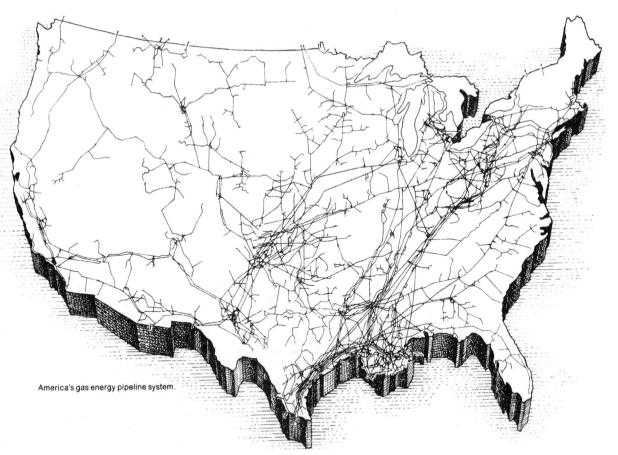

America's gas energy pipeline system.

Figure 6–6   Intercity Natural Gas Pipeline System. Courtesy: American Gas Association.

tion, and customer distribution. There are several thousand producers of natural gas and about 1,600 customer distribution companies. Connecting these two are about 100 interstate natural gas pipeline companies that transport approximately 65 percent of total natural gas production. The remaining 35 percent is transported by intrastate pipelines.[11]

Some interstate pipeline companies purchase gas in the field, or from other pipelines, and sell it to their customers. Almost all of the largest interstate natural gas pipeline companies are involved in their own natural gas exploration and development programs. In addition, they are often involved in customer distribution. An example is the American Natural Resources Company headquartered in Detroit, with 1982 revenues of $3.41 billion. This firm owns the Michigan Consolidated Gas Company, which distributes natural gas to over one million local customers in 430 Michigan cities. It also owns the Michigan-Wisconsin Pipeline Company, which connects their Michigan service area to the gas production region of the southwestern United States. It also owns 50 percent of the Great Lakes Gas Transmission Pipeline Company.

The natural gas pipeline companies and their subsidiaries produce about 10 percent of the gas they transport; the other 90 percent is obtained from independent producers. Of the purchase price of natural gas to the ultimate customers, about 60 percent goes to the customer distribution company, 30 percent goes for intercity transportation via trunk pipeline, and 10 percent goes to the producer of the natural gas.

The Alaska Natural Gas Pipeline

The Alyeska, or TAPS, pipeline is now completed. It is expected to be followed by an even more expensive pipeline to carry natural gas from Alaska to the 48 states—a natural gas pipeline six times longer than the 800-mile crude oil Alyeska pipeline. Figure 6–7 shows the proposed route of this 4,800-mile pipeline from Alaska's Prudhoe Bay, across the Yukon and western Canada, to where it splits with an eastern leg to Chicago and a western leg to San Francisco. The Alyeska oil pipeline cost about $9 billion, and the Alaska natural gas pipeline is projected to cost a minimum of $35 billion, making it the most expensive privately-funded construction project ever attempted. Some estimates are that the project will cost $50 billion before its completion in 1989. Construction has started on 30

---

[11] *1974 National Transportation Report*, p. 342.

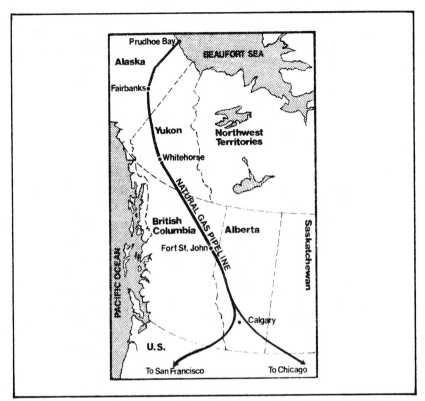

Figure 6–7 Proposed Alaskan Natural Gas Pipeline. Reproduced by permission of *The Wall Street Journal* (June 20, 1978), p. 40, © Dow Jones & Co., Inc.; all rights reserved.

percent of the pipeline in Canada and the United States. Funding for the Alaska portion of the pipeline—by far the most expensive segment at an expected cost of $27 billion—is still not finalized.[12] However, in 1981 funding took a giant step forward when three oil companies, Exxon, Sohio, and Atlantic Richfield, agreed to contribute $9 billion for a 30 percent interest in the Alaska portion of the natural gas line.[13]

The pipeline, when completed, will transport 2.5 billion cubic feet of natural gas *daily* to the United States. This is about 5 percent

[12] Richard D. James, "Alaskan Gas-Pipeline Promoters Ask: Buddy, Could You Spare $22 Billion?" *The Wall Street Journal* (July 2, 1981), p. 6. An article in *Time* (December 21, 1981) said the entire project cost "could exceed $43 billion. . . ."

[13] Richard D. James, "Three Oil Firms Get 30 Percent Stake in Alaska Gas Line," *The Wall Street Journal* (May 26, 1981), p. 2.

of the U.S. daily demand. The Reagan Administration favors construction of the line, but it is against the U.S. government's guaranteeing the construction loans. John McMillian, leader of the consortium of eleven gas transmission companies involved in the total project, acknowledged that it is not politically feasible to expect loan guarantees from the federal government. He quipped, "They'd lock me up if I asked our government to guarantee a debt of Exxon's when President Reagan is cutting food stamps."[14]

It is expected that this natural gas pipeline will experience fewer construction and environmental problems compared to the often delayed Alyeska crude oil pipeline. One reason is that many construction problems experienced during building the crude oil pipeline have now been solved. In addition, a natural gas pipeline, by its very nature, is less complex than a petroleum pipeline. The natural gas pipeline will be completely buried. Also, compressor stations to move gas through the pipeline are less complex and less costly compared to pumping facilities needed to move crude oil. The large oil collection "tank farm" at the terminus of TAPS at Valdez is not necessary for this natural gas pipeline. Finally—and very importantly—a buried natural gas pipeline presents fewer environmental problems.

Coal Slurry Pipelines

Coal slurry pipelines have been proven to be an efficient and economic way to transport coal over long distances. The coal slurry involves grinding coal into a powder, mixing it with water on a one-to-one ratio (by weight) and transporting the powdered coal-water mixture—the slurry—through a pipeline. At destination, the coal is separated from the water and is ready for use—typically as fuel for an electric generating plant.[15]

The slurry is designed to stay completely homogeneous at a normal operating flow speed of about three miles per hour. This flow rate is optimal—if the slurry flows faster or slower, the operating efficiency of the pipeline drops. At higher speeds, the solids held in suspension by water start to act like sandpaper, causing an abrasion that "eats away" at the pipe's insides. If the speed is too slow, the solids drop out of suspension, clogging the pipeline.

[14] "Pipe Dream: Agreement on a Gas Line," *Fortune* (June 29, 1981), p. 10.
[15] See: James C. Johnson and Kenneth C. Schneider, "Coal Slurry Pipelines: An Economic and Political Dilemma," *ICC Practitioners' Journal* (November–December, 1980), pp. 24–37; and Donald N. Beck, "Coal Slurry Pipelines—An Overview," *Annual Proceedings of the American Society of Traffic and Transportation* (1980), pp. 155–175.

Slurry pipelines can be thought of as having three major components. First, the slurry preparation plant, which involves grinding or crushing the solids into proper particle size. The particles are then mixed with the proper amount of water which has been already treated chemically to prevent pipe corrosion. The second component is the pipeline, with its required pumps and storage tanks. The third component is the dewatering facility, which typically involves a number of the following: storage tanks, filters, screens, centrifuges, thermal dryers, and water treatment facilities.

Coal slurry lines are massive users of water as a transportation medium—approximately 250 gallons of water per ton of coal transported—and are only economical if large quantities of coal are transported. The water used in slurry pipelines is usually measured in terms of an "acre-foot"—a volume equal to an acre (43,560 square feet) of water one foot deep, approximately 325,000 gallons. The water required for coal slurry pipelines is of great concern to environmentalists, especially in the arid western areas which are at the center of the largest U.S. coal reserves. It is possible to use underground water sources, but this could lead to detrimental environmental problems if it results in a drop in the level of the area's water table. For a proposed coal slurry pipeline from Wyoming to Arkan-

- *Water table* is the level of water below the surface of the ground which can be reached by individual landowners' pumps. If a coal slurry operation takes too much water, the level of the water table will drop which will mean that other wells in the area will become dry.

sas, the pipeline company—Energy Transportation Systems, Inc.—has signed an agreement with the State of Wyoming to use no more than 15,000 acre-feet of water per year. This water is pumped from deep wells at a geological formation level known as the Madison Formation. Wyoming has reserved the right to limit or curtail water pumping if it causes a significant drop in the area's water table.[16] In addition, Energy Transportation Systems, Inc., has arranged with the State of South Dakota to purchase water from their Oahe Reservoir to be used in the proposed slurry line. The water will be sent in a new 276-mile pipeline from near Pierre to Gillette, Wyoming.[17]

---

[16]*National Transportation Trends and Choices*, U.S. Department of Transportation (January, 1977), p. 128.

[17]"A Pipeline that Is Inciting a Water War," *Business Week* (October 26, 1981), p. 59.

Economic and cost aspects.   Studies conducted by the U.S. Department of Transportation have determined that, for a coal slurry line to be competitive with a coal unit-train, it should be at least 1,000 miles long with an annual throughput of 10 million tons. DOT studies estimate that to transport a ton-mile of coal via slurry pipeline requires about 650 to 750 BTUs; DOT also estimates that to transport

- *BTU* stands for British Thermal Unit, a measure of a specific amount of energy.

that same ton-mile via unit-train requires about 670 BTUs. Hence, DOT estimates suggest that it's a toss-up between slurry pipelines and coal unit-trains.[18] On the other hand, the Wyoming Department of Planning and Economic Development estimates that it will require 750 BTUs to transport a ton-mile of coal via slurry pipeline and only 350 BTUs via unit-train—definitely not a toss-up, and definitely an energy saving with the unit-train. Backing up this estimate is a study by the Burlington Northern Railroad which indicated that only 250 BTUs per ton-mile were consumed on its own coal unit-trains.[19]

It is similarly difficult to find agreement on the estimates of costs of transporting coal via these two alternative modes. There have been a number of studies; we'll take a look at two of them here. One cost study was done for the Bureau of Mines and the Federal Energy Administration by the Center For Advanced Computation of the University of Illinois. The researchers compared two coal slurry pipelines (one having no return of slurry water and the other which recycles the slurry water) and two alternatives for coal unit-trains (one operating at 80 percent of full capacity and another operating at full capacity). If the slurry water does not have to be returned, it is less costly to move coal by slurry pipelines than by unit-trains. (However, not returning and reusing the water may be ecologically undesirable.) If the slurry water must be returned, then unit-trains are the cheaper method for moving coal.[20]

The second study was conducted by the U.S. Congressional Office of Technology Assessment; the results were released in early 1978. This report concluded that railroads require less energy to transport a ton-mile of coal than a slurry pipeline. However, the report concluded that slurry pipelines appear to have an advantage

---

[18] *National Transportation Trends and Choices*, p. 128.
[19] Louis W. Menk, *A Railroad Man Looks at America* (St. Paul: Burlington Northern Railroad, 1976), p. 66.
[20] Tom Ichniowski, "Coal: Cheaper by Rail—If . . . ," *Railway Age* (November 28, 1977), pp. 34ff.

with respect to operating costs. The pipeline's cost advantage is based on the assumption of continued high rates of inflation. A slurry pipeline will incur high initial costs of construction, but once the pipeline is in the ground, its costs are fixed for the life of the project. Since railroads have a higher variable cost structure, the effects of inflation will impact on them much more than on the slurry pipelines.[21]

Existing and planned coal slurry pipelines.   Figure 6–8 illustrates the existing and proposed coal slurry lines. Notice that the map shows two *existing* coal slurry pipelines. One is the Ohio Pipeline and the other is the Black Mesa Pipeline in northern Arizona. The

[21] *Traffic World* (January 23, 1978), pp. 6, 24–29.

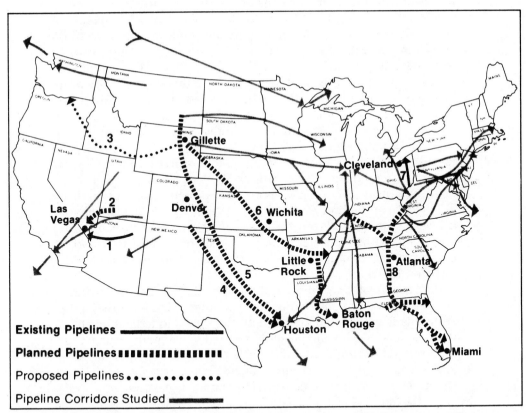

Figure 6–8   Existing and Planned Coal Slurry Pipelines. Source: *Traffic World* (May 18, 1981), p. 42. Used with permission.

Ohio pipeline was finished in 1957, is 108 miles long, and 10 inches in diameter. It connected a Hanna Coal Company coal mine to the Cleveland Electric Company power plant at Eastlake, Ohio. This line was successfully utilized until 1963, when it was closed down because newly initiated coal unit-train rates undercut the pipeline's rate.

At this writing, the only operating coal slurry line is the Black Mesa. Ironically, this pipeline is owned by the Southern Pacific Railroad, which built it in 1970 because the mountainous terrain made a coal unit-train impractical. The line is 273 miles long and uses 18-inch diameter pipe. It connects coal strip mines in northern Arizona to an electric generating plant on the Colorado River near Davis Dam in Nevada. It has four pump stations, each having 1,750-horsepower pumps which develop 1,600 pounds per square inch of pressure.

Rights-of-way problems. As the above discussion has noted, railroads are less than pleased with the large potential development of coal slurry pipelines. Naturally, railroads would be expected to do everything within their power—legally—to thwart the growth of this new competitor. One method of doing this is to prevent coal slurry companies from crossing railroad rights-of-way, which are privately-owned property. Since the railroad system literally criss-crosses the country, it is impossible for a slurry pipeline to establish a very long system before having to cross a railroad right-of-way.

A proposed coal slurry pipeline that is presently stymied by the railroad right-of-way issue is the 1,400-mile slurry line from Wyoming's coal-rich Powder River Basin to an electrical utility near Little Rock, Arkansas. (See Figure 6–8.) This pipeline is to be built by Energy Transportation Systems, Inc., (ETSI), which has already received authorization from the State of Wyoming to utilize the required quantities of water. The proposed line would transport 37 million tons of coal per year. There are even plans to extend it as far as Baton Rouge.

ETSI, and other proposed slurry pipeline firms, are trying to achieve the right of eminent domain in order to cross railroad property. This is being attempted at both the state and federal levels. At the state level, Oklahoma recently enacted a law giving slurry pipelines the right of eminent domain. North Dakota, Utah, Texas, Wyoming, Colorado, and Arkansas already have enacted such laws. Other western states are considering similar legislation.

At the federal level, legislation giving slurry pipelines the right of eminent domain was considered by Congress in 1978. One bill called for the Department of the Interior to issue the certificate of federal eminent domain if a slurry pipeline appears to be in the public interest. Two other similar bills were before Congress, and each of them called for the ICC to issue the certificate of federal eminent domain. Another bill would have the DOT determine if federal eminent domain is required. None of the bills passed, mainly because of railroad opposition.

In late 1981 and early 1982 Congress again held hearings on bills related to this issue. The ICC was to issue the certificate of federal eminent domain. Choice of the federal agency to be in charge of issuing the certificate of eminent domain is not a trivial issue. It is generally believed the Interior and Energy Departments would be more willing to issue the eminent domain certificates than would the ICC or the DOT, which would be more likely to specifically take into consideration the effect of the slurry pipelines on the long-run viability of the railroad industry. The Reagan Administration has opposed the federal government's granting of eminent domain to pipelines because they feel such a move would interfere with each state's right to control use of its own water resources.

Railroad Reaction to Coal Slurry Pipelines

Railroads believe that the development of coal slurry pipelines would create unfair competition.[22] Railroads are true common carriers and must transport a wide variety of products for customers within their service area. Coal slurry pipelines, on the other hand, are very specialized carriers—they transport only coal. If coal slurry pipelines are built, they will "skim-the-cream" of the railroads' most important single product—coal—and the effect will be that the railroads will lose a large portion of their revenues.

James R. Walker, an attorney for the Burlington Northern Railroad, noted that the development of western coal fields is important to the railroads because it is this traffic which, ". . . the railroads see as producing for themselves the economies-of-scale which will enable them to provide coal transport service to all coal users at low rates and, at the same time, it will enhance their ability to provide service to all shippers of all commodities. Indeed, new coal traffic has been characterized as the last, best hope of the railroads to avoid nationalization."[23]

---

[22] See: "Railway Labor Executives' Association Seeks to Sink Plan to Give Slurry Pipelines Eminent Domain," *Traffic World* (August 10, 1981), p. 39.

[23] James R. Walker, "Coal Slurry Pipelines and National Transportation Policy: A Critical Review," *The Logistics and Transportation Review*, Vol. 12, No. 4 (1976) p. 265.

Coal slurry pipeline development continues as one of the most highly debated issues in national transportation policy. Figure 6–9 contains excerpts from a 1982 editorial from *The Wall Street Journal* regarding this issue.

Additional Products Transported by Pipeline

Within cities, water and sewage are carried by pipelines. In downtown areas, steam for heating also moves through underground pipes. There are also three other broad categories of product pipelines: chemical pipelines; non-coal slurry pipelines; and various types of capsule pipelines and pneumatic pipelines.

Chemical pipelines. Three chemicals are transported in the United States by pipeline: liquid anhydrous ammonia (used in manufacturing fertilizers); ethylene (used in production of antifreeze); and propylene (used in manufacturing of detergents). The largest chemical pipelines include an 850-mile liquid anhydrous ammonia pipeline

Coal mining concerns and the railroads are locked in a classic feud pitting the principles of the competitive free market against the protection afforded by government regulation. The issue is whether pipelines should be allowed to compete with the railways for the expanding coal transport market. The Reagan administration, it's sad to say, is moving along the wrong track in this dispute.

What really seems to be on the administration's mind is the worry that support of eminent domain for coal pipelines would be perceived in the West as federal infringement in the sensitive area of water rights, even though this is not truly the case. So the administration drew back from the issue by making this false plea for states' rights. In the meantime coal producers must cope with transportation bottlenecks, and the railways are asking the Interstate Commerce Commission to lift price regulations on coal exports. This too has the coal mine companies up in arms.

Congress will soon have a chance to redress the balance. The House Public Works Committee soon will take up the pipeline issue. (The House Interior Committee has already approved the eminent domain legislation.) We hope that Congress shows more concern than the administration for introducing competition in the coal transport market and thus, it's hoped, encourages further development of our vast coal reserves.

Figure 6–9 *Wall Street Journal* Editorial on Coal Slurry Pipelines. Source: *The Wall Street Journal* (January 27, 1982). Used with permission.

from Texas to Iowa. There is a 1,100-mile liquid ammonia line from Louisiana to Nebraska and a 2,100-mile network transporting ethylene from Texas to Louisiana.

Non-coal slurry pipelines.   Three non-coal products commonly transported by slurry pipeline, especially in foreign countries, are iron concentrate, copper concentrate, and limestone. Other products shipped in limited quantities by slurry pipeline are magnetite concentrate, Gilsonite, phosphate, sulfur, and hematite.[24]

Capsule and pneumatic pipelines.   Capsule pipelines carry a product contained within capsules transported along the pipeline by either a pumped liquid or a gas. A *hydro-capsule* pipeline uses water or some other fluid as the carrying medium, while a *pneumo-capsule* pipeline uses either air or an inert gas. Pneumatic pipelines transport pulverized dry bulk materials such as cement or flour. They function in a manner similar to vacuum cleaners.

Pipeline Cost Structure

Pipelines have a high ratio of fixed costs to total costs. Fixed costs—those that do not vary with volume—include costs of the underground pipe system, pump and compressor stations, and tank farms at origins and destinations. Variable costs—those that vary directly with volume—include labor expenses, fuel to operate the pumps and compressors, and preventive maintenance. Fuel costs are estimated to be 25 percent of a typical oil pipeline's operating expenses. Labor costs are 10 to 15 percent of total operating expenses.[25] To illustrate the relatively low labor costs of a pipeline, the TAPS system cost $9.2 billion, yet this entire pipeline is operated, monitored, and maintained by only 450 workers. Therefore, it is generally believed that fixed costs for a pipeline are in the range of 60 to 70 percent of total costs.

Because of the pipeline industry's high fixed-cost structure, it is subject to significant increasing economies of scale. Another factor contributing to greatly lower costs per unit transported when vol-

[24] See: T. C. Aude, T. L. Thompson, and E. J. Wasp, "Economics of Slurry Pipeline Systems," *Transportation Research Forum Annual Proceedings* (Oxford, Indiana: Richard B. Cross, 1974), pp. 194–202; and E. J. Wasp and T. L. Thompson, "Coal Slurry Pipelines—Energy Movers of the Future," *Pipeline Industry* (May, 1974), pp. 26–29.

[25] Speech by Richard C. Hulbert, "Principles of Pipeline Economics," presented at the 1974 Association of Oil Pipe Lines Educators' Tour.

ume is high deals with the economics of pumping a fluid through a pipe. Professors Meyer, Peck, Stenason, and Zwick noted:

> Pumping horsepower is required to overcome friction created by the liquid touching the inside surface of the pipe. The larger the diameter of the pipe, the larger the volume per unit of pipe surface area. This means that the horsepower required to overcome a given amount of friction will propel more liquid through a larger than a smaller pipeline. This, in turn, gives rise to markedly increasing returns to scale, or reductions in unit costs as the throughput per day and the diameter of the pipeline is increased.[26]

This explains why many pipelines, such as TAPS, are jointly owned. It is more efficient to build one large-diameter pipeline than a number of smaller ones. An example of the significant scale economies in pipelining came out of a Congressional hearing in 1972. It was noted that a 36-inch oil pipeline costs about 3½ times as much to construct as does a 12-inch line. However, the 36-inch line can transport 17 times the volume of the 12-inch line.[27]

Regulatory Issues

The pipeline industry has not been subject to regulatory conflict to the extent found in the railroad and motor carrier industries. Nevertheless, there are three regulatory problems areas: minimum tenders, the "consent decree," and divestiture.

Minimum Tenders

In 1906 all oil pipelines were declared common carriers. Some pipeline firms which did not want to become common carriers thought they could avoid the issue by requiring a very large minimum tender. They claimed that handling small amounts of products

- *Minimum tender* is the smallest size of shipment or amount of oil or petroleum products a common carrier will accept from a shipper.

was inefficient because of the costs of doing paperwork and of monitoring the small shipments within the pipeline.

---

[26] John R. Meyer, Merton J. Peck, John Stenason, and Charles Zwick, *The Economics of Competition In The Transportation Industries* (Cambridge, Mass.: Harvard University Press, 1959), p. 126.

[27] *House Report No. 92-1617.* Hearings before the Subcommittee on Special Small Business Problems, House of Representatives (June, 1972), p. 142.

Even after petroleum pipelines were declared to be common carriers, they had large minimum tenders. Some were raised to 100,000 barrels which effectively stopped small independent oil companies from using the pipelines because they could never amass—at one time—that quantity of oil. In 1922 the ICC ruled that 100,000-barrel minimum tenders were unreasonable and stated that 10,000 barrels was more equitable. The latter figure is still a common minimum tender quantity of oil.

The "Consent Decree"

In 1939, both the Federal Trade Commission and the Department of Justice testified before Congress that the pipelines owned by the oil companies were paying dividends to their parent companies—this was a violation of the *Elkins Act* of 1903. The *Elkins Act* stated that a shipper is prohibited from receiving from a common carrier any sum of money or other consideration as a rebate or offset against the regular charges for transportation service. The Justice Department, alleging that the dividends were rebates, filed suit in September, 1940, in federal court against 20 major oil companies and 59 oil pipelines. The suit demanded that these 79 firms pay $1.5 to $2 billion in fines for their illegal actions. J. D. Durand, General Counsel of the Association of Oil Pipe Lines, later commented:

> Rebates and dividends are two distinctly different things. Rebates are pure gratuities paid to a shipper. Dividends are a fruit of stock ownership and are paid out of earnings. Never since the passage of the Elkins Act of 1903 had anyone contended that dividends constituted rebates under the Elkins Act. However, the rebate case brought by the Department of Justice, flimsy as it was, involved penalties so large that an adverse decision would have dealt a staggering blow to the entire oil industry. This together with the urgent necessity for the oil industry to make preparations for World War II, caused the pipeline and oil company defendants to agree to a consent decree, effective December 23, 1941.[28]

This consent decree, which is still in effect, limits the annual dividend payable by a pipeline to its oil company owners to 7 percent of the valuation of the carrier's property.

The Divestiture Issue

For sometime now, the U.S. Department of Justice has been considering having the pipeline companies be divested, or separated,

---

[28] Speech to 1974 Educators' Tour sponsored by the Association of Oil Pipe Lines, mimeographed, p. 33.

from their oil- and natural gas-producing parent firms. The theory of
the divestiture is that competition would be increased in the pipeline industry if they were not owned by producing companies.

This issue was hotly debated during the late 1950's and concluded with an extensive Congressional hearing. The Celler Subcommittee report (named after Congressman Emanuel Celler), which
was critical of some aspects of joint ownership, did *not* favor government action in ordering parent pipeline companies to divest themselves of their pipeline subsidiaries.

Pipeline Industry Future

The future of the pipeline industry is very favorable. The Department of Transportation estimates that between 1975 and 1990, crude
oil trunk lines will increase their ton-mileage by 105 percent. Refined petroleum products will increase 24 percent and natural gas
will be up 2 percent. Coal slurry lines, according to DOT estimates,
will achieve dramatically increased ton-mileage—up from 1.3 billion ton-miles in 1975 to 72 billion in 1990.

The primary factor explaining these projected increases in ton-
mileage is that pipelines enjoy a substantial energy-savings advantage over their competitive modes of transportation. (An exception is
the coal slurry pipeline versus rail unit-train controversy.)

Summary

Oil pipelines developed in the era of the Civil War. As the petroleum
industry grew, it relied on pipelines. John D. Rockefeller's Standard
Oil Company used pipelines as a method of controlling competition
in the oil industry. As a result, oil pipelines were placed under ICC
regulation by the 1906 *Hepburn Act*.

The *Hepburn Act* made the pipelines common carriers that had
to accept shipments from various independent oil shippers. In 1977,
control over the pipeline regulations was transferred to the Federal
Energy Regulatory Commission in the new Department of Energy.
The Federal Energy Regulatory Commission also regulates natural
gas lines.

There are three types of oil pipelines. Gathering pipelines are
small and lead from producing wells to gathering stations. Often
gathering lines are laid above the ground so that they can be moved
when needed at a different site. Crude oil trunk pipelines carry

crude petroleum from gathering stations to refineries. Refined products pipelines reach from refineries to major cities, where the products are used. The Trans-Alaska Pipeline System (TAPS) is an 800-mile-long crude oil trunk pipeline, 48 inches in diameter, which carries crude oil from Prudhoe Bay in northern Alaska to Valdez, a port in southern Alaska, where the crude oil is loaded aboard ships.

The most promising development for pipelines is the carriage of coal slurry, consisting of powdered coal carried along in a mixture of water. The principal obstacle the slurry pipelines are encountering is opposition from railroads, which will not allow the slurry pipelines to cross the rail lines. Railroads were successful in blocking proposed legislation in recent sessions of Congress that would have granted the right of eminent domain to slurry pipelines.

Pneumatic pipelines use air to transport dry bulk materials, such as cement. Capsule pipelines carry enclosed capsules in either fluid or a gas.

Pipelines enjoy increasing economies of scale, which is why oil companies join together to build large diameter pipelines. This is of some significance to regulators since it is difficult to maintain a competitive environment when there are savings in cost if "competing" firms can join together.

Questions for Discussion and Review

1. Discuss briefly the history of pipelines.

2. Discuss the role of Standard Oil in the history of pipelines.

3. Discuss the concept of eminent domain. In what segment of the pipeline industry has it become of crucial importance? Discuss.

4. What is the FERC?

5. Differentiate between an oil gathering line, trunk line, and product line.

6. Why was TAPS built?

7. Why did TAPS cost so much more than originally projected?

8. What is LNG? Why is it not shipped more frequently in this form?

9. Who owns the natural gas pipeline system?

10. Discuss, in general terms, the proposed Alaska Natural Gas Pipeline.

11. Explain the basic operation of a coal slurry pipeline.

12. Why do environmentalists often have qualms about coal slurry pipelines? Discuss.

13. Compare coal slurry pipelines to coal unit-trains in terms of energy efficiency.

14. What happened to the *first* coal slurry pipeline ever built?

15. Discuss the right-of-way problem involved in the development of coal slurry pipelines.

16. What has been the railroads' position toward the development of coal slurry pipelines? Discuss fully.

17. Take a position *for* or *against* coal slurry pipeline development and present a case supporting your position.

18. Figure 6–9 is an excerpt from a *Wall Street Journal* editorial dealing with coal slurry pipelines. What position did the editorial writer take? Why? Do you agree or not, and why?

19. What are the types of capsule pipelines? What is a pneumatic pipeline?

20. Discuss briefly these regulatory issues: minimum tenders, the "consent decree," and the divestiture issue.

Additional Chapter References

Bright, Donald B., "West Coast Crude Oil Pipeline System," *Annual Proceedings of the American Society of Traffic and Transportation* (1978), pp. 210–228.

Campbell, Thomas C., "Eminent Domain: Its Origin, Meaning, and Relevance to Coal Slurry Pipelines," *Transportation Journal* (Fall, 1977), pp. 5–21.

Courtney, J. L., "Arctic Natural Gas Transport Systems," *Annual Proceedings of the Transportation Research Forum* (1978), pp. 68–72.

Farris, Martin T., and David L. Shrock, "The Economics of Coal Slurry Pipelining: Transportation and Non-Transportation Factors," *Transportation Journal* (Fall, 1978), pp. 45–57.

Hyman, Eric L., "For Want of Water: Rail Versus Slurry Pipeline Transport of Coal in the Northern Great Plains," *Annual Proceedings of the Transportation Research Forum* (1978), pp. 533–542.

Johnson, James C., and Kenneth C. Schneider, "Coal Slurry Pipelines: An Economic and Political Dilemma," *ICC Practitioners' Journal*, Vol. 48, No. 1 (1980), pp. 24–37.

Rohleder, Gilbert V., "Pipelines—The Challenge of Regulation in a Free

Economy," *Annual Proceedings of the American Society of Traffic and Transportation* (1978), pp. 111–115.

Rose, Warren, "Facilitating U.S. Oil Imports: Deepwater Ports in the Gulf of Mexico," *Transportation Journal* (Winter, 1980), pp. 41–49.

Sims, Lee S., and Neal A. Irwin, "Transportation of LNG from the Arctic to Eastern Canada," *Annual Proceedings of the Transportation Research Forum* (1981) pp. 578–586.

Wald, Haskell P., "Rate Reform for Electric Utilities and Gas Pipeline Companies," *Transportation Journal* (Spring, 1975), pp. 30–41.

Weissbrod, Richard, and Stephen Vezeris, "Regulation of the Coal Slurry Industry," *Annual Proceedings of the Transportation Research Forum* (1978), pp. 83–92.

Case 6–1   Alaskan Haul Road Case*

Prior to building the Alaska oil pipeline, it was necessary to construct a "Haul Road" near the pipeline's intended route to carry pipe and construction equipment. The haul road, which had a gravel surface, stretched from Valdez to Prudhoe Bay and was 823 miles long. When the pipeline began pumping oil, ownership of the road and its 300-foot-wide right-of-way were deeded to the State of Alaska, although the pipeline company was given a permanent easement to use the road and the right-of-way for purposes of maintaining the pipeline and its pumping stations.

Peter Bowman had been graduated with high honors from the University of British Columbia, where he had majored in environmental policy. He had accepted a job with the Alaskan Department of Wildlife Management, and his first assignment was to help develop the Department's recommendations to the governor with respect to the Haul Road. The main issue was whether the Haul Road should be opened to public use.

Alaska's residents had assumed that the Haul Road would be opened to public use as soon as it had been turned over to the state by the pipeline company. Many families had their campers and four-wheel-drive vehicles packed and ready to move north on the road as soon as it was opened to public travel. They were annoyed to learn that the state government was not opening it immediately and was even wondering whether to open it at all. Both the governor and many state legislators were receiving angry phone calls and letters from Alaskan citizens demanding that the Haul Road be opened. The principal reason they gave was that since most of Alaska was inac-

---

*This case is based on material in an article by George Laycock, entitled "Main Drag to Prudhoe Bay," which appeared *Audubon Magazine* (March, 1979), pp. 36–43.

cessible because of rugged terrain, they felt that they should be given a chance to travel along the Haul Road route to see a portion of the state they had never seen before. Indeed, the route stretched north of the Arctic Circle, one of the few roads in the world to do so.

In addition to sightseers there were hunters, fishermen, and trappers who felt that the Haul Road would lead them to fish and game which, up to that time, had been fished and hunted only by the native Alaskans (Eskimos).

Bowman's supervisor told him that he should see conditions along the road for himself. He was told to take a four-wheel-drive vehicle from the department's motor pool, and to check out a sleeping bag, camping gear, and some dried food from the department's supply room. He was to supplement the food with groceries bought at local stores in Valdez. A route and timetable for the 1,646-mile trip were laid out for him. His vehicle had a radio, and he was to check in with his home office or with other points along the route at least once a day. He was given 15 days to complete his journey and was instructed to stop at least once every 10 miles to inspect the road, its drainage, and whether it had any noticeable impact on the adjoining environment.

For maps, Bowman was given U.S. Geological Survey maps, which showed topography and streams of the area before pipeline construction. Bowman was especially interested in what had happened to streams that the Haul Road crossed since many of them supported numerous forms of fish and other wildlife—the larger ones were even used by migrating salmon. The night before he left Valdez, Bowman used a felt-tipped pen to mark the points where the Haul Road intersected streams. He decided to check those points as he moved north. He would wait until he reached the north end of the road to decide what points to check on his return trip south.

The next morning Bowman started out and at the first three sites where the Haul Road crossed streams, he was pleased to see that bridges had been built with a minimum of disruption to the streambed and its surroundings. A few miles north of the third stop, the road pavement ended, and Bowman was driving on gravel, very dusty gravel, as he could see from the trail in his rearview mirror. At the next stream crossing, that of the Yellow Jack River, Bowman found no bridge. Instead, two 48-inch-diameter culvert pipes had been laid under the road to carry the water. Unfortunately, graders had pushed the gravel off the edge of the road, partially blocking both culvert pipes. Water flowed through the culverts, but the gravel served as a dam that would block any migrating fish. In addition, Bowman wondered whether the culverts could handle the water from a massive spring thaw. Already a few branches and twigs had accumulated at the upstream culvert. All the way north, this pattern of culverts, rather than bridges, continued. In most instances the culverts were partially blocked by gravel which had been pushed off the edge of the road, either by graders or by trucks which had traveled too close to the edge. Once, when Bowman had parked off the road and was walking along the stream's edge, a heavy pipeline company truck had roared by, leaving a cloud of dust and spray of pebbles in its wake. Bowman had seen some of the small stones hit the stream. He returned to his parked vehicle fearing that the windshield had been broken. It wasn't, although it was covered with a fresh, thick layer of dust.

Later that same day, as the angle of the sun changed, Bowman noticed that many plants along the Haul Road had been coated with dust and were gray rather than green. He wondered whether this coating of dust would be harmful. At one streambed, he walked over 300 feet away from the road's edge and still found that plants were heavily coated with dust. Upon closer inspection, he observed that some of the most heavily coated plants, near the road, appeared to be dying.

Bowman had hoped to see some of the wildlife for which the area was noted. He saw one or two wolves cross the road, and one night some black bears visited his campsite in search of food. He had heard that during the construction of the pipeline the bears had started living off of the garbage disposed of by the workers. Three nights later, when it was possible for Bowman to drive some distance from the pipeline and Haul Road, he did so and camped in isolation, although he could not escape the noise of the occasional pipeline truck as it roared along the Haul Road. While camped away from the road, Bowman was able to see owls and teal and, once, some caribou. He had hoped to see some Alaskan grizzly bears (from a distance) but was unsuccessful.

Bowman completed his round trip and concluded that the Haul Road was having three adverse impacts upon the environment: the poorly installed culverts were being filled with gravel from the road; the dust from the road was hurting plant life; and the Haul Road and its traffic were driving the natural wildlife away. The Haul Road and the pipeline which it paralleled were creating a barrier that game would not cross. He also believed that if the road were open to traffic, owners of four-wheel-drive vehicles would drive off the road and contribute additional damage to the surrounding environment.

After Bowman returned to Valdez he went to Fairbanks, where state highway officials told him that they were concerned about costs of patrolling the road if it were open to general traffic. The reason was that the road had been designed for heavy trucks, and many smaller vehicles, especially with inexperienced drivers, would have difficulty driving along some sections. Weather was unpredictable and, especially along the northern stretches of the road, could be much more severe than most people—including Alaskans—had encountered. Services along the road were few and far between. Maintaining patrol vehicles along the Haul Road would cost between five and seven million dollars per year. Road maintenance costs were also expected to be high since gravel must be continually replaced. If the road were to be opened, there was disagreement as to who should pay the costs. Some thought the users should pay tolls for being allowed on the road. Others felt that Alaskan motorists in general should pay the costs in the same manner as they paid for other roads. The pipeline company announced that the road was of limited value to it since helicopters were more useful to them for inspecting and maintaining the pipeline.

Question One: Is the damage Bowman found attributable to the pipeline? If so, who is—or will be—paying for it?

Question Two: Should the Haul Road be opened to the public? Why?

Question Three: If the Haul Road is opened, what restrictions should be placed on its use?

Question Four: If the road is opened, who should pay the costs of operating patrol vehicles along it? Why?

Question Five: Does government have an obligation to "open up" wilderness areas, or to protect them? Discuss.

Question Six: What other information would be useful to Bowman before he makes his recommendations?

Case 6–2   Panhandle Pipeline Company Case

Incorporated under Texas laws in 1927, the Panhandle Pipeline Company was now—in 1980—contemplating construction of a small pipeline between its refinery in Texas and Hiccup, Arkansas. A small tank farm would be built at Hiccup, and refined products would be distributed in the Hiccup area by truck.

As a company policy, Panhandle would build a pipeline only if a flow of products for at least 20 years was assured. Panhandle's market research staff concluded that the company could safely assume that there was a 20-year demand for 1,400 to 1,500 barrels of petroleum products to be shipped each day. This demand (1,400 to 1,500 barrels per day) was considered to be constant over the 20 years, since the Hiccup area's economy was not expected to grow.

Panhandle already owned the right-of-way, and the only choice its managers had to make dealt with the diameter of pipe to be used in the pipeline. Larger diameters of pipe cost more initially but, once in place, required less energy to pump a given amount of fluid from one end of the system to the other.

The pipeline costs consisted of only two items: fixed costs and variable costs. The fixed costs of an 8-inch-diameter pipeline were—when spread over the 20-year life of the project—$365,000 per year (in 1980 dollars). Comparable fixed costs for 10-inch-diameter pipe were $511,000 per year; for the 12-inch-diameter pipe, they were $657,000 per year. Variable costs were mainly those of electricity to drive the pumps. It was possible to increase the flow of product through an existing pipeline by increasing the speed of the pumps, but the costs of the electricity would usually increase faster than the volume of product handled.

Case Table 6–2–1 shows the estimated variable costs—using 1980 prices—for pumping 1,000 barrels to 2,000 barrels per day through three pipelines of different diameters.

Question One: What diameter of pipe do you think Panhandle should use?

CASE TABLE 6–2–1   Estimates of Variable Costs
of Operating Proposed Products Pipeline to Hiccup

Pipeline "Through-Put" in Barrels Per Day	Variable Pipeline Costs in Dollars Per Day		
	8″ Pipeline	10″ Pipeline	12″ Pipeline
1000	620	450	200
1100	690	500	220
1200	770	550	240
1300	860	600	260
1400	970	660	290
1500	1110	730	320
1600	1280	810	370
1700	1450	900	430
1800	1625	1000	520
1900	1850	1140	620
2000	1985	1290	730

Question Two: If the market for petroleum products in the vicinity of Hiccup is expected to grow, how would this change your decision, if at all?

Question Three: What if there was a good chance that the market near Hiccup would decline? How would this affect your decision?

Question Four: Panhandle's directors worry that the price of electricity will continue to increase. They ask you to assume that electricity costs increase and that the variable costs will be 1.5 times those shown in the table. How would this influence your recommendation?

Question Five: One of the company's directors fears that electricity costs will increase so much that the variable costs will be twice those shown in Case Table 6–2–1. She asks you to determine the "best" size of pipeline on the basis of this assumption.

Question Six: What effect does a high rate of inflation have on the selection of projects where there is a choice *between* high initial, fixed costs or high future, variable costs?

A business jet climbs after taking off from a small airport in the Pacific Northwest logging country.

Photo courtesy Citation Marketing Division, Cessna Aircraft Company.

7 Domestic Aviation

I asked American Airlines whether it could make money selling seats on transcontinental flights for $149. American said it costs about $45,000 to fly a DC-10 across the country, $13,000 in fuel costs alone. To get that money back, at these new low prices, American would just about have to fill all 225 coach seats and all 44 first-class seats. A plane flying with two out of every three seats filled is losing heaps of money.

MILTON MOSKOWITZ
San Francisco Chronicle
March 3, 1982

To drive home its price message, Peoples Express is putting on a mischievous ad campaign poking fun at other airlines and their patchwork quilt of fares. In one TV commercial, a reservation clerk at a fictitious competitor tells a customer: "You want the BSA Airlines super low-price special. OK? You simply fly one-way, and pay the price you pay the other way if you fly two ways. OK? Simply put, each way costs half of either way, both ways, some days. OK?"

Fortune
March 22, 1982

Because Skytrain is a small commuter airline, its pilots also put in time as ticket agents, schedulers, sales representatives, and go-fers. After landing one of Skytrain's two Chieftains at Ft. Wayne the other day, Capt. Ryan deplaned with a paper towel and bottle of Windex, hopped onto the starboard wing, and began to polish the windshield. Just before takeoff, he and Capt. Pendleton got out to help the Fort Wayne ticket agent push the plane from its parking space, blocked by another plane, back to the taxiway. This sort of thing can be unnerving to passengers accustomed to flying the major commercial airlines, and more than one has wondered aloud if Skytrain had been the inspiration for Bob Newhart's "Grace L. Ferguson Airline and Storm Door Company" routine.

Chicago Tribune
August 26, 1981

Introduction

To many readers, aviation is the most exciting form of transportation. Airplanes, an invention of this century, have developed extensively during the past half-century. No other form of transport still has as much potential for further development.

While all modes of transportation have been regulated, airline transportation was the first to begin to experience deregulation. And that's one reason why the airline industry is being watched very closely. U.S. aviation has been buffeted by three other factors: increases in the prices of fuel (by most measures aircraft are the least fuel efficient of all modes); the strike and subsequent dismissal of air traffic controllers in 1981; and the 1980–82 recession.

This chapter will cover the development of domestic airlines and the structure of the industry. Airports and the air navigation system will then be discussed, followed by a discussion of general aviation. Two related aviation topics, international airlines and the supersonic air transport (SST), will be covered in chapter 9.

Development of Aviation

There was great interest in the development of powered aircraft at the turn of the century in both the United States and in Europe. The first successful flight was in late 1903 at Kitty Hawk, North Carolina. This feat was accomplished by Wilbur and Orville Wright, two brothers who had a bicycle business in Dayton, Ohio. Their first flight lasted just under a minute, but by 1905, the Wright Brothers were making flights lasting as long as 30 minutes. They then decided to sell rights to their invention, and it was not until 1908 that they had concluded contracts with the U.S. government. By 1910, a number of aircraft had been developed both here and in Europe. Governments subsidized early aircraft development because they felt the real "value" of aircraft would be for military purposes.

In the early days of World War I, aircraft were used primarily for observation. But, by the end of the war, aircraft of opposing nations were fighting each other in the air—fighter planes—and carrying and dropping bombs—bombers. Few technological advances in the field of aeronautics are associated with World War I, except that for the first time aircraft were mass-produced. Wartime also saw the beginning of pilot training. Fighter pilots received considerable publicity, perhaps because of the fact that for several years the ground war was at a near stalemate.

In the mid, and late, 1920's, the domestic airline industry began. The government provided subsidies to the airline companies to carry mail. Mail transport was the beginning of the airline industry. Passenger business developed as an afterthought to the carriage of mail. The first U.S. aircraft designed primarily to carry passengers was the Ford Trimotor, introduced in 1926. It was an all-metal aircraft, capable of flying at 85 knots, nicknamed the "Tin Goose" and "one of the

- A *knot* is a measure of speed used for ships and planes. One knot is equal to about 1.15 miles per hour.

most uncomfortable airplanes ever to beset a paying passenger."[1] In 1930, Postmaster General Walter Folger Brown decided to place more emphasis on use of airmail subsidies to generate passenger business, so he restructured the airmail subsidy format so that only a relatively small number of airline operators could qualify. This was believed necessary to achieve growth. The firms that won the contracts in 1930 are the direct forebearers of today's major air carriers. Brown's plan appeared to be successful until 1934, when, under a different administration, it was disclosed that there had been many irregularities associated with the contract-awarding procedures. The contracts were cancelled, and it was decided that prior contract holders would be banned from bidding for the new business. Hence, then-existing airlines had to reorganize, and American, Eastern, TWA, United Air Lines, and others, were born.

Passenger aircraft technology burgeoned during the 1930's. Fuselages were streamlined, and a number of aircraft models were introduced. By far the most important and successful passenger aircraft was the Douglas DC-3, designed in response to specifications written by American Airlines. The DC-3 contributed enormously to the development of airline aviation in both the United States and other countries. The DC-3 did for aviation what Ford's Model-T car did for auto and truck users. Both the DC-3 and the Model-T were produced in large quantities, they were the dominant vehicle in their modes, and supporting transport facilities were designed to complement them. At the end of their reigns as "popular" models, the transport world they served was much different than it had been when they were introduced; and they were responsible for causing much of that change.

In the late 1930's there were many developments that improved the dependability and safety of the air navigation system—an essential step for air travel to become popular.

- The *air navigation system* is a nationwide (nearly worldwide) system of radio signals, personnel on the ground providing communication, and visual markings—beacons, etc.—all of which help guide the pilot on his or her course.

In the late 1930's there were two things that concerned Congress about airline transportation: its future and the degree to which gov-

[1] Robert J. Serling, "America's Airlines," *Flying* (September, 1977), p. 224.

ernment should be involved in both its promotion and regulation. President Roosevelt wanted the airlines to be subject to regulation by the Interstate Commerce Commission. Congress balked at this suggestion and was able to convince the President to approve a new regulatory agency, initially known as the Civil Aeronautics Authority, created by the *Civil Aeronautics Act*, signed into law on June 23, 1938. This new Authority took over some of the air safety responsibilities of the Department of Commerce, and it also had the power to determine the compensation paid to airlines for the carriage of mail. The new Authority could regulate the rates and services offered by the airlines in a manner similar to that used by the Interstate Commerce Commission in its regulation of railroads.[2] In 1940 the Civil Aeronautics Authority's name was changed to Civil Aeronautics Board (CAB).

Influence of World War II

World War II had a much greater influence upon the development of commercial aviation than did World War I. For the first time, vast numbers of aircraft were produced—the United States alone manufactured 30,000 four-engined bombers—and thousands of pilots were trained.

The usefulness of aircraft in maintaining supply lines was recognized. Often, aircraft were the only method of transporting men and materials to battle areas. Numerous advances in air navigation equipment made it possible to pilot a plane when visibility didn't permit the pilot to see much. The major technological development, which was introduced by the Germans late in the war, was the jet-powered aircraft.

Post-World War II Airlines

At the end of World War II, a number of new airlines were formed. Some were recognized by the Civil Aeronautics Board as "local service" airlines whose role was to serve small communities and "feed" passengers into the major airports served by the larger airlines. Hundreds of small firms went into the air freight business, often flying only one aircraft. "Non-scheduled" passenger airlines

- *Non-scheduled airlines* ("non-skeds") were restricted to offering *charter service*, i.e., allowing one group to charter, or rent,

[2]D. Philip Locklin, *Economics of Transportation*, 7th ed. (Homewood, Ill.: Richard D. Irwin, 1972), pp. 798–802.

the plane for a single trip. They were prohibited from offering scheduled service, although a number of them evaded this prohibition through use of various subterfuges.

were also formed, operating just outside the scope of the CAB's regular jurisdiction. In the 1950's, both the CAB and Congress took steps to "stabilize" the structure of the airline industry; the number of air freight airlines was reduced to four, and the opportunities available to non-scheduled airlines were sharply reduced.

Jet aircraft were introduced into commercial aviation in the 1950's. They operated at two to three times the speed of propeller aircraft and were much smoother. When introduced into markets formerly served by propeller-driven planes, jets attracted approximately 30 percent more passengers.[3]

During the 1960's fares remained relatively constant, despite inflation, and the number of passenger-miles traveled quadrupled.

Introduction of Jumbo Jets

At the end of the 1960's three models of "jumbo" jet aircraft (now called "wide body jets"), led by the Boeing 747, were introduced into passenger airline service. The 747, with a dense seating arrangement could accommodate 490 passengers, over three times the seating capacity of aircraft in use up until that time. Lockheed and Douglas introduced models with about two-thirds the passenger carrying capacity of the 747; they were intended for markets that could not generate enough passengers to fully load a 747. The airline industry's total passenger carrying capacity, measured in terms of available seats, increased dramatically.

The airline industry and its customers were affected in many ways. First, the *numbers* of scheduled flights were reduced, which relieved some problems of airport congestion. New York's Kennedy Airport handled 303,009 airline flights, with 18,856,073 passengers, in 1969. In 1972, the number of airline flights decreased by about 20 percent to 239,400, while the number of passengers increased by more than 10 percent to 20,069,949.[4] The reduction in flights forced some passengers into traveling "with the herd" and having less choice of flight times. The 747 also was able to carry substantial amounts of air freight in addition to passengers. This enabled several airlines to reduce their all-cargo flights, which had usually been flown at night. Many air cargo shippers had to use daytime passen-

[3]Estimate of Robert L. Banks, a Washington, D.C., transportation consultant.
[4]The Boeing Company, *747 In-Service Review* (Seattle, July, 1973).

ger flight schedules, thereby losing the advantage of "overnight" cargo service to many points.

- *Overnight freight service* is important to users of air freight. For most of them, it means that late in the afternoon, at the close of their business day, a truck picks up their outbound air freight and carries it to the airport where it's loaded aboard aircraft. The planes move at night, arriving in the destination city before daylight. It is then delivered by truck to the customer at the start of the business day. Users of air freight desire overnight service because—in the sense of scheduling work at different locations and shipments between them—virtually no working time is lost.

In the period when the jumbo jets were being introduced, there was little price competition allowed by the CAB. Instead of fare or rate competition, airlines competed in terms of service—which meant that they were all forced to buy substantial numbers of the new jets. The costs of the new aircraft, coupled with a leveling-off in the growth of passenger traffic caused by a slight recession in the late 1960's, had a disastrous effect on airline earnings. In 1970, the industry had a net operating income of $43 million on revenues of $9.3 billion, compared with the 1968 net operating income of $504 million on revenues of $7.7 billion.[5] In the early 1970's, the industry slowly recovered, mainly because the continual growth trend for airline passengers finally produced enough customers to fill the carriers' empty seats. The first fuel "crisis" in 1973–74 hurt the airlines badly, and they had to cut back on service. Once again, they slowly recovered.

Starting in 1977, steps were taken by both Congress and the CAB to "deregulate" the industry. The airlines have been responding to deregulation in a number of ways which will be discussed later in this chapter.

Airports and Airways

Not only have there been developments in aircraft, there have also been parallel developments in airports and in air navigation equipment which have accommodated the increased size, sophistication, and dependability of aircraft. A "chicken-egg" relationship has always existed between airports and the planes they serve. "The surplus [World War I] Jennies with their requirements for large, out-

---

[5] Air Transport Association of America, *Air Transport 1978* (Washington, D.C., the Association, 1978), p. 17.

lying airports . . . set the pattern upon which all subsequent private flying has developed.''[6] Hence a World War I–vintage aircraft influenced the initial size requirements for U.S. airports. In the late 1930's, as federal funds for airport and airport terminal construction became available under public works programs, many communities built public airports with paved runways and a passenger terminal designed to handle the DC-3. Subsequent generations of larger aircraft required runway and terminal expansion; in many communities it became necessary to relocate the entire airport to a larger site farther from the community it served. In the late 1960's, buoyed by the prosperity of the airlines they served and anticipating the need to serve both jumbo jets and SSTs, many new airports were on the drawing boards. A few, such as the one at Dallas-Fort Worth, were completed. Many others were blocked by pressures from environmental protection interests.

The nation's air navigation system has also improved. Air navigation systems were once merely a series of lighted beacons which the lonely aviator would try to follow at night. It is now a sophisticated system that allows pilots to take off and land enormous aircraft under conditions of nearly no visibility. Air travel is very safe, and—occasionally—there are no fatalities of passengers on U.S. domestic air carriers for an entire year.

General Aviation

There are about 215,000 general aviation aircraft in the U.S., compared with about 3,000 airline aircraft. General aviation aircraft pro-

- *General aviation* applies to all aircraft *except* those used by the airlines and by the armed forces. The phrase is synonymous with *private flying*. Most planes used for general aviation flying are small, single- or twin-engine, propeller-driven aircraft, although an airline-sized jet owned by a manufacturing corporation for carrying its top executives would be considered as a general aviation aircraft. It would be a *corporate jet*, engaged in business flying.

vide flight service to communities without scheduled airline service. At present, only about 700 airports receive scheduled airline service; there are approximately 11,000 airports (although many are unpaved

[6]Lynn L. Bollinger and Arthur H. Tully, Jr., *Personal Aircraft Business at Airports* (Boston: Harvard Graduate School of Business Administration, 1948), p. 41. The "Jenny" was a single-engine aircraft used for training military pilots.

and unlighted). General aviation and commercial airlines compete with each other for air space and runway usage at major airports.

Structure of the U.S. Airline Industry

The structure of the U.S. airline industry was influenced by the way it was regulated, and deregulated. This book will use the somewhat traditional categories of airlines although, as deregulation continues, the distinctions between them become increasingly difficult to discern. The following discussion is based mainly upon the historic origins of the various classifications of carriers. Those categories mentioned first are not necessarily the "biggest." Also, since deregulation there have been mergers between carrier firms belonging to different classifications, so one cannot be certain into which category the new firm fits.

In 1981, the Civil Aeronautics Board reclassified scheduled carriers according to their annual revenues. The largest airlines (by revenues) are called "majors," then "nationals," "large regionals," "medium regionals," and so on. In the following discussion, brief mention will be made of the new categories.

International Air Carriers

Initially, there were two principal U.S. international air carriers: Pan American World Airways and Trans World Airlines. Pan American operated in international markets only, while Trans World developed both a domestic and international route structure. Gradually, other domestic airlines were allowed to expand their domestic route structures to include points outside the United States. For local service airlines, this generally meant adding a stop or two in either Canada or in Mexico. However, for trunk airlines, the addition of service to points outside the United States generally meant major extensions to overseas continents.

Pan American was hurt by this expansion of domestic air carriers into the international market because these carriers all had domestic route structures which they could use to connect with their overseas flights. After trying for over 30 years to obtain some domestic route segments, Pan American was finally allowed to add some domestic legs to its international route structure in late 1977. In late 1979, Pan American and a domestic airline merged. The two airlines' route structures complemented each other. The distinction between international and domestic airlines has ended, at least in terms of discussing structure of the U.S. airline industry.

Domestic Trunk Lines

Created in 1934, the "trunks" include the best-known airlines: United, American, Eastern, Delta, Northwest, Western, and Continental. They have been operating without direct subsidies since about 1940. Their pre-deregulation route structures included flights from coast to coast, or between New York and Florida, and so on, connecting, say, the largest one hundred U.S. cities.

Using the CAB's new category of "major" air carriers, the eight mentioned in the previous paragraph, plus Pan American and TWA were all included for 1981, as were Republic and USAir from the local service ranks (to be discussed next). Ranked in terms of domestic passenger-miles, the busiest airline in 1981 was United, followed by American, Eastern, Delta, TWA, and Republic.

Local Service Airlines

After World War II the CAB allowed the formation of a new strata of airlines, local service airlines, known as "feeders." It was their role to "feed" passengers into and out of major "hub" airports served by trunk airlines. Initially, these airlines flew DC-3s. As late as the mid-1960's they were still flying a total of nearly 100 DC-3s, although these were matched by equal numbers of larger propeller craft and small jets.

Initially, the route structures of local service airlines were easy to describe. They usually fanned out like spokes, whose hub was one of the major airports: Atlanta, Chicago, Denver, Minneapolis–St. Paul, Pittsburgh, Roanoke, St. Louis, San Antonio, or Seattle. In 1950, these local service airlines' route structures did not overlap and did not compete with major routes flown by the trunks. The DC-3 had excellent characteristics for short-haul traffic, and many feeder routes were a series of stops 50 to 100 miles apart. The DC-3's only disadvantage was its small passenger capacity, 26 to 30, which became inadequate for many feeder routes. However, the local service airlines replaced the DC-3s with larger aircraft (usually propeller-driven Convairs carrying 45 to 50 passengers). But these larger planes developed mechanical problems which the airlines said were caused by too many short hops. The management of local service airlines also looked with envy at the trunk airlines who were changing their fleets to jets. Local service airline management realized that their route structures were inappropriate for jets, since jets could be used advantageously only in markets with large numbers of passengers and relatively long distances between airports.

Deciding that they did not want to be bound by literal definitions of the phrase "local service," the management of many local service airlines embarked upon a massive campaign to broaden their areas of operations. They wanted to fly larger equipment between fewer points and they attempted, with some success, to terminate service at smaller communities.

The management of local service airlines also convinced the CAB to grant them several longer routes into major city-pair markets. This happened in the late 1960's when airline revenues and profits were high. At that time, the granting of long routes to local service carriers was opposed by the trunk lines because it would mean direct competition between trunks and local service carriers. However, the CAB gave the routes to the local service carriers because trunk airline profits were becoming embarrassingly high, and it was hinted that if the local service carriers could obtain enough long-haul routes, they might be able to be weaned from their local service subsidies. (The CAB had a long history of awarding "profitable" new routes to the financially-weakest carriers in hopes of injecting revenues where they were needed most.)

In addition to Republic and USAir (both formed by mergers of other local service airlines), the local service carriers are Frontier, Ozark, Piedmont, and Texas International. Airlines operating within Hawaii (Aloha and Hawaiian Airlines) and within Alaska (Alaska Airlines, Inc., Kodiak Western Alaska, Munz-Northern, Reeve-Aleutian Airways, and Wien Air Alaska) serve functions similar to local service airlines.

One other carrier should be mentioned at this point because it probably fits into this category as well as any. The firm, Pacific Southwest Airlines (PSA) operated solely within California and, as an intrastate carrier, was subject to rate regulation by the California Public Utilities Commission. PSA's major market is between Los Angeles and San Francisco, although it also serves other points in California. In 1979, after all airlines were "deregulated," PSA expanded its route structure to serve points outside California.

The CAB's new category of "national" air carrier includes many local service airlines. In 1981 the busiest, in terms of domestic passenger-miles, was Frontier, followed by Piedmont, World (formerly a "supplemental" carrier), and PSA.

Commuter Airlines

The previous section discussed how "local service" airlines, in an attempt to be more like trunk airlines, dropped their obligation to serve some points. As the local service airlines dropped service, a new form of air carrier, virtually unregulated by the CAB provided they flew small enough planes, came into existence. At first they were known as scheduled air taxis. They were often owned and operated by the small airport's fixed base operator. Small twin-engine

- An airport's *fixed base operator (FBO)* is a private businessman who rents out spaces in the hangar to aircraft owners, sells fuel, has an aircraft maintenance shop, gives flying lessons, and owns a fleet of small planes which he leases or charters out to private parties.

aircraft soon began to operate between communities, which had lost their airline service, and major trunk airports. At first, the trunk airlines refused to cooperate with the new carriers; for example, the trunk airlines at major airports refused to agree to transfer baggage or to allow "through tickets" to be written for connecting flights on both airlines.

- A *through ticket* is good for an *entire* trip involving connections between two or more carriers.

However, passengers on these early commuter airlines began insisting that trunk airlines interchange baggage and tickets. The trunks finally agreed to do so, but at the risk of offending local service airlines with whom the scheduled air taxis were sometimes competing.

The relationship between local service carriers and the scheduled air taxis was not always hostile. A few local service carriers contracted with the scheduled air taxis to perform services at points where the local service carrier wanted to abandon service but was prevented by the CAB from doing so (or where smaller equipment of the size used by the air taxis was more suitable, thus allowing the local service carrier to move to larger planes).

The scheduled air taxis were not subsidized by the federal government, although some did have contracts for carrying mail at night. In addition, local businesses in the communities they served would agree to buy a certain number of tickets each month (and these agreements made it easier for the airline to obtain financing). Eventually the industry changed its name from "scheduled air taxis" to "commuter airlines." The size of equipment they fly has also increased. In 1979 the CAB allowed them to fly aircraft with as many as 60 seats.

Commuter airlines are generally small firms, tightly controlled by a single individual. Passenger comforts are on the Spartan side. Employee productivity is high, and wages, especially those of pilots, relatively low. The reason for this is the small number of pilots' positions open with major airlines; hence individuals who want to fly for a living and maintain their current "flight" status[7] may settle for jobs as commuter airline pilots.

Since airline deregulation, the commuter airline industry has really blossomed. One monthly trade journal reported:

> The act of creation is getting popular in the deregulated U.S. airline industry, and another wave of new airlines are being prepared for their first breaths of life. In the U.S. southwest Jetwest International Airways, Arizona Pacific Airline and American West Airlines are trying to launch service. Jetwest, formed by a group including former Bonanza Airlines' officials and headed by President Larry Decker, plans to operate a hub from Las Vegas, but with headquarters in Phoenix. Decker hopes to raise more than $30 million through stock and securities offerings. If the capital is secured, the airline plans to begin service in the spring, probably with six DC-9s, on underserved routes in the area. Fares will be below normal coach rates.[8]

At present, there are about 300 commuter airlines in the United States.[9] Most are very small, serving relatively unknown markets. A few, however, are large. Best known, perhaps, is Midway Airlines, based in Chicago with the hub of its operations being Midway Airport (which was Chicago's major airport before the opening of O'Hare). Started in 1979, the firm grew so quickly that by 1981 it was ranked 28th among U.S. airlines in terms of the number of passengers carried. In 1981 it also earned a small profit. Flying DC-9s, the firm connects Chicago's Midway Airport with Omaha, Kansas City, St. Louis, Minneapolis–St. Paul, Cleveland, Columbus, Detroit, New York (La Guardia), Philadelphia, and Washington, D.C. (National). The company also started service between Chicago and Boston in late 1981, but the major trunk airlines already in the market added more flights, which diminished Midway's market share to the point where it withdrew service in January, 1982.

Within the industry, the new commuter airlines are often called the "upstart airlines." A. Gerald Peters, an airline consultant and

---

[7]Pilots must fly regularly in order to keep their licenses current. Also, hours of flight experience is given heavy weight when one is hiring pilots.

[8]*Air Transport World* (November, 1981), p. 9.

[9]*Chicago Tribune* (August 23, 1981), p. 1 of the business section.

one-time commuter airline executive wrote a scenario that he believes describes the life (and not infrequent death) of a commuter airline firm. His description is reproduced in Figure 7–1.

Traffic statistics for U.S. commuter airlines, published by *Air Transport World*, indicate that in 1981 Ransome (based in Pennsylvania) had the most passengers, with 730,908 boardings. Semo (based in Missouri), which boarded 6,079, had the fewest passengers.[10] Ranging between these two were Air Illinois, Air Virginia, Atlantis, Bar Harbor, Big Sky, Cascade, Chaparral, Chautauqua, Cochise, Coral Air, and on through the alphabet of commuter airlines.

All Cargo and Parcel Express Airlines

Freight is carried on all types of passenger airlines; some trunk airlines have all-cargo planes devoted solely to carrying freight between important markets. The CAB recognizes *all-cargo airlines* as a special category of carrier. Shortly after World War II, a number of airlines that carried freight exclusively were formed, but their ranks have dwindled to the point that Flying Tigers is the sole survivor of the original all-freight carriers. Other air freight companies have more recent origins, with most starting as "commuters" which specialized in freight. Best known of these is Federal Express which provides overnight service for small parcels between several hundred U.S. cities. Other airlines that specialize in carrying air cargo are Summit, Blackhawk, Millers Air Transporters, Pee Dee Air Express, Purolater Sky Courier, etc.

This category of carrier is no longer as exclusive as it once was, since any of these carriers could legally carry passengers, if they cared to. Existing passenger airlines also could decide to specialize in freight. In addition, several large air freight forwarders have acquired their own planes and entered the freight carrier market.

Supplemental (Charter) Carriers

Supplemental carriers (now called "charter" airlines) came into being after World War II when there was a surplus of transport aircraft and trained pilots. At least 150 firms were formed that attempted to survive by carrying passengers and freight on a "charter" basis (meaning the entire plane was contracted out to a single party). For a while, these carriers were called "non-skeds" because of their apparent lack of schedules although, in fact, many of them operated

[10] *Air Transport World* (March, 1982), pp. 84–89.

Development Stage	Time Period	Characteristics
I. Excitement	1st–8th month	Shiny new airplanes, new ramp equipment, attractive offices, excited employees, enthusiastic passengers and travel agents, proud city fathers, beaming owners. A fat treasury, a new route every week. Everyone works long hours, at low pay and loves it ("we have a great future"). Loads of ego trips. Growth. Excitement.
*II. Trouble	3rd–12th month	Dirty airplanes, mechanical problems, late flights, cancellations, frequent schedule changes, customers bitching and complaining; the FAA is everywhere. Piles of lost baggage, irate travel agents, sullen employees (lots of resignations), city fathers are driving—not flying. Owners are frustrated; losses are high; everyone is tired, worn out, complaining about the low pay, working overtime and hating it. Trouble.
*III. Gloom	10th–18th month	Schedules cut, routes dropped, airplanes sold, managers fired, employees laid off, even faster schedule changes ("forget the OAG,† we have to change the schedule now!"). Bills pile up, creditors call, no parts, no raises, no ego, no morale, no overtime. Everyone's looking for a new job. The owners are desperate. Gloom.
IV. Death	12th–24th month	FAA pulls the certificate. IRS padlocks the doors. City fathers say, "I knew they couldn't make it." Bankruptcy. Collapse. Tears. Death.
	OR	
V. Peace	12th–24th month	Planning starts, statistics are prepared, organizational plan instituted, controls installed, marketing begins, fewer schedule changes, passengers return, complaints drop, flights run on time, costs meet revenues, owners relax, and a small profit appears. . . . . peace at last.

*Often an accident may occur at Stage II or III in which case the airline goes directly to Stage IV or V.

†OAG refers to the Official Airline Guide, which lists airline schedules and is used by the travel industry for reference.

Figure 7–1 The Life Cycle of a Commuter Airline: "Aerolinus Commuterus Observed." Source: A. Gerald Peters. Used with permission.

on a scheduled basis. They offered low fares, spartan service, and began attracting large numbers of passengers. Both the CAB and the scheduled air carriers wished to restrict the non-skeds and limit their share of the market. When several non-sked airlines experienced plane crashes, Congress reacted with stricter controls. By 1962, the number of firms was reduced to 30.[11] Supplemental airline carriers were no longer allowed to perform on "schedules" that shadowed the schedules of trunk carriers. For the most part, they had to rely on plane-load quantities of charter business.

The 1960's were fairly prosperous for those supplemental carriers which remained in business. The Department of Defense utilized them extensively for carrying war material and troops to Southeast Asia. The supplemental airlines were allowed to carry tour "groups" organized by tour operators and travel agents who would put together a "package" fare consisting of hotels, a few on-the-ground tours, airport-to-hotel transfers, and air fares. The tour operator would negotiate the price for each part of the "package" and then sell it to various interested groups. Thus, the tour operator provided the retailing function for the supplemental air carriers and filled their planes.

In the 1970's, the supplemental air carriers experienced more intense fare competition from the regulated airlines. The supplemental carriers also carried less military traffic to Southeast Asia as our involvement in the war lessened. By the late 1970's, only six supplemental air carrier firms remained.

Once the domestic airline industry was "deregulated" these firms could function as scheduled airlines; and other airlines could "charter" out equipment for single flights. Hence, today, there is no longer a specific category of supplemental airline.

Air Travel Agents and Freight Forwarders

Airlines have their own salespeople for both freight and passenger service. However, for much of their retail sales activity, they rely upon travel agencies and air freight forwarders. Both travel agencies and air freight forwarders are subject to minimal regulation by the CAB; also, they both usually deal in both domestic and international air transportation.

Travel agencies sell travel services to individuals and groups. The service they provide to travelers is to find desired combinations

---

[11] This early discussion is based on *U.S. Supplemental Air Carriers* (Long Beach: McDonnell Douglas Corporation, Nov. 1968).

of air service, hotel reservations, rental cars, and other travel needs. A travel agent's commission on airline ticket sales is about 7 to 8 percent; and commission on hotel space and car rentals is about 10 percent. The travel agent is not tied to a specific airline and tries to pick the one that best serves the traveler's needs.

There are also "wholesale" travel agents who put together "package" tours, such as "Eleven fun-filled days in Hawaii!" In advance, they tentatively book airline space and hotel rooms. They print brochures and distribute them to both local travel agents for retail sale and to various organizations whose members are likely to travel together. The wholesale travel agent's agreements with hotels and airlines allow for cancellations in case sales are insufficient for the agent to make a profit.

Air freight forwarders perform functions similar to surface forwarders. Airline air freight rates encourage large shipments—there are lower rates per pound for heavier shipments than for light shipments. This encourages the forwarders to scour the market each day, picking up enough small parcels so that they can tender large lots to the airlines and enjoy the lower per-pound rates. At the flight's destination, the forwarder's office will deliver each shipment to its consignee. Again, this relieves the airline from the routine details of the business. Forwarders have no particular loyalty to specific airlines; they deal with those who give them the best combination of flights and rates. However, since airline deregulation, several large forwarders have bought their own fleets of airplanes.

Both travel agents and air freight forwarders assume additional significance as the airline industry is deregulated. If some airlines decide they wish to avoid the retail aspects of their business, they can rely on travel agents and freight forwarders to deal with customers and to fill their planes. Airline deregulation extended directly to air freight forwarders, and they are no longer required to file their tariffs with the CAB.

- A carrier's *tariff* is a document listing his charges for carrying passengers or freight and for performing other services for his customers.

Regulation of the Domestic Airline Industry, 1938–1978

To understand better how deregulation is affecting the domestic airline industry, we should first know what regulation was and how it controlled the industry. Regulatory concepts initially used by the

ICC were followed fairly closely by the CAB, which paid attention to such issues as entry and exit control, adequacy of service, levels of rates, earnings, and specific rates.

Critics of the system of regulating our nation's transportation accused the CAB (as well as the ICC) of acting like cartels. That is, the critics accused the regulatory agencies of giving priority to serving the needs of the industry they were supposed to regulate rather than pursuing the "public interest." The regulatory bodies forgot that the public interest doesn't always coincide with the interests of the regulated carriers. It would be fair to say that for many years the CAB did act to protect "its" industry from many of the rigors of competition.

Nevertheless, under the protection of the CAB, the domestic airline industry progressed in its service to the public. There were technological advances such as the 747, which is 50 to 60 times more productive (in terms of passenger-miles per hour) than the DC-3. Under CAB regulation the number of airports receiving trunk and local service declined,[12] but the development of commuter airlines offset much of this loss. And by many measures, the number of airports with some form of scheduled service increased.

Entry-Exit Control

For many years the CAB had effective control over the number of airline firms. Very few of the small cargo or supplemental airlines formed after World War II survived. The number of trunk airlines in 1938 was 16; by 1978 it was 11. The one segment that did grow during the 1970's was commuter airlines, and the argument could be made that they were allowed only because they served the trunk and local service airlines in two ways: they fed passengers into and out of the larger carriers' systems, and they made it easier for the larger carriers to abandon the obligation to serve small communities.

Exit and entry can also be thought of in terms of points served. For the most part, the CAB allowed trunk and local service carriers to abandon small communities unless the community put up extensive objections. As carriers moved toward larger planes with longer ranges, abandonment of points has been facilitated by the availability of other categories of airlines—flying smaller planes—that are willing and able to continue service to the community in question.

---

[12] In 1955 trunk and local service carriers called at 539 airports in the 48 contiguous states. By 1975, the number declined to 394. See: Paul W. MacAvoy and John W. Snow, editors, *Regulation of Passenger Fares and Competition Among the Airlines* (Washington, D.C.: American Enterprise Institute for Public Policy Research, 1977), p. 84.

The airlines and the CAB often thought in terms of service between city-pairs, or routes. Individual airlines continually sought to "strengthen" their route structures, complementing their purchase of larger aircraft by adding distant cities with large populations (or other trip-generating potential, such as tourists to Hawaii). Simultaneously, they attempted to abandon routes to communities that generated few passengers or of such short distance between airports that the newer aircraft's operating advantages were lost. In the industry's "go-go" decade of the '60's, the CAB was continually adding new routes between various city-pairs, and airlines responded by submitting proposals to serve them. The CAB followed a number of criteria in awarding the new routes; one criteria was to strengthen the weakest carriers (analogous to pro football clubs' draft choice priority being in reverse order of their league standing).

Fares and Fare Levels

Specific fares were originally set in the days of the DC-3 and reflected the DC-3's cost of operations. As the airlines moved to larger equipment, the fare structures did not change and failed to reflect the improved operating efficiencies of the aircraft over longer distances. Since the newer equipment could carry larger loads for longer distances, the airlines found that the excess of revenues over costs in long-haul, heavily-traveled markets was high. At the same time, their costs per passenger for service in and out of small communities or on short hops was very high, and often less than revenues. Fortunately for the industry, overall revenues exceeded costs, and the firms were able to operate at a profit. However, they engaged in a form of cross-subsidy—taking high earnings from the long-haul markets between large cities and using them to offset losses in the small community/short-haul market. The CAB did not discourage this cross-subsidy practice.

As an example of the consequences of cross-subsidization, comparisons were often made between the San Francisco-Los Angeles market and the Boston-Washington, D.C., market, which had many similar characteristics. In the former market, PSA, a California intrastate carrier with cost-based rates and little need to cross-subsidize routes elsewhere, had fares that were about half those in the Boston-Washington, D.C. market, which was under CAB jurisdiction.

Up until about 1970, the overall level of fares was sufficiently high that the industry's needs were satisfied, even though fares rose much less than the overall cost of living. However, early in the 1970's, the rate of increase in traffic growth lessened, and airlines were saddled first with costs of the new jumbo jets and then with higher prices for fuel. Initially, they tried raising all fares; that didn't help much because higher fares discouraged vacation travel. In the late '70's, with the prodding of congressional committees and the CAB, a large number of lower promotional fares were offered to passengers who were willing to settle for slightly less service.

Domestic Airline Deregulation

The domestic airline industry was deregulated in two phases. In late 1977, all-cargo aircraft operations were deregulated, and in late 1978, the remainder of the industry was deregulated. In both instances, the statutes provided for a number of steps that would gradually unfetter the industry over a period of years.

Air Cargo Deregulation—1977

On November 9, 1977, President Carter signed into law a bill that freed all-cargo aircraft operations from CAB regulations. Passenger

- *All-cargo aircraft* operations included operations of the all-cargo airlines and of Federal Express. It also included the freight operations of a few trunk airlines and commuter airlines that had developed sufficient cargo business to permit them to operate some flights for cargo or mail only, without passengers.

operations—and the carriage of cargo aboard passenger-carrying flights—were not covered by this 1977 law. The 1977 law had three basic provisions:

1. For a period of one year (up until November 9, 1978), any certified air carrier that had offered scheduled all-cargo service during 1977 could apply for "grandfather" rights to provide *all-cargo* service. This all-cargo service could be offered at any time and to any place within the 50 states, Puerto Rico, and the Virgin Islands. After November 9, 1978, any firm could become an all-cargo carrier.
2. Any size aircraft could be flown in all-cargo service—a particularly important provision to Federal Express and commuter airlines which up until this time had been under aircraft size restrictions.
3. Airlines could establish whatever freight rates they chose although they could not be unjustly discriminatory. As of March, 1979, air carriers no longer had to file tariffs of freight charges with the CAB.

Passenger Airline Deregulation—1978

Deregulation of all-cargo service, however important, was overshadowed by anticipation that Congress would deregulate the entire domestic airline industry. Early in 1978, the CAB encouraged airlines to engage in fare competition. The airlines did so with vigor and air fare bargains blossomed in the summer of 1978. At the same time, Congress was debating various bills to deregulate the entire industry. A bill was finally enacted and sent to President Carter, who signed it on October 24, 1978. The new law had several major provisions.

1. Airline fares could be increased to keep up with the rate of inflation, plus 5 percent a year, or decreased by up to 50 percent each year. CAB regulation on rates would end in 1983.
2. Airlines were permitted to expand immediately into "dormant" routes, i.e., routes over which the CAB had once approved service but from which the original carrier had withdrawn, leaving no active carrier serving on the route.
3. Through 1981, existing carriers could add service to one entirely new market each year. Also, they could protect one route each year, meaning that no other carrier could enter into competition with them on that specific route. CAB route authority would end in 1981.
4. Carriers were allowed to abandon service in existing markets, although the last carrier serving a particular point will encounter some delays in its attempts to end service. Provisions are available for subsidizing carriers to continue the service, if necessary.
5. Airline industry use of the mutual-aid pact (by which an airline experiencing a strike was reimbursed financially by non-struck carriers whose business had increased because of the first carrier's strike) was severely limited. The federal government also assumed responsibility for reimbursing up to six years former airline employees who were laid off by carriers who had reduced their work force by more than 7.5 percent in any year because of deregulation.
6. The CAB would be abolished in 1985; whatever functions remained would be transferred to other agencies.

The Impact of Airline Deregulation

As was stated in chapter 3, it is difficult to separate the impact of deregulation from that of other factors, such as a sluggish economy.

By any standards and for whatever reason, however, 1981 was a bad year for the U.S. airline industry. Several major airlines, including Braniff, Continental, Eastern, Pan American, and United, had net losses for the year, and profit as a percentage of revenues ranged from about 2 to 6 percent for most other major airlines.

Braniff Airlines went bankrupt in the spring of 1982 and, as of this writing, a few other airlines are considered to be precariously close to bankruptcy, as well. The management of many airlines and many in the financial community believe that the *industry* would be better off if these bankruptcies took place. One trade journal reported in March, 1982, that several airlines were delaying their current equipment acquisitions since they were waiting for a "fire sale" on airplanes as soon as other airlines went bankrupt.[13] There were accusations that a competitor of one of the near-bankrupt lines had engaged in "dirty tricks" which caused a severe, although not fatal, cash squeeze on the troubled airline.[14] Smaller airlines, including the commuters, also are encountering their share of financial difficulties. Many firms, including some listed in the 1980 edition of this book, have disappeared.

In the "olden" (and, to some, "golden") days of CAB protective regulation, one would not have seen as many carriers in such deep financial difficulty. It is possible that deregulation opened the gates to more competition too quickly. Major airlines have not had a chance to react to the route and fare competition offered by both established rivals, as well as the "upstart" commuters. Consider these opening paragraphs in a trade journal article about United Airlines:

> United Airlines is a study in frustration in this, the fourth year since passage of deregulation. Instead of successful headway through rough transitional waters, the company is still floundering in financial losses and appears to lack a consistent strategy.
>
> That isn't to say that the largest U.S. airline hasn't accomplished some minor miracles. It has reduced its size, in both manpower and aircraft fleet; reorganized its management, pared costs, and realigned routes, all in an effort to become more efficient. But, the anticipated profitability that was expected to take only three, perhaps four years, has been delayed by major, uncontrollable factors. . . .
>
> United Chairman and Chief Executive Officer Richard J. Ferris is sitting on a very hot seat. After some initial hesitation, United became an outspoken proponent of deregulation, much to the dismay of its competitors, who feared they would be gobbled up by the giant airline. And Ferris, as United's chief, became the most visible airline proponent, willing to promote the benefits to any who would listen.

[13] *Aviation Week and Space Technology* (March 22, 1982), p. 25.
[14] *Time* (March 22, 1982), p. 52.

Now, as a result of such surprises as a 58-day mechanics' strike, the DC-10 grounding, a recessionary economy, rapid fuel price escalation and, finally, the limits on operations caused by the air controllers' strike, United has had to accept what could be a third losing year in a row. And the fact that some opponents of deregulation are doing better than United doesn't help matters.[15]

Aside from the airlines, one can also look at the effect of airline deregulation upon customers. Professors Stephenson and Vann surveyed a large number of air cargo shippers and found few negative impacts.[16] As for passenger traffic, there has been considerable competition in some markets while in others, usually involving shorter hauls, the fares have remained high and inflexible. For example, the coast-to-coast air fare has dropped to as little as $99 on occasion, while—at the same time—air fares between points on either coast and points within the Midwest were often twice as much. Alert travelers with some flexibility for scheduling have enjoyed many "bargain" rates. Each airline has had its own scheme. Figure 7–2 describes how passengers on American Airlines can earn "points" toward "free" first-class tickets. Note the special incentives to fly during certain periods or on certain routes.

The effects of airline deregulation on smaller communities are difficult to analyze because the "quality" of service has many dimensions. The following excerpts from a newspaper article about changes in air service to La Crosse, Wisconsin, a community of about 50,000 located on the Mississippi River, suggests that deregulation has not been beneficial.

A few years ago when G. Heileman Brewing Co. sales were running at a $500 million a year pace, La Crosse had 18 daily airline flights on Mississippi Valley and North Central airlines.

In 1981, Heileman may be on the verge of becoming a $2 billion company with the acquisition of Milwaukee's Jos. Schlitz Brewing Co.

But while Heileman has been growing, airline service has been shrinking. Mississippi Valley has pulled out of La Crosse and the 18 flights are down to eight, a situation that could affect Heileman employment in La Crosse, according to Russell G. Cleary, the company's chief executive officer.

Earlier this week, the effects of the reduced service became apparent when Cleary said some Heileman departments might be moved to the Milwaukee Schlitz headquarters if a merger between the two companies goes through. Cleary noted the extent of the move would depend on the level of airline service.

[15] *Air Transport World* (January, 1981), pp. 46–54.
[16] Frederick J. Stephenson and John W. Vann, "Deregulation: The Elimination of Air Cargo Tariff Filing Requirements," *Journal of Business Logistics* (March, 1982), pp. 59–72.

More reasons than ever to use A'Advantage.℠

American Airlines is dedicated to keeping AAdvantage the best frequent flier program in the airline industry. So we are pleased to inform you of these AAdvantages from American Airlines.

Special Holiday Bonus trip.

As an AAdvantage member, American is offering you a special bonus. If you travel 7,000 miles or more on American between November 15, 1981 and January 31, 1982 using your AAdvantage number—with a minimum of five flight segments—you'll receive a free First Class round-trip ticket to any destination in American's system! A certificate for your free trip will be sent to you by March 1, 1982 for use any time thereafter.

And when you earn your special AAdvantage Holiday Bonus, you get to keep all the mileage flown so that you can apply it toward a future AAdvantage award.

For more details, contact your Travel Agent or call American Airlines and ask for the AAdvantage desk.

The American/Lufthansa 2-for-1 pass!

Now if you fly American Airlines within the continental U.S., from November 20 to December 31, 1981 inclusive, you will be eligible for a Lufthansa 2-for-1 pass to Germany! The offer lasts from November 20, 1981 through March 31, 1982, except between December 15, 1981 and January 14, 1982. Check with your Travel Agent, an American Airlines representative or Lufthansa for more details.

Get two free First Class tickets at the 75,000-mile level.

As an AAdvantage participant, you are eligible to receive two free First Class round-trip tickets to any American Airlines destination, when you fly 75,000 miles or more with the AAdvantage program. So start taking AAdvantage!

Special double-bonus mileage segments.

Receive double-mileage credit on all flights to and from the following American cities:
December 1, 1981 through January 15, 1982:
- **Harlingen, Texas/Rio Grande Valley**
- **Mobile** and **Huntsville, Alabama**
- **Cancun, Cozumel,** and **Zihuatanejo/Ixtapa, Mexico**
December 1, 1981 through January 31, 1982:
- **Albany**
December 15, 1981 through January 15, 1982:
- **Dallas/Fort Worth** to **San Juan, St. Maarten, Nassau** and **Montego Bay**
- **Miami** to **Montego Bay**
- **Chicago** or **Dallas/Fort Worth** to **Palm Springs**
December 15, 1981 through January 31, 1982:
- **Dallas/Fort Worth** to **Toronto** or **Montreal**
Now through December 15, 1981:
- **Denver**
- **Detroit** to **Phoenix** or **Tucson**
For more information or reservations, contact your Travel Agent or American Airlines.

Figure 7–2   American Airlines Incentives. This was one side of a postcard. Courtesy: American Airlines.

"What we need is good morning and afternoon service from Minneapolis and Chicago," Cleary said Wednesday. "We need to get people in here and get them back out at night."[17]

At the present time, two programs exist to subsidize airline operations at small communities. The first, known as the "Section 406" program, has been in existence since the late 1930's and involves payments to the "local service" category of airlines. In 1980, five carriers—Frontier, Republic West (formerly Hughes Airwest), Ozark, Piedmont, and Republic—received $143 million in subsidies for serving 127 communities. "Section 419," enacted as part of the airline deregulation program in 1978, provides subsidies to the "last" airline serving a community in danger of losing all service. In 1980, 17 commuter airlines received $7.7 million to serve 34 communities.[18] A study of the "Section 419" programs concluded that they "generally have been successful in selecting reliable replacement carriers and preventing lapses in small community service."[19]

[17] *La Crosse Tribune* (August 20, 1981).
[18] *Aviation Week and Space Technology* (February 16, 1981), pp. 29–30.
[19] Arnold I. Havens and David A. Heymsfeld, "Small Community Air Service under the Airline Deregulation Act of 1978," *Journal of Air Law and Commerce* (Spring, 1981), pp. 641–677.

One last observation into deregulation's impact deals with the sizes of aircraft. After the all-cargo deregulation, the many new entrants into the freight market bought all existing used aircraft that could possibly be outfitted to carry air cargo. As for passenger aircraft, the commuter airlines, which have expanded since deregulation, usually fly relatively small, twin-engine, propeller-driven planes. The demand for wide-bodied jets, however, has dropped off because the markets in which they are used are not expanding. In addition, some major airlines are either cancelling orders or asking for delayed deliveries since they lack the ability to pay for the new planes.

Airports and Airways

In domestic aviation the aircraft are usually owned by private parties, either airlines or general aviation aircraft operators. The airports to and from which they operate are typically publicly-owned, and the air navigation system they rely upon while airborne is provided by the federal government.

Airports

There are many types of airports, ranging from sophisticated airports found near major cities to small grass strips looking like no more than hayfields. Heliports, which can accommodate helicopters, can be found on the tops of buildings in large cities. Seaplane bases service seaplanes and amphibious aircraft; these bases are found in areas where conventional landing strips are unavailable.

A conventional all-weather airport capable of handling a medium-size twin-engined aircraft like a DC-3 would need two paved runways, one about 4,500 feet long, the other a cross runway about 3,600 feet long for use when high crosswinds prevent use of the main runway. The main runway would be 100 feet wide. Also needed would be an apron for parking planes; taxiways parallel to the runways and leading to the apron (on which aircraft taxi to and from the hangar freeing the runways for take-offs and landings); a wind cone (or "sock"); a beacon light which identifies the airport at night; and runway lights along and at the ends of runways. Access roads, auto parking, buildings for airport users and their planes, and a few other modest structures would be provided as well.

Land requirements are great, especially off the ends of the runways, where approach paths must be kept clear of obstacles to aircraft flight or the pilot's vision. Ground level noise near take-off paths can be very bothersome, although the noise level varies by size of aircraft and its form of power. Light twin-engine aircraft will produce undesirable noise levels for a quarter mile beyond the runway's end; for a DC-3, this increases to at least a mile, while for a jet of the size used by local service airlines, the distance is one to two miles.[20] Hence, large amounts of land in addition to what is needed for actual runways must be purchased by the airport and kept uninhabited in order to minimize complaints about noise as well as to provide room for airport expansion. (An airport handling large jets would require runways 7,000 to 9,500 feet long, with a corresponding increase in all other dimensions as well.)[21]

Noise in the vicinity of airports continues to be a problem. Most airports were built many years ago, just outside of metropolitan areas. The airports were small and were built to handle the planes of that time which were not very big. Then, everything grew—the population in the immediate vicinity of the airport, the planes, air travel, and air freight. Now, these busy airports are in the middle of heavily-populated areas, and people living near airports are complaining about the noise. In late 1978, it was reported that "people who live within a three-mile radius of the Los Angeles International Airport have a 19 percent higher death rate than people who live six miles away. Most of the difference was in stress-related disease."[22]

Pressures from individuals living near airports have forced flight operations to limited departure and approach paths, often different from the ones that the pilots would prefer to use. Some cities now have "curfews" on flight operations during nighttime hours. Such actions would have an adverse affect on other airports as well, those to or from which flights would not be allowed.

Much of the opposition directed at the Concorde SST aircraft operating into New York's Kennedy airport was because of the noise it generates. The conventional jets that domestic airlines will be buying in the 1980's will come equipped with quieter engines. In a sense, the problem will never be solved since residents living near airports will continue to press for less noise.

Airline airports have passenger terminals capable of handling

---

[20] State Airport Planning: Technical Supplement (Madison: Wisconsin Department of Transportation, 1968), chapter 2. Newer airline aircraft are required to have quieter engines.

[21] Figures given are at sea level. At higher elevations, runways must be longer because the aircraft's landing and take-off distances increase since the air is not as dense.

[22] Time (September 18, 1978), p. 106. See also: "The Airports' Space Squeeze," Business Week (March 29, 1982), pp. 62–66.

TABLE 7–1 Top 20 U.S. Airports—1981
(Passengers Arriving and Departing)

Chicago O'Hare	37,992,151	Honolulu	14,344,225
Atlanta	37,594,073	Washington, D.C. (DCA)	13,870,905
Los Angeles	32,722,534	Houston	11,601,315
New York (JFK)	25,752,719	St. Louis	10,632,429
Dallas/Ft. Worth	25,533,929	Newark	10,181,865
Denver	22,601,877	Pittsburgh	10,112,266
Miami	19,848,593	Seattle	9,194,957
San Francisco	19,848,491	Las Vegas	9,138,268
New York (LGA)	18,146,191	Detroit	9,106,614
Boston	14,827,684	Philadelphia	9,008,529

SOURCE: AOCI

large numbers of passengers, aircraft, and baggage. Table 7–1 ranks the top 20 U.S. airports in terms of passenger arrivals and departures.

The two most modern passenger terminals in the United States are Dulles, serving Washington, D.C., where large bus-like vehicles carry passengers between the parked plane and the terminal; and Dallas-Fort Worth, the major new U.S. airport to open in the 1970's. A cross-section view of one of the Dallas-Fort Worth airport's several identical terminals is shown in Figure 7–3. New airports benefit from the mistakes or oversights at other airports which have had to expand on a piecemeal and panic basis, overcoming the latest bottleneck in parking, docking, ticketing, or baggage handling.

Early airports were developed with private funds; the larger passenger-handling airports were owned by either airlines or aircraft manufacturing companies. The situation changed in the mid-1930's

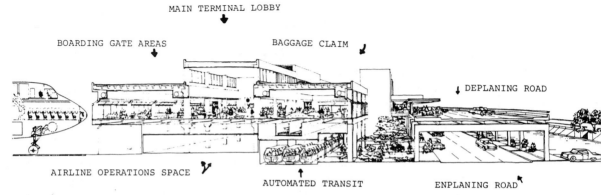

Figure 7–3 Cross-Sectional View of Terminal at Dallas-Fort Worth Airport.
Courtesy: Dallas-Fort Worth Airport Board.

when communities used federal public works programs for airport construction. During World War II many military airfields were built, some of which later reverted to civilian use. The *Federal Airport Act of 1946* established a federal aid program that matched construction funds supplied by local and state interests. In 1970, the federal program was increased, with part of the increased funding coming from user fees paid by both airlines and general aviation.

Slightly over 3,000 airports in the United States are paved and lighted, and nearly all of these are in public ownership. Another 2,000 are publicly-owned but lack paving, lighting, or both. Between 6,000 and 7,000 airports and air strips are privately-owned, and most of them are unlighted and unpaved. Only 500 U.S. airports have control towers which are manned by FAA personnel.

Public airports are owned and operated by city governments or special airport districts or boards. They attempt to recover their costs from the users of the airports. In very general terms, the half-dozen or so "busiest" airline airports cover all of their costs. Principal revenue sources for them are landing fees and space rental to airlines and concessionaires in and around the terminal building. Each passenger who uses the airport as well as those "meeters and greeters" present at his or her arrival are charged in a number of ways to raise funds to meet the airport's costs. Aside from these few very busy airports, most public airports do not cover costs. Most of them strive to meet "operating" expenses but cover little or none of their fixed, or capital, costs.

- Public agency budgets have two components: an *operating costs budget* and a *capital costs budget*. Both usually cover a 12-month period. Operating costs include personnel costs, rent, supplies, and equipment with a relatively short useful life. Capital costs are investments in land, buildings, and equipment with a longer useful life.

Public airports usually enter into a contract with a fixed base operator, who sells, services, and leases out aircraft. The contract with the fixed base operator would require payment of rent, some percentage of gross revenue, and a cent or two on each gallon of fuel sold. If an airline uses the airport, it will be charged rental for counter and office space within the terminal, and "landing fees" for each time one of its aircraft uses the airport.

The Airway System

The most elementary pilot rating licenses a general aviation pilot to fly only under conditions of clear visibility ("VFR" conditions).

- VFR stands for visual flight rules, or "clear weather," flying. *IFR* stands for instrument flight rules, which take effect whenever there is not clear visibility. A pilot needs to be "instrument-rated" to fly during IFR conditions.

More sophisticated pilot ratings allow the pilot to fly under conditions of limited visibility, relying on contact with land-based communications stations for guidance. Aircraft used for instrument flying require considerable additional air navigation equipment.

Figure 7–4 depicts the air navigation system. The components of an air navigation system are: control towers at specific airports; regional traffic control centers, which control the operations of airborne aircraft that have just taken off from or are waiting to land at an airport within the region; and en-route navigation aids, which are a nationwide network of very-high-frequency radio stations—called "Omni's," for *omni-directional*—emitting unique signals which allow pilots flying on instrument-equipped planes to determine their true location. (The pilot does this by determining his compass direction to *two different* radio signals, whose stations are shown on a flight chart, or map.) Nearly all of these services are provided by the Federal Aviation Administration.[23] Two additional FAA services are to provide "weather briefings," which allow a departing pilot to phone and learn of the weather conditions along his intended flight path, and a "flight plan" surveillance service. Before departing, the pilot telephones an FAA station and tells them his destination and intended arrival time. Upon reaching his destination, he must again call the FAA and "close" his flight plan, meaning he has landed safely. If he does not do so within a certain time, search procedures are begun.

One of the results of the air traffic controllers' strike and subsequent dismissal was a focusing of public attention on our nation's air traffic control system. The Reagan Administration has decided to install a much more highly automated system which will require a smaller number of controllers to operate.[24]

A serious problem in much of the nation is airspace congestion above metropolitan areas, especially on low visibility days when airline and other aircraft saturate the sky in holding patterns, waiting for their turn to land. On clear days there is less of a problem because

---

[23] Location of FAA navigational aids are usually justified on some form of activity count. Sometimes, a state, local airport, or private firm—an airline or general aviation user—will build and maintain some automated signaling device or landing aid at a locality where it is needed, but not justified by FAA criteria.

[24] *Business Week* (January 18, 1982), pp. 100–101.

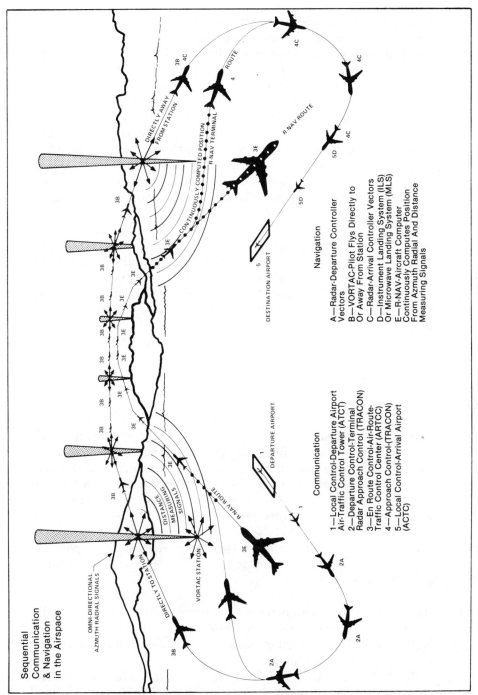

Figure 7–4 Air Traffic Control Sequencing. Courtesy: *Management Focus* (July–August, 1977), copyright Peat, Marwick, Mitchell & Co.

airports can handle more departures and arrivals per hour since it is not necessary to "guide" an arriving pilot down through layers of clouds to a point where he can see the runway. At the nation's busiest airline airports, the number of airline flights that can be scheduled for any one-hour period is limited by the airport's ability to handle traffic under conditions of restricted visibility. Figure 7–5 shows the pattern of scheduled airline operations at the major Los Angeles airport, which for several hours each day is operated close to its theoretical capacity for IFR conditions. Over 87 percent of its operations are by scheduled carriers. General aviation must be handled during off-peak periods. This limits the usefulness of the airport for transfers of passengers between airline and general aviation aircraft.

There are conflicts between the airlines and general aviation pilots as to who should obtain priority to use the air navigation system. There are also disagreements as to who benefits the most and who should pay. Most of the costs of the air navigation system have little to do with the size of a plane. (This is in contrast to airport costs, where larger planes require distinctly more expensive facilities.)

General Aviation Flying

General aviation includes all aviation except scheduled commercial airlines' activities and military flights. Commercial airlines and general aviation have a relationship that is both complementary and competitive. They often must share space in the air or on the runway; commercial airlines feel that, because they are carrying more passengers, their operations deserve priority. At one time, general aviation operators retorted that highway rules gave no preference to vehicles with more passengers. However, they have dropped that argument as special lanes and ramps have been set aside for buses and car pools.

Just under 80 percent of the aircraft used in general aviation are single-engine piston; 15 percent are multi-engine piston; the remainder are either helicopters or large conventional turbo-prop and turbojet aircraft. The larger, more expensive general aviation aircraft are typically flown more hours per year.

Table 7–2 is based on an FAA survey of general aviation activity conducted at 250 airports for two days during 1975. The left-hand

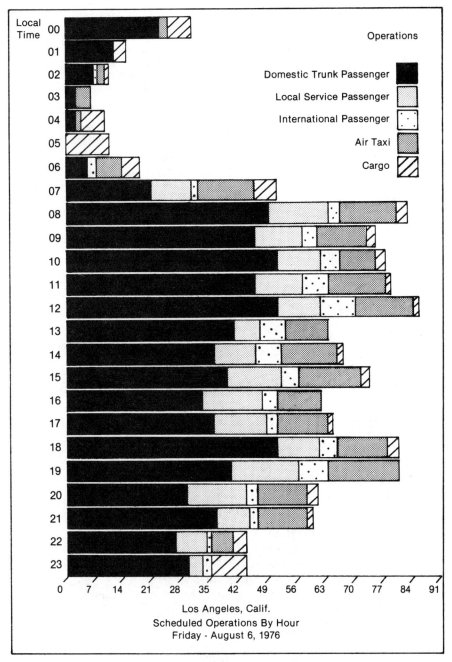

Figure 7–5 Scheduled Operations by Hour at Los Angeles Airport on Friday, August 6, 1976. The "air taxi" is similar to a commuter airline. "Scheduled operations" refers to the number of departures and arrivals. Source: *Profiles of Scheduled Air Carrier Departure and Arrival Operations for Top U.S. Airports* (Washington, D.C.: Federal Aviation Administration, 1976).

TABLE 7–2   General Aviation Aircraft Use

Itinerant (Cross-Country) Flight and Aircraft Use				
Aircraft Use	Average Flight Time* (minutes)	Average Flight Distance* (nautical miles)	Average Seats Available	Average Seats Occupied
Personal	82	173	4.0	2.5
Business	79	205	5.0	2.5
Executive	76	297	8.1	4.3
Commuter Air Carrier	47	134	10.1	5.5
Air Taxi	68	186	5.8	3.0
Instructional	58	102	3.5	1.9
Aerial Application	81	75	2.0	1.5
Industrial/Special	84	131	3.6	1.7
Other (research/development, demonstration, sport parachuting, etc.)	68	147	5.0	2.2
Overall	76	186	5.0	2.8

SOURCE: *1975 General Aviation Activity Survey* (Washington, D.C.: FAA, September 1976).

*Between takeoff and landing

column shows several categories of general aviation flying, as defined for that survey. Explanations of these categories follow:

Personal flying. The pilot of the plane is flying for some nonbusiness reason, such as going with some friends to a ski resort.

Business flying. The pilot and passengers, if any, are flying for a specific purpose, for example, a consulting engineer on his or her way to meet with clients.

Executive flying. The pilot is a professional pilot; his passengers are traveling on business, and the plane is owned by a corporation which uses it to carry personnel.

Commuter air carriers. These are the commuter airlines discussed earlier in this chapter. At the time of the survey, they were considered as a general aviation use.

Air taxi. A plane, often owned by the airport's fixed based operator, that is rented out on a single-trip basis to one or more passengers.

Instructional. This is flight instruction, i.e., people learning to fly.

Aerial application. This is crop dusting.

Industrial/Special uses. These are applications for which an airplane is ideally suited such as aerial photography; pipeline or power line patrol (flying at low speed to look for damage); or using helicopters as mobile cranes.

Table 7–2 deals only with itinerant (from one airport to another airport) flights which accounted for only 30 percent of the general aviation activity at the airports surveyed. Seventy percent of flights were "local" which meant the plane returned to the airport from which it departed without intermediate stops. The reason for this is that many flights are for instructional purposes.

The data on itinerant flights in Table 7–2 were also grouped according to the size of the airplane. The average distances of one-way itinerant flights, by size of plane were as follows: single-engine piston, one-three seats, 104 nautical miles; single-engine piston, four seats and over, 166 nautical miles; multi-engine piston, 228 nautical miles; turboprop, 274 nautical miles; turbo-jet, 481 nautical miles; and helicopter, 102 nautical miles.[25]

Business and Executive Flying

Business flying is conducted by individuals pursuing their own trades or professions who also are qualified pilots. They own or rent planes and use them in a manner similar to autos. Veterinarians use small planes to make "house calls" at various ranches. Salespeople find that use of a private aircraft increases the radius of the market area they can reach and also increases the number of hours they can spend in "face-to-face" contact with customers. Accurate statistics on business flying are difficult to obtain since individuals who enjoy flying try to justify their aircraft's expenses on the basis of business use. Executive flying is conducted by conventional business firms which own fleets of planes and employ professional pilots to fly them:

> . . . more than half of the nation's top 1000 industrial firms (such as General Electric, IBM, Xerox and Mobil Oil) have found good reason for operating their own aircraft—everything from modest piston-powered planes to multi-million-dollar jets outfitted with air-to-ground telephones, beds, pull-down conference tables and other in-flight "necessities."[26]

The principal purpose for these aircraft is corporate travel to and between points that do not receive scheduled airline service. Most companies require their executive personnel to indicate why it is not

[25] *1975 General Aviation Activity Survey* (Washington, D.C.: FAA, September, 1976) p. 20. A nautical mile is 6,076 feet.

[26] "The Corporate Jet Set," *San Francisco Chronicle* (June 1, 1978). The article indicated "more than 50,000 business aircraft now fly the corporate skies of America—up from 35,000 in 1972." See also: "Future for Small-Plane Sales Seems Bright As Companies Continue to Enlarge Fleets," *The Wall Street Journal* (August 4, 1978), p. 26.

possible or practical to use scheduled airline service for a particular trip before allowing them to use the company plane. General aviation becomes more advantageous when a number of employees are making the same trip (although company policy sometimes prohibits certain combinations of high-level executives to be on the same flight).[27] Some firms operate the equivalent of their own scheduled air taxi service to and from trunk airline airports. The firm's small plane may leave its home community each morning at 7 A.M., carrying employees who need to make flight connections at the trunk airport (or have business in the city near the trunk airport). During the day, the plane may be used for other company business and late in the afternoon it returns to the trunk airport and collects employees who have flown in on various airlines and returns them home. This combines several flights into one.

Corporate aviation has certain elements of luxury and has sometimes been the focus of embarrassing questions at stockholders' meetings. As a result, the majority of firms with corporate fleets "assume a low profile," and few of their planes carry corporate markings.

Summary

Aviation is a development of this century. Domestic airline operations began in the 1920's, but it was not until the introduction of the Douglas DC-3 in 1935 that the industry developed its present-day characteristics. World War II had a vast impact on aviation, in terms of developing equipment, training large numbers of pilots, and producing large numbers of aircraft which were declared surplus at the War's end. The jet-powered aircraft was also introduced during World War II.

Jet aircraft were introduced to the airlines during the 1950's. "Jumbo" jets, seating as many as 490 passengers, were introduced in the late 1960's. At that time, the airlines were competing in terms of service only and felt that they needed the jumbo models. As a result, they overbought aircraft. Early in the 1970's, passenger growth slowed, and several of the airlines were in precarious financial condition. Gradually, the growth in airline passenger travel filled the empty planes. In the late 1970's, the CAB and Congress deregulated the industry. The CAB itself is destined for elimination in 1985. In part because of deregulation, many airlines are losing money.

[27] This same prohibition would apply to airlines flights. See: *Business Aviation Practices* (New York: The National Industrial Conference Board, Inc., 1970). The reason for these restrictions is to protect a company from sudden loss of all its leadership.

There are several categories of air carriers. Initially, Pan Am was the nation's only international carrier, but now many trunks and local service airlines have some international operations. Trunk airlines were formed before World War II and have become the nation's major airlines, flying large numbers of passengers long distances. Local service carriers were created after World War II and initially were known as "feeders" since it was their job to feed passengers from small airports to the trunk line carriers at major airports. In the 1960's, the local service carriers wanted to buy jets, which meant that they would have to drop service at some of the smaller airports where jets could not operate. Communities lost the local service carriers' service, but in most communities this was assumed by a new form of carrier, known as a commuter airline.

General aviation serves those many thousands of airports that do not receive scheduled airline service. Small general aviation aircraft are propeller driven, carry two passengers, and cost about the same as large autos. Some business jets operate at the same speeds as airline aircraft. Owners of business aircraft usually use them for flights between areas not connected by scheduled airline service. Other business uses of general aviation include pilot training, crop dusting, and aerial photography. While general aviation complements airline operations, the two conflict in areas where airspace congestion is a problem. Extremely busy airports schedule airline flights throughout the desirable hours of the day, leaving no times available for general aviation aircraft.

Questions for Discussion and Review

1. Describe the development of U.S. domestic aviation up until World War II.

2. What influence did World War II have on commercial developments in aviation?

3. What changes were caused by the trunk airlines' introduction of jumbo (wide-bodied) jet aircraft in the late 1960's?

4. What is general aviation?

5. List and discuss the various categories of airline firms.

6. How do trunk airlines differ from local service airlines?

7. What market is served by commuter airlines? Do you think they are today's "local service" carriers? Why or why not?

8. Discuss the impact of deregulation on the commuter airline industry.

9. Figure 7–1 examines *AeroLinus Commuterus Observed*. Is this the Latin name of an exotic bird? Discuss.

10. What are the similarities between travel agents and air freight forwarders? Why do airlines encourage these businesses?

11. Discuss regulation of the domestic airline industry from 1938 until 1977.

12. What are the provisions of the 1978 law that deregulated the domestic airline passenger industry?

13. Why is it difficult to analyze the effects of deregulation in the airline industry?

14. Discuss major changes that deregulation has brought to the airline industry.

15. Do you believe airline deregulation was a good idea? Defend your answer.

16. Discuss airline passenger subsidy programs of the federal government. Do you believe these subsidies are prudent expenditures of federal funds? Why?

17. List the features and facilities at a modern airport.

18. Who is the fixed-based operator? What are his functions?

19. How does the domestic air navigation system function?

20. For what purposes are general aviation aircraft flown?

Additional Chapter References

Allen, Benjamin J., Roger D. Stover, and Leslie A. Cavarra, "The Capital Market Effects of Airline Deregulation," *Transportation Journal* (Spring, 1981), pp. 73–78.

Allen, Benjamin J. and David B. Vellenga, "Airline Deregulation and its Impact on Air Service to Selected Midwestern States," *Annual Proceedings of the Transportation Research Forum* (1980), pp. 136–146.

Cunningham, Lawrence F., Frank W. Davis, Jr., and Benjamin Tabor, "The Impact of Regulatory Reform and Other Uncertainties on the Airline Stocks: An Analysis of Recent Investor Sentiment," *Annual Proceedings of the Transportation Research Forum* (1980), pp. 157–164.

Dick, G. William, "National Airport System Plan Entry Criteria for General Aviation Airports," *Annual Proceedings of the Transportation Research Forum* (1979), pp. 481–487.

Ellison, Anthony P., "The Structural Change of the Airline Industry Following Deregulation," *Transportation Journal*, (Spring, 1982), pp. 58–69.

Glenn, C. H., "Energy for Air Transportation in the 1980's," *The Logistics and Transportation Review*, Vol. 17, No. 2 (1981), pp. 143–152.

Hendrickson, Hildegard R., and Craig L. Mathison, "Concentration in the Air Freight Forwarding Industry," *Transportation Journal* (Summer, 1976), pp. 58–62.

Hulet, John, and Gordon P. Fisher, "An Isolation-Usage Index for Rational Allocation of Air Service to Small Communities," *Annual Proceedings of the Transportation Research Forum* (1981), pp. 239–247.

Hunsakes, James Kirk, "The Changing Shape of America's Airline Industry: An Analysis of the Deregulation Strategies of Five Airlines," *Annual Proceedings of the Transportation Research Forum* (1981), pp. 449–456.

Jampolsky, Robin, "Fixed-Wing Aircraft and the Resource Industry—A Human Resources Issue," *Annual Proceedings of the Transportation Research Forum* (1981), pp. 665–676.

Jones, J. Richard, and Julie A. Stratford, "The Hidden Impact of Airline Deregulation: The Case of the Travel Agent," *Annual Proceedings of the Transportation Research Forum* (1980), pp. 165–171.

Karam, Gregory L., "Night Coach Fares and Airport Delays: A Fresh Look," *Transportation Journal* (Summer, 1978), pp. 33–39.

La Mond, A. M., "An Evaluation of Intrastate Airline Regulation in California," *The Bell Journal of Economics* (Autumn, 1976), pp. 641–657.

Rose, Warren, "Three Years After Airline Passenger Deregulation in the United States: A Report Card on Trunkline Carriers," *Transportation Journal* (Winter, 1981), pp. 51–58.

Stephenson, Frederick J., and Frederick J. Beier, "The Effects of Airline Deregulation on Air Service to Small Communities," *Transportation Journal* (Summer, 1981), pp. 54–62.

Taneja, Nawal K., *The Commercial Airline Industry: Managerial Practices and Policies* (Lexington, Mass.: Lexington Books, 1976).

Thornton, Robert L., "Channel Structure Changes and Passenger Air Deregulation," *Annual Proceedings of the Transportation Research Forum* (1981), pp. 285–293.

Voorhees, Roy D., and John Coppett, "New Competition for the Airlines," *Transportation Journal* (Summer, 1981), pp. 78–85.

Williamson, Kenneth C., and Lawrence F. Cunningham, "Commuter Air Carriers and Federal Equipment Loan Guarantees: History Repeating Itself?" *Annual Proceedings of the Transportation Research Forum* (1981), pp. 230–238.

Wyckoff, D. Daryl, and David H. Maister, *The Domestic Airline Industry* (Lexington, Mass.: Lexington Books, 1977).

Case 7–1   Mayday Air Express Case

After air cargo deregulation in 1977, Mayday Air Express, a small commuter airline flying between St. Louis and Springfield, Missouri, expanded rapidly into an overnight air parcel service. By 1983, it was connecting Atlanta, Boston, Chicago, Denver, Detroit, Houston, Los Angeles, Miami, Minneapolis/St. Paul, St. Louis, and

San Francisco. Trucks would pick up parcels in each city during the afternoon, where they would be loaded aboard small jets which would depart between 6 P.M. and 9 P.M. (depending upon time zone) and fly to St. Louis where they arrived between 11 P.M. and midnight (St. Louis time) and be completely unloaded. While the planes were being serviced and refueled, all the parcels would be routed through the terminal, re-sorted, and then loaded aboard the planes which would return to the other 11 cities, arriving by dawn. The parcels would then be delivered, by truck, in the morning. At noon, they would start picking up outbound packages again, and the cycle would be repeated.

St. Louis was the "hub" of the operation, and routes to and from St. Louis were "spokes." Through careful planning and selective marketing, Mayday was able to have fairly balanced loads in and out. Before arrival of the inbound planes, the destination of all parcels was known, and in case more than a full load of freight was destined for one city, either loads could be reshuffled on several planes, requiring them to make two stops the following morning; or else a reserve plane would be called into service. However, over 99 percent of the time, the inbound and outbound loads were sufficiently balanced that the same plane could be used both to and from St. Louis.

Mayday's management was debating whether to install a satellite terminal at Denver. Terminal rental and operation there would cost $500 per night (although this would be slightly offset by savings of $200 per night at St. Louis). The proposed system would have planes from Los Angeles, San Francisco, and Seattle land at Denver where the freight they were carrying would be sorted into five categories: freight for (a) Denver, (b) Los Angeles, (c) San Francisco, (d) Seattle, and (e) St. Louis and all other points which would be served through the St. Louis terminal. Freight in category (e) would be loaded aboard a much larger jet, which could carry over four times as much freight as the jets Mayday was presently using, but which cost three times as much per mile to operate. This large jet would fly from Denver to St. Louis, arriving just after midnight and would discharge all of its freight, which would then move through the St. Louis terminal and be added to the loads of planes bound for Atlanta, Boston, Chicago, etc. The large jet would take on freight at St. Louis which was destined for Denver, Los Angeles, San Francisco, and Seattle. It would fly to Denver, where the freight would be placed aboard the three jets which would carry it to the West Coast cities, and aboard trucks for delivery within Denver.

In terms of scheduling, the proposal was feasible. It would allow for later departure times at a few markets, as well as earlier delivery times the next morning, in others. In two markets, the scheduling changes were believed to be disadvantageous, although not seriously so.

The small jets used by Mayday cost $1.00 per mile to fly; the large jet proposed for the Denver-St. Louis shuttle would cost $3.00 per mile. Case Figure 7–1–1 shows the air-mile distances between the various points served by Mayday Air Express.

Question One: What are the nightly costs of flying small jets on the present system?

Question Two: Based on information given, does the satellite terminal at Denver seem to be feasible? Why?

Question Three: Assume that Mayday opened the satellite terminal in Denver, but after a few months, because of growth, the terminal in St. Louis was becoming congested. What is the next city the company presently serves that should be handled through the Denver terminal, i.e., transferred from the St. Louis terminal? Why?

Question Four: Assume that the Denver hub is now in operation. However, the lease on the building Mayday uses at St. Louis to transfer freight between its flights will expire at the year's end. Mayday's management wants to know the costs of moving the main transfer point from St. Louis to Detroit, where rents are very cheap because of the depressed economy. What are the nightly flying costs of a two-terminal (Denver and Detroit) system with a large jet shuttling between Denver and Detroit, with small jets connecting Denver with Seattle, San Francisco, and Los Angeles; and small jets connecting Detroit with Chicago, Houston, Minneapolis/St. Paul, St. Louis, Boston, Atlanta, and Miami? Ignore costs of operating the terminal(s).

Question Five: This is a continuation of Question Four. Assume instead that the St. Louis transfer operation is shifted to Chicago. What are the nightly flying costs of a two-terminal system (Denver and Chicago) with a large jet shuttling between Denver and Chicago, with small jets connecting Denver with Seattle, San Francisco, and Los Angeles; and small jets connecting Chicago with Detroit, Houston, Minneapolis/St. Paul, St. Louis, Boston, Atlanta, and Miami?

Question Six: What other information would be useful to Mayday's managers as they attempt to determine the best number and locations of terminals?

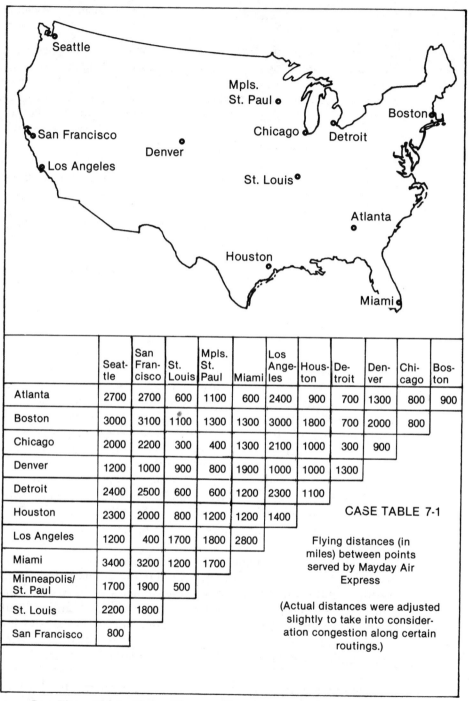

	Seat-tle	San Fran-cisco	St. Louis	Mpls. St. Paul	Miami	Los Ange-les	Hous-ton	De-troit	Den-ver	Chi-cago	Bos-ton
Atlanta	2700	2700	600	1100	600	2400	900	700	1300	800	900
Boston	3000	3100	1100	1300	1300	3000	1800	700	2000	800	
Chicago	2000	2200	300	400	1300	2100	1000	300	900		
Denver	1200	1000	900	800	1900	1000	1000	1300			
Detroit	2400	2500	600	600	1200	2300	1100				
Houston	2300	2000	800	1200	1200	1400					
Los Angeles	1200	400	1700	1800	2800						
Miami	3400	3200	1200	1700							
Minneapolis/ St. Paul	1700	1900	500								
St. Louis	2200	1800									
San Francisco	800										

CASE TABLE 7-1

Flying distances (in miles) between points served by Mayday Air Express

(Actual distances were adjusted slightly to take into consideration congestion along certain routings.)

Case Figure 7-1-1 Flying Distances Between Points Served by Mayday Air Express.

Case 7–2   Global Airlines Case

Peter Crosland was vice-president for air cargo with Global Airlines, Inc., a Dallas-based carrier which operated on both domestic and international routes. In 1977 domestic air cargo was deregulated; in 1978 domestic passenger service was deregulated, and IATA abandoned, for a while, its international airline rate-making activities. The net result of all this deregulation was that Global Airlines (and its competitors) could no longer internally subsidize losing operations with excess earnings from other operations (or routes). The reason was that, because of relaxed rules on entry, a competing carrier would be attracted into routes where Global's rates—and revenues—were higher than average.

Global's management decided that it wanted to place all of its stations, offices, and other activities on a "profit center" basis. This meant that each profit center was responsible for collecting receipts that were greater than its allocated costs. The performance of each manager would be monitored, and he or she would be rewarded according to the ability to earn "profits." Intra-company transactions had to be handled as purchases by one office from another. Care would be exercised to ensure that intra-firm charges for services and materials would be no higher than those of outside vendors.

A related problem was that Global was contemplating the purchase of several jumbo jets which had been used by Braniff Airlines. These planes were to have their main decks altered. They would, then, have removable seats and a movable bulkhead so that the main deck could be in an all-passenger, an all-freight, or various combinations of seat and cargo configurations. Before passenger deregulation, passenger fares were sufficiently high that passengers were always considered to be higher priority than freight. Since deregulation, some passenger fares were so low that it was not clear—to Crosland, at least—that the airline benefited from dumping freight in order to carry passengers paying very low promotional fares.

On Thursday, Crosland attended a staff meeting with several other vice-presidents and the firm's controller where more heat than light was generated. In the discussion several points—all valid—were made, although little agreement was reached. Some of the points made were:

▲ Most cargo moved on passenger flights, but some moved on all-cargo planes.
▲ Every night Global repositioned several planes from the West Coast back to the East Coast so they could be placed into pas-

senger service early the next morning. (The East Coast is three time zones ahead of the West.) These planes, being repositioned, carried no passengers—in order to avoid cabin service costs—but they always carried freight. At holiday times, when other night flights were filling, these planes would also carry passengers on their "repositioning" flight.

▲ Sometimes a plane's cargo space would "cube-out" (meaning the space would fill before the weight capacity would be reached) while most of the time the plane would "weigh out" first. This varied by model of plane and by season since some agricultural products, such as lettuce or cut flowers, were bulky.

▲ On long flights, the weight of fuel, rather than of passengers and their baggage, would displace the plane's freight-carrying capability.

▲ Passenger and freight movements fluctuated independently of each other by route, season, and time of day.

▲ At some of Global's smaller stations, the same personnel handled both passengers and freight, while at large stations the functions were separated.

▲ Opinions differed concerning strategies for adding new flights. One strategy was to serve as many additional points (airports) as possible. The other was to increase the number of flights in certain existing airport to airport markets in order to become the best-known carrier in those specific markets.

Question One: Assume you work for Global and are told to allocate costs between passenger and freight operations at a small airport terminal where the same personnel handle both passengers and freight. How would you go about doing this?

Question Two: Assume you work for Global and are told to allocate costs between passenger and freight operations of Global Flight 703, which flies daily from Dallas to New Orleans, carrying both passengers and freight. How would you go about doing this?

Question Three: How do you think Global Airlines should go about determining whether its air cargo operations are profitable?

Question Four: In situations where needs for passenger service and air cargo conflict, how should the conflict be resolved?

Question Five: If the profit center concept is adopted by Global Airlines' management, on what basis should air cargo operations be considered responsible for (1) its use of all-cargo planes and (2) its space on passenger flights?

Question Six: The case mentions two strategies for adding flights. One is to add service to as many additional airports as possible; the second is to add more flights in existing airport to airport markets with the goal of becoming the best-known (possibly dominant) carrier. List and discuss the reasons why cargo salespeople might prefer a different strategy than passenger salespeople.

A lock and dam, built by the U.S. Army Corps of Engineers, at Willow Island on the Ohio River, near Marietta, Ohio, and Parkersburg, West Virginia. The lock is 110 feet wide and 1,200 feet long; it will lift the entering barge about 20 feet.

Photo courtesy U.S. Army Corps of Engineers, Huntington District.

8 Domestic Water Carriers

Subsidy. The very word strikes a sour note for most participants in the free enterprise system. Most who take part in the free enterprise system say that subsidies should only be granted for brief periods of time in order to aid a necessary industry's initial development, or for the performance of necessary public services that otherwise would not be performed.

One industry looks on the question of subsidy differently. It regards subsidy as its natural right.

That industry is made up of the nation's inland water carriers—the barge industry.

ASSOCIATION OF AMERICAN RAILROADS
Background Report, February 25, 1981

The carriage of Alaskan oil is reserved for American tankers which have been constructed without a building differential subsidy. This has meant that about five million dwt. of U.S. flag vessels have been gainfully employed carrying Prudhoe Bay oil from Valdez, the terminal at the end of the Trans-Alaska pipeline, to other U.S. ports. If these ships had been out in the "real" world, it is doubtful if profits would have been at even half the level currently being obtained.

Lloyd's Shipping Economist
July, 1980

Introduction

In terms of technology, water transportation dates from ancient times. Even prior to the American Revolution, much of the trade and commerce between the 13 colonies was carried on small ships which traveled up and down the Atlantic Coast. Early in the nineteenth century, improvements were made along some of the rivers leading to the Atlantic so that they could carry waterborne commerce, and by 1850 much of the United States east of the Mississippi River was served by an elaborate network of barge canals. These are shown on Figure 8–1. Many were constructed before the railroads; others were built later to compete directly with the rails. They did not fare well competing with railroads because many of the railroads' business practices were aimed directly at driving the water carriers out of business. By the end of the nineteenth century, domestic water transportation had virtually disappeared, except for that on the Great Lakes. Not until the 1930's did inland waterways again begin to flourish. Several things happened at the same time to revive the inland waterway transportation system: massive federal improve-

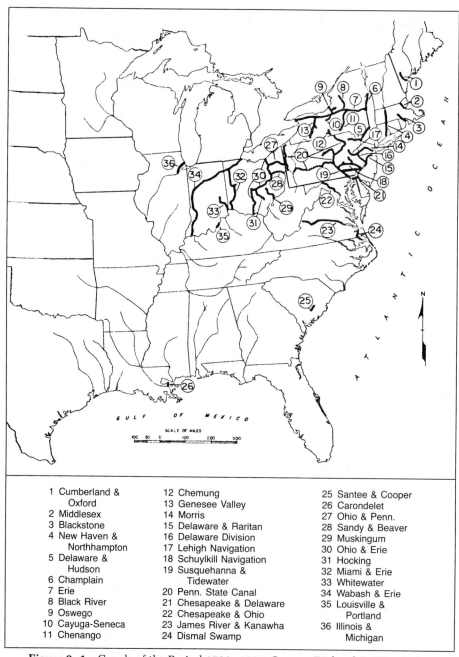

1 Cumberland & Oxford	12 Chemung	25 Santee & Cooper
2 Middlesex	13 Genesee Valley	26 Carondelet
3 Blackstone	14 Morris	27 Ohio & Penn.
4 New Haven & Northhampton	15 Delaware & Raritan	28 Sandy & Beaver
	16 Delaware Division	29 Muskingum
5 Delaware & Hudson	17 Lehigh Navigation	30 Ohio & Erie
	18 Schuylkill Navigation	31 Hocking
6 Champlain	19 Susquehanna & Tidewater	32 Miami & Erie
7 Erie		33 Whitewater
8 Black River	20 Penn. State Canal	34 Wabash & Erie
9 Oswego	21 Chesapeake & Delaware	35 Louisville & Portland
10 Cayuga-Seneca	22 Chesapeake & Ohio	
11 Chenango	23 James River & Kanawha	36 Illinois & Michigan
	24 Dismal Swamp	

Figure 8–1   Canals of the Period 1786–1851. Source: Richard G. Waugh, Jr., *Canal Development in Early America* (Fort Belvoir, Virginia: Board of Engineers for Rivers and Harbors).

ments to the Tennessee and Mississippi Rivers which included dams for flood control and power generation, and locks for passage of barges; a government owned and operated barge line (sold in 1953); and enforcement of laws on the books aimed at railroad predatory practices.

This chapter deals with domestic water transportation operating in several different navigational systems. Each uses different vessels according to type of navigation and the type of traffic. *Inland water carriers* are barges operating in the Mississippi River basin, basins to the east, and in a few other areas which will be listed subsequently.

- A *river basin* is a specific river, all other rivers and streams which flow into it, and the land area it drains.

Great Lakes carriers operate in the Great Lakes system, although they sometimes navigate down the St. Lawrence River to the point where it reaches the ocean. *Intracoastal* (along one coastline, such as the Gulf Coast) and *intercoastal* (between two coasts) *carriers* operate between various U.S. ports in the contiguous 48 states and use the ocean(s) as their waterway. *Non-contiguous domestic* carriers operate between the 48 states and Alaska, Hawaii, Puerto Rico, or Guam and other U.S. territories.

Statistics indicate that both Great Lakes shipping and domestic ocean shipping are not growing, while inland waterways transportation is. According to the Transportation Association of America, in 1939, Great Lakes shipping moved 76 billion ton-miles, accounting for 14 percent of all domestic ton-mileage. In 1980, Great Lakes shipping totaled 113 billion ton-miles, which was only 5 percent of all domestic ton-mileage. Domestic ocean commerce was estimated to be 242 billion ton-miles in 1939, but only 218 billion ton-miles in 1976. Freight carried on the inland waterways system has grown. In 1939 only 20 billion ton-miles, representing less than 4 percent of all domestic ton-mileage, was carried. By 1980 the inland water carriers handled 307 billion ton-miles of freight, 12 percent of the nation's total.[1]

Table 8–1 shows the number of tons of cargo carried by the inland waterways, the Great Lakes, and the domestic ocean carriers in

- *Tons*, rather than ton-miles, is sometimes a more meaningful comparative measure of waterborne commerce because of the

---

[1] *Transportation Facts & Trends*, 1978, and quarterly supplements (Washington, D.C.: Transportation Association of America, 1978 and 1979).

TABLE 8–1   U.S. Domestic Waterborne Commerce—1979
(in Millions of Tons)

The Inland Waterways System		
1. Waterways in the northeastern U.S. and along the Atlantic Intercoastal Waterway	129	
2. Waterways along the Gulf of Mexico	119	
3. Waterways in the Mississippi River and the Ohio River systems	317	
4. California waterways	5	
5. Waterways in the Pacific Northwest	47	
6. Other	6	
		623
The Great Lakes System (Commerce between U.S. Great Lakes ports only)*		151
Domestic Ocean Commerce		
1. Intercoastal (via Panama Canal)	4	
2. Coastwise (between mainland Ocean ports but not moving through the Panama Canal)	163	
3. Noncontiguous trade (between the mainland U.S. and Alaska, Hawaii, Puerto Rico, the Virgin Islands, etc.)	147	
		314
		1,088

SOURCE: U.S. Maritime Administration, *Domestic Waterborne Trade of the United States, 1975–1979* (Washington, D.C. 1981).

*In addition to the 151 million tons of domestic Great Lakes commerce, there are 57 million tons of cargo moving between U.S. and Canadian Great Lakes ports.

circuity involved in some water routes (for example from Chicago to Detroit via Lakes Michigan and Huron).

1979. One other statistic of interest is the percentage of domestic waterborne commerce that is subject to federal economic regulation. The Transportation Association of America estimates that only 16.3 percent of inland waterway traffic, 3.7 percent of domestic ocean traffic, and 0.2 percent of domestic Great Lakes traffic is subject to regulation.[2] This is in contrast to the other modes of domestic transportation discussed in earlier chapters of this book. This uneven coverage of regulation poses one of the most serious problems in domestic regulatory policy.

As for waterborne transport in the future, there are forecasts that by the year 2000 it will be nearly double its present volume. Domestic ocean shipping is expected to increase the most, mainly because of increased shipments of Alaskan oil to mainland U.S. ports. Inland waterways tonnages of coal, other products of mines, manufactured items, and chemicals are expected to increase, as are Great Lakes

[2] *Ibid.* The percentages here are total ton-miles of waterborne traffic.

movements of iron ore and coal.[3] Many of these forecasts were made before the 1979 increases in fuel prices. Since transportation by water is fuel efficient, its share of the market may increase by even more than was originally anticipated.

Inland Water Carriers

In this section, we will discuss the inland water carriers, describing their equipment and examining their markets; and we will also look at the generous role of government in providing the inland water navigation facilities—improved channels and locks—which make it

- *An improved channel* is a river bed which is dredged (deepened) to a certain depth so that loaded barges can travel through the channel without becoming stuck on the bottom. Often it is necessary to perform maintenance dredging to remove newly accumulated silt and sedimentation.

possible for the inland water carriers to serve their markets. Inland waterway carriers are sometimes called "barge operators," although the term "barge" means a non-self-propelled vessel and can be applied to barges which are used on the Great Lakes or the oceans. Barges used on the inland waterways have flat bottoms and shallow drafts and cannot be used safely on the Great Lakes or oceans because they would flip over in a storm.

- A vessel's *draft* is the distance between water level and the vessel's bottom. Barges used on domestic waterways have a draft— when loaded—of 9 to 12 feet.

The inland waterways industry operates about 24,000 dry cargo barges, 4,000 tank barges, and just over 4,400 towboats and tugboats.[4] In the decade from 1965 to 1975, the average horsepower of the towboats and tugs increased from 2,980 to 5,088 and the average tonnage capacity of dry cargo barges increased from 1,026 to 1,167 short tons. Note that each individual barge can carry at least 10 times the weight that can be carried in a rail car. Figure 8–2 shows above-

[3] See: *Domestic Waterborne Shipping Market Analysis, Executive Summary* (Chicago: prepared by Kearney Management Consultants for the Maritime Administration, 1974).

[4] *Water Carriers and Inland Waterways in Agricultural Transportation*, Agricultural Economic Report No. 379 (Washington, D.C.: Economic Research Service, U.S. Department of Agriculture, August, 1979), p. 6; and *The Barge and Towing Industry—A Statistical Profile* (Arlington, Va.: The American Waterways Operators, Inc., July, 1981).

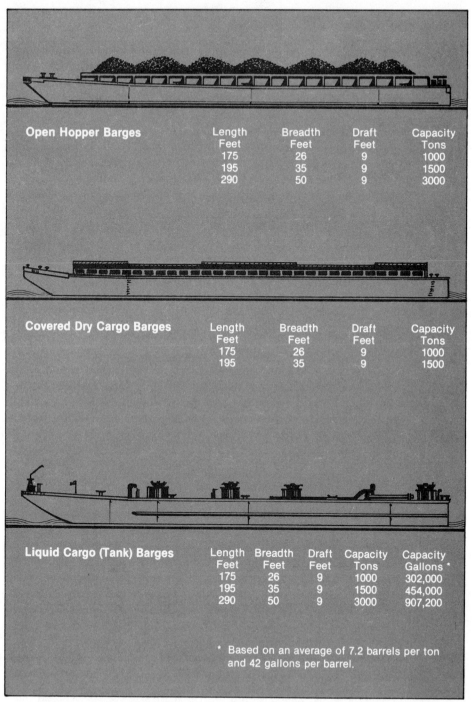

Open Hopper Barges

Length Feet	Breadth Feet	Draft Feet	Capacity Tons
175	26	9	1000
195	35	9	1500
290	50	9	3000

Covered Dry Cargo Barges

Length Feet	Breadth Feet	Draft Feet	Capacity Tons
175	26	9	1000
195	35	9	1500

Liquid Cargo (Tank) Barges

Length Feet	Breadth Feet	Draft Feet	Capacity Tons	Capacity Gallons *
175	26	9	1000	302,000
195	35	9	1500	454,000
290	50	9	3000	907,200

* Based on an average of 7.2 barrels per ton and 42 gallons per barrel.

Figure 8–2 Typical Barges Used on Inland Waterways. Courtesy: The American Waterways Operators, Inc.

the-water side views of three commonly-used types of inland water-way barges. Open hopper barges carry dry bulk cargoes such as coal, sand, gravel, and limestone. The covered dry cargo barges carry primarily grains. The tank barge illustrated is for carrying petroleum. There are also technically complex tank barges designed to carry liquids or gases under pressure or at high temperatures (so they will not lose their viscosity and be difficult to pump). Some barges come with flat decks for carrying vehicles or construction equipment. Since clearances above waterways are higher and less obstructed than for transport via rail or highway modes, barges are sometimes used to transport large, oversized items.

The phrase "towboat" is a misnomer, since they invariably *push* the "tow" of barges. Towboats have square prows (fronts) and flat bottoms and can only be used on inland waterways. They are illustrated in Figure 8–3, along with tugboats. Tugboats can be used on the oceans and the Great Lakes and are used for *pulling* single deep-water vessels. They are also the common workhorses in and around harbor areas, helping ocean liners dock, and pulling construction equipment.

Government's Role in Providing Facilities

The federal government has been involved in waterway improvement since shortly after the War of 1812 when it was decided that our nation needed protected routes for moving troops so that they could repel enemy forces invading from the ocean. West Point was one of the few schools at that time training engineers, and it was these young army engineers who worked out a plan to integrate and improve such an internal system of navigation. Part of the army engineers' plan was to fortify defenses around our major ports and harbors. Many of the improvements the engineers provided were also of great value to commercial navigation; once that value was recognized, states and port cities clamored for river and harbor improvements to be provided by the U.S. Army Corps of Engineers. By the beginning of this century, it had also become apparent that waterways and rivers could be used for purposes in addition to navigation, such as generating electric power, reducing flood damage, and providing water for irrigation. In 1925, Congress authorized the Army Corps of Engineers to look at the total spectrum of surface water uses in its studies of river basins.[5]

[5] Ellis L. Armstrong, ed., *History of Public Works in the United States, 1776–1976* (Chicago: American Public Works Association, 1976), p. 31.

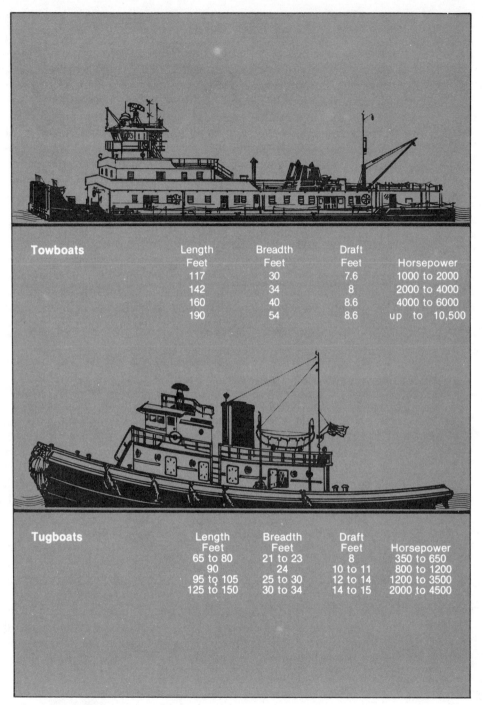

Towboats

	Length Feet	Breadth Feet	Draft Feet	Horsepower
	117	30	7.6	1000 to 2000
	142	34	8	2000 to 4000
	160	40	8.6	4000 to 6000
	190	54	8.6	up to 10,500

Tugboats

	Length Feet	Breadth Feet	Draft Feet	Horsepower
	65 to 80	21 to 23	8	350 to 650
	90	24	10 to 11	800 to 1200
	95 to 105	25 to 30	12 to 14	1200 to 3500
	125 to 150	30 to 34	14 to 15	2000 to 4500

Figure 8–3 Towboats and Tugboats. Courtesy: The American Waterways Operators, Inc.

The U.S. Army Corps of Engineers continues today to be the agency that provides most of the federal expenditures for river and harbor improvements. The Corps of Engineers' civilian functions are for the most part, separated from its military assignments. Commissioned Army officers are trained to command nearly all Corps' civil functions, as well as perform military duties.

The Corps of Engineers has a very close relationship to Congress when it comes to obtaining appropriations for funding its civil works functions. The term "pork barrel" legislation was—and is—frequently applied to the annual appropriations bill which funds the Corps' civil programs.

A typical Corps of Engineers project must clear four separate hurdles, each involving an action by Congress. First, Congress must authorize study of a problem, such as deepening a channel on the Allegheny River. Second, the study must be funded, which usually doesn't happen until a later Congress. If the Corps, in its study, finds the project is feasible (meaning its benefits will exceed costs), the project can then be authorized by Congress. The last step is to have funds appropriated by Congress so that the Corps can begin construction.

An illustration of these relationships is the Tennessee-Tombigbee Waterway, currently under construction. It connects the Tennessee River to Demopolis, Alabama, a total of 232 miles. Congress authorized the construction of the Tenn-Tom in 1946, but initial funding was not authorized until 1971. Why was funding initiated at that time? *Business Week* noted: "A powerful contingent of Southern senators and representatives pushed the money through with strong backing from then-President Richard M. Nixon, who was courting Southern conservative support for his reelection bid."[6]

In 1971, this waterway was predicted to cost $323 million. Today, $1.1 billion has been spent, and it is only 60 percent completed. It is now projected to cost about $3 billion in total to complete the Tenn-Tom. In 1981 Congress almost stopped funding the project! One opponent called it, "The granddaddy of the pork barrel projects." Senator Daniel P. Moynihan of New York declared, "The U.S. Army Corps of Engineers is trying to clone the Mississippi."[7]

With its cost overruns and other problems, why is the Tenn-Tom project still being funded? Again *Business Week* observed:

Senate Majority Leader Howard H. Baker Jr. (R-Tenn.) cannot afford to oppose a project that could increase trade through his state, say Senate

[6]"The Growing Clamor To Halt The Tenn-Tom," *Business Week,* (October 26, 1981), p. 56.
[7]*Ibid.*

staffers. And a longtime backer of Tenn-Tom, former Senate Armed Services Committee chairman and now ranking minority member John C. Stennis (D-Miss.), has helped save the project many times and is in a position to do so again. In the House, both Appropriations Committee Chairman Jamie L. Whitten (D-Miss.) and Tom Bevill (D-Ala.), chairman of the energy and water development subcommittee, represent districts that Tenn-Tom crosses.[8]

[8] *Ibid.*

All locks on the St. Lawrence Seaway are filled or emptied by gravity. To raise a vessel, for example, the upstream valves are opened and the water simply flows into the chamber through openings at the bottom of the walls. The following diagram illustrates the procedure:

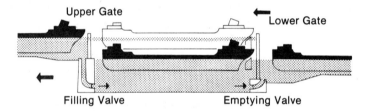

The diagram portrays the following steps:

1: From the lower level the ship sails through the open gates into the lock. The vessel secures itself to bollards on the side of the walls. The gates are closed.

2: The valves are opened and water is allowed to flow in, lifting the ship.

3: When the vessel reaches the higher level the upper gates are opened and the ship sails out.

To lower a vessel the above steps are reversed. It takes less than ten minutes to raise or lower the water level with more than 20 million gallons used for each lockage. Additional time, however, is required for the vessel to carefully maneuver in and out of the chambers. The average lockage requires approximately 33 minutes from the time the bow passes the approach wall until the stern is cleared of the outermost boom.

Figure 8-4   Locking Procedures on the St. Lawrence Seaway. These locks can accommodate vessels drawing 27 feet. Inland waterway locks are not as deep; often they can accommodate barges drawing only 9 to 12 feet. Courtesy: St. Lawrence Seaway Development Corporation.

Under separate, but related programs, the Corps also maintains the projects it has built. In waterways this means continual maintenance dredging of channels to remove accumulated silt and other debris.

The U.S. Coast Guard is primarily concerned with providing for the safety of water vessels. However, the Corps and the Coast Guard cooperate to provide various navigation aids, wherever needed, to guide vessels on their proper courses. For example, the Coast Guard maintains two buoy tenders at its St. Louis base—one for the Missouri River and one for the lower Mississippi—just to maintain navigation buoys (which are anchored, floating markers) and to replace those that have been sheared or crushed by passing vessels.[9]

The Tennessee Valley Authority (TVA) is an independent federal agency established in 1933 to develop the multiple-purpose potential of the Tennessee River. Dams were built on the river for three purposes: to control flooding, to generate hydroelectric power, and to aid navigation. Locks were built around each dam, and a 9-foot-deep navigation channel was provided along the 652-mile Tennessee River.

The flow of rivers makes it difficult for vessels to navigate upstream. One way to overcome this problem is to turn the river into a series of steps, each being a pool that lies behind a dam that crosses the river. Locks (see Figure 8–4) are built adjacent to dams to allow vessels to climb from one pool to another.

Figure 8–5 is a side view of the Ohio River, which drops about 450 feet in the nearly 1,000 miles from Pittsburgh to the Mississippi River. The steps shown on the drawing are—or have been—created by dams. The older system, with the smaller steps, consisted of nearly 50 dams. This system is being replaced by about 19 larger dams (and locks) which are the big steps in the figure. Fewer dams and locks speed up navigation because moving through a lock consumes considerable time.[10] The photo at this chapter's beginning shows one of the locks and dams on the Ohio River system, at Willow Island, above Parkersburg, West Virginia.

---

[9] *Transportation/USA* (Winter, 1978), p. 10. At very busy ports, the Coast Guard is installing vessel control procedures which are somewhat similar to air traffic control systems in the vicinity of airports.

[10] Other types of river users might prefer a different policy for using the river's water. Each time a lock opens, for example, the water passing through it is lost for purposes of power generation. The dry months may also be the time when demands for electric power are the greatest, and users of hydroelectric power would rather not save the water for navigation. See: Charles W. Howe and others, *Inland Waterway Transportation, Studies in Public and Private Management and Investment Decisions* (Washington, D.C.: Resources for the Future, 1969), pp. 21–22.

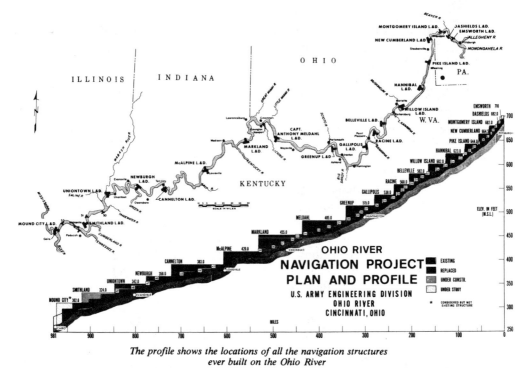

*The profile shows the locations of all the navigation structures
ever built on the Ohio River*

Figure 8–5 "Side" View of the Ohio River Showing Old and New Lock and
Dam Systems. Courtesy: U.S. Army Corps of Engineers, Huntington, West
Virginia District.

Barge Operations

Some inland waterways can handle barges drawing 12 feet of
water, others can handle barges drawing only 9 feet. Horizontal dimensions of locks also vary for different waterway systems; along
each waterway they are usually uniform. On the Illinois Waterway
(extending from Chicago southwesterly toward the Mississippi
River) the lock dimensions are 110 feet wide by 600 feet long. On the
Allegheny River (between East Brady, Pennsylvania, and Pittsburgh)
the lock dimensions are 56 feet wide by 360 feet long. On the Ohio
River, one of the nation's busiest waterways, the locks that are 110
feet by 600 feet are being replaced by fewer locks that are 110 feet by
1,200 feet.[11] This will speed the flow of traffic since barge "tows" are

[11] *Big Load Afloat* (Arlington, Va.: The American Waterways Operators, Inc.,
1973), pp. 126–127.

made up of many barges, lashed together, and the longer locks make it possible for a larger entire "tow" to pass through without having to be separated before reaching the lock, being moved through in segments, and being rejoined after passage through the lock.

While barges can be towed individually, as they often are near the sites where they are loaded and unloaded, their hulls are designed so that they can be lashed together into one large tow of many barges. Barges have rectangular shapes and are designed so that a block of them, say, nine, arranged three abreast and three long, can just fit inside a lock. A complete tow might be three abreast and six barges long; such an 18-barge tow would be split in two for passage through a lock. Actually, instead of containing 18 barges, one of the rear slots would be left empty so that the towboat would have space to fit in one of the two lock passages.

There are about 1,850 firms that provide inland waterways transportation of goods. Of these, 185 are ICC-certificated common carriers providing service over specified routes. For example, one East Coast firm advertised that it served "ports on the Atlantic Intracoastal Waterway and tributaries from Philadelphia, Pennsylvania to Jacksonville, Florida" and was "permitted under ICC authority to operate as far north as New York City and as far south as Palatka, Florida."[12] The firm listed as its equipment, four towboats and 20 dry cargo barges. It operated terminals at Paulsboro, New Jersey, (across the Delaware River from Philadelphia) and Jacksonville, Florida. Both sites contained warehouses and spaces for outside storage. The firm also used public port terminals at points in between Philadelphia and Jacksonville. The firm's sailing schedule was simply to leave Paulsboro each Wednesday, heading south.

The ICC has also issued permits to 31 firms to serve as contract water carriers, which means they contract with specific shippers, for one or more loads. There are 1,629 carriers exempt from economic regulation. Lastly, about 400 firms own their own barges and use them for private carriage of their own products.[13]

The Inland Waterways System

The inland waterways system of the United States is shown in Figure 8–6. The inland waterway system is concentrated in the Mississippi River Basin. However, note on the map that there are two waterways connecting to the Pacific Ocean: one barge waterway fol-

---

[12] Advertisement of the C. G. Willis, Inc. firm of Paulsboro, New Jersey.
[13] *Big Load Afloat*, p. 3.

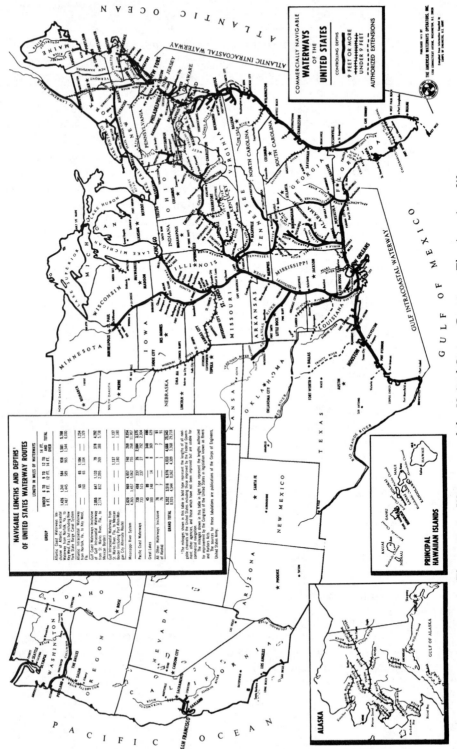

Figure 8–6 Waterways of the United States. Courtesy: The American Waterways Operators, Inc.

lows the Columbia River and reaches Idaho; the other waterway leads inward from San Francisco Bay, and barges and even moderate-size ocean vessels can sail as far inland as Sacramento. Along the Atlantic and Gulf Coasts are *intracoastal* waterways which provide sheltered navigation routes for barges along these two stretches of coastline. They are also heavily used by recreational boaters (as are other inland waterways). The Gulf and Atlantic intracoastal waterways are not linked. This was to have been accomplished by the "Cross-Florida" barge canal which was started in 1964 but halted several years later because of objections from environmental protection interests (who claimed that the construction was hurting the drainage patterns of central Florida). The intended route of the Cross-Florida project is shown in detail in Figure 8–7, which shows other inland waterways in Florida as well.

As the cancellation of the Cross-Florida waterway indicates, environmental issues are frequently present when new waterway projects are contemplated. The basic issue involves what to do with the dredged material from the river's bottom. According to two environmental groups, the Sierra Club and the Izaak Walton League, the dredged material is usually deposited in fertile backwater lakes and marshes along rivers, and this causes irreparable damage to both fish and wildlife habitat.[14]

In Figure 8–6 note the large number of very short waterways leading inland from both oceans, the Gulf, and the Great Lakes. Many of these waterways are deeper than conventional inland waterways; they were provided to allow deep-draft ocean and Great Lakes vessels to reach marine terminals and waterfront industrial sites in major cities. Most of these improvements are provided by programs administered by the U.S. Army Corps of Engineers. Inside large cities, a certain amount of freight transportation is moved by barges. Passenger ferry boats sometimes use a city's waterways to provide either commuter transportation or sightseeing cruises. Figure 8–8 shows the channels provided and maintained by the U.S. Army Corps of Engineers in the New York City area.

Barges and Their Competitive Position

Figure 8–9 is an interesting and informative way of comparing the various modes of domestic transport against each other. Many of the controversies in national transportation policy occur in situa-

[14] See: Dean Rebuffoni, "Mississippi Basin Commission's New Master Plan Draws Fire," *Minneapolis Tribune* (January 6, 1982), p. 5A.

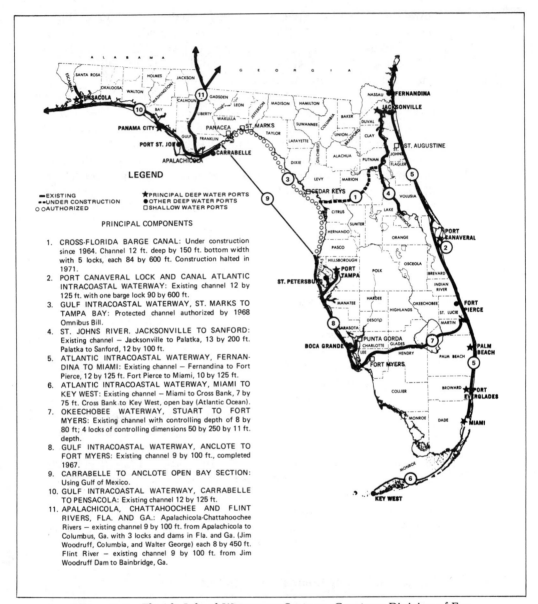

LEGEND

■ EXISTING
■ UNDER CONSTRUCTION
○ O AUTHORIZED

★ PRINCIPAL DEEP WATER PORTS
● OTHER DEEP WATER PORTS
□ SHALLOW WATER PORTS

PRINCIPAL COMPONENTS

1. **CROSS-FLORIDA BARGE CANAL:** Under construction since 1964. Channel 12 ft. deep by 150 ft. bottom width with 5 locks, each 84 by 600 ft. Construction halted in 1971.

2. **PORT CANAVERAL LOCK AND CANAL ATLANTIC INTRACOASTAL WATERWAY:** Existing channel 12 by 125 ft. with one barge lock 90 by 600 ft.

3. **GULF INTRACOASTAL WATERWAY, ST. MARKS TO TAMPA BAY:** Protected channel authorized by 1968 Omnibus Bill.

4. **ST. JOHNS RIVER, JACKSONVILLE TO SANFORD:** Existing channel — Jacksonville to Palatka, 13 by 200 ft. Palatka to Sanford, 12 by 100 ft.

5. **ATLANTIC INTRACOASTAL WATERWAY, FERNANDINA TO MIAMI:** Existing channel — Fernandina to Fort Pierce, 12 by 125 ft. Fort Pierce to Miami, 10 by 125 ft.

6. **ATLANTIC INTRACOASTAL WATERWAY, MIAMI TO KEY WEST:** Existing channel — Miami to Cross Bank, 7 by 75 ft. Cross Bank to Key West, open bay (Atlantic Ocean).

7. **OKEECHOBEE WATERWAY, STUART TO FORT MYERS:** Existing channel with controlling depth of 8 by 80 ft; 4 locks of controlling dimensions 50 by 250 by 11 ft. depth.

8. **GULF INTRACOASTAL WATERWAY, ANCLOTE TO FORT MYERS:** Existing channel 9 by 100 ft., completed 1967.

9. **CARRABELLE TO ANCLOTE OPEN BAY SECTION:** Using Gulf of Mexico.

10. **GULF INTRACOASTAL WATERWAY, CARRABELLE TO PENSACOLA:** Existing channel 12 by 125 ft.

11. **APALACHICOLA, CHATTAHOOCHEE AND FLINT RIVERS, FLA. AND GA.:** Apalachicola-Chattahoochee Rivers — existing channel 9 by 100 ft. from Apalachicola to Columbus, Ga. with 3 locks and dams in Fla. and Ga. (Jim Woodruff, Columbia, and Walter George) each 8 by 450 ft. Flint River — existing channel 9 by 100 ft. from Jim Woodruff Dam to Bainbridge, Ga.

Figure 8–7   Florida Inland Waterways Systems. Courtesy: Division of Economic Development, Florida Department of Commerce. Reproduced from the Division's *Florida Ports and Waterways Directory, 1973.*

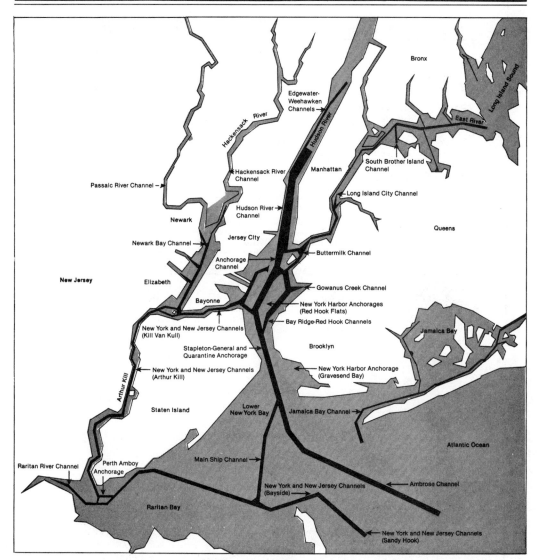

Figure 8–8 Federally-Provided Channels in the New York City Region. Courtesy: *1981 New York Port Handbook*, Port Authority of New York and New Jersey.

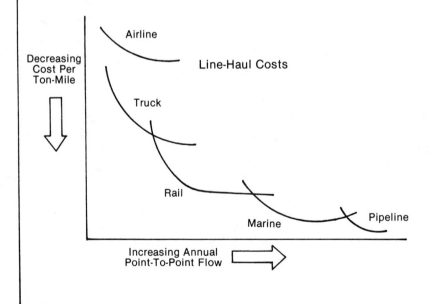

Inherent Line-Haul Characteristics of Domestic Modes

Mode	Flexibility	Typical Unit Capacity (Tons)	Speed (mph)	Cost (Cents per Ton-Mile)
Marine	Many Cargos Between Ports	1,000 to 60,000	3 to 30	0.1 to 1.1
Pipeline	Limited Cargos Between Terminals	30,000 to 2,500,000	3 to 6	0.1 to 0.25
Rail	All Cargos Between Rail Sidings	50 to 12,000	20 to 45	0.5 to 2.5
Truck	All Cargos Between All Points	10 to 25	40 to 60	2.0 to 4.0
Airline	Many Cargos	5 to 125	300 to 600	15 to 20

Competitive Advantage

High Flexibility	High Capacity	High Speed	Low Cost
1. Truck	1. Pipeline	1. Airline	1. Pipeline
2. Rail	2. Marine	2. Truck	2. Marine
3. Marine	3. Rail	3. Rail	3. Rail
4. Pipeline	4. Truck	4. Marine	4. Truck
5. Airline	5. Airline	5. Pipeline	5. Airline

Figure 8–9 Line-Haul Characteristics of Domestic Modes. Courtesy: Kearney Management Consultants (from a study performed for the Maritime Administration).

tions where two or more modes have similar or overlapping capabilities. Obviously, pipelines and airlines do not cross each other on the chart at the bottom of Figure 8–9. Hence there are few, if any, policy issues between them. But on the chart there are overlaps between railroads and barges (labeled "marine"), and there are many policy conflicts between those two modes.

LASH/Seabee Services

LASH (Lighter Aboard Ship) and Seabee vessels carry floating barges, aboard an ocean-going "mother" ship. The "mother" ship can moor offshore and discharge individual barges which tugs take to each consignee's dock for unloading. Such a system can make good use of shallow connecting waterways. In the United States, the system is widely used on the Mississippi River and on the rivers in Alabama which connect with Mobile. The difference between LASH and Seabee vessels is in the size of the barges they carry. A typical LASH barge is about 60 feet long, 30 feet wide, and 13 feet deep. Seabee barges are about 100 feet long, 35 feet wide, and 13 feet deep. Figure 8–10 shows an artist's rendering of future LASH vessels. Note that they carry conventional containers as well as barges.

LASH and Seabee vessels are believed to be the best-suited vessels for carrying cargo to and from less-developed areas of the world because they require the least in shoreside vessel handling facilities. Even water depths would not be a problem since the main vessel would be offshore and individual barges could be towed up the river.

Great Lakes Transportation

The five Great Lakes penetrate the industrial and agricultural heartland of the North American continent. They are part of the St. Lawrence River basin, which flows into the Atlantic Ocean between the Canadian provinces of Nova Scotia and Newfoundland. Four of the five Great Lakes and portions of the St. Lawrence River form a boundary between the United States and Canada. Figure 8–11 shows the system as well as an elevational profile.

Great Lakes vessels—called "lakers"—have long, low profiles and are not considered seaworthy for operation on ocean waters where storms can be more severe. They are designed and suitable for operating within the Great Lakes—St. Lawrence Seaway system.

Figure 8–10   Future LASH Vessels. Courtesy: Naval architect Jerome L. Goldman, president of Friede and Goldman, Ltd., and LASH Systems, Inc.

Until recently, all locks in the connecting channels between the Great Lakes and along the St. Lawrence Seaway were the same size and could accommodate vessels 730 feet long. In the late 1960's, the Poe Lock at Sault St. Marie was enlarged to accommodate vessels up to 1,000 feet long (and of proportionally greater width and depth, with a carrying capacity of about 65,000 tons—over twice that of the 730-foot-long lakers). Several new 1,000-foot-long lakers have been constructed; however, they are confined to the four upper Great Lakes because they cannot pass through the Welland Canal.

Ocean vessels can navigate on the Great Lakes although lock sizes prohibit many of the newer, larger "salties" from entering. As a result, some outbound overseas traffic is carried down by "laker" vessels to transfer points on the St. Lawrence River below the Seaway, such as at Montreal, and then loaded aboard larger ocean vessels.

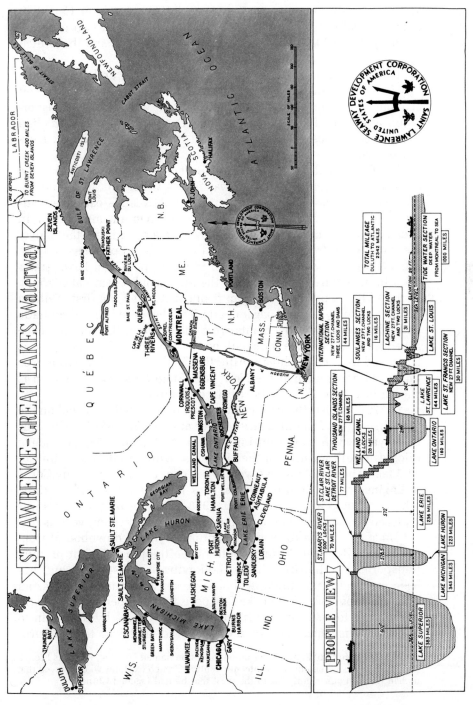

Figure 8–11   St. Lawrence–Great Lakes Waterway. Courtesy: St. Lawrence Seaway Development Corporation.

Most traffic through the St. Lawrence Seaway is either Canadian domestic traffic or international commerce (between two different nations). The St. Lawrence Seaway, built by Canada and the United States, is an international waterway.

The St. Lawrence—Great Lakes route has a long and colorful history.[15] It has been especially important in the social, political, and economic development of Canada, because it was the only transportation artery linking Canada together. Even today, most Canadian population is located along either the Great Lakes or the St. Lawrence River.

The Erie Canal—from Albany to Buffalo—was a real boon to the Great Lakes system since there was now a water link to the ocean. Most cargoes were transhipped (changed between Great Lakes sailing ships and canal barges) at Buffalo. Western grains moved east, in exchange for manufactured items. However, a more important movement westward from Buffalo was not products but people—settlers. The majority of whites who settled in the Upper Great Lakes states prior to the Civil War arrived via the Erie Canal–Great Lakes route. In the 1840's a private Canadian firm constructed the first Welland Canal, which bypassed Niagara Falls. This benefited Canadian trade and, after some improvements were made along the St. Lawrence River, made it possible for small, ocean-going vessels to navigate as far inland as Lake Michigan. After the Civil War, the Erie Canal was improved and renamed the New York State Barge Canal, which is shown in Figure 8–11. It is still in operation.

In 1797, the Northwest Fur Company built a shallow canal on the Canadian side of the St. Mary's River at Sault Ste. Marie. This was destroyed by U.S. troops during the War of 1812. In 1855, the State of Michigan built a canal on the U.S. side, with an allowable draft of 11.5 feet. These state works were taken over by the U.S. Army Corps of Engineers, which built a larger lock in 1888. Subsequently three other U.S. locks were built, and in 1968 one of the original locks was replaced by one that can accommodate 1,000-foot-long vessels.

Since before the turn of the century, iron ore downbound from the Mesabi Range in Minnesota has been the predominant product transported on the Great Lakes. Following at a distant second has been grain, also moving downbound; coal, which formerly was an upbound movement from Lake Erie ports to the upper Lakes, now (in the form of low-sulfur coal from Wyoming) moves by unit-train to Superior, Wisconsin, and then downbound via lakers to coal-burn-

---

[15] At the bottom of Figure 8–11 note the section named *Lachine*, which is French for *China*. It was named by a seventeenth-century French explorer who believed that he had traveled sufficiently far to the west that he had reached China.

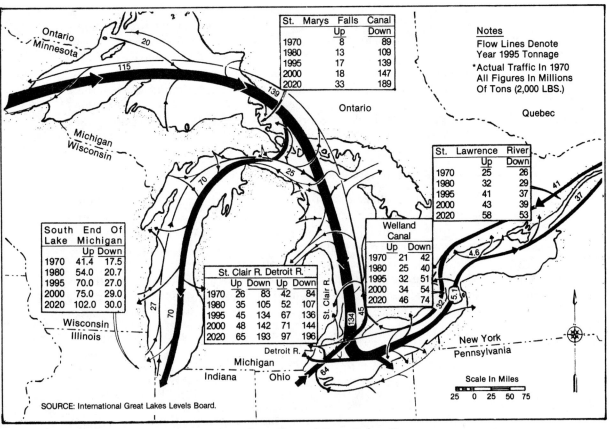

St. Marys Falls Canal

	Up	Down
1970	8	89
1980	13	109
1995	17	139
2000	18	147
2020	33	189

Notes
Flow Lines Denote
Year 1995 Tonnage
*Actual Traffic In 1970
All Figures In Millions
Of Tons (2,000 LBS.)

St. Lawrence River

	Up	Down
1970	25	26
1980	32	29
1995	41	37
2000	43	39
2020	58	53

South End Of Lake Michigan

	Up	Down
1970	41.4	17.5
1980	54.0	20.7
1995	70.0	27.0
2000	75.0	29.0
2020	102.0	30.0

Welland Canal

	Up	Down
1970	21	42
1980	25	40
1995	32	51
2000	34	54
2020	46	74

St. Clair R. | **Detroit R.**

	Up	Down	Up	Down
1970	26	83	42	84
1980	35	105	52	107
1995	45	134	67	136
2000	48	142	71	144
2020	65	193	97	196

Scale In Miles
25 0 25 50 75

SOURCE: International Great Lakes Levels Board.

Figure 8–12   Flow Chart of Great Lakes Commerce.

ing utilities on the lower lakes; and limestone, used in construction and in the manufacture of cement and steel.

Prior to World War II there were domestic freighters that carried miscellaneous shipments between Great Lakes ports. Until the 1950's some specially-converted lakers carried new automobiles from Detroit to other Great Lakes port cities. Passenger ferries once operated on the lakes, the last one connecting Milwaukee with Muskegon, Michigan. Several railroads operate rail-car ferries across Lake Michigan, but they are attempting to abandon the ferries, alleging that the technology for handling rail cars in this manner is obsolete.[16]

[16]Harold M. Mayer, *Wisconsin's Great Lakes Ports: Background and Future Alternatives* (Milwaukee: The University of Wisconsin Center for Great Lakes Studies, 1975), p. 55.

A generalized flow chart of Great Lakes traffic is shown in Figure 8–12, which includes actual figures for 1970 and projections for several future years. Numbers on the thick flow chart lines are estimates for 1995. Iron ore accounts for about one-half of tonnage carried on the lakes; grain, coal, and limestone together account for another 35 percent. This traffic does not move during winter months, when the locks at Sault Ste. Marie close. Navigation is carried on a limited basis on the southerly portions of Lakes Michigan and Erie during winter months.

Great Lakes Carriers

The fleet of "lakers" is old and difficult to analyze; many older Great Lakes vessels have been out of service for years, and yet, potentially, they could be called back into service. Some smaller vessels are kept in service so that they can make deliveries to customers at sites where the larger, newer vessels cannot reach.

The average age of U.S. vessels in the Great Lakes fleet is about 45 years old, although frequently old hulls are equipped with new propulsion units or self-unloading gear.[17] The majority of U.S. lakers are

- *Self-unloading* means that the vessel permanently carries equipment with which to unload its cargo. Receiving docks do not need machinery for unloading the vessel.

over 600 feet long and 12 of them are in the 700- to 730-foot category. Three new U.S. lakers are approximately 1,000 feet long and have been built since the opening of the new Poe Lock. The Canadian Great Lakes fleet is about half as numerous as that of the United States. Its average vessel age is much less and it contains 36 vessels in the 700- to 730-foot category. All but one of these large Canadian lakers were constructed in the decade after the St. Lawrence Seaway opened (1958) to serve Canada's domestic Great Lakes trade.

A truncated side view of one of the newest lakers is shown in Figure 8–13. The 1,000-foot-long vessel is named the *Mesabi Miner* and was built for Pickands Mather & Co., of Cleveland, a subsidiary of Moore McCormack Resources, Inc. Pickands Mather & Co. is a

[17] The self-unloader concept illustrates a practice in transportation of the carrier, rather than the receiver, providing the unloading capability. The vessel costs more, and has less capacity, than if it needed no self-unloading gear. One Canadian Great Lakes operator explained: "We've actually put a number of people in business with our self-loaders—people who don't have any docking facilities. The method sounds almost crude, but if we can get the ship to within 100 feet of shore, we can literally tie up to a tree stump. . . ." From interview with Peter R. Cresswell in *Surveyer* (quarterly journal of the American Bureau of Shipping, February, 1978), p. 15.

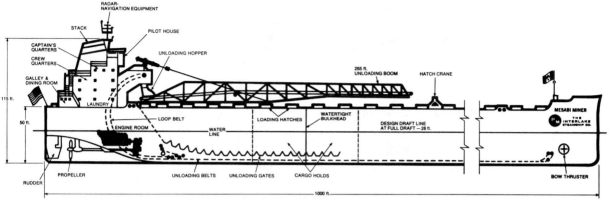

Figure 8–13 The Laker *Mesabi Miner.* Courtesy: The Interlake Steamship Company, operated by Pickands Mather & Co.

longtime iron ore producer on the Mesabi Range. This is the second of three similarly-sized vessels being built for them. The vessel is a self-unloader. At the bottom of the hull is a conveyor belt which carries the iron ore pellets toward the stern where they are lifted to the conveyor belt system which is connected as part of the unloading boom. The unloading boom can swing to either side and can extend about 200 feet over the dock's edge. The aging Great Lakes fleet is expected to be replaced by ships of this size and capability. Possibly they will be larger if a lock at Sault Ste. Marie is enlarged so that it can accommodate them.[18]

About 125 U.S. firms operate vessels on the Great Lakes. These firms had 638 vessels registered in 1980, although not all of those vessels were in active service.[19] Only 7 of these firms, controlling 55 vessels, were subject to ICC regulation as common carriers (and these 7 included 4 railroads who were operating rail-car ferries). Hence, very little Great Lakes transportation is regulated in economic terms. Of the 118 nonregulated firms, 34 are classified as "private" carriers, handling their own materials; and 84 firms are "for-hire" but are exempt from ICC controls. There are 140 vessels in the fleet which are 500 feet or longer, and these are owned by 14 companies. Steel or iron ore mining companies own 90 of these vessels. U.S. Steel Corporation alone owns 43 vessels. There are few Great

[18] John O. Greenwood, "Impressive New Tonnages are Coming. . . ." *Seaway Review* (Summer, 1975), pp. 23–25.

[19] Figures in this paragraph are taken from: U.S. Army Corps of Engineers, *Transportation Lines on the Great Lakes System, 1980* (New Orleans: Corps' Waterborne Commerce Statistics Center, 1981).

Lakes vessels 400 to 500 feet long. The remainder of the fleet consists of much smaller vessels, usually between 40 and 200 feet in length, and includes vessels used as tugboats, dredges, passenger ferries, and excursion boats.

The St. Lawrence Seaway

The St. Lawrence Seaway and the Great Lakes system were shown in Figure 8–11. While the Seaway is an international waterway built by two nations and open to all commercial vessels of the world, it is discussed in this chapter because of its close relationship to the Great Lakes navigation system. In addition it functions as a domestic waterway for substantial portions of Canada's domestic commerce and as a domestic waterway for a small amount of U.S. domestic commerce. The St. Lawrence Seaway allows vessels to sail between the Great Lakes and the Atlantic Ocean. An equally important waterway needed to bypass Niagara Falls, the Welland Canal, is built on Canadian soil and links Lake Ontario to the upper four Great Lakes.

The present St. Lawrence Seaway was constructed during the 1950's and was opened to navigation in 1959. It consists of seven locks, five built by Canada at an approximate cost of $340 million, and two built by the U.S. at an approximate cost of $126 million. In addition, the United States deepened the connecting channels between the Great Lakes to Seaway depths (27 feet) at a cost of $257 million; and—from 1967 to 1973—Canada spent $188 million to overcome a bottleneck that had developed at the Welland Canal, between Lake Erie and Ontario.

Tolls are collected for the use of the St. Lawrence Seaway, although this has been a source of disagreement between the United States and Canada. Canada was always much more interested in the Seaway project than was the United States, where the idea faced fierce opposition from East Coast ports and the railroads connecting them with the Midwest. In a 1951 meeting in Washington, D.C., Canadian Prime Minister St. Laurent informed President Truman that Canada was prepared to build the Seaway with or without the participation of the United States. Later, President Eisenhower was able to convince Congress to participate, but Seaway opponents in Congress insisted that the Seaway "pay for itself" out of toll collections. (Prior agreements between the U.S. and Canada provided that either nation could charge tolls for the navigation facilities they constructed, provided citizens and vessels of both countries were treated equally.)[20] When the Seaway opened in 1959, tolls of 90¢ per ton on general cargo, 40¢ per ton on bulk cargo, plus 4¢ per ton on the gross registered weight of the vessel were assessed. Toll receipts were split between the United States and Canada in proportion to their share of the costs in constructing the seven locks. At the same time, tolls were instituted for use of the Welland Canal and were collected by Canada. Tolls on the Welland Canal were unpopular with Canadians, who were used to paying nothing, and in 1963 Prime Minister Diefenbaker, as a campaign gesture toward Canadian wheat growers, removed tolls on the Welland Canal.

Seaway traffic did not grow as quickly as projected, and both the U.S. and Canadian Seaway authorities accumulated huge obligations of unpaid interest owed to their respective national treasuries. The burden on Canada was especially great; in the late 1960's Canada attempted unsuccessfully to renegotiate a higher toll structure for the Seaway. The United States opposed any increase but did agree to increase Canada's share of Seaway toll receipts from 71 to 73 percent. In 1970, Congress excused the St. Lawrence Seaway Development Corporation from any interest payments on outstanding debt.[21] Inflationary pressures during the 1970's forced Seaway operating costs up so much that toll receipts could not cover them. This caused serious political problems for both the U.S. and Canadian Seaway agencies since it meant they would have to go to their respective legislatures for annual appropriations to cover operating expenses. In 1978 both governments agreed to raise tolls.[22]

The issue of Seaway tolls was always less controversial in the United States than it was in Canada. The controversy in Canada includes arguments about who are really the "beneficiaries" of transport subsidies, and the trade and political relations between the two nations. Canadian wheat growers and shippers and Canadian ship operators, who carried 90 percent of the cargo between U.S. and Canadian ports (because they had lower costs than U.S. flag competitors), were beneficiaries of the Seaway and were responsible for

[20] This was a provision in the 1909 Boundary Waters Treaty between the U.S. and Great Britain (and subsequently adopted by the independent Canadian government).

[21] This was included in the *Merchant Marine Act of 1970*. More recently, the Canadian government excused its Seaway Development Authority from paying accrued interest.

[22] Toll increases were phased in over three years with 1980 tolls being: 68¢ per ton on bulk cargo (except grain which would be charged 41¢ per ton); $1.65 per ton on general cargo; and 68¢ per ton on containerized cargo. In addition, the vessel would be assessed 7¢ per ton for its gross registered weight. Pleasure craft would be charged $4 for each lock transited. See: *Federal Register*, Vol. 43, No. 54, March 20, 1978, p. 11673.

some of the delays by the Canadian government in raising the tolls. At the same time, however, Canadians believed that their mounting Seaway debts were a form of subsidy paid by them for the enjoyment of U.S. firms.

In the Canadian debate over whether to raise Seaway tolls appeared this statement (from an individual in Winnipeg) which indicates the multitude of considerations involved:

> The cost of moving eastern Canadian iron ore to U.S. Great Lakes ports by the Seaway is only marginally below the cost of moving it down the east coast of the U.S. and inland by rail. Similarly, U.S. grains carried for export through the Seaway could easily be re-routed down the Mississippi River system. The competitive position of Canadian Seaway carriers is dependent on carrying grain east and backhauling ore west. Lose one of these commodities and you lose the other. Lose both and there is not much left to carry.[23]

In 1980, the Seaway handled 27 million tons of grain (mostly downbound) and 11 million tons of ore (mostly upbound). Ore and grain accounted for 81 percent of the Seaway's 1980 traffic; other bulk cargo accounted for 14 percent; and higher value general cargo accounted for the remainder.

- *Bulk cargo* is in solid or liquid state, handled with scoops, shovels, conveyors, or pumps, and generally occupies an entire vessel (or barge or rail car or truck trailer). *General cargo* is of higher value per unit of weight than bulk cargo and usually consists of manufactured or packaged, processed items. It is handled by the piece or inside containers.

The significance of the St. Lawrence Seaway to the Great Lakes area of the United States and Canada probably cannot be overestimated. Its major value to the U.S. is that it allowed the Great Lakes-based steel industry to utilize the iron ores of eastern Canada, taking the place of the diminishing Mesabi reserves in Minnesota. Without the Seaway, much of this nation's steel-making capacity would have had to relocate outside the Great Lakes area. Also the Seaway has reduced transportation costs for export shipments of wheat grown by both U.S. and Canadian farmers.

The 1980's have continued to be unkind to the tonnage growth of the Seaway. With the increased emphasis on keeping ships at sea as

---

[23] Statement was by John MacDonald, Chairman of the Great Lakes Development Association, which appeared as a "comment" in a September, 1977, issue of the Canadian *Weekend Magazine,* a tabloid appearing in several Canadian Sunday newspapers, including *The Albertan.* It was in response to an article appearing in the August 6, 1977, issue entitled "Salvaging the Seaway."

much as possible in order to increase their revenue-producing ability, the Seaway's slow system of lockage travel has proven highly detrimental. *The Wall Street Journal* noted:

> Most of the large container ships can't fit in the seaway's locks, and, anyway, international shippers concerned about quick turnarounds for their vessels aren't interested in the slow process of negotiating the seaway's numerous locks. The 48-hour trip to Toronto from Montreal is an extra cost that container lines aren't eager to bear. . . .
>
> As a result, according to the Dominion Marine Association, a Canadian shipping group, while New York handled 1.8 million containers in 1979, Toronto handled just 10,000 and Chicago only 8,000.
>
> When the Greater Cleveland Regional Transit Authority recently ordered 48 light rail vehicles from an Italian manufacturer, Cleveland port officials hoped the shipments would come their way; they lost out. "It's cheaper to bring them into Baltimore and truck them the rest of the way," explains a spokesman for the transit authority.[24]

Further exacerbating the Seaway's problems has been constant pressure on Seaway officials to raise tolls on the waterway because tonnage has not been growing while costs of operating the Seaway have rapidly escalated because of inflation. Seaway tolls doubled from 1978 to 1981. In late 1981 the U.S. and Canadian Seaway executives issued their 1982 and 1983 Joint Seaway Tariff of Tolls. Rates are scheduled to increase 18 percent in 1982 and another 10 percent in 1983.[25]

The result of these rate increases will undoubtedly be to further depress tonnage figures for the Seaway. Ray F. Hoffman, Milwaukee port director, concisely summarized the problem:

> We've priced ourselves out of the market. The Seaway is the only waterway in American history compelled to pay its way, including the cost of construction, out of toll revenues. An average toll of a 12,000 GRT ocean-going general cargo ship transiting through the Seaway to Chicago and returning pays $72,000 for ship and cargo tolls plus pilotage using 1981 rates, or about 9% of the steamship company's total operating and administrative costs for this transit. There are no U.S. tidewater ports that share this encumbrance—because all other U.S. navigational waterways are constructed, maintained, and operated with 100 percent federal funding.[26]

[24] Alan Freeman, "St. Lawrence Seaway Pins Hope of Rebirth On a Longer Season," *The Wall Street Journal* (March 24, 1981), p. 1.

[25] "U.S.-Canadian Seaway Agencies Agree To Proposed Toll Revisions," *Traffic World* (September 14, 1981), p. 20.

[26] Julie Whitmore, "Seaway Hopes," *American Shipper* (December, 1981), p. 54. See also: Henry W. Vanderleest, "Great Lakes Ports and General Cargo Export Traffic: A Current Assessment," *Annual Proceedings of the Transportation Research Forum* (1981), pp. 96–101; and Joedy W. Cambridge, "The Great Lakes/St. Lawrence Seaway System: Can Cooperative Marketing Improve Its Prospects for the Future?" *Annual Proceedings of the Transportation Research Forum* (1981), pp. 102–111.

Domestic Ocean Shipping

In the early history of the United States, domestic ocean shipping was the most important form of freight transportation. Colonial American cities were linked commercially by small vessels sailing up and down the Atlantic coastline. U.S. domestic ocean transportation is generally thought of as having been an important form of commercial transportation until World War II. For example, before World War II, new automobiles from assembly plants in both Atlantic and Pacific coastal cities were distributed up and down the coasts by small, ocean-going vessels.

While coastal shipping has declined, its influence lives on in the form of the much lower rail rates it forces railroads to charge between coastal cities where the possibility of all-water transport exists.[27] (These are called "water-compelled" rates; see Figure 3–4.) Railroads cut rates when competing with water carriers and frequently operated their own vessel lines at a loss merely to drive out the legitimate water carriers. The railroads attempted to continue this practice as the Panama Canal was opening; Congress responded by passing the *Panama Canal Act* in 1912 which prohibits railroads from owning or controlling or having any interest in water carriers that pass through the Panama Canal.

The general patterns of domestic ocean transportation are shown in Table 8–2, with origins of the traffic listed on the left-hand column and destinations across the top.[28] Three-quarters of the tonnage shown in that table consists of gasoline, petroleum, and other petroleum products. Other cargos moving are sand and gravel, building cement, sulphur, phosphate rock, and sugar. In the Pacific Northwest, lumber is shipped by water.

The figures given emphasize tonnage, rather than value. In the case of traffic between the 48 states and Hawaii, most high-value cargo (manufactured items and foods) moves in ocean-going container ships. Traffic to and from Alaska and to and from Puerto Rico/Virgin Islands moves on single or multi-deck barges carrying railroad cars or truck trailers. One line operating out of Florida for

[27] For a discussion of the influence of water competition on transcontinental rail rates, see Stuart Daggett and John P. Carter, *The Structure of Transcontinental Railroad Rates* (Berkeley: University of California Press, 1947.) Domestic rail rates are much lower between cities on the Pacific Coast and those on the Atlantic Coast than they are from the same cities to inland points, the reason being that intercoastal water carriers (or their potential) kept rail rates low.

[28] Not shown in Table 8–2 are 175,432 tons of cargo that moved as domestic commerce between U.S. ocean ports and U.S. Great Lakes ports in 1977 via the St. Lawrence Seaway.

TABLE 8–2 Domestic Oceanborne Commerce of the U.S.—1977 (in Thousands of Short Tons)

Area of Shipping	Total Tons	Area of Receiving*								
		North Atlantic	South Atlantic	Gulf	California	Pacific N.W.	Hawaiian Islands	Alaska	Puerto Rico & Virgin Islands	Other Pacific Islands
North Atlantic	51,941	45,648	2,134	1,944	275	1	54	—	1,852	8
South Atlantic	2,828	714	546	631	161	—	5	—	770	1
Gulf	100,845	46,623	20,077	30,997	1,364	238	—	—	1,392	—
California	31,077	708	39	345	19,240	6,445	3,069	812	219	179
Pacific Northwest	6,177	116	10	15	2,940	714	470	1,882	—	8
Hawaiian Islands	5,268	25	—	136	2,530	251	2,322	8	—	5
Alaska	17,649	54	—	158	11,618	4,335	—	1,544	—	—
Puerto Rico & Virgin Islands	33,059	21,482	5,380	2,350	160	27	—	—	3,654	—
Other Pacific Islands & Trust Territories	91	—	—	—	56	—	8	—	—	27
TOTALS**	248,936	115,376	28,187	36,595	38,345	12,011	5,948	4,240	7,907	228

SOURCE: U.S. Department of Commerce, *Domestic Waterborne Trade of the United States, 1973–1977.*

* North Atlantic is that coastal area north of the Virginia/North Carolina state line. Gulf is from Key West, Florida, west to the border of Mexico. Alaska also includes the Aleutian Islands. Other Pacific Islands include Wake, Guam, Midway, and other island possessions and protectorates in the Pacific. When the source area is listed as both shipping and receiving, it means trade between ports within the same area.

**Totals may not add because of rounding.

Note: Data were unavailable to update this table completely. However, another source indicated that 73 million tons of oil were shipped from Alaska in 1980, of which nearly 80 percent went to California or Washington ports. Another 15 percent went to Puerto Armuelles, on the Pacific side of the Panama Canal, where it was transferred to smaller tankers for movement through the Canal to the East Coast. (Lloyd's Shipping Economics, July, 1981).

the Puerto Rico/Virgin Islands operates a triple-deck barge for carrying truck trailers. The vessel is 580 feet long, 105 feet wide, and can carry up to 374 forty-foot trailers.

Regular trade between the Atlantic and Pacific Coast via the Panama Canal all but died in World War II. In the early 1960's Sea-Land Service, Inc., inaugurated containership service between the two coasts, utilizing the Panama Canal. Sea-Land is also an important international containership operator and its domestic service complemented its international operations, as well as its service to Alaska, Puerto Rico, and the Virgin Islands. However, in early 1978, the firm announced that it was withdrawing from intercoastal service. A company spokesman said: "With the competition we faced from railroads for intercoastal traffic, our earnings were not adequate even to replace the vessels we had operating in the trade."[29] United States Lines, another U.S. flag vessel operator engaged in both international and domestic ocean shipping, continues to offer container service between the two coasts via the Panama Canal. After snow storms paralyzed surface traffic in the Northeast in early 1979, a United States Lines' advertisement said ". . . Send your goods south for the winter via U.S. Lines' all-water service."

Waterborne Passenger Transportation

Viewed from the national perspective, domestic passenger transportation by water is not significant, yet in a few areas it is important. The American Public Transit Association estimates that there are now 68 ferry boats in operation in the United States.[30] At one time there were many more, but the ferries have been replaced by bridges.

Many passengers are carried on "harbor tour" vessels in most port communities. Boat tours are a popular form of sightseeing and recreation. Several tour boat operators near New Orleans have built present-day replicas of sternwheeler paddleboats, like those used over a century ago. Some of these vessels have overnight accommodations and take tourists up and down the river.

In a few spots in the U.S., vessels are a necessary form of transportation to reach offshore islands. They carry passengers, mail, fuel, food, and other supplies. Examples of such offshore islands are Martha's Vineyard off Massachusetts; Tangier Island in Chesapeake Bay; Washington Island, off the Door County Peninsula in Lake

[29] *American Shipper* (January, 1978), p. 36. The company denied that the revised Panama Canal treaties, then under consideration, affected its decision.

[30] *Transit Fact Book, 1981 Edition* (Washington, D.C.: American Public Transit Association, 1981), p. 41.

Michigan; the Apostle Islands in Lake Superior; and Catalina Island off Southern California. In other areas, a few wealthy suburbs can be reached only by water, which is also true of many recreational areas.

Daily commuter traffic also moves in a few cities by water. The Staten Island Ferries are the best-known example. An extensive passenger and auto/passenger ferry system is operated by the State of Washington in the Seattle area. The Mississippi River Bridge Authority operates four ferry boats in the New Orleans area, carrying 10,000 individuals daily.[31] In Chicago, use is made of the Chicago River to carry commuters from Union Station (a terminal for many commuter trains) to the North Michigan Avenue area (where there are many new office buildings).

Figure 8–14 illustrates an attempt by the Golden Gate Bridge District to operate a ferry service which will serve to reduce automobile congestion on the Golden Gate Bridge. The famous Golden Gate Bridge connects San Francisco to Marin County on the north. Marin County's population is clustered along U.S. Highway 101; San Rafael is the largest city in Marin County. Other concentrations of population are to the north. The Golden Gate Bridge District, which finished paying for the bridge in 1970, uses a portion of the tolls collected from autos to subsidize four ferries operating on two routes connecting Marin County to downtown San Francisco. The San Francisco terminal is the Ferry Building (a pre-earthquake structure which once accommodated passengers to all points in the San Francisco Bay area before the bridges were built). The Sausalito terminal in Marin County serves a compact, affluent community, and the Sausalito ferry carries many tourists during the mid-day and on weekends. The Larkspur terminal has a large parking lot, serves mainly commuters, and is served by faster commuter ferries. Both ferry routes are designed so that the commuting time via ferry is less than the comparable time by auto. The ferries provide a high quality of service although they also require large subsidies enabling them to lower fares and thus to attract passengers. Some federal subsidies are also involved, and there has been great interest in this ferry service shown by the mass transit industry to see whether it can successfully attract commuters away from their autos.[32] A private operator pro-

---

[31] See: Richard D. James, "On Alaska's Coast, the 'Blue Canoe' Is the Only Way to Go," *The Wall Street Journal* (August 7, 1979), p. 27.

[32] The Golden Gate Bridge District also subsidizes bus operations between Marin County and downtown San Francisco and provides bus service to and from the Marin ferry terminal sites. In addition, it subsidizes van pools by providing vans for groups of commuters.

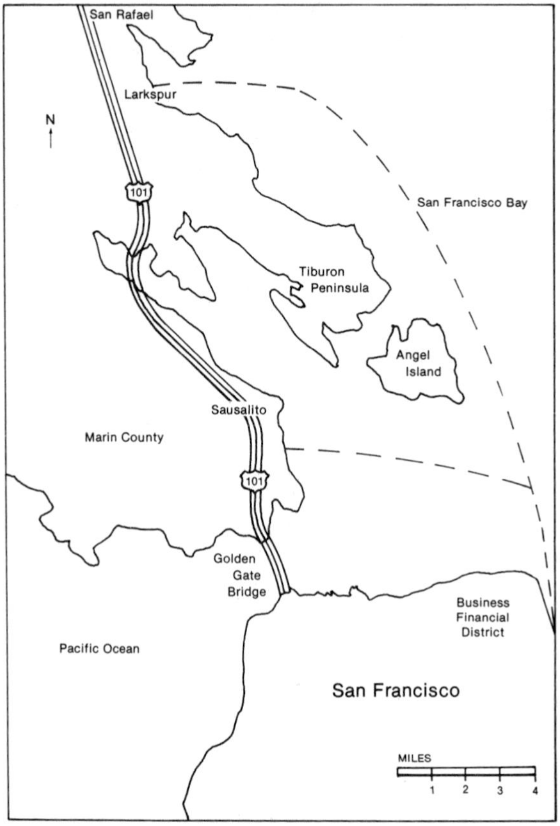

Figure 8–14 Routes of Ferries Operated by the Golden Gate Bridge District.

vides service between downtown San Francisco and a terminal on the Tiburon Peninsula, with an intermediate stop at the Angel Island Park. This same private operator also has a fleet of tour boats operating in the Bay area and is critical of the Golden Gate Bridge District's highly-subsidized ferry system since it hurts his tour boat business.

Two new passenger vessel technologies are the hydrofoil and hovercraft; neither is in widespread use in this country. The *hydrofoil* is a conventional vessel with water-ski-like foils attached to its hull. As the vessel picks up speed, it rises partially out of the water and travels on the foils at nearly 50 miles per hour, much faster than a vessel could travel if its hull were in the water. Hydrofoils are used commercially in other parts of the world and have been introduced into inter-island travel in Hawaii. *Hovercraft* travel on a thin cushion of air and can reach speeds of 95 miles per hour. They are in commercial use elsewhere in the world; their use in the United States is primarily limited to the Coast Guard and to the armed services.

Domestic Ports

Harbors are protected areas of water where vessels can be safe from storms; ports are usually located inside harbors (either natural or man-made) and contain facilities for the transfer of cargo between vessels and land. Ports attract other forms of trade and commerce, and cities grew around the nucleus of a port. Indeed, with only a few exceptions, most major U.S. cities are either ocean ports, inland waterway ports, or Great Lakes ports. Some port functions will be discussed here, although those functions related to international commerce will be covered in chapter 9.

Intermodal Connections

Ports are important to all modes of domestic transportation for several reasons. First, they are the sites where cargo must be transferred between modes of transport. Hence, many carriers want to serve ports because of the likelihood of sharing in the flow of traffic to and from the ports. Second, carrier offices must be located at ports to facilitate the smooth interchange of cargo between modes. Also, unless the flow of traffic through the port is evenly balanced in both directions, there will be an imbalance of empty vessel holds, rail cars, or trucks, in one direction or the other, and carrier management will be under continual pressure to develop new movements of traffic which will fill up the empty backhaul capacity. Lastly, carriers work closely with the operators of marine terminals and docks in the design and operation of the cargo unloading, transfer, and reloading facilities.

Often carriers serve competing ports and will have to choose the port through which they prefer to route traffic. In making this decision, a carrier will be guided by two principles:

1. It will carry as much of the traffic as it can over its own routes without having to interconnect with other carriers. This reduces delays and having to share revenues with other carriers.
2. It will choose a port where transfer costs and equipment delays are the least. The carrier does not want his equipment waiting to be handled; he wants it moving and earning revenue.

Large shippers are also attracted to locate their offices in major ports for some of the same reasons that attract carriers. They must be able to both accumulate large, and often fluctuating, inventories and accommodate surges in the movements of the product. As an example of the capacity needed, in a coal terminal intended for San Francisco's port, 100-car unit-trains would unload twice a day while 80,000- to 100,000-ton capacity ocean bulk carriers would load every two or three days. To accommodate these differences in flows, plus irregularities such as the mines' closing for vacation, possible dock or rail strikes, and delays in either rail or vessel schedules, it is necessary to have a coal facility with a storage capacity of at least 10 million tons.[33]

Because of surge situations, many firms dealing in commodities or manufactured items find that they have large inventories of their goods at port locations. The large number of water and land carriers

- Surge, when applied to bulk materials handling, is the fluctuation in the amount of materials received, or shipped, or the balance between them, i.e., materials on hand.

serving port cities makes this location an ideal spot to store and manage an inventory, since it is relatively easy to arrange for transportation in any direction.

Hence both surface carriers and many shippers choose port cities as the sites from which to manage their transportation operations. These port-related functions create jobs at all levels of employment, and port cities compete with each other in their efforts to attract port-related activities.

Waterfront Industrial Development

Water carriers frequently carry large tonnages of bulk raw materials which are inputs to various manufacturing and processing operations. Waterways are often the sites of heavy industry which is dependent upon low-cost water transportation. Location along a navigable waterway allows the firm to bargain with the railroad for lower "water-compelled" rail rates,[34] which gives the site lower rail rates than would be enjoyed by a site that cost the railroad an equal

---

[33] *The Proposed Coal Facility for San Francisco's Port* (San Francisco State University: Center for World Business, 1977).

[34] Water competition is an allowable reason for a railroad to seek relief from Section 4 of the Interstate Commerce Act. See Figure 3–4 and see also: D. Philip Locklin, *Economics of Transportation*, 7th ed., chapter 21; and John Guandolo, *Transportation Law* (Dubuque: Wm. C. Brown, 1973), chapter 28.

amount to serve, but which was not adjacent to the waterway. Waterfront sites have additional advantages. The surface water can be used for cooling machinery or condensers or for certain other manufacturing processes. Plant wastes, after proper treatment to remove pollutants, can be discharged into an adjacent stream.

A waterfront industrial site has several characteristics, depending upon the use to which it would be put. One list of characteristics follows:

1. The site must be close to commercial navigation channels, which is often measured in feet from the channel which is maintained by the U.S. Army Corps of Engineers. This distance must either be dredged by some non-federal party, or the facilities on shore must extend out toward it. For example, a navigation channel that is close to shore would be easy to reach, but would leave no room toward the channel upon which the firm could expand by reclaiming (filling submerged) land. The firm must also consider the cost of maintaining the channel between the industrial site and the Corps channel.

2. The industrial site must be above the level of floods or other water fluctuations. In a flood plain some types of facilities can be located on low land. Cargo-handling equipment may require placement in a flood plain merely to be close enough to the water to function.

3. The waterfront industrial site must be relatively level.

4. The soil at the site must be stable and capable of bearing the load of both the cargo being handled and stored and the buildings. Since soils near the water are often relatively infirm, any proposed site should be tested by making borings.

5. The site should have ready access to both rail tracks and highways and to high-voltage power.

6. The shape of the waterfront industrial site is difficult to specify. Much would depend upon the cost of maintaining water frontage. The site should have sufficient water frontage so that a vessel can tie up parallel to the shore for discharging cargo. For plants that receive barges, often a string of barges is tied parallel to the shore and then moved by a barge puller (a system of cables) so that each barge is placed under an unloading device.

7. The size of the site can vary. If the plant receives bulk materials, there must be adequate storage area to handle more than a vessel load at one time. There must also be sufficient space to

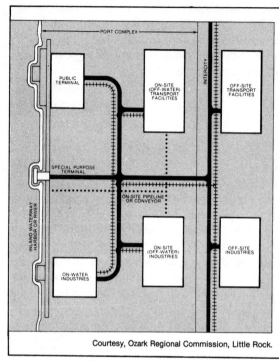

Basic Development Model for Ozarks Region Ports.

Whether large or small, the port cities within the Ozarks Region have adopted the kind of integrated waterside planning shown in this model. The interrelationship between modes of transportation and waterfront, off waterfront and off site industrial facilities is taken into account; development is in stages to insure orderly growth. The waterway is on the left and the rail line and highway are on the right.

Courtesy, Ozark Regional Commission, Little Rock.

Figure 8–15   Industrial Waterfront Layout.

stockpile the amount of material normally kept in storage by the manufacturer. The space required for storing 10,000 tons of coal would be at least 150 feet by 150 feet (assuming a pile 50 feet high and a 45-degree slope on the sides). In addition, the manufacturer would need space for the equipment to move it from the stockpiles into his hoppers. A manufacturer using barge transportation would have to think in terms of storing thousand-ton lots, and those using Great Lakes or ocean vessels would need storage for at least 15,000- to 100,000-ton lots.[35]

The layout of a waterways industrial site, intended for several different users, is shown on Figure 8–15. Equipment and buildings needed to load and unload the cargo must be close to the water; other uses can be located farther away. Some of the users of sites not on the

[35] Adapted and updated from: Wisconsin Department of Resource Development, *Waterfront Renewal: Technical Supplement* (Madison, 1964), pp. 22–23.

water can rely on pipes or conveyer belts to connect them with pumps or cargo-handling equipment on the water's edge.

Industrial waterways often attract a large concentration of heavy industries. Examples are the Rouge River in Detroit, where Henry Ford located his manufacturing colossus; the Chicago Ship and Sanitary Canal, along which much of that city's early heavy industry located;[36] and the Houston Ship Canal which contains many chemical- and petroleum-related operations. Most areas with waterfront sites advertise them to potential developers. The Ozarks Regional Commission (representing Arkansas, Kansas, Louisiana, Missouri, and Oklahoma) issued a promotional booklet showing the four waterways serving the area (the Arkansas, the Lower Mississippi, the Missouri, and the Ouachita). The booklet also contains descriptions of the 23 river posts and describes the sites for industrial growth along the 2,500 miles of navigable waterways in the region. The introduction to the brochure includes this statement:

> In an era in which environmental impacts have become a major factor in plant site selections, the fact the Ozarks waterways have been completed within the past few years means a great deal of comprehensive planning has occurred as construction went along. Virtually every county facing a navigable stream has in-depth land use research at hand. By including this input in their industrial packages, each state and city can offer relatively less "hassle" in finalizing a site and effecting early start-up.[37]

Domestic Waterways Issues

User Charges

Over the past decade, the most important domestic waterways issue has been that inland water carriers, domestic ocean carriers, and Great Lakes carriers (operating above the Welland Canal) were paying no user charges. By almost any measure devised by either accountants or economists, water carriers are our nation's most heavily-subsidized form of transportation, benefiting from massive federal expenditures.

[36]David M. Solzman, *Waterway Industrial Sites: A Chicago Case Study* (University of Chicago Department of Geography Research Paper 107, 1966). See also James B. Kenyon, *Georgia's Navigable Waterways and Industrialization* (University of Georgia Institute of Community and Area Development Monograph No. 15, 1964).

[37]*Inland Waterways Investment Guide* (Little Rock: Ozarks Regional Commission, 1977), p. 1. See also: *Tennessee's Opportunities on Its Waterways System* (University of Tennessee Transportation Center, 1974).

In the mid-1970's congestion developed at Lock and Dam #26 on the Mississippi River at Alton, Illinois, near St. Louis. This bottleneck affected the movement of barge traffic above this point on both the Upper Mississippi (leading to St. Paul) and on the Illinois Waterway (leading to Chicago). Some time before, in the late 1960's, the U.S. Army Corps of Engineers had proposed elimination of this then-potential bottleneck by replacing the locks with new ones having twice the capacity. Construction was not authorized, however, because of political opposition generated by the railroad industry, in particular, which also received some support from various groups of environmentalists.

The fact that the general taxpayer was being asked to build an expensive improvement for the free use of the barge industry was emphasized by the project's opponents. Eventually a number of diverse interest groups indicated that they would relax their opposition to expanding the lock if the waterway users would relax some of their opposition to the concept of waterways user charges. In 1978 Congress passed a bill which the President signed; it authorized the Alton project and imposed a fuel tax of 4 cents per gallon on fuel used by inland waterways carriers. The rate of tax will increase until it reaches 10 cents per gallon in 1985.

While the tax is a short step in the right direction, it has one apparent drawback: it provides no guidance as to where waterways improvements are needed. That is, it is merely an industry-wide tax giving no indication as to which waterways improvements make economic sense and which ones do not. A consequence to the public of providing waterways improvements which were "free" to the inland waterways operators is that there was often little solid economic justification for specific improvements. Several studies have shown that some waterways improvements made sense, while others did not. Table 8–3 shows estimates of what would happen if costs of taxpayer-provided improvements along each were calculated and then assessed as user charges against barges operating each of these specific waterways. As examples, 7.4 percent of the Mississippi River traffic between Minneapolis and Cairo, Illinois, would be lost, while *all* traffic on the Arkansas River would be lost, meaning that no barge traffic presently using the Arkansas could afford to pay its share of the costs presently borne by the taxpayers.

Section 205: Study on Waterway User Charges

In 1978, when Congress enacted the first user charge for the inland waterway system, Section 205 of the law provided that a mas-

TABLE 8–3   Amounts of Traffic Each Domestic Waterway Route is Estimated to Lose if the Federal Government Applied Specific Tolls to Each Waterway to Recover Public Funds Spent on That Waterway

Name of Segment	Percent of Ton-Miles Diverted
Mississippi River—Cairo to Baton Rouge	10.5
Mississippi River—Minneapolis to Cairo	7.4
Arkansas River	100.0
White River	.1
Ohio River	6.8
Monongahela River	2.6
Allegheny River	100.0
Tennessee River	6.5
Cumberland River	21.3
Kanawha River	3.0
Green and Barren River	.4
Kentucky River	100.0
Illinois Waterway	6.2
Gulf Intercoastal Waterway—West	7.7
Morgan City—Port Allen Route	9.5
Gulf Intercoastal Waterway—East	7.2
Pearl River	100.0
Alabama—Coosa River	43.9
Warrior—Tombigbee—Mobile River	.8
Missouri River	100.0
Apalachicola—Chattahoochee River	100.0
Atchafalaya River	20.0
Red River	—
Black and Ouachita River	100.0
Mississippi River—Baton Rouge to Mouth of Passes	11.5

Source: U.S. Department of Transportation, Transportation Systems Center, *Modal Traffic Impacts of Waterway User Charges*, Volume 1 (Cambridge, Mass), p. VIII-9, as reported in Congressional Budget Office, *Financing Waterway Development: The User Charge Debate*, (Washington, D.C.: July 1977), p. 26.

sive study be conducted to determine the long-run impact of user charges on inland water carriers. This study was conducted by the U.S. Departments of Commerce and Transportation and their report was finished in November, 1981. It noted that in 1981 the tolls collected equaled 11 percent of the costs of maintaining the waterway system. The report noted that inland water carriers *can* and *should* pay higher user charges in order to achieve governmental equality of treatment between modes. One major conclusion of the Section 205 Report was that the inland waterways will continue to show strong economic growth to the year 2000 *with* or *without* additional federal user charges. The governmental study observed:

> The more traffic there is moving on the river, the lower the user-charge per ton of traffic and the less the impact of the user-charge. Much of the

traffic growth is in coal. In tonnage terms, coal is by far the largest single commodity moving on the waterways. It accounted for approximately 27 per cent of total tons in 1977, and is forecast to be very close to 50 per cent by the year 2000, with or without user charges. There is also very strong growth in corn, soybeans, fertilizer, chemicals and steel.[38]

Since inland water carriers are not significantly affected by higher levels of user charges, the federal researchers advocated that user charges should be increased to full-cost recovery levels. Specifically, user charges should pay for 100 percent of all federal expenditures for *maintenance* of the existing inland waterway system. In addition, all *future* new waterway projects would have user charges set at cost-recovery levels to recoup both construction and maintenance costs. The report stated that at this level of user charges, probably no new capital improvement projects would be built before the year 2000. (However, two major semi-completed capital projects should continue—the Tenn-Tom waterway and Locks and Dam #26—because construction is well along on both projects.)[39] The Section 205 Report concluded:

> All subsidies to freight movement are to be eliminated, either through reduction or termination of spending programs or through the imposition of user charges where programs are retained. With respect to waterway operations, the Administration has already proposed legislation to institute full cost recovery from commercial users of the inland waterways and of deep-draft channels.
>   In sum, then, the Executive Branch has adopted a clear and consistent policy towards financial support for the freight modes. The era in which promotional or developmental goals were pursued is long gone. Efficient, self-sustaining operation of the freight systems is the objective now. All freight subsidies are to be eliminated.[40]

The Reagan Administration, in accordance with this philosophy, proposed an increase in inland waterway user charges. The plan keeps the existing schedule of fuel tax per gallon (which increased to 6¢ per gallon on October 1, 1981) and adds an additional ton-mile tax which will generate about $600 million its first year in operation. Furthermore, other services now provided free will be paid for on a usage basis. An example would be the port and channel navigation aids provided by the Coast Guard.[41]

---

[38] Cited in "Sharp Growth in River Traffic Expected Despite User Charges," *Traffic World* (November 9, 1981), p. 26.

[39] National Waterways Conference, Inc., *Newsletter* (December 11, 1981), p. 3.

[40] Cited in "DOT, Commerce Dep't Finish Study of Impact of Waterway User Fees," *Traffic World* (November 30, 1981), p. 21.

[41] The American Waterways Operators, Inc., *Weekly Letter* (February 12, 1982), p. 3.

Extension of Navigation System in Winter Months

This issue affects navigation on the Great Lakes, the St. Lawrence Seaway, and portions of the Upper Mississippi and its tributaries. Each winter, depending upon the severity of the weather, navigation usually comes to a halt along these waterways. Locks become difficult to operate, or ice blocks endanger navigation and bulk cargos freeze so that they cannot be handled. Compounding the problem is that winter is the time when two bulk products carried by vessel—petroleum and coal—are in greatest demand. The low temperatures which freeze waterways and locks also increase the consumption of and demand for fuels.

Traditionally, many of these cargos moved only during the open navigation season and were stockpiled for wintertime use. However, current physical distribution logistics thinking has held that inventories and accompanying inventory-carrying costs should be considered.[42]

Extending the operating season of a waterway which would otherwise freeze requires a number of actions by the parties maintaining and using the locks. At locks, the gates must be kept in a movable condition and ice jams must be broken up before they reach a lock. Vessel operators also must take special precautions. On the Great Lakes, they carry lighter loads so that they do not ride as low in the water.[43] On rivers, the barges in tows are arranged in a manner that the tankers—which might be punctured by ice—are inside, protected by a ring of barges carrying solid cargo. Shippers and receivers of cargo usually need additional cargo handling equipment to accommodate the frozen bulk cargo. Loading and unloading takes much longer. Lastly, an agency, such as the Coast Guard, must maintain surveillance over large accumulations of ice and must warn vessels of their locations and assist in breaking them up before they reach navigation locks where they might cause massive ice jams.

During much of the 1970's, the U.S. Army Corps of Engineers, the St. Lawrence Seaway Development Corporation, the Coast Guard,

[42] See: James C. Johnson and Donald F. Wood, 2nd edition, *Contemporary Physical Distribution and Logistics* (Tulsa: PennWell Books, 1982), Chapter 7.

[43] Vessels are assigned "load lines"—one for each season—which are painted on the side of the hull. Depending upon the season in which they are sailing, they may not load so deeply that the seasonal line is submerged. (On ocean-going vessels, these lines are called "Plimsoll" marks.) On November 10, 1975, the laker *Edmund Fitzgerald* sank into 530 feet of water in eastern Lake Superior with its crew of 29 during a severe storm. A Coast Guard Board of Inquiry "while admitting it could not positively identify the cause . . . , indicated the flooding of the cargo hold took place through ineffective hatch covers." (*Seaway Review*, Autumn, 1977), pp. 21–24.

and several other agencies explored the problems of extending the commercial navigation season on both the Great Lakes and the St. Lawrence Seaway. Tentative conclusions of their studies are that it will be advantageous to extend the open season by increments (i.e., keeping it open later in the fall and opening it earlier in the spring). The incremental costs and advantages can be evaluated for each additional extension.[44]

Alaskan shipping would also benefit from technologies that extend navigation seasons. In 1969 the tanker *Manhattan*, with a special ice-breaking hull, sailed from the East Coast to the North Slope of Alaska and returned via the Northwest Passage north of Canada. After the voyage was completed, the decision was reached that it was not an economically feasible way of moving oil from the North Slope. Canada would also benefit from extensions of navigation seasons and cooperates with the United States in water routes where both nations share interests. Figure 8–16 shows a unique "team" of Canadian icebreakers and the caption explains how they work together.

Changing Water Levels

Vessel technology dictates that larger hulls, loaded to deeper drafts, are more efficient. Since rivers and harbors, in their natural state, tend to have many shallow spots, it is necessary to continually dredge away at the shallow sites so that laden vessels can pass. Often, a single deepening operation is not sufficient since spring floods may carry down another load of suspended solid material which it will dump, usually, at the location where the flowing water's velocity is suddenly slowed. The silt-carrying capacity of flowing water is proportional to its speed. Often a river's speed is slowed when it suddenly reaches a large body of water, such as one of the Great Lakes or the ocean. In a natural state, this would be where a sandbar would form, blocking the river's mouth to navigation. Therefore, in some areas the Corps of Engineers must continually operate dredges to maintain a passable depth for an authorized project.

Dredged material, whether from new dredging or from maintenance dredging, must be discharged at some site, either in deep water or on land. In recent years, environmental protection interests

---

[44] *Water Resources Development by the U.S. Army Corps of Engineers in Michigan, 1977* (Chicago: Office of the Division Engineer, North Central, 1977), pp. 13–16. See also: Deborah F. Silver, "Environmental Conflict Clouds Future of Seaway's Winter Navigation Plan," *Traffic World* (April 2, 1979), pp. 27–29.

Figure 8–16 The Canadian Coast Guard Icebreaker *Alexander Henry*. This 210-foot vessel has a hovercraft attached to the bow. As the hovercraft moves onto the edge of an ice sheet, the air it is discharging depresses the water level by a few inches. Water flows out from under the ice, removing the buoyant support it had given to the ice, which then collapses. This form of operation consumes much less fuel than the older method in which a conventional icebreaker "plows its way" through the ice. Courtesy: Canadian Department of Transport.

have objected to many proposed dumping sites, making it necessary for the dredged material to be carried farther and farther away for dumping. This has increased the cost of the operation, and—since the Corps of Engineers uses a "benefit-to-cost" ratio to analyze projects—makes deepening to accommodate larger vessels more difficult to justify.

In addition, various demands for water remove some "off-of-the-top" which has a negative effect on navigation. Chicago and its sanitary district divert water from Lake Michigan at the rate of 3,200 cubic feet per second. This water is used for domestic purposes, and the treated and diluted sewage is then discharged into the Illinois River, which flows into the Mississippi and out of the Great Lakes

Basin.[45] As a result of this diversion, Lake Michigan is three inches lower than it would otherwise be—and for a laker which is operating in waters where its draft is a concern, this three-inch loss of water level cuts about 300 tons from its payload. Note, however, that the barges operating on the Illinois River enjoy deeper water. At present, studies are underway to determine whether the amount of diversion should be increased.[46] Lower surface levels also have an adverse effect on waterfront dock operators because they make the vessel loading and unloading operation more difficult.

Hydroelectric power plants compete with navigation for the same water. Every time a vessel passes through a lock which bypasses a dam used to generate hydroelectric power, that amount of water passing with the vessel is lost for purposes of power generation. In addition, in studies regarding the extension of navigation on the Great Lakes–St. Lawrence system, one "problem is the fact that hydroelectric companies need a stable ice cover to avoid the possibility of broken ice entering turbine inlets."[47] Hence they would prefer not to see ice-breaking operations take place above power dams.

In ocean tidal areas, environmental protection interests have shown increased concern with changes in the "mixing" of salt and fresh waters, as tides move in and out. These groups tend to oppose engineering improvements designed to maintain levels of water for navigation which—as a side effect—create changes in the tidal "zone" where fresh and salt waters meet and mix.

Summary

Water transportation is the oldest technology of transport, yet it still requires heavy subsidies. By many measures, it is the most heavily-subsidized form of domestic transportation in the United States.

There are three categories of domestic water transportation: inland waterways (or barge); Great Lakes; and ocean transportation between U.S. ports. Inland waterways transportation is growing in volume; the other two are declining.

The federal government is deeply involved in the provision of

[45] Some of the water is diverted to increase the flow of the treated sewage effluent down the Illinois Waterway.

[46] The American Waterways Operators, Inc., *Weekly Letter*, (Dec. 10, 1977). The study, authorized by Congress, is being conducted by the Army Corps of Engineers.

[47] "Canada's Hard-Worked Icebreaking Fleet," *Surveyer* (quarterly journal of the American Bureau of Shipping, November, 1977), pp. 18–25.

waterway improvements which are then used by commercial navigation firms. The specific government agency involved is the civil works branch of the U.S. Army Corps of Engineers. The Corps' involvement dates from the 1820's when West Point was one of the few sources of trained civil engineers.

The main volume of inland waterway traffic is on the Mississippi River and its tributaries. "Tows" of barges are lashed together and pushed by towboats. At locks, the tows are broken down, passed through the lock, and reassembled on the other side. There are also barge operations in the following regions: the Pacific Northwest, the Columbia River Basin; the San Francisco Bay region; and coastal waterways along the Atlantic and Gulf Coasts. A "cross-Florida" barge canal, designed to connect the Atlantic and the Gulf coastal waterways, was stopped from being completed by environmental protection interests.

Great Lakes shipping is carried on special vessels, known as "lakers." The primary domestic movement on the Great Lakes is of iron ore from Minnesota to the steel mills along southern Lake Michigan and Lake Erie. Completion of a new lock at Sault Ste. Marie has permitted a larger size of laker, approximately 1,000 feet in length, to be placed into service. Several have been built, but they are "bottled up" in the upper four Great Lakes by the Welland Canal which cannot accommodate them. Smaller lakers and ocean-going ships can move through the Welland Canal and through the St. Lawrence Seaway.

Domestic ocean shipping never really recovered from World War II. Its main use is to connect the 48 states with Alaska, Hawaii, and Puerto Rico/Virgin Islands. Movements of oil from Alaska to other U.S. ports fall into this category. The volume of coast-to-coast water transportation via the Panama Canal is small and declining; however just because the Panama route is there, transcontinental rail rates are lower than similar rail rates from either coast to inland points.

Water vessels also are used for carrying passengers, including tourists, sightseers, and—in a few areas—weekday commuters to and from work. In San Francisco, the Golden Gate Bridge District uses auto fares to subsidize ferries which provide commuter service to individuals who would otherwise drive on the Golden Gate Bridge.

Domestic ports were discussed in terms of their significance as interchange points between transport modes and as sites for industrial activity. Industrial waterways are stretches of water that attract large numbers of heavy industrial firms.

Questions for Discussion and Review

1. Discuss the amount of traffic carried by the various components of our domestic waterways system.

2. Why is the U.S. Army Corps of Engineers involved in providing facilities for use by domestic water carriers?

3. Discuss the controversy involving the "Tenn-Tom" waterway. Do you believe this project should be completed? Defend your answer.

4. Describe how vessel locks work.

5. Where are the major waterways routes used by inland water carriers? Which carry the most traffic?

6. Compare Figure 8–1 to Figure 8–6. What major alterations have taken place in the U.S. waterways system during the last 130 years? Why have these changes taken place?

7. What are LASH vessels? How do they function?

8. What are the principal cargos carried by Great Lakes carriers?

9. What is a self-unloading vessel? What advantages does it offer to prospective users?

10. Describe the laker fleet and its ownership.

11. Why did Canada and the United States cooperate in building the St. Lawrence Seaway?

12. How successful has the St. Lawrence Seaway been in collecting tolls? Have all costs been covered?

13. What is the current status of the St. Lawrence Seaway in terms of traffic growth? Why?

14. Discuss the patterns of domestic ocean commerce.

15. Describe the passenger ferry operations of the Golden Gate Bridge District. Do you think the District is justified in using a portion of tolls, collected from motorists who use the bridge, to subsidize the ferries? Why or why not?

16. Why do carrier firms locate significant parts of their operations in port cities?

17. What is a "water-compelled" railroad rate?

18. List the characteristics that a waterfront site intended for industrial development should possess.

19. Discuss the findings of the Section 205 study conducted by the U.S. Departments of Commerce and Transportation. Do you agree with the conclusions? Why?

20. What major issues face our domestic waterways industries?

Additional Chapter References

Bahn, Henry M., and James R. Jones, "Transshipment of Containerized Agricultural Exports Via the Columbia Snake River System," *Annual Proceedings of the Transportation Research Forum* (1978), pp. 34–41.

Carroll, Joseph L., and Srikanth Rao, "Locks and Dam 26: Critique of Corps' Forecasts and Capacity Analysis," *Annual Proceedings of the Transportation Research Forum* (1976), pp. 101–109.

Casavant, Ken L., "Impacts of User Fees and Dam Development on Energy Consumption in Transporting Pacific Northwest Wheat," *Annual Proceedings of the Transportation Research Forum* (1981), pp. 441–447.

Cook, Peter D., "An Approach to the Analysis of Multi-Purpose Water Use Impacts of Commercial Navigation on the U.S. Waterway System," *Annual Proceedings of the Transportation Research Forum* (1979), pp. 145–150.

Cook, Peter D., Philip Roark, and David C. McGaw, "Water Flow, Light Loading, and Transport Cost on the Missouri, Apalachicola, and Alabama Rivers," *Annual Proceedings of the Transportation Research Forum* (1980), pp. 311–318.

Creelman, W. A., "The Outlook for Water Carriers in the 80's," *Annual Proceedings of the National Council of Physical Distribution Management* (1980), pp. 223–230.

Crew, James G., and Kevin H. Horn, "The Impact of Rail Rates or Costs Upon Waterway Project Planning: An Uncertain Future," *Annual Proceedings of the Transportation Research Forum* (1981), pp. 432–440.

DeRoche, Edward H., "Transportation on Canada's Waterways—Some Fuel Considerations," *The Logistics and Transportation Review*, Vol. 17, No. 2 (1981), pp. 129–134.

Eastman, Samuel Ewer, "Expanded Inland Water Transportation: Preliminary Estimates of Potential Fuel Savings and Accompanying Initial Costs," *Annual Proceedings of the Transportation Research Forum* (1981), pp. 413–422.

Gladwell, David M., "The Barge Freight Call Session of the Merchants Exchange of St. Louis: An Innovation in Transportation Pricing," *Transportation Journal* (Fall, 1980), pp. 5–18.

Hauff, Alan F., "Barge Fleeting . . . A Classic Battle Between the Barge and Towing Industry and the Environmentalists," *Annual Proceedings of the Transportation Research Forum* (1981), p. 448.

Howe, Charles W., and others. *Inland Waterway Transportation, Studies in*

Public and Private Management and Investment Decisions. (Baltimore: The John Hopkins Press, 1969).

Iowa Department of Transportation, *River Transportation In Iowa.* (Ames, Iowa: Office of Advance Planning, Planning Research Division, May, 1978).

Johnson, James C., and Donald L. Berger, "Waterway User-Charges: An Economic and Political Dilemma," *Transportation Journal* (Summer, 1977), pp. 20–29.

Mayer, Harold M., *Wisconsin's Great Lakes Ports: Background and Future Alternatives* (Milwaukee: Center for Great Lakes Studies, The University of Wisconsin-Milwaukee, July, 1975).

Shaw, Gordon C., "Changes in Canadian Great Lakes Shipping Since the Opening of the St. Lawrence Seaway in 1959," *Annual Proceedings of the Transportation Research Forum* (1978), pp. 571–591.

Tennessee's Opportunities On Its Waterways System, prepared for the Tennessee Department of Transportation and Appalachian Regional Commission, Bureau of Business and Economic Research, Memphis State University and Transportation Center, The University of Tennessee, Knoxville (1974).

U.S. Department of Agriculture, Economic Research Service, *Water Carriers and Inland Waterways in Agricultural Transportation.* Agricultural Economic Report No. 379 (Washington D.C.: August, 1977).

Van Cook, Charles F., and Stewart Rog, "Capacity of the Mid-America Inland Waterway System," *Annual Proceedings of the Transportation Research Forum* (1978), pp. 463–470.

Vanderleest, Henry W., "Great Lakes Ports and General Cargo Export Traffic: A Current Assessment," *Annual Proceedings of the Transportation Research Forum* (1981), pp. 96–101.

Wolfe, K. Eric, "An Evaluation of Inland Waterway Tax Collection Mechanisms," *Annual Proceedings of the Transportation Research Forum* (1981), pp. 423–431.

Wood, Donald F., "The St. Lawrence Seaway: Some Considerations of Its Impact," *Land Economics* (February, 1958), pp. 61–73.

Case 8–1 Guadeloupe Guano Company, Ltd., Case

Rodney Ciganovich was plant engineer for the Guadeloupe Guano Co., Ltd., a firm with a large guano processing and bagging plant located at a coastal port in Guadeloupe, which received guano from several sources. The plant had three unloading docks, one which could accommodate vessels drawing 40 feet, one accommodating vessels drawing 30 feet, and one accommodating vessels drawing only 20 feet. The docks could handle vessels drawing less water than just indicated, but not more. Shore-based unloading equipment was used to remove the guano from the vessels' holds. Clamshell buckets on overhead cranes were used. At present, the crane at the 40-foot dock could unload guano at a rate of 500 tons per hour; the crane at the 30-foot dock, 400 tons per hour; and the crane at the 20-foot dock, 300 tons per hour. Once a crane started unloading a vessel, it was not feasible to move the vessel to another dock to continue the unloading. This was because of union rules regarding the ships' crews. Port traffic and shoreside work practices dictated that vessel unloading would begin only at 8 A.M. and then would continue until the vessel was light (empty).

Three sizes of vessels were used in the guano trade, and their sizes were strictly limited by the available depths at the points where the unprocessed guano was loaded. The *Macomber* class of vessel was converted World War II cargo ships and could draw only 20 feet of water when fully loaded at 10,000 tons. The *Mandel* class, converted from Korean War attack supply ships, carried 25,000 tons maximum and drew 30 feet. The *Mead* class, originally built for use by the military in southeast Asia in the late 1960's, drew 40 feet while carrying a maximum load of 50,000 tons.

Recently, Ciganovich had been troubled by declining profit margins caused, in part, by the fact that the vessels were chartered on a time basis and bills for chartering were climbing faster than the amount of tonnage handled. In addition, Chloe Soroquere, owner of the firm, had sent him a note from the Bahamas indicating that every time she yachted in the vicinity of the Guadeloupe dock, it was either empty or else had a backlog of ships waiting for dock space.

The note from Ms. Soroquere indicated that Ciganovich should consider scheduling arrivals so as to minimize waiting time. After careful investigation, Ciganovich and David Norton, his assistant, concluded that they could not control the loading of the vessels or their time en route. Hence, if unloading times were scheduled, there would be no net improvement in the ability of the chartered fleet to carry a certain tonnage annually. Norton had carefully charted the arrival patterns of the vessels for the past two years, a pattern that was not expected to change.

There were 200 arrivals each year of *Macomber*-size vessels. This was on a fairly regular basis, and on any one day there was a 200/365 chance a vessel would arrive.

There were 122 arrivals each year of *Mandel*-size vessels, also on a fairly regular basis.

There was only one *Mead*-size vessel in use, and it sailed back and forth. It would return to Guadeloupe one or two days after departing. It made 60 round trips per year.

Charter rates for vessels varied with shifts in world markets. After some consultation with Jay Wiharja, the vessel chartering agent the firm used, Norton and Ciganovich estimated that vessel delay times cost $300 per hour for *Macomber*-class vessels; $500 per hour for *Mandel*-class vessels; and $800 for the *Mead*-size. Wiharja made one further suggestion. He asked: "Could the bucket and crane at the 20-foot dock be relocated to the 40-foot dock? The cranes could work simultaneously, each unloading a different hold in the same vessel." Wiharja assured them this would not affect the vessels' stability. However, he added that only two cranes could be used simultaneously to unload a vessel; three would be too many.

Ciganovich and Norton then carefully examined the three cranes and clamshell buckets and determined that the 300-ton-per-hour crane could be placed on the 40-foot dock and used alongside the 500-ton crane, increasing the dock's unloading speed to 800 tons per hour. The 20-foot dock would then not be used. Ciganovich then decided to move the crane, if the move could be justified. His only objective would be to minimize the costs of vessel time in port, either unloading or waiting to dock.

Question One: Should the 300-ton crane be moved from the 20-foot pier to the 40-foot pier where it would work alongside the 500-ton crane, and the 20-foot dock be closed? Why?

Question Two: Is there an even more efficient manner of rearranging the three cranes on the two deeper docks (while closing the 20-foot dock)? If "yes," what is it?

Question Three: At the present time, are the proper cranes at each dock? Should they be rearranged, still keeping one crane at each dock? Why?

Question Four: Should a new, additional crane be purchased? What should its capacity be and how much should Guadeloupe Guano Company be willing to pay for it? At which dock should it be located?

Question Five: Another alternative would be to dredge alongside either or both the 20-foot dock and the 30-foot dock so they could handle larger vessels. How would you determine the value of such work?

Question Six: How much should Guadeloupe Guano Company be willing to pay the local unions to overcome the current work practices which "dictated that vessel unloading would begin only at 8 A.M. and then would continue until the vessel was light (empty)"?

Question Seven: Would it be easier to rely on different sizes of vessels to deliver the guano? How could one determine this?

Case 8–2   Van Bemmel Steamship Company Case

Van Bemmel Steamship Company was a small U.S. flag carrier, operating only one vessel on a regular route between the East Coast and Japan via the Panama Canal with intermediate stops, in both directions, at San Juan, Long Beach, and Honolulu. Its approximate route is shown on the map. A round trip would be New York, San Juan, Long Beach, Honolulu, Osaka, Honolulu, Long Beach, San Juan, and back to New York. At each port of call, the vessel spent an entire day discharging and taking on containers. Time at sea between ports (in either direction) was: New York–San Juan, 2 days; San Juan–Long Beach, 5 days; Long Beach–Honolulu, 4 days; and Honolulu–Osaka, 6 days. (These days are in addition to the single day spent in each port, whenever the vessel stopped.) The vessel made about nine round trips per year, and it could carry 1,200 containers, either full or empty. The route is shown in Case Figure 8–2–1.

The vessel's operating costs were $8,000 per day while sailing and $6,000 per day while in port. Its fixed costs were $10,000 per day. The vessel handled only containers, and the port terminal operator charged $100 for either loading or unloading a container (full or empty).

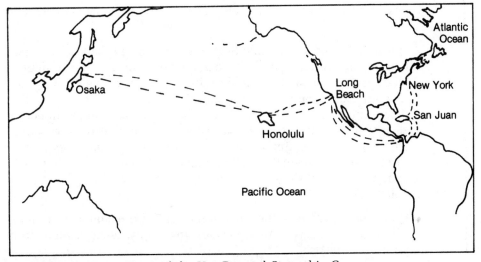

Case Figure 8–2–1   Route of the Van Bemmel Steamship Company

CASE TABLE 8–2–1 Number of Full Containers Carried
on the Van Bemmel Company's Route

Full Containers from Port Listed Below to Port Listed Across Top	New York	San Juan	TO Long Beach	Honolulu	Osaka
F New York		100	100	200	100
R San Juan	100				100
O Long Beach	100	200		300	200
M Honolulu	100	100	100		
Osaka	200		100	100	

Case Table 8–2–1 shows the number of full containers that the Van Bemmel vessel carried between the ports on its route. At present the firm is attempting to determine its costs of carrying containers between the different ports it serves.

Question One: Assume that the Van Bemmel Company wants to use its own containers exclusively. Any containers it picks up at a port (either full or empty) will have to have been left at the port on a previous voyage. Using Case Table 8–2–1, calculate the minimum number of containers the company must own. Show your work.

Question Two: How much ship space could be saved if, instead of owning its own containers, Van Bemmel Company leased them for one-way hauls only, and thereby carried only containers loaded with freight?

Question Three: Case Table 8–2–1 shows 16 different origin-destination pairs, or markets, for loaded container movements. Calculate all costs that the Van Bemmel firm incurs during a single voyage and then allocate them per *loaded container* for each of the 16 markets where the firm carries loaded containers. (When you are done, for each of the 16 markets with loaded containers, multiply the average cost per container times the number of loaded containers carried from origin to destination. When you add the costs of serving all 16 markets, the total should equal total costs for a single voyage.) Show your work.

Question Four: Given the facts in the case, if the company wants to fill up containers it currently is carrying empty, what markets (from point to point) should it emphasize?

Question Five: Assuming business is increasing uniformly, between which ports will the vessel's capacity first be reached? Once this happens, what should the firm do?

Question Six: Conrail and the Santa Fe Railroad approach Van Bemmel with a proposal for land-bridge service, using rail to carry containers between Long Beach and New York, rather than water. Outline how you would determine the value to Van Bemmel of this proposal.

This Dutch vessel, Super Servant I, built in 1979, submerges in protected water so that a load can be floated above its deck. Visible in this photo are the vessel's front superstructure and two structures at the stern.

Photo courtesy Wijsmuller B.V.

Shown here on the Mississippi River, the Super Servant I is carrying a French-built generator. At Baton Rouge, the vessel submerged, and the load (which was built to float) was moved by towboats to Vanceburg, Kentucky.

Photo courtesy Port of New Orleans.

9 International Transportation

Secret cash rebates and direct financial concessions, pernicious as they are, probably represent but the tip of the malpractice iceberg in ocean commerce.

FEDERAL MARITIME COMMISSIONER KARL BAKKE
in Transport 2000
February, 1979

We must be aware of the example of the Soviet Union, which has grasped the value and relevance of a coherent, focused, and consistent national maritime policy. Their maritime activities are carefully orchestrated; their maritime resources supplement and reinforce one another. The time has come for the United States to undertake a similar commitment.

RONALD REAGAN
1980

The Motor Carrier Act of 1980 not only eased entry requirements for domestic truckers, but Canadian and Mexican truckers, as well. Truckers wishing to compete for cross-border trucking find Canadian authority hard to get and Mexican authority impossible, while their foreign counterparts take advantage of the relaxed U.S. laws, claims the American Trucking Associations.

American Trucker
March, 1982

The Carter Administration's unilateral move to deregulate international air fares to increase airline competition was an act of "colossal stupidity," Italy's most powerful airline executive said yesterday.

From interview with Umberto Nordio,
chairman of the board and president of
Alitalia Airline
San Francisco Chronicle
March 17, 1982

Introduction

International carriers operate between nations, carrying freight or passengers. In technological terms, they are similar to U.S. domestic carriers. That is, the airplane, the ship, or train is just about the same, wherever it travels. However, the legal framework within which they operate is different. Since international carriers move between nations, no single nation can regulate them. Trading nations have had to enter into agreements concerning matters that protect and promote international trade, for example, measures relating to safety of vessels at sea.

In recent years, the United Nations has assumed a coordinating role, and it has under its jurisdiction a number of agencies involved with international transportation. The International Civil Aviation Organization (ICAO) has functions similar to those of the U.S. Federal Aviation Administration; the ICAO is concerned with the technical and safety aspects of international flying. Another organization of the U.N., the Intergovernmental Maritime Consultive Organization (IMCO), is concerned with international navigation and other technical maritime matters. The U.N.'s Conference of Trade and Development (UNCTAD) is involved with promoting international trade and assisting the developing nations. UNCTAD is concerned with commercial and legal aspects of trade development.

Documentation

One thing that makes international transportation different from domestic transportation is that movements between countries are accompanied by many more documents than is the case for domestic shipments. The amount of documentation required is determined by the product being shipped, its origin, and its destination. Figure 9–1 indicates common documents needed for export shipments from the United States. Note especially item 5, a letter of credit, and item 9, an

- A *letter of credit* is an international trade document in which the buyer's bank guarantees payment for the goods once they are received. Sellers desire this guarantee since they have little recourse to courts in case the buyer refuses to pay for the goods.

insurance certificate. The insurance certificate indicates the goods are insured by either the carrier or an insurance company; foreign shipments require specific insurance coverage, which is often not the required practice for domestic movements.

Additional documents are required for international transport of livestock or agricultural products, which usually must be accompanied by a certificate of inspection stating that they are free of certain diseases.

Figure 9–2 lists the documents needed to import shipments into the U.S. The principal hurdle for imported materials is to pass through customs, where duties (or fees) are assessed and collected. Major ports have land set aside in an area known as a *foreign trade zone* into which goods from inbound ships or planes can be trans-

Common Export Documents

1. Ocean Bill-of-Lading

A receipt for the cargo and a contract for transportation between a shipper and the ocean carrier. It may also be used as an instrument of ownership which can be bought, sold or traded while the goods are in transit. To be used in this manner, it must be a negotiable "Order" Bill-of-Lading. Abbreviations: Blading, B/L.

A *clean Bill-of-Lading* is issued when the shipment is received in good order. If damage or a shortage is noted, a clean bill-of-lading will not be issued. An *On Board Bill-of-Lading* certifies that the cargo has been placed aboard the named vessel and is signed by the master of the vessel or his representative. On letter of credit transactions, an On Board Bill-of-Lading is usually necessary for the shipper to obtain payment from the bank. When all Bills-of-Lading are processed a *ships manifest* is prepared by the steamship line. This summarizes all cargo aboard the vessel by port of loading and discharge.

Inland Bill-of-Lading—Also known as a waybill on rail or the "pro forma" bill-of-lading in trucking. It is used to document the transportation of the goods between the port and the point of origin or destination. It should contain information such as marks, numbers, steamship line, etc. to match with a dock receipt. Abbreviate "pro" or "pro ticket", waybill.

2. Dock Receipt

Used to transfer accountability for the cargo between domestic and international carriers at the ocean terminal. This is the document, prepared by the shipper or forwarder, which the ocean carrier signs and returns to the delivering inland carrier, acknowledging receipt of the cargo.

3. Delivery Instructions

Provides specific information to the inland carrier concerning the arrangement made by the forwarder to deliver the merchandise to a particular pier or steamship line. Not to be confused with *Delivery Order* which is used for import cargo.

4. Export Declaration

Required by the U.S. Department of Commerce to control exports and act as a source document for export statistics. It includes complete particulars on the shipment. Common abbreviation is Export Dec.

5. Letter of Credit

A financial document issued by a bank at the request of the consignee guaranteeing payment to the shipper for cargo if certain terms and conditions are fulfilled. Normally it contains a brief description of the goods, documents required, a shipping date, and an expiration date after which payment will no longer be made.

6. Consular Invoice

Required by some countries, this document is used to control and identify goods shipped to them. It usually must be prepared on special forms and may require legalization by their Consul.

7. Commercial Invoice

A bill for the goods from the seller to the buyer. It is often used by governments to determine the true value of goods for the assessment of customs duties. It is also used in the preparation of consular documentation. Governments using the commercial invoice to control imports often specify its form, content, number of copies, language to be used, etc.

8. Certificate of Origin

A document which is used to assure the buying country precisely in which country the goods were produced. The certification of the origin of the merchandise is usually performed by a recognized Chamber of Commerce.

9. Insurance Certificate

Assures the consignee that insurance is provided to cover loss or damage to the cargo while in transit.

10. Transmittal Letter

A list of the particulars of the shipment and a record of the documents being transmitted together with instructions for disposition of documents. Any special instructions are also included.

Figure 9–1 Common Export Documents. Prepared by The Port Authority of New York and New Jersey, Port Service Improvement Committee, One World Trade Center, New York, New York. Courtesy: The Port Authority of New York and New Jersey.

Common Import Documents

1. Arrival Notice

Sent by the carrier, it informs the notify party of the estimated arrival date of the vessel, identifies the shipment with some details, such as number of packages, weight, etc., and indicates when free time expires. Often is also a freight bill.

2. Customs Entries

a) Consumption Entry—A form required by U.S. Customs for entering goods into the United States. The form contains information as to the origin of the cargo, a description of the merchandise and estimated duties applicable to the particular commodity. Estimated duties must be paid when the entry is filed.

b) Immediate Delivery Entry—used to expedite the clearance of cargo. (It allows up to ten days for the payment of estimated duty and processing of the consumption entry. In addition, it permits delivery of the cargo prior to payment of the estimated duty and then allows subsequent filing of the consumption entry and duty.) Also known as I.D. entry.

c) Immediate Transportation Entry—allows the cargo to be moved from the pier to an inland destination via a bonded carrier without the payment of duties or finalization of the entry at the port of arrival. Known as an I.T. entry.

d) Transportation and Exportation Entry—allows goods coming from or going to a third country, such as Canada or Mexico, to enter the U.S. for the purpose of trans-shipment. Known as T&E entry.

3. Carriers Certificate and Release Order

Used to advise Customs of the details of the shipment, its ownership, port of lading, etc. By means of this document, the carrier certifies that the firm or individual named in the certificate is the owner or consignee of the cargo. Commonly known as the Carrier Certificate.

4. Delivery Order

Issued by the consignee or his customs broker to the ocean carrier as authority to release the cargo to the inland carrier. Includes all data necessary for the pier delivery clerk to determine that the cargo can be released to the domestic carrier. May also be known as a Pier Release.

5. Freight Release

Evidence that the freight charges for the cargo have been paid. If in writing, it may be presented at the pier to obtain release of the cargo. (Normally, once the freight is paid, releases are usually arranged without additional documentation.) Also known as Freight Bill Receipt.

6. Special Customs Invoice

An official form usually required by U.S. Customs if the rate of duty is based upon the value and the value of the shipment exceeds $500. This document is usually prepared by the foreign exporter or his forwarder and is used by Customs in determining the value of the shipment. The exporter or his agent must attest to the authenticity of the data furnished.

Figure 9–2   Common Import Documents. Prepared by The Port Authority of New York and New Jersey, Port Service Improvement Committee, One World Trade Center, New York, New York. Courtesy: The Port Authority of New York and New Jersey.

ferred prior to moving through customs. Imported goods with high duties or excise taxes, such as alcoholic beverages, are kept in foreign trade zones until they are needed by the distributors for their retail outlets. When they are needed, they are moved from the foreign trade zone through customs where duties are paid and tax stamps are affixed; then the goods can be marketed. Foreign trade zones are also used for assembling products and holding goods made in other countries until they are relabeled to meet U.S. consumer safety standards.

The United States, as well as other nations, has established *import quotas* which restrict the movements of specific goods. There are two kinds of import quotas: absolute quotas and tariff-rate quotas. Some goods have quotas that are absolute—once the quota is reached, no additional imports of the specific commodity are allowed. Tariff-rate quotas allow certain amounts to enter a country at a given level of customs duties; additional amounts are allowed to enter, but at a higher duty rate. Import quotas protect local growers and manufacturers from foreign competition.

Foreign Trade "Specialists"

Because of the paperwork requirements of foreign trade and the large number of regulations which must be followed, specialized firms have developed that handle many aspects of a manufacturing or wholesaling firm's export or import shipments. The *international freight forwarder* assumes complete responsibility for documenting all of his customers' export shipments and seeing that the shipments and documents reach the departing vessel or airplane. Figure 9–3 is a widely-used document known as a "Shipper's Letter of Instructions" by which the shipper outlines how a shipment should be handled; a forwarder then handles the details of documentation, shipping, and clearance through customs.

The international forwarder earns his revenues from several sources. First—and similar to domestic forwarders—he consolidates small shipments of many customers into a single large shipment that enjoys a lower rate per pound charged for larger shipments. Second, forwarders collect specific charges for each document they prepare. Third, many international carriers give "commissions," a form of rebate, to good customers (U.S. carriers are not supposed to give these kinds of rebates.)

International freight forwarders have close ties with overseas firms, called *customshouse brokers*, which facilitate the movement

ɯ. j. byrnes & co. / BYrnesAIR

custom brokers • ocean & air freight forwarders

1610 rollins road • burlingame, ca 94010 • 415/692-1142

SHIPPER'S REF. NO.	DATE	SHIP VIA			
		☐ AIR ☐ OCEAN	☐ CONSOLIDATE		☐ DIRECT

SHIPPER'S LETTER OF INSTRUCTIONS

NOTE: ① IF YOU ARE UNCERTAIN OF THE SCHEDULE B COMMODITY NO. - DO NOT TYPE IT IN - WE WILL COMPLETE WHEN PROCESSING 7525-V.
② IF YOU HAVE SHIPPED THIS MATERIAL TO US VIA AN INLAND CARRIER - PLEASE GIVE US THE INLAND CARRIER'S NAME, SHIPPING DATE, AND RECEIPT OR PRO. NO. (IF AVAILABLE). THIS WILL HELP US EXPEDITE YOUR SHIPMENT WITH THE INLAND CARRIER.
③ BE SURE TO PICK UP TOP SHEET AND SIGN THE FIRST YELLOW EXPORT DECLARATION WITH PEN AND INK.

SHIPPER _____ ADDRESS _____

AGENT OF SHIPPER *(Forwarding agent)* ADDRESS
W.J. BYRNES & CO./BYrnesAIR **P. O. BOX 4185, BURLINGAME, CA 94010**

ULTIMATE CONSIGNEE ADDRESS

INTERMEDIATE CONSIGNEE ADDRESS

PLACE AND COUNTRY OF ULTIMATE DESTINATION

SHIPPER MUST CHECK ▶	☐ PREPAID OR	☐ COLLECT	C.O.D. AMOUNT $

SHIPPER'S INSTRUCTIONS IN CASE OF INABILITY TO DELIVER CONSIGNMENT AS CONSIGNED: ☐ ABANDON ☐ RETURN TO SHIPPER ☐ DELIVER TO

SHIPPER REQUESTS INSURANCE ☐ NO ☐ YES $

If Shipper has requested insurance as provided for at the left hereof, shipment is insured in the amount indicated (recovery is limited to actual loss) in accordance with the provisions as specified in the Carrier's Tariffs. Insurance is payable to Shipper unless payee is designated in writing by the shipper.

ꜰKS & NUMBERS	NUMBER & KIND OF PACKAGES, ETC.	GROSS POUNDS	D/F	SCHED. B No.	NET QUANTITY	DECLARED VALUE - CUSTOMS

These commodities licensed by U.S. for ultimate destination .... Diversion contrary to U.S. law prohibited.
VALIDATED LICENSE NO.   OR GENERAL LICENSE SYMBOL

BE SURE TO PICK UP TOP SHEET AND SIGN THE FIRST YELLOW EXPORT DECLARATION WITH PEN & INK.

18. THE UNDERSIGNED HEREBY AUTHORIZES____ **W.J. BYRNES & CO./BYrnesAIR, 1610 ROLLINS RD., BURLINGAME, CA 94010**
TO ACT AS FORWARDING AGENT FOR EXPORT CONTROL AND CUSTOMS PURPOSES.   (Name and address—Number, street, place, State)

(DULY AUTHORIZED
EXPORTER_____ BY OFFICER OR EMPLOYEE)_____

DOCUMENTS ENCLOSED:

FORWARDING AGENT DESIGNATED BY EXPORTER ——————▶ _____
(Name of corporation or firm, and capacity of signer; e.g., secretary, export manager, etc.)

'ress _____

SᴘᴇCIAL INSTRUCTIONS:

NOTE: The Shipper or his Authorized Agent hereby authorizes the above named Company, in his name and on his behalf, to prepare any export documents, to sign and accept any documents relating to said shipment and forward this shipment in accordance with the conditions of carriage and the tariffs of the carriers employed. The shipper guarantees payment of all collect charges in the event the consignee refuses payment. Hereunder the sole responsibility of the Company
ABF-5 is to use reasonable care in the selection of carriers, forwarders, agents and others to whom it may entrust the shipment.

Figure 9–3 Shipper's Letter of Instructions. Courtesy: W. J. Byrnes & Co./BYrnesAIR, Burlingame, California.

of the goods through the importing nation's customs. The primary function of customshouse brokers is to see that the goods move through customs, paying the smallest applicable duty.

Export packers work in conjunction with international freight forwarders (often sharing the same quarters). The export packer serves as a consolidation point for physically assembling export shipments that originate at several points, stuffs (packs) an ocean-going container, and then tenders it to the steamship line.

A modified form of forwarder operation, which has developed in recent years, is the *non-vessel operating common carrier* (NVOCC). The Federal Maritime Commission (FMC), which regulates U.S. international maritime activities, recognizes NVOCCs as common carriers to the extent it allows them to enter into joint rates with ocean

- A *joint rate* is a single rate between origin and destination offered by two or more connecting carriers.

carriers. At present, however, the ICC does not allow NVOCCs to enter into joint rate agreements with domestic rail or motor carriers (nor does it allow joint rates between carriers it regulates and ocean carriers). However, some motor carrier and freight forwarding firms also happen to possess NVOCC authority so they are able to handle the domestic U.S. leg of the movement as well.

In a general sense, the NVOCC performs forwarder functions and is able to enter into "joint" rates with water carriers (meaning lower overall costs to the shipper). The NVOCC's services can include picking up export goods at the shipper's dock, combining them with other LCL shipments from other customers, filling a container with the various customers' goods, and shipping it overseas. The NVOCC takes responsibility for getting the goods from the shipper's warehouse to his customer's premises.[1]

- *LCL* means less than carload, when speaking of rail traffic, or less than containerload, when speaking of container traffic.

One of the restrictions that international carriers must face is that foreign nations will only allow shipments to enter at points where customs and immigration officers are stationed. Carriers must provide additional time in their schedules to allow for passage through such checkpoints. Some nations will require incoming vessels and vehicles to be inspected for cleanliness before being allowed to

---

[1]"A Freight Forwarder Offensive," *Distribution Worldwide* (October, 1978), pp. 53–54. There are about 400 NVOCCs operating in the U.S. In 1981, the ICC, acting under a provision in the *Motor Carrier Act of 1980*, allowed forwarders to enter into joint rate agreements with ocean carriers.

enter; they may also require the carriers to apply for special permits before allowing them to continue. Carriers operating in foreign countries retain local agents to make all necessary arrangements and "smooth the way" (by whatever means necessary) to ensure that the carrier's vehicle is not detained for unusually long periods of time.

International Balance of Trade Concerns

International transportation directly involves each nation's balance of trade. That is probably the *main* policy difference between domestic transportation and international transportation matters. Nations trade with each other, and whenever a nation buys or borrows from another more than it sells, the *balance*, or the difference, must eventually be settled with "hard" currency. Ideally, each nation's im-

- A *"hard"* currency is one that is widely acceptable to nations and traders throughout the world. "Soft" or "weak" currencies may be useful within certain nations, but sellers from other countries are reluctant to accept them.

ports and exports would be balanced; in reality this does not occur. Nations with adverse trade balances (i.e., imports greater than exports) must take steps to restore the balance. The following account illustrates one way of improving a trade balance:

> In an attempt to slow the pace of imports, Chile has slashed in half, to 90 days, the period of import letters of credit. The move is part of the Chilean government's effort to equalize its two-way foreign trade at around $300 million a month and to reduce a current account deficit that will reach a record $4.65 billion for 1981. Importers now have only three months to buy, ship and sell their foreign merchandise before they have to pay for it, either with the sales proceeds or with money borrowed at rates that can be as high as 5 percent a month.[2]

The governments of all nations are concerned with their "balance of payments" position and encourage—often through subsidies—involvement of their nation's citizens and firms in international transport ventures because they think this will improve their nation's balance of payments position. Each international carrier "flies the flag" of some nation, which means that the vessel or aircraft is registered in that particular nation and is subject to that nation's taxes, laws, and safety regulations. From the standpoint of international trade, all revenues that a firm earns from customers of other

[2] *Pacific Traffic* (February, 1982), p. 36.

nations are considered sales to foreigners, or *exports*. Not only goods can be exported, so can services. For example, a nation that has few raw materials or manufactured goods to export can, instead, export transportation services. Conversely, a nation that does not have merchant ships or international airlines "flying its flag" must pay *foreign* firms to carry its imports and exports. In an international transactions sense, this nation must *import* its international transportation needs.

Export of Transportation Equipment

Nations can also export the transportation vehicles, vessels, and aircraft they manufacture. One area where the United States has been particularly successful is the export of commercial aircraft, starting with the Douglas DC-3 prior to World War II and continuing to this day. In addition to helping the balance of trade, export aircraft sales allow manufacturers to increase the total numbers of any model produced, reducing the average costs per unit.

U.S. aircraft manufacturers dominate the free world market for commercial airline aircraft (and even have made sales to Red China). European aircraft manufacturers have had continual trouble selling large numbers of planes, although in 1978 a French-German-British-Spanish consortium, *Airbus Industrie*, sold 23 A-300-B Whisperline

- A *consortium* is a joining together of firms to undertake a project where the resource requirements (or the risks) are too great for any single firm to assume.

jets to Eastern Airlines. This was the first major sale of foreign-built jet aircraft to U.S. carriers since the 1950's.

Russia supplies most Communist-bloc nations with their commercial airline aircraft. Russia also builds merchant ships, floating dry-docks, dredges, tugs, and fishing boats for its own use and for sale to other Communist nations. It is one of the few manufacturers of hydrofoils, and as of 1977 the Russians had exported over 100 hydrofoils to 40 nations, including many outside the Communist bloc.[3]

The United States exports very few new commercial ships, primarily because of the high labor costs of building ships in this country. Japan is the world's principal ship-building nation and—by some measures of ship-building output—produces half of the new vessel tonnage in the non-Communist world.

[3] *Soviet Export* (Moscow, vol, 20, 1977), pp. 8–9.

Cross-Trading

Cross-trading occurs when a nation's planes or ships carry passengers or cargos between two other nations. This is very closely regulated in international aviation (as will be discussed later), and permission must be obtained in advance by any foreign firm desiring to land at a nation's airports for purposes of discharging or taking on passengers or freight. Nations reserve to their own carriers the rights to carry all domestic commerce. This practice is known as *cabotage*.

Maritime trade is much less restricted; in theory, a vessel flying one nation's flag may freely enter any nation's commercial ports to take on or discharge passengers or cargo of other nations. The nation that supplies the ship carrying traffic between other nations is said to be involved in *cross-trading*. In the non-Communist world, the nations that earn the most from carrying the commerce of other nations are Norway, United Kingdom, Japan, West Germany, and Denmark. Shipping is important to the Norwegian economy; in 1976 Norway exported approximately $3.5 billion of goods and $2.8 billion of shipping services. At the other extreme, in 1976 the United States "imported" a net amount of $1.6 billion in shipping services performed by carriers of other nations, representing about 15 percent of our trade deficit for that year.[4]

In the past decade, the single most important change in the balance of world shipping has been the dramatic increase in Soviet-flag merchant vessels. They sail mainly in trades between other nations, and it seems that their only goal is to earn "hard" western currencies.[5] These Russian ships make as few purchases as necessary in foreign ports in order to minimize their expenditures of Western currencies. They are even refueled at sea by Russian tankers.

Carrying a Nation's Own Foreign Trade

Each nation also tries to carry a large portion of its own exports and imports. Several devices are used to encourage the use of one's own ships and planes. In the case of international airlines, two nations agree to exchange airline service; then each selects its own carrier to connect it with the other nation. The market, or amount of business, is shared on a 50/50 basis, and should the share of one

---

[4] *American Shipper* (July, 1978), pp. 38–39. A "trade deficit" is similar to an adverse "balance of payments" position.

[5] Russians need to earn "hard" Western currencies in order to buy goods from non-Communist-bloc nations. See: Robert E. Athay, *The Economics of Soviet Merchant-Shipping Policy* (Chapel Hill: The University of North Carolina Press, 1971).

nation's carrier fall much below 50 percent, the nation is likely to protest. When jet aircraft were being introduced into international service, those nations whose airlines were not yet equipped with jets would not let the other nation's airlines use jets in the market they had agreed to share because jets would draw considerable traffic away from the airline still using propeller-driven aircraft.

Nations also can earn foreign currency by having marine insurance cargo coverage purchased within their own country. Russia buys its imports by asking the bidder to submit a bid that excludes insurance costs, and a Russian agency then provides the insurance; and Russia sells its exports on a "delivered" basis including insurance costs. Hence, Russia insures the movements of both its imports and exports, which means marine insurance companies in other nations are excluded from this business. Russia has the most stringent insurance purchasing requirements. However, approximately 45 other nations have enacted measures that give preference to their own insurance industry. Typically, they insist that all imports be insured by their own nation's firms, or else they place a tax on import insurance purchased in other nations.[6]

Nations with very "weak" economies must discourage imports because they cannot afford the outflow of "hard" currencies to pay for imports. They will require that an "import permit" be issued in advance by their government before an import sales transaction can be completed. (The import permit is needed when the buyer attempts to move the goods through his nation's customs.) Often, a condition of the permit is that the goods move on a carrier flying the importing nation's flag.

Cargo preference is a device by which a nation can have a certain portion of its commercial shipments carried on its own flag carriers. For example, U.S. laws require that three categories of cargo must be carried on U.S. flag vessels. They are: military supplies used by U.S. armed forces, shipments resulting from loans made by the Reconstruction Finance Corporation (both of these types of shipments must move exclusively on U.S. ships), and other cargos resulting from U.S. government appropriations (50 percent of which must move in U.S. flag vessels). This last category is the largest and includes foodstuffs bought under farm price-support programs and then made available to charitable organizations for distribution overseas. The U.S. Maritime Administration monitors these shipping transactions and requires a copy of the bill-of-lading for shipping these cargos for audit purposes. They will grant waivers from the

---

[6] *American Shipper* (October, 1981), p. 50.

requirement in instances where the shipper cannot find a U.S. flag vessel to carry the cargo; this might happen if the ports of discharge can handle only very shallow-draft vessels.

International Cargo-Sharing Agreements

Another way a nation can increase the amount of foreign trade carried on its own flag vessels is to enter into a "pooling" agreement with some other nation with whom it trades. Such a pooling agreement will require that part or all of the cargo moving between the two countries is carried on their own merchant fleets. These agreements are common between many nations, although the U.S. Department of Justice has some reservations as to how legal they are. (Some of the pooling agreements even distribute the share of traffic to specific vessel lines.)

In the grain sale to Russia in the early 1970's, one aspect of the sale-purchase agreement dealt with which nation's vessels were to carry the grain. It was decided that one-third would be carried by U.S. flag vessels, one-third by Russian flag vessels, and one-third by whatever other vessels of any flag could be chartered to carry the cargo. A trade agreement between the United States and the People's Republic of China, entered into in late 1980, contained a provision guaranteeing to the merchant marine of each nation a minimum of one-third the traffic between them. The remaining one-third was available to third-flag carriers.[7]

Less-developed nations also desire to carry more of their own traffic but seem unable to penetrate the existing shipping market, which is dominated by vessel lines from developed countries. In 1974, working through the United Nations' Conference on Trade and Development, an international agreement was drafted that allocated all "liner" traffic between nations on a 40/40/20 split. The exporting

- Ocean *liners* which carry cargo call on a regularly-scheduled basis and carry "less-than-shipload" lots of relatively high value general cargo.

and importing nations would each have 40 percent of the business and "cross-traders" would be restricted to 20 percent. If interpreted literally, the 20-percent limitation on cross-traders is severe since in many markets it would represent insufficient cargo to keep them in business. As of early 1982, 45 nations had ratified the agreement, with more expected to follow. (Technically, the code will go into

---

[7] *Handling and Shipping Management* (April, 1981), p. 16.

effect when it is approved by 24 nations controlling, among themselves, a cumulative total of 25 percent of the world's merchant tonnage—a measure of vessel capacity.) The code is expected to go into effect soon, although whether, where, and how it will be enforced are matters of conjecture.[8]

Less-Developed Countries

Less-developed countries (LDCs) are those which trail the world in terms of industrialization and other forms of progress. Many of them are new nations formed since World War II and are located in Africa or Asia.

The LDCs that were formed since World War II were once political colonies of the major European powers. Somewhat to their surprise, most LDCs discovered that becoming politically independent of the European power was not the same as becoming economically independent. Financial interests of European countries (as well as the U.S.) still had considerable influence over the economy of the emerging LDC. For example, a new nation may discover that its rail system did *not* link together all regions in the nation. Instead, the railroad was located so that it could carry mineral and other natural resources to ports where they had been loaded for shipment to the former "mother" country. The case was similar for local airlines which also had been developed as "children" of the major power's airline. The route structure of the new nation's airline was such that it served only to feed passengers into and from the international routes of the major power's airline. The local airline did little to tie together the new nation.

The LDCs had no merchant fleets of their own and had to continue to rely on vessel operators that were headquartered in Europe. To date, the LDCs have been relatively unsuccessful in developing their own merchant fleet; they continue to depend upon shipping firms based in developed countries which aggravates their balance of payments position. These LDCs view the international ocean carrier industries as cartels run by and for the major nations of the world.

- A *cartel* is an organization of businesses that formerly competed with each other but now have joined together to control production and prices and fight outside competitors.

LDCs also feel that they have little choice but to accept technological "improvements" which are of little value to them. Examples are

---

[8] *Traffic World* (January 18, 1982), pp. 16–17.

the "jumbo" jet airliner, which holds many more passengers than any LDC could hope to generate, and containerization in the maritime industry, which substitutes very expensive equipment for labor (this substitution is economically justified in developed countries but not in LDCs).

Developed nations realize that it is only a matter of time before the LDCs enact sufficient regulations so that they can participate in carrying more of their own foreign trade. Developed nations recognize this will happen and are attempting to sell ships and planes to the LDCs. An example of this is shown on Figure 9–4, a cartoon accompanying an article in a 1977 British shipping journal which was critical of the shipbuilding industry for selling vessels to LDCs at very low cost.

> Few potential buyers are to be found amongst the domestic owners of the main shipbuilding countries, so that a major part of the (sales) offensive is being directed towards the shipowners of the developing world. . . . Indeed, so attractive are the terms now being offered to, and accepted by, export buyers that they are now sometimes actually exceeding the terms available to domestic buyers in the shipbuilder's own country.[9]

To some LDCs, participation in the international transportation market is also a matter of pride. "An airline is a status symbol in the Third World. Next to the flag, the tail fin is the most eloquent statement of a country's sovereignty."[10]

Flags of Convenience

How can a ship-operating firm avoid the restrictions and regulations of its own nation and find an easier set of rules to follow? The answer is simple: Register the ship in another nation. The vessel flies the flag of this other nation, and it is called a "flag of convenience." U.S. firms, especially petroleum firms with large tanker fleets, own and operate many vessels under foreign flags of convenience. They do this to avoid the high labor costs associated with manning a U.S. flag vessel with a U.S. crew, which would be required if the vessel was registered in the U.S.

The concept and practices of using "flags of convenience" is old, dating to at least the sixteenth century, when English merchants

---

[9]"Gift Wrapping Shows No Sign of Stopping," *Seatrade* (September, 1977), pp. 3–4.

[10]*The Wall Street Journal* (August 25, 1981). The same article quoted Sassy N'Diaye, the African director of IATA, "An airline isn't a luxury. It's a foreign-currency earner; it's vital to communications; it's vital to development, and in a crisis . . . , it's your link with the world."

'We only paid for one ship. The other was a free sample.'

Figure 9–4 Shipbuilders May Offer Generous Terms to Buyers in Less-Developed Countries. Courtesy: *Seatrade*.

used Spain as a flag of convenience in order to participate in the Spanish West Indies trade, which, at that time, was monopolized by Spanish vessels. In this century, prior to World War II, U.S. vessels were transferred to foreign registry so they could carry supplies to Britain without violating neutrality pacts. In the early 1950's, when a Communist takeover of Greece was threatened, many Greek ship-owners transferred their vessels to Liberian registry in order to avoid having to relinquish their vessels.[11] Until the mid-1970's, mainland China operated many vessels under flags of convenience. The main reason was that many western nations were wary of doing business directly with Red China or Red Chinese agencies.

It is often believed that nations which are flag of convenience havens have lax maritime safety standards. (See Figure 9–5.) Many of the tanker oil spills occurring in 1970's were from vessels registered in flag of convenience nations.

National Defense Concerns

There are many relationships between the commercial and military aspects of international transportation. At one time merchant vessels were armed and could be used for fighting purposes. The phrase "gunboat diplomacy" meant using a nation's navy to assist in negotiating trade treaties with nations having little, or at least less, military power. There is still considerable exchange between civilian and military transportation technologies.

In an uneasy world, commercial transportation can serve as a "cover" for espionage purposes. Vessels visiting foreign ports or fishing trawlers operating offshore often are equipped with electronic equipment more sopisticated than would appear necessary. Commercial airline flights can be used to supply ammunitions and carry mercenaries. In the winter of 1981–82, as relations between the United States and Russia became strained because of the latter's involvement in Poland, the U.S. rerouted the flights of Aeroflot, the Russian airline, so that they would not fly over a nuclear submarine base in Connecticut. At one point during the winter, when Russian invasion of Poland seemed imminent, Aeroflot canceled all of its outbound flights from Moscow, causing international travelers to switch to non-Russian airlines. It was rumored that the Aeroflot aircraft were to be used to transport Russian troops.

[11]David Bess, *Marine Transportation* (Danville, Ill.: Interstate Printers & Publishers, Inc., 1976), pp. 158–159.

Our Man Hoppe

A Super Spill

Arthur Hoppe

THE REPUBLIC of Phynkia apologized yesterday for the damage caused when a supertanker flying its flag went aground in Atlantic City.

A Phynkian spokesman said the apology included the loss of the Steel Pier, the demolition of the lobby of the Traymore Hotel and "the unfortunate oil slick" which now covers the East Coast from Bangor to Key West. He disavowed any responsibility, however, for the chimpanzees.

Phynkia has recently passed Liberia and Panama as one of the world's leading maritime nations with a fleet of more than 2300 vessels flying its flag (a cross of gold rampant on a field of oil).

Despite being landlocked, it offers foreign ship owners a number of advantages including a flat $19.95 fee for license plates and free road maps.

★ ★ ★

THE SPOKESMAN emphasized yesterday, however, that the tanker involved in the Atlantic City mishap, the S.S. Augean Surprise, "met the highest Phynkian standards of marine safety." And the vessel's captain, Alfred M. (Crazy Al) Feck, he added, had "passed every conceivable test of Phynikan seamanship."

Captain Feck agreed about the condition of the Augean Surprise. "It was a great little boat and I'll sure miss it," he said.

Feck attributed the accident to a number of factors over which he had little control, one being that he was somewhat off course. "I was aiming at Long Beach, but I missed that danged Panama Canal again," he explained.

"The consarned thing can't be more'n 50 feet wide."

Captain Feck had nothing but praise for his crew of 38. "Don't blame 'em a bit for jumping ship when we arrived in the lobby of the Traymore," he said. "You know how sailors are after they hit the beach, not to mention the Boardwalk, too."

Feck was asked if his crew was comprised of native Phynkians. "No, they're chimpanzees," he said. "My Assyrian owners found out that chimps will work even cheaper than Phynkians. You give 'em a couple of bananas a day and show 'em a Tarzan movie on Saturday nights and you got yourself a real happy boat."

A reporter noted that it must have been difficult for Feck to teach his bandy-legged little sailors the difference between port and starboard.

"Port?" inquired Feck. "Starboard?"

★ ★ ★

AN AGENT for The Assyrian Steamship, Player Piano & War Surplus Line, which may or may not own the vessel, said he was sure sorry, too, for the 1500-mile long oil slick.

"To make amends, Atlantic City can keep the ship," he said magnanimously. "It was getting pretty rusty and, what the hell, it's insured anyway."

In Washington, a spokesman for the Coast Guard said there were no plans to close American ports to Phynkian tankers.

"What good would it do?" he said. "They haven't hit one yet."

Figure 9–5   Satire on Flags of Convenience. Courtesy: Art Hoppe, copyright 1977, *San Francisco Chronicle.*

In case of war, a nation's commercial carriers would be expected to help assist its military operations. In the very early days of World War II, U.S. commercial airline aircraft were used to ferry troops to Alaska and the Aleutians, where a Japanese attack was expected. At the same time, about 160 U.S. transport ships, utilized in the domestic intercoastal trades, were taken over by the military and used to supply British troops in the Middle East.[12] During the Falkland Islands dispute in 1982, Britain placed some of her commercial cargo and passenger ships into military service.

Neutral nations are also affected by conflicts involving other nations since their vessels may be subject to attack if attempting to carry on trade with either of the belligerents. Or the existing market for shipping may be upset, as occurred when the Suez Canal was closed suddenly, and commercial vessels were required to travel longer distances.

Both the U.S. Air Force and Navy run an equivalent of civilian air and merchant ship service throughout much of the world. They use military crews to carry personnel and supply military bases. Commercial air and sea transportation firms continually criticize the military for operating these services since they are carrying people or goods who otherwise would move on U.S. flag commercial carriers. The military respond that they need to use some of their own carriers because of needs for security, training, and ability to rely on military discipline in case the ship or plane is suddenly required for use in a "warlike" situation.

In wartime, trained aviation and maritime personnel would be needed. This has sometimes been used as an argument to encourage pilot training and general aviation. At graduation, cadets at merchant marine academies receive concurrent reserve commissions in either the Coast Guard or Navy. Subsequent sections of this chapter will discuss subsidies for shipbuilding and for operating merchant vessels in commercial trades. Part of the justification of these programs is that they allow us to maintain a pool of trained shipyard workers, sailors, and vessel officers who would be needed in wartime.

A military or semi-military capability can be useful in peacetime. In 1948 both commercial and military aircraft were used to supply Berlin during the blockade imposed by Russia. In the 1973 Middle

---

[12]Thomas B. Crowley, cited in *Sea Power Forum*, March 3, 1978 (San Francisco: Maritime Administration, Western Region, 1978), p. 58. At the war's end, the intercoastal shipping firms were unable to recapture many of their previous markets.

East War, the U.S. Military Airlift Command flew to Israel 20,000 tons of supplies, including self-propelled guns and tanks. Their efforts were supplemented by Israeli commercial aircraft.[13]

International Commodity Flows

Precise data regarding volume of international commerce are difficult to find. There is no central clearinghouse for reporting all sales transactions and vessel movements among all nations of the world. Some bulk movements are repeated every year, such as the shipments of agricultural products from the tropics to the United States or Europe. Other movements are irregular and occur because yields in grain crops are greater in one country than in another; the most current example is the movement of U.S. and Canadian wheat to China. The costs to transport bulk materials or petroleum on ships are determined by a "bid and ask" market, which fluctuates widely and is a function of the anticipated need for ship capacity. Traders in commodities—such as grain or sugar—also keep a close eye on the rates needed to charter (lease) a vessel. Whenever the traders notice that the spread, or difference, between prices of a commodity in two separate areas is more than the costs of chartering a vessel to carry the commodity, they will simultaneously (1) buy the commodity where it is available at the low price; (2) agree to sell it in the country willing to pay the high price with a later delivery date; and (3) charter a vessel to make the voyage.

One measure of the relative volumes of ocean trade is the tonnages of ships available for carrying different commodities. In mid-1978, the capacity of the world's existing bulk carriage fleet equaled 505 million long tons. Of this, 64 percent represented petroleum tankers, 10 percent represented combined carriers, and 26 percent

- *Combined carriers* are ocean ships that can carry *either* liquid products *or* dry bulk materials.

represented carriers of dry bulk products. There was an additional 40 million tons of capacity on order, divided in the same proportion.[14] Figure 9–6 shows the patterns of *international* petroleum

---

[13]Clinton H. Whitehurst, Jr., *The Defense Transportation System: Competitor or Complement to the Private Sector?* (Washington, D.C., American Enterprise Institute for Public Policy Research, 1976), p. 22.

[14]*Shipping Statistics and Economics* (London: H. P. Drewry, May, 1978), p. 49.

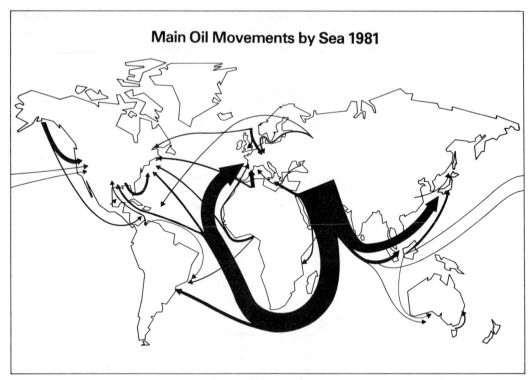

Figure 9–6   Movement of Oil by Water Carriers. Courtesy: "BP Statistical Review of the World Oil Industry, 1981."

movements by water, the single largest tonnage to move in international waterborne commerce.

In addition to bulk carriers, there are vessels which carry general cargo, i.e., items which must be handled on a piece-by-piece basis (or in containers). The capacity of this fleet is approximately 70 million tons, although only limited comparisons should be made with the bulk fleet since the general cargo vessels operate at faster speeds.[15] General cargo is much more valuable on a per-ton basis—that is, a 40-ton generator (general cargo) is worth more than 40 tons of rice (bulk cargo)—and its owners are willing to pay higher transport costs in order to reduce the amount of time their investment is tied up in transit.

An indication of the relative importance of non-petroleum bulk

---

[15] General cargo vessels try to obtain as much general cargo as they can. They then fill unused capacity with bulk cargo. This is known as "topping off." For this bulk cargo, they would charge the same rates as the bulk carriers' charter rates.

cargos can be obtained by tallying the charter contracts for a specific period of time, since the contracts indicate the type of cargo to be carried. Using figures for May 1978, a summary of 205 specific charter agreements was examined.[16] The majority of the agreements, 112 involving 128 vessel loads, were for the carriage of grains, including corn, sorghum, soy beans, and maize. One agreement was for citrus pellets (26,000 pounds from Tampa to Amsterdam); 4 were for rice (to be carried on 5 vessels); 5 were seeds (on 6 vessels); 25 were for sugar (on 27 vessels); and 1 was for tallow. There were 10 agreements for the carriage of iron ore; 9 (involving 11 vessels) for carrying coal; 8 for carrying iron and steel; 7 (involving 10 vessels) for carrying fertilizer; 5 each for carrying phosphates and scrap; and 1 each for carrying new autos, pipe, cement, sulfur, and alumina. The average tonnage for each type of commodity varied. For iron ore, the average shipload was 70,000 tons; for coal, it was 58,000 tons. For agricultural products, the average was much lower; for sugar, the average vessel load was under 10,000 tons.

There are no worldwide statistics concerning the movements of higher-value processed and manufactured items. However, there are some statistics concerning the movements of containerized cargoes between U.S. ports and ports elsewhere in the world. Cargo moving in containers is of higher value per ton than cargoes that move in bulk. Table 9–1 shows the 20 nations with which the United States traded the most containerized cargo during the year 1979.

Trade Routes

Commerce has moved by water since long before the time of Christ. Vessels would sail great distances, carrying products for exchange. As distant markets became linked on a somewhat regular basis, the path the vessel traveled became known as a trade route. At each end of the trade route there was cargo needed at the other end, and the cargo was of sufficient value that it could be sold at a price that covered the cost of transportation. Cities and ports along the paths of the trade routes benefited because the shipping vessels would stop at them as well as take on supplies. Thus, trade also developed at intermediate ports along the trade route. The idea of regional or national self-sufficiency was tempered by the desire to enjoy products that one could not produce "at home." In a trading world, each nation

---

[16] *Shipping Statistics and Economics* (May, 1978), pp. 29–38. Transactions involving shipments between Communist nations are not reported.

TABLE 9–1   U.S. Oceanborne Containerized Foreign Trade—1980
(In Commercial Tons)

Top Twenty Countries Ranked by Total Trade with U.S.	Inbound*	Percent of Total	Outbound*	Percent of Total	Total In & Out	Percent of Total
Japan	3,052,094	23.9	4,756,320	22.9	7,808,414	23.3
Netherlands	1,313,834	10.3	2,157,543	10.4	3,471,377	10.4
Republic of China (Taiwan)	1,181,569	9.3	1,639,919	7.9	2,821,488	8.4
Hong Kong	871,404	6.8	1,735,623	8.4	2,607,027	7.8
West Germany	1,047,640	8.2	1,383,655	6.7	2,431,295	7.2
United Kingdom	731,935	5.7	1,010,704	4.9	1,742,639	5.2
Italy	707,189	5.5	690,200	3.3	1,397,389	4.2
Australia	488,783	3.8	677,446	3.3	1,166,229	3.5
France	456,725	3.6	619,519	3.0	1,076,244	3.2
Belgium	303,728	2.4	562,193	2.7	865,921	2.6
Republic of Korea (S. Korea)	105,445	0.8	714,656	3.4	820,101	2.4
Singapore	235,147	1.8	569,697	2.7	804,844	2.4
Spain	248,467	2.0	359,408	1.7	607,875	1.8
Jamaica	260,384	2.0	303,791	1.5	564,175	1.7
Sweden	131,231	1.0	293,946	1.4	425,177	1.3
New Zealand	251,896	2.0	134,825	0.6	386,721	1.2
Venezuela	16,466	0.1	351,192	1.7	367,658	1.1
Brazil	198,101	1.6	165,828	0.8	363,929	1.1
Saudi Arabia	6,490	0.1	294,073	1.4	300,563	0.9
Honduras	201,934	1.6	74,688	0.4	276,622	0.8

SOURCE: U.S. Department of Commerce, *Containerized Cargo Statistics, Calendar Year 1980.*

*Inbound refers to cargo entering the U.S.; outbound to cargo leaving the U.S.

could specialize in growing or manufacturing whatever it could do best, trading its surplus with other nations.

Nineteenth-century European powers aggressively developed systems of colonies with which they could trade. They bought the colonies' raw materials and, in turn, sold them manufactured products. Of course, the colonies weren't able to transport the goods; the European powers transported the goods both ways on their own ships, earning additional profits on the transportation of the trade.

The concept of trade routes still holds. Cargo-carrying vessels travel back and forth on regular routes. Some travel only between major ports while others call on a regular, although less frequent, basis at smaller ports.

Canals

As international trade developed, ships' captains continually looked for the shortest navigable courses. Canal-building technology, first used domestically within England and the United States, was eventually employed on a grand scale to reduce sailing distances around both the African and the South American continents. The Suez Canal, completed a century ago, made it possible to save so much shipping capacity that an actual surplus of ships was created. In a Middle East dispute in the late 1960's, the Suez Canal was closed. Because the Suez was closed, many additional large tankers were built to carry petroleum the longer distances. These new "supertankers" were too large to pass through the Canal even if it had been open. When the Suez did reopen in 1975, the world's fleet of supertankers had to bypass it or else use it only for their return voyage, when they were riding light (or high in the water).

> Gulf Oil moves crude oil from Kuwait to Bantry Bay, Ireland, via the Cape of Good Hope using 326,000 dwt tankers, and then transships via 100,000-ton "shuttle" tankers to refining areas throughout Europe. Although the route is 13,000 miles longer than the Suez Canal route, the operating cost per barrel . . . is about half the unit cost of transporting the oil through the Suez in 50,000-ton tankers.[17]

Hence, closure of the Canal may have had an effect other than that anticipated.

- *Deadweight tonnage* (dwt) is the weight in long tons (2,240 pounds) which a vessel can carry. It includes the weight of the cargo, bunkers (which is fuel), and ship's stores.

The Panama Canal was completed by the United States early in this century.[18] The recent ratification of the new treaty between the United States and Panama once again focused attention on the Canal, its history, and its usefulness. Like the Suez Canal, the Panama Canal also is unable to accommodate the largest merchant (and naval) vessels. The phrase "Panamax" refers to a vessel, about 75,000 tons in capacity, that can just clear the Canal. As an example of how this size restriction works: Tankers carrying Alaskan oil sail south and moor just off the Pacific entrance to the Panama Canal, where they then transfer oil to smaller ships which carry it through the Canal and northward to the U.S. East Coast. Traffic through the Panama Canal has also been hurt by the U.S. railroad-containership innovation—the land bridge (or container-train), which carries traffic that otherwise would have moved through the Panama Canal. There is also railroad land-bridge traffic moving through Russia and

---

[17] Leon L. Smith, "Deepwater Port Crisis on the U.S. East Coast," *Naval Engineers Journal* (February, 1973), p. 18.
[18] See: David McCullough, *The Path Between the Seas* (New York: Simon and Schuster, 1978).

Siberia, connecting Western Europe with Japan. This Siberian land-bridge serves as an alternative to shipping through the Suez Canal.

International Rail and Truck Movements

Figure 9–7 is from an advertisement for the port of Halifax, Nova Scotia, as a "mini-bridge" container-handling port for cargo originating or terminating in the Midwest. The ad extols use of the St. Lawrence "route" for traffic but believes that rail, rather than water, is the mode to be used. In the early 1980's, U.S. East Coast port interests were attempting to have Congress pass a law that would discourage the movement of container traffic originating or terminating within the Midwest from moving through the Canadian ports of Montreal and Halifax. (One reason the cargo was moving through these Canadian ports was that their labor costs per container handled were in the range of $12 to $16 per container, while comparable costs for moving through U.S. East Coast ports were between $30 and $40.)[19]

Canadian shippers also route some containers through U.S. ports. One reason, seldom publicized, why shippers route some traffic through another nation's ports is that shippers like to have an alternative port they can use in case the ports in their own country are closed by a strike. By being a somewhat "regular" customer of the

[19]*American Shipper* (March, 1982), p. 3.

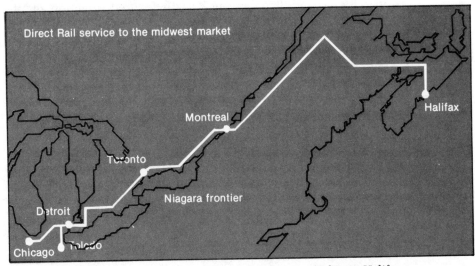

Figure 9–7   Port of Halifax Ad. Courtesy: Halicon, Halifax.

port which is still open, their cargo will receive preference in handling over cargo which other shippers try to divert from the strikebound ports. Rail and motor carrier freight traffic moves very easily across the U.S.-Canadian border, although it must pass through customs inspection. Highway vehicles and railroad equipment used in both countries are interchangeable.

Surface traffic at the Mexican-U.S. border often does not flow as smoothly. Congestion and delays are often a problem. For example, in December, 1980, the National Railways of Mexico placed an embargo (meaning they refused to accept) rail shipments from the United States. This was because there was a backlog of 40,000 U.S. freight cars waiting to be unloaded in Mexico.[20] U.S. truckers complain that it is almost impossible for them to operate within Mexico, while Mexican truckers have less trouble operating in the U.S.[21]

Ports

In the preceding chapter we discussed ports, and how they functioned to interchange traffic between land and water carriers. Ports handling international commerce perform the same physical transfer function and, in addition, contain firms that perform all of the "paperwork" functions associated with international business transactions.

Economic Impact of Ports

Handling cargo in ports consists of many tasks, especially when it is international cargo. A study by the Port of New York estimated that every 600 tons of foreign trade handled annually creates the equivalent of one job within the economy.[22] Figure 9–8 depicts all of the activities that occur within a port and attempts to place them in relationship to each other. After studying the figure, you should be able to appreciate the many mechanisms which must be coordinated in order for cargo to flow.

One problem created by containerships is the reduced need for longshoremen. "Prior to 1966, when containers entered foreign

---

[20] *Rail News Update* (July 1, 1981), p. 3.
[21] *Go West Magazine* (March, 1982), pp. 23–24.
[22] Jerome Gilbert, Nai-Ching Sun, and Amos Ilan, *What U.S. Ports Mean to the Economy* (Washington, D.C.: Maritime Administration, September 1978). The study, paid for by the Maritime Administration, was conducted by the staff of the Port Authority of New York and New Jersey.

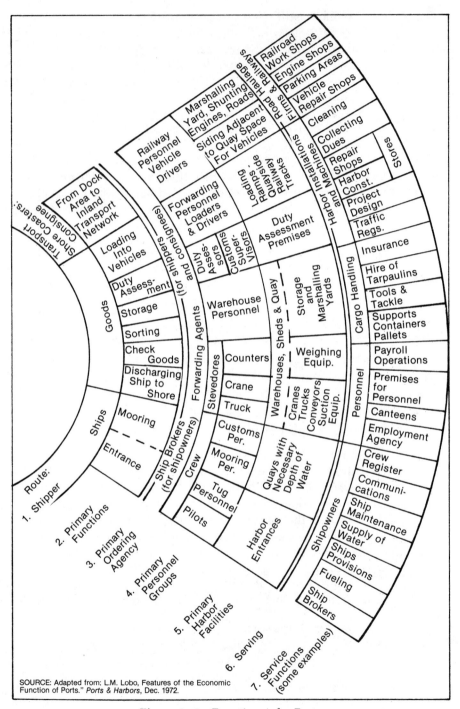

SOURCE: Adapted from: L.M. Lobo, Features of the Economic Function of Ports." *Ports & Harbors*, Dec. 1972.

Figure 9–8 Functions of a Port.

trade, dock productivity averaged one ton a manhour. With containerization, productivity can reach 200 or 300 tons a manhour."[23]

In the 20-year period, 1958 to 1978, the number of longshoremen working in the Port of New York dropped from 31,600 to 11,800,[24] although the longshoremen's own uninspiring work practices were one of the reasons that justified the move toward containerization. (Longshoremen on the West Coast have been somewhat more receptive to containers than has been the case for unions on the Atlantic and Gulf Coasts.) Longshoremen and Teamsters are in continual jurisdictional disputes to determine which union's members have the right to perform certain tasks. This includes the area away from the pier where ocean-going containers may be stuffed and unstuffed, and the area at the piers where the cargo is transferred between ocean vessels and trucks.

Inadequate Depths

A problem facing many ports in the United States—as well as in other countries—is that they aren't deep enough to accommodate the new, large vessels. "At the turn of the century channels 30 feet were adequate for virtually all ships in the world."[25] Today, half-million-ton supertankers draw 90 feet of water. The additional draft requirements of the larger vessels must be met by digging and maintaining deeper depths in the channels between the port facilities and the open sea.

Under present arrangements, the U.S. government, acting through the Army Corps of Engineers, dredges and maintains the channel depths; the dock owners are responsible for maintaining depths alongside their property. One way to recover some of the costs of providing deeper drafts would be to assess "user charges" on vessels using the deeper channels. Some nations do this.

The Reagan Administration is attempting to reduce—if not eliminate—the federal government's financial responsibility for dredging costs. East Coast ports that want to handle more coal traffic need greater depths. In early 1982, the federal government offered to loan $105 million to the State of Maryland to cover approximately 25 percent of the costs of deepening the channel near Baltimore from 42 to 50 feet. The state would have to cover the other 75 percent of the costs. As of this writing, the state has apparently refused the offer.[26]

[23] *American Shipper* (November, 1977), p. 41.
[24] *Ibid.*
[25] Richard W. Barsness, "Maritime Activity and Port Development in the United States Since 1900: A Survey," *Journal of Transport History* (February, 1974), p. 174.
[26] *American Shipper* (March, 1982), p. 38.

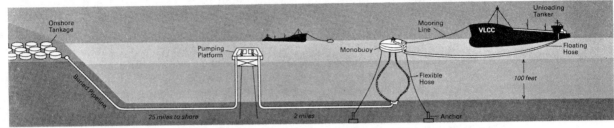

Diagram shows how ocean-going tanker moors to anchored monobuoy and delivers oil through floating hose to monobouy. Flexible hoses connect monobuoy to pipeline manifold on ocean floor, and oil then moves through undersea pipeline to control platform, which serves several monobuoys. From platform, oil is pumped via submarine pipeline to onshore tankage some 25 miles away. Installation will withstand 110-knot-winds and 65-foot waves.

Figure 9–9   Offshore Oil Discharge Mooring Facility. Courtesy: *Span* Magazine, Standard Oil Company (Indiana).

Offshore Facilities

Tankers are at less of a disadvantage than dry-cargo carriers when it comes to draft limitations, since it is possible for tankers to moor offshore and load or discharge their cargo through flexible pipelines. An example of this is shown on Figure 9–9. Another method is to moor the large tanker offshore and pump oil to or from smaller tankers which can be handled in shallower ports.

Several large oil companies joined together in a venture named "Seadock" to build an offshore mooring and oil-unloading facility about 25 miles south of Freeport, Texas, in water approximately 100 feet deep. Legally, the venture would have been considered as an oil pipeline and subject to Department of Energy regulations. In late 1976, outgoing Secretary of Transportation William Coleman approved a license for the facility but with so many restrictions that the consortium of oil companies decided not to move ahead with the project.[27] Another one has been built off the Louisiana coast.

Dry bulk materials can be handled in slurry form and also pumped to and from vessels moored offshore. Iron ore is handled this way in vessels with special holds containing pumps and agitators for reintroducing water to the mixture and stirring it until its consistency is sufficiently liquid that it can be pumped.

Ocean Carriers

Vessels are classified by the type of cargo they carry. Bulk carriers are built for handling only one type of cargo; the principal categories

[27] *The Wall Street Journal* (July 27, 1977), p. 4.

are tankers, dry bulk carriers, and—recently—the LNG (liquified natural gas) ships. General cargo vessels (including containerships) carry assorted cargo, usually worth more on a per-ton basis. Examples are: LASH (Lighter/Aboard/Ship) vessels, RoRo (Roll on/Roll off) ships, and "Combo" ships (which combine aspects of container and RoRo vessels). Specialized vessels are built to serve the needs of larger shippers. For example, Japanese automakers own several ships on which the space between decks is just high enough to clear roofs of the new autos being shipped. On the return voyage to Japan, the vessels carry soybeans from the U.S.

Tankers and Bulk Carriers

In terms of tonnage, tankers dominate the world's commercial fleet. Petroleum companies own their own tankers and also charter others either for a specific voyage or for a given period of time. In mid-1978 there were in the world approximately 3,200 tankers of which 1,465 belonged to oil companies.[28]

Modern tankers are extremely large.

> Guiding and steering a ship from a bridge set nearly a quarter of a mile from the bows is frightening enough to a man unaccustomed to it, but he also is one hundred feet above the water and has to walk one hundred and fifty feet from port to starboard to see what is happening on the other side. . . .[29]

If anything, the tankers are too large. Since 1974, the increase in prices of petroleum has reduced many worldwide movements of petroleum and, as a result, many large tankers have been withdrawn from service.

We have become aware of the large size and the enormous capacity of modern supertankers from their accidents causing large oil spills and fouling large stretches of shoreline throughout the world. Whether the larger tankers are more or less accident-prone than smaller ones is unknown. West Coast states have been reluctant to admit supertankers into their ports, fearing oil spills. The State of Washington attempted to limit the size of loaded tankers entering Puget Sound, but the U.S. Supreme Court overturned the state law, saying that the regulations should be controlled by federal authorities.[30]

A very specialized type of vessel has been developed in recent years to carry liquified natural gas, mainly from other areas of the

[28] *Shipping Statistics and Economics* (May, 1978), p. 15.
[29] Noël Mostert, *Supership* (New York: Alfred A. Knopf, 1974), p. 30.
[30] *The Wall Street Journal* (March 7, 1978), p. 4.

world to the United States. The gas is compressed to ¹⁄₆₃₀th of its volume, at which point it becomes liquid.

The kinds of commodities carried in dry bulk vessels were listed earlier in this chapter. The largest vessels are used for carrying iron ore, which moves in regular patterns. Many of these vessels are owned by either the steel company or the ore producer. The two areas of the world that receive the largest tonnages of ore by sea are Western Europe and Japan. Ore is a dense cargo and depths along-side ore-handling facilities have to be quite deep. Two-thirds of the world's ore movements in the mid-1970's were on vessels of 50,000 dwt, or greater.[31]

Coal moves on smaller bulk carriers than those that carry iron ore. The United States is the world's principal exporter of coal; Japan is the principal importer. In the mid-1970's half of the world's coal movements were on vessels of 50,000 dwt capacity or larger. In other bulk trades, such as the carriage of grain, bauxite, or phosphate, smaller vessels tend to be used. About 75 percent of the world's grain trade was carried on vessels of 35,000 dwt, or less; almost none moved on vessels over 50,000 dwt. In the bauxite trades, cargos move on vessels ranging from 20,000 to 50,000 tons, while for phosphates, 80 percent of the traffic was carried on vessels of 35,000 dwt capacity or more.[32]

Several factors dictate the size of vessel used in bulk trades. In ore trades, the routes are regular, and high-speed loading and discharge facilities are installed at each end of the route. This yields a quick "turn-around" time, lessens costs in-port (when the vessel is not productive), and favors employment of a larger vessel.

Smaller vessels are, and will continue to be, used in many trades. Available depths in many ports, canals, and alongside cargo-handling facilities, all impose a limit on the size of vessel they can accommodate. The grain trade, while "regular" in the sense that it employs many vessels on a worldwide basis each year, is "irregular" in that the patterns of trade shift, depending upon the success and failure of crops in various parts of the world. Hence, the grain trade to or from any single facility or port may be quite irregular, and it is this irregularity that makes it difficult to justify and invest in improvements for handling larger vessels. There will always be a need for smaller vessels because of draft limitations in many parts of the world and because smaller businesses can invest in only so much

---

[31] *Ports and Terminals for Large Bulk Carriers* (London: H. P. Drewry, report #46, October, 1976), p. 9.
[32] *Ibid.*, p. 79.

cargo at any one time. That is, they cannot afford to accumulate an entire "vessel load" for a giant-sized ship.

Figure 9–10 shows an ocean-going 27,500-dwt vessel for carrying dry bulk cargo. It happens to be called an "open-hatch" carrier because it is built to allow the entire hatch to be uncovered, making it easy to load or unload a cargo such as lumber.

"Tramp" shipping is used to describe a large segment of the dry-cargo bulk market. One writer defined a "tramp ship" as:

> Any vessel with a tonnage of 4,000 dwt or above which *in the long run* does not have a fixed itinerary, and which carries mainly dry-cargoes in bulk over relatively long distances and from one or more ports to one or more ports. . . .[33]

The market for tramp services is competitive; tramp vessels are chartered for a trip or for a period of time. Vessel chartering agreements specify the port of loading and the port of discharge, the rates (in tons per hour) at which the cargo will be loaded and unloaded, a daily charge for delays encountered by the vessel, and any other responsibilities that either the shipper or shipowner must assume. Tramp vessel owners are very concerned about finding another cargo at their port of destination, and they will charge less for a voyage to a port with available outbound cargos (such as New Orleans where grain is shipped continually) than to ports with few or no outbound bulk cargos.

General Cargo Vessels

General cargo is of higher value per ton than bulk cargo and usually consists of manufactured or processed items. It is handled by the piece, or on pallets, or in containers. Since the mid-1960's, the principal vessel employed in the carriage of general cargo has been the containership. While containers are usually 8 ft. wide, 8 ft. high, and 20 to 40 ft. long, there is no "standard" length; various ship lines use their own lengths which are dictated by highway or railroad car length limits in countries. Most containerships require shore-based equipment to load or unload, although a few have their own cranes.

In 1979 there were an estimated 2,000,000 containers (in TEUs) throughout the world, compared with only 300,000 in 1970.[34] About half are owned by container leasing companies. In mid-1978 there

---

[33] B. N. Metaxas, "The Future of the Tramp Shipping Industry," *Journal of Transport Economics and Policy* (September, 1972), p. 271.

[34] "The State of Containerization—1979," *Transport 2000* (Nov./Dec., 1978), pp. 1–48.

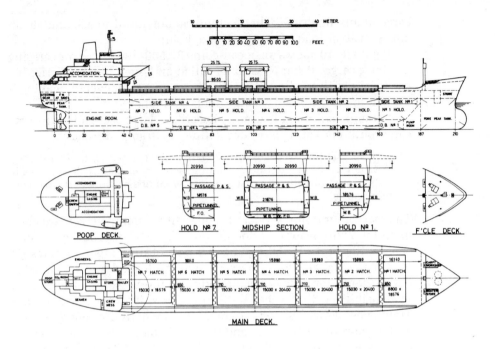

Principal dimensions: L.o.a.: 564' 0'' L.p.p.: 530' 0'' B.mld.: 85' 0'' D.mld.: 48' 3''

Capacities:

HATCH	HATCH SIZES	HOLDS	CU.FT. GRAIN	SQUARE BALE CU.FT.
1	28' 10½'' x 60' 11¼''	1	108.096	84.685
2	49' 3¾'' x 66' 11¼''	2	183.244	177.127
3	49' 3¾'' x 66' 11¼''	3	184.410	177.291
4	49' 3¾'' x 66' 11¼''	4	184.410	177.291
5	49' 3¾'' x 66' 11¼''	5	184.410	177.291
6	49' 3¾'' x 66' 11¼''	6	183.268	177.291
7	49' 3¾'' x 66' 11¼''	7	137.830	135.370
		Total cargo space	1.166.668	1.106.346

27.450 t.dw. — 34' 1¾'' salt water draft.

Figure 9–10   Open-Hatch Ocean Vessel. Courtesy: Star Shipping (U.S.W.C.) Inc.

were 340 vessels in the world equipped to carry only containers, and 204 equipped to carry both containers and non-containerized cargo.

- *TEU* stands for an equivalent of a 20 foot long container 8 feet wide and 8 feet high. A 40-foot container would equal two TEUs.

There were also 75 containerships and 261 partial containerships on order.[35] Table 9–2 shows the number of containers handled in 1980 foreign trade by U.S. ports.

RoRo (Roll On/Roll Off) vessels have sufficient space between decks to enable conventional highway trailers to be carried on all the vessel's decks. RoRo carriers specialize in oversized cargo, such as construction machinery, buses, etc., which can be driven or towed

---

[35] *Shipping Statistics and Economics* (May, 1978), p. 54.

TABLE 9–2 Foreign Container Traffic Handled by U.S. Ports —1980
(In TEUs)

Ports Ranked by Volume of Traffic	TEUs (in thousands)
New York	750
Los Angeles	445
Oakland	342
Seattle	329
Long Beach	295
Baltimore	262
Norfolk	201
Houston	136
Miami	132
Charleston	118
New Orleans	93
Savannah	92
San Francisco	90
Philadelphia	69
San Juan	46
Boston	40
Portland, Oregon	38
Jacksonville	36
Galveston	21
Gulfport	20
Tacoma	19
Port Everglades	18

SOURCE: U.S. Department of Commerce, *Containerized Cargo Statistics, Calendar Year 1980.*

Note: The ports listed above accounted for a total of over 96 percent of the ocean-going foreign trade of the U.S. moving in containers (or trailers, i.e., as RoRo).

aboard. Loading and unloading RoRo's is much easier than for other types of vessels because only a ramp is needed to load and unload; this means the RoRo vessel is more flexible than containerships because it can call at ports that do not have extensive container-handling equipment. RoRo vessels also carry conventional containers on their top deck. A cut-away side view of a RoRo vessel would look like a multi-level city parking garage, each level connected to the others with an up and down ramp.

Barges

LASH and Seabee vessels, large "mother" ships that carry barges, were discussed in chapter 8. A LASH vessel, which carried both barges and conventional containers, was illustrated in Figure 8–10. LASH and Seabee ships carry both general cargo and bulk cargo.

Figure 9–11 shows a Japanese development, the "Industrial Plat-

Figure 9–11 Pulp Plant on Platform Barge Deck. In background is the power plant, also built permanently above a platform barge deck. Photo was taken in Japanese yard as the pulp and power plants started their voyage to Brazil. Courtesy: Ishikawajima-Harima Heavy Industries, Co., Ltd., Tokyo.

form System," used to tow two halves of a woodpulp-processing plant, built in Japan, to a site in Brazil's Amazon River Basin. Two barges first were built in the Japanese yard and then the pulp plant and the accompanying power plant were built on top of each barge. Very careful attention was paid to determining how the weight of the pulp and power plants would be distributed on their respective barges. The plants were then towed by tugs the entire way to the Jari River in Brazil to a site that had been partially enclosed by a dike. At the places inside the diked area, where the pulp and power plants were destined to be placed, wooden pilings had been driven into the bottom. When the two barges with the plants arrived, they were towed inside the diked area and moored next to the pilings. The dike was then extended to completely enclose the area, and water was pumped in to raise the barges. The barges were then floated directly above the piles, the water level was lowered, and the barges holding the two plants were then resting on top of the piles. Windows were cut in the sides of the barges, and the barges became the lower floors of the pulp and power plants. It was estimated that construction costs were reduced by 20 percent and two years of time was saved by having the plant built in Japan and towed to Brazil rather than having it constructed at the Brazilian site.[36]

Ocean-going barges are also being developed to carry bulk cargo. Their advantage over conventional vessels is that the tug or towboat propelling the barge has a much much smaller crew.

Passenger Ships

Passenger travel by ship has lost out to passenger travel by airplane. Today, there remain passenger ships, but few are used for direct travel; they offer vacation "cruise" service. The most common vacation cruise service offered in the U.S. is at Miami, where numerous foreign-flag vessels offer cruises among the Bahamas. Less frequent cruise service is offered along the West Coast, although there are cruises along the coast and to Hawaii. Worldwide, there are about 75 to 100 vacation cruise ships in operation.

Cargo-carrying liners sometimes are outfitted with passenger accommodations for carrying up to 12 passengers. (Vessel insurance requires that a medical doctor be carried on board if there are more than 12 passengers.) Modern containerships are less likely to have

---

[36] "Shipbuilder in Japan Delivers Completed Pulp Plant to Brazil," *Surveyor* (quarterly journal of the American Bureau of Shipping, May, 1978), pp. 14–18.

passenger accommodations because the time they spend in each port is very brief, and passengers have very little time to go ashore.

Cruise ships fly foreign flags because U.S. labor costs are high, and cruise ships require large crews. At one time, the U.S. government subsidized passenger ships, but their owners chose to drop out of the passenger business, although several U.S. carriers—whose vessels carry both cargo and passengers—do receive subsidies from the U.S. Maritime Administration.

Steamship Liner Conferences

Shippers of petroleum and large quantities of bulk materials own many of their own vessels. For the rest of their needs they lease or charter vessels in very competitive markets, where forces of supply and demand can be relied upon to establish the day's price for shipping and to allocate the available tonnage to those willing to pay. This type of competitive market, with relatively equal bargaining strength between buyers and sellers, does not hold for general cargo shipments. This is because most general cargo shipments tendered are small, weighing only a few tons each. The relative bargaining power of any one shipper, when contrasted to that of the vessel owner, is small.

Rules of international maritime commerce allow ships flying any flag to call at a nation's port and offer whatever rates are necessary to obtain cargo. Without the conference system, these vessels would appear only when large tonnages of cargo were available for shipping; they would not be interested in small shipments or in providing the regular service which many shippers needed.

The *conference system* was devised to "tie" shippers and vessel operators together, the shippers agreeing to use only conference vessels, the conferences agreeing to provide conference shippers lower rates than the rates charged shippers not agreeing to use conference vessels exclusively. The conference would also agree to provide regular sailings on a scheduled basis, despite the fact that during certain seasons, the total amount of cargo offered by all shippers might be small. Liner companies from different nations can belong to the same conference.

The word "conference" denotes no single system but is a generic term covering a wide variety of common services and common obligations undertaken by shipowners serving particular trades. Broadly speaking, the term denotes a meeting of lines . . . serving any particular route, aimed at agreement on uniform and stable rates of freight and the provision of services, under stated working conditions in that trade. It ranges from a very informal association to a well developed organization with a permanent secretariat behind it. The obligations the parties to such agreements undertake towards one another will vary as widely as do the agreements themselves.[37]

There are several hundred conferences in the world, including over one hundred that serve to connect U.S. ports with foreign ports. Examples of conferences would be Australia to Japan, or Israel to the U.S.-North Atlantic region. Usually conferences serve trade moving in one direction only since some members may return by a triangular, rather than straight route. The same vessel company usually belongs to several conferences, including some that might compete with each other, such as from South Atlantic ports to the U.K., and from Gulf ports to the U.K.

The membership of most conferences is "closed," which means that additional lines are not welcome. At one time, when faced with competition from an outsider, the conferences would assign one of their vessels to be a "fighting ship," which would follow the outside line's vessel from port to port, offering to carry the cargo for less than whatever the outsider would charge. Recently, developing nations have forced conferences serving their ports to allow native-flag vessels to enter the conference, since one of the developing nations' complaints has been that conferences represented the established powers' commercial needs.

Conference members attempt to eliminate competition among themselves as much as possible. They do this by "pooling" or sharing. An example would be for three lines to agree to sail from A to B, with the first line's vessel to leave now; line 2's vessel to leave a week from now; line 3's, two weeks from now; and then repeat the sequence with line 1's vessel leaving again in three weeks. All lines would agree to charge the same rates for cargo, pay similar commissions to forwarders, etc. Nonetheless, because of vagaries in the flow of cargo, it may be that in the course of a year the traffic carried was not divided into equal thirds carried by each line. At the end of the year, the conference would examine the books of all three members and redistribute the revenues or profits according to some previously agreed upon formula. For example, each line might have been guaranteed a minimum of 25 percent of the revenue from *all* of the traffic; at the year's end, if one line earned less, the other line(s)

---

[37] *The Liner Conference System* (New York: United Nations Conference of Trade and Development, 1970). p. 3. See also: B. M. Deakin, *Shipping Conferences, A Study of Their Origins, Developmental, and Economic Practices* (Cambridge, England: Cambridge University Press, 1973), p. 3.

which earned more would reimburse the one earning less. This reimbursement could be justified by the belief that the line that earned less than 25 percent, while carrying less than its share of traffic, actually contributed to the well-being of the entire conference since it offered its share of scheduled sailings—one every three weeks—and was available to those shippers who had contracted with the conference and were dependent upon it for service.

Shippers' contracts with conferences vary with the conference and its relative monopoly position. In general terms, the shippers agree to give the conference vessel lines all of their business in the area served by the conference. The two common exceptions are when the conference has no vessel or vessel space available or when the shipment is larger than a certain size, i.e., so large that it might be feasible for the shipper to charter an entire vessel. In turn, shippers who sign contracts with the conference pay rates that are 10 to 15 percent lower than would be charged to non-contracting shippers. In many conferences, a deferred rebate is used, meaning the shipper has on deposit with the conference a 10 to 15 percent rebate for using the conference vessels exclusively for some past period. The rebate is paid, although never immediately, so the shipper always has on deposit with the conference some money which he risks forfeiting any time he strays from giving the conference members his exclusive patronage.

Shippers Councils

In many countries, shippers join together in *shippers councils* to exercise countervailing power against the conferences. Membership in councils consists of shippers of a single commodity or similar overseas markets. Their strength comes from the fact that they represent enough cargo tonnage that they could, if necessary, bypass the conference and charter a vessel or two for their own exclusive use. The shippers councils' main success has been in convincing conferences to "open up their books" when trying to justify rate increases.

For the most part, shippers councils are not permitted in the United States because of anti-trust considerations. The principal argument in favor of allowing shippers councils in the U.S. is that overseas firms, competing with U.S.-based firms, are able to meet as councils and exert more downward pressure on the ocean freight rates they pay.

United States Policies Regarding Conferences

In the United States, public opinion and many of the laws are based more on fear of monopolies and collusive agreements between competitors than is the case in many other nations. This is reflected in our legislation regarding steamship conferences in which we attempt to reconcile our own "anti-trust" outlook with the realities of international shipping and the inability of any single nation to decide "what is right" for the world.

The basic U.S. statute that regulates international conferences calling at U.S. ports is the *Shipping Act of 1916* (as amended). The Act was based on findings of a congressional committee, commonly known as the Alexander Report. At present, the federal regulatory body concerned with carrying out the law is the Federal Maritime Commission (FMC). It functions as do other U.S. transportation regulatory agencies, and its decisions may be appealed to Federal courts.[38]

Conferences and their members must be "approved" by the FMC in order to obtain immunity from our anti-trust statutes. What follows is a list of requirements unique to conferences serving U.S. ports. Deferred rebates are prohibited. Instead, "dual rate" contracts are allowed, meaning that shippers who contract with the conference pay lower rates. Conferences must be "open" in the sense they cannot exclude members and cannot use "fighting ships" to undercut potential competitors. Conferences serving U.S. ports must also employ neutral "self-policing" bodies to ensure that all conference members are correct in describing and weighing the cargo tendered to them by shippers (i.e., not cheating by carrying more freight than is indicated on the shipping documents).

"Cheating" by conference member lines is an important problem throughout the world. In many areas of the world, it is a "way of life" especially appropriate to ocean shipping where the operator is scheduled to sail and may have to give some additional incentives to reluctant shippers so that he can fill his vessel. These practices are not unknown within the U.S.

> A steamship company official and an exporter meet on the golf course for their regular Sunday round. . . .
> "Tell you what," says Joe, from the shipping firm, "today I'll give you three strokes on the side." Al the exporter agrees. They also decide to sweeten the bet.
> Al, as usual, comes up the big winner. At the 19th hole, instead of the dollar or two he'd normally collect, Joe hands him $1,000—of company money.
> In the company books, it will go down as convention expenses.
> This is one of the more intriguing ways of making illegal cash kick-

---

[38] The Federal Maritime Commission also regulates rates and services of domestic offshore carriers, i.e., between the 48 states and Alaska, Hawaii, Guam, Puerto Rico and the Virgin Islands.

backs in the shipping industry, a payoff to the exporter for selecting a particular line to ship his products.[39]

In June 1979 a new U.S. law was enacted that strengthened the power of the Federal Maritime Commission in combating illegal rebates given by ship operators carrying U.S. foreign trade. The new law gives the FMC the right to suspend tariffs of any conference serving U.S. ports that refuses a subpoena request by the FMC in connection with a rebating investigation. Also, in late-1978 a law was enacted allowing the FMC to suspend rates charged by state-owned vessel lines (meaning Russian-flag) serving as "cross-traders" in the carriage of U.S. foreign trade. The FMC could suspend rates for up to 180 days, if they were found to be unreasonably low. The purpose of the law is to prevent Russian and other Communist-bloc vessels from charging very low rates for the purpose of earning Western currencies.

U.S. Maritime Administration Programs

When compared with other countries, the United States is a "high-cost" shipbuilder and a "high-cost" vessel operator. Government subsidies are required to keep our shipbuilders and ship operators competitive, although the subsidies often seem to be administered in a way that only further drives up costs, fueling the cry for even higher subsidies.

The rationale for subsidizing merchant marine activities is two-fold. In wartime the ships and shipbuilding and sailing skills would be needed. In peacetime, a merchant marine is necessary so that a trading nation can earn foreign exchange from transporting its own imports and exports. The United States is not the only nation that subsidizes its merchant marine; Communist-bloc nations and many Western industrial nations do so as well.

The remainder of this section will discuss various U.S. shipping subsidy programs, all of which are administered by the Maritime Administration, a part of the U.S. Department of Transportation.

Shipbuilding subsidies reflect an attempt to make the prices of ships purchased in U.S. yards similar to the prices of ships built elsewhere. Most purchasers of ships built in U.S. yards are U.S. firms who request a subsidy, after they receive a bid from a U.S. shipyard, which can be compared to bids from foreign yards. (If the

[39] H. W. Kusserow, "How Shippers Kick Back," *San Francisco Examiner/Chronicle* (June 8, 1975).

vessel has any special features that would be necessary for its use in wartime, the federal government will pay for them directly.) The Reagan Administration eliminated funds for this program, saying that it was "rethinking" its maritime aid program. Whether the funds will be restored is unknown at this writing. U.S. vessel operators are presently placing orders for new ships to be built in foreign yards. Two other forms of shipbuilding subsidies are loan guarantees and special tax incentives on funds that shipowners reserve for new vessel construction.

Operating-differential subsidies are paid to vessel operators, mainly of liner vessels. In fiscal 1977 there were 21 U.S. flag carriers, operating a total of 186 vessels, that had operating subsidy contracts with the Federal Maritime Administration. Also, subsidies were paid to 79 vessels carrying wheat to Russia.[40] To be eligible to receive operating-differential subsidies, vessels usually must be built in U.S. yards and manned by U.S. crews. Liner subsidies are calculated to offset the higher costs the U.S. flag operator must pay, when compared with costs paid by competitors on the same route. "Essential U.S. Foreign Trade Routes" are established and U.S. flag vessels serving these routes then apply for operating-differential subsidies. Sometimes more than one operator is subsidized to provide service on a route. An example of a route description is:

> Trade route 18, U.S. Atlantic and Gulf/India, Persian Gulf, and Red Sea. Between U.S. Atlantic and Gulf ports (Maine-Texas, inclusive) and ports in Southwest Asia from Suez to Burma, inclusive, and Africa on the Red Sea and Gulf of Aden.[41]

About 35 routes have been designated, although at some times they may lack any U.S. flag lines serving them. One example was a Great Lakes-Caribbean route via the St. Lawrence Seaway where the U.S. flag operator dropped out after Castro became the leader of Cuba and U.S.-Cuban trade was eliminated.

While most U.S. flag liner operators are subsidized, a few are not. The best known of these is Sea-Land Service, a large containership operator which apparently feels it prefers to be free of Maritime Administration restrictions (and is still able to operate at a profit). In 1978 Sea-Land placed a single order with Japanese and Korean shipyards of $385 million for 12 new containerships. (In 1981, Sea-Land

---

[40] *Marad '77*, The Annual Report of the Maritime Administration for Fiscal 1977 (Washington, D.C., 1978), p. 2.

[41] *Essential United States Foreign Trade Routes* (Washington, D.C.: Maritime Administration, 1975), p. 5.

sold to the U.S. Navy six of its fleet of SL-7s, which it had purchased new from Dutch and German shipyards in the early 1970s. The SL-7s were high-speed containerships, powered by fuel-inefficient steam turbine engines. The Navy will convert the SL-7s to "fast-deployment" RoRo vessels, and each will be able to carry the equipment for a heavy mechanized Army Division. The money Sea-Land received, $207 million, has to be spent by the firm for construction in U.S. shipyards.)[42]

Other programs, also administered through the Maritime Administration, help the industry. The U.S. Merchant Marine Academy, at Kings Point, New York, and six state maritime academies (in California, Maine, Massachusetts, Michigan, New York, and Texas) are subsidized. They train merchant marine officers. The Maritime Administration maintains the "reserve fleet" of mothballed commercial ships, which have been retired from active service. While these are maintained primarily for military emergencies, they can be—and have been—released for use by commercial operators.

Research into maritime problems is sponsored by the Maritime Administration. A matter of continual concern is the adaptability of cargo ships presently in use to wartime situations.[43] The agency is also involved in some "market development" and "port planning" activities, although the effectiveness of its efforts in these two areas is difficult to evaluate. Lastly, the Maritime Administration ensures that cargo preference requirements—i.e., that certain percentages of government sponsored cargos move on U.S.-flag vessels—are met.[44] The agency also has a limited involvement in some aspects of domestic shipping.

International Travel and Tourism

Before discussing international air transport, some mention should be made of international travel and tourism. Travel is the movement of people for business, family, personal, or vacation purposes. Tourism is associated with travel for pleasure, and the tourist industry

---

[42] *American Shipper* (October, 1981), p. 38. The vessels had cost about $53 million each in 1972, and were sold for $35 million each in 1981. They could travel at 33 knots (38 mph).

[43] *American Shipper* (February 1977), pp. 16–17; see also; "The Containership in a National Emergency," *Transport 2000* (March/April, 1977), pp. 34–38.

[44] Another subsidy to the maritime industry, totaling nearly $100 million per year, is paid by the U.S. Department of Agriculture to U.S. bulk carriers to haul grain—purchased from U.S. farmers under price-support programs—to developing nations. See: *American Shipper* (March, 1979), pp. 8–9, 45–46.

provides food, lodging, and other services to the pleasure-seeking traveler.

In addition to representing business for carriers, these international travelers take money they earn in their home country and they spend it in another. This has an impact on each nation's balance of payments. In 1978, citizens of other countries spent $7.3 billion while traveling within the United States, while U.S. citizens traveling in other countries spent $8.5 billion.[45] In other words, we spent (or imported) 1.16 times what we received (exported). Ten years earlier, in 1968, the ratio had been much higher, we spent 1.7 times what we had received. The reason for the change has been that as other countries have become more prosperous (in comparison to the U.S.) more of their citizens have chosen to visit this country.

In 1978, approximately 20 million trips were made by foreigners to the United States. Most, about 60 percent, were from Canada. Sixteen percent came from Latin America, 12 percent from Europe, and 5 percent from Japan. In the same year, there were about 19 million trips made by U.S. citizens to other countries, including 11.3 million to Canada, and 4.1 million to Europe and the Mediterranean.

The $7.3 billion of services and goods sold in 1978 to tourists traveling in the U.S. represented only 3.3 percent of our total exports for that year. For some nations, the percentage is much higher. Examples are Spain, where expenditures by tourists were 24 percent of all exports; and Austria, Greece, and Portugal, where the percentage ranged between 16 and 22. Thus we have seen, and will see, efforts by many governments—including our own—to attract additional visitors. In many instances, international air carriers will be beneficiaries of these efforts.

International Airlines

The history of international aviation is much briefer than the history of international ocean shipping. There was a limited amount of international aviation between the two world wars, but it did not become significant until after World War II. In terms of technology and operations, the international airline industry does not differ much from the domestic trunk airline industry, which was discussed in chapter 7. Indeed, the international carriers went through a phase of

---

[45] All data in this section are from *Tourism Policy and International Tourism in OECD Member Countries, 1980* (Paris: The Organization for Economic Co-Operation and Development, 1980).

fare deregulation, which followed the U.S. decision to deregulate its domestic airlines.

Compared with the domestic U.S. airline industry of today, the international airline industry differs in three major respects. First, except for U.S. carriers, nearly all international air carriers are owned, in whole or in part, by their respective national governments. Second, exchange of flight service between any two nations must be agreed upon in advance by both nations; this often means that a minimum of two carriers, one from each nation, fly the same route. Third, unlike shipbuilding, the airline aircraft manufacturing industry in the United States is the major supplier of new aircraft to most nations in the free world. Hence, our nation's international aviation policy must promote the health of *both* our international air carriers and our airline aircraft manufacturing industry.

Development of International Airlines

There was relatively little international aviation prior to World War II, and the aircraft then had limited capability. Initially, trans-oceanic air passenger service was provided by dirigibles, operated by Germany to both the United States and Brazil. The *Hindenburg* was 808 feet long, 135 feet in diameter, and could carry 72 passengers. After it was accidentally destroyed by explosion and fire at Lakehurst, New Jersey, in 1937, the remaining German dirigibles were withdrawn from commercial service.[46]

A parallel development was the flying boat, built separately by both British and U.S. aircraft manufacturers. Initial routes for U.S. planes were to South America while British planes attempted to connect various segments of the British Empire. Flying boats did not require airports, and the hull would keep the plane afloat at sea in case it had to make an emergency landing. The Boeing 314 *Clipper*, introduced in the late 1930's, was a beautiful airplane and "ahead of its time" in terms of technology. It could carry 72 passengers for a maximum range of 5,200 miles. The plane had two decks, connected by a spiral staircase, and tunnels in its wings to allow mechanics inflight to reach the four engines to make minor repairs. The immense commercial potential of these planes was never realized because World War II intervened.

World War II was responsible for determining the structure of the international airline industry as we know it today. This was for several reasons. Development of land-based bombers and military trans-

---

[46]Henry R. Palmer, Jr., *This Was Air Travel* (New York: Bonanza, 1962), p. 168.

port aircraft, as well as the building of airstrips throughout most of the world to accommodate them, accelerated the transition from flying boats to land-based craft for long-distance flying. (Aerodynamically, the flying boat is less efficient than a land-based craft because of the shape of its bottom hull and the additional weight of the bracing needed to reinforce it.) Flying boats enjoyed a short revival after the war's end, but by about 1950, four-engine propeller-driven land-based aircraft were used on most trans-oceanic flights.

World War II also solidified the position of the United States as a manufacturer of airline aircraft. During the war, aircraft production facilities of most other nations were destroyed. Early in the war, U.S. and British leaders agreed to allocate production of many war materials, and it was decided that during the war, remaining aircraft manufacturing facilities in Great Britain would be used for building fighter aircraft, while U.S. facilities would be used for producing bombers, military transports, and some fighters.[47] At the war's end, there was a large surplus of U.S.-built military transport aircraft throughout the world, and they were converted and equipped for use in commercial airline fleets.

World War II also demonstrated the ability of aircraft to carry men and materials, and it became obvious that, after the war, airlines would become a much more important mode of transportation. Recognizing this, the "Allies" (nations that were fighting Germany-Japan-Italy) met in Chicago in 1944 and in Bermuda in 1946 to establish the postwar rules under which international aviation would be conducted.[48] The U.S.S.R. had been invited to attend but did not (its delegates to the conference were stopped by the Russian government while en route). Hence, the structure developed at the Chicago and Bermuda conferences applies to the non-Communist world only, although Communist-bloc national airlines make some adaptations to Western rules when they exchange flights with Western nations.

The Bermuda Agreement

The 1946 conference in Bermuda continued the agenda of the 1944 Chicago meeting.[49] The net effect of both conferences was to establish mechanisms to provide for air safety, to establish airline

---

[47] Robert L. Thornton, *International Airlines and Politics* (Ann Arbor: University of Michigan Bureau of Business Research, 1970), p. 23.

[48] *Ibid.*, chapter 2.

[49] At the risk of over-simplification, no distinction will be made here between agreements at the Chicago and at the Bermuda conventions. A more accurate description can be found in Thornton, chapter 2.

routes between nations, and to regulate fares. The International Civil Aviation Organization (ICAO) was organized at this conference.

The ICAO, now part of the United Nations and headquartered in Montreal, has several functions: develop techniques of international air navigation; encourage international air travel safety; and encourage the development of airports, airways, and air navigation facilities for commercial international aviation.[50] The ICAO is interested in issues such as the following: licensing of operating and maintenance personnel; rules of air navigation; meteorology; aeronautical charts; aircraft airworthiness; registration markings; air traffic control services; communication systems (as they affect navigation); search and rescue; and aircraft accident investigation. The ICAO has been especially helpful in establishing civil aviation in the newly developing areas of the world. Through various programs, it has encouraged high levels of technical proficiency with the result being a very high level of safety in all aspects of international air transport.

The Chicago and Bermuda conferences also adopted a set of principles, commonly known as "the five freedoms." They are:

1. The freedom of any nation's commercial aircraft to fly over other nations.
2. The freedom of any nation's commercial aircraft to land in other countries for purposes of taking on fuel or repairs.
3. The freedom of any nation's airline to deliver passengers and freight from that nation to other countries.
4. The freedom of any nation's airline to pick up from other countries passengers and freight bound for that nation.
5. The freedom of any nation's airline to pick up traffic in one foreign country destined for another foreign country along trunk routes.

The fifth freedom is the most significant since it allows airlines to construct "round-the-world" routes, carrying traffic between other nations (and earning foreign exchange).

The "freedoms" are, in fact, a statement of principles; the actual air service between nations comes into being only after careful negotiations. For example, advance permission must be sought to fly over another nation's airspace, and one may sometimes read of a nation's refusing to allow certain commercial flights between other nations to pass over.

---

[50]Richard N. Gariepy and David L. Botsford, "The Effectiveness of the International Civil Aviation Organization's Adjudicating Machinery," *Journal of Air Law and Commerce* (September, 1976), pp. 352–353.

Bilateral Negotiations

Bilateral negotiations are conducted between nations wishing to exchange airline service. Airports to be served are agreed upon in advance, and the agreement contains provisions for monitoring and controlling the amount of service offered by each airline (this can be in terms of flights, type of aircraft, number of seats, etc.). Each nation then designates one of its international airlines to provide service on the route. This has yielded a route structure that is somewhat less than ideal, especially for small nations that have only one major airport where the routes look like double-thick spokes on a wheel, connecting with capital cities of other countries. In addition, the markets are served by a minimum of two carriers (one from each of the two nations), even though there may not be enough traffic to support both.

Negotiations involve trading of proposed service aren't always successful. For example, a newspaper report on some negotiations between Japan and the United States, stated that Japanese "Transport Minister Tokusaburo Kosaka warned Japan would restrict U.S. commercial carriers' service to Japan unless the United States accepts Japanese demands to fly cargo to the hub of the American market in Chicago and expand service to other cities."[51] The same article continued that other items on the agenda dealt with the Japanese wanting "beyond rights"—that is, the right for the Japanese airline that currently flies from Japan to Los Angeles to pick up passengers in Los Angeles and fly them to South America. (This is an example of a "fifth freedom" operation.) The Japanese also sought to limit additional flights by U.S. air carriers in Asian markets.

The International Air Transport Association (IATA) was established at the Bermuda Conference. Its function was to establish passenger fares and freight rates for international air movements. Membership in IATA is open to any international airline licensed to provide scheduled air service by a government eligible for membership in the ICAO.[52] IATA was a cartel which controlled rates and service competition (such as inflight drinks and meals). IATA's ability to enforce its rules slowly disintegrated as more and more airlines (many from the emerging nations) sought to escape from its restrictions. In late 1978, IATA abandoned some of its rate-making and enforcing duties, leaving the void to be filled by bilateral negotia-

---

[51] *San Francisco Chronicle* (April 22, 1982).
[52] Alan Stratford, *Air Transport in the Supersonic Era* (London: St. Martin's Press, 1967), p. 24.

tions between nations.[53] At the same time the U.S. government was suggesting to the newly-deregulated U.S. airlines that their membership in any international rate-making body might make them vulnerable to prosecution under anti-trust statutes. Chaos followed, and there was open rate competition in many markets. Foreign governments, most of which owned their own airlines, put pressure on the U.S. government to withdraw its opposition to IATA. Our government did, and today most U.S. international scheduled carriers participate in IATA's rate-making procedures.

Because routes between two countries are established through negotiations between the two countries, it is necessary to mention two points related to U.S. airlines with international operations. First, in international matters the roles of the President of the United States and the State Department become more important. When negotiations are carried on with other nations, State Department personnel represent the United States and the agenda of items to be discussed is usually long, with air service, often a lonely item, low on the list. If State Department negotiators do well on other agenda matters, they may feel obligated to be less forceful on aviation issues, or vice versa. Second, international airlines of other nations are owned in whole or in part by their respective governments, which means that diplomats from foreign governments when negotiating on an international air service issue are representing another governmental entity. This does not hold for the U.S., where the State Department personnel may be negotiating a service matter without having a specific U.S. airline in mind.

U.S. Aircraft Exports

Also a factor in international negotiations is the role of U.S. airline aircraft manufacturers as suppliers to most of the free world's airline fleets.

> . . . At Nixon's request, [Japanese Prime Minister] Tanaka agreed to make special purchases of about seven hundred and twenty million dollars' worth of products to reduce the trade imbalance between the two countries, and that this was to include three hundred and twenty million dollars' worth of large commercial aircraft. . . .[54]

[53] *Aviation Week and Space Technology* (November 27, 1978), p. 35; and (December 4, 1978), p. 30. See also: "A Global Drive for Freer Flying," *Business Week* (January 29, 1979), pp. 66–68.

[54] Robert Shaplen, "The Lockheed Incident," *The New Yorker* (January 23, 1978), p. 58. The meeting referred to took place in 1972. Another example of Japanese efforts to offset the balance of payments deficit of the U.S. was the loan, made by a consortium of nine Japanese leasing companies at several percentage points below the market rate of interest, to Singapore Airlines to purchase five Douglas DC-10s. *San Francisco Chronicle* (December 1, 1978), p. 35.

TABLE 9–3   Sales and Deliveries of All Boeing Jets Through 1981

Model	Announced Orders			Deliveries		
	Foreign	Domestic	Total	Foreign	Domestic	Total
707	353	609	962	336	605	941
727	545	1,280	1,825	531	1,255	1,786
737	624	366	990	548	275	823
747	417	169	586	376	164	540
757	31	105	136	—	—	—
767	66	107	173	—	—	—
All models	2,036	2,636	4,672	1,791	2,299	4,090

Source: Adapted from Boeing Jetliner Monthly Summary, December 31, 1981, Boeing Commercial Airplane Co.

Not only is the sale of aircraft quite important as an export, in addition to the initial sale, there is a continuing commitment of the importer to buy parts and, often, maintenance service as well. In terms of number of aircraft, of the 400 Boeing 747s in service or on order as of mid-1978, 254 had been sold to foreign airlines. Many foreign airlines are equipped exclusively with U.S.-built planes.

Foreign markets for U.S.-built aircraft will become increasingly important since foreign airlines' traffic is growing more quickly than the traffic handled by U.S. carriers. This is illustrated in the following figures which include both international and domestic operations of all airlines and also include those of Russia and the Peoples' Republic of China. In 1960, all airlines in the world flew an estimated 82 billion revenue passenger-miles, of which 51 percent was performed by U.S. carriers. In 1978, the world figure had climbed to 667 billion revenue passenger-miles, although the share flown by U.S. carriers dropped to 33 percent.[55]

Another bit of data showing the pre-eminence of U.S.-built airline aircraft is that over the 21-year period, 1958–1978, of all the new planes delivered to non-Communist bloc airlines, over half were built in the U.S. by Boeing. Hence, a single U.S. firm supplied over half of the free world's commercial airline aircraft. (When making sales abroad, Boeing often agrees to buy a certain amount of component parts from the nation whose airline is ordering the planes.) Table 9–3 shows all Boeing sales and deliveries, through the end of 1981. Note the large volume of foreign sales.

Figure 9–12 is from a Lufthansa brochure and indicates the vari-

[55] *Dimensions of Airline Growth* (Seattle: The Boeing Commercial Airplane Company, 1979).

A glance at the fleet

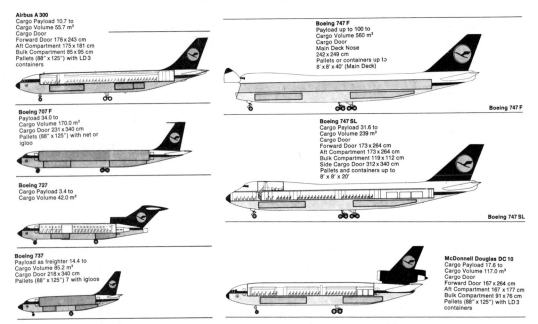

Airbus A 300
Cargo Payload 10.7 to
Cargo Volume 55.7 m³
Cargo Door
Forward Door 178 x 243 cm
Aft Compartment 175 x 181 cm
Bulk Compartment 85 x 95 cm
Pallets (88" x 125") with LD 3
containers

Boeing 747 F
Payload up to 100 to
Cargo Volume 560 m³
Cargo Door
Main Deck Nose
242 x 249 cm
Pallets or containers up to
8' x 8' x 40' (Main Deck)

Boeing 747 F

Boeing 707 F
Payload 34.0 to
Cargo Volume 170.0 m³
Cargo Door 231 x 340 cm
Pallets (88" x 125") with net or
igloo

Boeing 747 SL
Cargo Payload 31.6 to
Cargo Volume 239 m³
Cargo Door
Forward Door 173 x 264 cm
Aft Compartment 173 x 264 cm
Bulk Compartment 119 x 112 cm
Side Cargo Door 312 x 340 cm
Pallets and containers up to
8' x 8' x 20'

Boeing 747 SL

Boeing 727
Cargo Payload 3.4 to
Cargo Volume 42.0 m³

Boeing 737
Payload as freighter 14.4 to
Cargo Volume 85.2 m³
Cargo Door 218 x 340 cm
Pallets (88" x 125") 7 with igloos

McDonnell Douglas DC 10
Cargo Payload 17.6 to
Cargo Volume 117.0 m³
Cargo Door
Forward Door 167 x 264 cm
Aft Compartment 167 x 177 cm
Bulk Compartment 91 x 76 cm
Pallets (88" x 125") with LD 3
containers

Figure 9–12   Planes in the Lufthansa Fleet. Courtesy: Lufthansa German Airlines.

ous planes in their fleet. Five are built by Boeing, one by McDonnell Douglas, both U.S. firms; and the Airbus is manufactured in Western Europe.

International Charter Air Carriers

Scheduled international airlines operate much the same way as U.S. trunk carriers, often using the same types of equipment. The only differences in their operations come from the complications and delays that occur because their passengers and freight are moving from the jurisdiction of one nation to that of another. In the U.S. domestic market, charter (or supplemental) air carriers are relatively insignificant in terms of market share. (In 1977, supplementals received only 2.5 percent of the U.S. airlines' total revenues.)[56] In international markets, the role of the charter carriers is much more

[56] *National Air Carriers Association Annual Report 1978* (Washington, D.C.: the Association, 1978), p. 10.

important. They have developed substantial market shares in major markets; the best example is the market between the U.S. and Europe, where over 30 percent of the passengers in 1977 moved on charter flights.[57] Activity by chartered carriers in this and other major airline markets helped undermine the "established order" of scheduled airlines' rates. One individual associated with the success of the international charter airlines is an Englishman, Sir Freddie Laker. His firm, Laker Airways, had soared to success on the basis of introducing cut-rate fares. However, it went bankrupt in February, 1982, and since then Laker has been stymied in his attempts to form another airline. Laker blames the rival, existing airlines, saying: "All the other airlines are interested in getting my two million passengers, putting them in a seat, and ripping them off. . . ."[58]

The Chicago and Bermuda conferences ignored the role of charters, and their acceptance was mainly through bilateral negotiations between nations. Much of the structure of the airline industry provided by the Bermuda agreement is giving way. The most recent air service agreements negotiated by the U.S., with the United Kingdom and the Netherlands, recognize charter flights as a segment of the market; the negotiations included markets to be served by both the scheduled and the charter carriers.

Most international charter flights conducted today are still outside the scope of existing bilateral agreements. The rules of both the originating and terminating nation apply, with the stricter rules controlling. In theory, a concept of reciprocity exists; i.e., a nation will accept about as many charter flights from a foreign nation as that nation has accepted or will accept in return.

> Israel banned for more than 10 years all U.S. charter flights to and from Israel, even while its state airline, El Al, operated a substantial charter program over U.S. routes. Recently, El Al was required to obtain CAB's prior approval for charters on U.S. routes, and Israel has since granted U.S. carriers a limited number of U.S.-originated charter flights.[59]

Two complexities are involved in bilateral negotiations regarding charter flights.

The first is the relationship between a nation's scheduled and trunk carriers. In the U.S., the firms are separate, although scheduled carriers can operate chartered flights. In some nations, the two are closely linked; when a charter airline manages to sell a flight, it can borrow planes from a scheduled airline.

---

[57] *Ibid.*

[58] *San Francisco Chronicle* (March 22, 1982).

[59] *The Critical Role of Government in International Air Transport* (Washington, D.C.: The Comptroller General, March 17, 1978), p. 47.

The second complexity results from some nations deciding to have very lax rules regarding charter flights; what this means is that charter airlines from all nations will be encouraged to send flights to the nation with lax rules, discharging large numbers of tourists and their money! Some European nations do this, apparently feeling that they can earn more foreign exchange from the tourists than they can by protecting the markets of scheduled carriers.

The Supersonic Transport (SST)

The supersonic transport (SST) is currently used exclusively in international flight operations.[60] In a technological sense, it was the logical "next step" in the development of transport aircraft. In the early 1960s, Britain and France (working together), the United States, and Russia each undertook the development of a commercial passenger craft that could travel at supersonic speeds (1300 to 1400 mph). Heavy government subsidies were required to develop this aircraft; the subsidies were justifed on the basis of national prestige the aircraft would gain.

In 1970, the U.S. Congress decided to abandon further funding of the SST project. This happened for several reasons.

1. There was a fear that the plane's operations would pollute some of the outer areas of the atmosphere.
2. U.S. airlines had just accepted delivery of the new wide-bodied "jumbo" jets and did not want the financial burdens of having to accept delivery of another series of new planes.
3. The SST designs developed through 1970 did not appear to be profitable to operate. Seating and range were very limited, while operating costs would be so high that either operating costs could not be covered by fares or else fares would have to be so high as to severely limit the market.

Hence, the U.S. dropped out of the race to build a commercial SST.

Russia and Britain/France completed theirs. One of the Russian models crashed at a Paris airshow. It is rumored that others were placed into domestic Russian service but withdrawn after additional

---

[60]During the early 1960's, when the U.S. was funding the development of the commercial SST transport, it had been intended for the plane to connect major domestic U.S. markets. However, when traveling at supersonic speeds, the planes leave in their wake a "sonic boom" which is like a rolling roar of thunder. A law was passed prohibiting commercial transports from flying at supersonic speeds across the U.S. land mass (which cut heavily into the planes' potential market).

crashes. The British-French consortium built 16 SSTs, known as Concordes. Air France bought four, and British Airways bought five; trans-Atlantic service is offered to the United States on these planes. Seven Concordes were never sold. Losses on operating the Concorde are very large, in part because the plane is very fuel *inefficient.* "A Concorde consumes four times the fuel that a Boeing 747 does on the New York-Paris run."[61]

A factor limiting the Concorde's success is that its routes tend to be East-West rather than North-South in nature, which means that passengers suffer from jet lag (or, more accurately, "supersonic jet lag"). "Jet lag" is a phenomenon that occurs to one's body as it is moved swiftly through several time zones. Physically, the body cannot easily adjust to the change in time and one feels fatigued. The net result is to offset a portion of the time-saving advantages of the faster flight.[62]

In late 1979 Britain and France ended their commercial SST development programs. The commercial SST is an interesting aviation development but ahead of its time. In a commercial sense, we may have reached several limits of aircraft development. The lack of success of the SST means that there is little demand for faster planes. The Boeing 747 may also be the largest plane in commercial service for many years.

Competition Between Air and Ocean Carriers

Trans-ocean flights by airlines have all but destroyed the passenger-carrying ocean vessel trade. It appears that the international airlines are also in the process of capturing much of the high-value cargo which was once carried by the ocean vessels. One study, by Port of New York economists, found that in 1974 international airlines carried just under one percent of the tonnage of this nation's international general cargo trade. Tonnage is not the only measure, however. In terms of value, this tonnage accounted for 26 percent of the total value of U.S. general cargo exports and imports.[63]

In the late 1970's, the most significant international air cargo development was the introduction into numerous foreign trade routes

[61] "High Fuel Cost and Empty Seats Put Concorde's Future in Doubt," *The New York Times* (August 11, 1979).

[62] Vicki Goldberg, "What Can We Do About Jet Lag?" *Psychology Today* (August, 1977), pp. 69–72.

[63] See Jerome Gilbert and others, "Future Developments in International Air Cargo Transportation," in *Proceedings—Seventeenth Annual Meeting of the Transportation Research Forum* (Oxford, Indiana: Richard B. Cross, 1976), pp. 398–403.

of Boeing 747s with main-deck cargo configurations. The three different 747 models that can carry cargo on their main deck are the 747-200F, an all-freighter, and the 747-200C and the 747-200B, both of which can have their main deck in all passenger, all cargo, or various combinations of seating and cargo-carrying configurations. To give an idea as to how this main-deck cargo service has grown, in 1974 only three cities in the world were served by scheduled flights of 747s which had main-deck cargo-carrying space. By mid-1978, the number of cities receiving this scheduled service had increased to 46.

Figures are not available showing the degree to which these air freighters have penetrated the various cargo markets within which they operate. In an all-cargo configuration, the 747 can carry over 100 tons, which is about 1 percent of the tonnage capacity of a small ocean-going freighter. However, within an hour, the 747 can cover 25 to 35 times as much distance as the ocean vessel. Hence, if ton-miles per hour were the only criterion, three or four 747s can displace the need for one entire small freighter.

"According to some recent reports by Boeing, some 95 main deck cargo-carrying 747 aircraft have been delivered to various airlines to date and are serving most of the world. Twenty-five more will be delivered each year well into the 1980's."[64] An air fleet of this size will assume a significant part of the traffic now carried by ocean vessels.

Even though they are in competition, there is some coordination between ocean and air carriers. In the tourist trades, travel "packages" are put together combining an air trip to a site where connections are made with cruise vessels. An example would be a flight from New York to Athens, where passengers would board a cruise vessel touring the Aegean Sea. At our coastal ports, shipments arriving by sea are sometimes transferred to an airport and flown to some inland destinations. The procedure is reversed for exports. These intermodal transfers occur only in instances where demand for transportation service is somewhat more than could be satisfied by a water-land carrier routing and somewhat less than necessary to justify an all-air routing. An example is Hawaiian pineapples which move by water to San Francisco or Los Angeles and then are carried to inland and East Coast cities by air.

---

[64]Fred H. McCusker, "New Dimensions in Air Cargo Traffic," *Transport 2000* (September/October, 1978), p. 24. See also: "Freight Traffic Expected to Grow 8% This Year," *Air Transport World* (February, 1982), pp. 42–44.

Summary

The single most important objective of a nation's international transportation policy is to help that nation achieve a favorable "balance of payments" position in its economic relations with other nations. Whenever a nation's foreign trade moves on ships or planes of another nation, that nation is "importing" the transportation service supplied by another. Exporting transportation equipment, as well as transportation service, is a way to earn foreign exchange. The United States is the principal supplier of airline aircraft to the non-Communist world.

A second major reason nations are interested in international transportation is their concern for national defense. In both World War I and World War II we found that we needed a much larger shipbuilding capacity than peacetime needs alone would justify.

The single most important commodity in world shipping is petroleum, which is carried by tankers. Dry bulk cargos of importance are iron ore, coal, and grain. General cargo is non-bulk in nature, and it is more valuable per ton than bulk cargo. It once moved exclusively on break-bulk liners, but cargo-handling technology has yielded several new types of cargo-handling vessels: the containership, the LASH vessels, and the RoRo carriers. Rates for the carriage of shiploads of petroleum and dry bulk products are established competitively through the bidding process of the vessel charter market. Rates for general cargo are usually established by liner conferences, which are organizations or *cartels* of vessel owners operating in a specific market. The conferences tie shippers to exclusive use of the conference vessels. In return, the shipper pays rates which are about 10 percent less than rates charged to shippers who will not bind themselves to exclusive use of conference vessels.

Ports are important cargo-transfer points; U.S. ports face two major problems. Containerization of ocean cargos and unit-trains carrying nothing but containers across the country to and from a small number of major ports threaten the existence of many smaller ports. The second problem is inadequate depths of water within ports to handle the large sizes of ships now being built. The problem for handling tankers is a bit less crucial, since the tankers can moor at offshore buoys and pump their cargo inland.

International air carriers represent a much newer technology. Their operating characteristics and equipment are generally similar to those of U.S. trunk airlines. International airlines of other countries are owned in whole or in part by their respective national governments; U.S. international airlines are privately owned.

The framework for regulating international aviation was established at two conferences, one in Chicago in 1944 and one in Bermuda in 1946. The ICAO was established as a branch of the United Nations to handle matters of air safety and air navigation. Exchange of airline service between two nations is dependent upon bilateral negotiations between the two governments.

Boeing supplies over half of the non-Communist world's airline aircraft needs. Air travel outside the U.S. is increasing faster than domestic air travel. Of particular significance in the late 1970's was the introduction of numerous Boeing 747s with main-deck cargo space into principal trade routes throughout the world. The net result will be to take away from the ocean vessel lines a significant portion of their high-valued cargo. Trans-oceanic airlines have already eliminated conventional passenger vessels from most markets.

Questions for Discussion and Review

1. What are the various documents likely to accompany an export shipment?

2. What are the various documents likely to accompany an import shipment?

3. What services does an international freight forwarder provide and what are his sources of revenue?

4. What is the difference between a "hard" currency and a "soft" currency?

5. What is "cross-trading"?

6. Why does a nation attempt to transport a large portion of its own imports and exports?

7. What is a "flag of convenience"? Why would one be used?

8. Discuss the national defense implications of the U.S. merchant marine and overseas airlines.

9. Discuss the present status of U.S. ports handling international trade. What problems do they face? What are their opportunities?

10. Discuss the basic types of ocean vessels. Which type of vessel is dominant in terms of tonnage? Why?

11. What is the ocean liner conference system? How does it function?

12. What are shippers' councils? Do you think that U.S. shippers should be allowed to form them? Why or why not?

13. What is the U.S. position regarding shipping conferences? Do you agree with this position? Defend your answer.

14. What subsidies and other forms of assistance are provided by the U.S. government to the U.S. merchant marine?

15. Why do countries actively seek foreign tourists?

16. Discuss the development of international airlines through 1946.

17. What are the "five freedoms"?   *PAGE 414*

18. What is the difference between the success of our shipbuilding industry and the success of our commercial aircraft building industry?

19. Discuss the role of international charter air carriers.

20. Discuss the commercial SST. Do you think it has been a success?

Additional Chapter References

Allen, Benjamin J., "The Economic Regulatory Scheme for Deepwater Ports," *Transportation Journal* (Winter, 1977), pp. 5–16.

Athay, Robert, *The Economics of Soviet Merchant-Shipping Policy*, (Chapel Hill: Univ. of North Carolina Press, 1971).

Bess, David, *Marine Transportation* (Danville, Ill: Interstate Publishers, 1976).

Dicer, Gary N., and Gerald D. Sentell, "Economic Modeling of Changing Maritime Transport Patterns in the 80's: A New Approach," *Annual Proceedings of the Transportation Research Forum* (1979), pp. 151–158.

Dowd, Laurence P., *Introduction to Export Management* (Burlingame, Calif.: Eljay Press, 3047 Hillside Drive, 1977).

Gamble, John King, Daniel B. Charter, Jr., Charles I. Cook, Charlene Quinn Dunn, Maria Kazanowska, Christopher B. Llana, and Edwin F. Stein, Jr., *Marine Policy: A Comparative Approach* (Lexington, Mass.: Lexington Books, 1977).

Goss, R. O., *Studies in Maritime Economics* (London: Cambridge University Press, 1968)

Hedden, Walter P., *Mission: Port Development* (Washington, D.C.: The American Association of Port Authorities, 1967).

Jacobs, Clyde, "Ocean Shipping and Fuel Realities," *The Logistics and Transportation Review*, Vol. 17, No. 2 (1981), pp. 135–142.

James, Leonard G., "Rebating on the High Seas," *ICC Practitioners' Journal*, Vol. 47, No. 2 (1980), pp. 174–193.

Jansson, Jan Owen, "Intra-Tariff Cross-Subsidization in Liner Shipping," *Journal of Transport Economics and Policy* (September, 1974) pp. 294–311.

Jantscher, Gerald R., *Bread Upon the Waters, Federal Aids to the Maritime Industries* (Washington, D.C.: The Brookings Institution, 1975).

Johnson, James C., James P. Rakowski, and Kenneth Schneider, "U.S. Coal Exports: Problems and Prospects," *Colorado Business Review* (April, 1982), pp. 2–4.

Keesling, Garland, "An Analysis of the West Coast Longshoring Productivity Trends," *Annual Proceedings of the Transportation Research Forum* (1979), pp. 424–431.

Kilgour, John G., "The Cargo Preference Program and the Cabotage Restrictions: Effectiveness and Cost," *Transportation Journal* (Spring, 1976), pp. 63–73.

Markes, Gerald, "Export Paper," *Annual Proceedings of the National Council of Physical Distribution Managment* (1981), pp. 839–850.

Marshall, Robert B., and Gunnar K. Sletmo, *Analysis of Competitive Practices in the Maritime Industry* (Glen Cove, New York: Center for Maritime Studies, Webb Institute of Naval Architecture, 1978).

Mayer, Harold M., *Wisconsin's Great Lakes Ports: Background and Future Alternatives* (Milwaukee: University of Wisconsin-Milwaukee, Center for Great Lakes Studies, 1975.)

O'Loughlin, Carleen, *The Economics of Sea Transport*, (London: Pergamon Press, 1967).

Peterson, Roger A., "Cargo Preference Legislation and the U.S. Tanker Fleet," *Transportation Journal* (Summer, 1980), pp. 15–22.

Port Development in the United States, report prepared by the Panel on Future Port Requirements of the United States, Maritime Transportation Research Board (Washington, D.C.: National Academy of Sciences, 1976).

Rosenberg, L. Joseph, and Grant M. Davis, "A Pragmatic Analysis of the U.S. Maritime Policy: Its Impact on Marketing Costs," *Annual Proceedings of the Transportation Research Forum* (1977), pp. 341–345.

St. Joer, C. E., "Geography—The Last Barrier to International Trade," *Annual Proceedings of the National Council of Physical Distribution Management* (1977), pp. 435–440.

Whitman, Michael J., "Foreign Management of U.S. Labor," *Annual Proceedings of the National Council of Physical Distribution Management* (1981), pp. 788–795.

Zannetos, Zenon S., *The Theory of Oil Tankship Rates* (Cambridge: The M.I.T. Press, 1966).

Case 9–1   The Coals to Newcastle Case

The Blizzard Steamship Company, headquartered in Hampton Roads, Virginia, had been asked to bid on the carriage of coal that

CASE TABLE 9–1–1   Fuel Consumption Per Road Trip for
Jennifer Young Between Hampton Roads and Newcastle

Duration of Trip in Days*	Total Fuel in Tons
14	650
16	500
18	400
20	320
22	250
24	220

*Includes 2 days in port

would be loaded at Hampton Roads and carried by vessel to a port in England, where it would move by rail to a point near Newcastle. Scott Blizzard was president of the company and, after determining that the bid required commitment of one vessel for an entire year, noted that the only vessel he had available was the *Jennifer Young*, an aging vessel named after the granddaughter of its original owner.

Fernando Escobar, Blizzard's assistant, told Blizzard that the usual terms for coal-carrying charter contracts had variances of a few percentage points around performance figures, so that all calculations could be rounded to the nearest full number of round trips carrying a full load. Escobar also said that there were few "backhaul" cargos available from England that would be compatible with coal shipments in the other direction, so calculations should be made for carrying coal to England and returning light (empty).

At present it cost Blizzard's firm $1,000 per day in port and $2,000 per day at sea to operate the *Jennifer Young*. These costs are exclusive of bunkers (fuel oil needed to power the ship) which, in recent years had been broken out as a separate item. The current cost of bunkers is $100 per ton. Escobar had prepared estimates of fuel consumption to show the effects on fuel consumption of varying the vessel's speed. All calculations assume a full day in port on each end of the voyage, and full numbers of days at sea. While the vessel is returning light, it is traveling against prevailing weather, so the number of days is the same, in each direction. Escobar's estimates are shown in Case Table 9–1–1.

The *Jennifer Young* can carry 20,000 tons, *including* the weight of bunkers. Before loading with coal at Hampton Roads, the vessel takes on enough fuel for the entire round trip, and the weight of this fuel must be subtracted from the vessel's 20,000-ton capacity.

Question One: Calculate the cost per ton for carrying coal on a 14-day round trip.

Question Two: Calculate the cost per ton for carrying coal on a 16-day round trip.

Question Three: Calculate the cost per ton for carrying coal on an 18-day round trip.

Question Four: Calculate the cost per ton for carrying coal on a 20-day round trip.

Question Five: Calculate the cost per ton for carrying coal on a 22-day round trip.

Question Six: Calculate the cost per ton for carrying coal on a 24-day round trip.

Question Seven: Jeff Drimmer, of the Drimmer Marine Equipment Supply Company, has been trying to interest Blizzard in installing a loading/unloading device on the *Jennifer Young* which would reduce time in each port to one-half day, thus cutting one day off each round trip. However, the new equipment weighs 250 tons and reduces the vessel's carrying capacity from 20,000 tons to 19,750 tons (both including fuel). Blizzard knows that Drimmer's claims are true; he also believes that the most likely use for the *Jennifer Young* for many years will be carriage of coal from the United States to Europe. Given the present costs, how much per year would Drimmer's device save Blizzard's firm?

Question Eight: Ignore Question Seven. After determining costs, Blizzard calls his old schoolmate Martin Sato for advice as to "what to bid." Sato says that a bid of $6.00 per ton will probably be accepted. If the *Jennifer Young* is the only vessel Blizzard anticipates having available, about how many tons per year should he offer to carry at $6.00 per ton? About how many round trips per year will maximize his profit (defined as total revenue minus total cost) at this rate?

Question Nine: Assume the loading/unloading device mentioned in Question Seven has been installed on the *Jennifer Young*. Now answer the questions posed in Question Eight.

Question Ten: Taking into account your answers to Questions Eight and Nine, how much—if anything—would the loading/unloading device be worth to the Blizzard Steamship Company for a one-year period in terms of changing profits? (This answer may ignore the cost of purchasing and installing the loading/unloading device. The answer should only influence the decision whether to equip the *Jennifer Young* with the new equipment.)

Case 9–2   The Hong Kong Basket Case

At the end of the war in Vietnam, Michael Machado settled in Hong Kong, where he soon became involved in the manufacture of metal wastebaskets. At present, the one style he made had a cylindrical shape and, when packaged, weighed 10 pounds and measured exactly two cubic feet in volume. The wastebaskets sold well, mainly because of the unique silk-screen patterns painted on the sides.

One day, a Ms. Linda Hernandez, whose business card indicated she was a buyer for a large U.S. chain store, appeared at Machado's office and said her firm might be interested in purchasing a large number of the wastebaskets. Since her firm distributed a nationwide catalog, they would need a large number in their initial order. Ms. Hernandez indicated that if a sales contract was offered, it would be for 10,000 wastebaskets, plus an option for buying an additional 10,000 at the same price within one year. She further indicated that her firm would like to select certain colors for the silkscreen application since the wastebaskets would be one part of a larger home-furnishings sales promotion.

Machado took Ms. Hernandez on a tour of his plant where he showed her how the circular bottoms were cut out and attached to the rectangular shaped sheet of metal which became the side. "Rectangular?" asked Ms. Hernandez. "That means your baskets are cylinders and can't be placed inside each other."

"So?" said Machado. "I could have told you that an hour ago."

"If they can't be 'nested'—the term for placing one item inside the other—they'll cost an arm and a leg to ship," said Ms. Hernandez, "and I doubt that we could price them competitively with all those shipping charges. What you should do is taper your wastebaskets so that when they're packed, one can be slipped inside another and so on. The tapering wouldn't affect the silk-screen patterns, which is the feature we want."

Machado agreed to make some cost calculations, and Ms. Hernandez said she had several days of business in Hong Kong and would return to his office on Thursday. She left and Machado called Cameron Wong, an overseas freight forwarder with whom Machado did business. Machado explained the problem to Wong, and Wong quoted him an hourly wage rate for performing the rate research to determine shipping charges. Machado also asked Henry Ng, his plant foreman, to make some cost calculations regarding the manufacture of cone-shaped, rather than cylindrical, wastebaskets. Both Wong and Ng agreed to have the figures by Wednesday.

At 9 A.M. Wednesday they met. Ng explained that the machinery could be modified to cut and assemble wastebaskets with three different amounts of taper, and he referred to them as styles A, B, and C. Production costs differed because of trim and fitting. For conventional, non-tapered wastebaskets, the costs of production were $10,000 for 10,000 units. For style A they would be $11,500 for the same number of units; style B, $14,000; and style C, $15,000. All could be silk-screened. The conventional wastebaskets weighed 10 pounds each; style A, 9½ pounds; style B, 9 pounds; and style C, 8½ pounds. The amount of taper determined how many wrapped baskets could be placed inside each other. Shipping volume, in cubic feet per 100 wastebaskets, would be: conventional, non-tapered 200 cubic feet; style A, 150 cubic feet; style B, 100 cubic feet; and style C, 90 cubic feet.

Machado then turned to Wong and asked: "What about transport costs?"

Wong replied: "There are several components. First, you have to get the packed wastebaskets from here to port. The best rate I can find is from Joseph Wong who will charge $25 per trip from your factory to the pier. His truck will carry 800 cubic feet each trip, in this instance we don't have to worry about weight. The ocean freight rate on wastebaskets such as yours is $13.00 per ton (2,000 lbs.), except that if they can get more revenue by considering every 40 cubic feet as a ton, they charge you that way. The rail rate in the United States to Ms. Hernandez's company warehouse is $4.00 per hundred pounds unless they're 'nested,' in which case the rate is $3.00 per hundred pounds."

"How do they define 'nested'?" asked Ng.

"The freight classification I read indicated that the volume (cubic feet divided by weight) has to be reduced by at least 33⅓ percent over shipping the goods in un-nested condition," answered Wong.

"Are there other charges?" inquired Machado.

"Only one," answered Wong. "You, actually the importer, has to pay a 10 percent import duty, based on your cost of production here. Actually, it's more complicated than that, but I think what I said will hold for your calculations. Sorry I didn't make all these exact calculations before coming, but I needed to hear what Ng had to say."

"Okay," said Machado. "Now, let's figure out whether we can afford to taper 10,000 wastebaskets. I won't do it unless the total costs, including transportation, are less than what they would be for our present style. Let's get some sharp pencils and go to work."

Question One: Calculate the total costs of the cylindrical wastebaskets. Assume all relevant costs—including allowance for profit—

have been given and that Machado is interested in the "delivered" cost of the goods to the warehouse in the United States where Ms. Hernandez would want the goods shipped.

Question Two: Do the same for style A wastebaskets.

Question Three: Do the same for style B wastebaskets.

Question Four: Do the same for style C wastebaskets.

Question Five: Which style, if any, should Machado offer to sell to Ms. Hernandez? Why?

Question Six: What other, real-world factors do you think would be involved in determining the total costs of this transaction?

These three photos show changes over the past half century in truck-trailers used to carry new autos. Top picture shows a 1929 White tractor with four Chevrolets on a trailer that was built before states started regulating trailer dimensions. Middle picture shows a GMC tractor and 1955 Oldsmobiles. The bottom picture is of a Ford trailer with a load of Renaults and illustrates the combined results of small cars and large trailers allowed by West Coast states.

Photos courtesy White Motor Corp., Fruehauf Corporation, and Convoy Company.

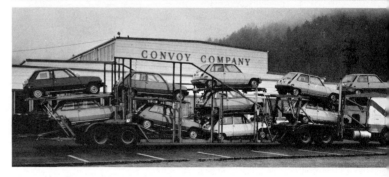

10 Physical Distribution and Logistics Management

Prior to recent years, American management's philosophy has typically been: "If you're smart enough to make it, aggressive enough to sell it, then any dummy can get it there." And now we're paying for it.

BERNARD J. LALONDE
Remarks, Harvard Business School
April, 1978

In the 1970's, inventory profits from inflation tended to offset financing charges. Because interest rates now exceed inflation, inventories have become the most volatile element in the cost of production. . . .

Fortune
July 27, 1981

Sushi may be sweeping the West Coast, but here in Motor City the latest craze is Kanban.

Kanban is the word for Japanese auto manufacturers' precise methods of controlling inventories so that suppliers deliver needed parts to the assembly line "just in time." Holding inventories of engines, axles and other parts to an absolute minimum saves Japanese auto makers hundreds of dollars per car in storage and carrying costs.

American car makers would dearly love such savings, but, like raw fish, Kanban may be difficult to swallow. As they get deeper into it, the domestic auto companies are finding that their system of manufacturing cars favors large stockpiles of parts. Changing that system is going to be a difficult and expensive process.

The Wall Street Journal
April 7, 1982

"Our order pickers can select over 33,000 orders a day manually, onto four-wheel carts, directed by a sophisticated software program that gives us precise control over work flow and people." L. L. Bean's director of distribution, Tom Day, called it "A simple system that works. We get high productivity with relatively low capital investment in equipment. The computer generates pick lists which tell pickers how to set up shelves on these carts to handle each order, making the best use of cart space. It also batches orders into the most efficient picking route. When the carts arrive at packing stations, the computer-sequenced orders need no further sorting."

Modern Materials Handling
February 5, 1982

Introduction

Chapters 5 through 9 dealt with specific modes of transportation. This chapter, and the following two, are written from the viewpoint of the shipper or receiver of freight. This chapter deals with physical distribution and logistics, and describes where and how these functions fit into the overall operations and structure of the manufacturing or the wholesaling or the retailing firm. Chapter 11 will deal with traffic management, the aspect of physical distribution that handles transportation. Chapter 12 covers carrier rates, that portion of the traffic management function which determines actual carrier charges.

The National Council of Physical Distribution Management defines *physical distribution* as:

> The integration of two or more activities for the purpose of planning, implementing, and controlling the efficient flow of raw materials, in-process inventory, and finished goods from point of origin to point of consumption. These activities may include, but are not limited to, customer service, demand forecasting, distribution communications, inventory control, material handling, order processing, parts and service support, plant and warehouse site selection, procurement, packaging, return goods handling, salvage and scrap disposal, traffic and transportation, and warehousing and storage.

As the definition indicates, transportation is only one of many activities that fall within the scope of physical distribution.

Some people draw a distinction between *physical distribution* and *logistics*. Others say only semantics separate them. Figure 10–1 is a diagram that attempts to represent the distinctions in terminology. In the diagram, the flow from left to right represents the sequence of activities in producing a good from the raw material stage through finished products delivered to the customer or user.

PD/L management is a diverse, challenging, and fundamental aspect of business. It is a "growth area" for people interested in careers related to transportation. This chapter will present an overview of PD/L, which will reflect the shipper's viewpoint in the handling, storing, and transporting of products.

PD/L Concept

The PD/L concept uses the *systems approach* to solve a problem. This means that instead of concentrating on *one* aspect of a problem, *all factors* that affect and impact on the problem are analyzed and evaluated. Assume a problem develops with a distributor that involves slow and erratic delivery service to retail customers. The distributor's PD/L manager, using the systems approach, would first determine which aspects of PD/L were possibly causing the system

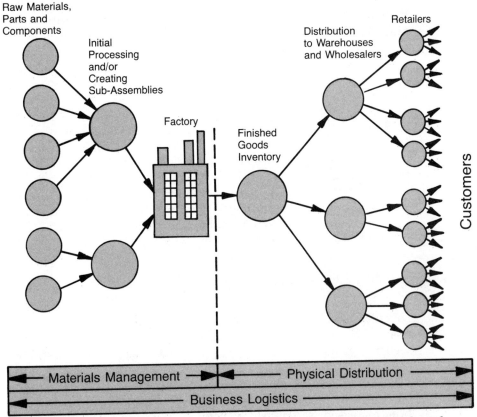

Raw Materials, Parts and Components

Initial Processing and/or Creating Sub-Assemblies

Factory

Finished Goods Inventory

Distribution to Warehouses and Wholesalers

Retailers

Customers

Materials Management

Physical Distribution

Business Logistics

Figure 10–1   Controls over Materials and Products Flow. Source: Adapted from Richard A. Lancioni, "The Physical Distribution Concept and Its Implementation," *Papers, NCPDM Annual Meeting* (Chicago, 1978), p. 102; and Alan J. Stenger and Joseph L. Cavinato, "Adapting MRP to the Outbound Side," *Production and Inventory Management* (Fall, 1979), pp. 2–4.

to malfunction. Likely candidates would be transportation (unreliable carrier service); inventory control (inability to determine location of the product at the warehouse closest to the customer); warehousing (inability to accurately and rapidly "pick" the product from the warehouse and tender it to the carrier); and/or order processing (excessive time to prepare the necessary documents so the order can be processed for shipment). Each potential problem area would be analyzed and evaluated to determine how it related to the problem. In this way, factors that might be the possible cause would be located and corrective action could be taken.

More specifically, the systems approach suggests that there are three basic components of the PD/L concept and, hence, three components which must be examined when exploring any PD/L situation. The three components are: *total-cost analysis, avoidance of sub-optimization,* and *use of cost trade-offs.*

The Total-Cost Approach

This means that the PD/L manager must be aware of all costs, both individually and as a total. The PD/L manager cannot tinker randomly with one or two components of the entire system without taking into account how any of the changes resulting from the tinkering will affect the overall cost of the firm's distribution. PD/L decisions and policies can influence the firm's total sales as well as its costs of operations. One must be concerned with costs of both inbound and outbound movements.

Avoiding Sub-Optimization

Sub-optimization occurs when one component of the system "overachieves," in a sense, and—by so doing—works to the detriment of the entire operation. An example would be a warehouse security system that initially was believed to be very successful because it eliminated thefts. Yet, many honest employees may find the new system to be so oppressive that they quit their jobs. Possibly the costs of losing experienced employees are greater than the savings from increased warehouse security.

Cost Trade-Offs

The third component of the PD/L concept is cost trade-off. The idea of cost trade-off is to allow some functional costs to increase, but only if this will bring about a greater saving in costs of performing some other function. The net effect is that total costs are less after the changes take place.

Montgomery Ward provides an example of cost trade-offs. Montgomery Ward wants to provide a high level of customer service for repair parts for their products. However, many repair parts—especially for older products—are requested infrequently. To stock these "slow-moving" parts in *all* Montgomery Ward's service centers would result in an excessive amount of inventory in relationship to actual demand or need for the parts. This is a serious problem because inventory holding costs (to be discussed later in this chapter) are high. To avoid these high inventory holding costs, Montgomery Ward consolidated all their slow-moving products into one central warehouse located seven miles from Chicago's O'Hare Airport. When a slow-moving product or part is needed in the field, the Chicago warehouse is notified via telephone or some other form of electronic communication, and the item is shipped by air within a few hours. Air freight is much more expensive than surface transportation, but this extra cost for air shipping is more than offset by the overall decrease in Ward's inventory holding costs. The net effect is that customer service standards are not compromised while the cost trade-off achieved reduced total costs of Ward's repair parts distribution function.

Why the Growing Importance of PD/L

In the decade of the 1970's, PD/L was increasingly recognized as a significant management function. Five trends can be identified that all worked together to make this happen. The first is a general result of the evolution of American business. The Industrial Revolution of the previous century had stressed the importance of production efficiency. Starting in this century, when the quantity produced began to exceed the quantity demanded, the importance of sales and marketing emerged. Sales and marketing efforts increased demand. By the early 1970's both production and marketing in many firms had become about as effective as they could. There were fewer "breakthroughs" in production efficiency, and products were being marketed to their fullest. The previous successes and barriers to further successes in these two areas led to the recognition of PD/L which, to quote Peter Drucker, became ". . . today's frontier in business. It is the one area where managerial results of great magnitude can be achieved. And it is still largely unexplored territory."[1]

A second factor resulted from marketing policies that encouraged "product proliferation," e.g., colored and patterned tissue in addition to the utilitarian white. Each color and pattern of tissue requires its own inputs and packages and must be kept track of individually as it moves through the distribution channels. As we move toward computer-controlled production lines, it will be possible to have smaller production runs of slightly different items. Marshall McLuhan and George Leonard said: "When automated electronic pro-

---

[1] Peter F. Drucker, "Physical Distribution: The Frontier of Modern Management," in Donald J. Bowersox, Bernard J. LaLonde, and Edward W. Smykay, eds., *Readings in Physical Distribution Management* (New York: The Macmillan Co., 1969), p. 8.

duction reaches full production, it will be just about as cheap to turn out a million different objectives as a million exact duplicates."[2]

The third factor that helped the development of PD/L has been the emergence of computer technology. PD/L is highly dependent on data—massive quantities of data! The following is an illustrative list (not comprehensive by any means) of data required to manipulate the costs of the three basic components of the PD/L concept: (a) location of each customer; (b) variation in size of each customer's order based on business climate and seasonality; (c) location of each vendor of raw materials; (d) location of production facilities, warehouses, and distribution centers; (e) transportation costs from each vendor to each production plant and from each plant to each customer; (f) available carriers and the service levels they provide; and

- Customer *service levels*, as used in PD/L, are objectives set by management for the firm's distribution function to achieve. An example would be to insist that 98 percent of all orders be filled accurately; i.e., the firm did not want more than 2 percent of the orders returned by the customers because of errors.

(g) inventory levels currently available in each warehouse and distribution center. This massive amount of required data—in many cases needing to be updated every day—would render PD/L analysis impossible if the data had to be collected, tallied, and analyzed "by hand." Luckily, just as the PD/L concept was "blossoming" in the late 1950's, the business computer was being extensively marketed. Without the computer to process the prodigious quantities of required data, the PD/L concept would have stayed just that—an academically interesting idea with few "real-world" applications.

The fourth factor is also related to the emergence of computer technology. Historically, large retailing, wholesaling, and manufacturing firms, which often had hundreds of vendors, found it very difficult to isolate those suppliers who provided either very good or very poor levels of customer service. Therefore, suppliers with only adequate or sub-standard levels of customer service were secure in the sense that their customers probably were not able to pinpoint specific suppliers' faults. However, with the use of computers to prepare purchase orders, bills-of-lading, carrier claim requests, etc., customers became better able to identify vendors who provided superior, average, and inadequate levels of customer service. Offending suppliers were often singled out and notified that if their per-

[2] Marshall McLuhan and George B. Leonard, "The Future of Education: The Class of 1989," *Look* (February 21, 1967), p. 24.

formance did not improve, they would receive no new orders. Many suppliers were awakened and learned for the first time that their service was poor, and they were forced to upgrade it.

The final factor contributing to management's increased regard for PD/L has been that transportation costs are rising. This has been especially true since fuel prices began skyrocketing. Hence management is concerned about finding methods to minimize the adverse impact of rapidly increasing transportation costs. Carrier deregulation has also changed the "established" rules of transportation which for many years had guided management's decisions.

Logistics Functions

Because of the diverse functions within the PD/L concept, PD/L management personnel must be both *technical experts* and *generalists*. In the first capacity, the PD/L manager must be knowledgeable about specific things, such as freight tariffs, inventory models, purchasing, production, warehouse location analysis, and transportation rates and regulations.

As a generalist, the PD/L manager must be able to conceptualize the relationships among the various functional area components. The PD/L manager must be able to recognize situations where suboptimizing is limiting the PD/L system's effectiveness and also to recognize opportunities for cost trade-offs. Finally, the PD/L manager must be able to relate his or her function to other operations of the firm:

> The emphasis is on the importance of the *modern* distribution man thinking in terms of the whole business system with which he is concerned. He must not only think of a flow of materials within his company, his thoughts must go beyond the shipping dock to the customer's doorstep . . . sometimes backward to the sources of supply. His thinking must cut across traditional organization lines. It must reach out to include competitors, potential markets . . . in short, the physical distribution manager must think big.[3]

Figure 10–2 presents an estimate of the relative costs of each of the activities involved in distributing finished products, that is, each of the activities that often are included within the PD/L function. While it is somewhat dated, its pie shape is useful for demonstrating two PD/L concepts. Total cost involves the size of the entire pie, while cost trade-offs involve the relative size of each slice. Table

---

[3] Harry J. Bruce, "Distribution History in the Making," *Pacific Traffic* (November, 1973), p. 50.

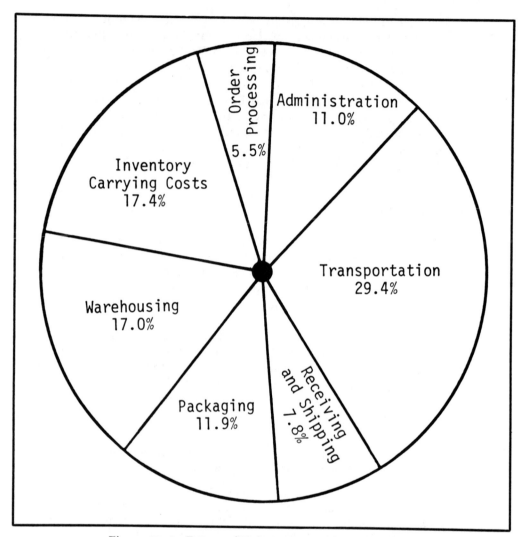

Figure 10–2 Estimated Relative Costs of Each Component of PD/L. This chart is based on 1971 data and shows how a typical firm would have divided its distribution dollar then. Since 1971, interest costs for borrowing money have increased, which would affect the inventory carrying costs; fuel costs also are higher now, which would increase transportation costs. A study cited in the American Trucking Association's *Research Review* (August 15, 1979) indicated that transportation costs accounted for 45 percent of distribution costs in the late 1970's. Source: *Air Cargo from A to Z* (Air Transportation Association, 1971), p. 5.

TABLE 10–1 Distribution Costs by Industry

Industry group	Distribution costs	
	as % of sales	per hundred weight
Industrial non-durables	8.61	19.14
chemicals and plastics	7.64	5.78
other products	9.11	26.17
Industrial durables	7.61	22.96
Consumer non-durables	7.90	16.21
pharmaceuticals	5.13	48.57
household products	6.73	27.27
toiletries	7.29	20.32
general merchandise	10.09	20.78
food products	7.93	6.55
dry and packaged	8.24	8.00
canned and processed	8.72	4.54
temp.-controlled	6.88	6.76
Consumer durables	8.54	33.21
appliances	8.33	17.15
other	9.86	44.09

SOURCE: Herbert W. Davis and Company's *1981 Cost Database*. Note: This table is based on a survey of over 200 firms, with at least ten in each category. It appears that these costs are for the physical distribution portion of the respondents' activities.

10–1 shows, for 1981, the distribution costs as a percent of sales for a number of industries. The same table also compares these costs to the weight of product shipped, with the highest cost-per-hundred-pounds being for pharmaceuticals, and the lowest for canned and processed foods.

Traffic Management

PD/L is responsible for the transportation of (1) all raw materials, (2) goods-in-process between production plants, and (3) finished products. For most companies, transportation represents the largest single cost item in the PD/L system. How well all the other aspects of PD/L hang together depends on how effectively and how successfully the transportation aspects are managed. The following list illustrates the interdependency between transportation and the other aspects of PD/L.

1. Transportation costs are directly affected by the location and number of a firm's plants, warehouses, vendors, and customers.

2. Inventory levels at each stocking point are influenced by the mode of transportation used for both inbound and outbound shipments. The faster and more reliable the transportation, the less inventory required at each warehouse location.
3. Packaging requirements are directly influenced by the transport mode used. For example, international shipments by water require more extensive protective packaging than do shipments by air.
4. The transport mode utilized influences the material handling equipment at each production plant and warehouse.
5. If the order processing system is designed to encourage large orders at specified times, the result will be maximum consolidation of shipments between common points. Larger shipments result in lower per-unit transportation charges, measured in dollars per unit of weight.
6. The customer service standards established by the firm will directly influence the mode of transportation selected.

The topic of traffic management is covered more fully in the next chapter.

Purchasing

It is generally believed that personnel employed in purchasing goods, materials, and services are inadequately trained in the complexities of transportation and traffic management.[4] For improved efficiency in the purchasing function, there should be close liaison between traffic and purchasing personnel. When this is accomplished, significant improvements can be achieved in both reducing costs and improving carrier delivery schedules. The role of the traffic department is to advise and assist purchasing people on the transportation aspects of a purchase and to advise them of possible savings in transport costs.

An illustration of this cooperation is the liaison between the purchasing department and the traffic department at Kaiser Aluminum and Chemical Corporation. The purchasing department, when issuing a purchase order to a vendor, attaches the name, address, and phone number of the manager of Kaiser's private truck fleet. Before the vendor ships the products to Kaiser, the manager of Kaiser's private truck fleet is contacted to determine whether he can transport

---

[4] See: Jeffrey G. Miller and Linda G. Sprague, "Behind the Growth in Materials Requirements Planning," *Harvard Business Review* (September–October, 1975), pp. 83–91, and "Physical Supply—The Purchasing Side of Physical Distribution," *Handling and Shipping* (December, 1976), p. 52.

the product on Kaiser trucks. The key factor is whether the shipment fits into their private truck schedule. Kaiser's Manager of Warehousing and Transportation, James P. Falk, noted that when Kaiser's trucks are utilized, a savings of 35 percent is accomplished compared to motor common carrier rates.[5]

Falk also indicated that whenever possible, he requests that the purchasing department buy F.O.B. (Free on Board) Origin. This indicates that the seller's or vendor's price for a product does *not* include any transportation to the buyer's receiving dock. (An alternative price quotation is F.O.B. Destination. It is known as a delivered price, because the price quotation includes both the merchandise and transportation costs to the buyer's specified receiving dock.[6]) F.O.B. Origin purchasing requires more work for the purchaser; he must arrange for transportation service from the seller. However, in many cases, the extra effort results in significant cost savings. Falk remarked:

> We forever communicate the philosophy that any purchase has a transportation cost, regardless of the terms of sale. We often go to our purchasing people at Kaiser Aluminum requesting that the terms be changed, for a couple of reasons. If it is a large capital purchase, or a continuing purchase, we will want to control the transportation from a service and cost standpoint. It may be that we will seek to attack the rate, but you cannot do that unless you control or pay for the transportation. As a general rule, we try to get terms of sale on an F.O.B.—Origin basis.[7]

Materials Requirements Planning

Materials requirements planning (MRP) is used by manufacturing firms to purchase and schedule the deliveries of parts and components.

> The system, called material-requirements planning, is almost always referred to in the trade by its initials, MRP. It starts with an annual-sales forecast, usually based on what economists expect. But frequent revisions based on actual sales enable companies to alter the myriad details of ordering and manufacturing to avoid under- or overproduction. In big companies, the interlocking schedules are so complex that the adjustments would be impossible without a computer, explains William E. Mullin, director of systems at Pfizer. When the system works correctly, companies can avert costly ripple effects from either an abrupt drop in

[5] Jack W. Farrell, "Inbound Logistics," *Traffic Management* (September, 1977), p. 62.

[6] See: James C. Johnson and Louis E. Boone, "How Competitive Is Delivered Pricing?" *Journal of Purchasing and Material Management* (Summer, 1976), pp. 26–30.

[7] Jack W. Farrell, *loc. cit.*, p. 65.

sales or problems with deliveries by their suppliers. "In a pinch, the locomotive can be halted much quicker," says Mullin.[8]

A firm's logistics staff fits into production scheduling and MRP processes in the following ways. First, order processing often gives the firm its most accurate data regarding actual sales. This information can be read by skilled market analysts in a manner similar to that of a physician listening to a pulse or heartbeat. For example, Snap-on Tools Corporation receives orders from its branches via WATS telephone lines. The information on the order forms is processed so that goods will be shipped and, of interest here, the data on the order are fed into the firm's forecasting equations and then into its master production scheduling process. This then triggers raw materials purchase orders for materials needed to either manufacture the precise items that the customer has just ordered or to replenish stocks that will be depleted once his order is filled.[9]

Second, the logistics staff is concerned with scheduling and managing inbound products that have unique handling or storage characteristics. The logistics staff might also have contingency plans for finding and moving critical parts in cases where the initial source of supply proves to be inadequate or unsatisfactory. Lastly, the logistics staff is responsible for all movements of materials between a firm's plants and warehouses.

Customer Service/Product Support

Customer service can be defined as those activities designed to keep a customer "happy." Management consultant Harvey N. Shycon noted the essence of customer service when he remarked:

> We in distribution have recognized that providing a proper level of service to the customer is one of the major objectives of the physical distribution operation. Getting the product to the customer when he wants it and where he wants it is the most important thing that we do. And performing this operation at a reasonable cost is the primary objective of every good distribution operation.[10]

Many firms recognize customer service as an excellent competitive weapon in marketing a product because, unlike price competition, which can be rapidly emulated by competitors, customer service improvements—which are often time-consuming and difficult to

---

[8] "A Big Payoff from Inventory Controls," *Fortune* (July 27, 1981), p. 78.

[9] See: "Fitting It All Together," *Handling and Shipping Management Presidential Issue, 1978–1979*, pp. 4–9.

[10] Harvey N. Shycon, "Customer Service: Measuring Its Value," *Annual Proceedings of the National Council of Physical Distribution Management* (1973), p. 420.

establish—cannot be copied as rapidly. Furthermore, inadequate customer service can be highly detrimental to the marketing efforts of a company. If poor customer service persists, the company can find itself classified as an "unacceptable vendor" by its customers.

The most common customer service complaint is the inability of the seller to provide on-time delivery.[11] This problem can be over-

- *On-time delivery* means that the goods arrived when promised. Often, this is interpreted to mean during working hours (from 8 A.M. to 5 P.M.) of a specific day. The receiver does not want the goods any earlier than this because he may not have room to store them. If the goods are later than expected, the receiver may suffer a *stock-out*, meaning he has a buyer wanting an item which is out of stock.

come by an efficient PD/L system. Because the marketing department is directly concerned with the firm's customer service standards, the way to integrate marketing and customer service is through PD/L. The marketing department should establish the level of customer service standards because it is in daily contact with the firm's customers and therefore knows what level of customer service is traditional in the industry, what specific customers require, and more important, what the firm's competitors are offering. The role of PD/L management is to be an "advisor" to the marketing department regarding the costs associated with each potential level of customer service. Remember that relatively small increases in the overall level of customer service can substantially increase the costs of providing the increased service. Marketing and PD/L management often compromise on the level of customer service to be provided.

Customer service *goals* are also established as a means of improving and maintaining service levels. Sometimes, a supervisor's year-end "bonus" is based on his or her record in meeting the goals. Examples of goals for one firm were that (1) all orders received by 11 A.M. would be shipped the same day; (2) 95 percent of the phone calls at the order processing desk would be answered within 48 seconds; (3) debit/credit memos (issued to correct mistakes) should be less than 1 percent of all orders; and (4) customer inquiries should not exceed 7 percent of all invoices.[12]

Product support is a form of customer service that takes place

---

[11] See: James R. Stock, "How Shippers Judge Carriers," *Distribution Worldwide* (August, 1976), pp. 32–35.

[12] Peter E. Reisner, "Impact of Systems Design and Systems Integration on Abbott Laboratories' Customer Service," *Papers, 1981 NCPDM Annual Meeting*, p. 637.

after the sale and delivery of products. It might involve service and repair, replenishment of used, expendable materials, etc. An example would be a machinery manufacturer who maintained a stock of repair manuals for his product and would send them to customers who mislaid their original copy.

Order Processing

Order processing is an integral part of customer service. The seller defines order processing as beginning the moment he *receives* an order and ending the moment his warehouse is *notified to ship* the order. (The buyer defines the process more broadly, usually from the time he places the order until the goods are delivered to his dock. He holds the vendor responsible for all delays.) This time period—which can vary from a few hours to many days—typically involves the following activities: (1) the credit department verifies the credit standing of the customer; (2) the marketing department credits the salesperson with the sale; (3) the accounting department records the transaction; (4) the inventory control people locate the closest warehouse to the customer that stocks the product and notifies that warehouse to ship the product; and (5) the firm's master inventory file is updated reflecting the decrease in inventory.

Each firm has its own order processing system. Figure 10–3 diagrams a system showing the linkages between a firm's order receiving, finance, inventory records, traffic, and warehouse functions. In the figure, at the warehouse function stage, note the step indicating "verify completeness of order." In this hypothetical example, there was a discrepancy between the firm's inventory records and what could actually be found in the warehouse; hence a number of adjustments have to be made.

Many firms have placed the order processing function in the PD/L system for two reasons. First, a primary activity of order processing involves both inventory control and warehousing—both functional areas contained in the PD/L system. Therefore, the logic is to assign order processing to the management group that it works most closely with—in this case PD/L. Second, and more important, is that PD/L is directly involved in providing a consistent and reliable on-time delivery service to customers. If order processing often involves unreasonable delays, it becomes difficult for the PD/L system to compensate for these delays. Therefore, *all* activities that interact with a firm's ability to provide a timely and consistent delivery schedule should be controlled by the group responsible.

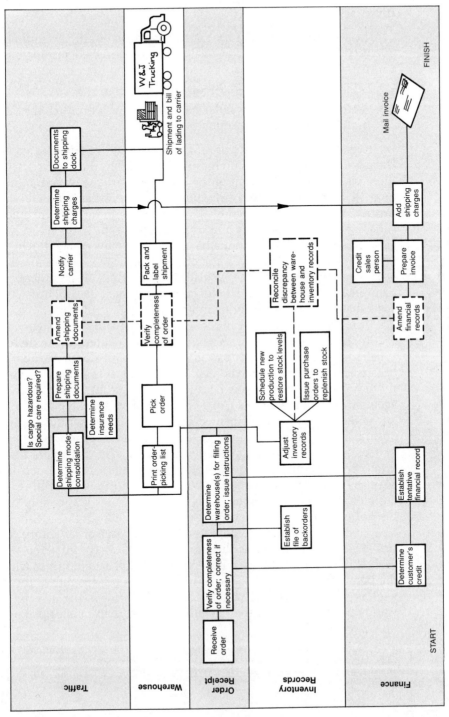

Figure 10–3 Flow Chart of Order Processing System.

Inventory Control

The function of inventory control is to maintain the optimum quantity of goods—both raw materials and finished products—at various sites. There are costs associated with holding inventory and costs incurred with a stock-out.

- A *stock-out* is when a seller has a buyer for a product but finds that his stock of the product is exhausted.

Inventory holding costs are high, especially for finished goods. During discussion of the auto industry's problems during the 1970's, there was frequent mention of the financial burdens of maintaining huge inventories of unsold automobiles. In *Air Freight and Reduced Inventories*, a booklet issued by Air Canada Cargo in 1980, inventory carrying costs estimated as a percentage of merchandise value averaged 34 percent. The components of these costs were as follows: interest on borrowed money, 18%; obsolescence, 7½%; deterioration, 4%; warehouse storage, 1½%; materials handling, 1%; clerical and administrative, 1½%; and taxes and insurance, ½%. These high costs discourage firms from maintaining large inventories; however, if a firm keeps inventories too low, the risk of stock-outs increases.

Stock-outs can be costly. A stock-out of raw materials can involve substantial expense if the firm is forced to shut down production because a key input is unavailable. Union contracts sometimes specify that if production ceases because of a stock-out caused by management error, the workers can go home and still receive their regular wages. A stock-out of finished goods can also be serious because customers are forced to buy and try competitors' products.

Computer models are available that help PD/L managers determine the optimum level of inventory to maintain. The models balance the costs of holding an inventory against the probabilities and costs of stock-out situations.[13] Figure 10–4 shows graphically how the volume of inventory changes day to day.

In most firms, the PD/L department is in charge of inventory control. The reason for this is that inventory is directly involved with each of the other PD/L functions; location analysis determines where the inventories will be located; transportation service moves the inventory into and out of warehouses; order processing selects the warehouse from which the customer's order is to be shipped; and

[13] See: Kenneth A. Miller, "Simplifying Inventory Control," *Distribution Worldwide* (January, 1978), pp. 52–53; and James Don Edwards and Roger A. Roemonich, "Scientific Inventory Management," *MSU Business Topics* (Autumn, 1975), pp. 41–45.

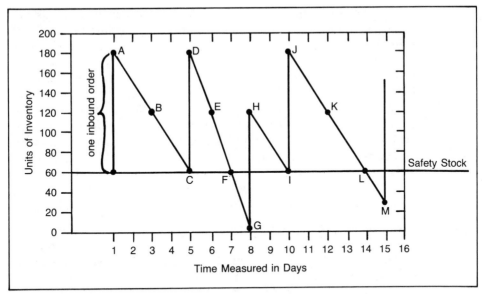

Figure 10–4 Inventory Flow Diagram. Commonly referred to as a "saw-tooth" diagram, this drawing plots inventories over time. The safety stock is selected to minimize the possibilities of stock-outs; one inbound order of 120 units is routinely ordered whenever stock levels (excluding safety stocks) reach 60 units. Average demand is 30 units per day, and it takes two days to receive an order using the normal mode of transport. At points B, E, H, and K (called reorder points), a new order of 120 units is placed; two days later the 120 units are added to the stock on hand. Slope AC is the normal cycle; slope DG shows that when demand suddenly doubles to 60 units per day, the safety stock is just barely sufficient. At point L, delivery of the inbound shipment is late, by one day. See: James C. Johnson and Donald F. Wood, *Contemporary Physical Distribution and Logistics*, 2nd ed., (Tulsa: PennWell Books, 1982), pp. 263–273.

customer service is related to deciding the location and size of the firm's entire inventory.

Warehousing

Warehousing involves the *place* for storing raw materials or finished products until needed. "A typical manufacturing concern has 30 percent to 35 percent of its total space under roof devoted to the storage of raw material or finished goods inventory," and for "most manufacturers, warehousing costs (for both raw materials and finished goods) constitute six to eight percent of the sales dollar."[14]

[14]Kenneth B. Ackerman and Bernard J. LaLonde, "Making the Warehouse More Efficient," *Harvard Business Review* (March–April, 1980), p. 94.

The length of time the raw materials or finished products are expected to be in the warehouse generally determines the type of warehouse operation. A *storage warehouse,* as the name implies, is used to store raw materials or finished products until they are needed at a later date. Storage warehouses are commonly used to hold products produced on a seasonal basis which enjoy regular sales, such as canned fruits and vegetables. Some goods would be held nearly a year. *Distribution centers,* or *distribution warehouses,* on the other hand, stress rapid throughput—the products arriving and departing the warehouse within 72 hours or so. Typically, when utilized for raw materials and production inputs, the distribution center is used as a "make-bulk" distribution center. For finished products inventory, a "break-bulk" center is more likely to be used.

- A *make-bulk* operation receives and consolidates many small shipments and builds them up into truck-trailer loads, or rail-car loads, or vessel loads. This larger load then travels at a lower rate per pound.

- A *break-bulk* center receives full trailer, rail-car, or vessel loads which have been traveling at relatively low rates because carriers charge lower rates per pound on larger shipments. At the break-bulk center the shipment is broken down into smaller lots and delivered, often by truck, to individual customers.

Storage and distribution warehouses are privately owned. The term "public warehouse" means it is for use by others. Private warehouses are used exclusively by their owners.

Plant and Warehouse Location Analysis

Analyzing where to locate plants and warehouses is a PD/L function because facility location can have an impact upon transportation, customer service standards in terms of delivery reliability, and inventory analysis regarding the proper level of inventory at each location. For example, James D. Murphy, Jr., President of American Buildings Company, remarked, "The strategy in selecting locations for our plants was to serve a 500-mile radius, permitting overnight delivery of orders. . . . Eighty percent of the major U.S. market is within 500 miles or overnight by truck from one of our plants."[15]

Location analysis involves successively more detailed examina-

---

[15] Jack W. Farrell, "Controlled Scheduling Cuts Inventories," *Traffic Management* (July, 1976), p. 26.

tion of smaller and smaller geographic areas. There are available a number of computer programs to assist in the initial steps, determining the best general region in which to locate. Later steps involve actual examination of sites, and the final step, determining the specific site, is so unique to each situation that management judgment and thought are the deciding factors.

Each of the following factors is typically considered in a location decision: (a) energy supplies and cost, (b) labor force availability, (c) natural resource availability, (d) location of existing and potential customers, (e) tax structure, (f) transportation costs and service, (g) environmental protection requirements, (h) land-use zoning, and (i) community services.[16]

Packaging

There are two general functions performed by packaging. One involves the advertising put on the exterior of the package for customers to see. The advertising on packages is designed by the marketing department; and it is becoming more and more important because of the trend to self-service retailing. The advertising on packages generates sales; this kind of selling is called "silent selling."

The second function of the package is to protect the contents. Protective packaging, which is commonly incorporated into the PD/L system, requires large annual expenditures. In 1982, shippers spent $49 billion for protective packaging materials. An effective protective packaging program helps reduce loss and damage claims, as well as reduce customer annoyance.

The objective of the packaging engineer is to design a package that meets the carriers' requirements and neither overprotects nor underprotects the product. The problems of underprotection are obvious. The main problem with overprotection is the wasteful expense. Dennis E. Young, a packaging engineer, remarked, "Overpackaging is several times more costly than damage, and it's insidious because you don't know that you have problems. You can at least see damage, but overpackaging remains a hidden waste."[17]

The protective packaging function is integrated into PD/L because it is closely associated with transportation, customer service,

[16] See: *Traffic Management* (February, 1977) for a number of articles on computer applications in site location decisions. Also, see: Roy D. Voorhees, "Communications: A New Logistics Factor in Location Decisions and Patterns of Regional and National Development," *Transportation Journal* (Summer, 1976), pp. 73–84.
[17] Bill Moore, "Protective Packaging Impacts on PDM," *Handling and Shipping* (October, 1976), p. 50.

warehousing, and materials handling.[18] The transportation interface is a key one, because common carriers have a legal right to specify the minimum packaging requirements that they will accept. Carrier packaging requirements are becoming more detailed and highly complex. A current issue with common carriers is whether they should replace detailed specifications with *performance standards*. The latter specifies what the package must be able to withstand in regard to shock, humidity, vibration, etc., but leaves each shipper free to determine what materials to use in order to achieve the required performance.

Materials Handling

Materials handling is closely related to protective packaging, although materials handling is concerned with both raw materials and finished products. The materials handling system moves products and raw materials into and out of (a) the production plant, (b) warehouses, and (c) the vehicles that move between them.

For finished products, materials handling commonly uses the *unit-load* concept. Unit loading involves combining individual boxes (which have been protectively packaged) into larger units that can be moved more efficiently. A common unit-load is a pallet-load (a pallet is a flat wooden platform, usually 48 inches by 40 inches, and 6 inches high). Many boxes can be stacked and secured to the pallet, often to a height of 4 to 6 feet. A loaded pallet can be transported by a forklift truck, which has two long "arms" that slide under the pallet and pick up the entire "unit" load. Unitizing loads via pallets—which results in faster handling and reduced per-unit labor costs—is growing at an 8-percent annual rate. In 1977 about 236 million wooden pallets were manufactured, according to the National Wood Pallet and Container Association.[19]

The unit-load system can also be thought of as a series of "building blocks," with loads being built up from individual items to truck or rail-car loads. This is illustrated in Figure 10–5. Because of the cost savings in handling unit-loads, sellers often price their product in a manner that strongly encourages buyers to order in unit-load quantities.

[18] See: Edward J. Bardi and Larry G. Kelly, "Organizing For Effective Packaging Management," *Transportation Journal* (Winter, 1974), pp. 53–57; Michael A. McGinnis and Charles J. Hollon, "Responsibilities of the Packaging Organization," *Transportation Journal* (Summer, 1977), pp. 30–35; and Dennis E. Young, "Packaging: Shake it Till it Breaks," *Traffic World* (April 9, 1979), pp. 73–76.

[19] See: Jack W. Farrell, "Pallet Interchange: Troubled Progress," *Traffic Management* (May, 1978), pp. 71, 73ff.

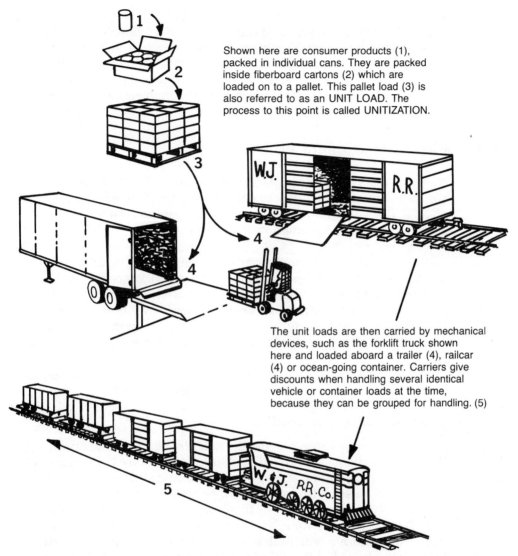

Shown here are consumer products (1), packed in individual cans. They are packed inside fiberboard cartons (2) which are loaded on to a pallet. This pallet load (3) is also referred to as an UNIT LOAD. The process to this point is called UNITIZATION.

The unit loads are then carried by mechanical devices, such as the forklift truck shown here and loaded aboard a trailer (4), railcar (4) or ocean-going container. Carriers give discounts when handling several identical vehicle or container loads at the time, because they can be grouped for handling. (5)

Figure 10–5   Summary of the "Building Block" Concept of Packaging.

A perplexing problem for materials handling management is hazardous commodities, which may be radioactive, corrosive, poisonous, explosive, toxic, or flammable. These products must be properly marked for easy identification. Numerous federal regulations specify such safety factors as strength and type of shipping container, materials that cannot be stored and transported together, proper descriptions of the hazardous materials to be transported, how to prepare unit-loads of dangerous materials, how to properly store hazardous commodities in warehouses, how to load, block, and brace hazardous materials in transport vehicles, and warning placards which must be placed on rail cars or trucks. Placards are of great importance if a fire takes place, so the fire fighters know what is burning and how best to put it out.

Organizational Structure for PD/L

Now that we have outlined the functions within the PD/L concept, we will discuss how these functions are organizationally implemented. We will examine a number of key organizational issues that are involved when one attempts to determine how to "fit" the PD/L concept into the firm.

The organizational problem arises because PD/L functions are spread throughout the firm. The value of the PD/L concept is that it orchestrates many widely-dispersed functions to ensure a smooth flow of inputs and outputs. However, to remove all of these functions from the control of others and place them under the control of a new PD/L manager is too big a reorganizational step for most firms to undertake. Existing managers would be reluctant to surrender their functions to the new PD/L manager, and any cooperation they give to the new PD/L concept would be lukewarm, at best.

Two Organizational Alternatives

Two approaches to achieving the coordination needed between PD/L functional areas will be offered here. One approach, known as the "status-quo" option, attempts to minimize resistance within an organization to establishing the PD/L concept. It involves keeping the various functional areas in their respective, existing organizations but, at the same time, encourages each functional area to actively communicate with each other on both a formal and informal basis. Only through this kind of communication can such a system utilize the total-cost approach, make cost trade-offs, and ensure that sub-optimization is avoided.

In this status-quo approach, unilateral actions affecting other PD/L functional areas should not be permitted. Instead, each functional area will coordinate its various activities as well as maintain a continual dialogue regarding problems, proposals, etc., with other functional areas.

It has been found that the status-quo approach to achieving the PD/L concept within an organization has been most effective when

TABLE 10–2   Organizational Structure of
Physical Distribution/Logistics Function

Organizational Alternative	Percentage of Respondents
PD/L is headed by a VP	22.3%
PD/L reports to the VP—corporate staff	18.8
PD/L reports to the VP—production	15.8
PD/L reports to the VP—marketing	10.8
PD/L reports to the VP—finance	3.3
Other	29.0
Total	100.0

SOURCE: Adapted from James C. Johnson and Donald L.
Berger, "Physical Distribution: Has It Reached Maturity?"
International Journal of Physical Distribution Management
(Vol. 7, No. 5, 1977), p. 287.

the overall size of the firm is small and there is only a small number
of employees trying to communicate and coordinate. For many
firms, the status-quo approach has worked, and has avoided the
trauma of actually transferring and reassigning functional areas.[20]

There are two major problems with the status-quo organizational
alternative. First, larger companies have found that interdepartmen-
tal communications between the functional areas of PD/L have often
not been successful because of organizational rigidities. A second
problem of the status-quo approach is that the overall philosophy of
the PD/L concept never gets an opportunity to be fully implemented.
Since PD/L functional personnel are scattered throughout the firm's
organizational structure, they find that they are always subservient
to the main objectives of the senior departments (i.e., production,
marketing, and finance) in which they are assigned.

The second organizational alternative—and generally preferred
by PD/L "believers"—is the unified PD/L department. This solution
is believed to be better, since each functional area of PD/L is assigned
to the new PD/L department. Communication is more efficient and
more effective because the personnel in each of the functional areas
work in offices close to one another. Furthermore, because the PD/L
group is solely devoted to achieving an optimum combination of
good customer service standards and low costs of moving raw materials and finished products, the functional areas can better contribute to these goals. A recent survey of large firms found that almost all
of them had or were in the process of establishing PD/L departments.
Table 10–2 indicates that a common organizational structure has a
separate PD/L department which is headed by a vice-president.

[20]Robert S. Jeffries, Jr., "Distribution Management—Failures and Solutions,"
Business Horizons (April, 1974), p. 56.

The PD/L Concept: Has It Reached Maturity?

This chapter has implied that the PD/L concept is an accepted business philosophy. To test this hypothesis, a survey was conducted of firms that had members in either the National Council of Physical Distribution Management or the American Society of Traffic and Transportation.[21] There were 358 firms that responded.

The first question asked which PD/L functional areas were presently assigned to the PD/L department. Table 10–3 presents a summary of the findings. Notice that transportation, warehousing, inventory control, and materials handling have been incorporated into about half of the PD/L departments.

TABLE 10–3   Functional Areas Presently
Included in PD/L Departments of
358 Firms

Functional Areas	Percentage Located in PD/L Departments
Transportation/Traffic	92.2%
Warehousing	74.9
Inventory control	51.1
Materials handling	49.7
Order processing	45.0
Protective packaging	43.6
Customer service	42.2
Purchasing	24.0
Other	11.2

SOURCE: Adapted from: James C. Johnson and Donald L. Berger, "Physical Distribution: Has It Reached Maturity?," *International Journal of Physical Distribution* (Vol. 7, No. 5, 1977), p. 287.

Respondents were also asked what problems currently existed in their firms. For respondents in *marketing*, one problem appeared six times more frequently than any other—the lack of appreciation and understanding of the marketing function by PD/L executives. Typical verbatim statements were:

▲ ". . . Failure to understand people resources as thoroughly as physical resources. . . ."
▲ ". . . Inability to relate to customer needs—too oriented to production requirements. . . ."

[21] James C. Johnson and Donald L. Berger, "Physical Distribution: Has It Reached Maturity?" *International Journal of Physical Distribution* (Vol. 7, No. 5, 1977), pp. 283–293.

▲ ". . . Wrong priorities—over emphasis on operating cost control at expense of customer service. . . ."

▲ ". . . Mired in the *details* of transportation management. . . ."

PD/L executives were also asked what problems they were experiencing. They believed, as is typical of any emerging business discipline, that their function was not fully appreciated by senior management. Representative statements included:

▲ ". . . Lack of understanding of what our group can contribute to company goals. . . ."

▲ ". . . We still talk our own language and I sometimes feel other departments don't understand us and consequently they do not include PD in their management thinking. . . ."

▲ ". . . Inability to convince top management to more completely unify PD because of toes which would be stepped on. . . ."

It is the opinion of the authors (who have coauthored a text dealing with physical distribution and logistics)[22] that the PD/L concept still has not achieved maturity. From the standpoint of a college student thinking of career opportunities, this opinion should be interpreted positively, since it means that the PD/L field still offers many opportunities to talented, aggressive individuals.

Summary

From the shipper's viewpoint, transportation is only a component of physical distribution/logistics (PD/L). Therefore, a brief overview of PD/L is necessary so the transportation function can be seen in its proper prospective. PD/L involves the "total package" of related activities in physically moving raw materials, goods-in-process, and finished goods inventory.

PD/L management is a relatively new area that utilizes the PD/L concept to solve distribution problems. The PD/L concept is comprised of three subparts: (a) using a total-cost approach, (b) avoiding sub-optimization, and (c) recognizing cost trade-offs.

The PD/L concept integrates ten functions: (a) traffic management, (b) purchasing, (c) materials requirements planning, (d) customer service/product support, (e) order processing, (f) inventory control, (g) warehousing, (h) plant and warehouse location analysis, (i) packaging, and (j) materials handling.

[22]James C. Johnson and Donald F. Wood, *Contemporary Physical Distribution and Logistics*, 2nd ed. (Tulsa: PennWell Books, 1982).

Because PD/L is relatively new, there are many organizational issues that have yet to be resolved. A basic problem is that PD/L functions are located in all parts of a firm's existing organization. There are two approaches—the "status quo" and the "unified"—to integrating PD/L functional areas into a firm's organizational structure.

Questions for Discussion and Review

1. What is the PD/L concept? Do you believe it is practical? Support your answer.

2. Discuss the "total-cost" approach.

3. What is the logic of trying to avoid sub-optimization?

4. Define cost trade-offs and discuss how they relate to the PD/L concept.

5. Why has PD/L become more important to firms in recent years?

6. Why must the PD/L manager be both a specialist and a generalist?

7. Which of the functional areas of PD/L appears to have the largest cost? Which is the second highest? Discuss.

8. Discuss implications of purchasing F.O.B.-origin and F.O.B.-destination.

9. Discuss the concept of materials requirements planning. How does it interact with the firm's PD/L system?

10. Discuss customer service and why it is important to both the marketing and PD/L departments.

11. What is order processing? Why is it considered part of PD/L? Discuss.

12. Discuss the components of inventory-holding costs.

13. What is a stock-out? Why are they not considered beneficial?

14. Distinguish between a storage warehouse and a distribution warehouse.

15. Discuss a number of factors relevant to a locational analysis study.

16. What are the two general functions performed by packaging?

17. What is the building-block concept of packaging?

18. Discuss two organizational alternatives for PD/L management.

19. Is the PD/L function in most firms considered a "mature" area? Defend your answer.

20. Table 10–3 indicates which functional areas were included in the PD/L departments of 358 firms. Why was the traffic and transportation function most commonly included?

Additional Chapter References

Ackerman, Kenneth B., "Common Sense is Warehousing Cost Reduction," *Annual Proceedings of the National Council of Physical Distribution Management* (1981), pp. 296–312.

Barnett, G. Lane, "Improved Customer Service Versus Reduced Distribution Costs an Integrated Approach Through 'Pre-sell' Techniques," *Annual Proceedings of the National Council of Physical Distribution Management* (1981), pp. 603–616.

Blanding, Warren, *Blanding's Practical Physical Distribution* (Washington, D.C.: Traffic Service Corp., 1979).

Browne, William G., and E. D. (Pat) Reiten, "Auditing Distribution Channels," *Journal of Marketing* (July, 1978), pp. 38–42.

Buffa, Frank P., and John I. Reynolds, "A Graphical Total Cost Model for Inventory-Transport Decisions," *Journal of Business Logistics* (1979), pp. 120–142.

Erb, Norman H., "A Note on the Meaning of Physical Distribution Management (PDM)," *Transportation Journal* (Summer, 1975), pp. 56–57.

Finch, George E., and Charles H. Powell, "Ragu' Foods Customer Service Program," *Annual Proceedings of the National Council of Physical Distribution Management* (1981), pp. 617–634.

House, Robert G., "Measuring the Impact of Alternative Market Classification Systems in Distribution Planning," *Journal of Business Logistics*, Vol. 2, No. 2 (1981), pp. 1–31.

Johnson, James C., and Donald F. Wood, *Contemporary Physical Distribution & Logistics*, 2nd ed. (Tulsa: PennWell Books, 1982).

Kerin, Roger A., and Michael Harvey, "Contingency Planning for Product Recall," *MSU Business Topics* (Summer, 1975), pp. 5–12.

Lambert, Douglas M., and John T. Mentzer, "Is Integrated Physical Distribution Management a Reality?," *Journal of Business Logistics*, Vol. 2, No. 1 (1980), pp. 18–34.

Lambert, Douglas M., and James R. Stock, "Physical Distribution and Consumer Demands," *MSU Business Topics* (Spring, 1978), pp. 49–56.

Langley, C. John, Jr., and William D. Morice, "Strategies for Logistics Management: Reactions to a Changing Environment," *Journal of Business Logistics*, Vol. 3, No. 1 (1982), pp. 1–16.

McCaughey, William C., "Shippers and Carriers Can Benefit By Working Together," *Annual Proceedings of the National Council of Physical Distribution Management* (1978), pp. 147–154.

McDermott, Dennis R., and James R. Stock, "An Application of the Project Delphi Forecasting Method to Logistics Management," *Journal of Business Logistics*, Vol. 2, No. 1 (1980), pp. 1–17.

McGinnis, Michael A., and Charles J. Hollon, "Packaging: Organization, Objectives, and Interactions," *Journal of Business Logistics*, Vol. 1, No. 1 (1978), pp. 45–62.

Mello, Sheila, and Janice H. Kempf, "Integrating Logistics with Information Systems," *Annual Proceedings of the National Council of Physical Distribution Management* (1981), pp. 887–897.

Miller, John A., "Survey of Software for Physical Distribution," *Annual Proceedings of the National Council of Physical Distribution Management* (1981), pp. 60–162.

Morgan, F. W., and William B. Wagner, "The Backorder: Role and Relevance in Distribution Service," *International Journal of Physical Distribution and Materials Management* (1978), pp. 298–307.

Nelson, Paul T., and Gadi Toledano, "Challenges for International Logistics Management," *Journal of Business Logistics* Vol. 1, No. 2 (1979), pp. 1–21.

Rose, Warren, *Logistics Management: Systems and Components* (Dubuque, Iowa: Wm. C. Brown, 1979).

Schary, Philip B., and Boris W. Becker, "The Impact of Stock-Out and Market Share: Temporal Effects," *Journal of Business Logistics*, Vol. 1, No. 1 (1978), pp. 31–44.

Speh, Thomas W., and George D. Wagenheim, "Demand and Lead-Time Uncertainty: The Impacts on Physical Distribution Performance and Management," *Journal of Business Logistics*, Vol. 1, No. 1 (1978), pp. 95–114.

Schuster, Allan D., "The Economics of Shipment Consolidation," *Journal of Business Logistics* Vol. 1, No. 2 (1979), pp. 22–35.

Stenger, Alan J., "Productivity Improvement in Physical Distribution: The NCPDM Study and Beyond," *Transportation Journal* (Fall, 1980), pp. 19–32.

Voorhees, Roy Dale, and Merrill Kim Sharp, "The Principles of Logistics Revisited," *Transportation Journal* (Fall, 1978), pp. 69–84.

Yaros, Ronald S., and Donald F. Wood, "Recalling Products in the Drug and Cosmetic Industry," *Journal of Business Logistics*, Vol. 1, No. 2 (1979), pp. 48–59.

Case 10–1   Birmingham Steel Corporation Case

Susan Boyer graduated from Auburn University in 1947. Her first position with the Birmingham Steel Corporation was in public relations. When a management position in the traffic department opened in 1951, Susan applied and was accepted. Although the only female among more than 40 employees in the traffic department, Susan liked her work and because of her enthusiasm and drive, she was rapidly promoted. In 1959, the company had privately selected her as a candidate for a possible senior management position.

In 1960 the company promoted Susan to traffic manager of the $680 million-a-year company. Her operating budget was $32 million. By 1963 she was named transportation manager because the firm had started an extensive private trucking operation.

Because of her interest in transportation law, she had taken and passed the ICC Practitioner's test in 1958. She realized the importance of regulation in traffic and in 1961 started attending night law school. In 1968 she received her law degree and was admitted to the Alabama Bar. Her employer encouraged her continued education and paid all of Susan's educational expenses. In 1970 she was named vice-president for transportation. She was the highest ranking female in the firm. By 1982 the firm had $3.7 billion in sales, and her budget was in excess of $247 million.

Birmingham Steel reorganized its senior corporate officers in late 1981. Three new positions were created: senior vice-president for marketing; senior vice-president for finance; and senior vice-president for logistics. Boyer, who was appointed to the latter position, was now in charge of these function areas: (a) transportation, (b) warehousing, (c) materials handling, (d) customer service, and (e) inventory management. In addition, she and other senior corporate officers were occasionally asked to work on special projects that did not necessarily fall within their normal areas of expertise. This case involves one of those situations.

On October 19, 1982, Boyer received an inter-office memo from the president of Birmingham Steel, Herbert L. Hughes. The memo is reproduced as Case Figure 10–1–1 and the letter referred to in the memo is Case Figure 10–1–2.

Boyer then asked the personnel department to give her a list of recent MBA's hired by Birmingham Steel. Boyer decided there were four main issues and she asked each person to research one issue. The people and issues were:

1. Emmy Lou MacDonald (MBA—Memphis State University, presently working in the accounting department): Examine the "quality of life" in Minnesota.
2. Ed Haley (MBA—Iowa State University, presently working in the transportation department): Research the cost of relocating the Research Center to Fargo.
3. Buchan MacDonald (MBA—University of Missouri, J.D.—

BIRMINGHAM STEEL
OFFICE OF THE PRESIDENT

Inter-Office Memo

TO: Sue Boyer

FROM: Herb Hughes H. H.

SUBJECT: Research Center Relocation Study

DATE: October 19, 1982

Sue, our research employees in Duluth, Minnesota, are "on the warpath" again. Please see the attached letter from Dr. Brown. As you know, this is the third year in a row that they have requested a relocation of the research facility to Fargo, North Dakota. In past years, I have told our Duluth people that we were "studying their request," but in fact I have taken only cursory action hoping the issue would eventually subside. It has not and therefore I believe it is time to conduct a thorough investigation of the issues raised in Dr. Brown's most recent letter.

A related issue deals with Minnesota as a possible site for our proposed midwestern finished-goods storage warehouse. One member of our Board of Directors -- Swen Swenson, III (who also happens to be the largest shareholder in the company) -- is a native Minnesotan and he is strongly arguing for the new facility to be located in Minnesota. It is estimated that this warehouse will employ approximately 150 new employees when it's completed in the late 1980's.

Please do the following:

a.   Contact Dr. Brown and tell her that you are in charge of a special task force to study the relocation issue.

b.   Appoint appropriate task force members to help you in this project. I would be pleased if you would select a number of our recent (within the last five years) MBA employees from various departments. (This will help to "broaden" their exposure to additional types of problems.)

c.   Present to me a written recommendation by January 14, 1983, dealing with: (1) relocation of the Research Center and (2) should Minnesota be considered for the proposed mid-western finished-goods warehouse.

Case Figure 10-1-1   Memo from Birmingham Steel President About Relocation of Research Center.

Birmingham Steel
Research Center
4900 Montana Street
Duluth, Minnesota 55806

October 7, 1982

Mr. Herbert L. Hughes
President and Chief Executive Officer
Birmingham Steel Corporate Headquarters
Birmingham, AL 35207

Dear Herb:

Our research facility now employs 114 people: 47 scientists who all hold
advanced graduate degrees; 49 technicians, most of who are college graduates,
who assist in our labs, program computers, etc.; and 18 people in clerical
and secretarial positions. Recently, all employees at the research center
voted on whether to recommend to corporate headquarters that we stay in
Duluth or move to Fargo, North Dakota. The primary issue is the high
personal income taxes in Minnesota. As an example, in 1981 I paid $2,742
in Minnesota taxes; if I had resided in Fargo, my North Dakota state taxes
would have been $835. The vote totals were as follows: 79 for moving;
21 for staying; and 14 with no opinion.

Let me provide you with a brief historical background on why the Research
Center is located in Duluth, of all places. In 1896, Swen Swenson discovered
rich iron ore deposits in northern Minnesota. He purchased approximately
76,000 acres of this land at minimal prices because it was considered
worthless property. In 1923, the son of the founder of Swenson Iron Ore
Company, Swen Swenson, Jr., merged his company with Birmingham Steel. One
condition of the merger was that Birmingham Steel had to always maintain a
major facility in Minnesota. When Birmingham Steel sold its Minnesota ore
properties to Republic Steel in 1963, Board of Director member Swen Swenson, III
(grandson of the founder) insisted that his father's mandate about a "major"
facility in Minnesota be honored. Therefore, the Research Center was moved
from Pittsburgh, PA to Duluth in 1963.

Our present employees, in most cases, enjoy the vitality of living in a
northern climate. There is no desire, for example, to relocate to the
corporate headquarters. We believe that there are two possible solutions to
allowing us to relocate in Fargo. First, move another Birmingham facility to
Minnesota, or second, find some legal "loophole" to void the Minnesota major
facility clause in the 1923 agreement.

Please give serious and prompt consideration to our request. Employee
morale is low, and it will get lower as April 15 (tax time) approaches.

Sincerely yours,

Kathy

Kathy Brown Curran, Ph.D.
Director, Research

dm

Case Figure 10-1-2   Letter from Research Director About Relocation of Research Center.

University of San Diego, presently in the law department): Determine the business climate in Minnesota, excluding taxation.
4. Annalee Hanson (MBA—Eastern Kentucky University, presently in public relations): Examine the business and personal tax environment in Minnesota.

Each person was asked to finish his or her research by December 6, 1982. December 7 and 8 were devoted to oral reports and discussion between Boyer and her four research associates. She concluded the second day-long session by requesting each person to prepare a *succinct* summary of their research. These reports were due by December 20, 1982 and are reproduced as Case Figures 10–1–3 to 10–1–6. (See also Case Figure 10–1–7.)

Question One: What should Boyer recommend concerning relocation of the Research Center? Why?

Question Two: What should be Boyer's position regarding Minnesota as a potential location for the proposed finished-goods storage warehouse? Why?

Question Three: Regarding the warehouse location question, which of the four issues examined do you believe: (a) Is the *most* important? Why? (b) Is the *least* important? Why?

Question Four: Do you believe the Research Center employees were impertinent in asking to be relocated to Fargo? Why?

Question Five: What additional information should be gathered to address the two issues involved in this case?

Question Six: Regarding relocation of the Research Center, should Brown or someone else from Duluth have been involved in the study? Why?

Question Seven: Draft a brief statement (300 words or less) from Boyer to Hughes outlining her decision and rationale regarding the relocation issue.

Case 10–2   Excelsior Manufacturing Company Case

Rufe Jefferson founded the Excelsior Manufacturing Company in 1952 in Excelsior, Minnesota. Although a geologist by education, Rufe's first love was cross-country skiing. Since existing equipment was primitive at that time—it typically involved the usage of modified down-hill ski equipment—Rufe designed and built skis that

Quality of Life in Minnesota

Emmy Lou MacDonald

The quality of life issue is difficult to examine because it is a
nebulous sugject. Does quality of life involve: (a) year-round warm weather,
(b) professional sports availability, (c) excellent medical and dental care,
(d) ample cultural events, (e) good roads, (f) adequate public transportation,
(g) readily available higher educational opportunities, (h) low crime rates,
(i) cheap alcoholic beverages, (j) high welfare payments, etc.? As this list
indicates, it is difficult to find a consensus about which items should be
evaluated when deciding if a state possesses a high "quality of life."

Minnesota generally ranks in the top third of all states when examined
in terms of "quality of life" issues. In regard to the above factors,
Minnesota ranks favorably on all points except (a) and (i).

National Geographic magazine made the following observations about the
quality of life in Minnesota and its two main Cities, Minneapolis and St. Paul:

* The Cities, almost more suburban than urban in layout and personality,
  suffer less than most American metropolises from traffic jams, human
  congestion, poverty, and violent crime. The Cities are far more
  congenial to the Muses. Wealthy underwriters of the arts live there, and
  over the years they have contributed half a billion dollars to cultural
  and other civic development in the Cities as well as throughout
  the state.

* From all over Minnesota people pour into the Cities for such cultural
  amenities as theater, music, dance, art, and education. But they take
  pride in their state's rugged outdoor image as well. On radio and TV
  they are often reminded of it by the haunting voice of the loon,
  Minnesota's state bird, which inhabits its wilderness lakes.

* St. Paul is the seat of the state's liberal government--marked, perhaps,
  by high taxes, but also by notable results in education and social
  services, and in balancing the protection of the environment with the
  promotion of industry.

* Minnesotans have always lavished money and concern on a more important
  resource, their children. The state has a major university and
  58 colleges, 47 of them founded as church schools. With the earliest
  Minnesota immigrants had come commitments to learning as well as
  to God.

Case Figure 10-1-3 Summary Report on Quality of Life in Minnesota.

COST OF RELOCATING FROM
DULUTH TO FARGO

By Ed Haley

There are many cost factors -- some tangible and others intangible -- involved in moving a major research facility. Below are highlighted a number of the pertinent factors involved:

a. Personal moving expenses of 114 people from Duluth to Fargo.

b. Transportation of equipment and supplies between the two locations.

c. Selling the existing facility in Duluth. Note that at present the Duluth area is economically depressed because (a) iron-ore sales are low because of the recession, (b) one of Duluth's largest employers moved its production facilities, and (c) the U.S. Air Force recently closed a major facility in the area.

d. The Fargo economy is booming because (a) many businesses from Minnesota are moving to Fargo for tax reasons and (b) North Dakota's economy has been greatly buoyed up by large oil discoveries in the Williston Basin area.

e. North Dakota and Fargo are very business-development oriented. They will issue industrial revenue bonds for the new location, limit initial property tax payments, help to pay for retraining of any new employees, etc.

f. It is estimated that the Research Center would be inoperative for about 45 days during the relocation.

Case Figure 10-1-4   Summary Report on Cost of Relocating Research Center.

OVERALL BUSINESS CLIMATE IN MINNESOTA

By Buchan MacDonald

The State of Minnesota has, at best, a neutral environment towards business development -- and many observers believe it is <u>antagonistic</u>. In 1981, William Shapiro, an executive of the Fantus Company, a large Chicago-based plant location consulting firm, noted that his firm has made hundreds of plant location studies, and that Minnesota is the <u>only</u> state that his firm has <u>never</u> recommended favorably for a new plant location facility.

Some factors are beyond the state's control. These would include a harsh winter climate and the absence of indigenous petroleum, coal, or natural gas resources. Stephen Keating, former chairman of Honeywell, Inc., has stated: "There's no way Minnesota can match the attractiveness of the Sunbelt states today. Many of the big companies have gravitated to the sun states because of their obvious appeals, now increasingly appealing because so many of them have energy bases that produce major state revenues without increasing business taxes -- as a matter of fact, while <u>lessening</u> business taxes. Unless we make some special efforts, we're going to fall further behind."

Besides high taxes, Minnesota is a labor-dominated state in terms of legislative action. No where is this more clearly seen than in the Workmen's Compensation insurance rates. Data from <u>Minnesota Corporate Report</u> (Nov. 1981) show that annual costs to employers for workmen's compensation in seven job categories (such as carpenters, plumbers, truck drivers) are on the average 7 to 8 times higher in Minnesota than in North Dakota.

A 1981 survey of chief executive officers of Minnesota's largest corporations was revealing about the state's business climate. When asked their opinion about Minnesota's business environment, 46 percent of the executives said it was "below average," and 30 percent said it was "worst than average." Fully 85 percent thought their firms would be more profitable if they were located in another state, while 15 percent thought it would make no difference. Only 12 percent of the executives would today locate a new enterprise, in the same industry as their present companies, in Minnesota; whereas 88 percent would seek another location.

Because of Minnesota's unfavorable business climate, it is estimated that up to 1,000 firms have left the state in recent years. This has greatly angered Minnesota's labor unions. Their reaction to this exodus is a bill before the state legislature known as the "Hostage Shop" or "Plant Closing Law." It would require all companies with 100 or more employees to notify employees two years in advance of management's intent to greatly reduce or cease operations. In addition, the employer would have to make a payment to the community of 10 percent of its annual payroll to help the community offset the effects of decreased employment. Finally, each severed employee, for a period of time based on his or her longevity with the firm, would receive relocation expenses, severance pay, and company-paid health insurance. This bill is again before the legislature in late 1982.

A final indication of the strength of labor unions in Minnesota is the Strikebreaker Bill currently before the Minnesota legislature. According to <u>Minnesota Corporate Report</u>, "This bill prohibits employers from using their own personnel to operate struck plants during the course of a labor dispute. Promoted by labor as a means of bringing labor disputes to a speedy conclusion, such legislation would make it impossible, businesses argue, for management to withstand labor's demands."

Case Figure 10-1-5   Summary Report on Business Climate in Minnesota.

<u>Minnesota's Tax Climate</u>

by Annalee Hanson

Minnesota is a high-tax state. Twenty years ago in 1961 the Minnesota Chambers of Commerce declared:

"Taxes, especially on the state level, are a serious threat to present industry, to future industrial expansion and a deterrent factor in securing new industry."

Today, Minnesota has the highest marginal personal income tax rate, 16 percent, in the United States. The corporate income tax rate at 12 percent is also the highest in the country. Finally, Minnesota has one of the highest unemployment compensation taxes in the U.S. State sales and property taxes are at an average rate.

In a 1980 study by Alexander Grant and Company for the Conference of State Manufacturers' Associations, Minnesota was found to be the 13th most expensive state in which to conduct business.

An example of the effect of the high personal income tax can be seen in Moorhead, Minnesota, which is across the Red River from Fargo, North Dakota. Dave Wachal, vice-president for finance of American Crystal Sugar, which is located in Moorhead, lives in Fargo. Why? Because he can save over $2,500 in state income taxes. Of American Crystal's nine senior executives, six live in Fargo. Wachal noted, "I decided to live in North Dakota before I moved, strictly due to taxes. I was a loyal Minnesotan and I felt bad about it, but I'm crying all the way to the bank.

Case Figure 10-1-6   Summary Report on Business and Personal Taxes in Minnesota.

Case Figure 10-1-7   North Dakota Ad About Low Workmen's Compensation Rates.

were narrower and longer than cross-country equipment available in stores. Cross-country enthusiasts were impressed by Jefferson's refinements and clamored to purchase skis from him. Rufe started to make them on weekends and evenings, but he was receiving 20 orders for every pair of skis completed. In 1952 he decided to manufacture skis full-time, and he incorporated his business (although he owned all the common stock).

Sales continued to grow because Rufe was fanatical about quality control. Each ski did not receive one coat of varnish, or 5, but 22! (Rufe never disclosed how this magic number was determined.) By 1979, sales were about $22 million per year, and Excelsior Manufacturing employed about 600 people—each of whom had to be a devoted cross-country skier as a condition of employment. Sales were concentrated in the northern one-third of the United States and in Canada.

In 1972, Rufe turned over the day-to-day operations of the firm to "Slippery" Dan Kelly, from Miles City, Montana. "Slippery" acquired his nickname because of his unique ability to wax his skis most advantageously in any type of snow conditions. Slippery was concerned about the "invasion" of cross-country equipment in the latter half of the 1970's from Norway and Finland. Although this equipment was generally of good quality, it did not compare to the superb workmanship found in Excelsior Skis. The imported equipment also had a lower price and Slippery believed this was directly affecting the sales of Excelsior. From 1975 to 1979, total unit sales of cross-country skiing equipment were growing at the unbelievable rate of 27 percent per year, while Excelsior's sales were growing at a modest 3 percent. This sluggish growth trend had to be arrested.

Slippery decided a thorough analysis of Excelsior's total operation was in order. Two well-known management consultants—Frank McDonald and Lowell Miller—were hired. They lurked around the facility on and off for six weeks. Another two months passed by.

Tuesday, May 13th, finally arrived. Rufe and Slippery were to meet the consultants at 9:00 A.M. to receive a three-hour executive summary. The consultants were told to be brutally frank if necessary—but both Rufe and Slippery hoped that none of the serious problem areas would be directly related to their management policies and philosophies.

It was now about 11:45 A.M., and Miller was presenting a summary: "In general, your operation has few basic flaws. Our market research studies indicate that among connoisseurs of cross-country skiing, the name of Excelsior is always at the top. Your target market appreciates your attention to detail and is willing to pay your premium price. Your accounting records were weak, but we've noted they can be corrected with relative ease. Your most serious problem, then, is customer service relations. Many of your retailers have complained of 'stock-outs' of your equipment during the critical sales period of October to December. In fact, as we mentioned, a number of your most important retailers have threatened to drop the Excelsior line if you 'don't get your customer service act together.' We recommend that Lyders be replaced with a person who better appreciates the physical distribution or logistics concept. He indeed has kept transportation costs at an unbelievably low per-unit cost—but at a great cost to customer service relations."

What to do with "Shifty" Steve Lyder? (Nicknamed because of his unique ability to shift his weight and, therefore, execute very sharp turns when going downhill on skis.) Shifty was the oldest member of the management team. He was a *traffic man* and proud of it! He frequently told Rufe and Slippery, "All this talk about physical distribution is a bunch of foolishness dreamed up by ivory-towered eggheads who have never driven a truck or cut a bill-of-lading."

Shifty stressed *low* transportation costs. All skis were currently delivered to customers by four private trucks which followed an established route. Deliveries were made every three to four weeks, and *no exceptions* to this schedule were tolerated. If stores ran out of Excelsior equipment—it was their fault for not forecasting sales correctly! They would just have to wait until the next regularly scheduled Excelsior truck arrived.

Question One: List and discuss the *costs* to Excelsior Manufacturing Company of its present physical distribution system outlined in the last paragraph of the case.

Question Two: List and discuss the *benefits* to Excelsior of its present physical distribution system.

Question Three: Do you think that Shifty's policy about deliveries is well suited to a cross-country ski manufacturer? Why?

Question Four: Should Excelsior change its marketing system and work through wholesalers, forcing the wholesalers to maintain large inventories and make quick deliveries to retailers? Why?

Question Five: What additional information do you need to help analyze this case? Why?

Question Six: What action(s) should Rufe and Slippery take in this situation? Defend your answer.

Question Seven: Should Shifty be separated from the company? Why? What alternative courses of action are feasible? Discuss each.

The shape of the wind deflector above the cab may have contributed the idea for the sign painted on the side of this private truck. The nose cone is manufactured by Nose Cone Mfg. Co.

Photo courtesy Trucking Equipment Supply Co., San Francisco, Calif.

In late 1981 Fruehauf developed this tractor-trailer combination with a design that reduces aerodynamic drag.

Photo courtesy Fruehauf Division, Fruehauf Corporation.

11 Traffic Management

With deregulation, managers of "traffic," "transportation," "physical distribution" or "logistics"—whatever you term it—are going to have to put aside their green eyeshades and tariffs and become "wheeler-dealers" to survive. Top managers in companies where the transportation bill is significant are going to have to spend some time understanding the opportunities (and risks) brought about by transportation deregulation, and they may have to find new managers for the buying of transportation who can seize the opportunities and avoid the risks.

CHARLES W. HOPPE
Traffic World
February 23, 1981

James Edler, corporate traffic manager of American Greetings Company remarked: "The president of American Greetings came to me and said, 'We can't afford to pay our freight rates anymore.' All of a sudden the traffic manager is a significant member of the management team."

Handling and Shipping Management
May, 1981

Bob Tannenbaum, an executive of East-West Shippers Association, noted that trucking deregulation has made the motor carrier industry more price aggressive: "These trucks are cost-competitive and they have a lot of advantages the railroads can't offer. I'm enjoying deregulation. It keeps me up at night thinking about ways to save money."

Distribution
November, 1980

Introduction

This chapter will examine how users and the suppliers of freight transportation services interact from the transportation users' viewpoint. Looking at this user-supplier relationship from the users' viewpoint is known as *traffic management.*

Traffic management involves purchasing transportation service, trying to obtain the desired level of service at the lowest cost. Traffic management is a complex, detailed, and challenging aspect of business. Top management's respect for this function has grown in recent years as the PD/L concept has become recognized as an essential business strategy.

Senior management is becoming more interested and more involved in traffic management. The basic reason is that the nation's freight bill is estimated at nearly 8 percent of GNP. This means that, on the average, 8 percent of the cost of everything we purchase goes to cover transportation costs. The same would hold for a typical firm; i.e., 8 percent of its expenditures also go for freight transportation. Because transportation costs are escalating due to increased energy costs, top management has recognized that transportation costs represent a significant—and increasing—cost of doing business.

Since the various functional areas of PD/L function as a chain, the system can be no stronger than its weakest link. Therefore, a successful PD/L system must possess a competent and professional traffic management department.

> The purchase of transportation demands a high degree of skill and care. Intelligently and imaginatively administered, this function can make a material contribution to a company's profit and prestige. If its importance is not fully understood at top levels of management or if it is in the hands of incompetent personnel, however, the transportation responsibility can degenerate into chaos and financial loss.[1]

History of Traffic Management

The development of traffic management has had its ups and downs. Prior to the 1887 *Act To Regulate Commerce*, the role of the traffic manager was important. The traffic manager dealt primarily with the railroads since there were no other means of long-distance land carriage. The traffic manager's primary responsibility was to negotiate the largest "kickbacks," or rebates, from the railroad. Often the traffic manager was a former employee of the railroad and, presumably, "better trained" to negotiate a deal from his former railroad cronies.

Federal railroad regulation in 1887 dealt a crippling blow to the traffic management function. Rebates and other forms of discriminatory service were suddenly illegal, and therefore the "special services" of the traffic manager were unnecessary. The traffic manager's role declined, and managers became little more than clerks who would notify the railroads when a shipment was ready to be picked up. (They also attempted to collect loss and damage claims for goods damaged in transit.)

Because of the development and growing use of the motor truck, the 1920's marked a renewal of the importance of the traffic management function. The railroad's transportation monopoly was broken, and competition became feasible in both the freight market—via

---

[1]Charles H. Wager, Richard C. Colton, and Edmund S. Ward, *Industrial Traffic Management*, 5th ed. (Washington, D.C.: Traffic Service Corp., 1973), p. 1.

trucking and barges—and, later, in the passenger business—via commercial aviation. In addition, the federal government became a significant provider of rights-of-way for railroad competitors. The highway, waterway, and airway systems were all expanded with federal aid. Freight forwarders and shippers' cooperatives were also emerging as transportation alternatives. In addition, Congress, by the early 1920's, had enacted many amendments to the *Act To Regulate Commerce*, and that is when transportation regulation started becoming complex. Finally, all modes of transport were experimenting with new and innovative pricing techniques. All of these factors complicated the job of the traffic manager. A "clerk-type" traffic manager could not cope with the large array of transport alternatives, and the traffic management function was upgraded to become a more important corporate function. Its personnel were upgraded, and this function today—because of the PD/L concept—is a respected part of the corporate management team.

Deregulation of transportation has made further demands upon the traffic manager. Prior to deregulation, many of the carriers with whom the traffic manager dealt were "regulated," charging identical rates and competing only in terms of variations in service. With deregulation, more carriers are competing in terms of *both* costs and service, which complicates the carrier-selection process since more variables must be taken into account. Thus, not only will the traffic manager of the 1980's have to be familiar with all the traditional means of dealing with regulated carriers (as outlined in this and the following chapter), but he or she also must become astute at bargaining in a market where some carriers' charges will fluctuate by the hour. Despite all the stresses and strains carrier deregulation is causing today's traffic manager,[2] it will serve as the single most important catalyst for *upgrading* the status of the traffic management profession during the decade of the 1980's.

Edward Kammerer, director of transportation for Celanese Chemical, noted the above trends and observed, "We have more than doubled the years of advanced education in our department."[3] A similar trend is occurring at Bordon Chemical according to William A. Talmadge, distribution manager for industrial operations. "We need people with broader experience, not just in traffic. We're looking for a lot more college graduates, including those with advanced degrees, and many of those in our department without degrees are going back to school to get them—we need broader business experience."[4]

[2] Roger Jerman, Ronald Anderson, and James Constantin, "The Traffic Manager: Alive and Well," *Distribution Worldwide* (May, 1979), pp. 57–61.

[3] "For Transport People, More Status," *Chemical Week* (August 5, 1981).

[4] *Ibid.*

Duties of the Traffic Manager

The traffic manager is responsible for a large number of activities. To get some idea of the range of these activities, see Figure 11–1, which is a statement of the traffic manager's goals and objectives at the Motorola Corporation. It should be studied carefully because it contains an overview of this chapter and examines many of the relationships that exist in transportation between users, carriers, and government.

Organizational Structure for Traffic Management

Traffic management involves so many *specialized activities* that there is no one standard or conventional organizational structure. Instead, each firm evolves an organizational structure that best serves its needs. However, there are a few common elements in organizational planning. Figure 11–2 illustrates an organizational structure that is "hybrid" of a number of actual traffic departments. In describing responsibilities of positions in that figure some new terms are used, which will be explained later in the chapter. The general traffic manager (GTM) has an assistant general traffic manager (AGTM) who supervises the barrage of daily activities occurring in a traffic department. This frees the GTM to represent his department in corporate-level activities. Supervision of specific traffic department functions is the job of the assistant general traffic manager. The AGTM also monitors the daily activities of each traffic section and presents a daily or weekly report to the GTM noting problem areas where established goals and objectives are not being met. The GTM and AGTM are also the "contact" people with individuals in the firm's other physical distribution functional activities.

The chief pilot is in charge of scheduling the corporate fleet of private aircraft and its staff of pilots. He is also responsible for insuring proper aircraft maintenance and compliance with all federal and state safety regulations.

The traffic manager of transportation services supervises a number of activities including loss and damage claims against carriers, demurrage, detention, tracing, expediting, household moving for company employees, and siding and weight agreements with railroads.

The rates manager is concerned with determining the lowest applicable freight rate. Negotiation of favorable freight rates is also his or her job. Other typical responsibilities include reparations, "auditing" of carriers' charges, and collecting overcharges.

MOTOROLA'S TRAFFIC OBJECTIVES

1. Direct and control the purchase of adequate domestic and international freight and passenger and employee household goods transportation and public warehouse space at the lowest cost consistent with the overall good of the company.

2. Aid in the elimination of wasteful practices and needless expense such as incurred through loss and damage in transit, car demurrage and truck detention, the use of improper bill of lading descriptions and uneconomical routings, the shipping and receiving of uneconomical quantities, the use of unnecessary premium cost transportation, and the payment of excess duties and Customs penalties.

3. Remain familiar with transportation and Customs laws and, regulations to insure that the company's traffic operations are conducted accordingly and that all benefits to which we may be entitled are secured. Keep company and division management informed of any changes that may affect the company.

4. Operating either independently for Motorola or through our local and national Traffic Committee and Association Memberships, support or oppose carrier and shipper proposals as well as local, state and federal legislation affecting transportation in general or Motorola in particular; also negotiate with carriers, their Freight Rate Making Bureaus, and Classification Committees for adjustment of rates, ratings, rules and regulations to reduce transportation costs and/or improve services.

5. Formulate, standardize, recommend and coordinate corporate traffic and transportation policies regarding public warehousing and the company's movement of materials, supplies, finished goods and personnel. Cooperate and work with all Divisions, departments, and sales areas to make sure that these policies are complied with and that there is no relaxing of control procedures.

6. Assist all Divisions in solving local and field problems involving domestic and international traffic and transportation activities, including Customs problems, and serve as liaison between those Divisions, the carriers, and Customs personnel.

7. Analyze and keep abreast of the constant changes, trends, methods, services, equipment, and technological advances in the domestic and international transportation field and when practical and economical, apply them to the company's operation.

8. Study transportation economies with respect to our domestic and foreign distribution and marketing methods; also with respect to plant, warehouse and distributor locations. Make recommendations based on such studies.

9. Study and develop current and long-range plans and programs involving the organization and functions of the Corporate, Canadian, and Western Area Traffic Departments so that changes can and will be made as needed to be sensitive and responsive to the requirements of all Divisions, and the company overall.

10. Operate the department at minimum cost consistent and compatible with the department's essential space and people requirements if its Objectives and Goals are to be achieved in all areas of the company operations. Includes the necessity to maintain standards as high as our budget permits when hiring personnel to insure a maximum level of proficiency within the department.

11. Encourage personal development and self-improvement; counsel and advise Traffic personnel in the development of their technical and managerial abilities so as to enable them to deal more effectively with associates and others, and to improve their overall capacity for advancement to positions of greater responsibility.

12. Cooperate with traffic and transportation organizations to promote the transportation industry and to make it more attractive to prospective employees.

13. *All things being equal,* use and promote the use of carriers who are customers and/or potential customers of the company; also secure an interest in and promote the use of company products by the carriers.

14. Promote, foster and maintain good relations with all carriers, warehousemen, suppliers, and customers—with the best interests of the company foremost at all times.

Figure 11–1 Example of Traffic Management Objectives. Source: Janet Bosworth Dower, "How Top Management Evaluates the Traffic/Distribution Function," *Distribution Worldwide* (May, 1973), p. 56.

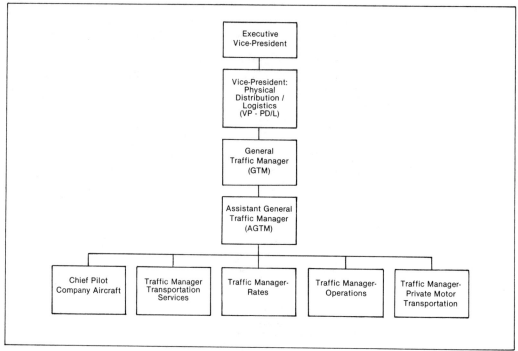

Figure 11–2   Traffic Department Organizational Structure.

The operations manager determines the transport mode for each shipment and the specific carrier. He or she also prepares the shipment documentation, determines the shipment's routing, administers the transit privilege accounting, and uses reconsignment and diversion options, if necessary. The firm's private truck fleet is also handled within the traffic department. The fleet manager supervises the scheduling of the truck fleet, its maintenance and insurance requirements, and sees to it that the fleet operates legally. In addition, if the firm operates a fleet of automobiles, their maintenance is handled by this section.

Rate Determination and Negotiation with Common Carriers

Much of this chapter deals with the traffic manager's dealings with common carriers. What is described are traditional practices. Since deregulation, however, common carriers (and other carriers as well) have more options to conduct portions of their business on a "contract" basis with shippers. Understanding the common carrier "obligations" is still important since many new contracts are written so that they contain all of the routine provisions with only one or two exceptions, which are negotiated. Hence a shipper's traffic manager may enter into negotiations with a carrier and insist that all provisions of the usual common carrier agreement be maintained with, say, only two exceptions. For example, the shipper's traffic manager might commit his firm to ship a certain volume of traffic with the carrier in return for a new, lower, rate from the carrier.

Much of this chapter up until the section about negotiating contract rates describes the activities of a traffic manager who relies on common carriers. Remember, however, that many of these activities may also relate to the traffic manager's dealings with contract carriers as well. In today's world, the common carrier and the contract carrier may, in fact, be the same firm.

Traditional common carrier rate determination is one of the most complex aspects of traffic management.

> To the uninitiated it [a freight tariff] has become a bogie understandable only to the trained specialist. . . . In fact, it would appear to some that the tariff compiler has succeeded in creating something in the nature of a *Frankenstein* which he may alter only by the addition of further complexities.[5]

Rate Analysis

Many beginning students of transportation and traffic management wonder why the *shipper* should determine common carrier freight rates in the first place. They argue that since the *Interstate Commerce Act* (Section 6 and strengthened by the 1903 *Elkins Act*) requires common carriers to determine the lowest legal or correct rate—why should the shipper waste time determining the applicable rate? The answer to this question is that while it is possible to leave rate determination *exclusively* up to the carrier, this is a naive solution fraught with economic danger. As will be seen in chapter 12, because of the redundancy of freight rates, there typically are several rates that are applicable for any specific shipment. When the carrier's personnel are asked to determine the freight rate, they have no incentive to systematically search the applicable tariffs to find the *lowest* rate. They will cite the rate that is the *easiest* to find. Many shippers believe that if the carrier is responsible for rate determination, the rate will be about 10 percent higher than the rate the ship-

---

[5] Edward A. Starr, *The Interpretation of Freight Tariffs* (Fort Worth: The Transportation Press, 1961), p. 1.

per will find—after an exhaustive search of rate tariffs. The 10-percent difference is what makes freight rate determination a key aspect of traffic management.

Freight rate determination is typically performed by specialists, formerly called *rate clerks* but now known as *rate analysts*. Their work is sophisticated, intricate, and demanding.

Rate Negotiation

Another aspect of rates involves *negotiation* to change existing rates which are not favorable to the firm. Although common carrier freight tariffs may seem to be cast in concrete—they are not! Given sufficient analysis, patience, determination, and bargaining strength, the traffic manager can frequently lower existing freight rates or change a tariff rule—which has the effect of reducing the total freight charges. Rule changes could involve lowering the minimum weight that qualifies for the lowest rate or allowing a less expensive form of protective packaging. Howard Gabriel, general traffic manager of Hershey Foods, noted that more than half of his time involves negotiating favorable rates.[6]

Deregulation has made it possible for carriers to be more flexible about changing rates within the common carrier framework because rate bureaus now have less restraining influence on the rate adjustments made by individual carriers. *Forbes* magazine noted, "Traffic managers are already negotiating over tariffs much as institutional investors squared off with their brokers when Wall Street's fixed commissions were abolished six years ago."[7] *Forbes* reported that in the first seven months of 1981, Lever Brothers estimated it had saved $4 million in reduced freight rates because of increased carrier competition.[8]

Figures 11–3 and 11–4 illustrate briefly how an international traffic manager would approach vessel lines and conferences in order to have rates adjusted. Only one of the two rate modification forms referred to in Figure 11–3 is reproduced here, as Figure 11–4.

Astute traffic managers are constantly alert to situations that will support their case when negotiating with common carriers and carrier rate bureaus to lower existing freight rates. There are four rationales for requesting lower rates. The first—and the one with the highest percentage of success—involves a situation where a lower

[6]Janet Bosworth, "What Does a Traffic Manager Do?" *Distribution Worldwide* (March, 1971).

[7]"Computers on the Loading Dock," *Forbes* (August 31, 1981), p. 94.

[8]*Ibid.*

THE PORT AUTHORITY OF NY & NJ

One World Trade Center
New York, N.Y. 10048

(212) 466-7000
(201) 622-6600

Transportation Management Division
Suite 64-East
April 15, 1982

Professor Donald Wood
School of Business
San Francisco State University
San Francisco, CA 94132

Dear Professor Wood:

Subsequent to our telephone conversation of April 7th, I am writing this letter to you. Enclosed please find rate modification forms from Trans Freight Lines (an independent) and the Continental North Atlantic Westbound Freight Conference (conference).

Adjusting ocean freight rates can be a time-consuming process. Rate increases or new items in tariffs become effective only after 30-days' notice. Rate decreases on already published tariff rates become effective on 1-day's notice. New tariff items may become effective on 1-day's notice if the result is a decrease in rates as compared to the "general cargo n.o.s." rate, if that were the only applicable rate on commodities prior to publication of the new item.

In order to initiate a rate modification, it is necessary to contact the steamship conference or the office of the independent carrier. A sales representative from either type carrier will be able to advise you of the procedures. The procedure with a conference carrier is somewhat more complex than dealing with an independent. Should you contact a conference line for a rate adjustment, he will send you a conference form. After filling out the form, it would be sent to the conference office rather than back to the carrier with whom initial contact was made. At the next regularly scheduled meeting of the conference rate committee, your proposal will be discussed and voted upon. Should your proposal be accepted, the rate or classification will be published in the conference tariff and will apply to all steamship lines in that conference. You can imagine that getting the proposal to the conference as early as possible would be to your benefit.

Independent carriers could logically act more expeditiously on shipper requests. They could decide almost immediately whether to accept or reject your proposal.

For reference, consult Title 46, Parts 527 and 536, of the Code of Federal Regulations. If further questions arise, please do not hesitate to contact me. Thank you for your interest in the Port of New York and New Jersey.

Yours truly,

James A. Cline

James A. Cline
Logistics & Regulatory Affairs Analyst

Writer's direct dial telephone: (212) 466-8328

Figure 11–3 Modification of Ocean Freight Rates. Courtesy: *Via Port New York–New Jersey.*

TFL TRANS FREIGHT LINES, INC.		FMC NO.	ORIG REV	PAGE
			ORIGINAL	29
			CANCELS	PAGE
FREIGHT TARIFF NO. 32		**32**		
FROM: PORTS IN GREAT BRITAIN, NORTHERN IRELAND AND THE REPUBLIC OF IRELAND AS SHOWN IN RULE 1	TO: UNITED STATES ATLANTIC COAST PORTS IN THE EASTPORT, MAINE/KEY WEST, FLORIDA RANGE AS SHOWN IN RULE 1		EFFECTIVE DATE September 4, 1981	
			CORR NO.	

RULES AND REGULATIONS	RULE

SHIPPER'S REQUESTS AND COMPLAINTS (Continued)

REQUEST FOR ESTABLISHMENT OF OCEAN RATE OR MODIFICATION OF EXISTING RATE

19 (Cont'd)

RETURN TO: TRANS FREIGHT LINES, INC.
P.O. BOX 1520
SECAUCUS, NEW JERSEY 07094

1. NAME AND ADDRESS OF SHIPPER _____

2. NAME AND ADDRESS OF CONSIGNEE _____

3. NAME AND ADDRESS OF FORWARDING AGENT (IF ANY) _____

4. PORT OF SHIPMENT _____   b. PORT OF DESTINATION _____

5. POINT OF ORIGIN _____   b. ULTIMATE DESTINATION _____

6. COMMODITY (GIVE COMPLETE DESCRIPTION AND TRADE NAME IF APPLICABLE) IF POSSIBLE ATTACH EXPLANATORY LITERATURE AND BROCHURE. _____

7. SITC AND/OR B.T.N. CODE NUMBER(S): _____

8. IF HAZARDOUS CARGO STATE NATURE OF HAZARD GIVING FLASHPOINT AND IMCO, (INTER-GOVERNMENTAL MARITIME CONSULTATIVE ORGANIZATION) OR CFR CODE

9. PRESENT RATE: _____

PROPOSED RATE: _____

10. PARTICULARS OF COMMODITY: _____

TYPE OF PACKING: _____

a)LENGTH (CM) _____ b)WIDTH _____ c) _____ d) CUBE _____

e)WEIGHT PER PIECE OR PKG. (KILOS) _____ f)CUBIC METERS PER 1000 KILOS _____

g)F.A.S. VALUE IN U.S. $ PER 1000 KILOS _____ h)WILL COMMODITY BE PALLETIZED OR UNITIZED _____

i)IF IN BULK STATE WHETHER LINER BAG USED OR REQUIRED _____

11. IF ALTERNATIVE TRANSPORTATION IS BY AIR, STATE RATE APPLICABLE PER KILO: _____

12. TOTAL WEIGHT SHIPPED DURING LAST CALENDAR YEAR IN 1000 KILOS: _____

13. ANTICIPATED ANNUAL MOVEMENT IN WEIGHT TONS IF REQUEST GRANTED: _____

14. SPECIFY ANTICIPATED TOTAL WEIGHT IN KILOS AND TOTAL MEASUREMENT IN CUBIC METERS TO BE STOWED IN A CONTAINER·

20' CONTAINER: KILOS _____ CUBIC METERS _____ 35/40' CONTAINER: KILOS _____ CUBIC METERS _____

15. SPECIFY TYPE OF CONTAINER (E.G. STANDARD DRY/REEFER/INSULATED/OPEN TOP/HALF, HEIGHT, ETC.)

16. REASON FOR RATE MODIFICATION REQUEST: _____

PLEASE COMPLETE AS MANY OF THE QUESTIONS AS POSSIBLE. IF WE CAN HELP YOU IN THIS MATTER, PLEASE CONTACT US.

APPLICANT'S NAME AND DEPARTMENT: _____

ADDRESS: _____

TELEX _____   TELEPHONE _____

SIGNATURE _____   DATE _____

FULL NAME AND TITLE (BLOCK CAPITALS) _____

FOR EXPLANATION OF ABBREVIATIONS, REFERENCE MARKS AND SYMBOLS, SEE PAGE 2.   ITS(202)347-8770

(ITS)

Figure 11–4 Rate Modification Form from Ocean Carrier Tariff Rules. Courtesy: Trans Freight Lines, Inc.

freight rate will significantly increase the volume of freight the carriers will transport. Assume that the motor common carrier rate on leather moccasins from Bemidji, Minnesota, to Los Angeles is $46.20 per CWT. Because of the relatively high freight rates, Bemidji-

- *CWT* is an abbreviation standing for century weight or hundred weight, or 100 pounds.

produced moccasins retail in Los Angeles for $14.00 per pair, while comparable moccasins produced in Hermosillo, Mexico, retail in Los Angeles for $12.00. If the truck rate from Minnesota can be reduced to $27.00 per CWT, it might be projected that Bemidji moccasins would be price competitive with those produced in Hermosillo. Let's assume that the Bemidji moccasin producers can convince the truckers that—with the lower rate—annual shipments would increase from 17,000 pounds to 134,000 pounds per year. The motor common carrier involved would undoubtedly favor the lower freight rate—assuming it covered the variable costs of carriage—because the carrier's revenues would increase from $7,854 ($46.20 × 170) to $36,180 ($27.00 × 1,340).

A second situation warranting a reduced rate involves an increased volume which is *not* precipitated by the carrier lowering its rate. Edward Jordan, supervisor of transportation at Scott Paper Company, stated that his company constantly monitored its shipments looking for increased tonnage to specific destinations. Jordan remarked, "If we notice that our shipments are increasing at a better than normal rate to a certain destination, then we'll study the volume to see if it merits a point-to-point rate."[9] The logic of such a request for a lower rate is that carriers can operate more efficiently when handling large volumes of shipments between two locations. Because their costs are lower on a per-unit basis, carriers can afford to share these savings with their customers who provide them with the high-volume business.

A third condition for arguing for lower rates is when existing rates on comparable products are significantly dissimilar. Assume the rail rate on clay flowerpots from Hattiesburg, Mississippi, to Billings, Montana, is $7.84 per CWT. Let's further assume that the rate for cement flowerpots between the same points is $5.92. The traffic manager for the firm producing the clay flowerpots should assert to the carriers and rate bureaus that the clay and cement flowerpots are competitive and exhibit the same transportation characteristics (i.e.,

---

[9]Janet Bosworth, *loc. cit.*

they weigh about the same, are subject to the same breakage rates, etc.), therefore they should also pay the same transportation rate. If the railroad resists changing the clay rate closer to the concrete rate, the traffic manager can go to the ICC and request that it order the carrier to lower the rate, alleging that Sections 1 and 3 of the *Interstate Commerce Act* have been violated.

Competition between transportation modes is the fourth rationale for seeking rate reductions. If railroads are exclusively transporting a product, the traffic manager may desire some intermodal competition to insure the railroad continues to provide good service. In addition, the traffic manager may not want to be completely tied to one mode of transportation in case it might be shut down by a strike. Therefore, he or she will negotiate with motor carriers or water carriers to lower their existing rates in order to be competitive. Astute traffic managers also threaten to use or expand their private truck fleet in cases where common carrier rates seem "high."

Carrier Selection

The initial choice of modes (barge, air, etc.) is made by the firm's PD/L manager who attempts to minimize the costs of achieving a certain standard of delivering raw materials, components, finished products, etc. Choice of which carriers within a mode to use is often made by the firm's traffic manager.

Table 11–1 presents the findings of a recent survey of how industrial shippers select their carriers. Each traffic manager was asked to rate the criteria that contributed to his selection, assigning each criterion a number from 0 (least important) to 100 (most important). Notice that the most important criterion was *consistent, on-time pickup and delivery.* Freight charges and time in transit (speed of delivery) were also important. (This survey was conducted *before* the 1980 deregulation of the trucking and railroad industries. Because of the increased level of rate competition precipitated by deregulation, a similar survey *today* would show that carrier freight charges are now a more important consideration than in previous years.)

In this section we will examine these three selection criteria and will also look at the advantages of one-carrier service from origin to destination. Other listed criteria, such as loss and damage and tracing, are discussed in later sections of this chapter.

TABLE 11-1   Carrier Selection Criteria

Selection Criteria	Mean Importance Score	Selection Criteria	Mean Importance Score
Consistent, On-Time Pickup and Delivery	92.4 (N = 79)	Serviceability (pick-ups and deliveries) at Off-Line Points	50.2 (N = 71)
Freight Charges	79.8 (N = 80)	Local Reputation of Carrier Firm(s)	47.1 (N = 71)
Time-in-Transit	79.1 (N = 74)	Availability of Special Transportation Equipment and Services	41.0 (N = 71)
Points Served by Mode, Including Routing Authority	73.9 (N = 74)	Possible Future Rate Increases by Mode Due to Higher Fuel Costs	36.2 (N = 70)
Frequency of Service	72.1 (N = 70)	Information Services Offered to Customers	35.0 (N = 69)
Loss and/or Damage Claim Settlement History	69.2 (N = 74)	Consolidation and/or Breakbulk Services	33.9 (N = 70)
Timely Acceptance of Shipments of All Sizes	65.6 (N = 70)	Vulnerability of Mode to Current or Future Energy/Ecology Problems	25.1 (N = 69)
Door-to-Door Delivery	61.9 (N = 70)	Competence of Carrier's Solicitors	24.5 (N = 69)
Shipment Tracing Capability (finding "lost" shipments)	61.8 (N = 73)	Acceptability of Other Organization Members	22.6 (N = 68)
Prompt Claim Service	60.8 (N = 72)	Energy Efficiency (e.g., Fuel Economy) of Mode	21.1 (N = 67)
Adaptability to Specific Shipper Needs	55.5 (N = 72)	Environmental Impact(s) of Mode	11.7 (N = 69)
Availability of Standard Transportation Equipment	50.6 (N = 69)		

SOURCE: Adapted from James R. Stock and Bernard J. LaLonde, "The Transportation Mode Decision Revisited," *Transportation Journal* (Winter, 1977), p. 56.

Note: N stands for sample size, or the number of respondents who selected and ranked a particular criterion.

Consistency of Service

Consistency of service—indicating that the carrier picked up and delivered when promised—is demanded by suppliers because it is an essential aspect of the suppliers' marketing efforts.[10] If the sup-

---

[10] See: P. Ronald Stephenson and Ronald P. Willett, "Consistency: The Carrier's Ace in the Hole," *Transportation Journal* (Spring, 1969), pp. 28–33; Bernard J. LaLonde, John Grabner, and James Robeson, "The Motor Carrier Selection Decision," *National Council of Physical Distribution Management Annual Proceedings* (1971), Section 13; Tom Foster, "How To Grade Your Carriers," *Distribution Worldwide* (June, 1978), pp. 34–39; and James M. Daley and Zarrel V. Lamberg, "Toward Assessing Trade-Offs by Shippers in Carrier Selection Decisions," *Journal of Business Logistics* (Vol. 2, No. 1, 1980), pp. 35–54.

plier does *not* provide delivery to customers when promised, then customers will search for *new* suppliers who will consistently meet delivery promises. (Note the customer blames the seller for the carrier's faults.) On-time delivery is important to customers because inventory holding costs are expensive and consistent delivery schedules allow retailers and other customers to carry smaller inventories.

Freight Charges

Freight rates are an important consideration when choosing among transportation modes. The first edition of this text stated, "They (freight rates) are less critical when selecting a specific carrier within one mode. All regulated carriers within a single mode usually charge the same rate, and they can do so legally." Deregulation has altered the validity of this statement. Today, traffic managers are inundated with carriers willing to quote a lower rate than other regulated carriers in the same mode. This action is known as taking "independent action." Alert traffic managers constantly monitor rate tariffs so that they can quickly detect rate "flag-outs" that they can take advantage of.

- *Independent action,* allowed by laws that authorize carrier rate bureaus, means that the rate set by a bureau *cannot* be made binding on all member carriers. A carrier who sets or maintains a rate different from that set by the bureau is said to be taking independent action or *flagging out* (meaning a "flag" or footnote symbol appears in the bureau's tariff, indicating that a particular carrier is not charging the bureau's rate).

Sears, Roebuck and Company illustrates the advantages to a large shipper of the current rate competition in the transportation industry. George F. Tidmarch, vice-president of physical distribution, stated that Sears has frequently been offered trucking rate discounts of 15 to 20 percent below the standard rate bureau rates. Sears has taken advantage of all rate reductions whenever the quality of carrier service is acceptable. *Business Week* observed, "In a move typical of the new trends in U.S. shipping, Sears has decided to centralize its freight operation and keep track of carriers via computer to make sure it gets the best deals. The expected result will be a cutback to 200 truckers and 10 air forwarders."[11]

---

[11] "Tiger International: Is Its Grand Transportation Plan More Than A Dream?," *Business Week* (April 27, 1981), p. 92.

Delivery Speed

Speed of service is a measure of the time from when a shipment is tendered to a carrier to when the shipment is delivered to the consignee's receiving dock. If there are two competing carriers and both offer consistent service, then a deciding factor will often be the delivery speed. Examples of shipments that require rapid delivery speed are perishable products and emergency shipments of repair parts.

Single-Carrier Service from Origin to Destination

As was mentioned in chapter 5, end-to-end mergers of railroads were occurring in the latter half of the 1970's and the early 1980's. One factor explaining this trend is that shippers prefer single-carrier service and responsibility for the entire shipment. Tracing and collecting loss and damage claims are simpler when only one carrier has handled the haul. Also, single-carrier service typically results in more consistent and faster service than when interlining is nec-

- *Interlining* is movement on one or more connecting lines. It is sometimes called a through movement.

essary. A comprehensive survey of trucking mergers found that single-carrier service and responsibility was a key factor in a shipper's selection of a specific motor common carrier.[12]

Equipment Availability

Equipment availability can be a critical factor when selecting a specific carrier, especially in the railroad industry. When shipping unique products, such as exceptionally large products or heavy machinery, the *Official Railway Equipment Register* is helpful in determining which railroads possess the rail cars capable of doing the job. (See Table 11–2.)

Regular railroad equipment is often in short supply during certain times of the year. In the spring of 1978, there was a serious shortage of freight cars to transport grain and fertilizer. In March, 1978, the railroads had, on a daily average, requests for 13,000 more boxcars, and for 27,000 more covered hopper cars than they could supply.[13] During these shortages, the railroad that can "find" a few

[12] James C. Johnson, *Trucking Mergers* (Lexington, Mass.: D. C. Heath & Co., 1973), Chapters 4 and 5.

[13] Albert Karr, "Railroads, Shippers, ICC Are Wrestling With Worst Grain-Car Shortage in Years," *The Wall Street Journal* (April 10, 1978), p. 16.

TABLE 11–2 Sample Page from Official Railway Equipment Register Showing Car Dimensions and Capacity

					DIMENSIONS										CAPACITY		
				INSIDE			OUTSIDE							DOORS				
							Length	Width		Height from Rail				Side				
A.A.R. Mech. Desig.	DESCRIPTION	A.A.R. Car Type Code	NUMBERS	Length	Width	Height	At Eaves or Top of Sides or Platform	Extreme Width	To Extreme Width	To Eaves or Top of Sides or Platform	To Extreme Height	Width of Open'g	Height of Open'g	Cubic Feet Level Full	Lbs. (000)	No. of Cars
	See Explanation Pages for Abbreviations & Symbols		▶*Change from Previous Issue*	ft. in.	ft. in.	ft. in.	ft. in.	ft. in.	ft. in.	ft. in.	ft. in.	ft. in.	ft. in.			
	"GM&O"															
HTS	Hop., Wood Chip . . . . E	K240	▶ 866300–866399	56 1	10 1	. . . .	59 9	10 3	10 8	14 8	15	15	16	10	5748	154	97
	"IC"															
LP	Wood Rack, Axle Spac. 5'8", Truck Ctrs. 43'10"	L027	1000–1999	50	9 3	8	57 5	9 2	9 3	4	12	12				162	974
GBS	Gond., Sides & Ends Height Increased, (Corn Cobs), 25K, Axle Spac. 5'6", Truck Ctrs. 30'6 1/4" . . . . F	E130	2100–2199	41	9 6	11 1	45 4	10 4	10 5	9 4	15 6	15 6	. . . .		4337	110	78
GBS	Gond., Sides & Ends Height Increased, (Corn Cobs), 25K, Axle Spac. 5'6", Truck Ctrs. 30'6 1/4" . . . . ■C	E130	2200–2236	41	9 6	10	45 4	10 4	10 5	9 4	14 6	14 6	. . . .		3923	110	16
GBS	Gond., Sides & Ends Height Increased, (Scrap Auto Bodies), 25K, Axle Spac. 5'6", Truck Ctrs. 30'6 1/4" C	E130	2220	41	9 6	10	45 4	10 4	10 5	9 4	14 6	14 6	. . . .		3923	110	1
GBS	Gond., Sides & Ends Height Increased, (Corn Cobs), 25K, Axle Spac. 5'6", Truck Ctrs. 30'6 1/4" . . . . F	E130	2250–2299	41	9 6	11 1	45 4	10 4	10 5	9 4	15 6	15 6	. . . .		4337	110	36
GB	Gond., Fixed Ends, (Logs), 25K, Axle Spac. 5'6", Truck Ctrs. 30'6 1/4"	G112	2300–2499	41	9 6	4 7	45 4	10 4	10 5	4 4	9 4	9 4	. . . .		1785	100	134
XM	Box, 25K . . . . ■	B107	▶ 3000–4999	40 6	9 2	10 6	44 4	9 5	10 8	5 8	14 6	15 1	8	9 10	3898	100	104

SOURCE: Courtesy, *The Official Railway Equipment Register* ® and © 1977 N.R.P. Co.

extra cars for the shipper will be favorably remembered at a later, and less hectic, time.

One solution to periodic rail-car shortages is for the traffic manager to negotiate with the railroad for the railroad to provide specific cars that are designated only for use by the particular shipper.[14] These cars are then said to be in "exclusive service" and become known as "assigned cars." An example of this is the 190 new, 62½-foot, fully-insulated rail cars that Conrail purchased to serve exclusively the Joseph Schlitz Brewing Company. These 190 special cars cost Conrail $9.3 million and brought Conrail's fleet of Schlitz assigned equipment to 2,413 cars. From the railroad's viewpoint, the advantage of exclusive usage cars is better car utilization. The shipper must prove to the carrier that with exclusive usage cars, it will be able to schedule shipments that will result in each car moving more loaded miles than would be the case without exclusive equipment. Railroads are impressed with this argument, because it allows them to use their car fleet more efficiently.

[14] James E. Hendricks, "A Study of Exclusive Use Service," *Transportation Journal* (Fall, 1967), pp. 50–56.

Transit Privileges

Transit privileges allow a load of traffic to be stopped en route between its initial origin and ultimate destination, and to be unloaded, stored, and/or processed and then reloaded for shipment to its final destination. The key to understanding transit privileges is the concept of *tapering rates*, which apply to all modes of transport. As seen

- *Tapering rates*, expressed in terms of cents per ton or per passenger, increase as distance increases, but not as much. That is, in terms of percentage increases, they increase less than the increase in miles.

in Figure 11–5 the rate increases with distance, but increases at a slower rate. A shipment from City A to City B, 200 miles, pays a rate of $2.90 per hundred weight, while a shipment twice as long from City A to City C pays only $4.10 per hundred weight instead of double the 200-mile rate. The logic of tapering rates is that some costs do not increase with distance. This would include most terminal operation costs, billing costs, and pickup and delivery costs. Therefore, as distance increases, these costs are spread over more miles, allowing the rate to increase proportionately less than the distance.

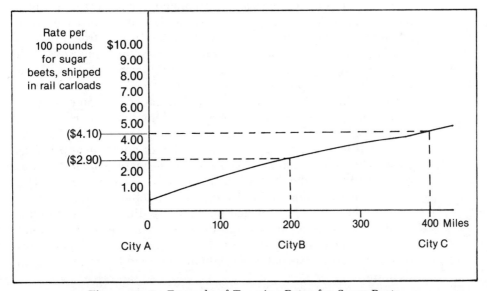

Figure 11–5   Example of Tapering Rates for Sugar Beets.

Assume City A in Figure 11–5 is in the center of a sugar beet producing area. A sugar beet dealer purchases sugar beets at relatively low prices in City A during harvest time, stores them, and then is lucky enough to resell them at City C where prices are much higher. The merchant must decide where to store the sugar beets. Figure 11–5 illustrates that logically the storage point should be either City A or City C but *not* in between. Why? Because with tapering rates, one long shipment is less costly than two shorter trips equal in distance to the long trip. Notice that storage in City A or City C results in one long shipment at $4.10 per CWT. If storage were at City B, the result would be a 200-mile shipment at $2.90. When the storage period ended, a second 200-mile shipment to City C would also cost $2.90 for a total transportation cost of $5.80. In other words, a decision to store at City B and ship twice would cost $1.70 per CWT more than storing at either City A or City C and shipping only once.

The result of the tapering rate structure is to keep freight moving and to discourage stopping, storing, or doing anything to the freight en route. This discourages producing intermediate goods or otherwise processing the product at any point between City A and City C. Railroads, in an attempt to disperse storage and other activities— often onto land that they own because of the federal land grant program—initiated the *transit privilege* concept. It allows products or raw materials to be shipped to an intermediate location, where they can be stored, compressed, blended, mixed, milled, inspected, refined, reconditioned, fabricated, assembled, etc. The regular freight rate is the rate from origin to the intermediate location. Then, generally up to one year later, the products can be shipped from this intermediate location to destination and only pay the *remainder* of the long-haul through rate. In Figure 11–5, $2.90 per CWT is paid from City A to City B. Upon shipment from City B to City C, only $1.20 per CWT is paid, so that eventually the total transportation cost equals $4.10 per CWT, which is the same as the long-haul rate from City A to City C.

This is a *greatly simplified* explanation of how transit privileges work. They are a complex aspect of traffic management; there are traffic managers who work exclusively in this demanding area. (Just three of many complicating factors are rate changes during the interim period; rates for finished products are different than the rates for the raw materials used as production inputs; or the total weight of the products leaving the intermediate point can be significantly less or greater than what was originally shipped to the intermediate location.)

Documentation

The traffic department prepares all the documentation involved in transporting the firm's products. By far the most important single document is the *bill-of-lading*—which is the basic document when shipping by common carriers.

The bill-of-lading performs three functions. First, it is the *receipt* for shipments tendered to the carrier. The carrier's driver after receiving the freight, signs the bill-of-lading and gives the original to the shipper. This signed receipt is the shipper's proof that the carrier received the freight.

The second function of the bill-of-lading is that it contains the *contract* specifying the duties and obligations of both the carrier and the shipper. By law, the bill-of-lading contract for surface common carriers is *standardized,* which of course helps simplify the traffic manager's job because he or she knows the obligations of the shipper and the duties of the carrier.

The third function is that in some forms the bill-of-lading serves as evidence of title to the goods described and being shipped. On an order *bill-of-lading,* the name of the consignee is not specified. When an order bill-of-lading is used, it also serves as *evidence of title* to the goods. As an example, consider an agricultural cooperative in Jacksonville, Florida, which has loaded a boxcar of oranges it had not yet sold. The cooperative would use an order bill-of-lading, tender the shipment to the Southern Railway, and would ask that the car be sent toward Cincinnati. The cooperative would try to sell the oranges and once a buyer for the oranges was found, the cooperative would send via first class mail the original copy of the order bill to a bank near the buyer and would simultaneously notify the buyer as to the name of the bank. The buyer would go to the bank and upon his paying for the oranges the bank would surrender to him the original copy of the order bill-of-lading. The buyer would take it to the Southern Railway, which would then deliver the carload of oranges to the holder of the order bill. Order bills-of-lading are *negotiable instruments*—this means that the purchaser can sell the products to another party and surrender the original copy of the order bill to transfer title to the products. (Order bills are used in one other situation, that involving slow-paying customers, because the order bill-of-lading guarantees that the customer pays for the products prior to receipt.)

Another bill-of-lading is called the *straight bill of lading.* On a straight bill (Figure 11–6) the name of the consignee is entered in the

UNIFORM FREIGHT CLASSIFICATION 7

(Uniform Domestic Straight Bill of Lading, adopted by Carriers in Official and Western Classification territories, March 15, 1922, as amended August 1, 1930, and June 15, 1941.)

UNIFORM STRAIGHT BILL OF LADING

Original—Not Negotiable

Shipper's No..........

(To be Printed on "White" Paper)

Agent's No............

Company

RECEIVED, subject to the classifications and tariffs in effect on the date of the issue of this Bill of Lading,

at.., 19...

from...

the property described below, in apparent good order, except as noted (contents and condition of contents of packages unknown), marked, consigned, and destined as indicated below, which said company (the word company being understood throughout this contract as meaning any person or corporation in possession of the property under the contract) agrees to carry to its usual place of delivery at said destination, if on its own road or its own water line, otherwise to deliver to another carrier on the route to said destination. It is mutually agreed, as to each carrier of all or any of said property over all or any portion of said route to destination, and as to each party at any time interested in all or any of said property, that every service to be performed hereunder shall be subject to all the conditions not prohibited by law, whether printed or written, herein contained, including the conditions on back hereof, which are hereby agreed to by the shipper and accepted for himself and his assigns.

(Mail or street address of consignee—For purposes of notification only.)

Consigned to...

Destination...State of.........................County of....................

Route..

Delivering Carrier.............................Car Initial.....................Car No.................

No. Pack-ages	Description of Articles, Special Marks, and Exceptions	*Weight (Subject to Correction)	Class or Rate	Check Column	Subject to Section 7 of conditions, if this shipment is to be delivered to the consignee without recourse on the consignor, the consignor shall sign the following statement:
					The carrier shall not make delivery of this shipment without payment of freight and all other lawful charges.
					(Signature of consignor.)
					If charges are to be prepaid, write or stamp here, "To be Prepaid."
					Received $............ to apply in prepayment of the charges on the property described hereon.
					Agent or Cashier.
					Per.................... (The signature here acknowledges only the amount prepaid.)

*If the shipment moves between two ports by a carrier by water, the law requires that the bill of lading shall state whether it is "carrier's or shipper's weight."

Note.—Where the rate is dependent on value, shippers are required to state specifically in writing the agreed or declared value of the property.

The agreed or declared value of the property is hereby specifically stated by the shipper to be not exceeding

Charges advanced:

$......................

....per.

....Shipper.   ....Agent.

Per..   Per..

Permanent postoffice address of shipper...

Reproduced by permission of tariff publisher.

Figure 11–6   A Long-Form Straight Bill-of-Lading (Front Side). Reproduced by permission of the Uniform Classification Committee.

appropriate place and the carrier is under a strict legal obligation to deliver the freight to the named consignee, and to no one else. Ownership of the goods is neither stated nor implied.

An additional classification of bills is the specific form—long, short, and preprinted. The *long-form bill-of-lading*, which may be either an order or straight bill, contains the standard information; that is, the particulars to be written in, on the front of the bill; the reverse side contains the entire contract. Because of the difficulty of reading the long-form contract and the high printing costs of including the contract on all bills, the railroads and motor carriers in 1949 adopted the *short-form bill-of-lading*. Instead of printing the entire contract on the back of the bill, the short form has the following statement on its face: "Every service to be performed hereunder shall be subject to all terms and conditions of the Uniform Domestic Straight Bill of Lading. . . ."

Another type of bill, which may be a long, short, order, or straight, is *preprinted*. In theory, the bill-of-lading is prepared and issued by the carrier. In fact, however, many shippers buy their bills and then have them preprinted with a list of the products that they regularly ship. Figure 11–7 illustrates a preprinted, short-form, straight bill-of-lading. Why would shippers go to the expense of buying and printing their own bills? The answer is that in practice, shippers frequently prepare their own bills before notifying the carrier. The preprinted bill can be prepared more rapidly and with less chance for error. The shipper can insert the correct classification or rate rather than let the carrier determine it. Preprinted forms may also be designed to be compatible with the shipper's computerized records system, which is the purpose of the small boxes at the bottom of Figure 11–7. Note that there is also a column for indicating whether the product is "hazardous."

The other basic document that the traffic manager must be familiar with is the *freight bill*. It is an invoice, submitted by the carrier, requesting payment. Usually the traffic manager approves each freight bill before it is paid by the accounting department.

The discussion in this section focused on common carrier documents. When using "contract" carriers, which will happen more frequently under deregulated transportation, it is likely that two bargaining options will evolve. The first will be that the bill-of-lading contract conditions hold, and the only item to be bargained is the transportation charges. The second option would be bargaining to include *both* the charges and the other elements in the contract dealing mainly with the carrier's other obligations (such as liability for damaged goods).

NAME OF CARRIER	SHIPPERS NUMBER MUST APPEAR ON ALL FREIGHT BILLS ▼

STRAIGHT BILL OF LADING – SHORT FORM – ORIGINAL – Not Negotiable

RECEIVED, subject to the classifications and tariffs in effect on the date of the issue of this Bill of Lading.

SHIPPER'S NO.
104214
CARRIER'S NO.

FROM **Scherer** MEDICAL AND SCIENTIFIC   AT   DATE   19
(Mail or street address of consignee---For purposes of notification only.)

CONSIGNED TO

DESTINATION   STATE   COUNTY
(To be filled in only when shipper desires and governing tariffs provide for delivery thereat.)

DELIVERY ADDRESS

ROUTE   DELIVERING CARRIER   VEHICLE OR CAR INITIAL & NO.

No. Packages	HAZ MAT.	KIND OF PACKAGE, DESCRIPTION OF ARTICLES, SPECIAL MARKS, AND EXCEPTIONS	*Weight (Sub. to Corr.)	Class or Rate	Ck. Col.
	NMFC				
	42690	Alcohol, including Isopropyl		65	
	56480	Bandages or Dressings		100	
	56490	Bandages or Splints, plaster of paris		70	
	56560	Containers, blood collecting, Vacutainers		70	
	56600	Crutches		100	
	56710	Drapes, Sheets, Pillow Cases, Towels, disposable		77½	
	56835	Pads or Swabs, saturated with rubbing alcohol		70	
	56950	Swabs, not medicated, wood, paper, plastic or cotton		70	
	56960	Syringes, expendable, plastic, with or w/o needles		100	
	56970	Tape, adhesive, in rolls		77½	
	56980	Tongue depressing blades or Swab applicators		70	
	57260	Diapers, Diaper Liners, Bedding Pads, cellulose		100	
	59380	Solutions or distilled water, intravenous		55	
	60000	Drugs, Medicines, Toilet Preps, release value 50¢/lb.		70	
	60000	Chemicals, NOI, release value 50¢/lb.		70	
	86770	Glass, microscopical slide or cover		70	
	88120	Glassware, laboratory		100	
	98375	Caps or hats, paper, folded flat		85	
	153900	Paper goods, folded flat		85	
	156720	Containers, plastic, nested, under 16 oz. capacity		77½	
	156850	Gloves, plastic or rubber		85	

Subject to Section 7 of Conditions of applicable bill of lading, if this shipment is to be delivered to the consignee without recourse on the consignor, the consignor shall sign the following statement:
The carrier shall not make delivery of this shipment without payment of freight and all other lawful charges.

_____
(Signature of Consignor.)

If charges are to be prepaid, write or stamp here, "To be Prepaid."

TO BE PREPAID

Rec'd $ _____ to apply in prepayment of the charges on the property described hereon.

_____
Agent or Cashier

Per _____
(The signature here acknowledges only the amount prepaid.)

Charges Advanced $ _____

"Shipper's imprint in lieu of stamp; not a part of bill of lading approved by the Interstate Commerce Commission."

The Fibre Boxes used for this shipment conform to the specifications set forth in the box maker's certificate thereon, and all other requirements of Rule 41 of the Consolidated Freight Classification.

C.O.D.

*If the shipment moves between two ports by a carrier by water, the law requires that the bill of lading shall state whether it is "carrier's or shipper's weight."
NOTE—Where the rate is dependent on value, shippers are required to state specifically in writing the agreed or declared value of the property.
The agreed or declared value of the property is hereby specifically stated by the shipper to be not exceeding
per

Scherer MEDICAL AND SCIENTIFIC Shipper, Per _____   Agent, Per _____

CHECK & FILL IN ONE: →	FREIGHT TO CUSTOMER 62 77450	FREIGHT RETURN TO MANUFACTURER 62 77550	INTERHOUSE FREIGHT 62 77650	FILL IN: →	REGION NO.
FORM 6012	ACCOUNT NUMBER		9 9 9 ACCOUNT NUMBER		

Figure 11–7 Preprinted Bill-of-Lading. Courtesy: William C. McCaughey, Director of Traffic and Transportation, Bergen Brunswig Corporation.

Carrier Routing

The top sections of the forms shown in Figures 11–6 and 11–7 have a line entitled *route*. A rail shipper has an absolute right to route shipments to their destinations; that is, he can select the carriers for the shipment's entire route. This provision was added to the original 1887 *Act To Regulate Commerce* by the *Mann-Elkins Act* in 1910. The purpose was to permit the shipper to patronize certain rail carriers that did not happen to serve the origin city. The rule for routing via common carrier truckers is slightly different. The trucker can refuse to accept a shipment with specific routing instructions. However, if a trucker signs the bill which specifies routing, the instructions must be followed.

Should the traffic manager specify routing instructions on the bill-of-lading? A helpful rule in determining whether to specify routing is that in the absence of any shipping directions, the carrier is legally obligated to use the least expensive route. As a general statement, it is best *not* to specify routing instructions unless there is a good reason to do so. Railroads often work out expeditious interchange agreements with other railways at junction points which insure rapid transfer of the freight from one carrier to the next. This is also true of motor carriers.[15]

Shippers generally choose routings to give business to carriers they prefer. Some years ago, General Motors routed its traffic over lines that had purchased GM-built diesel locomotives. Shippers also may pick a slow routing if they have a temporary oversupply of inventory moving through their distribution system.

Loss and Damage Claim Processing

"Cargo loss and damage has been the bane of the transportation industry since the invention of the wheel."[16] Claims for lost and damaged freight cost the carriers and shippers annually somewhere between $8 *billion* and $13 *billion*.[17] Direct carrier to shipper payments for losses are, by mode: trucking (common, contract, private and exempt)—66 percent; rail—25 percent; maritime—7 per-

---

[15] Kenneth U. Flood, *Traffic Management*, 3rd ed. (Dubuque, Iowa: Wm. C. Brown Company, 1975), Chapter 9. See also: Tom Dulaney, "Computers Turn On To Rating and Routing," *Distribution* (March, 1981), pp. 55–58.

[16] Carlo J. Salzano, *Traffic World* (April 7, 1975).

[17] U.S. Senate Select Committee on Small Business, Cargo Theft Joint Conference, Part 4 (1971).

cent; and air—2 percent.[18] Many of the "paperwork" costs fall on the shipper's traffic department.

Both carriers and shippers want to reduce freight loss and damage claims. For carriers, claims are a serious profit drain. H. D. Knudson of the Burlington Northern Railroad noted, "Every dollar that carriers pay out in loss and damage claims is a profit dollar. Figuring at a six percent profit, for every $100 paid out in claims the marketing department has to generate approximately $1,700 of new business."[19] Shippers dislike loss and damage claims because they are expensive to process and, more importantly, frequently cause stock-outs.

An alarming aspect of loss and damage (L&D) is that from 1969 to 1978, losses from theft, pilferage, and vandalism for the nation's carriers increased 480 percent! This parallels the recent national trend in all kinds of crime which is increasing at a rate many times faster than the population increase.

Common carriers traditionally were slow in handling loss and damage claims. Therefore, in 1972 the ICC issued a new regulation which placed three requirements on all surface common carriers: (1) common carriers must acknowledge receipt of each claim within 30 days; (2) carriers are charged with the responsibility of promptly investigating the claim; and (3) all claims either must be resolved within 120 days of their receipt, or the claimant must be given a written explanation as to the reasons why the carrier has neither paid nor officially rejected it.

Assume that the carrier and the shipper are not able to resolve a dispute regarding a surface carrier loss and damage claim. What then? Loss and damage claims are handled by the court system, not by the ICC. The law states that the claimant has nine months from the date the shipment is delivered to file a claim with a carrier. If the carrier and claimant cannot settle the issue, then the claimant has two years and one day from the date the claim is denied (in whole or in part) to file a claim in the appropriate Federal District Court. If the claim is not filed within this time period, no further action can be taken against the carrier. Table 11–3 is a summary of the time limits for filing loss and damage claims on all types of freight shipments.

---

[18] W. Bruce Allen, "The Impact of Transport Loss and Damage on Transportation Demand," *Transportation Research Forum Annual Proceedings* (Oxford, Indiana: Richard B. Cross, 1973), p. 605.

[19] "Freight Loss and Damage and Carrier Profits," *Traffic World* (August 7, 1978), p. 1.

TABLE 11–3 Time Limits for Filing Freight Claims

Time Limits For Filing on Shipments Moving in Interstate or Foreign Commerce						
	Claims				Suits	
VIA	Loss Damage or Delay	Concealed Damage	Non-Delivery	Overcharges	Loss, Damage or Delay	Overcharges f/
Air Freight (Domestic)	9 months & 9 days from shipping date (see exceptions) a/	Report in Writing within 15 days of delivery	9 months & 9 days from shipping date (see exceptions) a/	2 years from shipping date (see exceptions) a/	2 years from disallowance of claim	2 years from delivery or 6 months from disallowance, whichever is later
Air Freight (International)	Damage 7 days from delivery Delay 14 days	7 days from delivery	120 days from shipping date. b/	2 years from arrival or scheduled arrival	2 years from arrival or scheduled arrival	2 years from arrival or scheduled arrival
		NOTE: Under Investigation by CAB.				
Air Freight Forwarder	No Uniform Rules—Consult Individual Tariffs of Forwarder Used Before Selecting Forwarder				No Uniform Rules—Consult Individual Tariffs of Forwarder Used Before Selecting Forwarder	
Bus	9 months from delivery	If written notice not given within 15 days of delivery, claimant has burden of proving it did not cause the damage. c/	9 months and 15 days from shipping date	3 years from delivery	2 years plus 1 day from disallowance of claim	3 years from delivery or 6 months from disallowance, whichever is later. h/
Rail	9 months from delivery	If written notice not given within 15 days of delivery, claimant has burden of proving it did not cause the damage. c/	9 months after a "reasonable time" for delivery	3 years from delivery	2 years plus 1 day from disallowance of claim	3 years from delivery or 6 months from disallowance, whichever is later. h/
Steamship	1 year from delivery or scheduled delivery	Report in Writing within 3 days of delivery	1 year from scheduled delivery	2 years from shipping date or payment of charges whichever is later. d/	1 year from delivery unless extended in writing	6 months from shipping date or payment of charges, whichever is later, unless formal complaint filed with Federal Maritime Commission within 2 yrs. d/
Truck and Freight Forwarders	9 months from delivery	If written notice not given within 15 days of delivery, claimant has burden of proving it did not cause the damage. c/	9 months after a "reasonable time" for delivery	3 years from delivery	2 years plus 1 day from disallowance of claim	3 years from delivery or 6 months from disallowance, whichever is later. h/
UPS	9 months from acceptance by UPS	If written notice n..t given within 15 days of delivery, claimant has burden of proving it did not cause the damage. c/	9 months from acceptance by UPS	3 years from delivery	2 years plus 1 day from disallowance of claim	3 years from delivery or 6 months from disallowance, whichever is later. h/

a/Exceptions filed for account of individual airlines in CAB No. 96, Official Air Freight Rules Tariff No. 1-B, Rule 60.
b/Airbill provision, but not authorized in Warsaw Convention.

c/Former rules requiring notice in writing within 15 days held UNLAWFUL in Ex Parte 263, 340 ICC 515,536-7.
d/Tariff rule requiring claims for adjustment of weights or measurement errors to be made before shipment leaves custody of carrier held UNLAWFUL by U.S. Coun .f Appeals in Dist. of Col. 7/13/76.
e/Applies only to common carriers. For contract carriers and exempt commodity shipments, see individual contracts, if any, and/or state statutes.
f/Also applies to filing complaints with the ICC against surface carriers.
h/The extra 6 month period starts from the first disallowance by the carrier following the last resubmission of the claim by the claimant within the claim filing period. If the carrier brings an action to collect charges or collects same, an additional 90 days is granted from that date.

SOURCE: Courtesy, *Distribution Worldwide* (June, 1977), pp. 38–39.

Determination of Freight Claim Damage

One of the most difficult aspects of claims work is determining the exact dollar amount of the damage. The law states that the common carrier is responsible for the *full actual loss* sustained by the shipper or consignee. How can this figure be determined? A common rule of thumb is:

> The basic thought underlying the federal statutes which define the liability and prescribe the measure of damages in cases of this kind is that the owner shall be made whole by receiving the proper money equivalent for what he has actually lost, or, in other words *to restore him to the position he would have occupied, had the carrier performed its contract.* (Emphasis added.)[20]

[20] Richard R. Sigmon, *Miller's Law of Freight Loss and Damage Claims*, 3rd ed. (Dubuque, Iowa: Wm. C. Brown Co., 1967), p. 141.

A key factor in determining the value of the "full actual loss" is the word *earned*. Assume that a retailer owned the products shipped via a surface common carrier and that they were damaged beyond repair. The question arises, Should the retailer recover the wholesale price or the retail price? If the products destroyed were going into a general inventory replacement stock, the retailer would receive only the wholesale price plus freight costs (if they were paid) because the retail price had not been *earned*. Assume, instead, that a product is ordered especially for a customer. When the product arrives, it turns out to be damaged, and the retailer's customer cancels the order. In this situation, the retailer is entitled to the retail price because the profit would have been *earned* if the carrier had properly performed its service.

Concealed Loss and Damage

Another difficult area for shippers and carriers alike involves *concealed* loss or damage. If a shipment arrives in obviously damaged condition, the consignee either refuses the goods or makes a notation of the damage on the delivery receipt. Because the damage is clearly evident, the issue is not whether the carrier is liable but the dollar amount of the claim that the carrier must pay. However, concealed loss and damage situations are more difficult to determine; often the exterior package does not appear to be damaged or tampered with but the damage is within the package. Only when the consignee opens the package is the damage or loss discovered. As can be appreciated, carriers are reluctant to pay all concealed loss and damage claims for two reasons. If the package came through the shipment with no exterior damage, then there is a strong possibility that the product was improperly protected within the package. If this is the case, the carrier is exempted from liability, since improper packaging is a *fault of the shipper*. Another reason for the carrier's reluctance is the possibility that the consignee's employees broke or stole the products.

Freight Claim Prevention

Another important aspect of the traffic manager's job is to see that the freight is packaged, handled, and transported in such a way that loss and damage claims won't occur. The traffic manager has a very willing partner in the effort—the carrier who would have to pay loss and damage claims.

The railroad industry has been active in assisting traffic managers to solve this joint problem. Their efforts have been successful. In 1975, railroads paid out 1.83 percent of their total freight revenues for freight claims; this ratio dropped to 1.36 percent in 1976 and to 1.29 percent in 1977. The Soo Line Railroad is a leader in L&D prevention. Jim Leaf, manager of freight damage prevention, noted, "We concentrate just about our entire effort on the shippers. We know the shippers well enough that they'll call us when they have a problem. We're constantly reviewing our shippers to find out where we should spend our time."[21] In the first third of 1978 the Soo Line had a pay-out ratio on freight claims of 0.48 percent of total revenues.

Another example of joint cooperation to reduce freight claims is a major food shipper who was experiencing more than 100 damaged cartons per carload on the Southern Railway. Jim Cox, director of freight claim services for the Southern, and the shipper's traffic manager jointly analyzed the problem and decided to change the product's protective packaging. While each new carton was somewhat more expensive than those previously utilized, the result was that only two cartons were damaged in the first five carloads. The shipper was more than satisfied, recognizing that a classic PD/L cost trade-off had been utilized. Packaging costs increased, but the savings from reduced loss and damage was greater than the increased costs.

Motor common carriers are also striving to reduce loss and damage. Ninety percent of common carrier trucking company losses happen at freight terminals. While hijackings of entire trucks are dramatic events, these in-transit thefts amount to only 10 percent of total losses. Terminal theft, according to insurance company claim records, is concentrated in nine commodity categories which account for 80 percent of losses. These categories are clothing, electrical appliances, automotive parts, food products, hardware, jewelry, tobacco products, scientific instruments, and alcoholic beverages.[22] In order to thwart theft from terminals, trucking companies are using more electronic technology, such as closed-circuit television surveillance equipment, ultrasonic and microwave alarm systems which detect movement, and limited-access control systems.

Shippers are also actively involved in reducing loss and damage claims. They are using better protective packaging and are blocking and bracing their products more effectively within rail cars or trail-

---

[21] "How Rail-Shipper and Rail-Rail Cooperation Cuts Damage Losses," *Railway Age* (June 26, 1978), p. 39.

[22] Miklos B. Korodi, "Stop Thief!" *Distribution Worldwide* (December, 1974), p. 47.

ers to prevent them from moving and shifting during transportation. For this purpose inflatable dunnage bags are often utilized. In addi-

- *Dunnage* is any material used to brace a load into place and to keep products from shifting while being carried. An *inflatable dunnage bag* looks like a heavy-duty air mattress. After an entire rail car or trailer is loaded with cartons or loaded pallets, an uninflated dunnage bag is slipped between two rows of cartons, and then is inflated. When inflated, it expands to a size where it exerts pressure on the entire load of cartons, making them "keep in their place" during the entire trip. At the consignee's dock, the air bag is deflated before unloading can begin.

tion, many shippers are using sophisticated computer programs to spot situations where repetitive incidents of damage occur. Sometimes a flaw in the packaging is discovered, although in one instance a defect in rail track was discovered. The track defect set up a pattern of damaging vibrations within the rail cars if the train traveled at certain speeds.

Freight Claim Arbitration

As was stated previously, if the shipper and carrier cannot satisfactorily resolve a claim, the shipper's only recourse is to start a legal action against the carrier in the appropriate state or federal court. Lawsuits, by their nature, are expensive and time-consuming. An alternative that is growing in acceptance is *binding arbitration*. A 1978 survey indicated that 16 percent of traffic managers had used arbitration to settle rail loss and damage claims.[23]

- An *arbitrator* is an outsider who is retained by both parties to a dispute. He listens to both sides and renders a decision which he believes is "fair" to both parties. In *binding arbitration*, the disputing parties agree beforehand to abide by the arbitrator's decision.

Railroads use the American Arbitration Association, which randomly assigns an arbitrator to each dispute. Once both parties to the dispute agree to arbitration, the arbitrator's decision is final. Motor common carriers created the Transportation Arbitration Board (TAB) in November, 1976. Unlike rail arbitration, the truckers use two arbitrators per dispute, one from the shipper's side and one from the carrier's. Anthony Quattrochi, corporate claims supervisor at Pfizer,

---

[23]"What Shippers Are Saying About L & D," *Railway Age* (May 29, 1978), p. 46.

Inc., and cochairman of TAB, notes that arbitration appears to be working—although perhaps not exactly in the way it was planned.

> Quite frankly, we are surprised that we are not deluged with claims. In assessing this situation we found that when shippers requested arbitration, carriers paid the claims in question soon after the suggestion was made. Similarly, carriers heard nothing more after they suggested arbitration when they reached an impasse with shippers. So TAB is working—if not by resolving claim disputes directly then in an indirect manner.[24]

When TAB decisions are finalized, a summary of the case is made available to the public. Figure 11–8 is a summary of a TAB case involving missing car stereo/tape players.

Tracing and Expediting

Tracing is a procedure to locate lost or late shipments. When it is determined that a shipment has not arrived at destination on time, the traffic department will contact the carrier to whom it tendered the shipment and ask them to "trace" it. This is a no-cost service offered by common carriers. Tracing should be requested only when a shipment is unusually late. Many of the airlines, large trucking companies, and almost all of the railroads have computer systems that monitor the progress of all freight movements throughout their systems or at least know where it "should" be. Figure 11–9 is an advertisement for the Southern Pacific railroad illustrating direct shipper-to-railroad communication via computer.

Expediting is another no-cost service of common carriers. It involves the shipper notifying the carrier as far in advance as possible of the need to "expedite" a shipment, which means that the shipper wants a specific shipment to move through a carrier's system as quickly as possible and with no delays. The carrier must have sufficient lead time to alert its employees regarding the specific shipment being expedited. For the railroads this involves alerting the yardmaster at each classification yard so that the expedited car can be singled out when it arrives and immediately switched to the proper outbound train. Motor carriers generally notify the operations manager of each freight terminal to make certain that he personally sees that the shipment is transferred directly to the next outbound truck.

---

[24]Stephen Tinghitella, "Freight Claims: An Overview," *Traffic Management* (September, 1977), p. 59. See also: William J. Augello, "Is Arbitration Working?" *Distribution Worldwide* (August, 1979), pp. 38–39.

A CLEAR DELIVERY RECEIPT WON THE CASE (TAB Case 138)

FACTS: On October 6, 1978 Pickwick International (P.I.) shipped 15 cartons to Musicland, Joliet, IL on their bill of lading #10037 via Mid-American Lines. The shipment was picked up without exception and delivered on October 10, 1978 without exception on Mid-American pro #302087821. The following day the driver was asked to verify the discrepancy. An inspection was performed on October 17, 1978. P.I. filed a claim for $728.85 representing the loss of 5 car stereo/tape players missing from three cartons that had been retaped with non-pilfer proof tape. The carrier declined the claim and both parties agreed to arbitration.

CONTENTIONS: The claimant contends that the delivery records were not clear. According to an affidavit signed by William Sletteland, Store Manager, he personally observed 3 cartons had been tampered with and retaped with non-pilfer tape. He noted his receipt, "called for inspection for concealed pilferage." Musicland also contends the signature on the carrier's receipt is not recognized as a representative of the Joliet, IL Musicland. Based on these assumptions, they claim the carrier's premise of alleged clear delivery is not sustainable. Other affidavits establish that the cartons were each sealed with P.I.'s pilfer proof tape at time of pick up. And at time of delivery, 3 of the 15 cartons were resealed with non-pilfer proof tape.

The carrier contends that the shipment was picked up and delivered without exceptions. Their receipt signed by Jodi Dranak and the driver, E. Joslin on October 10, 1978 was clear of exceptions. Their brief explains the tape used to recouper the tampered cartons is not that used by Mid-American. They have a program of using two types of tape which is kept under a controlled situation and a policy of dismissing employees using any other type of tape. They feel P.I.'s concern for pilferage of their products should have resulted in exceptions at time of delivery if they were evident. Although Mid-American Lines does not know when or where the shortage occurred, they do hold that it did not occur while in their possession.

DISCUSSION: Both briefs are filled with discrepancies as to the dates involved, particularly on the date of shipment. The date has no bearing on the outcome nor do any other mistaken dates. The important fact is the clear receipt at time of delivery. The delivery accomplished on October 10, 1978 was signed without exception as evidenced by the carrier's record of delivery. Their receipt signed by Jodi Dranak (for consignee) and E. Joslin (driver) and dated is complete without any notation. The consignee's record shows a notation that they called for inspection for concealed damage but is not signed by the driver.

William Sletteland's affidavit attempts to establish that exceptions were taken at the time of delivery. Mr. Sletteland's name does not appear on the carrier's receipt which would indicate he was not present at that time. The wording on the recipt, "called for inspection for concealed pilferage" has the connotation of being placed on their copy some time after delivery. A more appropriate notation at the time of delivery would be something more descriptive of the situation such as "3 cartons tampered and resealed" or "3 cartons opened and resealed before delivery."

A consignee noting possible pilferage or damage has the right to open those pieces showing evidence of loss or damage in the presence of the driver. It would seem as the store manager so noting tampered cartons would insist on this being performed before signing rather than waiting until the following day, as the facts indicate. P.I. seems highly concerned about pilferage as evidenced by the use of pilter proof tape. Also, the affidavit of the shipping clerk further substantiates this concern. It seems strange that immediate inspection was not requested. Further, the briefs nor inspection report indicate when the inspection was requested, as it was performed on October 17, 1978.

The claimant's brief attempts to disclaim the signature of Jodi Dranak as a representative of Musicland. Yet, they do not state that Jodi Dranak is not employed by Musicland.

CONCLUSION: Based on the discrepancies between the copies of the delivery receipts, the fact that the consignee failed to request an immediate inspection, the arbitrators are of the opinion that the carrier's prima facie case of non-negligence has not been offset.

DECISION: The arbitrators find the carrier, Mid-American Lines, not responsible for the alleged shortage and that both parties absorb their own arbitration costs.

Figure 11–8 A Transportation Arbitration Board Case. Source: *Distribution* (May, 1980), p. 62.

Demurrage and Detention

Demurrage is a penalty payment made by the shipper or consignee to a railroad for keeping a rail car beyond the specific length of time when it should be released back to the carrier. Demurrage is also collected by inland water carriers if their barges are kept by the shipper or consignee for a longer period than allowed. Pipelines are also

Figure 11–9 Ad About Carrier Tracing Via Computer. Courtesy: Southern Pacific Transportation Company, San Francisco, California.

involved with demurrage if oil stored in tanks at destination is not removed within specified time limits.

Detention is basically the same concept as demurrage, except that detention usually refers to the trucking industry. Users of containers owned by the airlines are subject to similar charges.

For many traffic managers, handling demurrage and detention are important responsibilities. The rail demurrage tariffs typically state that demurrage payments will start after the expiration of the applicable "free-time." For most cars, the receiver or consignee has 48 hours of free-time (starting at the first 7:00 A.M. after the car has been delivered) to *unload* the freight car. The "free-time" for *loading* a car is 24 hours. "Free-time" does not count Saturdays, Sundays, or holidays. For example, if a rail car is delivered to the consignee at 10:00 A.M. on Thursday, the first day of free-time starts on Friday at 7:00 A.M., Saturday and Sunday are not counted, and then the second day starts at 7:00 A.M. on Monday. The consignee must release the car to the carrier by 7:00 A.M. Tuesday or else pay demurrage charges. The ICC-authorized demurrage payment schedule was changed in early 1981 to $10 per day or any part of a day for the first four penalty days. During *penalty* days, all days, including weekends and holidays, are counted. For the next two penalty days the payment is $20 per day, and thereafter it is $30 per day. The railroad collecting the demurrage can keep only $10 per day if it is not the railroad which owns the car, with the remainder over $10 per day going to the railroad which owns the rail car.

Many traffic managers who are large users of rail cars have found it advantageous to enter into *averaging agreements* with the railroads. In an averaging agreement an accounting system of debits and credits is established. Every time the shipper or consignee releases a car one day early, a credit is received. Each time a car is surrendered to a carrier one day late, a debit is recorded. Debits and credits can only be applied to the loading of the car, or to the unloading, but they cannot be transposed; i.e., credits earned for rapid loading cannot be applied against debits charged for slow unloading. At the end of each month the debits and credits are added. If there is a credit balance, the carrier does not pay the shipper or consignee. If, however, there is a debit balance, the shipper or consignee will pay the carrier the appropriate payment based on the size of the debit balance. Each month the average agreement starts again; credits from a prior month cannot be brought forward.

Detention, as mentioned earlier, is the similar penalty payment assessed by the motor common carriers. In the case where the driver waits with the vehicle, the detention penalty often starts after one or two hours. If the trucker delivers a trailer for loading, the "free-time" before detention begins is generally less than the railroads offer. This reflects the "faster pace" of the trucking industry.

Reparations

The preceding discussion illustrated instances where the traffic manager should work closely with carriers to solve mutual problems. In other cases, the traffic manager must be assertive to protect the interests of his or her company, even at the risk of alienating the carriers. Such is the case with *reparations*. Reparations are payments made by a carrier to a shipper who had been paying unlawfully high rates to the common carrier.

To understand the procedure involved in securing a reparation payment, it is necessary to distinguish between a *legal* rate and a *lawful* rate. A *legal* rate is any rate that is filed with the ICC and subsequently published in a tariff. If a rate can be located in an official tariff then, by definition, it is legal. A *lawful* rate, on the other hand, is a legal rate that does not violate provisions of the *Interstate Commerce Act*. Since the ICC processes thousands of rate changes daily, it is not possible for the Commission to determine whether each rate change is lawful. Therefore, it is possible to have a legal rate which is not lawful.

Assume that a traffic manager shipping ketchup is paying the legal commodity rail rate of $4.75 per CWT from Fresno to Cleveland. However, he has located in another tariff that bottled mustard transported between the same cities pays only $2.97. The traffic manager believes that since there is no substantial difference between the two products, there is rate discrimination against the ketchup. Therefore, a complaint is filed with the ICC, alleging that the $4.75 rate violates Sections 1 and 3 of the *Interstate Commerce Act*. Assume further that the ICC rules that the ketchup rate is unlawful. In this case only, the ICC will determine what the lawful rate should be. Because ketchup and mustard have similar transportation and demand characteristics, the ICC might determine that a lawful rate for ketchup is also $2.97 per CWT.

At this point, the traffic manager's firm is eligible to receive a reparation from the railroad because the carrier has been unlawfully overcharging the shipper. The shipper or consignee can be reimbursed for the difference between the past legal rate and the new lawful rate for all shipments during the previous 24 months.[25]

---

[25] See, for example: "Dresser Wins Reparation On Rail Shipments of Clay," *Traffic World* (June 15, 1981), p. 47.

Starting in 1965, reparations also became available from motor common carriers, but the federal court system must be used to gain these reparations.[26]

Bank Payment Plan

The ICC requires that rail carriers be paid within five working days of receipt of the freight bill and that motor common carriers be paid within seven working days. To meet these time limits many traffic managers participate in *bank payment plans.*

The idea is simple: both the shipper and the carrier agree to use a bank that will treat freight bills as checks drawn on the shipper's freight account. The bank pays the carriers by transferring funds out of the shipper's account into the carrier's account. Each day the bank sends the shipper the freight bills paid that day.

Bank payment plans are experiencing substantial growth because shippers appreciate the convenience of the bank handling the paperwork involved in paying freight bills. Carriers support the concept because of the speed with which they are compensated for their transportation service.[27]

Over and Under Charges

The traffic manager is charged with the responsibility of not overpaying freight bills. Likewise, the carriers are legally bound not to undercharge their customers (if they did, it would be discriminatory). Therefore, each attempts to ensure that the correct freight rate is assessed the first time. However, due to the labyrinthine system of common carrier rates in the United States, the probability of errors is high. The *Interstate Commerce Act* states that both over and under charge claims must be presented within three years of the delivery of the freight to the consignee. (See right-hand portion of Table 11–3.)

The primary technique used to determine carrier overcharges (few traffic managers actively look for undercharges) is the freight-bill audit. There are two basic types of freight-bill auditing. The *internal audit,* as the name implies, is conducted by the shipper itself. The *external audit* is performed by independent companies, which

[26]Peter Lynagh, "Motor Carrier Reparations, A Settled Issue?" *Transportation Journal* (Winter, 1973), pp. 27–33.

[27]See: "Cash Management Plans Draw Shipper Interest," *Distribution* (January, 1980), p. 22.

typically charge 50 percent of any recovered overcharge. Almost all knowledgeable traffic managers utilize external freight-bill auditors because there is no cost if the auditor does not find any overcharges. Some shippers have their freight bills audited *three* times! First, an internal audit conducted by the firm's own employees. Second, an external audit firm is used on a 50-percent fee basis for all billing errors recovered. The third time, an external auditor is again utilized—but this time they receive 75 percent of any money collected from the carriers.[28]

Another error both internal and external auditors check for is the *duplicate payment* of freight charges. In late 1977, the ICC sued 12 motor common carriers for purposely keeping from shippers payments that were known to be duplicates.[29] More recently the ICC has estimated that common carrier truckers received approximately $2 billion in excess revenue from duplicate billings.[30] Double freight bills for the *same* service can occur for a number of reasons—some accidental and others fraudulent. On an interlined shipment, both the originating and terminating carriers can bill the shipper or consignee, or the originating carrier can bill the shipper and the final delivering carrier can bill the consignee. Another common situation is to bill the consignee for freight charges when the products were sold FOB-Destination, which indicates the shipper paid the freight charges. A final reason, and probably the most common explanation for duplicate billing, is that the carrier has not been paid in a timely manner and therefore a second "rebill" is sent to the shipper.

Appearances Before Rate Bureaus, Regulatory Commissions, Courts, and Congress

The traffic manager is often called on to present testimony before rate bureaus, regulatory hearings, and, occasionally, courts or legislative committees. Appearances before rate bureaus is a common activity for most traffic managers, especially for traffic managers who are actively trying to lower rates, alter packaging requirements, or lower ratings or classifications (which will be discussed in chapter 12). Traffic managers also appear at ICC hearings to argue for pro-

---

[28] See: Colin Barrett and J. S. Traunig, "Overpaying Freight Bills," *Distribution* (May, 1980), pp. 71–74; "Freight Bill Auditing By Computer Used To Stem Shipper Overpayments," *Traffic World* (July 27, 1981), pp. 23–24; and "Computers on the Loading Dock," *Forbes* (August 31, 1981).

[29] "ICC Sues 12 Truckers on Charges of Keeping Duplicate Payments," *The Wall Street Journal* (November 4, 1977), p. 11.

[30] Colin Barrett and J. S. Traunig, *loc. cit.,* p. 71.

posed changes that would benefit their company. Carrier representatives will also be present, arguing for the carriers' interests. If some issue is appealed from the regulatory body into a state or federal court, the traffic manager would again be expected to testify (although in this situation the traffic manager probably would be accompanied by the firm's legal counsel).

Despite the trend toward deregulation in recent years, the transportation industry is still regulated by the federal government. Transportation laws are far from static. Almost weekly, a subcommittee of the Senate or House of Representatives holds a hearing on some proposed change in the *Interstate Commerce Act*. Frequently, key witnesses for or against the proposed legislation are traffic managers and others who work daily with the present transportation regulatory system. They are in an excellent position to comment on the workability of the present situation and why the proposed change is needed or not.

Small Shipment Problem

Truckers believe that shipments between 50 and 500 pounds[31] do not generate sufficient revenue to warrant common carrier service. They have urged the ICC to allow significantly higher rates on small shipments. Deregulation may increase the "small shipment" problem because carriers may have more freedom to abandon markets. Traffic managers must continuously search for solutions to the problem that small shipments typically receive inadequate service, even at relatively high rates.[32]

Three concepts have proven helpful in solving this problem. First, multi-shipper freight consolidation via non-profit shipper cooperatives may be feasible. Non-profit shipper cooperatives are organizations that act as freight forwarders (they consolidate small shipments and tender them to carriers in large-volume shipments), except that they are not privately owned for-profit firms. As cooperatives, all "profits" earned are returned to their members. Historically, non-profit shipper cooperatives were not allowed to advertise their service. However, in May 1981, the ICC ruled that cooperatives can now utilize sales representatives who can call on shippers. The

---

[31] For transportation alternatives for shipments under 50 pounds, see: Linda Bolt, "The Growing World of Small Shipments," *Distribution Worldwide* (April, 1978), pp. 51–56.

[32] See: "Saving Money on Small Shipments," *Traffic Management* (August, 1980), pp. 64–66.

purpose of the sales calls is to generate new shipper members for the cooperative.[33]

Shipper cooperatives appear to be growing in acceptance, and it is estimated there are between 300 to 500 in operation. They typically utilize railroad and motor common carriers for the line-haul segment of the transportation.

A second answer to the small shipment problem is *intra-firm* consolidation of shipments. Computer assistance is especially helpful in locating company-wide consolidation opportunities. The computer can search bill-of-lading information for previous periods and locate situations where the firm could have consolidated shipments without significant decreases in customer service levels.[34] Both make-bulk and break-bulk warehouses (discussed in chapter 10) can be utilized in the consolidation program.

The final alternative to the small shipments problem is "do-it-yourself" private transportation, which will be discussed later in this chapter.

Embargoes

An embargo is a situation where a common carrier can legally refuse to accept shipments destined for a certain location. This usually happens when excessive congestion is found at a destination or when delivery is impeded because of storm-related damage to the carrier's right-of-way or terminals. In December, 1980, the ICC authorized a rail embargo for shipments bound for Mexico. The Mexican economy was robust because of their massive oil exports. Therefore, Mexicans were ordering massive quantities of U.S. grain and manufactured products. The result was that the Mexican rail system could not absorb the great influx of loaded rail cars. At the time of the embargo, over 46,000 loaded U.S. rail cars were standing idle in Mexico.[35]

Embargoes do *not* violate common carrier obligations when they have been approved by the Interstate Commerce Commission. The ICC has noted, "Carriers have the right, in order to prevent complete

[33] "Shippers' Groups May Advertise without Losing Exempt Status with ICC," *Traffic World* (May 25, 1981), p. 53.

[34] See: Warren Blanding, "Creative Computerization," *Traffic World* (January 16, 1978), pp. 41–44; Theodore Pollock, "A Management Guide to LTL Consolidation," *Traffic World* (April 3, 1978), pp. 29–35; James M. Masters, "The Effects of Freight Consolidation on Customer Service," *Journal of Business Logistics*, Vol. 2, No. 1 (1980), pp. 55–74.

[35] "Boxcars Snarl Mexican Trade, *Business Week* (February 9, 1981), p. 46.

paralysis of their operating facilities, to protect themselves by embargo against acceptance of freight."[36] Embargoes are common in international shipments. Even mail to Canada will not be accepted if there is a Canadian postal workers' strike.

Traffic managers, when informed that carrier embargoes are in effect, must be able to rapidly reroute their freight to (a) other carriers within the same mode, (b) a different mode, or (c) alternative destination cities. Alert traffic managers often have contingency plans in anticipation of carrier embargoes. Over the years, they also give traffic to other modes and to a number of carriers within each mode, so that they do not become overly dependent on any mode or carrier.

Diversion and Reconsignment

Diversion and reconsignment are almost exclusively railroad services that are commonly utilized with order bills-of-lading. Both terms today are used interchangeably, although technically there is a difference. Diversion involves notifying the railroad *before* delivery to the specified city to reroute the car to another destination. Reconsignment is also rerouting, but it takes place *after* the rail car has been delivered to the original destination city.

Both of these services are frequently used in the transportation of foods and other perishable products where markets quickly change. Diversion and reconsignment tariffs specify the charges for each reroute, and in some cases a specified number of diversions or reconsignments is included at no extra charge in the rate.

Side Track and Weight Agreements

Side track agreements involve negotiating (with the help of the firm's attorney) with the railroad that has connecting trackage to a production plant, warehouse, or distribution center. The general pattern is that the railroad builds and maintains the trackage on *their* property and the shipper is responsible for building and maintaining the side track on its property. However, since the shipper has neither construction nor maintenance equipment for the track, the track is often built and maintained by the connecting railroad. The side track agreement sets forth the obligations and responsibilities of each party. Often the railroad will waive track charges if the shipper provides it with more than a certain amount of business. Figure 11–10 is

[36] 73 ICC 749, 752 (1922).

Peter F. Walstad

ATTORNEY AT LAW _____

4900 IDS TOWER
MINNEAPOLIS, MINNESOTA 55402
PHONE (612) 333-4171

May 7, 1982

Dear Professors Wood and Johnson:

Frustration! It is the key word that describes dealing with railroads relative to side tracks and side track agreements.

To build a few feet of spur track, to sign a standard construction agreement and to sign a standard operating agreement seems simple, doesn't it? But it is not! Frankly, railroads are so top heavy with personnel who must check, recheck, initial and approve (but not for final approval) standard construction agreements and side track agreements that months go by before agreements are ready for signing.

I have represented clients before Eastern, Western and Central railroads and they're all alike--a mass amount of delaying protocol.

After submitting an initial request for a standard spur track construction agreement and a standard side track agreement, I begin the "Great Wait." The construction agreement begins its slow journey from traffic to operations, from surveyors to engineers, from desk to desk in the local office then to division office for checking and initialling, approval and possibly rejection, and would you believe it, to the home office for approval, redraft or rejection.

After several weeks of empty promises to deliver an executed copy of the agreement and many phone calls, I receive an executed copy of the construction agreement. This is not to say the actual commencement of construction has begun; several months often pass and so does the deadline for completion. Weeks after a promised deadline, barring strikes of the railroad employees or 'out of stock' materials, the track is said to be completed; only to find out that the frog is missing or needs replacement or that the spur track has been completed but not up to the side track. The construction procedure starts again.

When the track is finally in, the formal side track agreement starts its slow journey through the railroad maze just as the construction agreement did!

For this letter I reviewed a typical file. It happened to involve a Western railroad. We started the procedure in November of 1977 to obtain a simple construction and industrial side track agreement. We did not get the matter resolved and the executed agreement until January of 1979! In the meantime, my client designed a new factory, let the contracts, built the plant, put in production equipment, trained a work force and started operations in June of 1978. In the interim period my client was forced to substitute truck service for shipping incoming raw materials and outgoing finished product. Do draw your own conclusion!

Very truly yours,

Peter F. Walstad

Peter F. Walstad

Figure 11-10   Side Track Agreement Problems.

a statement from Peter F. Walstad, general counsel of Flexsteel Industries, in which he discusses frustrations in dealing with railroad side track agreements.

Weight agreements are commonly utilized by all modes of transportation. Since freight rates are typically quoted in regard to weight, exact weight determination is important. Weighing each vehicle before and after loading is an expensive and time-consuming process for both carrier and shipper. For repetitive shipments, a weight agreement is typically utilized. An independent (of carrier and shipper) weighing and inspecting bureau certifies that each bag, box, pallet-load, etc., has a specific average weight which is used to determine freight rates.

Transit Insurance

As discussed in chapter 3, while surface common carriers have a strict liability, there are *five* exemptions which release the common carrier from liability. Many shippers, to protect themselves from these exemptions, possess transit insurance. In addition, transit insurance is recommended when using contract carriers and is essential when using private carriers or when making international shipments. Since deregulation of the domestic air cargo industry, the airlines have reduced the amount of insurance coverage they provide for shippers, so shippers may need to supplement their insurance coverage for these shipments also. The firm's traffic manager works with its insurance personnel to determine the type and amount of transit insurance the company needs.

Negotiating Contract Rates

Contracts with carriers are entered into when both parties are willing to forego some or all of the protections offered by the standard common carrier contract provisions appearing in the long-form bill-of-lading. Contract carriage was and is widely used by motor and water modes; and, in 1978, the ICC allowed railroads to enter into contracts with shippers. The *Staggers Rail Act of 1980* reaffirmed this. Examples of contract terms in agreements that have been negotiated between railroads and individual shippers are summarized below:

▲ In an agreement between the Western Pacific Railroad and Sierra Pacific Industries involving the movement of woodchips moving to California ports for export, the shipper agreed to pay an additional $150 per month per car in return for the railroad's agreement to assign 25 cars for the exclusive use of the shipper.

▲ In an agreement between the Chicago and Northwestern and General Foods Corporation involving the carriage of grocery products from Northlake, Illinois, to eight consignees in the St. Louis area, the shipper agreed to pay the railroad an additional amount (ranging from $117 to $159 per car) when the car was delivered on a precise, previously scheduled, day.

▲ In an agreement between Ford Motor Company and the Missouri Pacific Railroad involving the movements of new autos and auto parts between several specified points, the railroad agreed to give the shipper an allowance if 30 or more cars were tendered at one time or if the cars arrived at their destinations late. In return, Ford agreed to ship 95 percent of this business via Missouri Pacific.

▲ In an agreement between Del Monte Corporation and the Western Pacific Railroad, the railroad agreed to grant allowances ranging from $50 to $125 per car if the customer utilized the cars in both directions to carry canned goods. The shipments had to be routed via the Western Pacific Railroad, and established tariff rates (less the allowance) would apply.

▲ In an agreement between the Norfolk and Western Railroad and an export coal shipper, the railroad agreed to provide better service in supplying and moving cars and the shipper agreed to load and unload the cars more promptly. The purpose of the agreement was to reduce congestion at an East Coast coal port.

▲ In an agreement between General Motors and the Santa Fe Railroad involving the utilization of specialized equipment used exclusively by GM, it was agreed that at the end of each month the miles which each car had traveled loaded and empty would be calculated. If it traveled more miles loaded than empty, the Santa Fe would pay GM $.20 for each mile loaded in excess of each mile empty. If the car traveled more empty miles than loaded miles, GM would pay the Santa Fe $.20 for each mile empty in excess of each mile loaded. (All these adjustments would be made to GM's freight bill. The incentive to them was to make better use of the cars.)[37]

The burden of monitoring the carrier's performance in agreements such as these falls upon the shipper's traffic manager.

[37] ICC Contract Advisory Service releases (July 11, 1980 and January 28, 1981).

Contracts involving other modes of transport may seek some of the same objectives indicated in the rail examples just given. Sometimes a carrier will assign one or more vehicles to the exclusive use of the shipper for a specified amount of time. A retail store may contract with one or more truckers to help with holiday deliveries, or an auto manufacturer may contract for exclusive use of several cargo aircraft during the time it is retooling for a new year's models.

Short-term contracts are entered into for single hauls for certain commodities, such as agricultural products. The most frequent example occurs with motor carriers. In this instance, the shipper must not only know how to bargain for rates and service, he or she must also be able to judge the individual carrier's reliability.

Private Transportation

Private motor carriers are the main form of trucking activity. In 1978, the Transportation Association of America estimated that ICC-regulated truckers—both common and contract—performed 16.1 percent of all intercity freight tonnage. By comparison, non-ICC regulated trucking—private and exempt—accounted for 23.2 percent. By this measure, non-regulated trucking transports 44 percent more intercity tonnage than regulated truckers. The 1977 Census of Transportation noted that there are approximately 1.4 million trucks with three, four, or five axles (these large vehicles are used almost exclusively for freight hauling). Of this number, 74 percent are used for *private carriage* and 26 percent are used by for-hire carriers. In a recent Department of Transportation survey, it was found that 49.2 percent of the shipper respondents were engaged in private transportation. When queried why they started using private transportation, the most common response (43.2 percent) was *service* considerations.[38]

A 1980 survey by Drake Sheahan management consultants found that 68 percent of private carrier management respondents indicated that their private fleets had expanded their operations in the previous three years. Of these respondents, they indicated that their fleets operated empty—deadheaded—for 27 percent of their mileage. They hoped that recent regulatory changes would enable them to significantly reduce this quantity of deadheading.[39]

[38] J. Richard Jones, *Industrial Shipper Survey*, U.S. Department of Transportation, (September, 1975), pp. 85–92.

[39] R. Stanley Chapman, "Study Shows Few Private Carriers Interested in 'Toto' Operations," *Traffic World* (April 21, 1980), p. 36.

Advantages of Private Carriage

The demand for better service is the primary factor explaining the growth of private transportation. William L. Robinson, traffic manager for Sears, Roebuck & Company in Memphis, noted that motor common carrier service to three catalog sales offices ranging up to 350 miles away was both unreliable and took too long. "The big reason we switched to our own trucks was because we found we could cut delivery time to only 12 hours from the average 48 hours it took the common carrier."[40]

The traffic manager of a major plastics producer was more blunt when explaining his switch to private trucking:

> We just couldn't pound it into the trucking company that what we needed was fast service. What would often happen was that the trucker would pick up 75 percent of a truckload at our plant but before the truck would leave his terminal he would try to fill it up completely. Sometimes this would take a week or more. While we can understand his desire for a full load, we just couldn't live with that in today's competitive market. All things considered, we're not saving anything in freight costs, but service to our customers is much improved.[41]

Cost advantages are also feasible for private carriage, especially if the return haul does not have to be "deadheaded," i.e., traveled with no load. Two recent studies have concluded that private truckers will consistently experience lower per-unit costs than for-hire carriers because of certain advantages they possess. These advantages include (a) no terminal expense (because the freight terminal aspects of the shipper's production plants and warehouses would have to exist if the shipper utilized for-hire carriers), (b) no pickup and delivery expenses from the main terminal, (c) no billing and collecting costs, (d) no advertising or marketing expenses, (e) no carrier rate quotation department, and (f) reduced loss and damage because the freight is handled less. One other advantage of the private operator, to quote Bernard V. Sigg, "To survive, the for-hire carrier must make a profit—the private carrier merely break even."[42]

Three additional benefits of private motor carriage can be mentioned.

---

[40] James R. MacDonald, "Captive Carriers," *The Wall Street Journal* (November 11, 1964). See also: Robert M. Butler, "Private Carriage 'Feast of Facts' Featured at PCC Mid-Year Meeting," *Traffic World* (June 1, 1981), pp. 50–56.

[41] James R. MacDonald, *loc. cit.*

[42] Bernard V. Sigg, "The Economic Efficiency of Private Motor Transportation," *Transportation Research Forum Annual Proceedings* (Oxford, Indiana: Richard B. Cross, 1974), pp. 439–442; and Dwight Stuessy, "Cost Structure of Private and For-Hire Motor Carriage," *Transportation Journal* (Spring, 1976), pp. 40–48.

First, trailers can be utilized as mobile warehouses. Products can be produced and immediately loaded into truck-trailers. They can then be transported to destination and remain in the trailer if the firm's warehouse is temporarily full. Detention charges are avoided. It is not uncommon for a private fleet operator to own 45 trailers and only 8 or 9 tractors.

Second, the trailers can be attactively painted and function as rolling billboards. Figure 11–11 shows two examples; one from Gerber's Baby Foods in the late 1930's and a present-day one from

Figure 11–11   Trucks As Traveling Billboards. Courtesy: Gerber Products Co., and Levi Strauss & Co.

Levi Strauss. (Interestingly, one of the reasons Levi Strauss returned to decorated trailers was to deter hijacking, since the decorations would make a stolen trailer easier to spot. The firm formerly used plain trailers.)

Finally, the private truck fleet can be helpful in negotiating rates with other carriers. The threat of traffic diversion to private transportation will insure that the carriers will quote their lowest reasonable rate.

Problems of Private Carriage

Two major potential problems are often overlooked when deciding if a firm should invest in private transportation.

Often the traffic manager, in his or her zeal for the new operation (and the larger budget and increased responsibility), fails to consider who is actually going to manage the private carrier operation. The traffic manager assumes that he or she will assume the additional work. However, for all but the simplest operations, an additional manager must be assigned the responsibility for scheduling, maintenance, labor negotiating, and all the other details that require managerial attention.[43] This can be a significant cost item that was not originally budgeted. And if drivers belong to the Teamsters Union, which is very successful in obtaining high wages for its members, the firm's other laborers, who do not belong to the Teamsters, might wonder why their wages are not as generous.

There is a second problem. To appreciate it, consider this: In chapter 3 we learned that the *common carrier* is supposed to serve everyone without discrimination. Common carriers, presumably, are especially beneficial to small firms and firms located in rural areas. For this reason, common carriers are sometimes referred to as the "backbone" of the American transportation system.[44] Private carriage grows only at the expense of common carriage, and private carriage is harmful to the economic health of the common carrier system. Therefore a traffic manager is faced with a difficult ethical issue—should he or she consider the potential negative effects on the common carrier system when contemplating private carriage?

One ardent supporter of the common carrier system has attacked the position that the "public" (i.e., traffic managers) has a right to use all forms of available transportation.

[43] See: Francis J. Quinn, "Maintaining and Controlling the Private Fleet," *Traffic Management* (July, 1980), pp. 37–43 and Jack W. Farrell, "What's Really Happening To Private Fleets," *Traffic Management* (July, 1981), pp. 33–56.

[44] Martin T. Farris, "The Role of the Common Carrier," *Transportation Journal* (Summer, 1967), pp. 28–34.

The "public" behind the private carriage I am talking about is, at most, a few hundred, perhaps a thousand companies, who are putting hundreds of thousands of trucks on our already crowded highways, and thousands of barges in our inland waterway systems. Private operators of such trucks and barges benefit in two ways: They confer cost benefits to themselves, and impose higher costs on everyone who uses common carrier service. The withholding of high-rated tonnage from common carriage which is usually what moves to private carriage, enables the private carrier to "make" money by lowering his costs, while the average charges of the common carrier have to rise to compensate for the loss of such revenues. This benefit to a few, results in higher charges for many.[45]

Warren Blanding, a highly-respected transportation consultant, has even suggested that it is time to consider the feasibility of a federal law rendering private carriage illegal.[46] He believes such a drastic step may be necessary if the common carrier system is to survive.

Deregulation and Private Carriage

The recent deregulation trend in trucking has significantly impacted on the operations of private carriage in two ways: (a) "Toto" operations and (b) intercorporate transportation. Each will be examined.

In late 1978 the ICC allowed private truckers to become for-hire carriers.[47] This controversial decision, known as the "Toto Case," was previously discussed in chapter 4. While each private carrier must apply to the ICC for operating rights (requiring a certificate to be a common carrier and a permit to be a contract carrier), the Commission has noted that in most cases they will automatically be issued. Therefore, private truckers desiring to avoid "deadheading" can now legally reduce this problem. Notice that deregulation has made the traffic management function more complex and challenging. The manager of the private truck fleet must weigh the advantage of a loaded truck on the return haul versus possible service interruption caused by transporting products for others.[48]

How have traffic managers reacted to the Toto decision? The pre-

---

[45] Paul H. Reistrup, "How 'Common' Need Public Carriage Be In This Automotive Era?" *Transportation Research Forum Annual Proceedings* (Oxford, Indiana: Richard B. Cross, 1973), p. 811.

[46] Warren Blanding, "The Shipper's Dilemma," *Transportation and Distribution Management* (October, 1973), pp. 16–17.

[47] See: "For-Hire Rights For Private Carriers Upheld by ICC," *Traffic World* (November 27, 1978), pp. 9–10.

[48] Colin Barrett, "In the Wake of 'Toto'," *Traffic World* (January 15, 1979), pp. 139–142.

viously-noted 1980 Drake Sheahan survey found that only one out of four private fleet managers anticipated studying the possibility of applying to the ICC for operating rights.[49] The reason for this cool reception was a "Catch 22" type provision in the present regulatory laws for for-hire carriers. Specifically, all for-hire carriers must receive ICC authorization before engaging in major financial transactions, such as borrowing, issuing bonds and common stock, etc. Therefore, any firm that obtained "Toto-type" operating rights would become subject to ICC control of the firm's entire financial operations. This would be true even though only a very small percentage of a firm's operation was that of a for-hire carrier. Needless to say, many firms found this financial control by the ICC to be totally unacceptable! Private carriers tried to have this aspect of the Toto decision changed in the *1980 Motor Carrier Act*. However, for-hire carriers argued strongly not to exempt "Toto" for-hire carriers from ICC financial regulation—and this position prevailed. Can this problem be solved? Colin Barrett, a transportation management consultant, suggests a solution. The firm "spins off" the private carriage operation into a wholly-owned corporate subsidiary. This subsidiary then provides intercorporate transportation service to the main corporation. The subsidiary trucking company can then apply for "Toto" operating rights and the ICC's financial jurisdiction applies only to the trucking subsidiary and not the entire corporation.[50]

Prior to the *1980 Motor Carrier Act*, the ICC had not authorized private trucking operations to be involved in "intercorporate" trucking operations. This meant that one fully-owned subsidiary of a corporation could not provide transportation service to another fully-owned subsidiary of the same corporation. Thus, a truck owned by the Goodmark subsidiary of General Mills, Inc., could transport General Mills food products from Raleigh, North Carolina, to Minneapolis. The truck, however, could *not* legally transport the products of the Parker Brothers Game Company—also a subsidiary of General Mills—from Minneapolis to Raleigh on the return haul. The result of this ICC interpretation of the *Interstate Commerce Act* was that substantial numbers of private truck operations were forced to run empty on backhauls. This was both frustrating to the managers of private truck fleets and it resulted in significant quantities of fuel being wasted by "deadheading" trucks. The *1980 Motor Carrier Act* corrected this situation.

The 1980 Act specifies that a corporation wishing to engage in

[49] Stanley Chapman, *loc. cit.*

[50] Colin Barrett, "Boom Times For Private Carriage," *Distribution* (March, 1981), p. 52.

intercorporate transportation must file a "notice" with the ICC. By March 1981, approximately 500 parent corporations had done so. These companies represented over 5,000 wholly-owned subsidiary corporations.[51] One firm benefiting from intercorporate hauling is Combustion Engineering. Intercorporate transportation allowed this company to reduce empty mileage for its private trucking fleet from 20 percent of total mileage to 8 percent. This will result in an estimated annual transportation savings of $800,000.[52] Another firm that has benefited from intercorporate hauling is Mobil Corporation. Each of Mobil's four major subsidiaries—Montgomery Wards, Mobil Chemical, Container Corporation of America, and Mobil Oil—has participated in transporting products for the other subsidiaries. Ray J. Gestaut, fleet manager for Wards noted the results of intercorporate transportation. "We see better utilization of our fleet and even a diminishing of total fleet equipment, plus those precious fuel savings."[53]

In closing this discussion of private carriage, mention should be made of the fact that the terms *common*, *contract*, and *private* carriage refer to legal forms of carrier activity. To confuse the issue slightly, shippers may contract with truck (or other modal) equipment supplying companies to lease from them equipment to operate as private carriers. Shippers may also "lease" drivers from other firms to drive their trucks. A second fact to be mentioned is that the carriage of most agricultural products by motor carrier or fresh fruits and vegetables by rail is usually exempt from ICC regulation. Therefore the traffic manager of a firm moving these goods would contract with trucks or railroads, or rely on private carriage.

The remainder of the chapter deals with two other traffic management functions which are common to many firms. One deals with movements of hazardous materials, and the other deals with the "employee services" offered by the traffic department.

Transportation of Hazardous Materials

Traffic managers, along with carrier and government representatives, are working to reduce transportation accidents involving hazardous materials. The problem is serious. Table 11–4 shows the number of hazardous materials "incidents" or accidents involving hazardous

[51] *Ibid.*, p. 51.
[52] *Traffic World* (December 22, 1980), p. 24.
[53] Robert M. Butler, *loc. cit.*, pp. 51–52.

TABLE 11–4   Hazardous Materials Transportation Incidents—1979

Mode	Incidents Reported	Deaths	Injuries
Air	284	0	13
Highway (for hire)	15,355	14	608
Highway (private)	623	6	89
Rail	1,215	26	228
Water	34	0	1
Freight forwarders	2	0	0
Other	11	0	2
	17,524	46	941

SOURCE: U.S. Department of Transportation, *10th Annual Report, Hazardous Materials Transportation* (Washington: Government Printing Office, 1980).

materials reported to the U.S. Department of Transportation in 1979.

The most important recent change in federal regulations dealing with hazardous materials was passage of the *Hazardous Materials Transportation Act*, a subpart of the *Transportation Safety Act of 1974*. This law consolidated the regulation of hazardous materials into one DOT agency, the Materials Transportation Bureau. Major aspects of the 1974 law include authorizing (a) the DOT to regulate additional aspects of the transportation of hazardous materials, such as unloading procedures and the routing of shipments; (b) establishing training requirements for carriers, shippers, and manufacturers of hazardous materials, and (c) increasing penalties for violating the law.

The training mandate in the 1974 act is a basic requirement for both shippers and carriers. Specifically, the DOT regulations state: "It is the duty of each person who offers hazardous materials for transportation to instruct each of his officers, agents, and employees having any responsibility for preparing hazardous materials for shipment as to the applicable regulations."

DuPont Corporation has been a leader in training its employees regarding hazardous materials. DuPont Corporation delivers six million tons of hazardous goods each year. It established the RHYTHM educational program to ship these products safely. It is an acronym for "Remember How You Treat Hazardous Materials." Donald Brown, manager for hazardous materials at DuPont, said:

> We set up a computerized system to take all our products and list the flash point, type of label required, type of package needed, and so forth. It also tells what happens if the material is exposed to a person's skin,

what happens if it is ingested, and what kind of emergency response should be made if there is a leak in the container.[54]

The Manufacturing Chemists Association and other similar trade organizations have established toll free "800" numbers which have knowledgeable people available 24 hours per day. These phone numbers are made available to all local police and fire departments. Figure 11–12 illustrates the organizations involved in a chemical emergency.

An additional safety requirement dealing with hazardous materials became effective November 1, 1981. The Materials Transportation Bureau of the DOT required *all* carriers of hazardous materials to carry a placard whose color indicates the *general* type of commodity; a four-digit number on the placard indicates *specifically* the exact hazardous substance involved. This information is helpful to police, fire fighters, and others at an accident site. For example, a red placard on a vehicle indicates a flammable liquid or gas and the number "1781" identifies the substance as "hexadecyltrichlorosilane."[55]

Employee Services of the Traffic Department

Traffic departments, especially in larger firms, typically provide a number of transportation-related employee services. These services generally include:

1. The traffic manager is responsible for purchase and maintenance of the firm's fleet of automobiles used by sales and service personnel. In addition, senior officers of the firm are typically provided with automobiles; the traffic department is charged with keeping these cars clean, gassed, and properly maintained.

2. The traffic department issues commercial airline tickets to employees. This activity is generally restricted to large firms that, in effect, have their own "travel agency." This service will often reserve and issue tickets for employees' business and vacation trips. The in-house travel agency often pays for

[54]*Distribution Worldwide* (November, 1978), p. 31. See also: Perry A. Trunick, "Hazardous Materials: The Perils of Hauling," *Handling and Shipping Management* (November, 1980), pp. 70–78.
[55]*Traffic World* (October 12, 1981), p. 35.

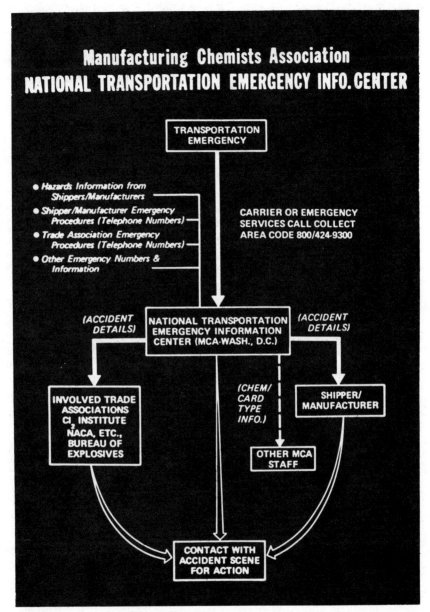

Figure 11–12   Hazardous Materials Emergency Procedures. Courtesy: Manufacturing Chemists Association.

itself because it qualifies for the airline sales commission that is granted to regular travel agencies.[56]

3. Another employee-related function of the traffic department involves purchase, scheduling, and maintenance of the firm's private airplane fleet. In large companies, this can involve 10 or 20 aircraft, including some jets. Because of its highly-specialized nature, the *chief pilot* is often administratively in charge of the pilots and aircraft, as was shown in Figure 11–2. Because of the energy shortage of the 1970's, many firms restricted the use of their private aircraft in order to demonstrate their social responsibility. General Mills, Inc., in Minneapolis asks their executives *not* to request a private plane if there are five or more daily commercial nonstop flights from the Twin Cities airport to their destination. Administratively, many corporations have an internal policy of not allowing an excessive number of their senior officers to travel in the same aircraft. They want to avoid the problem that Texasgulf Corporation experienced in February, 1981, when one of their company jets crashed. The death toll included the chairman of the corporation and four other top executives.[57]

4. One more employee function performed by the traffic department is arranging to move a transferred employee's household possessions.[58] Ironically, many traffic departments are apprehensive about this function. They point out that it is a "no-win" activity! If the moving company performs perfectly, the employee involved assumes this is a typical situation and no accolades are presented to the traffic department. Alternatively, if the moving company fails to deliver the household possessions on time, the employee may blame the problem on the traffic department for failing to plan the move adequately.

Many traffic departments have been breathing sighs of relief because many corporations are now utilizing *relocation management companies*, such as Homequity, to relocate employees. These firms specialize in helping transferred employees move; typically they perform three services: (a) purchase the employee's present home at

[56] See: "The CAB Makes An Illegal Rebate Legal," *Business Week* (March 2, 1981), pp. 137, 141.

[57] Maria Shao, "Texasgulf Snaps Back From Tragedy With New Team But Same Philosophy," *The Wall Street Journal* (March 24, 1981), p. 14.

[58] For further information, see: Paul E. Jamison, "How to Establish a Moving Policy," *Transportation and Distribution Management* (April, 1968), pp. 35–42; "Corporate Moving Policies," *Distribution Worldwide* (September, 1977), pp. 58–62; and Steve Frazier, "Relocation Firms Find Housing Slump Spurs Business and Troubles," *The Wall Street Journal* (January 6, 1982), p. 1.

fair market value, (b) assist the employees' search for a home at their new location, and (c) arrange all moving of the employee's household possessions.

Summary

Traffic management is a challenging, detailed, and diverse aspect of physical distribution/logistics. The essence of traffic management is purchasing transportation for a company—always trying to obtain the best possible service at the lowest cost consistent with the firm's specified level of customer service.

Organizationally, the firm's general traffic manager is in the PD/L department, and his activities must be coordinated with the firm's other distribution and logistics goals. Within the traffic function, there are many responsibilities, including determining the correct rate to pay for a shipment and negotiating with carriers to achieve better rates in the future.

The traffic department also selects specific carriers to use and monitors their performance. A continual problem is that the firm's customers often hold it responsible for the quality of service provided by carriers it uses.

There are many detailed functions performed by the traffic operation. They must prepare shipping documents, select the "route" the shipment must follow, and file "loss and damage" claims in case something happens to the shipment while it is in the hands of the carrier. They also work with the carriers to reduce the incidence and amount of future loss and damage claims.

Deregulation is increasing the responsibilities of the firm's traffic manager. There are more individual negotiations with carriers to obtain better rates and service. If the shipper has his own fleet of trucks, he may also now solicit business from other shippers in order to utilize otherwise empty backhaul capacity.

The traffic function within the firm also arranges for employee transportation, supervises use of the firm's own aircraft, maintains the firm's fleet of private automobiles, and provides household goods moving service for employees being transferred.

Questions for Discussion and Review

1. Why is traffic management considered such an essential aspect of PD/L?

2. Trace briefly the history of the traffic management function.

3. "Deregulation has created an ideal environment for the traffic management function to be fully appreciated by senior management." Discuss the validity of this statement.

4. Study the traffic management corporate objectives in Figure 11–1. Which do you believe is the: (a) most important? Why? and (b) least important? Why?

5. Discuss a composite organizational structure for the traffic department.

6. Why not let the common carrier determine the correct freight rate?

7. Discuss three situations in which the carrier may be willing to negotiate a lower rate to the shipper.

8. Why is rate negotiation a more important aspect of traffic management in today's deregulated environment than it was before deregulation?

9. Discuss various criteria used by traffic managers in selecting a carrier.

10. What is "flagging-out" a rate?

11. Why do many shippers believe that single carrier service from origin to destination is preferable to an interlined shipment?

12. What is a transit privilege? Why are tapering rates important to this concept?

13. Discuss how an order bill-of-lading is used.

14. Discuss, in general terms, the freight loss and damage situation.

15. Discuss how freight claim damages are determined.

16. Why are concealed loss and damage claims so difficult from the carriers' viewpoint?

17. Discuss the function of the Transportation Arbitration Board. Do you agree with their decision in the case examined in Figure 11–8? Why?

18. Discuss the concept of a reparation.

19. Discuss the service provided by freight bill auditors. How are they compensated?

20. Discuss the problem of duplicate payment. What causes this problem?

21. Discuss a number of rail contract provisions that have been negotiated between traffic managers and the railroads.

22. Discuss the advantages and disadvantages of using private carriage rather than common carriers.

23. How have (a) "Toto" operations and (b) intercorporate transportation affected the traffic management function? Discuss.

24. Discuss the role of the traffic manager when shipping hazardous materials.

25. Discuss four employee services often performed by the traffic department.

Additional Chapter References

Anderson, Ronald D., Roger E. Jerman, and James A. Constantin, "AST & T Membership Profile," *Transportation Journal* (Summer, 1977), pp. 54–60.

Arizzi, Vincent J., "The Role of the Corporate Staff Transportation Group," *Transportation Journal* (Winter, 1974), pp. 41–52.

Bardi, Edward J., "Carrier Selection From One Mode," *Transportation Journal* (Fall, 1973), pp. 23–29.

Bardi, Edward J., and Larry G. Kelly, "Organizing for Effective Packaging Management," *Transportation Journal* (Winter, 1974), pp. 53–57.

Brown, Terence A., "Shippers' Associations: Operations, Trends, and Comparative Prices," *Transportation Journal* (Fall, 1981), pp. 54–66.

Calabro, Pat J., and Thomas W. Speh, "Historical Perspectives On The Freight Car Supply Problem: The Role of Demurrage," *ICC Practitioners' Journal* (May–June, 1976), pp. 470–481.

Campbell, John H., "From Traffic Manager to Logistician," *MSU Business Topics* (Autumn, 1980), pp. 25–30.

Corsi, Thomas M., Michael A. McGinnis, and Merrill J. Roberts, "A Multiple Criteria Analysis of Modal Choice," *Journal of Business Logistics*, Vol. 2, No. 2 (1981), pp. 48–68.

Davis, Bob J., "Reebie Associates: Transguide, A Guide to Sources of Freight Transportation Information," *Transportation Journal* (Summer, 1981), pp. 98–99.

Davis, Frank W., Jr., Kenneth W. Heathington, Richard T. Symons, and Stephen C. Griese, "Bus and Taxi Package Express—A Major Component of Urban Goods Movement," *Annual Proceedings of the Transportation Research Forum* (1974), pp. 145–152.

DeHayes, Daniel W., Jr., and Robert L. Taylor, "Moving Beyond the Physical Distribution Organization," *Transportation Journal* (Spring, 1974), pp. 30–41.

Hill, Stephan G., "Contract Rates: Increasing Rail Profitability," *ICC Practitioners' Journal* (January–February, 1979), pp. 222–232.

Kaminski, Peter F., and David R. Rink, "Industrial Transportation Management in a Systems Perspective," *Transportation Journal* (Fall, 1981), pp. 67–76.

Meyers, Norman A., "The Portland, Oregon, Metropolitan Motor Carrier Rate Problem: A Proposed Solution," *Transportation Journal* (Winter, 1975), pp. 13–27.

Piercy, John E., "Lost, Damaged and Astray Freight Shipments: Some Explanatory Factors," *Transportation Journal* (Summer, 1980), pp. 33–37.

Vann, John W., and Frederick J. Stephenson, "Purchasing Agents' Views of Different Air Cargo Services," *Annual Proceedings of the Transportation Research Forum* (1981), pp. 294–301.

Wheeler, Alan D., "The Computer: Triumph or Terror for Transportation Managers," *Transportation Journal* (Summer, 1976), pp. 39–47.

Case 11–1   O'Toole Tool Company Case

Located in the Detroit area, the O'Toole Tool Company used plants that had formerly been occupied by automakers and their suppliers. It occupied plants in seven locations, in an approximate 3 × 3 grid, and travel time (one-way) between each plant and those nearest to it was just under one hour. Because of the street system, and barriers created by Huron, Rouge, and Detroit Rivers, it was possible to travel in only north-south or east-west paths between the O'Toole plants. For purposes of discussion here, rather than referring to the plants by the names they were known as locally, we shall call them A, B, C, D, E, F, and G. The relative locations of the plants are diagrammed in Case Figure 11–1–1.

Plants were open 24 hours per day and there was a continual flow of messages between them. Case Figure 11–1–2 shows the numbers of messages that left each plant, destined for another, per hour. Two messengers traveled back and forth between each plant, leaving on the hour. There was enough time so that messages could be sorted and resorted at each point just before the hour ended. Those going beyond the first stop would move to the next plant in the second hour. Alternate routes could be followed. For example, messages from plant A to plant F could follow three routes: A–B–C–F, A–B–E–F, or A–D–E–F, and each route took three hours.

Question One: Calculate the *average* length of time it takes a message to move to its final destination.

Question Two: Without increasing the time it takes any message to move from its origin to final destination, lay out a routing system

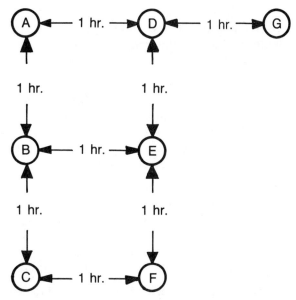

Case Figure 11-1-1   Location of and One-Way Travel Time Between O'Toole Plants.

From Plant

		A	B	C	D	E	F	G
	A	—	0	1	13	2	4	16
	B	3	—	10	1	1	12	2
To Plant	C	0	11	—	4	3	13	0
	D	15	2	2	—	0	2	17
	E	4	2	3	0	—	3	5
	F	2	14	13	1	3	—	4
	G	17	4	4	14	1	2	—

Case Figure 11-1-2   The Number of Messages Leaving Each Plant Per Hour Destined for Other Plants.

that equalizes, as best it can, the number of messages carried between any two plants. However, all messages between any two plants must follow the same route. Do not worry about an imbalance in the direction of messages between any two plants.

Question Three: Try to do an even better job of evening the workload. You may route messages between two plants on two or more routes (for example, of the four messages from A to E, they may all travel A–B–E or A–D–E, or some may travel one route while the balance may travel the other). You still don't need to worry about directional imbalance between plants.

Question Four: You want to cut costs by eliminating completely messenger service on one of the links, and rerouting those messages. For example, if the A–D link were dropped, messages from A to D would follow the route A–B–E–D. Which link could be dropped with the least impact on the average amount of time it took for all messages in the system to reach their final destination?

Question Five: Assume instead, you want to drop service completely to (and from) one of the seven plants. First-class mail will be used to serve the plant where you no longer have messengers call. Since costs of dropping messenger service to and from any one of the plants is the same, which plant should be dropped if the criteria is smallest increase in average length of time it takes a message to move through the new six-plant system?

Question Six: Returning to the situation in Question One, assume the Rouge River floods and cuts links A–D and C–F. Now calculate the average amount of time it will take for messages in your system to reach their final destinations.

Case 11–2   The Alhambra Ocean-Going Barge Case

The Alhambra Steamship Company (ASC) operated a number of tug-boat subsidiary firms in East Coast and Gulf Coast ports. In addition, it operated as a regulated water carrier in the New York-San Juan market. Several competing carriers were also in this market and, in recent years, they had introduced RoRo (Roll-on, Roll-off) vessels for carrying truck trailers (without tractors) between New York and Puerto Rico. The vessels that ASC was operating in this market were old, conventional "break-bulk" freighters and could not compete with the "RoRo" service. ASC management concluded that the firm would either have to go into "RoRo" service, or else drop out of the market completely.

Since ASC was also in the tugboat business, the managers viewed with interest the increased use of ocean-going tug and barge combinations. When compared with conventional vessels, the tug-barge combinations required smaller crews and were more flexible in terms of scheduling. If necessary, the tugs could be interchanged with other ASC tugs, and ASC tugs could be used to assist in the docking of the ocean-going barges.

Three sizes of ocean-going barges were under consideration. The dimensions of ASC's slip limited the barges to a certain length of keel and beam; however, naval architects suggested multi-deck barges. Both double-deck and triple-deck barges appeared feasible. A single-deck barge could hold 100 trailers, a double-deck barge could hold 200 trailers, and a triple-deck barge could hold 300 trailers. Costs also differed, with single-deck barges costing $2 million each; double-deck barges, $4 million each; and triple-deck barges, $8 million each. If double-deck barges were used, ASC would have to invest $300,000, in total, for loading/unloading ramps at both New York and San Juan. The triple-deck barges would require larger ramps, costing a total of $800,000. Single-deck barges would not require these types of ramps.

The ocean-going tugs needed to pull the barges also differed in size and in price. Tugs needed for single-deck barges cost $2 million each, while those needed to pull double-deck barges would cost $2.5 million each. Tugs for pulling the tri-level barges would cost $3 million each. It was felt that a commitment would have to be restricted to a single size of barge and tug. (Mismatched tug and barge combinations would be fuel-inefficient, and operating different sizes of barges would lead to traffic imbalances since ASC would want to move the same number of trailers in each direction.)

Nine alternatives appeared feasible in terms of scheduling and allocation of capacity. They are shown in Case Table 11–2–1 and labeled A, B, C, D, E, F, G, H, and I. Different ratios of tugs to barges are shown because of different scheduling of equipment. For example, alternatives B and C offer high-frequency service, and tugs would be towing loaded barges while other barges were in port, being loaded or unloaded. Alternatives with less frequent sailings would have the barges and tugs remain linked but would require faster trailer loading and unloading procedures while the tug-barge combination was in port.

The total market (for all carriers) was estimated to be 30,000 trailers moved per year (round trips). Demand fluctuated seasonally with

CASE TABLE 11–2–1   Equipment Alternatives

	A	B	C	D	E	F	G	H	I
	Single-Deck Barges			Double-Deck Barges			Triple-Deck Barges		
Number of barges	3	8	10	3	4	6	2	3	4
Number of tugs	3	4	5	3	3	4	2	3	3
Number of sailings (round trips)	30	80	100	30	40	60	20	30	40
Annual capacity (in numbers of trailers) (round trips)	3,000	8,000	10,000	6,000	8,000	12,000	6,000	9,000	12,000
ANNUAL COSTS Depreciation on barges, tugs, and ramps	10% per year, straight line on barges, tugs, and ramps, for all alternatives								
Fuel (in $1,000's)	2,000	4,000	5,500	2,500	3,300	5,000	2,000	3,000	4,000
Crew costs (in $1,000's)	1,200	3,200	3,200	1,200	1,600	2,400	800	1,200	1,600
Port costs (in $1,000's)	200	300	400	200	250	300	300	400	500
PROJECTED TRAFFIC (in numbers of trailers—round trips) Traffic attracted by number of sailings, estimated at .3 percent of market, per sailing	9%	24%	30%	9%	12%	18%	6%	9%	12%
Traffic attracted by capacity, each thousand of trailer capacity over 5,000 attracts 3 percent	—	9%	15%	3%	9%	21%	3%	12%	21%
Total Market Share Expected	9%	33%	45%	12%	21%	39%	9%	21%	33%

peaks resulting from Puerto Rican crop harvests and heavy shipments of merchandise in the pre-Christmas season. The rate per trailer carried on a round trip was $1,300. The volume of trade and its patterns were not expected to change. Nor was the rate, aside for adjustments caused by inflation. Hence the ASC management felt it could use "constant" dollars for their analysis.

Since the rates were fixed, ASC management felt that it could be the "low-cost" operator in the market and offer a higher level of service, measured in terms of frequency of sailings, dependability, quick "turnaround" of the shippers' trailers, capacity to handle "peak" traffic, etc. Outside consultants warned ASC managers of the dilemma they would face when attempting to find the right mix of equipment and schedules to penetrate the existing market. Some of the San Juan-New York traffic was time-sensitive, and those shippers would favor whatever carrier had a schedule with frequent, dependable sailings. Other traffic, occurring at "peak" periods, would favor whatever carrier happened to have the greatest capacity for handling a large number of trailers. The consultants devised two formulas that they believed were applicable to the market in question. They are shown at the bottom of Case Table 11–2–1. Since ASC was considering scheduled service, the net impact of both factors (or results of both formulas) should be added, although it is possible that the amount of traffic generated by *both* factors will exceed ASC's projected capacity.

Four cost items are listed. Port costs include mooring of the barge, loading, and discharging the trailers. Larger barges incur higher port costs because they are more difficult to maneuver in port and require more "back-up" land for parking trailers.

Question One: Assume ASC wanted to maximize its return on its new investment in barges, tugs, and—if used—the ramps. Which alternative is best?

Question Two: Assume, temporarily, that all nine alternatives appear equally profitable. From a scheduling standpoint which would be *most susceptible* to service competition, say, by an operation that used trucks between New York and Miami, and barges between Miami and San Juan? Assume that the competitor's service would be faster and as dependable.

Question Three: Which alternative would be *most susceptible* to industry deregulation that would permit outside carriers to enter the market for a short period during peak seasons and help carry the large amounts of traffic?

Question Four: Which alternative would be *most susceptible* in case existing competitors decided to fight back by changing schedules, equipment mix, etc., making it difficult for ASC to achieve as much market penetration as the consultant had predicted? Why?

Question Five: Assume you were a shipper who used the service on a regular basis. Which alternative would you prefer to see ASC adopt? Why?

Question Six: What other real-world factors should ASC management take into account in making this decision?

Logistics sometimes involves interplant movement of materials. This new Great Lakes vessel, M/V American Republic, was designed to carry iron ore pellets from Republic Steel Corporation's plant in Lorain, Ohio, out into Lake Erie to Cleveland, and then up the narrow Cuyahoga River for delivery to steel plants. The vessel then returns to Lorain and can complete one round trip every day. Its size (630 feet long) is small for a modern laker but was dictated by the bridges, channel dimensions, etc., along the Cuyahoga.

Photo courtesy Lake Carriers' Association.

12 Common Carrier Transportation Rates

Without a knowledge of a rational and stable rate structure, many of the existing physical distribution systems in place today may be in jeopardy.
    CHARLES S. SHERWOOD
    Testimony before Motor Carrier Ratemaking Study Commission, 1982

There are certain things, spiritual and material, in the presence of which ordinary mortals stand dumb. When I stood at the tomb of Napoleon, first viewed the Washington Monument, gazed into the Grand Canyon, words were superfluous.
    Feeling akin to this arises within me when I contemplate a freight tariff, with its exceptions, items, notes, commodities, distances, proportionals, disproportionals, gateways, basing points, arbitraries, and God knows what. If the thing itself amazes, what must be the feeling when one views from afar the mind that conceived it?
    I can approach a Superintendent, a General Manager, a General Solicitor, or a President, if you will, with a certain amount of assurance, and composure; but when I approach the portals of a Traffic Expert's office, I not only remove my hat, but also my shoes, and like the devout Moslem, chant as I near the throne:
    Great is Mohammed, but greater is the man who understands the freight tariff.
    Quotation from an anonymous railroad attorney cited in
    PAUL T. MCELHINEY and CHARLES L. HILTON's
    Introduction to Logistics and Traffic Management,
    1968

In two separate decisions . . . , the Interstate Commerce Commission gave the National Motor Freight Tariff Assn. and Roadway Express permission to use the U.S. Postal Service ZIP Code Directory as a means of identifying locations in motor carrier tariffs.
    Transport Topics
    March 15, 1982

Introduction

Common carrier rates are established by the carriers or by carrier rate bureaus, after taking into account the needs of the shippers. To understand how common carrier rates are determined, one must understand the interactions between shippers and carriers. One objective of this chapter is to describe the important factors between shippers and carriers that determine what the rates will be. The chapter will also contain some detailed rates.

Our chapter's title needs some qualification because, as earlier chapters indicated, the "common carrier concept" is eroding as a result of deregulation. This makes it more difficult than it was before deregulation to neatly categorize carriers into common, contract, or exempt classifications. Common carrier rates *once* were nearly synonymous with "rate bureau" (or "collective") rates; that is no longer so, since the deregulation statutes are reducing the number of rate-making situations where rate bureaus can be utilized.

For shippers fortunate to possess some bargaining power with carriers, the rates as determined by the documents described in this chapter are *still used*, although they often can be changed more easily than was once the case. Indeed, these "established" rates may serve as the point of departure from which serious bargaining with the carrier begins. The final contract negotiated may make many references to the various published classifications, tariffs, etc., with the only deviation being, say, the rate charged per hundred pounds.

In chapter 11 we discussed how determining common carrier transportation rates is a highly complex, esoteric, and demanding activity. And it all begins with the freight tariff. In transportation, the term *freight tariff* refers to large paperback books, often 1,000 or more pages in length, that are used to determine the applicable rate on any shipment. These books are considered as "official publications" because they take on the force and effect of the law when carriers file them with the ICC, FMC, or FERC.

- Tariffs are *filed* with regulatory bodies by carriers or rate bureaus which means they are sent to the Washington, D.C. office of the regulatory board. Usually the tariffs are to take effect on some future date, and other parties have a certain number of days to file protests with the regulatory board, asking that the new tariff be suspended until the regulatory board can set a date to hear reasons why the new tariff should or should not be allowed to go into effect.

Today there are more than 350,000 active tariffs on file with the ICC, and according to the ICC's 1981 *Annual Report*, 2,478 new tariffs were received by the Commission *every working day!* Each tariff contains many rates. In 1960, transportation consultant Herbert O. Whitten estimated there were over 43,000,000,000,000 (43 trillion!) rates on file with the ICC.[1]

---

[1] Herbert O. Whitten, "Why Freight Rates Must Be Computerized," *Distribution Age* (March, 1966), p. 30.

Determining common carrier freight rates is so complex that an entire profession—external freight bill auditing—has emerged just to detect errors made in the initial rate determination. We discussed rate auditing firms in chapter 11.)

Full-Cost vs. Value-of-Service Pricing

In *full-cost* pricing each rate is set to cover both fixed and variable costs of the haul plus a profit. Full-cost pricing has an inherent logic to it—"No elaborate economic reasoning is necessary to demonstrate that any privately owned business must at least recover its full costs on its aggregate business if it is to continue long-term operations. The alternatives are bankruptcy or some form of subsidy or government ownership."[2] Nevertheless, there are two basic problems in trying to price each rate at the full (fixed plus variable) cost of production. First, full-cost pricing necessarily involves an *allocation* of fixed costs to each movement of traffic. This allocation, however, must be somewhat *arbitrary*.

> Fully-distributed cost, measured by some kind of arbitrary statistical apportionment of the unallocable costs among the various units or classes of traffic, is an economically invalid criterion. . . . No particular category of traffic can be held economically responsible for any given share of the unallocable costs.[3]

A second problem with full-cost pricing is that it tends to involve *circular reasoning*. To price a product, fixed costs for a given future time period must be allocated to *forecasted* traffic volume for that time period. However, the volume forecasted will affect the allocation of fixed costs per unit. A high volume forecast will result in low per unit fixed-cost allocation and thus a lower total cost rate. This may well result in higher transportation volume because the lower freight rate encourages additional traffic. Alternatively, a low volume forecast results in a higher per unit allocation of fixed costs, resulting in higher freight rates which may stifle traffic volume. There is only one way to accurately determine full costs—and that is to accurately allocate fixed costs—and the only way to do that is know beforehand exactly what the total volume of business will

---

[2]Roy J. Sampson, "The Case For Full Cost Ratemaking," *ICC Practitioners' Journal* (March, 1966), p. 493.

[3]Association of American Railroads, "The Role of Cost In The Minimum Pricing of Railroad Services," *Chicago University Journal of Business* (October, 1962), p. 7; see also: John J. Coyle, "Dissimilar Pricing: A Logical Approach To Regulated Rates," *Public Utilities Fortnightly* (September 15, 1966).

be. However, the *volume* of business is directly affected by the level of freight rates. But the level of freight rates is determined by the expected freight volume! To summarize—freight rates determine volume and volume determines freight rates. This enigma prevents full-cost pricing from being a valid approach to freight rate pricing for most carriers. Only those carriers who can correctly predict future traffic, such as those who are entering into long-term contracts with shippers, can use full-cost pricing for their services. Pipelines are another example since they will not be built until a sufficient number of commitments are received from potential users.

Carriers who cannot use full-cost pricing rely on another type of pricing, called *value-of-service* pricing. Also known as *discriminatory* pricing, *differential* pricing, and *"charging what the traffic will bear"* pricing, this method involves using variable costs to establish a floor that serves as the minimum for rates. Actual rates are usually set higher than variable costs and the objective is to set rates that will maximize the difference between revenues received over the variable costs incurred for carrying each shipment. (See Table 12–1.) The

TABLE 12–1 Value-of-Service Pricing Example

Assume that the railroad's variable costs of carrying carloads of bricks between Tucson, Arizona, and Des Moines, Iowa, were $800 per carload. Assume further that, through experience, they can estimate fairly well the number of cars of bricks they will haul given different rates. The rates, and volumes of traffic are shown here:

(1) Rate per carload of bricks	(2) Number of carloads which will be shipped at rate in (1)	(3) Gross revenues to railroad	(4) Railroad's variable costs	(5) (3) minus (4)
$800	100	$80,000	$80,000	0
$850	90	$76,500	$72,000	$4,500
$900	80	$72,000	$64,000	$8,000
$950	70	$66,500	$56,000	$10,500
$1000	60	$60,000	$48,000	$12,000
$1050	50	$52,500	$40,000	$12,500
$1100	40	$44,000	$32,000	$12,000
$1150	30	$34,500	$24,000	$10,500
$1200	20	$24,000	$16,000	$8,000

Based on these data, the railroad would prefer a rate of $1,050 per carload, which would maximize the difference of gross revenues less variable costs.

Fixed costs are not of concern here. However, when using this sort of pricing, two rules apply. First, the variable or marginal revenue (MR) must be greater than variable or marginal cost (MC). Second, for the firm's entire operation, the average revenue (AR) per shipment carried must be greater than the average cost (AC) of carrying each shipment. Otherwise, the carrier will be losing money.

result is that a ton of stainless steel, a ton of sand, a ton of cigarettes, a ton of books, and a ton of carpet, each moving from Indianapolis to Tallahassee, each pays different rates. One commodity may pay just above variable costs and another will pay 200 to 300 percent of full costs. (Recall also the Piranha River Barge Company Case, which appeared in chapter 3. The Barge company had to charge different amounts from each user in order to collect enough money to run the barge.)

Professors Wilson and Smerk noted that value-of-service pricing allows carriers to ask, "What is this service worth to shippers? We can think of this as the *demand* of the shippers for railroad service. The demand for transportation service is different for each commodity; therefore, if the railroad places the same price on its services for all commodities, it will find that it discourages some shippers from moving their goods."[4] By way of analogy, a meat market that priced all cuts of meat at the same price per pound would run out of steaks and have ox-tails left over.

Value-of-service pricing became extensively utilized as a result of the precedent established by the railroads during the 1800's. The railroads, which had no effective surface competition during this period, established a pricing structure that called for high rates for relatively high-valued commodities (i.e., liquor, tobacco products, watches, etc.) and low charges for products of lower value (sand, gravel, scrap iron, etc.). This pricing system was both sanctioned and encouraged by the ICC. Paul M. Zeis notes the rationale, "The theory behind this method of pricing was to maximize the total movement of goods in the United States, and profits derived from the transportation of high valued . . . commodities were expected to offset the carriage of other commodities at less than their full cost."[5] (This pricing structure—which fully conforms to rational economic logic[6]—is a primary causal factor of many contemporary railroad problems since, over the years, they have lost their "high-value" business to other modes and are left carrying primarily bulk products which sometimes fail to cover full costs.)

Value-of-service pricing, which was started by the railroad industry, has been adopted by all common carrier modes of transportation.

[4]George W. Wilson and George M. Smerk, "Rate Theory," in Stanley J. Hille and Richard F. Poist, Jr., eds., *Transportation: Principles and Perspectives* (Danville, Ill.: Interstate Printers and Publishers, 1974), p. 186.

[5]Paul M. Zeis, "Competitive Rate Making in the United States," *Transportation Journal* (Summer, 1969), p. 36. See also: James C. Nelson, *Railroad Transportation and Public Policy* (Washington, D.C.: The Brookings Institution, 1959), Chapter 10.

[6]See: A. C. Pigou, *The Economics of Welfare* (London: Macmillan and Co., 1962), Chapter 18.

However, it is obvious that value-of-service pricing produces a very complex pricing structure—because each product between each origin and destination often has a unique rate based on demand. The present pricing system confuses the shipping public and it certainly has not produced a strong, growing, and vibrant common carrier system.

Collective Rate-Making

Almost all common carriers participate in collective rate-making via rate bureaus for setting some of their rates. (See chapter 3: rate bu-

- *Collective rate-making* is a description of the rate-making process of common carrier rate bureaus. The needs of both the carriers and their customers are taken into account. While the term implies equality in bargaining power between carriers and shippers, this is not always the case.

reaus for surface carriers were legalized by the 1948 *Reed-Bulwinkle Act*.) Each rate bureau generally works for the carriers in a specific "rate territory." There are approximately 10 rail rate bureaus, 7 do-

- *Rate territory* is the geographic area over which a rate bureau has jurisdiction to set rates. *Intra-territory rates* are established for hauls within that territory. For hauls between two territories, say, the Rocky Mountains and New England, another rate bureau has jurisdiction and it sets *inter-territory rates*. Each rate bureau has its own staff and a carrier can belong to several rate bureaus. Often a single employee of a carrier will serve as its representative to all rate bureaus to which it belongs.

mestic water rate bureaus, and 48 motor carrier rate bureaus. Air carriers also worked together to set rates, but under deregulation they are now subject to anti-trust statutes and it appears they can no longer work together to set prices.

We will trace through the typical procedure involved to establish a new rate or to change an existing rate. First, the shipper and carrier must tentatively agree on a rate that appears to be reasonable to both. Assume a shipper's traffic manager has negotiated with a motor carrier to lower an existing rate. (Various rationales for the lowering of existing rates were discussed in chapter 11.) The motor carrier would then notify the rate bureau having jurisdiction that a rate change is proposed. (If a carrier will not agree to the traffic manager's proposed rate change, the traffic manager has the option to go directly to the rate bureau to request the change.) The proposal for the lower rate is considered by the rate bureau's Standing Rate Committee. The proposal is assigned a docket number, and all bureau members and shippers are notified of the proposed rate change. Figure 12–1 is a flow chart of the rate bureau collective rate-making process. The Regular Procedure in Figure 12–1 is most frequently utilized. After the proposed change is properly advertised, the Standing Rate Committee—composed of rate bureau employees and representatives of the carriers who are members—conducts a hearing on the proposed rate change. Both shippers and carriers present their positions regarding the proposed change. After the hearing, the Standing Rate Committee can approve as proposed, approve with amendments, or disapprove the proposed change. Approval implies that *all* carrier members of the rate bureau agree to charge exactly the same rate as has been proposed.

If the Standing Rate Committee disapproves the rate change, the party initiating the change can appeal to the General Committee, composed of carrier members of the bureau. If this group (which may hold an additional hearing) votes to not authorize the rate change, then any carrier member has one additional—and very important—option: to take *independent action*. This option is a guaranteed right of the *Reed-Bulwinkle Act*. It allows an individual carrier, or a group of carriers, to have its own rate different from that charged by the rest of the bureau members. At this point, the proposed rate—either with the bureau's approval or as an independent action—is filed with the ICC. (ICC handling of a proposed rate change will be discussed shortly.)

Recent Changes in the Reed-Bulwinkle Act

The *Reed-Bulwinkle Act* has been amended a number of times in recent years. The ICC conducted an extensive investigation into the operations of rate bureaus, and its findings were issued in a report in June, 1975. The report was basically tolerant and supportive of rate bureau activities, although the ICC declared that if a rate bureau desired to maintain its exemption from the antitrust laws, then it must henceforth cease—as a rate bureau—from protesting to the Commission whenever a member decided to take independent action. (Individual rate bureau members can still protest independent action if they believe the proposed rate violates the Interstate Commerce Act.)

The second significant change in the *Reed-Bulwinkle Act* was contained in the *Railroad Revitalization and Regulatory Reform Act*

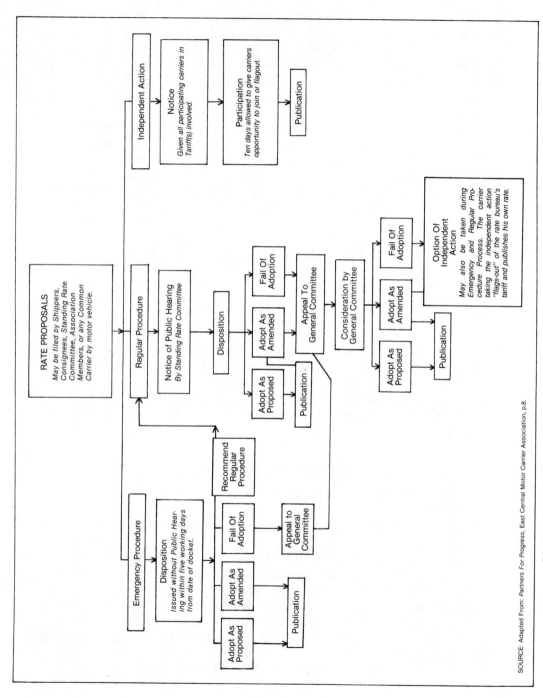

Figure 12–1 Rate Bureau Collective Rate-Making Process. Since deregulation of surface carriers, there are certain situations in which rate bureaus cannot be used for setting common carrier rates.

SOURCE: Adapted From: *Partners For Progress*, East Central Motor Carrier Association, p.8.

of 1976—commonly known as the *4-R Act*. The *4-R Act* restricts railroad rate bureau activities in two situations. First, a proposal by a railroad to establish or change an existing rate for traffic that moves exclusively on the proposing carrier's track cannot be protested at the rate bureau by other railroads. Second, when through-routes and joint-rates (involving a movement handled by connecting carriers) are involved, only carriers that can "practically participate" in the traffic involved are allowed to vote on the rate bureau's acceptance or rejection of the proposed change. G. J. Rooney notes that the phrase "practically participates" apparently means: a carrier would be allowed "voting eligibility on interline proposals if such carrier participates in any commodity rate from an origin involved in the proposal to a destination involved in the proposal."[7]

In 1980, both the motor carrier and the railroad deregulation laws addressed collective rate-making procedures. The *Staggers Rail Act* reaffirmed the previously mentioned two provisions of the *1976 4-R Act*.

The *1980 Motor Carrier Act* made two major changes in motor carrier rate bureau activity. First, when a rate is discussed and voted upon at a rate bureau only those carriers that can participate in the transportation service can vote on it. This involves both single-line (one carrier) and joint-line (multiple carrier) rates. Secondly, and of great importance to the trucking industry, starting in 1984, no carrier may vote on or discuss single-line rate proposals. Since there are thousands of trucking companies, the latter provision would, in effect, eliminate collective rate-making in the trucking industry. Congress recognized that this provision was extremely controversial and, therefore, provided a mechanism to alter this aspect of the 1980 law. The law provided for a Motor Carrier Ratemaking Study Commission. It is to study the single-line rate concept and report its findings to Congress in 1983. *Traffic World* magazine noted:

> Only time will tell what the study commission will recommend to Congress when it issues its report in 1983. Although recommendations made by the commission will not be binding on Congress, there is little doubt that the panel's report will be very influential in determining a course of action for Congress regarding any further legislation on collective rate-making.[8]

If Congress does *not* act, single-line rates cannot be discussed in motor carrier rate bureaus starting in 1984. Therefore, the trucking

[7] G. J. Rooney, "The RRRR Act—Some Implications for Railroad Rate Bureaus," *Transportation Journal* (Winter, 1977), p. 28.

[8] Robert C. Dart, "Truck Rate Panel May Be Industry's Last Hope For Rate-making System," *Traffic World* (July 13, 1981), p. 21.

industry is actively preparing its case to present to the study commission. James C. Harkins, executive director of the National Motor Freight Traffic Association, believes the trucking industry position will prevail when the commission makes its report in 1983. "We're going to make it next to impossible for them to deny the public interest needs for a continuation of the collective process."[9] As this book is being revised, the motor common carrier industry is attempting to develop support for the idea of maintaining rate bureaus.

ICC Rate Procedures

From what has been discussed in preceding chapters it is easy to realize that the ICC is intricately involved in common carrier rate-making. Two important activities of the ICC when it becomes involved in the rate-making or the rate-approval process are:

1. The investigation and suspension procedure by which the ICC examines the legality of a specific rate.
2. The handling of general rate increases, by which carriers attempt to raise all rates in an effort to keep up with increased costs of labor or fuel, in particular, or inflation, in general.

Investigation and Suspension

The ICC is charged with the responsibility to insure that all surface common carriers under their jurisdiction charge rates that are just, reasonable, and not unduly discriminatory. (See chapter 3.) The *Interstate Commerce Act* requires common carriers to notify the ICC and shippers at least 30 days before any rate changes are to go into effect. During this period, any party who believes the proposed rate change violates the *Interstate Commerce Act* can protest the rate to the ICC. The protest, which must be in writing, must clearly specify which provisions of the *Interstate Commerce Act* will be violated.

Protests may come from a number of groups that are neither shippers nor carriers. For example, a city's Chamber of Commerce could protest a rate change believed to be detrimental to the commerce of that city. It would probably claim a violation of Section 3 (now sec-

---

[9] *Ibid.* For an excellent collection of articles that address this highly complex issue, see: Grant M. Davis, editor, *Collective Ratemaking In The Motor Carrier Industry* (Danville, Ill.: Interstate Printers and Publishers, 1980).

tion 10741) of the *Interstate Commerce Act*, which deals with a number of types of discriminatory rates, including illegal preference given to certain geographical areas. Similarly, a state's Director of Economic Development could file a protest, charging that the rate violation would slow the economic growth of his state.

Carriers were typically the group that issued the greatest number of rate change protests. This was ironic, because the clear legislative intent of allowing protests had been to protect *shippers*. Instead, carriers were the dominant protester—and some carriers automatically protested almost *all* proposed rate changes, especially if a competing mode of transportation were proposing a lower rate. Deregulation has reduced the opportunities for carriers to protest the rate actions of others.

When a proposed new rate is filed, the ICC publishes it, and if no protests are filed against the proposed new rate, it becomes effective within 30 days of the date it was filed. The ICC has the power to suspend a rate on its own initiative, even if no protests are filed. The ICC would do this if it believed there is a reasonable probability that the proposed new rate would violate the law. Occasionally, on rate changes that may establish important precedent, the ICC will suspend the rate on its own initiative, even if no group has protested.

When protests are filed, the ICC decides whether they are valid. In most cases, when a number of protests are filed, the Commission will suspend the rate—and this is known as a *I & S Proceeding*. It involves suspending the rate and then investigating its lawfulness. The ICC has seven months either to authorize the proposed rate or to reject it. During the I & S period, the ICC will hold public hearings to help determine the lawfulness of the rate. During the I & S proceeding the burden of proof is upon the carrier proposing the change to prove that the rate is just and reasonable and does not violate the *Interstate Commerce Act*. If any party is dissatisfied with the ICC's decision, they can appeal the ICC's decision to a federal court.

General Rate Increases

The railroad and motor common carrier industries often ask for a general rate increase, i.e., on all rates. In February, 1978, the major motor carrier rate bureaus requested a 7-percent rate increase to offset increased labor costs. In May, 1978, railroads requested a 4-percent rate increase in all regions of the country except the South where they requested only a 2 percent increase.

General rate-increase proposals always generate some opposition. This should be expected since they apply to *all* shippers, and at least a few can be expected to think of some reason to object. There are two grounds for objections.

The first is that a shipper will claim that the reasons given by the carrier industry for needing the increase do not apply to his shipments. For example, the rail carriers might claim that one reason they need a general rate increase is because they have been paying out more to shippers in loss and damage claims. The sand and gravel shippers would then argue that much of the general rate increase should not apply to them since the sand and gravel industry files few loss and damage claims. (This is because sand and gravel are seldom subject to damage or pilferage!)

The second type of objection will come from a shipper whose product is so sensitive to transportation charges that he fears losing all his markets if the general rate increase applies to him. Shippers of scrap metal and baled wastepaper are often in this situation. Transportation costs from their site to their buyers is the major cost of doing business.

If the protesters to general rate increases are successful, the general rate increase will be approved, but the protesters will benefit from either an exception or a hold-down.

- In this instance, an *exception* is a rate that is not increased at all. A *hold-down* is a rate that is increased, but not as much as the general rate increase. For example, the general rate increase might be 5 percent, but the increase on baled wastepaper would be held down to only 2 percent.

General rate-increase proposals are generally subject to I & S proceedings. However, the new deregulation statutes have given carriers more freedom to raise rate levels in order to keep up with inflation.

Basic Freight Rates

So far this chapter has been devoted to some of the larger issues involving common carrier rates and common carrier rate-making. From this point on, more detailed rates and their applications will be discussed.

The specific rate for shipping a product via common carrier from City A to City B is determined by the use of tariffs, which are books containing rules, regulations, and charges for shipping via common carrier.

Class rates can be thought of as standard rates for almost all products or commodities shipped. These rates are found with the help of a *classification tariff*. The *Uniform Freight Classification*, used by railroads, gives each shipment a *rating* or *class* number ranging from a high of 400 down to 13. It contains 30 separate ratings or classes, and it is used extensively by the railroads and many truckers and water carriers. The other widely used classification tariff is the *National Motor Freight Classification*, which has ratings or classes from 500 to 35, with 23 separate ratings. The higher the rating or class, the greater is the relative charge for transporting the commodity.

Among the many factors that are involved in determining a product's specific class or rating are the following:

1. Density of loading that is possible for each product.
2. Additional facilities and services that each product may require.
3. Specialized equipment that may be required.
4. Susceptibility of the product to loss and damage claims.
5. Probability that the product may cause damage to other products being shipped because of spoilage, leakage, etc.
6. Type of packaging used.
7. Value of the commodity being transported.
8. Competition from other carriers of the same mode.
9. Competition from other modes of transport.
10. Transportation rates that are currently charged for similar products.
11. Projected volume of traffic for the product involved.
12. The stage in the manufacturing process that the product represents; that is, a finished product, a component part, etc.
13. The current economic conditions of the industry in which the product is used.[10]

In 1981, the ICC proposed a significant revision in the classification considerations to be utilized by the National Motor Freight Classification. The commission proposed to simplify the procedures. In addition, the proposed revision removes value-of-service considerations that now exist, such as factors 7 to 13 listed above.

The purpose of this change is to encourage common carrier trucking companies to establish rates that closely parallel the costs of providing the transportation service involved. The Commission believes this proposal will have the effect of lowering most trucking rates, which it believes is consistent with the legislative intent of the

[10]Charles A. Taff, *Management of Physical Distribution and Transportation* (Homewood, Ill.: Richard D. Irwin, Inc., 1972), p. 297.

1980 Motor Carrier Act. The ICC proposal would involve only four classification factors: (a) density of the article, (b) stowability, (c) ease or difficulty of handling, and (d) liability.[11]

The classification of a product has no relationship to the shipment's origin, destination, or route. A second document is used to establish the *rate basis* number. This number is the *approximate* distance in miles between the pair of cities in question. With (1) the commodity rating or class and (2) the rate basis number, the specific rate per hundred pounds can be located in (3) another tariff. Finally, (4) to establish the specific cost of moving commodity A between City B and City C, the following formula must be used.

SPECIFIC RATE × WEIGHT = TRANSPORTATION CHARGES
(per hundred)   (in hundreds)
pounds)   of pounds)

This example shows how this formula works. Assume a brewery in Pittsburgh has an order for 1,000 cases of beer (each weighing 12 pounds) to be shipped to Winston-Salem. Because the size of the order is relatively small, it will be sent via motor common carrier. The truckers certified to operate between these cities use the National Motor Freight Classification (NMFC). To establish the commodity classification, the NMFC index is first consulted. Figure 12–2 illustrates an index page showing beers are item 111470. We next must locate this item number in the NMFC, and this is shown in Figure 12–3. Notice that the tariff specifies in detail the acceptable packaging containers for beer. The rating or class is found in the right hand column. It is 65 for an LTL (less than truck-load) shipment.

The TL (truck-load) rating or class is 35, and to qualify for this lower rating, the MW (minimum weight) is specified, 50.2 hundredweight (or 50,200 pounds). Since only 12,000 pounds are being transported, the proper classification is 65. Next the rate basis number must be located in the tariff that is concerned with the traffic's origin and destination. Figure 12–4 is the proper page from a rate basis tariff, and the applicable number for our example—Pittsburgh to Winston-Salem is 490. Next, with the class or rating of 65 and the rate basis number of 490, we proceed to a Table of Class Rates, which is illustrated in Figure 12–5. The rate basis numbers are in the right hand column, and since our number is 490 we use the column designated 481 to 500. In the second right hand column is the *weight*

---

[11] See: "ICC Calls For Revision of Trucking Commodity Classification System," *Traffic World* (May 25, 1981), pp. 46–47.

INDEX TO ARTICLES

This index has no effect upon the application of the classes provided on Pages 242 to 649. It is to be used only as a guide to the location of the item containing the classification of an article.

ARTICLE	ITEM	ARTICLE	ITEM	ARTICLE	ITEM
A		Boat(s):		Cups:	
Acetadol.	42610	Outboard motor.	24700	Turpentine,zinc.	201000
Acetaldehyde.	42610	Boots:			
Acetanilid.	42620	Leather	28220	**D**	
Acetates:		NOI.	28160	Diffusers:	
Sodium.	46090	Wooden.	28220	Lamp,NOI	109090
Acetone, NOI.	42640	Borings:		Lighting fixture,NOI	109090
Acids:		Zinc.	200580	Diggers:	
Abietic.	3000	Boxes:		Post hole.	131710
Acetic.	3020	Shadow.	79195	Discs:	
Acetylsalicylic	58520	Bromide:		Road grader.	122060,v122500
Boric.	4020	Sodium.	46200	Drags,road.	v122440
Carbolic.	4040	Butter:		Drivers:	
Acrylate:		Dehydrated.	55380	Post	131706
Butyl	42650	NOI.	55380	Drops,cough.	58730
Ethyl	42650			Dyestuffs,NOI.	60280
Ethylhexyl.	42650	**C**			
Hydroxyethyl.	42650	Cabinets:		**E**	
Hydroxypropyl.	42650	Filing,steel and fibreboard		Edge(s):	
Isobutyl.	42650	combined	79220	Cutting,grader.	122020
Methyl.	42650	Canoes.	24700	Cutting,road grader.	v122500
Aerials:		Carriers:		Cutting,scraper.	122020
Aircraft.	60530	Tool bar.	131720	Enclosures:	
Automobile radio.	60520	Cars:		Antenna.	14440
Ale	111470	Dump.	v122500	Engines:	
Anchors:		Carts:		Traction	v122500
Brass,bronze or copper,NOI.	30120	Concrete.	v122500	Extender(s):	
Anhydride,acetic.	42630	Dump.	v122500	Zinc oxide	201080
Animals:		Cases:		Extinguishers,fire	
Stuffed	14400	Filing.	79220	69180,69185,69190,69220	
Annunciators.	14420	Charges:			
Anodes:		Fire extinguisher	69160	**F**	
Brass,bronze or copper.	30140	Cheese.	55470	Fat(s):	
Zinc.	200500	Chloride:		Anhydrous butter	55380
Antennae:		Sodium.	74660	Butter,frozen.	v55430
Aircraft.	60530	Clips:		Films,moving picture	39700
Apparatus:		Nose,swimming	69120	Findings,boot.	28140
Household or home		Clocks,neon illumination.	48710	Findings,shoe.	28140
playground	15510	Clocks,NOI.	48720	Fins,swimming.	69120
Arresters:		Cloth(s):		Fixtures:	
Dust.	60140	Abrasive.	1030	Electric floodlighting.	109480
Articles:		Clothing:		Flitters,aluminum.	149520
Plastic or rubber,NOI.	156600	NOI.	49880	Flitters,bronze.	149520
Zinc,NOI.	201040	Coffee:		Food:	
Ash(es):		Condensed	72600,72620	Cheese	55470
Zinc.	200520	Extract of.	72600,72620	Furniture:	
Aspirin	58520	Green	72660	Bamboo.	79050
Assemblies:		Instant.	72600	Cane.	79050
Tractor-grader power		Roasted	72680	Fibre.	79050
control.	v122500	Soluble	72600	Grass.	79050
Attachments:		Unground.	72680	Rattan	79050
Bulldozer	122040	Collectors:		Reed	79050
Augers:		Dust.	60140	Willow	79050
Post hole	131710	Compound(s):			
		Fire extinguisher	69160	**G**	
B		Water softening,medicated.	58540	Globes:	
Barrows:		Water softening,perfumed.	58540	Lamp,NOI	109090
Concrete.	v122500	Cradles:		Lighting fixture,NOI	109090
Bar(s):		Bamboo.	79070	Goggles,swimming	69120
Tool,tractor attachment	131720	Cane.	79070	Graders and levelers	
Zinc.	200540	Fibre.	79070	combined	v122100
Base(s):		Grass	79070	Graders and road rollers	
Fluorescent electric lamp.	109020	Rattan	79070	combined	v122120
Incandescent electric		Reed.	79070	Graders:	
lamp	109040	Willow.	79070	Drag.	122080
Bassinets	79070	Cream:		Levelers and road rollers	
Beers	111470	Frozen.	v55430	combined	122100
Belts:		Cribs:		Machinery.	v122440
NOI.	49800	Bamboo.	79070	Wheeled.	122140
Beverages:		Cane.	79070	Grids:	
Alcoholic	111420	Fibre.	79070	Resistance	62130
Cereal,non-intoxicating	111470	Grass	79070	Grindings:	
Bins:		Rattan	79070	Zinc.	200580
Stone	v122500	Reed.	79070		
Bisulphite:		Willow.	79070	**H**	
Sodium.	46180,46190	Crushers:		Harrows:	
Blades:		Stone	v122500	Machinery.	v122500
Grader.	122020	Crystals:		Heaters:	
Road grader	v122500	Bath.	58540	Asphalt road	
Scraper	122020	Cultivators:		construction	v122500
Blanks:		Machinery.	v122500	Road repairing	v122500
Zinc,NOI.	200560				

For explanation of abbreviations and reference marks,see last page of this tariff.

Figure 12–2 Index to National Motor Freight Classification. Reprinted with permission of the tariff publisher.

Item	ARTICLES	CLASSES		MW
		LTL	TL	
	LAMPS OR LIGHTING GROUP: subject to item 109000			
109139	**Globes, Shades, Diffusers, Refractors or Reflectors,** NOI, lamp or lighting fixture, in wooden boxes or in Packages 1289 or 37F:			
Sub 1	Not nested	300	300	AQ
Sub 2	Nested	250	250	AQ
109280	**Lamp or Lantern Parts,** NOI, finished, metal other than cast iron	85	70	16.2
109320	**Lamp Socket Tubes** (lining for incandescent electric lamp sockets), fibre, paper or pulpboard, in boxes or crates	150	100	10.2
109400	**Lamps,** baking oven, cast iron, in packages	92½	55	24.2
109440	**Lamps,** electric, arc, without globes or shades, in barrels or boxes	100	55	30.2
109460	**Lamps,** artificial sunlight, heat ray or therapeutic, electric, with or without electric incandescent lamps, in boxes or crates	125	85	12.2
109470	**Lamps,** blueprinting or photographic, NOI, electric, with or without metal reflectors or stands, in barrels boxes or crates	125	70	15.2
109475	**Lamps,** calcium carbide **(Lights),** in cans in boxes	100	70	20.2
109477	**Lamps,** cap, hat, head band or belt, battery operated, with or without battery, see Note, item 109478, in boxes	100	70	16.2
109478	NOTE—Applies on lamps consisting of head-piece, cable and other appurtenances for attaching to the battery.			
109500	**Lamps,** electric, gas or oil, NOI, portable, with or without globes, shades or reflectors, see Notes, items 109501, 109504 and 109512, in barrels or in Packages 794, 817, 970, 1424, 1467, 2204, 5F, or 30F, having a density of:			
Sub 1	Less than 8 pounds per cubic foot, see Note, item 109514	150	125	10.2
Sub 2	8 pounds per cubic foot or greater, see Note, item 109514	100	70	18.2
109501	NOTE—Applies only on portable lamps such as floor standing, desk, table, wall hanging (pin-ups) or pole lamps.			
109504	NOTE—One incandescent or flourescent lamp (bulb) for each socket may be included in same box with lamp.			
109512	NOTE—The quantity of globes, shades, reflectors or similar devices must not exceed the number required to equip the articles with which shipped.			
109514	NOTE—When lamps and their complement of globes, shades or reflectors are in separate packages, the density for determining the applicable provisions must be the result of the division of the total weight of all packages by the total cubage (cubic displacement) of all such packages.			
109550	**Lamps (Bulbs),** electric, incandescent, NOI; **or Photo Flash Lamps (Bulbs);** see Note, item 109604, in barrels or boxes, or Packages 256 or 257	150	125	10.2
109570	**Lamps (Bulbs),** electric, mercury vapor, see Note, item 109604, in barrels, boxes or in crates, or Package 547	150	100	10.2
109600	**Lamps (Bulbs or Tubes),** electric, fluorescent, other than neon, see Note, item 109604, in wooden boxes or in Packages 256, 257, 1161, 1417 or 1430	100	55	22.2
109604	NOTE—Applies only on the articles named which, when installed in lamps, lighting fixtures or other apparatus, function as sources of light or heat.			
109895	**Shades or Reflectors,** NOI, lamp or lighting fixture, iron, steel or tin, with or without equipment of sockets:			
Sub 1	Not nested, in barrels, boxes or crates	100	55	20.2
Sub 2	Nested, in barrels, boxes or crates	85	55	20.2
Sub 3	Nested solid, in barrels, boxes or crates	70	55	20.2
111400	**LIQUORS, BEVERAGE:**			
111420	**Beverages,** alcoholic, carbonated, containing not exceeding 6 percent of alcohol by volume, in glass containers or metal cans in boxes	65	35	30.2
111450	**Liquors,** alcoholic, NOI, in glass or in metal cans in barrels or boxes, see Note, item 111452: in Packages 1343 or 1352; or in bulk in barrels	100	50	40.2
111452	NOTE—Wooden boxes must be nailed with cement-coated nails; or must be encircled by two or more continuous metal or wooden straps; or must be encircled by one wire or metal strap around the center or by one wire or metal strap around each end, securely fastened to prevent removal; or all side joints must be sealed with metal seals and ends nailed.			
111470	**Liquors, Malt: Ale, Beers, Beer Tonic, Porter, Stout or non-intoxicating Cereal Beverage,** in glass in bottle carriers with tops securely fastened, see Note, item 111473, in glass or metal cans in barrels or boxes, in metal dispensing containers less than 5 gallons capacity in carriers made of 500 pound test solid fibreboard, in boxes enclosed in crates, or in bulk in barrels; also TL, in open top carriers, or in metal cans in fibre boxes, not sealed, or in Packages 174, 186, 238, 788, 1145, 1155, 1162, 1257, 1360, 1376, 1431 or 1447	65	35	50.2
111473	NOTE—Bottle carrier containers made of fibreboard need not meet the certificate requirements of item 222, but must be equipped with partitions full shoulder height of the bottles loaded therein. Such partitions must touch all four sides of the carrier. Inner packaging must comply with item 222-2 or Package 174.			
111490	**Vermouth,** in containers in barrels or boxes, or in bulk in barrels	100	50	40.2

For explanation of abbreviations and reference marks, see last page of this tariff.

Figure 12–3 Page from National Motor Freight Classification. Reprinted with permission of the tariff publisher.

TARIFF ICC SMC 530-A

RATE BASIS NUMBERS
(FOR APPLICATION, SEE ITEMS 70 AND 90)
(APPLY RATES OPPOSITE CORRESPONDING RATE BASIS NUMBERS IN SECTION ONE)

BETWEEN ♦ AND ♦	PENNSYLVANIA														
	LEWISTOWN	LIGONIER	LINESVILLE(N)	LYKENS	MACDONALDTON	MANSFIELD	MARIENVILLE	MEADVILLE	NEW BETHLEHEM	NEW FREEDOM,PA-MILLERS,MD	NIVERTON	OIL CITY	PATTON	PHILADELPHIA	PHOENIXVILLE
FLORIDA															
IMMOKALEE	1219	1375	1407	1203	1210	1366	1415	1415	1372	1109	1214	1415	1278	1174	1177
JACKSONVILLE	920	1075	1107	903	910	1066	1115	1115	1072	806	914	1115	978	874	887
JAMIESON	1019	1150	1040	1002	994	1165	1131	1048	1090	905	998	1069	1162	973	986
JASPER	946	1100	1074	929	936	1092	1141	1082	1098	832	940	1103	1004	900	913
JUPITER	1184	1350	1371	1167	1174	1330	1379	1379	1336	1070	1178	1379	1242	1138	1151
GEORGIA															
ABBEVILLE	897	1025	984	878	862	1044	1067	992	1024	783	866	1013	930	851	864
ALBANY	962	1000	985	943	927	1109	1076	993	1035	848	931	1014	995	916	929
ALMA	884	1050	1045	867	874	1030	1079	1053	1036	770	878	1074	942	838	851
AMERICUS	932	1050	950	913	897	1076	1041	958	1000	818	901	979	965	886	899
ARLINGTON	998	1000	1002	979	963	1142	1093	1010	1052	884	967	1031	1031	952	965
NORTH CAROLINA															
CARRBORO	475	600	653	458	456	621	660	661	617	361	459	660	523	429	437
CHARLOTTE	559	680	722	540	524	703	729	730	686	445	528	729	592	513	527
CLARKTON	575	740	777	558	580	721	784	785	744	450	594	784	647	529	542
CLIFFSIDE	620	740	718	601	585	767	790	726	747	512	589	747	653	574	587
CLINTON	501	680	722	484	523	647	711	729	670	387	526	712	591	455	468
SOUTH CAROLINA															
AIKEN	733	875	906	716	707	879	912	902	869	619	711	912	775	687	700
ALLENDALE	725	875	909	708	712	871	917	917	874	611	716	917	780	679	692
ANDERSON	702	825	804	683	667	846	872	812	829	588	671	833	735	656	669
ANDREWS	634	800	836	617	637	780	843	844	800	520	642	843	717	588	601
BARNWELL	710	875	893	693	696	856	901	901	858	596	700	901	764	664	677

BETWEEN ♦ AND ♦	PENNSYLVANIA														
	PITTSBURGH	PUNXSUTAWNEY	QUEEN JCT	READING	RENOVO	ROBERTSDALE	SALIX	SALTSBURG	SCHUYLKILL HAVEN	SCRANTON	SHAMOKIN	SHIPPENSBURG	SLATE RUN	STEWARTSTOWN	STONEBORO
ALABAMA															
ANNISTON	758	843	797	853	938	897	852	797	863	936	873	759	934	787	793
ATMORE	1001	1086	1040	1097	1181	1156	1095	1040	1122	1195	1132	1018	1193	1010	1036
BAYOU LA BATRE	1061	1146	1100	1167	1241	1216	1155	1100	1182	1255	1192	1078	1253	1080	1096
BIRMINGHAM	779	864	818	895	959	939	873	818	905	978	915	801	976	829	814
BLOCTON	816	901	855	932	996	976	910	855	942	1015	952	838	1013	866	851
GEORGIA															
ATHENS	818	823	860	731	838	793	781	807	760	833	770	656	831	644	877
ATLANTA	769	854	808	792	899	854	842	808	821	894	831	717	892	705	804
AUGUSTA	796	801	838	709	816	771	759	785	738	811	748	634	809	622	861
BAINBRIDGE	1006	1094	1045	992	1101	1054	1052	1045	1021	1096	1033	927	1094	905	1041
BAXLEY	941	946	983	843	952	905	904	930	872	947	884	779	945	756	1006
NORTH CAROLINA															
GOLDSBORO	576	581	618	432	541	494	539	565	461	536	473	397	534	345	660
GREENSBORO	526	531	568	439	546	501	489	515	468	541	478	364	539	352	610
GREENVILLE	565	570	607	411	530	483	528	554	441	523	462	387	523	334	649
HAMLET	634	646	676	526	635	588	597	623	555	630	567	472	628	439	718
HENDERSON	531	535	573	387	496	449	494	520	416	491	428	352	489	300	615
WHITEVILLE	589	760	810	572	611	735	799	817	758	475	614	800	679	543	556
WILMINGTON	543	720	764	526	565	689	753	771	712	429	568	754	633	497	510
WILSON	434	620	655	417	456	580	644	662	603	320	459	645	531	388	401
WINDSOR	442	620	663	425	464	588	657	670	611	328	467	653	522	339	355
WINSTON-SALEM	490	600	652	470	454	633	659	660	621	380	463	659	526	448	461

FOR EXPLANATION OF REFERENCE MARKS NOT EXPLAINED ON THIS PAGE, SEE LAST PAGE(S) OF TARIFF AND/OR EFFECTIVE SUPPLEMENTS THERETO.

Figure 12–4 Page from a Rate Basis Tariff. Reprinted with permission of the Southern Motor Carriers Rate Conference.

SECTION 1
TABLE OF CLASS RATES
FOR APPLICATION, SEE ITEM 5000 ON THE TITLE PAGE OF THIS SECTION

92½	85	77½	70	65	60	55	50	45	40	37½	35	WEIGHT GROUP	RATE BASIS NUMBERS INCLUSIVE
774	720	663	604	570	531	493	453	...	...	...	...	L5C	381 TO 400
688	635	580	521	482	445	410	372	...	...	...	...	5-1M	
586	539	493	444	416	383	348	316	...	...	...	...	1-2	
543	498	459	413	382	350	323	294	...	...	...	...	2-5	MC
452	415	379	341	317	293	271	243	...	...	...	...	5-10	1482
435	401	364	329	307	283	260	234	...	...	...	...	10M	
424	392	355	321	298	277	252	230	207	183	182	181	VT	
793	737	675	616	578	542	500	468	...	...	...	...	L5C	401 TO 420
700	644	587	532	495	460	418	381	...	...	...	...	5-1M	
601	550	505	455	422	389	358	323	...	...	...	...	1-2	
554	512	466	420	390	357	331	300	...	...	...	...	2-5	MC
460	425	388	348	323	298	275	251	...	...	...	...	5-10	1495
445	410	375	337	312	288	264	243	...	...	...	...	10M	
438	399	364	330	306	284	259	236	211	189	186	185	VT	
812	748	692	632	594	553	512	475	...	...	...	...	L5C	421 TO 440
724	661	600	545	509	466	430	391	...	...	...	...	5-1M	
617	568	517	465	434	400	364	336	...	...	...	...	1-2	
570	524	478	433	403	370	341	305	...	...	...	...	2-5	MC
472	431	397	359	331	304	279	257	...	...	...	...	5-10	1507
455	417	383	346	319	293	270	248	...	...	...	...	10M	
445	407	373	337	310	289	264	240	216	192	190	189	VT	
823	761	699	642	602	559	525	479	...	...	...	...	L5C	441 TO 460
734	676	616	557	517	476	435	397	...	...	...	...	5-1M	
627	576	522	476	440	406	370	339	...	...	...	...	1-2	
578	535	489	438	410	375	345	314	...	...	...	...	2-5	MC
481	441	404	365	338	312	286	262	...	...	...	...	5-10	1515
465	425	389	353	326	301	276	252	...	...	...	...	10M	
451	414	381	342	316	293	269	244	220	195	194	192	VT	
845	780	717	654	614	576	531	491	...	...	...	...	L5C	461 TO 480
753	696	632	569	529	487	449	410	...	...	...	...	5-1M	
643	590	538	489	452	420	384	347	...	...	...	...	1-2	
598	548	498	453	418	388	352	323	...	...	...	...	2-5	MC
496	456	414	373	346	321	293	269	...	...	...	...	5-10	1539
478	440	400	359	335	310	283	259	...	...	...	...	10M	
464	426	391	353	327	300	277	250	227	201	199	198	VT	
861	800	737	674	630	583	543	500	...	...	...	...	L5C	481 TO 500
775	709	647	586	543	504	462	420	...	...	...	...	5-1M	
658	607	554	501	461	431	393	359	...	...	...	...	1-2	
611	562	513	462	429	400	362	331	...	...	...	...	2-5	MC
507	465	425	386	357	329	299	275	...	...	...	...	5-10	1545
490	449	410	372	343	317	289	264	...	...	...	...	10M	
473	439	398	359	334	307	285	258	232	207	203	202	VT	
878	815	747	683	640	600	553	511	...	...	...	...	L5C	501 TO 520
785	724	659	594	552	512	466	429	...	...	...	...	5-1M	
671	617	562	509	470	435	398	363	...	...	...	...	1-2	
621	570	521	470	436	405	369	337	...	...	...	...	2-5	MC
514	473	430	392	363	334	304	277	...	...	...	...	5-10	1557
496	456	414	379	351	322	293	268	...	...	...	...	10M	
484	444	403	364	339	310	288	262	236	209	208	207	VT	
897	833	764	694	653	607	565	525	...	...	...	...	L5C	521 TO 540
804	741	676	609	567	521	480	435	...	...	...	...	5-1M	
690	636	576	519	485	445	408	370	...	...	...	...	1-2	
635	584	535	483	446	414	376	345	...	...	...	...	2-5	MC
528	489	443	399	371	343	315	286	...	...	...	...	5-10	1570
510	470	427	385	358	331	305	276	...	...	...	...	10M	
495	454	413	377	348	322	293	268	241	212	211	210	VT	
911	843	773	703	660	614	571	528	...	...	...	...	L5C	541 TO 560
815	752	683	618	574	529	483	441	...	...	...	...	5-1M	
697	642	584	530	491	452	419	374	...	...	...	...	1-2	
649	594	542	491	455	420	386	348	...	...	...	...	2-5	MC
536	494	447	409	378	346	318	291	...	...	...	...	5-10	1585
517	475	431	395	363	335	308	280	...	...	...	...	10M	
504	463	423	382	355	327	300	275	244	219	216	215	VT	

Figure 12–5 Table of Class Rates. Reprinted with permission of the Southern Motor Carriers Rate Conference.

group. We will use the 10M (M is the Roman numeral for 1,000) line. It is applicable for all shipments that weigh between 10,000 pounds to VT (volume or truck-load quantities, which for beer was 50,200 pounds). Finding the class of 65 on the top row, and using the column of 10M in the 481–500 range of rate basis numbers, we find the rate is 343. Rates are generally quoted in cents per hundred pounds, in this instance 343 cents or $3.43 per hundred pounds. The total charge can now be determined using this formula:

SPECIFIC RATE × WEIGHT = TRANSPORTATION CHARGES
(per hundred)   (in hundreds)
pounds)   of pounds)
$3.43   ×   120   = $411.60

An unusual aspect of class rates is that it is sometimes possible to pay a lower total charge by alleging to ship a higher weight than is actually transported.[12] To understand how this works, assume the same brewery now wanted to transport 40,000 pounds of beer between the same origin and destination. The rate using the 10M column and a class of 65 equals a charge of $1,372 ($3.43 × 400 = $1,372). However, if the motor carrier is told the shipment weighs 50,200 pounds (this is legal), the shipper qualifies for the VT line and a class of 35. The charge in this case is $1,014.04 ($2.02 × 502 = $1,014.04). This situation is obviously advantageous and would be used. Transportation people say the shipment involved 40,000 pounds of actual freight and 10,200 pounds of "wind." The point where it is cheaper to ship "wind" and qualify for the truck-load class is known as a *break-even point*. Break-even points must always be considered when using class rates.

One other item must also be checked when using class rates (and some other types of rate tariffs): the carriers' minimum charge for any shipment. Often a tariff, in its early pages, will contain a statement that the minimum charge for any shipment is, say, ten dollars. In that case the ten-dollar charge would prevail, even if the calculations through all the steps yielded a smaller amount.

Exception rates can best be thought of as modified class rates. They are designed to produce a less expensive rate than the class rate. The class rate formula, however, is still used to calculate the freight charge. The exception rate is lower than the class rate by taking "exception" to some aspect of the class rate. Thus, the exception tariff may provide for a lower rating or class than the class tariff,

[12] See: J. B. Sims, "Freight Rates and Their Break-Even Points," *Transportation Journal* (Winter, 1972), pp. 15–19.

it may provide for less expensive packaging requirements, or it may require a lower minimum weight to qualify for a TL or CL rate. Exceptions are generally the result of competitive factors, either between modes or between individual carriers of the same mode. They also are established because of unusual regional or local operating conditions.

Commodity rates (sometimes referred to as point-to-point rates) can be thought of as custom-made economy rates that a carrier makes available because a specific commodity is shipped in large quantities or at frequent intervals. These rates, which are found in commodity tariffs, are specific in nature. They typically state the commodity, the origins and destinations involved, and the minimum weight required for the commodity rate. Figure 12–6 illustrates a commodity rate tariff page. Commodity rates are lower than either class or exception rates and hence should be used whenever they are available.

Hierarchy of Rates

Class, exception, and commodity rates have been discussed. It is important to note that there is a priority or *hierarchy of rates* regarding which of these rates to use at any given time. The *Interstate Commerce Act* stated that *commodity* rates have the highest priority. In other words, whenever a shipment is tendered to a carrier, the commodity rate should be used if it is available. If it does not exist, then an *exception* rate should be used. If it is not available, the class rate can always be found for any product. (This is even true for new products that are not currently located in the class tariffs. A procedure known as the *rule of analogy* is used. This states that if a product is not described in the tariff, then the shipper and carrier will agree to use the rating or class of the most similar existing product in the tariff.) Eventually, the new product will be placed in the classification tariff. Having said all this, we conclude that the shipper may use whatever rate results in the lowest legitimate charges.

Additional Types of Freight Rates

Class, exception, and commodity rates are the basic transportation freight rates. However, there are a large number of additional aspects which are further used to classify commodity freight rates.

ITEM	COMMODITY	FROM (And points taking same rates as provided)	TO	LTL RATE	VOLUME RATE	VOLUME MIN WT (In lbs)
	RATES IN CENTS PER 100 POUNDS, EXCEPT AS OTHERWISE PROVIDED					

ITEM	COMMODITY	FROM (And points taking same rates as provided)	TO	LTL RATE	VOLUME RATE	VOLUME MIN WT (In lbs)
4060-A	BAGS, VIZ.: Burlap, new, lined or not lined, in machine pressed bales. Cotton, clayed or other than clayed, in machine pressed bales. Paper, NOI. CLOTH, DRY GOODS OR FABRICS, VIZ.:	Des Moines. . . Ia.	Decatur . . . .Ill.	...	① 125	20000
			Kansas City ... Mo.	...	93	
			St. Louis . . . Mo.	...	① 98	
		Kansas City . . Mo.	Des Moines . . Ia.	...	② 93	
			Farragut. . . . Ia. Shenandoah . . Ia.	...	85	

Bagging, Viz.:
Burlap, new, lined or not lined, in machine pressed bales.
Cotton, clayed, or other than clayed, in machine pressed bales.

① Applies only on Bags, cotton, clayed or other than clayed, in machine pressed bales.

② Will not apply on straight shipments of Bags, garment, paper.

ITEM	COMMODITY	FROM	TO	LTL RATE	VOLUME RATE	VOLUME MIN WT (In lbs)
▲ 12490-B	MACHINERY OR MACHINES, OR PARTS NAMED, VIZ.: Hydraulic Dumping Hoists (Farm Wagon), (See Note). Reducing Machines, gear or speed, and/or parts and Accessories (Wagon Unloaders), (See Note). VEHICLES, OTHER THAN SELF-PROPELLED, VIZ.: Farm Carts, Truck, Trailers or Wagons, Horsedrawn or Trailer, with or without bodies, KD. VEHICLE PARTS, VIZ.: Bodies, farm wagon, KD.	Quincy. . . . .Ill.	Des Moines. . . Ia.	...	71	20000
			Mason City. . . Ia.	...	84	
			Omaha . . . . .Neb.	...	① 105	20000
				...	① 99	24000
				...	① 93	30000
			Scotch Grove. . Ia.	...	67	20000
			Sioux City. . . Ia.	...	96	
			Sioux Falls . .S.D.	...	② 101	30000
			Spencer . . . . Ia.	...	94	20000

① Applies only on:
   Machinery or Machines,
      or Parts named, Viz.:
         Hydraulic Dumping Hoists (Farm Wagon).
   Vehicles, Other Than Self-Propelled, Viz.:
      Farm Carts, Trucks, Trailers or Wagons, Horse Drawn or Trailer, with or without bodies, KD.
   Vehicle Parts, Viz.:
      Bodies, farm wagon, KD.
② Applies only when the shipment is loaded into or onto the truck by the shipper and unloaded therefrom by the consignee.

NOTE - Weight of the Hydraulic Dumping Hoists and Reducing Machines, gear or speed, must not exceed 25 per cent of the weight of the shipment.

EXCEPTIONS:
Via A & B Transfer, Inc., rates will not apply.

ITEM	COMMODITY	FROM	TO	LTL RATE	VOLUME RATE	VOLUME MIN WT (In lbs)
14820-A	ADVERTISING MATTER, VIZ.: Catalogues and parts thereof. PRINTED MATTER, VIZ.: (See Notes 1 and 2). Magazines and Periodicals and Parts or Section thereof.	Des Moines. . . Ia.	Chicago . . . .Ill.	...	① 50	22000

Rate applies only on:
(1) Shipment originating at Des Moines, Ia., and consigned to Postmaster or post office for movement beyond Chicago, Illinois, or
(2) Shipments consigned for delivery to a railroad or motor carrier within the city limits of Chicago, Illinois, where such shipments are unloaded into freight cars a charge of 2 1/4 cents per 100 pounds will be assessed on actual weight or volume minimum weight whichever is greater, such charge to be in addition to all other applicable charges.

① Will also apply on split delivery, subject to the following (See Note 2):
   (a) Shipments moving on one bill of lading may be delivered to two addresses or locations at the same destination points.
   (b) Shipper must show on bill of lading the address or location and the number of pieces or packages and weight to be delivered at each address or location.
   (c) Where split delivery service is performed by the carrier a charge of 791 cents will be made in addition to all other rates and charges applicable to the shipment.

NOTE 1 - All charges on shipments moving under rate in this item must be prepaid.
NOTE 2 - NOT SUBJECT TO ITEM 1242.
EXCEPTIONS:
Via A & B Transfer, Inc., rate will not apply.

For explanation of abbreviations and reference marks see last page(s) of tariff.

Figure 12-6 Page from a Commodity Tariff. Reprinted with permission of the Middlewest Motor Freight Bureau.

Quantity-Oriented Rates

Many commodity rates are established on the basis of the quantity or volume of freight that is tendered to the carriers.

Volume rates are found in the trucking industry. They generally are used for shipments that are larger than the truck-load (TL) minimum and are designed to compete with railroad CL rates. A major difference between the rail CL rate and volume truck rates is that the volume truck rates include loading and unloading assistance by the truck driver. CL rates require that all loading and unloading is done by the shipper and consignee; i.e., the railroad merely "spots" the car on a siding, next to a warehouse door.

Incentive rates are primarily used by the railroad industry to encourage heavier loading of rail cars. Assume the CL minimum required weight is 30,000 pounds, yet the rail car itself (especially if it is newer) frequently has the physical capacity to hold 70,000 to 100,000 pounds. Since it costs the railroad very little more to haul a car with 30,000 pounds as opposed to the same car with 100,000 pounds, the railroads have initiated rates designed to provide an "incentive" to shippers to load more freight into each car. An incentive rate would be: 103 cents per 100 pounds for the first 30,000 pounds; 65 cents per 100 pounds from 30,000 pounds to 60,000 pounds; and 51 cents per 100 pounds for 60,000 to 100,000 pounds.[13]

Multiple-Car rates are used by railroads. Generally, multiple-car rates call for a minimum of 5 cars and maximum of 25 cars. The logic for the multiple-car rate reductions is that by moving cars in blocks, switching costs at terminal areas are reduced. These rates also specify the minimum weight that must be loaded into each car. Multiple-trailer rates are used in much the same way by the truckers to compete with the railroads' multiple-car rates.

Train-Load rates are the rail rates used with unit-trains, which specialize in entire train-load movements of coal, grain, etc. The train-load tariffs often specify the minimum tonnage to be transported via each unit-train and also the minimum number of trains that will be operated each week, month, or year.

Miscellaneous Rate Definitions

A *local rate* implies that a transportation service from City A to City B is performed by just one carrier. The term *local* has nothing to

[13] See: Thomas C. Campbell and Sidney Katell, "Railroad Volume Freight Rates: Evolution and Analysis," *ICC Practitioners' Journal* (January–February, 1977), pp. 146–160.

do with geographical consideration. It means only that a single carrier is used. A local rate on the Burlington Northern Railroad can apply from Chicago to Seattle. On the other hand, a *joint rate* extends over the line of two or more connecting carriers.

A *through rate* is one that applies from origin to destination for a shipment. It can be either a local through rate or a joint through rate. A through route is an arrangement between connecting carriers in which a transportation service is offered from origin on one carrier's line to a destination on the other carrier's line.

Combination rates exist when there are no joint or local rates from origin to destination. Therefore, the applicable rate is a combination of the local rate or joint rates. The latter is feasible, as shown in Figure 12–7. The shipment originates in City A and is bound for City E. If there are no joint rates, then the applicable rate will be a combination rate made up by adding local rates 1, 2, 3, and 4. However, assume a joint rate does exist from City B to City E. Then the applicable rate is also a combination rate, the sum of local rate 1 and joint rate 1.

All-commodity rates are also known as *freight, all kinds (FAK)*. These are commodity rates established by the railroads and motor carriers and are used to compete with private truck transportation. These rates are applied only on the basis of weight and without regard to the type of freight that is actually transported. The most frequent users of FAK rates are retail chain stores, forwarders, and shippers' cooperatives, all of which transport large shipments containing a variety of unrelated products. Another example of an "all-freight"

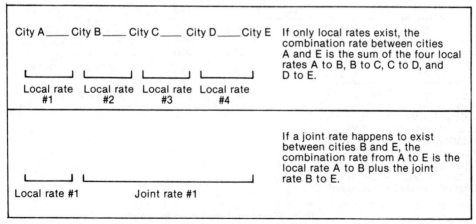

Figure 12–7 Combination Rates.

type of rate comes from the small parcel, or courier service, where the only concern is weight, origin, and destination. (However, the carrier may refuse to carry certain items, say, hazardous matter.) Figure 12–8 is a West Coast Air Carrier's simplified rate card.

It was noted earlier that common carriers are responsible for the "full actual loss" if they receive a valid loss or damage claim from a shipper or consignee. However, in the case of *released value rates*

✦IRCΛL Cargo

18025 SKY PARK E.
IRVINE, CA 92714
(213) 640-2491

NEW FREIGHT AND *JET-PAC* SERVICE BETWEEN

LOS ANGELES
and major cities in CALIFORNIA, NEVADA, OREGON, WASHINGTON

RATES (Airport to Airport)

FREIGHT—(213) 646-1284   *JET-PAC* —(213) 646-1477

Los Angeles to:	Min.	100 Lbs.	500 Lbs. (PER CWT)	1000 Lbs. (PER CWT)	1-50 Lbs.	51-70 Lbs.	*JET-PAC*
					PER SHIPMENT		GUARANTEED, SAME DAY SMALL PARCEL SERVICE
Fresno	$16	$16	$15	$14	$24	$30	
Monterey	$16	$16	$15	$14	$24	$30	PREPAID ONLY
Oakland	$16	$16	$15	$14	$24	$30	MAXIMUM WEIGHT—70 LBS. MAXIMUM VALUE—$500
Portland	$22	$22	$21	$20	$30	$40	Just Deliver Your Package To The AirCal Office
Reno	$16	$16	$15	$14	$24	$30	Baggage Claim Area At Least 30 Minutes'
San Francisco	$16	$16	$15	$14	$24	$30	Before Scheduled Departure Of Your Preferred Flight.
San Jose	$16	$16	$15	$14	$24	$30	For More Information Call:
Seattle	$22	$22	$21	$20	$30	$40	**(800) 638-7348**

- 24-Hour Door-To-Door Service
- Pick-up and Delivery Service
- **Maximum Weight—Per Piece: 300 Lbs.**
  (no limit on total weight per shipment)
- **NEW FREIGHT TERMINAL**
  10013 International Road (see map other side)
  Fully Staffed with AirCal Personnel

Figure 12–8 An Air Carrier's Simplified Rate Card. Courtesy: AirCal Cargo.

this is not true. This involves lower rates to the shipper in return for his or her agreeing to a limited liability for the common carrier. When released value rates are applicable, it is important that the shipper determine whether additional insurance is needed for the goods given to the carrier, that is, insurance for the value beyond the limit for which the carrier is liable.

A *paper rate* is one which is legally filed in a tariff but is seldom, if ever, used. That is, it exists on paper, but it has no real-world application. An example would be a rate on fresh bananas *from* Alaska *to* Brazil. (An early railroad abuse dealt with paper rates. The railroad would announce a list of rate changes, with a few increases and many decreases. The significance was that the increases were for traffic the railroad was currently handling, while the decreases were in the paper rates, i.e., involved non-existent business.)

A *blanket rate* is also known as *group rate*. It involves the same rate from one origin to a destination area in which all points therein pay the same rate. Thus a railroad rate on plywood from Seattle may have one and the same rate for all points east of the Mississippi River and north of the Ohio River to the Pennsylvania state line. Blanket rates are used most extensively in the railroad industry. A primary reason for the existence of blanket rates is that it greatly simplifies tariff preparation because the various locations in the blanketed area do not have to be individually named. The railroads also use blanket rates to prevent Section 4—long and short haul—violations. This is done by giving the intermediate locations the same rate as the more distant destinations.

It is also possible to group or blanket an originating area with traffic to a specific point or to blanket both an originating area and a terminating area. This is shown in Figure 12–9.

Section 22 (now section 10721) of the *Interstate Commerce Act* allows reduced rates for governmental organizations. Reduced rates under Section 22 are extensively used by the United States government.[14] The Department of Defense uses these rates for about 70 percent of its traffic by weight. The DOT has proposed that these rates only be available to the government during times of national emergency.

Export and import rates exist between inland points and international points, and they have priority over comparable domestic rates between the same two points. For example, the rail rate on grain

[14] See: James C. Johnson, "Section 22: Panacea or Parasite?" *Transportation Journal* (Summer, 1974), pp. 34–40 and Enrico DiGiammarino and Donald F. Wood, "Motor Carrier Section 22 Tenders: Do They Cover Variable Costs?" *The Transportation Law Journal* (July, 1975), pp. 155–176.

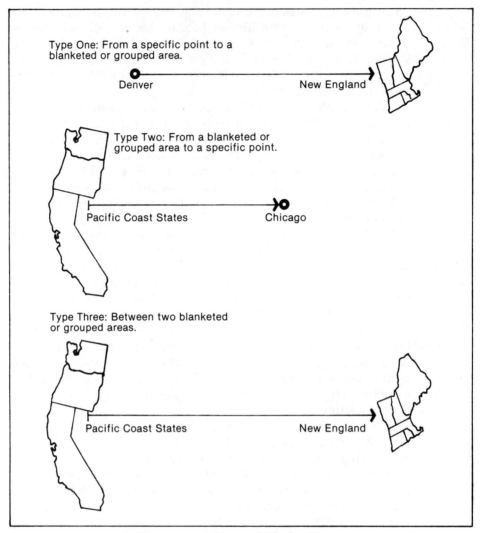

Type One: From a specific point to a blanketed or grouped area.

Denver   New England

Type Two: From a blanketed or grouped area to a specific point.

Pacific Coast States   Chicago

Type Three: Between two blanketed or grouped areas.

Pacific Coast States   New England

Figure 12–9   Types of Blanket Rates.

from Kansas City to New Orleans bound for overseas is less than the domestic rate for grain between these same two cities. The rationale for lower export and import rates is that without them, the traffic might not move at all because foreign competitors closer to the markets would have price advantage. An example of export rates is shown in Figure 12–10. International carriers or groups of carriers publish tariffs of transportation charges for ocean or international air movements.

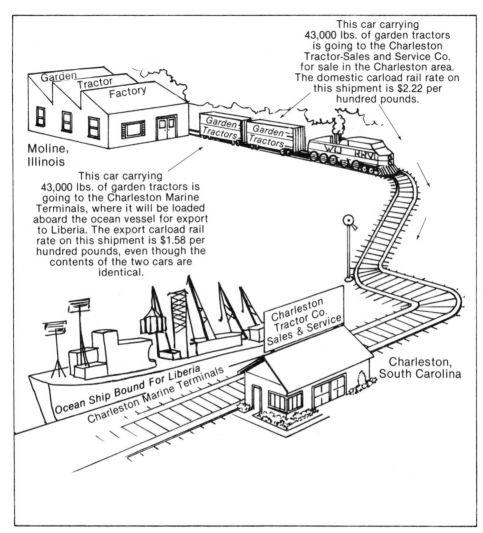

This car carrying 43,000 lbs. of garden tractors is going to the Charleston Tractor-Sales and Service Co. for sale in the Charleston area. The domestic carload rail rate on this shipment is $2.22 per hundred pounds.

This car carrying 43,000 lbs. of garden tractors is going to the Charleston Marine Terminals, where it will be loaded aboard the ocean vessel for export to Liberia. The export carload rail rate on this shipment is $1.58 per hundred pounds, even though the contents of the two cars are identical.

Figure 12–10 Example of Export Rates. As the picture shows, two identical movements of goods travel at different rail rates. The rail rate on the export shipment is less, and the Moline firm would claim that it needs the lower rate in order to compete in the export market with manufacturers from throughout the world. To qualify for the lower export rate, the Moline firm would have to show the railroad a copy of the ocean-shipping documents for the export shipment.

Computerized Freight Rates

One of the most dismal problems of our transportation system has been the enormousness and the complexity of its rate structure. So complex (and frequently illogical) is the system that it was once believed to be impossible to computerize. This meant that a shipper's traffic department was the last bastion within the firm to resist the time-saving advances that computers were providing to all other aspects of business enterprise.

Fortunately, things have begun to change. Considerable progress is finally being made to render carrier and rate bureau tariffs into a form that computers can accommodate. In general terms, the industry is revising its description of commodity items, its listing of routes and junctions, and its listing of geographic points, so that they are amenable to computer processing. Several precise steps include:

1. The removal of minor differences in the place and commodity descriptions used by different modes.
2. The removal of peculiarities in wording of tariffs and tariff rules that are difficult to convert to computerized format—one example being overuse of the word *except*.
3. The requirement that new tariff and tariff rule submissions to the ICC for approval be in a specific, computer-oriented format.

Much of the credit for creating the framework that will make computerized freight rates possible should go to the Transportation Data Coordinating Committee (TDCC). The TDCC was started in 1968 as a non-profit corporation designed to develop, foster and maintain a program of action to achieve coordination of transportation data and information systems by standardization of descriptions and codes, tariff formats, systems and procedures for transportation and distribution. Its membership is composed of both shippers and carriers, and its goals are endorsed by federal agencies, including the ICC and the DOT. Additional participating organizations include the National Industrial Traffic League, Transportation Association of America, Association of American Railroads, and the American Trucking Associations.

The initial thrust of the TDCC was to encourage further development of standardized code categories. Edward Guilbert, president of the TDCC, noted, "Code standardization is simply an attempt to get all parties with a common interest in transportation to speak a common language."[15] It is generally believed that if tariffs are to be *simplified* and *computerized*, standardized industry codes must be maintained by carriers and shippers in order that both have comparable data bases.[16]

Four codes will be briefly mentioned—each has been tentatively accepted by the TDCC. They will be the "building blocks" of the TDCC Tariff Modernization Program. The objectives of this program are to *simplify* and further *computerize* transportation documentation and rate determination.

1. *Commodity Code.* The Standard Transportation Commodity Code (STCC) is designed to accurately represent all products and commodities being transported.
2. *Carrier Code.* The Standard Carrier Alpha Code (SCAC) lists all common carriers by rail and motor carrier firm.
3. *Geographic Code.* The Standard Point Location Code (SPLC) is a six digit number that is a unique identifier to individual locations.
4. *Patron Code.* Patron codes identify both shipper and receivers. *Dun's Code,* based on Dun and Bradstreets' customer codes, is the choice of the TDCC because it provides an alphabetical listing of more than 2.4 million businesses in the United States.

Many large shippers and carriers have computerized certain aspects of their freight and passenger moving activities. One of the reasons that the TDCC exists is to encourage all these individual users of transportation-related computer applications to adopt a universally-used code system. This way, carriers and shippers could interchange computer-generated information. Also, if different transportation modes adopted similar coding, shippers would be more likely to introduce computers into their documentation and rate determination procedures.

Deregulation of the trucking and rail industries has also stimulated interest in computerizing freight rates. Why? Because transportation rates now change more rapidly to reflect market conditions. However, the astute traffic manager must devise a system to cope with this fluid rate situation. Computerization of rates has proven to be a successful solution. Walter W. Slaughter, Jr., manager of traffic

[15] General Information Pamphlet, Transportation Data Coordinating Committee (1968).
[16] *Traffic World* (January 21, 1980) contains a special feature on computers and freight rate determination.

services at Borg-Warner Corporation, noted one reason why his firm has moved rapidly to computerize rate determination: "Deregulation promises to make rates increasingly unstable. Competition may bring opportunities to cut costs, but only if traffic personnel have the timely knowledge to take advantage of fast-changing conditions."[17]

Assume that a traffic department decides to computerize the carrier rate determination function. Then a basic issue becomes: Should the computerization be performed internally or externally? An internal system implies that the firm will own or lease their own computer facilities and that the entire rate retrieval operation will be performed by employees of the company. The use of an outside contracting company is the key aspect of the external system. Here the computer itself (known as *hardware*) and its rate retrieval or other programs (known as *software*) are operated and continually updated by the contracting company. Their business is to provide accurate and expeditious rate determination for their traffic manager customers.

The general trend for firms first utilizing computer rate retrieval is to use the services of an external rate specialist. Illustrative of this situation is the General Tire and Rubber Company. This company prepares between 11,000 to 15,000 bills-of-lading per month and it utilizes the services of Distribution Sciences, Inc., a firm that has been a pioneer in computerized rate determination. Why did Joseph Vatalaro, General's corporate director of transportation, decide to utilize an outside firm? "The decision was made after General Tire researched the project of building its own data base and keeping it up to date. We didn't want to re-invent the wheel. Our study showed that tariff maintenance is a monumental task even after the gigantic effort of putting the tariff on system initially."[18]

Another reason many firms choose to use an external computerized rate service is that it is both less expensive to start up and can be operational in less time (a few months) than an internal service. Mr. Slaughter of Borg-Warner stated that it normally takes about two years to fully implement an internal automated rate system. In addition, the old manual system and new computerized system must operate in parallel for a few months. This is designed to insure that the new system has become fully "debugged," that is, all errors in the software have been located and corrected, before full reliance is placed on it. Slaughter noted, "Only larger companies are likely to

[17] "Traffic Computerization: Internal or External," *Traffic Management* (November, 1980), p. 64.
[18] Tom Dulaney, "Computers Turn On To Rating and Routing," *Distribution* (February, 1981), p. 36.

find the internal service a practical alternative since there will be a need for programmers who are tariff specialists, a complete and renewable tariff library, experienced data entry personnel, and priority access to company computers. Data storage capacity must be ample. Backup personnel must be available, so that if key personnel are absent the system does not break down." [19]

Firms that choose to have an internal rate automation system can purchase "canned" software packages. These involve detailed programs that have been fully checked for "bugs"—errors—and therefore they can be utilized almost immediately. In late 1980, the McDonnell Douglas Automation Company announced that it had developed and completely tested a computerized freight rate retrieval system. The program, known as FREIGHT, is designed for relatively large shippers. With this program, the shipper uses a centralized data base of transportation rates and routes. A McDonnell Douglas spokesman stated:

> Use of this system will lower a shipper's operating costs, reduce paperwork and prevent overbilling.
>
> Inquiry into the transportation data base can be either from a CRT terminal or by automated request from user-written programs. All inquiries for rates must include mode of shipment, date of shipment, weight, origin, destination and product. Optional inquiry data can include pallet weight, delivering carrier, container code and specific routes.
>
> FREIGHT searches the data base for a point-to-point rate. If none applies, a scale rate is calculated based on mileage and supplied to the requestor. Primary and alternate routes also can be furnished by the system if not specified with the inquiry.
>
> With FREIGHT, a shipper's traffic department can update the rate file from on-line CRT terminals immediately on receipt of new tariffs. This new rate data is available immediately to all company personnel having computer access through CRT terminals.[20]

The cost of the FREIGHT computer program, all necessary documentation, training materials and training of user's personnel is $125,000.

Summary

Common carrier rates are established either by the carriers themselves or carrier rate bureaus, which represent all common carriers

---

[19] "Traffic Computerization: Internal or External," p. 65.
[20] "Large Shippers Can Now Use Centralized Data in Computing Freight Charges," *Traffic World* (October 20, 1980), p. 43.

serving an area. Rate bureaus are permitted by the *Reed-Bulwinkle Act* (enacted in 1948), which exempts them from anti-trust laws. Recent deregulation laws in the railroad and trucking industries have lessened the importance of collective rate-making activities of rate bureaus.

There are two approaches to carrier rate-making. The first is known as the *full-cost* method, which means every movement covers its full cost of carriage. This is difficult to practice since one's future costs depend upon volume of traffic, and volume of traffic depends upon the rates one sets. In addition, many carriers—especially railroads—have heavy fixed costs, and one is never certain how to accurately allocate them to specific movements of goods.

The other approach to carrier pricing is *differential* pricing (also known as discriminatory pricing or value-of-service pricing), which means covering the carrier's variable cost for each haul plus an additional contribution toward meeting overhead or fixed expenses.

The ICC is involved in the common carrier rate-making process in the sense that it can determine whether the rates set by the carriers or carrier rate bureaus should be permitted to go into effect. The ICC is concerned with specific rates, general rate increases (applying to the level of *all* rates), and the adequacy of carrier and carrier industry earnings.

The precise rate on any shipment is determined by both the carrier's cost of service and the "value" of the service to the shippers. To determine the actual rate on a shipment, one must consult a number of carrier or rate bureau documents, known as tariffs.

The decade of the 1980's will see an explosive growth in computerized rate retrieval. This trend has been made possible by the pioneering efforts of the Transportation Data Coordinating Committee Tariff Modernization Project.

Questions for Discussion and Review

1. It is generally acknowledged that determining a freight rate is a highly complex process. Why is this true? What would you do to simplify the freight rate structure?

2. What is full-cost pricing? Why is it not used more extensively?

3. Discuss the circular reasoning problem that is found in the application of full-cost pricing.

4. What is value-of-service pricing? Why is it so extensively utilized?

5. Why did the railroads become early users of value-of-service pricing?

6. What is collective rate-making? Why is it legal in the transportation industry but *not* in other major industries?

7. Discuss the actions taken when a rate change is proposed to a rate bureau. Is this procedure excessively cumbersome? Discuss.

8. What is independent action? When is it used?

9. Discuss recent changes in the 1948 *Reed-Bulwinkle Act*.

10. What is an I & S proceeding?

11. Congress originally believed rate protests would be used in one manner, but in fact they have been typically used differently. Discuss.

12. What are general rate increases? Why are they commonly utilized?

13. Discuss the factors involved in determining a product's classification or rating.

14. In 1982 the ICC proposed to change the considerations involved in determining a product's class or rating. What was proposed? Do you agree with this proposal? Defend your answer.

15. What tariff information is needed to find a class rate? Discuss.

16. Discuss when it may be to the shippers advantage to ship "wind."

17. What are commodity rates? Why does the railroad industry use them more extensively than motor carriers?

18. Discuss three types of quantity-oriented rates.

19. Discuss the TDCC tariff modernization project. Do you believe it is a good idea? Why?

20. Discuss the impact of transportation deregulation on computerizing freight rates.

21. Assume a firm decides to computerize the freight rate determination function. What considerations should be examined? Discuss.

22. This chapter discussed many traffic management functions. Which two functions do you believe will change the most during the 1980's? Defend your answer.

Additional Chapter References

Cavinato, Joseph L., Alan J. Stenger, and Paul Novoshielski, "A Decision Model for Freight Rate Retrieval and Payment System Selection," *Transportation Journal* (Winter, 1981), pp. 5–15.

Harmatuck, Donald J., "Problems in Estimating the Social Cost of Minimum Rate Regulation," *Transportation Journal* (Winter, 1978), pp. 19–28.

Heaver, Trevor D., and James C. Nelson, "The Roles of Competition and Regulation in Transport Markets," *The Logistics and Transportation Review*, Vol. 14, No. 4 (1978), pp. 359–378.

Manning, Kenneth M., "Rates of Return in the Tank Motor Carrier Industry," *Annual Proceedings of the Transportation Research Forum* (1978), pp. 398–406.

Martin, Michael V., "Misallocative Effects of Value-of-Service Rail Grain Rates," *Transportation Journal* (Spring, 1979), pp. 74–83.

Miller, C. Joseph, and Edward J. Marien, "Rail Contracts—Is it the Way to Go?" *Annual Proceedings of the National Council of Physical Distribution Management* (1981) pp. 390–407.

Sampson, Roy L., "Are Motor Carrier Freight Rate Bureaus Really Necessary?" *Academics Talk To Motor Carriers* (Washington, D.C.: American Trucking Associations, 1978), pp. 95–103.

Schary, Philip B., "Transportation Rates and the Recycling Problem," *Transportation Journal* (Spring, 1977), pp. 46–56.

Schuster, Allan D., and Robert G. House, "An Analysis of the Determinants of Pickup and Delivery Cost," *Annual Proceedings of the Transportation Research Forum* (1978), pp. 387–397.

Case 12–1   Lewistown Coal Mine Case

Located in Lewistown, Pennsylvania, the Lewistown Coal Mine was contemplating the purchase of 78 electric arc lamps (without globes and packed in boxes) from a vendor in Clinton, North Carolina. The lamps weigh 421 pounds apiece and are sold F.O.B. source.

Use the tables that appear earlier in this chapter for answering some of the following questions.

Question One: What are the transportation costs if a motor common carrier is used?

Question Two: A vendor in Charlotte, North Carolina, makes similar lamps, weighing 399 pounds each. Assuming the price of the lamps is the same, what would be the difference in transportation costs, if any, to the Lewistown Coal Mine if it purchased the lamps from the Charlotte vendor?

Question Three: The Lewistown Coal Mine managers are worried about having to borrow money to pay for the lamps and their transport before they have use of the lamps. They are wondering whether this should influence their choice between the two vendors. List all the facts they would have to know in order to make these determinations.

Question Four: The Lewistown Coal Mine is also considering the purchase of 18,000 pounds of lamp or lantern parts (item 109280) from the vendor in Charlotte. What would the transportation costs be?

Question Five: Continuing with the situation mentioned in Question Four, only 15,000 pounds of parts are needed now; the balance will not be needed for three months. What are the total transportation costs if two shipments are made? What savings might offset part of these additional transportation costs?

Question Six: The phrase "shipping wind" means paying for the minimum truckload weight required to qualify for a TL classification. This is done in situations where the minimum truckload weight requirement times the TL class number yields a smaller number than the actual weight times the LTL class. It is a legal practice. Should this practice be applied in the situation described in Question Five? Why?

Case 12–2   Georgia Lamp Co. Case

Founded in Atlanta shortly after the Civil War, the Georgia Lamp Co. manufactured lamps and lampshades for use in the home. The styles of the company's products had changed little over the years, but sales had increased greatly in the past decade because of renewed interest in more traditional styles of furniture. The firm sold lamps in all fifty states, relying on motor common carrier (except for shipments to Hawaii and Alaska). Its distribution system was archaic and probably was not serving Georgia Lamp very efficiently.

Using some of the tables that appear earlier in this chapter, see if you can help answer these questions for the company.

Question One: Using a motor common carrier, the average transportation costs for a shipment of lamps from Atlanta to Pittsburgh is $1,000. What would the costs be for the same shipment if it went to Scranton, Pennsylvania, instead?

Question Two: Currently, the shades move under classification item 109895. By what percentage would the LTL freight charges be reduced if shades were shipped in nested, rather than unnested, form? What if the shades were "nested solid"?

Question Three: Can you think of other savings from shipping the shades in nested form? If so, what are they?

Question Four: Can you think of disadvantages of shipping the shades in nested form? If so, what are they?

Question Five: Many of the electric lamps the firm sells move under classification item 109500. The lamp is packaged in a carton measuring 1 foot by 1 foot by 5 feet, and weighing 30 pounds. The suggestion has been made to redesign the long, narrow stem of the lamp so that it can be disassembled for shipping. It would be in two pieces and the new carton would be 1 foot by 1 foot by 2.5 feet. Because of extra hardware required, the lamp in the smaller package would weigh 31 pounds. (Both weights given include weight of packaging.) By what percentage would the transportation costs be reduced if the new package was used and shipped by LTL common carrier trucking?

Question Six: Answer Question Five assuming that TL common carrier trucking is used.

Planes are sometimes used to advertise autos. In this 1970 photo, with Detroit in the background, a helicopter tows a sign with the name of a new model of Chevrolet.

Photo courtesy Chevrolet Motor Division.

Or autos can advertise flying. In this case, 72 Volkswagen beetles, which are going to be loaded on the 747, are used to spell out "Lufthansa Cargo."

Photo courtesy Lufthansa German Airlines.

13 Private Carrier Management

The qualities necessary for effective motor carrier management are basi-cally identical to other businesses but the industry is unique in that much of the non-professional work force operates outside direct supervision, dealing with the public and with goods of exceptionally high value.

LAURENCE A. PIERCE
Transport Topics
June 22, 1981

If you're a cargo airline, your lifeblood is aviation fuel. And when the cost of that fuel goes up by 900 percent in only eight years, you find a way to save.

Jet Cargo News
August, 1981

All too often the present carrier salesperson is not actively interested or involved. They say they have 30 years' experience but in reality they have one year's experience 30 times.

WILLIAM R. DONHAM
Standard Brands, Inc.
1978

Introduction

One of the career paths for individuals interested in transportation is employment with carriers. This chapter deals with the management of carriers that operate in the "private" sector of the economy. Chapter 14 will deal with management of carriers owned and operated by governmental bodies. Both chapters touch upon the cornerstones of any enterprise: finance, marketing, and general management. We present some examples from various modes and illustrate the wide spectrum of talents needed for the carrier to operate efficiently and, for any private carrier, to operate profitably.

Ownership Patterns

Large carriers are organized as corporations, with boards of direc-tors, officers, bondholders, common stock shareholders, etc. They are subject to all laws regarding corporate conduct, except that some-times the rules of a transportation regulatory body take the place of anti-trust laws or Security and Exchange Commission regulations.

There sometimes are restrictions on the common ownership of two competing carriers and on the acquisition of one carrier by another.

Smaller carriers are also corporations, but much more closely held, sometimes by members of a single family. Pipelines are mostly owned entirely by the oil companies that built them. A few attempts have been made in the direction of "employee-owned" carriers and today, one railroad—the Chicago and Northwestern—advertises itself as such. Some local taxicab companies are cooperatives with drivers owning a pool of vehicles.

In the motor carrier industry there are at least 100,000 "owner-operators"—individuals who function as small, independent businesses. They usually contract, on a trip basis, with shippers of exempt agricultural commodities or with other carriers or shippers who are in need of additional capacity. (While the larger motor carriers are unionized, their contract with the Teamsters generally allows them to employ owner-operators whenever all of their regular drivers are working.) The owner-operator is frequently victimized by truck brokers, who make their living by matching drivers to loads, because they make it their business to know the days' supply of and demand for trucks better than does any single owner-operator.[1] While there are many abuses in the owner-operator system in trucking, it functions as the competitive fringe of many forms of freight transportation, with the result being that rates are lower than they otherwise would be.[2]

Another area of concern regarding ownership of carriers, especially large regulated common carriers, had been the issue of conglomerates, i.e., large firms that acquire control of many others. Here the primary concern was that the conglomerate could combine products or services of both its regulated and unregulated spheres of business and thereby gain some sort of competitive advantage, outside the regulators' authority. The most frequently-cited example prior to airline deregulation had been the common ownership of airlines and resort hotels, with the sale of single price "package tours" including

[1] There is considerable turnover in numbers of owner-operators. In California about 3,000 individuals enter into the market as owner-operators each year although the number of active motor carriers in the state remains relatively constant, at about 20,000. There is much multiple counting, however, since often an owner-operator will fall behind on truck payments, the truck is repossessed, the owner-operator will take another job until he saves enough for the down payment on another used truck, and start all over again. Source: interview with Joseph C. Kaspar of the California Trucking Association, April 17, 1979.

[2] See D. Daryl Wyckoff and David H. Maiston, "The U.S. Owner-Operator Trucker: A Transportation Policy Based on Personal Bankruptcy," *Proceedings, 1977 Transportation Research Forum* (Oxford, Indiana: Richard B. Cross, 1977), pp. 291–297.

both regulated (airline) and unregulated (hotel) services. The second concern was that the conglomerate would transfer assets out of the common carrier operation into more profitable ventures.[3] (The concept of common carrier transportation had been to attain a balance between the common carrier's obligation to serve his customers and his need for some protection from competition. When a common carrier became a part of a diversified conglomerate, the conglomerate's owners could exploit the carrier's "protected" status for their short-term gain.)

Intramodal Relationships

Few carriers operate in isolation. They recognize that there are other carriers in their own mode as well as in other modes. There are both complementary and competitive relationships between carriers of the same mode and between carriers of different modes. This section will deal with the relationships among carriers of the same mode; the following section will deal with the relationships among carriers of different modes.

Intramodal Competition

There is considerable competition among carriers of the same mode within specific markets. The main evidence is advertising claiming that one carrier's rates or services are better than those of another carrier, and specifying that other carrier by name. Since deregulation of the air cargo industry, much of the advertising used by the airlines and air parcel services has become much more hard-hitting. Currently, many large city newspapers run airline ads detailing passenger fares and describing the options offered to passengers. Prospective users may compare prices in airline ads in the same way they can compare food prices in supermarket ads.

An example of service competition within the same mode occurred in the last few months of 1978 after airlines began reacting to complaints from their regular-fare coach passengers—typically men and women on business trips—about the quantity (and, possibly, quality) of the bargain-fare passengers who were crowding into the

---

[3]Railroads are especially vulnerable since an "outside" owner can enjoy many short-term savings by avoiding track maintenance. Losses occur much later, when trains derail. Connecting railroads also suffer loss of business. See: Lemont K. Richardson, "Would Diversification Put More Money into Railroads?" *Railway Age* (June 27, 1977).

coach section. Several airlines moved to three class (first class, full-fare coach class, and discount coach class) service with the full-fare coach passengers receiving preferential service over those paying the discount fares. These airlines advertised "full service for full fare" and that "the chances are much less that you'll have someone asking you to hold the baby while they find the baby food."[4] The idea of three classes of service was adopted by some airlines in mid-October. A major holdout was United Airlines which "apparently gained some discount passengers as a result."[5] Those airlines which had offered the three classes of service reversed themselves and reverted to two-class service in January 1979.[6]

Intramodal Cooperation

There is considerable cooperation within modes. Firms serving the same area often cooperated through rate bureaus to establish rates. In deciding the "proper" rate, the rate bureau members often took into account the financial "health" of all rate bureau members and tried to strike a balance between the needs of the individual carriers and the well-being of all carriers serving the region. They also discourage "cut-throat" rates. Since deregulation, which has

- *Cut-throat rates* in transportation are so low that they are considered injurious to the carrier industry. One cuts his competitor's throat only to find that his own throat has been cut also.

restricted the situations in which carriers can still rely on rate bureaus to establish rates, carriers, especially in the trucking industry, have sought to have the rate bureaus restored to their pre-deregulation status.

If a service offered by two connecting carriers becomes of considerable importance to both, they will go to great lengths to coordinate their operations. Examples are railroads which run trains over the other's tracks without changing engines or a trunk and feeder airlines which carefully consult with each other before altering schedules at connecting airports.

Carriers belong to trade groups which lobby for their interests before Congress and state legislatures, represent them in labor negotiations, and serve as a clearinghouse for information on new government programs. For example, the American Trucking Associations

---

[4] Cited in the *San Francisco Chronicle* (November 19, 1978).
[5] *San Francisco Chronicle* (December 27, 1978).
[6] *Ibid.* An additional problem had been the need to separate each of the three sections into smoking and non-smoking areas.

(ATA) represents the trucking industry and is also an "umbrella" over more specialized trucker groups such as those serving the moving industry, contract carriers, film carriers, heavy specialized haulers, new auto carriers, oilfield equipment carriers, tank truckers, steel carriers, etc. In addition, there are trucking associations in each state, which are affiliated with the ATA.

Carrier associations are also needed to divide and clear payments between connecting carriers hauling through traffic, and to collect and pay out charges on equipment of one carrier used by another. U.S. flag ocean carriers even support an organization that maintains employment and medical records on all U.S. seamen: these records are available to the ocean lines for review before hiring an individual to sail on a specific voyage. Shipowners and shipbuilders support ship classification societies which establish design and construction standards for all vessels.

Carriers also cooperate by exchanging equipment; the best example of this is the railroads. Cars belonging to many different railroads can be seen on almost any train. The railroad industry has found that it could obtain higher utilization of cars by cooperatively owning a fleet of cars that could be used anywhere and which need not be returned in the direction of the owning railroad. These cars are referred to as "free-runners." To accomplish this, the railroads formed the Trailer Train Company, which is now owned by 32 railroads and, in turn, owns nearly 100,000 trailer and container-carrying flatcars. The firm, formed in 1955, gave birth in 1974 to another company—Railbox—which now owns over 13,000 free-running boxcars.[7]

Intermodal Relationships

Intermodal relationships are complex compared to intramodal relationships. Nearly all moves are now dependent upon motor carriers to perform the initial and the final phases of the haul. Table 13–1 shows alternative methods for shipping goods eastward from Kobe, Japan, to Rotterdam, Holland. Three modes are sea, air, and rail (land bridge across the U.S.). The shipper has five alternatives. The carriers along this route have several choices of marketing strategy; if they decide that a part of a loaf is better than none, they must be willing to connect with other modes with which they normally compete.

[7]*Pullman Standard Carbuilder* (Winter, 1978), pp. 3–6.

TABLE 13–1   Alternative Modes and Intermodal Combinations for Shipping TV Receivers from Kobe, Japan, to Rotterdam—1977 Costs

Mode(s) Used	Carrier Charges for a 10,000 Pound Shipment with a Density of 10 Pounds Per Cubic Foot	Shipping Time (in Days)
All air, on a scheduled international airline	$17,000	2–3
All air, sharing space with other charter shipments, on a charter airline via Hong Kong	$12,000	5
Ocean (Kobe to Seattle); and then air from Seattle to New York to Amsterdam	$ 6,500	12
Ocean (Kobe to Seattle); then Rail "land bridge" from Seattle to New York; and then by ocean to Rotterdam	$ 3,000	19
Ocean from Kobe to Rotterdam	$ 2,000	28

SOURCE: Adapted from materials supplied by Boeing Commercial Airplane Company.

Intermodal Competition

Competition between modes is intense. Recall from the early chapters that the total freight market is changing in terms of the share carried by individual modes. Railroads have been especially vulnerable; a brief post-World War I history of transportation in the U.S. could be described as other modes developing at the expense of the railroads.

Modes compete with each other in terms of both service and price. Each mode has certain characteristics such as speed, minimum size of shipment, vehicle capacity, and dependability. If two different modes charge the same price for a similar haul, the user merely picks the mode offering preferable service characteristics. Usually the prices are not the same, and the shipper takes the price differences into account as he or she weighs the advantage of each mode. Figure 13–1 is an excerpt from an air cargo ad showing cost advantages of air cargo over truck.

Intermodal Cooperation

For years some of the "canons" of United States transportation policy have been to maintain a separation between modes, with cooperation between modes discouraged and ownership of one mode by another restricted. All this was in contrast to the policies of other

AMERICAN WILL SHOW YOU HOW WE'RE CHEAPER, FASTER AND BETTER, DOOR-TO-DOOR.

It may surprise you to learn that for many shipments, you can save time and money by using the American Airlines Freight System instead of LTL (Less than Truckload). The door-to-door cost comparisons below will give you some idea of what you can save in dollars. And when it comes to time, you'll save days... not just hours. In addition to saving you time and money, our service is convenient and reliable. When you ship door-to-door with American you have one carrier responsibility, one shipping document and one invoice. To find out just how much money, time and trouble you can save, call your American Airlines Freight System Representative. You'll find him in the Yellow Pages under Air Cargo.

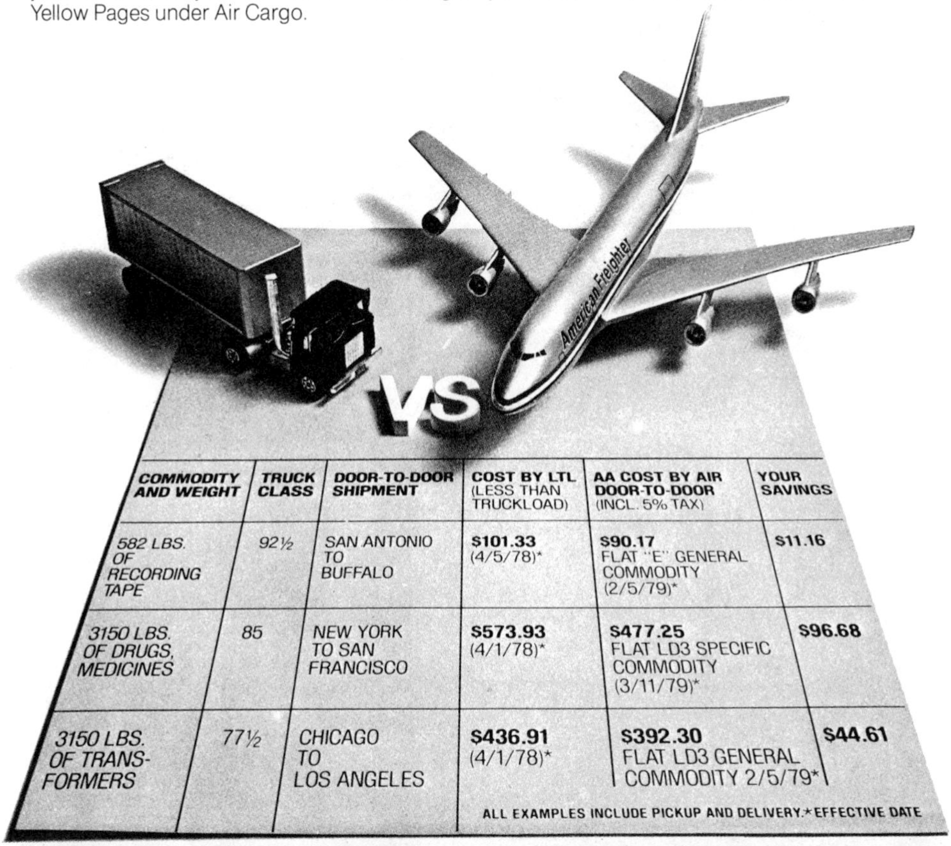

COMMODITY AND WEIGHT	TRUCK CLASS	DOOR-TO-DOOR SHIPMENT	COST BY LTL (LESS THAN TRUCKLOAD)	AA COST BY AIR DOOR-TO-DOOR (INCL. 5% TAX)	YOUR SAVINGS
582 LBS. OF RECORDING TAPE	92½	SAN ANTONIO TO BUFFALO	$101.33 (4/5/78)*	$90.17 FLAT "E" GENERAL COMMODITY (2/5/79)*	$11.16
3150 LBS. OF DRUGS, MEDICINES	85	NEW YORK TO SAN FRANCISCO	$573.93 (4/1/78)*	$477.25 FLAT LD3 SPECIFIC COMMODITY (3/11/79)*	$96.68
3150 LBS. OF TRANSFORMERS	77½	CHICAGO TO LOS ANGELES	$436.91 (4/1/78)*	$392.30 FLAT LD3 GENERAL COMMODITY 2/5/79*	$44.61

ALL EXAMPLES INCLUDE PICKUP AND DELIVERY. *EFFECTIVE DATE

GET IT ON AMERICAN

American Airlines Freight System

Figure 13–1 Ad Showing Advantage of One Transport Mode over Another. Courtesy: American Airlines Freight System.

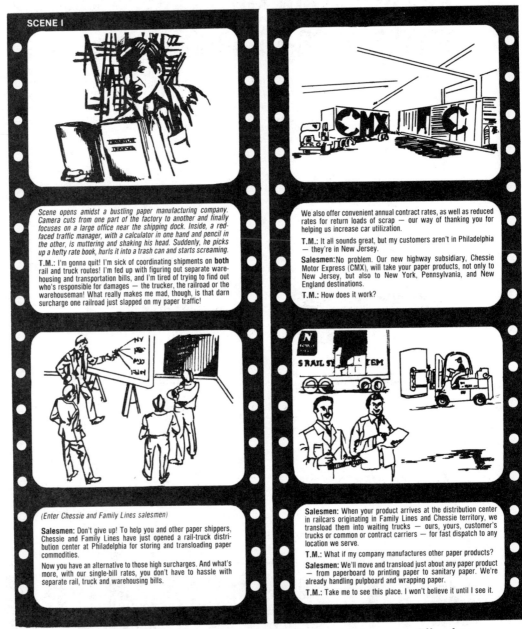

Figure 13–2 Ad for Multi-Modal (and Warehousing) Service Offered to Paper Shippers. Courtesy: Chessie System, excerpted from its brochure, *Great Paper Caper.*

countries which allow *total transportation companies*—companies that operate all modes of transport.

In the United States the restrictions against intermodal ownership are gradually giving way. The most typical example is the operation of motor trucks by airlines and railroads to perform pick-up and delivery service. Figure 13–2 is an excerpt from a Chessie System brochure indicating that it offers a combined rail-motor carrier-warehouse system for paper products. Another example of intermodal ownership is that some railroads own pipelines, mainly because the railroad already owns a right-of-way that can be used by the pipeline. Also as railroads attempt to abandon branch lines, they are sometimes more successful if they promise to substitute motor carrier service in place of the rails.

Traditional animosity between modes has not helped the development of intermodal business. One of the "surprises" following the fuel crises of 1974 and 1979 was that trailer-on-flatcar (TOFC) traffic did not increase significantly. Lack of cooperation between the two modes and the railroads' feeling that the traffic would be lost once fuel prices stabilized are two explanations given. Evidence that trailer-on-flatcar traffic falls short of being the "best of both worlds" can be seen in Table 13–2, taken from a consultant's report. In no instance do the shippers feel that TOFC is an improvement over all-truck service. When compared to rail, TOFC represents an improvement in only three of eight criteria; for the other five criteria, it is considered to be worse.

TABLE 13–2 Shippers' Evaluations of Rail, TOFC, and Truck Service

Evaluation Criteria	Ratings (1 = best; 5 = worst)		
	Boxcar	*TOFC*	*Truck*
Physical Service:			
Reliability	5	4	1
Transit time	5	3	1
Flexibility (adjustment to shipper's needs)	5	2	1
Administrative Support:			
Loss and damage claims	2	5	1
Convenience of use	4	5	1
Tracing	4	5	1
Equipment Characteristics:			
Cubic capacity	1	5	3
Economics:			
Freight rates	1	4	5

SOURCE: Adapted from Booz/Allen and Hamilton, *Piggyback: The Efficient Alternative for the 80's*, a report prepared for Transamerica Interway (March, 1980).

Nonetheless, the *container* is an intermodal piece of equipment and its successful employment requires close coordination and co-operation between connecting modes. The typical surface container is 8 feet high, 8 feet wide, and between 20 and 40 feet long, and can be interchanged between rail, water, and motor carriers. (The truck trailer itself has become intermodal as railroads developed special flatcars and ocean carriers developed RoRo vessels.) A lightweight 8 by 8 by 20 foot container can be easily interchanged between air-plane and truck. Other air cargo containers, especially those de-signed for carriage as belly cargo, are less interchangeable with other modes, although freight forwarders have special truck bodies to ac-commodate them.

- *Belly cargo* is carried below the main deck in either a passenger or all-cargo carrying aircraft.

In the past decade, container-leasing companies have sprung into existence to facilitate the interchange of container equipment be-tween the several modes and between carriers of different nations. Use of "neutral" or "free-running" containers is more efficient since there is less concern about returning containers to a specific carrier which owns them.

Carrier Cost Structures

In the decision-making process of the firm, costs under considera-tion fall into two categories: *fixed* and *variable*. *Fixed* costs are taken as given, meaning that they cannot be altered during the span of time being considered. *Variable* costs can be altered during that time span; often the "go" or "no go" decision is based entirely upon varia-ble costs. A store owner, debating whether to remain open on Sun-days, would consider only his or her variable costs; in this case the variable costs would be the additional selling help, utilities, and clean-up at the day's end. Those are the variable—or incremental—costs. These would have to be less than the additional—or incre-mental—sales receipts from Sunday.[8] In addition, for the firm to remain in business for a long time, its total receipts must be greater than the total of its variable and fixed costs.

There are extreme differences in the cost structures of individual transport modes. Pipelines and railroads are burdened with very

---

[8] The merchant would also want to make certain that the Sunday business repre-sented additional sales, not merely sales that would have taken place during the other hours the store was open.

high fixed costs, represented by right-of-way and pipes or tracks. The initial investment costs are high, and there are continual costs of maintenance and taxes. The investment has to be made in constructing an entire pipeline before any products can move.

At the other extreme of the cost spectrum is the small trucking company, using leased vehicles, the owner operating out of a phone booth, keeping notes and records on the back of envelopes. To this trucker, virtually all costs are variable. If his business falls off, his cost obligations vanish. Note the great advantage this trucker has. (While he may claim that his truck "pays its fair share of highway taxes," this happens only if the truck is operating.)

Economies of Scale

Most transportation enterprises enjoy increasing economies of scale, which means that as they increase their output, the average cost per unit of output decreases. A graphic example of increasing economies of scale, from the pipeline industry, is shown on Figure 13–3. The graph shows that larger-diameter pipes have lower throughput costs per barrel of oil.

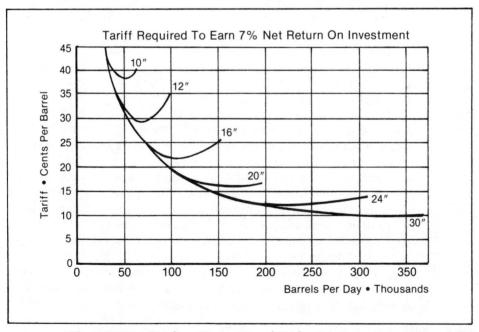

Figure 13–3 Pipeline Economies of Scale. Courtesy: Association of Oil Pipe Lines.

Diseconomies of scale set in when a firm becomes too large, and the costs of controlling an expanded operation are greater than whatever savings result from the larger size. This could be offered as a partial explanation of the Penn Central bankruptcy; the firm—by some financial measures the largest in the U.S.—was too large to manage.

Terminal and Line-Haul Costs

Related to the concept of scale economies is the concept of dividing a carrier's costs into *terminal* costs and *line-haul* costs. *Terminal* costs are costs associated with picking up the cargo or passenger and starting the transportation process, as well as similar costs at the trip's destination. For a railroad, the terminal costs are the costs of switch engines and crews that pick up and deliver cars at each customer's siding. After the outbound cars are collected, the switch engine takes them to the classification yard where they are sorted and placed on outbound trains for the *line-haul* portion of their trip. As the line-haul train reaches the destination city, the cars for that city are turned over to a switch engine which delivers them to customers' sidings while picking up outbound cars to repeat the process. For an airline, the terminal costs are the costs it must pay for its use of space at the airport terminal, for ground services, and for ticket offices.

Line-haul costs are the costs of flying the planes or moving the trains between cities. For railroads, the line-haul costs would also include costs of maintaining the right-of-way and track on main lines between major cities the railroad serves.

Trade-offs between terminal costs and line-haul costs are possible. The most typical example is an increase in terminal costs to speed loading and unloading of the plane, ship, or other vehicle so it can return to line-haul service more quickly.

Carrier costs can be allocated on the basis of whether they are terminal or line-haul in nature. Hence, an airline cost function per passenger might be $10 terminal cost ($6 at originating and $4 at terminating airport) plus 10 cents per mile line-haul cost. As the trip's length increases, the terminal costs are spread over a larger number of miles. This is called the *tapering principle*, which means that as distance increases, the total cost also increases, but at a slower rate. In the airline example just given, a 200-mile trip would cost $30 ($10 terminal costs plus $20 line-haul costs) for an average cost of 15¢ per mile. If the trip length were doubled to 400 miles, total trip costs would increase only 67 percent, to $50 ($10 terminal costs and $40 for line-haul costs). The new average cost per mile would be 12.5¢.

Example of Carrier Costs

Carrier costs can be allocated and reported in a variety of ways. Regulatory bodies are interested in knowing whether the carriers' earnings are adequate or excessive. Lending institutions want to know because they are concerned about the safety of their funds loaned to carriers. Stockholders want reports presented in a manner that they can compare with reports from other forms of investment.

Table 13–3 shows the average cost structure of some trucking firms, operating about 10 trucks apiece, headquartered in California, Florida, and Texas. The firms use refrigerated trailers for carrying agricultural products and some of them also had operating rights to carry other commodities. The data in Table 13–3 are arranged to show differences between fixed and variable costs.

Carrier Financing

The typical private carrier firm covers its expenses out of operating revenues, but it must look to other forms of financing for its equipment and terminal facility needs. Small trucking firms are often either sole proprietorships or partnerships, with the owner-operator supplying a portion of the capital and relying on vehicle finance companies to provide the balance of funds needed for the tractor and trailer. The owner-operator's personal and business finances are often mixed, and in slack transport periods, he may even take another form of temporary job to keep up the payments on his truck. At this stage of its life, the small trucking company or commuter airline is financed in part by "sweat" capital, meaning that the owners work extra-long hours at little or no pay in order to launch their business.

As carriers expand, they typically incorporate. This provides tax advantages and limits the firm's liability. It may also be easier for the incorporated firm to borrow money since it is less closely bound to the life (and health) of a single individual. A carrier corporation has several sources of capital funds. It can issue and sell both stocks and bonds, negotiate short-term and medium-term loans with "institutional" investors, enter into lease agreements with the manufacturers of vehicles, and rely on banks to provide short-term loans.

Investors scrutinize the carrier as closely as they would any other type of investment opportunity. They quickly distinguish between fixed assets, such as rights-of-way, which may be of limited resale value in case they are seized as collateral for a defaulted loan, and mobile assets which can be easily seized and resold. Railroads with dismal profits find it all but impossible to borrow money for improv-

TABLE 13–3 Typical Annual Costs of Operating a Trucking Firm—1976[1]

FIXED COSTS

Interest costs on 10 tractors and refrigerated trailers	$35,400
Depreciation and interest costs on land, terminal building, and non-revenue-earning equipment (such as in the office and in the maintenance shop)	8,378
General office expenses (legal and audit, telephone, office supplies, utilities, management travel)	11,100
Insurance[2]	33,300
Office salaries and fringe benefits	38,200
Vehicle licenses	9,800
Taxes	3,100
Total fixed costs	$139,278

DRIVER COMPENSATION

Base pay[3]	13 cents per mile
Social Security	5.85% of first $15,300 per driver
Unemployment Compensation insurance	2.65 of first $4,200 per driver
Workmen's Compensation insurance	7.96% of total salary
Health and welfare plan	2.4% of total salary
Living allowance	$10 per day on the road per driver

VARIABLE COSTS OF OPERATING A REFRIGERATED TRUCK/TRACTOR

	Cents per mile
Fuel	11.82
Tires	2.01
Maintenance	6.25
Telephone (long distance calls between drivers, terminals and brokers)	.58
Miscellaneous	1.84
	22.50 total cents per mile

DEPRECIATION[4]

Tractors	$3,040 for first 65,000 miles driven each year plus $.047 for each additional mile
Trailers	$1,680 for first 85,000 miles driven each year plus $.02 for each additional mile

SOURCE: Patrick P. Boles, *Cost of Operating Refrigerated Trucks for Hauling Fresh Fruits and Vegetables*, (Washington, D.C.: Economic Research Service of the U.S. Department of Agriculture, July, 1977). His sample consisted of nine firms.

[1] To give readers an idea as to how trucking costs have climbed since 1976, the *Research Review* of the American Trucking Associations (dated September 15, 1981) reported the following percentage increases in trucking costs since 1976: vehicle depreciation, 75%; driver costs, 63% and fuel, 153%;

[2] Over 95 percent of the insurance costs are for coverage on vehicles and cargo.

[3] Base pay differs depending upon whether one driver or two (with one sleeping) are used on a haul. To keep competent drivers the firms must provide them with a "steady" amount of work throughout the year.

[4] Depreciation is difficult to estimate since depreciation as calculated for tax purposes is not at the same rate as the vehicles "wear out."

ing their right-of-way, while they have no trouble in borrowing money for new rolling stock. They borrow through a financial instrument called an Equipment Trust Certificate (ETC); it allows the railroad to borrow 80 percent of the costs of new engines and cars and repay over 15 years at a rate of interest just above the prime rate.[9] One reason the ETCs are a desirable and relatively safe investment is that they are secured by the rolling stock, which can be easily repossessed and resold.

Investment in ETCs and outright purchase of rolling stock for long-term lease to the railroads is a desirable investment because of the tax benefits that come from the depreciation of capital investments. Until new tax laws were enacted in 1981, railroads were often unable to take the full tax advantages from depreciation because of their poor earnings. The 1981 law allows railroads (and some others) to "sell" the tax advantages from depreciation. The new law also allows railroads to begin depreciation. The new law also allows railroads to begin depreciating track. "If all railroads took the fastest, five-year track depreciation, they would get $1.5 billion in tax benefits in 1981. But overall the railroads, which paid only $600 million in federal taxes [in 1980] can't use such a huge one-time deduction."[10] So they will spread it over several years.

Equipment manufacturers also provide financing, especially if it will facilitate sales. In 1978, when Eastern Airlines purchased 23 A-300-B Whisperjets from the French-German Airbus Industries for $778 million, it required the seller to provide $391 million in financing. The $391 million came from three sources: $250 million from European banks which had a relationship with the seller; $96 million was loaned directly by the seller; and $45 million was loaned by General Electric, which manufactured the planes' engines.[11]

Inflation and high interest rates are as of much concern to carriers as they are to other forms of business. The new laws that "deregulated" transportation contained provisions allowing those rates still subject to regulation to be adjusted (without regulatory review) within the limits of changes in the cost-of-living indices.

R. J. Pfeiffer, chairman of Matson Navigation Company, commented in 1982:

> The containership S.S. Maui was built in 1978, at a cost of sixty-one million dollars. Its sister ship, the S.S. Kauai, was delivered in 1980, at a cost of seventy-eight million dollars—a 28-percent increase in two years. The

[9] See: Donald R. Hawks and Donald F. Wood, "Marketing Railroad Equipment Trust Certificates," *ICC Practitioners' Journal* (May–June, 1978), pp. 466–478.
[10] *The Wall Street Journal* (Oct. 27, 1981).
[11] *San Francisco Chronicle* (April 7, 1978).

average interest rate on bonds issued to finance the *Maui* construction was 7.5 percent; the *Kauai* debt rate doubled to 15.1 percent in those two years.[12]

Loan Guarantees

A loan guarantee involves an additional party "guaranteeing" repayment of a loan. In the period since World War II, the U.S. government has guaranteed some railroad loans, making it easier and less expensive for the railroads to borrow. The U.S. government also guarantees loans for the construction of vessels in U.S. shipyards.

Private parties also guarantee transportation loans. During the early days of the Penn Central bankruptcy, a railroad that connected with and was dependent upon the Penn Central for delivering some of its own traffic, guaranteed a loan by the Penn Central trustees to purchase some desperately-needed rolling stock. Some commuter airlines receive guarantees from business in small communities that want to see airline service established in their locale. Pipeline debts are often secured by the oil companies that own the pipelines.[13]

Carrier Marketing

Demand for freight transportation is often referred to as "derived demand," meaning that it is a function of the demand for the products carried. For example, there is a market for *carrying* pineapples from Hawaii to the mainland U.S. only because there is a market on the mainland for Hawaiian-grown pineapples. It also works the other way. Good transportation service can, of course, help develop markets; an example is the use of air freight to carry fresh produce and seafood, developing markets that couldn't exist if served by slower modes. The derived demand concept is also important to carrier pricing since the buyer of the product hauled by the carrier considers the total delivered price when making the decision whether to purchase. Carriers today are trying to obtain a better understanding of their customers' needs. Some railroads are reorganizing their market functions around "product" specialists who can work with various types of shippers.[14] Farrell Lines, an ocean carrier, is also using the "product management" approach to its sale of vessel space.

[12] R. J. Pfeiffer, comments to the Propeller Club of San Francisco (February 24, 1982).

[13] B. J. Bledsoe, paper presented at 1976 Association of Oil Pipelines Educators Conference, at Houston (July 25–28, 1976).

[14] Frederick J. Beier, in Donald V. Harper, *Transportation in America* (Englewood Cliffs, New Jersey: Prentice-Hall, 1978), p. 321.

The product management staff is responsible for pricing, booking, scheduling, and customer service. The product managers analyze data from the Dept. of Commerce, the *Journal of Commerce*, various shipping conferences, the Canadian government, and internal sources. They use the data to set market-share goals, identify key buying influences among shippers, freight forwarders, and consignees, and to make rolling quarterly forecasts. Based on these analyses, they allocate the space on board each vessel among Farrell's sales regions by setting quotas for the commodity mix and dollar revenues they want.

Farrell's regional managers set quotas for each of their salespeople, whom they call territory managers. Salespeople file weekly call reports and receive monthly reports showing where they stand against forecast. At the end of each quarter, they are required to explain in writing, variances from their forecasts. . . .

Product managers reinforce the field selling effort by putting together packages of services for customers. Typically, a package includes truck or rail transportation at both ends as well as the ocean voyage, all quoted at one price.[15]

Carriers of passengers serve both business and vacation travelers. Business travel is justified by having a sufficient reason to send an individual from one point to another, paying the travel expenses and compensating the individual for the time spent traveling. The rationale for vacation travel is different, and the individual purchasing this sort of service may be picking from a variety of other goods and services, all of which are competing for his or her discretionary income.

Product/Service Mix

Product mix is a marketing term describing the variety of products or services a seller chooses to sell in order to make the most profits. Since transportation is a service, one can speak of *service mix* to describe the range of services a carrier offers. A carrier's service mix offers service to various geographic markets, along different routes, and with a various frequency of schedules. A carrier with a given number of vehicles will try to schedule them on routes and with a frequency that satisfies the greatest amount of demand. Each vehicle itself can be divided up to provide various types of service. Buses operating on some rural routes have movable bulkheads (or partitions) which divide the freight and passenger compartments and which are adjusted to accommodate the "best" mix of passengers and freight on any particular haul. An airline aircraft contains first class and tourist class seating and carries passengers flying under one of many options of ticket prices. The same plane carries

---

[15] *Sales and Marketing Management* (August 17, 1981), p. 36.

freight in its belly compartment, and often there is a mix of freight, not only in terms of types of commodity, but in terms of the "priority plan" which the shipper chose—and paid for—to ensure that the shipment was handled by the carrier within a specified amount of time. (To give an example of the range of priorities, the highest is usually labelled "next flight out" which means, literally, what it says. At the other extreme, some air carriers that fly from coast to coast have contracts with household-goods movers to carry household goods from coast to coast within five days. The rate is about what it would cost the mover to use a truck; and the five days is barely time-competitive with use of a truck. However, the airline earns more revenue than if it were to fly with the space unused.)

Carriers can also look at the various price and service attributes potential buyers want. This is sometimes called *market segmentation*. Professor Michael McGinnis has conducted studies of shippers and concluded that they can be divided, or segmented, into seven categories: the competitive shipper who feels that he sells in a very competitive market and needs a carrier service/price mix to complement his own selling strategy; the price-oriented shipper; the service-oriented shipper; the "large" shipper, i.e., one who ships large quantities; the loss-and-damage oriented shipper; the externally-oriented shipper (one whose choice of transportation is determined by others); and the inventory-oriented shipper (one whose inventory policies or needs dictate choice of carrier).[16]

Sometimes, providing an intended good or service results in another product or service accompanying the intended one. These unintended but accompanying goods or services are either joint products or by-products. A by-product is of secoary importance and becomes available as a result of producing the primary product. The main thing that distinguishes a by-product from a joint product is that the firm producing the by-product is not dependent upon its sale. For example, empty rail cars being returned to a coal mine for another load are a by-product; if the carrier could find a shipper to use the empty hopper cars on their way back to the coal mine, this would be utilizing the by-product. Presumably, the railroad's rate for carrying the coal hoppers filled with coal from the mine would also cover the cost of moving the empty cars back toward the mine. So, if a shipper were found to use the capacity of the empty cars, he could be charged a very low rate, just enough to cover whatever incremen-

[16]Michael A. McGinnis, "Segmenting Freight Markets," in James M. Daley, ed., *Marketing Motor Transportation: Concepts and Applications* (Washington, D.C.: American Trucking Associations, 1981), pp. 59–72.

tal costs the railroad incurred in moving full cars, rather than empty cars toward the mine. This would be known as *by-product pricing*.[17]

Joint products are similar to by-products except that the producer or carrier is dependent upon the sale of *all* joint products for continued success in business. A bus company receiving 70 percent of its revenues from scheduled passenger service and 15 percent each from charter operations and parcel service would consider all three as joint products unless it could survive (literally) without one of them. The concepts of joint product and by-product permeate transportation since they are applicable whenever a mixed load, differing routes, or developing "backhaul" traffic is involved. Over time, the character of a product may change from a by-product to a joint product or it may even become a primary product. An example is airline passenger travel. Airlines began originally for the purpose of carrying mail and took along passengers on an incidental basis.

An extremely profitable transportation firm could consider many more of its services as by-products since it could exist without them. The carrier who is just hanging on financially cannot be as cavalier; it needs every product it is hauling in order to survive. Hence they are all joint products.

Just as shippers and passengers make cost and service "trade-offs" in buying transportation services, carriers make "trade-offs" of their own in trying to anticipate their customers' needs. Airlines change the seating configurations on their aircraft, devoting a certain number of spacious seats to first class passengers and using the remainder of the plane for denser seating for passengers paying lower fares.

Some carriers provide the same service but vary their prices according to demand. The best examples are "tramp" steamers or contract rail or motor carriers who are negotiating the rate for a one-time haul. Charter airlines also vary their rates according to the season. One estimate of charges for chartering an entire DC-8 to fly from the West Coast to Athens was $70,000 during the peak period, June 1–August 30; $45,000 during the low period, November 1–March 31; and $53,000 for periods in between.[18]

---

[17] The concepts of joint-product and by-product pricing as applied to transportation are discussed in: Frank M. Lewis, "Is Belly Cargo Profitable?" *Proceedings, 1971 Transportation Research Forum* (Oxford, Indiana: Richard B. Cross, 1971), pp. 101–107.

[18] In-between periods are referred to as "shoulders." Figures given here are for 1978 and 1979.

Carrier Marketing Goals

Firms establish marketing goals and then direct their marketing efforts toward achieving these goals. A typical firm would have as its goal to increase profits. This could be achieved by either increasing revenues, or decreasing costs, or both. In any particular transportation market, the goal of a carrier often is to increase sales volume or market share. Any carrier that operates regularly usually has a fixed commitment of expenses, that is, the cost of offices, terminals, equipment, and personnel, all needed to serve the market in which it operates. Additional business generated in the market produces more in incremental revenues without much increase in incremental costs.

Some carriers develop new markets. In the 1930's the Santa Fe Railroad and Fred Harvey developed motor coach (or bus) tours in Arizona and New Mexico in order to attract railroad passengers to the area.[19] Railroads promote industrial development along their tracks and even sell industrial or warehouse sites to potential rail users.[20] Figure 13–4 shows an advertisement for an industrial site south of Detroit, offered for sale to potential railroad users by the Detroit, Toledo & Ironton Railroad.

The main marketing goal of nearly all carriers is to increase equipment utilization. Carriers strive to sell the maximum services of their equipment for two basic reasons: (1) there are usually more facilities and equipment than are needed; and (2) the wide fluctuation in demand for transportation services creates many situations when equipment is underutilized. This goal is related to the general business goal of increasing return on investment (ROI); that is, transportation equipment represents an investment, and as additional traffic is found to use it, more revenues (and profits) are generated, increasing the "return" on the investment.

Yellow Freight System, a large motor carrier, attempts to increase use of its equipment by using a profit-center concept which encourages balanced loads in all directions. Each of the firm's numerous terminals is a profit center, and the profits at each center are calcu-

- The *profit center* approach to managing a large enterprise involves having each branch of the business operate somewhat like an independent business. It "buys" supplies and services from other branches of the same business and "sells" to them

---

[19] D. H. Thomas, *The Southwestern Indian Detours* (Phoenix, Arizona: Hunter Publishing Co., 1978).

[20] See: Frederick J. Beier, "Costs of Locating On-Rail: Perceptions of Shippers and Practices of Carriers," *Transportation Journal* (Fall, 1977), pp. 22–32.

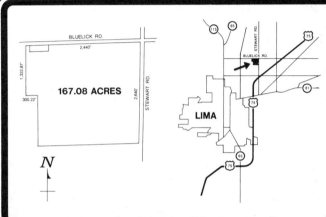
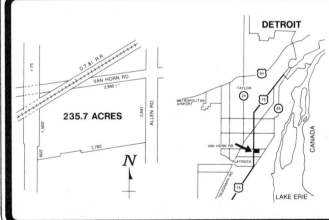

Figure 13–4 Railroad Industrial Development Ad. Courtesy: Detroit, Toledo & Ironton Railroad.

> whatever it can. These intra-firm transactions, plus *real* transactions with outside customers and suppliers, determine the profit center's "profitability."

lated as follows: (1) take the revenues earned on all freight originating or terminating at that terminal; (2) subtract from that revenue figure the total costs of handling that traffic (both line-haul and terminal costs and costs for transferring the freight at intermediate terminals); and (3) divide difference between the revenues and costs by two, to get the profit for that terminal. (Division by two is necessary since the traffic is counted twice, both at the terminal where it originates and the terminal where it terminates.)

Yellow Freight's method differs from the conventional motor (and other) carrier practice of giving complete credit to the originating terminal only. Under Yellow's system, the terminal manager and salespeople are as interested in soliciting inbound traffic as they are in finding outbound traffic. More importantly, the system encourages them to *balance* loads in all directions and to avoid business requiring numerous transfers at intermediate terminals.[21]

Before recent changes in the law, a common carrier's marketing goal often was to maneuver out of some of its common carrier obligations. While under a "duty to serve," the carrier avoided serving those accounts (i.e., those customers, those markets) where the costs outweighed the revenues. Certainly, this type of business was not solicited, and if pressed to provide it, carrier salespeople indicated that it would be of poor quality (a self-fulfilling prophecy). Common carriers continually try to direct their efforts toward business that is profitable and away from business that is not.

Carrier Advertising, Promotion, and Public Relations

Carriers advertise, promote their business, and are active in public relations for the same reasons as other firms which operate in a competitive marketplace: they are trying to win and keep customers. Carriers are also concerned about improving their industry's image.

While carriers within the same mode do compete in certain markets, in other markets they may connect with each other and be mutually dependent. This makes them hesitant about firing salvos of advertising directly at each other. Industry leaders would also discourage this type of intra-modal competition since it might backfire, sending users to other modes. Figure 13–5 is an ad from a Chicago-

---

[21]Information provided at the Yellow Freight System's Faculty Visitation Program, Shawnee Mission, Kansas (June, 1977).

Figure 13—5 Airport Limousine Flyer. The major portion of a flyer, printed on hard paper, is shown. At the top was an open loop by which the flyer could be hung on residential door knobs. Reproduced with permission of American Limousine; designed by Catherine Easter.

area airport limousine service; the ad was printed and trimmed in a manner so that it could be hung from doorknobs in the suburbs served by the limousines. Note that the service advertised exists to provide connections with another mode of transportation.

Carriers' sales promotional activities are aimed at a more specific audience than is general advertising. A freight carrier will attempt to learn enough about a shipper's business so that the carrier's sales staff can make a specific proposal for handling the shipper's business. Carrier representatives are always carrying "give-away" items such as ballpoint pens, calendars, ash trays, tie clips, or golf balls to give to existing or prospective shippers (and to beloved former college teachers). The idea, of course, is to keep the carrier's name in front of the shipper in hopes that the shipper will recall it just as he or she is ready to call a carrier to pick up some outbound freight. Gift bottles of liquor frequently achieved the same objective, and more than one traffic manager adopted the principle of letting "the route follow the loot." More sophisticated traffic managers, especially those guided by physical distribution/logistics objectives, are shrewder purchasers of carrier services. Carrier deregulation is resulting in more price competition and is requiring carrier sales representatives to rely more upon a "sharpened pencil" rather than gratuities. (The *sharpened pencil* is a selling term in trades where price competition is used.)

Large carriers have public relations departments which grind out favorable publicity concerning their firm and their industry. Several transportation trade magazines employ no news staffs of their own, and rely almost solely upon press releases received from carriers and equipment manufacturers, printing the press releases as news stories.

- A *press release* is written in the form of a news story and distributed widely to newspapers, trade magazines, radio and TV stations, with the hope that some of them will carry the story.

Large carriers and carrier organizations maintain offices in Washington, D.C., and in state capitals. The purpose of these offices is to monitor legislative proposals and to "lobby" with legislators and legislative staffs. While performing this function, the public relations staff works closely with either the firm's top management or its legal staff. When legislative hearings are held, the carrier's public relations and legal office will arrange for one of the firm's top executives or operating experts to prepare and deliver testimony before the legislative committee.

Because of the nature of the business, carriers' vehicles are sometimes involved in accidents which result in property damage, human injury and deaths. A carrier's public relations staff (again, in this instance, linked with top management or the firm's attorneys) issues whatever statements the company chooses to make regarding the accident; and the public relations staff is responsible for answering—or declining to answer—queries from the news media.

Carrier Customer Service and Sales

Customer service involves assisting customers; many carriers engage heavily in numerous customer service activities. For example, Western Airlines publishes for the use of its counter personnel a 125-page guide with answers to the many questions travelers will ask about their trip on Western. The booklet contains information on baggage allowances, carriage of personal sports gear, credit cards acceptance, airline and airport codes, ski information for all resort areas served by Western, seating configuration charts for various models of aircraft, maps of all airport terminals Western serves, and hotel/motel listings in the vicinity of these airport terminals.[22] Western's ticket agents also have direct access to computer terminals that supply other types of information the passenger may desire.

Freight carriers help shippers trace and expedite specific shipments. They also work closely with regular shippers to develop packaging methods which both reduce damage and increase vehicle utilization. A carrier will sometimes build special rail-car or truck trailers for a customer's needs. Within guidelines established by regulatory bodies, carriers can even "dedicate" specialized equipment to the specific use of some customers. The customers, in turn, agree to give the carrier a certain amount of business for as long as the vehicle is dedicated to their use.

Carrier salesmen are attempting to overcome the image of being a "gladhander" with bright slacks, a circus sideshow barker's striped coat, an expense account larger than his salary, and, unfortunately only a limited knowledge about transportation. More sophisticated traffic and logistics managers are demanding knowledgeable salespeople. Today's leading carriers are upgrading their sales forces, recruiting better educated and more skillful individuals. Carriers are also offering salespeople better support in terms of customer service and operating performance.

Two forms of transportation—airlines and ocean liners—rely

[22]*Reference Guide, March 1978 edition* (Los Angeles: Western Airlines, Inc., 1978).

heavily on the use of agents to sell their services and to book specific reservations for seats and space. For this service, the sales agents collect a commission. Agents thrive in markets where each carrier's service is limited, and the potential customer would prefer to pick a specific flight time or voyage date rather than be "brand-loyal" to a specific line. In the trucking field, brokers "match" loads to trucks and collect commissions from the trucker. Freight forwarders also relieve carriers from some of their retail selling and customer service duties. One of the consequences of deregulation is that carriers will rely more on these agents, brokers, and other "outside" firms to carry out retail sales functions, leaving the carriers to specialize in providing transportation. Don Garland, Traffic Department Manager for Zellerbach Paper Company, recently stated that the "travel agent" concept should be used by railroads to generate "trailer-on-flatcar" traffic.[23] (Trailers are loaded two to a rail car and shippers of single trailers must find "partners," to use the other half of the rail car.)

Examples of Railroad Marketing

In 1982, one of the co-authors of this book served as a judge in the *Modern Railroads* magazine's "Golden Freight Car" competition, which was designed to recognize successful railroad marketing efforts.[24] Here, with the permission of *Modern Railroads*, is a summary of some of the more interesting entries, illustrative of railroads' marketing efforts.

1. The Boston and Maine Railroad, in an attempt to recapture and develop new cement traffic, entered into a joint venture to provide a cement silo which would encourage shipment by rail to the silo, and at that point the cement would be transferred to the silo, and then to trucks.
2. Conrail felt that an initial step in developing new grain traffic would be to simplify its existing grain tariff documents. Over 4,000 pages of rules covering the carriage of grain were condensed to 37 pages.
3. CP Rail, in conjunction with a Thunder Bay terminal operator, developed a land-water route for the movement of potash. CP offered volume discounts, and coordinated the movements of trains with the arrivals of vessels.
4. The Delaware Otsego System took over track abandoned by

---

[23] "The TOFC Travel Agent," *Trains* (January, 1982), p. 70.
[24] The results of the survey are reported in *Modern Railroads* (June, 1982), pp. 32–39.

another railroad and, with the help of the New Jersey Department of Transportation, a federal grant, a loan from the New Jersey Economic Development Authority, a change in union work rules, and shipper commitments, managed to "revive" a dead railroad line.

5. The Family Lines Rail System established a new volume rate for the movement of phosphate rock from Florida to Illinois. This was done in conjunction with scheduling changes so that the same cars could be used for carrying grain in the opposite direction.

6. The GT Rail System (based in Detroit) was confronted with a surplus of idle auto-carrying rail boxcars, due to the slump in the domestic auto industry. They instituted new lower rates on cereal products to make use of the idle rail cars.

7. The Illinois Central Gulf developed barge-competitive rail rates from Illinois mines to Gulf ports for export shipments of coal. This move was to help develop the line's share of the anticipated increase in export movements of coal.

8. The Soo Line offered a "Spring Shoppers Special" which gave each of its grain shippers two free 100-ton loaded car movements (to either Minneapolis/St. Paul or Duluth/Superior) as a bonus for every ten carloads of grain the shipper moved at regular rates on the Soo Line.

Organizational Structure of Carriers

Most carriers are organized or structured in such a way as to focus on the performance and coordination of two functions. One function (the line-haul function) is the movement of vehicles between terminals, carrying freight and passengers. The other function is that of operating the terminals where freight and passengers are gathered for outbound movements or distributed or dispersed after arriving from another terminal. Terminal managers are given responsibility over vehicles used locally, such as to pick up and deliver freight. However, vehicles moving between terminals are controlled and supervised from a much higher level, often the carrier's home office. Only the home office knows the total demands its entire carrier fleet is facing, and can allocate vehicles to satisfy these demands.

Figure 13–6 is an organization chart for a hypothetical U.S. flag ocean carrier. Its vessel (and land bridge) operations are shown as the six boxes at the bottom representing the six activities from which the firm earns money. Terminals are considered by this carrier to be

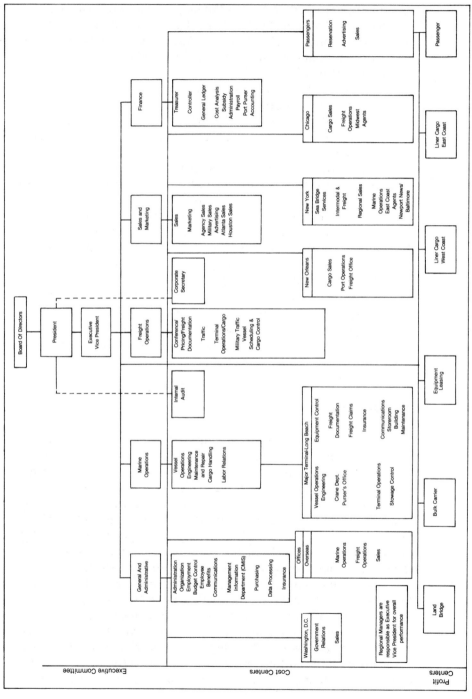

Figure 13–6　Organizational Chart of Hypothetical U.S. Flag Ocean Carrier.

cost centers, as are the higher level administrative activities. The duties of the carrier's terminal and sales organization in each major city vary, which is somewhat typical in the steamship industry, especially when concerning sales and terminal operations in foreign countries. This firm also has a Washington, D.C. office which handles government sales, negotiations with the Maritime Administration concerning subsidy contracts, and appearances before regulatory bodies and Congressional committees.

Carrier Planning

The carrier's planning function looks toward the future and helps top management make decisions which have long-range implications. Planning is closely allied with financing because a lender may want to know precisely how the carrier is planning on paying off a financial obligation. Investments in terminals have long-term implications because either the terminal is purchased or a long-term lease is required.

The manager of planning and economics for Mobil Pipe Line Company stated:

> . . . feasibility studies must start early to evaluate and forecast the forward 15 to 20 years considering such factors as: the state of the economy, product demand growth, new refinery construction, refinery expansions and shutdowns, domestic crude production levels, Canadian crude and product imports to the U.S., and debottlenecking of existing or construction of new crude and product pipelines. This planning effort has been made even tougher in recent years by extensive government interference in the free market. Now we must also forecast the effect of future government actions such as crude entitlement programs, price regulations, import regulations, crude and product allocation programs, taxation changes (depletion allowance, investment tax credit, foreign tax credit, excess earnings tax, accelerated depreciation allowances, etc.), environmental regulations, energy conservation programs, deep water port permits, leasing of frontier crude production areas, and vertical and horizontal divestiture actions.[25]

Carrier planning also has a geographic framework. Figure 13–7 shows the growth of Consolidated Freightways which started as a regional motor common carrier. Prior to deregulation, entry into and withdrawal from markets was controlled by regulatory processes, and was a slow and orderly procedure. Deregulation changed that for

[25] L. C. Daniels, Paper presented at 1976 Association of Oil Pipe Lines Educators Conference, at Houston, July 25–28, 1976.

Figure 13–7   Consolidated Freightways' Geographic Growth, 1930–1977. Courtesy: Consolidated Freightways.

many carriers, and today they may enter into, or drop, a market, as they choose.

This approach to carrier planning has several geographic elements, all of which are illustrated in Figure 13–8. The terminals are located near to users, and one measure of a carrier's size is the number of terminals it operates or serves. The hubs are large terminals

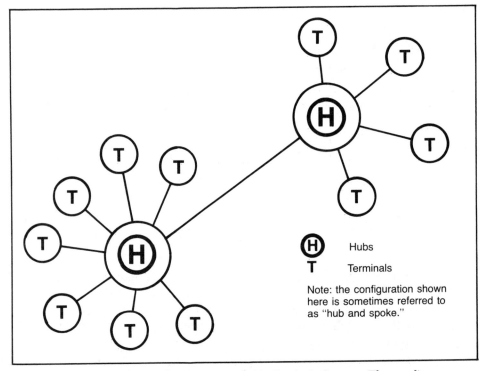

Figure 13–8   Geographic Diagram of Air Carrier's System. The configuration shown is sometimes referred to as "hub and spoke."

where traffic from smaller (satellite) terminals is collected and sorted for shipment outward to other terminals within the hub's service area, or to other hubs, for ultimate distribution to more distant terminals. The lines on Figure 13–8 are the routes followed by the carrier's vehicles. Routes between terminals and hubs are sometimes referred to as "collector routes" while routes between hubs are known as "line-haul routes." The term "lane" means traffic between two markets (route being the path followed). Whenever the traffic between two terminals surpasses a certain level (often a vehicle load), a new route between the two terminals will be established, bypassing the hubs.

Personnel are also considered by the carrier's planners. It may be that a certain union local is not highly regarded by the carrier's man-

- *Manning formulas,* often the result of labor agreements, although sometimes established by government safety regulations, specify the minimum number and classification (such as brakemen, firemen, conductor) required for a certain operation.

agement. In such a case, the carrier may choose to relocate its terminal to an area outside that local's jurisdiction. Union work rules and manning requirements also influence the carrier's investment in vehicle sizes and types.

At the administrative and management levels, it is necessary to hire professionals who have specialized backgrounds, such as in computers or sales. Table 13–4 shows the results of a survey of 30 carriers throughout the U.S.; the survey asked which specific fields of study carriers thought were desirable for Masters of Business Administration (MBA's) they hired. MBA's are likely to be placed on the carrier's management "fast track" and the contents of Table 13–4 indicate the carriers' viewpoint of those skills or fields of knowledge they feel are important to tomorrow's managers.

Carrier planning can be in terms of geographic markets and routes, equipment, or personnel. The planning can also be aimed at certain customers, certain hauls, or certain geographic service areas. Professors Daley and Cummings have suggested that carriers use several *strategic planning* tools so that they can make better managerial choices.[26] The two tools they recommend are *segmental analysis,* which helps focus on costs and revenues associated with each aspect (segment) of the business undertaking; and *portfolio analysis,* an

[26] James M. Daley and Wm. Theodore Cummings, "Implementation of Strategic Planning for Motor Carriers," in James M. Daley, ed., *Marketing Motor Transportation: Concepts and Applications* (Washington, D.C.: American Trucking Associations, 1981), pp. 74–88.

TABLE 13–4   Importance of Certain Fields of Study to MBA/MA's
Employed in the Transportation Industry: Industry View

Field of Study	Industry(%)		
	VI	D	NI
Computer hardware & programming	0	71.4	28.6
Computer applications	23.8	71.4	4.8
Practical aspects of transportation	38.1	57.1	4.8
World business environment	19.0	66.7	14.3
Traffic physical distribution	42.9	52.4	4.8
Government transportation policy	52.4	42.9	4.8
Operations research/quantitative methods	28.6	66.7	4.8
Accounting	33.3	52.4	14.3
Marketing	38.1	61.9	0
Insurance	0	52.4	47.6
Real Estate	0	23.8	76.2
Personnel and industrial relations	28.6	57.1	14.2
Office administration	9.5	66.7	23.8
Automation/cybernetics	14.3	76.2	9.5
Math/statistics	23.8	52.4	23.8
Social environments of business	28.6	61.9	9.5
Micro/macro economics	14.3	71.4	14.3
Psychology/human behavior in business	33.3	66.7	0
Public speaking/business writing	57.1	38.1	4.8
Business law	9.5	81.0	9.5

Legend: VI   Very Important
D   Desirable
NI   Not Important

SOURCES: Industry data from survey of 30 large carriers. Study is discussed in: Gus L. Keolanui and Donald F. Wood, "A Note on the 'Need' for Graduate Education in Transportation in the United States," *International Journal of Physical Distribution* (1975), pp. 294–297.

approach to looking at markets in a manner similar to that used by investors managing an investment portfolio (i.e., asking which markets represent stability, or growth potential, or freedom from certain risks, etc.).

Equipment Choice

An important aspect of the carrier planning function is to help decide which type of equipment should be acquired. Once that is decided, the next consideration is whether the equipment should be purchased or leased. One important advantage of leasing is that the carrier may have more flexibility over the long run because the leasing company may allow the carrier to switch equipment models in case a different size of vehicle becomes more appropriate.

For standardized equipment, the decisions evolve around the questions of "how much?" new equipment is needed. The first step is to estimate how much equipment is currently available to serve some need. A Conrail planner said that all of the following questions must be answered.

What will be the freight car retirements over the planning horizon?
What are corporate repair programs, by car segment?
Will there be any change in the level of foreign railroad or third party (e.g., railbox) participation in the traffic mix?
Can alternative equipment be substituted to enhance car supply?
How much will freight car utilization improve?
What acquisition programs are upcoming?[27]

When selecting a new style or size of equipment, many concerns must be taken into account. One such concern is *payload* which refers to the amount of revenue-producing cargo or passengers a vehicle can haul. Payload multiplied by speed yields a figure known as ton-miles per hour or passenger-miles per hour, a measure of output. Range is the distance of haul before needing to refuel. For aircraft, especially, carriage of additional fuel subtracts from the plane's payload of passengers and freight. Other concerns are compatibility with existing equipment, manufacturer's reputation, maintenance ease, loading and unloading capacity (in terms of dimensions of what can be handled and speed with which the vehicle can be loaded or unloaded), and operating costs under a variety of conditions. In recent years, fuel efficiency has become a very important concern. Vehicles must also meet certain environmental protection standards. Last, but not least, are safety and comfort. Unions may insist, as a part of a contract, on the provision of certain features in vehicles, such as air-conditioning in intercity trucks. Figure 13–9 shows three differing viewpoints as to the "ideal" truck.

Technology often leads to vehicles that are larger and faster than many carriers can use. An important consideration is to find the vehicle that is best suited for the market the carrier wishes to serve. Sometimes a few shippers will have very specialized needs, and the carrier must decide whether to invest in a unique vehicle to serve these needs. Figure 13–10 shows some very specialized equipment: collapsible cattle pens for use aboard an all-cargo DC-8. (The grille along the side of the plane is to protect the plane from the animals'

[27] Alan J. Montgomery, "Justifying Railroad Equipment Acquisitions," a talk given at the Carrier Management Conference, sponsored by the University of Minnesota, in Minneapolis, Sept. 10, 1979. "Foreign railroad" means other U.S. railroads; "third party" means some firm other than Conrail or the shipper(s).

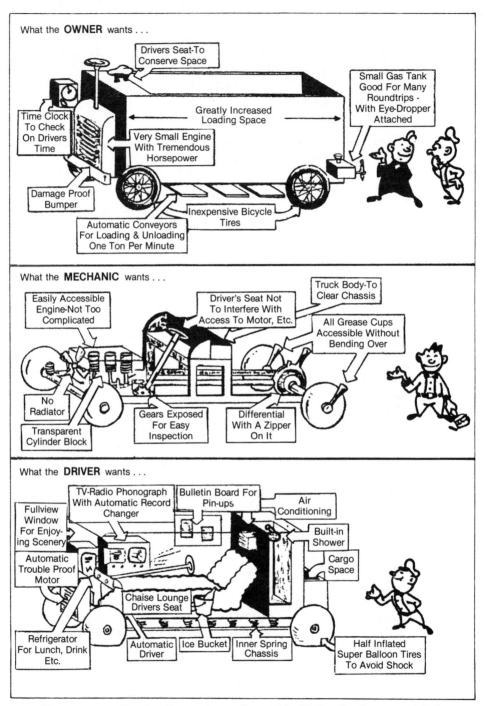

Figure 13–9 Varying Perceptions of an "Ideal" Truck. Courtesy: Mack Trucks, Inc.

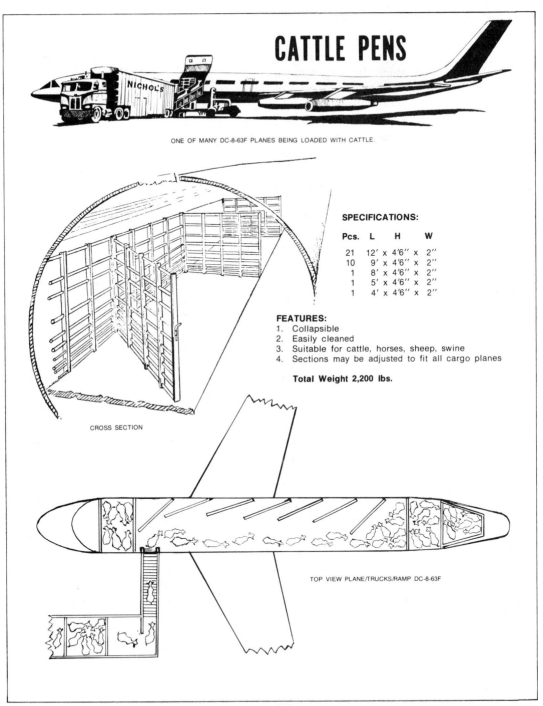

CATTLE PENS

ONE OF MANY DC-8-63F PLANES BEING LOADED WITH CATTLE.

SPECIFICATIONS:

Pcs.	L	H	W
21	12' x	4'6'' x	2''
10	9' x	4'6'' x	2''
1	8' x	4'6'' x	2''
1	5' x	4'6'' x	2''
1	4' x	4'6'' x	2''

FEATURES:
1. Collapsible
2. Easily cleaned
3. Suitable for cattle, horses, sheep, swine
4. Sections may be adjusted to fit all cargo planes

Total Weight 2,200 lbs.

CROSS SECTION

TOP VIEW PLANE/TRUCKS/RAMP DC-8-63F

Figure 13–10 Cattle Pen for All-Cargo DC-8. Courtesy: Alex Nichols Agency, Long Island, New York.

hoofs, and the right-angle gates distribute the weight of the herd along the length of the plane.)

Another concern of the carrier in buying equipment is whether it should contain the devices necessary for loading and unloading or whether the shipper and the consignee should provide the equipment. If a tank car or tank trailer must be equipped with a pump, the carrier must buy and maintain the pump, and consume energy by transporting the pump around for the entire life of the vehicle. In addition the pump may cut into the vehicle's payload. On the other hand, carrying the pump may allow the carrier to serve customers who lack pumping facilities of their own.

In recent years, because of the escalating prices of fuel, carriers have also replaced existing power units with units that burn either less fuel or less costly fuel. As an example of this, in March, 1979, Seatrain (an ocean carrier) decided to switch the engines on four of its freighters. The original engines, built in 1971, were high-speed gas turbines and burned a kerosene-like fuel which—in 1971—sold for only $3 more per ton than diesel fuel. By 1979, the fuel cost $65 more per ton than diesel fuel, so the ships are now being powered with diesel units.[28]

Resale value of vehicles is also an important concern in planning. Often vehicles pass through a series of owners. Sixty-year-old Great Lakes vessels, 40-year-old DC-3s, and 30-year-old trucks can still be found in active service. High resale value usually means the original buyer made a wise choice and maintained it well. A study of the determinants of prices of *used* airline aircraft found that the following aircraft features helped increase the plane model's resale value: payload, range, whether the model was "convertible" between passenger and freight service, speed, maximum seating capacity, how many of that model of aircraft were still in existence, and the inverse of the plane's runway requirements.[29] (Having a reasonable number of the existing model still in operation was important because the buyer then could be more certain of finding maintenance and parts. The inverse of runway requirements meant that a plane with short runway requirements was more flexible since it could operate in and out of more airports.) Figure 13–11, from a business jet manufacturer's brochure, shows the takeoff distance required by several competing aircraft. This illustrates the same principle, i.e., the ability of an aircraft to operate at a larger number of facilities is an asset.

[28] *The Wall Street Journal* (March 29, 1979), p. 24.

[29] David S. Christiansen and Donald F. Wood, "Determinants of Used Airline Aircraft Prices," *Proceedings, 1972 Transportation Research Forum* (Oxford, Indiana: Richard B. Cross, 1972), pp. 467–473.

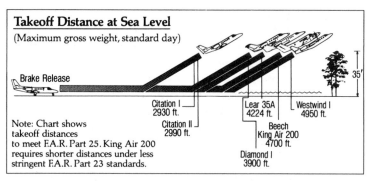

Figure 13–11   Takeoff Distances for Various Business Jets. Courtesy: Citation Marketing Division, Cessna Aircraft Company.

Personnel Administration

Hiring, training, and retaining of qualified personnel is a constant challenge for carriers. "Team work" is important because all of the carrier's personnel must work together if the carrier is to develop and maintain a reputation of providing a high level of service to its customers. Initial selection is important. One motor carrier "lays claim to hiring less than three percent of all applicants for driver positions."[30]

Management Level

Carriers hire management and professionally-trained individuals from among college graduates and away from other carriers (if some work experience is considered desirable). The career path for a management-oriented individual is to spend time in "the field," with both the terminal and line-haul functions, and to spend some time in the home office. Some individuals "jump" between working for carriers and working for shippers. An individual who has worked in carrier management can function well in a shipper's physical distribution, logistics, or traffic management activities.

Carriers also promote to management levels individuals who started "at the bottom" as drivers, mechanics, terminal employees, among others. The term "at the bottom" is only figurative since the promotion into management may mean an immediate pay cut for the individual who chooses to leave his unionized job.

[30] *Transport Topics* (June 22, 1981), p. 17.

Unions

Most carrier labor is unionized although there are three exceptions: the independent truckers (owner/operators), many of the small commuter airlines, and officers and crews on foreign-flag merchant vessels. Because these non-union operations have lower labor costs, they pose a continual threat to the carriers who must hire unionized labor. Many of the new carriers that have entered into business since deregulation are non-union, which gives them a distinct cost advantage.

Labor-management disputes in the railroad and domestic airline industry are handled under the provisions of the 1926 *Railway Labor Act*. Disputes in other modes are handled under conventional labor legislation, such as the *Taft-Hartley Act*. Until the recent deregulation of domestic airlines, the carriers were bound by a "mutual-aid pact" which meant that a carrier who was being struck received a portion of the excess earnings other carriers were enjoying because they were carrying traffic that otherwise would have moved on the strike-bound carrier. The airline unions did not like the pact and were successful in having its use severely restricted as one portion of the new airline deregulation law. (Such a pact would have been more difficult to justify in a "deregulated" industry since it is anti-competitive by its nature.)

The Teamsters are the best known of the transportation unions. Interestingly, the public distinguishes between its disgust for the union's leadership and its general admiration for individual truck drivers (whom many view as twentieth-century cowboys). James R. Hoffa, the former—and presumably late—head of the Teamsters was able to force together a "master" agreement, covering nearly all unionized trucking firms in the United States. This increased his bargaining power because of the threat of nation-wide strike. More important, it moved bargaining for management's position away from individual firms to large councils of truck firms which represent a "consensus" viewpoint.

In labor-management negotiations, the key bargaining features are typically wages and work rules. Work rules are becoming the more important of the two because they bind the carriers, as well as the mode, to particular combinations of labor and capital. Usually a competing mode is not similarly bound and can grasp and take advantage of a technological advance which makes it much more competitive. The inflexible attitude of railroad unions toward changing antiquated work rules is one of the prime reasons for the decline of railroads in the U.S., and the inability of Congress and the President to address this same issue while deciding to "rescue" the Northeastern railroads was one of the most significant and costly errors made in national transportation policy during the 1970's.

The management of any carrier is usually bound by contract agreements covering wages, fringe benefits, and some work rules, all of which have been negotiated by an industry-wide group of bargainers. The individual carrier has some input into the management group's decision, and may even have a representative on the management bargaining team. Some work rules are negotiated somewhat more individually, either with individual carriers or with a group of carriers in one geographic region. This is done because there often may be items that are unique to the firm or the firm's area. Examples might be work practices under severe climatic conditions, or the celebration of some locally-observed holiday. Grievance procedures are also covered in industry-wide contracts.

Training

Both new and long-term employees must be trained. This is a continuing function. Unlike a manufacturing firm whose employees work under one roof and can be closely supervised, the carrier's employees are at many locations, they are in constant contact with customers and the general public, and they must present a good image of the firm and of the mode.

New employees require additional training and close supervision. (See Figure 13–12.) Often they are on a "probationary" status for several months, which means they can be discharged if it appears they will not become useful workers.

Current employees are often requested to attend training sessions both to update and to reinforce their skills. These training sessions cover such topics as driving courtesy and safety, first aid, customer relations, understanding safety regulations, and so on. Training is a costly function, mainly because the employees attend the sessions during working time for which they are paid although they are not performing their work. However, it is justified because the benefits to the employer are great, even if only a small portion of the material covered is retained and put to use. While employees may grumble about having to attend the sessions, the sessions are a break in their regular routine. The programs demonstrate management's concern for the employee and dependence upon them for success.

Many transportation employees are licensed by government or professional bodies. Examples are pilots, aircraft mechanics, drivers, and ships' officers. Carriers expect these individuals to retain their professional ratings and licenses.

As new equipment is introduced, employees must become familiar with it. The manufacturer frequently assists in this training function. As one step in familiarizing airline pilots with the jumbo jets, mock cockpits were built on the beds of trucks the same height above the ground as the jumbo jet cockpits were above the runway surface. The purpose of this was to familiarize pilots with working at an elevation above ground that was different from the one they had been used to. Figure 13–13 is a "simulator" based on the same principle as a device many readers may have used in high school drivers' training courses. This simulator is used for training personnel to man the

"YOU MUST BE THE NEW MAN."

Figure 13–12 New Employees Require Training. Reproduced by permission of the artist and the Masters Agency.

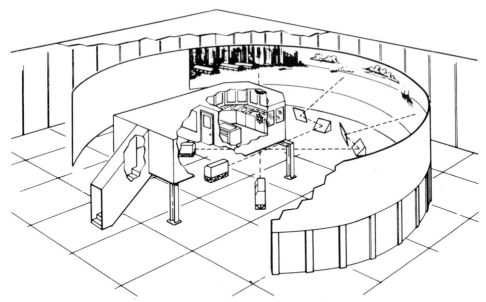

Figure 13-13   Training Room to Simulate Pilot House of Large Tanker. Courtesy: Sperry.

bridges of 250,000-dwt tankers. The panoramic screen is 12 feet high and 60 feet wide; projected on the screen are actual pictures of world ports the vessel is likely to enter. Various conditions, including emergencies, are simulated for the trainees to respond to.

Personnel at all levels are encouraged to take additional course work at community colleges and universities; in some cases, employers will pay for the courses taken. Part of the benefit is from the material actually learned while the other part of the benefit is that the individual exercises his mind, is exposed to other students and their thinking, and hears some new ideas or approaches from the instructor. Some professional groups, such as those listed at the end of chapter 1, also provide educational programs and seminars.

The Control Function

To execute successfully the organization's goals, a carrier manager must be able to control what happens in the organization. Some of the things a manager must deal with in exerting control are far-flung operations, sporadic communications with vehicles, product loads that differ each day, and continually changing customer needs. Financial control is also important: bills must be paid and collections made.

Equipment Scheduling and Control

The initial consideration in scheduling transportation equipment is to have it in a place and at a time so that it can earn as much revenue as possible from whatever market is being served. Given this objective, the next most important consideration is the influence of labor work rules (or governmentally-mandated safety standards). For example, airline schedules must take into account the rules concerning flight personnel, how they are paid, and travel allowances for when they lay over in a city that is not their home station. There are two additional considerations regarding airline schedules: (1) aircraft maintenance is performed at night, and there are economies of scale for maintenance operations if large numbers of planes can be handled at a small number of maintenance bases; (2) since most passengers like to fly during daylight hours, airlines flying between the East and West Coasts can obtain higher utilization of a plane by having it start its morning on the East Coast and end its day on the West Coast, and then be "repositioned" back to the East at night.

Carriers use computers to "test" hypothetical schedules to see how well they meet anticipated demands and how costly they would be to operate. Many large commercial airlines try to have their aircraft in the air 10 to 12 hours per day.

Improved utilization of equipment also increases the carrier's return on the funds it has invested in the equipment. A spokesman for Farrell Lines, a U.S. flag ocean carrier, estimated that if Farrell Lines could improve its efficiency annually on a worldwide basis so that it could squeeze *one* extra day's utilization out of each vessel, container, and other equipment under its control, the savings would equal $1.5 million per year.[31]

Carriers who interchange equipment with other carriers have the additional problem of meshing their schedules with each other. And as the volume of traffic changes, the size of the vehicle or vessel that can most efficiently carry the available traffic changes also. While users and connecting carriers want numerous arrivals and departures, it is less expensive for the carrier to make fewer trips and to utilize larger equipment. Equipment received from other carriers must also be inspected. Figure 13–14 is a form used by American President Lines for this purpose.

[31] Statement of William B. Weekley, assistant to the President of Farrell Lines, reported in *American Shipper* (June, 1979), p. 18.

AMERICAN PRESIDENT LINES, LTD.

EQUIPMENT INTERCHANGE RECEIPT AND SAFETY INSPECTION REPORT

No. 818294   OUT

CONTAINER NUMBER	TYPE	SIZE	STATUS	SEAL NO., REAR DOOR		Date/Time
		☐ 20 ☐ 40	☐ Full ☐ DMG ☐ Empty	Old	☐ Left Intact ☐ Rem'd By Customs ☐ Found Broken ☐ Other See Remarks	

CHASSIS NUMBER — SIZE ☐ 20 ☐ 40 ☐ 40/20 — CONDITION ☐ Good Order ☐ Bad Order — New

M.G. SET NUMBER	CHASSIS LICENSE	EXP. DATE	SEAL NO., SIDE DOOR		TRACTOR LICENSE NUMBER
			Old	☐ Left Intact ☐ Rem'd By Customs ☐ Found Broken ☐ Other See Remarks	

M.G. SET HRS. FUEL LEVEL | ACQUIRING CARRIER — New — CSC INSPECT DUE DATE MONTH YEAR

SCALE WGT.	TRACTOR WGT.	CHASSIS WGT.	CONT. GROSS WGT.	TARE WGT.	PLACE OF DELIVERY	
kilos lbs.	kilos lbs.	kilos lbs.	kilos lbs.	kilos lbs.		CONT. HEIGHT ☐ 8'-0" ☐ 8'-6" ☐ 9'-0" ☐ 9'6" ☐ Other

REEFER TEMP.	HAZARDOUS COMMODITY	CARGO	CUSTOMER ACCT.	REDELIVER CHASSIS TO:	REDELIVER CONTAINER TO:
°F	☐ Flam. Solid ☐ Flam. Gas ☐ Flam. Liq. ☐ Non-Flam. Gas ☐ Corrosive ☐ Radioactive ☐ Poison ☐ Org. Perox. ☐ Oxidizer ☐ Other	☐ Over Height ☐ Over Width			

SHIPPER/CONSIGNEE NAME | SHIPPER/CONSIGNEE LOCATION | NET WGT. kilos lbs.

☐ ON LEASE OFF LEASE ☐ | DESTINATION | PORT OF LOADING | EX VESSEL/VOY | D/R NO. - B/L NO.

TCN NUMBER | DODAD NUMBER | MSC. NO. | TYPE RECEIPT — REG. ☐ MIL. ☐ CFS ☐

CARGO RECEIVED SUBJECT TO TERMS AND CONDITIONS OF OCEAN CARRIER'S BILL OF LADING

MARK CLEARLY ALL DAMAGE OR DEFICIENCY FOUND BY INSPECTION SYMBOL.

CONTAINER

B = Bent   S = Scraped
Br = Broken   T = Torn
H = Hole   L = Leaking
C = Cut   F = Flat
D = Dented   O = Burned Out
M = Missing

☐ Temporary repairs affected.

INTERSTATE COMMERCE COMMISSION REGULATIONS REQUIRE EACH PART LISTED TO BE INSPECTED
If not defective, use check mark. If defective, describe defect.

LIGHTS	G	B	LIGHTS	G	B	REFLTRS.	G	B	MISC.	G	B	POSITION	BRAND NO. CONDITION	POSITION	BRAND NO. CONDITION
TAIL Rt.			MARKER Rt. Frt.			REAR Rt.			RIGHT MUD FLAP			L.O. Front		R.O. Front	
TAIL Lft.			MARKER Lft. Frt.			REAR Lft.			LEFT MUD FLAP			L.I. Front		R.I. Front	
STOP Rt.			MARKER Rt. Mid.			SIDE Frt. Rt.			GLAD HANDS Frt.			L.O. Rear		R.O. Rear	
STOP Lft.			MARKER Lft. Mid.			SIDE Frt. Lft.			GLAD HANDS Rear			L.I. Rear		R.I. Rear	
TURN Rt.			MARKER Rt. Rear			SIDE Mid. Rt.			PINTLEHOOK						
TURN Lft.			MARKER Lft. Rear			SIDE Mid. Lft.			7-WAY PLUG						
CLEAR Rt. Frt.			IDENT 3 LITE			SIDE R. Rt.			BRAKES, Air Leak						
CLEAR Lft. Frt.			LICENSE			SIDE Rr. Lft.									
CLEAR Rt. Rr.															
CLEAR Lft. Rr.															

(TIRES — column marked L.O. Front, L.I. Front, L.O. Rear, L.I. Rear)

MISC. DATA/REMARKS/EXCEPTIONS

INLAND CARRIER SIGN
By signature hereunder and on the date stated above, the receiving party accepts care, custody, and control of the container and chassis indicated above in accordance with American President Lines, Ltd. (APL) Standard Interchange Agreement. The terms and conditions of which are contained on the reverse side of carriers receipt. The carrier further acknowledges that the container and chassis has been duly inspected by the carrier and APL and that the condition of said equipment as stated herein is true and correct save as excepted in writing by me.

BY

APL CLERK OR REPRESENTATIVE SIGN
I hereby certify that on the date stated last above, I carefully inspected the equipment described above; that this is a true and correct report of the results of such inspection; and that possession of such equipment was taken on behalf of American President Lines, Ltd. at the place, date and time first indicated above. AMERICAN PRESIDENT LINES, LTD.

BY

Figure 13–14 Report Form for Equipment Received from Other Carriers. Courtesy: American President Lines, Ltd.

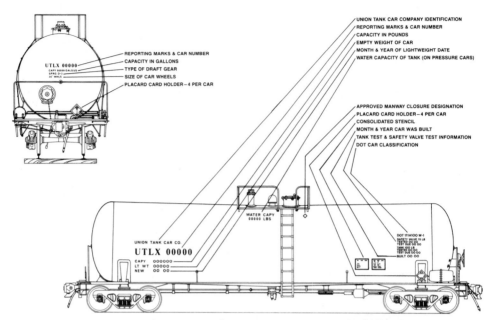

Figure 13–15 Tank Car Stenciling. Courtesy: Union Tank Car Company.

A carrier must schedule its own equipment; a carrier must schedule equipment that has been leased (under a variety of contractual arrangements which may specify where and when it must be released); and a carrier must also schedule equipment rented from connecting carriers on a per diem basis. Standard equipment and markings on equipment make it easier for shippers to interchange equipment. Figure 13–15 shows the stenciling that must appear on a rail tank car; all the items of information are useful to both the carrier and the user.

Equipment Maintenance

Airline aircraft are well maintained, and they are maintained at levels specified by government regulations. Maintenance periods are placed into each plane's schedule, as well as into the schedule of the airline's entire fleet. Maintenance of this sort is called *preventive* maintenance; it is a costly undertaking but is necessary to assure the lowest possible level of equipment malfunction. (Airline aircraft are designed to have "redundant" systems. That means everything is operated by at least two independent systems; if one malfunctions, there is another system which can be relied upon, at least temporarily.)

The other approach to maintenance is known as *corrective* maintenance. Corrective maintenance means taking care of a defect *after* it is discovered. While corrective maintenance is less costly than preventive maintenance, it may yield disastrous results. Relying on corrective maintenance only could result in fatal accidents or in accidents where people are injured, cargo destroyed, or the vehicle damaged beyond repair.

Most carriers, aside from the airlines, have maintenance policies that blend certain aspects of *preventive* and *corrective* programs. Components of equipment necessary for a vehicle's or vessel's safe operation should be subjected to preventive maintenance inspections. The decision whether to subject other components to preventive checks can be determined by statistical analysis which weighs costs and probabilities of breakdowns against the costs of checking and testing the equipment.[32]

The carrier also has to decide which maintenance to perform in its own shop and which to contract out. Another thing that must be decided is how often to rebuild (extensively overhaul) the fleet's trucks, trailers, containers, rail cars, etc. Sometimes older equipment can be placed in semi-retirement, that is, used only during seasonal peaks or for work around terminals. There is usually an extensive market for used transportation equipment, and the carrier must choose between selling used equipment or refurbishing it. Maintenance shops of some carriers contain a few "rainy day" overhaul projects which the shop crews work on when there is nothing else more urgent.

Railroads and pipelines must also maintain their rights-of-way. Most of this work is mechanized. Railroads have equipment that can move along track, pick up ballast, clean it (by breaking it up and passing it through screens) and redeposit it on the roadbed where a scraper plate shoves it back between the ties. Railroads also use a series of cars with finely-adjusted grinding wheels which keep the track "true." The quality of right-of-way maintenance performed by different railroads varies. Many railroads deferred essential maintenance for years, and the price is now being paid in terms of derailments and trains having to operate at slow speeds. The result of

[32]Charles R. Yager and Richard Bauer, "Huge Rewards Come from Managed Maintenance," *Management Focus* (New York: Peat, Marwick, Mitchell & Co., July/August 1978), pp. 23–29. See also: James A. Bausch and Richard R. Hooven, "Deferred Maintenance: A Profit Maximizing Approach," *Transportation Journal* (Winter, 1977), pp. 60–64.

this neglect now makes rail deliveries less dependable, slower, and less competitive with other modes.

Safety and Security

Safety and security are two issues of continual concern to carrier management. Safety of passengers and security of cargo are part of the common carrier's obligation. (One of the items of negotiation between a *contract* carrier and a shipper would be the carrier's liability to the shipper in case of a mishap.)

Airline hijackings and bombings were an alarming development; their incidence has been reduced substantially by enactment of numerous security measures. The measures are costly and paid for, in both money and time, by the air traveler.

Cargo is vulnerable to theft. Trucks are the usual targets, although every so often there is a spectacular robbery of high-valued air freight. Shippers are also concerned with theft since, even though the loss may be covered by the carrier, the disruption to the orderly flow of goods may be upsetting to the shipper's overall logistical scheduling.[33]

The following quotation from a railroad president speaking about security is an example of management techniques and how they should be used when confronting a serious problem:

> Critical also to an effective security program is top management's policy regarding a security department or force. Whether it be one officer or a part-time officer, or whether it be almost the equivalent of a small army such as Conrail has, top management's commitment to the security department is absolutely necessary.
>
> First, the security department must report at a rather high level, certainly at a vice-presidential level and preferably within the operating side. Definite instructions as to what management expects out of its security department must be formulated and agreed to with the head of the department. The quality of the people within the security force, the training (both initial and subsequent), the special skills that need to be developed, how and with what authority can security personnel act within the organization, . . . these are some of the things top management must define to the security department. On top of that, they must show their support with concrete and visible results, so that every supervisor and every employee knows exactly what support their security department has.[34]

[33] Distribution system security is discussed in: James C. Johnson and Donald F. Wood, 2nd ed., *Contemporary Physical Distribution & Logistics* (Tulsa: PennWell Books, 1982) pp. 579–587.

[34] Statement by John H. Burdakin, President of the Grand Trunk Western Railroad, in *Proceedings of the 1977 National Cargo Security Conference* (Washington, D.C.: Transportation Association of America, 1977), p. 36.

Theft is only one peril to which cargo is subjected; carrier management must be concerned about other perils as well. The Insurance Company of North American, which insures cargos on ocean vessels, tallied its claims for the 1975–79 period and found the following. Thirty percent of losses were considered as fortuitous and unpreventable, and they were caused by sinkings, strandings, collision at sea, and fire. Seventy percent were considered preventable and included theft and pilferage (21%), handling and stowage damage (39%), and water damage (10%). The 70-percent figure for preventable loss is high, although it represents an improvement over earlier periods, such as 1956–60, when it was 78 percent.[35] Carriers continually work with their regular shippers to reduce loss and damage claims. Better packaging, specially-designed vehicles, and more secure procedures for handling high-value cargo shipments, are examples of their mutual efforts.

As an employer, the carrier is responsible for protecting the safety of its employees. A number of federal transportation agencies are concerned with carrier safety, and the carriers are also subject to regulation by the *Occupational Safety and Health Act* (OSHA). The public is usually very concerned about the safety of carriers because carrier accidents often harm the general public. A topic of recent concern has been the transport of hazardous materials. Many new regulations are in effect, with a noticeable one being the use of colored placards on the sides of trucks and rail cars carrying hazardous cargo.

Carrier's Use of Computers

Computers are used in many aspects of a carrier's business and not solely for purposes of control. Various carriers have linked their computers so that they can communicate with each other. Large shippers even have access to portions of a carrier's computer network which can provide answers concerning the location and status of shipments. Larger carriers and carrier trade associations sell computer services and computer programs to smaller carriers. The American Trucking Associations has a computer service that matches available truckers with available backhauls. Pipelines use computers to schedule and monitor the flow of products. Steamship lines use computers to control the movements of containers and to plan the load arrangement of containers aboard a ship in a manner that both

[35] *Ports of the World, 12th edition, A Guide to Cargo Loss Control* (Philadelphia: Insurance Company of North America, 1981), pp. 44–47.

minimizes the vessel's time in port—spent unloading and loading containers—and provides a low center-of-gravity for the loaded vessel.

Airlines are probably the most highly computerized of all modes. In 1978, the trade magazine *Air Transport World* surveyed 92 air carriers, which together carry two-thirds of the world's air traffic; the survey asked about their use of computers. The larger carriers relied on computers to perform more functions than did the smaller ones. The survey found that over 80 percent of the airlines had computerized reservations systems; between 40 and 50 percent indicated they also used computers for recording passenger check-in, "writing" tickets, quoting fares, handling hotel and car rental reservations, and tracing baggage. About 25 percent of the airlines surveyed used computers to schedule aircraft and crews; 33 percent used the computer to "balance" the distribution of weight on an aircraft which was being loaded. Seventy percent of the carriers used computers to control the inventory of parts in the maintenance bases; 50 percent used computers to record the maintenance "history" of airframes and engines; and 43 percent used computers to schedule maintenance activities. Ninety-two percent used computers in their financial operations; 61 percent used computers to generate reports used by management to monitor various activities; and 31 percent used computers to control their air cargo operations. Other specific computer functions listed by individual airlines involved: credit verification, fuel management, sales analysis, quality assurance, field maintenance reliability, producing master timetables, agent cash control, catering requisitions, and pension contributions.[36]

In 1979 the Missouri Pacific Railroad announced that its new computerized service was installed to provide many elements of customer service, including assignment of empty cars to meet customers' requests; monitoring of every car on the Mo-Pac system; diversions of cars en route; planning and scheduling of extra-wide or high loads; and tracing and expediting. For repetitive business, Mo-Pac also uses its computer system to print waybills, and to simultaneously print work orders for the switch engine to pick up the loaded car(s) and plan to handle the cars as they move through the Mo-Pac system. In advertisements, Mo-Pac indicated that it took 10 years to design, develop, and test its new computer system, which they named TCS (standing for Transportation Control System).

More than 8,500 employees have been carefully trained to carry out the TCS missions. The hardware utilized in TCS forms a tightly integrated com-

---

[36] *Air Transport World* (April, 1978), pp. 20–35.

munications network throughout the Mo-Pac system and includes two massive central computers in St. Louis; more than 100 CRT devices within our general office, CRT printers in more than 44 traffic offices on and off our system; mini-computers keeping highly detailed inventories in 22 major yards; devices maintaining inventories in 81 medium size yards; and car device machines in some 48 small yards. Within this system are more than 1,000 interrelated programs.[37]

Carriers are now relying upon computers to assist them in reducing their consumption of fuel. Equipment scheduling, often handled by computers, takes fuel costs into consideration. Flying Tigers has installed small computers on its aircraft which pilots use to determine the most efficient operating altitudes and speeds.[38] Ocean vessels have similar equipment, which takes into account all the forces of the sea that the vessel is encountering and then determines the most fuel-efficient course for the vessel.

Carrier Leadership

To this point, the chapter has touched upon most aspects of carrier management except one, leadership. This includes top management, which must lead the entire enterprise, and all subordinate managers who have responsibilities for their respective sections. Small carriers are very dependent upon the leadership skills and entrepreneurial talents of one, or just a few, individuals. As the carrier firm grows, management and leadership responsibilities are shared by more persons.

There is probably no single formula for success at top management. Some of today's leading carriers are governed by committees of "low-profile" executives who stress teamwork and cooperation. Other carriers are still guided, if not ruled, by a single "strong" personality.

Carrier deregulation requires top managers who are capable of responding quickly to competitors' actions in the marketplace. The days of counting on the ICC to protect an established carrier's market share, and to automatically pass on to the shipper any new wage costs of the carrier's employees, are gone. The new generation of

[37] *Mo-Pac Guide to Our Transportation Control System*, a series of six booklets (St. Louis: Missouri Pacific Railroad, 1979). "CRT" stands for cathode ray tube, which looks like a TV screen. An individual sitting in front of the CRT would "ask" a question by using a typewriter-like device linked to a computer. The answer would be shown on the CRT screen.

[38] *Jet Cargo News* (August, 1981), p. 23.

carrier management needs more experience in competitive selling and quickly responsive pricing.

Alfred E. Perlman, one of the most highly-regarded executives in American railroading, was interviewed in 1978 and asked about what he felt were the keys to a successful organization. His answer, which is summarized here, while dealing with organization, reflects his highly-respected leadership style.

1. Set the company up by functions (operating, marketing, sales, legal, finance, executive, etc.). There should be a liaison department set up to help all of the departments communicate with each other.
2. Each department should have its responsibilities. Each individual should be aware of his or her job description.
3. Find the people with the necessary qualifications and put the right people in the right jobs. Remember the people who run an organization are critical.
4. Planning is a very important managerial function. Each department must formulate plans for one year and for the long term. The one-year plan must be continually updated. The plans of each department should be discussed in a major meeting.
5. The factors of communication and control are the other factors that are very critical to a successful organization.[39]

Summary

Business functions are frequently placed into three categories: finance, marketing, and management; all of these were covered in this chapter. While many carriers compete in some markets, in other markets they complement each other. The container is an intermodal device requiring cooperation between several modes.

Financing of carriers is similar to that of other private enterprises although lenders prefer having their loans secured by the carrier's mobile assets which can be more easily repossessed.

Demand for freight transportation is *derived* since it is a function of the demand for the product in another location. Carriers offer a variety of services and should determine whether a service is a "by-product" or a "joint product" in terms of its importance to them. Carriers have marketing goals, with a common one being to increase

[39]Alfred E. Perlman, interview conducted by Gary V. Hunter, Western Pacific Railroad, October 26, 1978. See also: "Perlman's People," *Modern Railroads* (August, 1982), pp. 37–38.

utilization of equipment. Carrier advertising primarily stresses service and rates. Customer service representatives attempt to keep existing customers happy with the carrier's service. Large carriers and carrier trade group maintain public relations departments.

The remainder of the chapter dealt with managerial functions, such as organization and planning. One of the key areas where a carrier's planners must advise management deals with the choice of equipment to be purchased. Personnel administration includes recruitment, training, and labor relations. The control function includes scheduling of equipment, personnel, maintenance, safety, and security. Computers are widely used by carriers.

Questions for Discussion and Review

1. Why is it sometimes difficult for a common carrier to meet his common carrier "obligation"?

2. Give some examples of intramodal *competition* and intramodal *cooperation*.

3. Give some examples of intermodal *competition* and intermodal *cooperation*.

4. It was stated in this chapter that "Traditional animosity between modes has not helped the development of intermodal business." Discuss why this statement is true and the implications of it.

5. How does a carrier's cost structure influence the prices he should charge?

6. Give examples of *increasing* economies of scale, and of diseconomies of scale.

7. Define *terminal* costs and *line-haul* costs. How are they related?

8. What is an Equipment Trust Certificate?

9. Discuss the utilization of the "product management" approach to carrier marketing.

10. Discuss the concept of market segmentation. How can carrier management utilize this concept?

11. What is the difference between a joint product and a by-product? Do you think that selling advertising placard space on the

back of buses is a by-product or a joint product of operating the bus? Why?

12. What types of marketing goals might a carrier have?

13. What are profit centers? Can carriers use the concept?

14. If a carrier group maintained an office in Washington, D.C., what functions do you think that office would perform?

15. Why must carrier firms plan for the future?

16. When might a common carrier choose to deliberately give poor service to a particular market? Is this consistent with his common carrier obligation? Why or why not?

17. What is a "manning" formula?

18. What facts influence a carrier's choice of equipment?

19. What are the two main items that are covered by collective bargaining between a carrier and its employees?

20. Why is continual training a necessary function?

21. What is the difference between preventive maintenance and corrective maintenance? If you own an automobile, which type do you practice? Why?

22. How are computers utilized by carriers?

Additional Chapter References

Ballou, Ronald H., "Computer Methods in Transportation—Distribution," *Transportation Journal* (Winter, 1976), pp. 72–85.

California Trucking Association, *Labor Relations Department Analysis, California and the National Master Freight Agreement* (Burlingame, Calif., 1979).

Casavant, Ken L., and Robert K. Stump, "An Economic Evaluation of the Regional Differences in Operating Problems and Structure of Agriculturally Exempt Motor Carriers," *Annual Proceedings of the Transportation Research Forum* (1978), pp. 416–422.

Chow, Garland, "The Status of Economies of Scale in Regulated Trucking: A Review of the Evidence and Future Directions," *Annual Proceedings of the Transportation Research Forum* (1978), pp. 365–373.

Davis, Grant M., Martin T. Farris, and Jack J. Holder, Jr., *Management of Transportation Carriers* (New York: Praeger Publishers, 1975).

Delaney, Robert V., "New Directions for Transportation Productivity—The New England Experience," *Journal of Business Logistics*, Vol. 2, No. 1 (1980), pp. 93–105.

Hammond, Phil B., "Applicability of the Fair Labor Standards Act to the Transportation Industry," *ICC Practitioners' Journal*, Vol. 48, No. 3 (1981), pp. 319–335.

Jaski, Ernest B., and Patrick J. Moody, Jr., "Career Education—School and Industry Working Together," *Transportation Journal* (Spring, 1977), pp. 57–64.

Kneafsey, James T., *The Economics of the Transportation Firm: Market Structure and Industrial Performance* (Lexington, Mass.: Lexington Books, 1974).

Langley, C. John, Jr., and Wallace R. Wood, "Managerial Perspectives on the Transportation Leasing Decision," *Transportation Journal* (Spring, 1979), pp. 36–48.

Lieb, Robert C., "A Review of the Federal Role in Transportation Labor Protection," *ICC Practitioners' Journal* (March–April, 1978), pp. 333–341.

Martineau, Doug, "How Can You Reduce Transportation Costs While Motivating the Professional Driver in a De-regulated World?" *Annual Proceedings of the National Council of Physical Distribution Management* (1981), pp. 408–420.

McKenzie, Patrick B., David L. Shrock, and Lonnie L. Ostrom, "Analysis of Motor Carrier Productivity Using Probability Plotting Techniques," *Transportation Journal* (Fall, 1979), pp. 71–77.

Maze, T. H., "The Value of Information in Unregulated Truck Service Markets," *Transportation Journal* (Winter, 1980), pp. 57–62.

Morash, Edward A., Stanley J. Hille, and Edward R. Bruning, "Marketing Rail Piggyback Services," *Transportation Journal* (Winter, 1977), pp. 40–50.

Mundy, Ray A., C. John Langley, Jr., and Thomas E. Gibson, "Industry Evaluation of a Transportation/Logistics Curriculum," *Transportation Journal* (Fall, 1977), pp. 33–39.

Nelson, Michael A., and Paul H. Banner, "Analysis of Alternative Railroad Cost Recovery Procedures," *Annual Proceedings of the Transportation Research Forum* (1981), pp. 465–471.

Paxson, David S., "Changes in Intercity Truckload Costs and Service 1950–1980," *Annual Proceedings of the Transportation Research Forum* (1981), pp. 508–515.

Prior, Robert L., "Manpower Planning, Performance Measurement, Increasing Productivity," *Annual Proceedings of the National Council of Physical Distribution Management* (1977), pp. 413–422.

Schuster, Allan D., "The Use of Run-Through TOFC Trains as a Substitute for Motor Carrier Service," *Annual Proceedings of the Transportation Research Forum* (1981), pp. 195–202.

Selva, Regina T., "Forces Influencing Fuel Procurement Planning by Motor Carriers," *Annual Proceedings of the Transportation Research Forum* (1981), pp. 516–522.

Steffes, Dale W., *A Study of The Optimum Speed of A Coal Unit Train* (Houston: Planning and Forecasting Consultants, February, 1976).

Stern, George L., "Railroad Car Productivity," *Annual Proceedings of the National Council of Physical Distribution Management* (1978), pp. 259–268.

Wagner, William B., and Rick Elam, "Changing Environment of Truck Equipment Leasing," *Transportation Journal* (Summer, 1977), pp. 86–96.

Wilson, Hoyt G., "Upgrading Transport Costing Methodology," *Transportation Journal* (Spring, 1979), pp. 49–55.

Case 13–1   Vancouver Pulpwood Co., Ltd., Case

After moving from Winnipeg, Rene Charbonneau found work as a cost accountant for the Vancouver Pulpwood Co., Ltd., a small firm employing 25 to 30 people, which purchased low grades of lumber and processed it into a form that could be utilized by pulp mills. Logs were purchased at various sites in British Columbia and floated down the Fraser River inside large floats of chained-together logs pulled by a tugboat. At certain times of the year logs were also collected from the Pacific Coast from points as far north as the Queen Charlotte Straits. The logs were taken to the company's pulpwood plant, located on the channel in New Westminster, B.C. (a suburb of Vancouver). Operators of small log-carrying vessels were contracted with to pick up the logs at various sources and deliver them to the Vancouver Pulpwood Company's dock. In recent years this service had become undependable, and twice the plant had to close down because the contractors were tardy in making deliveries.

Charbonneau's first day on the job included a tour of the office and the plant. He was told that his first assignment would be to look over cost figures for a converted vessel the firm was planning to buy to carry its own logs. Two alternate designs were available, and Charbonneau's boss was uncertain how to evaluate the differences. The vessel already existed; its former use had been as a ferry for carrying construction equipment needed for the Alaskan pipeline. It was shallow draft, but could be operated on ocean waters. Its length was 125 feet.

"How much will it carry?" asked Charbonneau, trying to think of an intelligent question.

"That's the problem we want you to answer," grinned Dawson Kilpatrick, Charbonneau's boss. "You see, we don't know whether to mount a crane in the middle of the vessel so she can load the logs herself or hire a floating crane to take the logs out of the water and load them on our vessel."

"How long do we plan on keeping the new vessel?" asked Charbonneau, who was secretly pleased with himself for saying "we" rather than "you" and hoping that Kilpatrick noticed.

"Twenty-five years," was the response.

"Over that long a period the crane would pay for itself, wouldn't it?" said Charbonneau, suddenly realizing that he knew nothing about the costs. He continued: "All we need to know is how much we can save in paying those blokes who supply us with the cranes to lift the logs, isn't that so?"

"That's only part of the calculation," responded Kilpatrick. "The crane itself won't cost much. The problem is that if we mount a crane on the vessel, we permanently reduce its available payload. I'm surprised you didn't think of that."

Charbonneau decided to say little more. Instead, he asked Kilpatrick for the figures to be analyzed.

Kilpatrick's response was to indicate that the vessel would cost $900,000 without a self-mounted crane and $1,000,000 with it. The vessel would be in continual operation except for the month of January, when it would undergo routine maintenance and the crew would be given vacation. The vessel's operating costs fell into two major categories: crew and fuel. Crew costs totaled $109,500 per year. Fuel costs were more difficult to predict since they were dependent upon the number of voyages performed and the weather conditions.

Charbonneau, on his tour of the plant, had noticed two shore-based cranes which were unloading vessels. He asked whether having a vessel-mounted crane would influence the need for the shore-based equipment and Kilpatrick answered "no." He explained that the shore-based equipment had higher capacity and would be needed to unload other vessels upon which the company would still be dependent for delivering a portion of their needs.

"By how much will carrying a permanent crane cut into our vessel's payload?" asked Charbonneau.

"About 50 tons," was Kilpatrick's reply. "With the crane, she'll carry 1,000 tons; without it, about 1,050."

"Is that the only difference?" queried Charbonneau.

"No," said Kilpatrick. "The rate at which logs can be picked out of the water also varies. Using her own crane she can pick up logs at the rate of 275–350 tons per hour. If she relies on a barge-mounted crane alongside, only 250 tons per hour can be loaded, and if barge-mounted cranes are on both sides, then 400 tons can be loaded per hour."

"I don't understand the differences between the three rates," said Charbonneau. "I would have thought that two would be twice as quick as one."

"In calm weather, that's true," said Kilpatrick, "but under rough conditions it's hard to coordinate the roll of the vessel with that of the cranes alongside. That's one reason why the vessel-mounted crane is the quickest."

"Do you have costs on renting the barge-mounted cranes to come alongside?" asked Charbonneau.

"Twenty-five dollars an hour each; two cost fifty dollars an hour."

"Well, from that I can make my calculations. Right?" queried Charbonneau.

"Not quite," was Kilpatrick's response. "Fuel costs are tricky to figure and hard to predict. They may double again."

Charbonneau asked: "How do you calculate them now?"

The response was, "At present fuel costs, the vessel without cranes will consume $200 worth of fuel on each round trip. With the self-mounted crane, she'll consume $210 worth each trip, the increase being because the vessel's power is needed to work the crane. However, since different loading rates are possible, the number of round trips the vessel can perform each year is affected. With a self-mounted crane, the vessel will make 75 round trips. If there is no self-mounted crane and we rely on barge-mounted cranes alongside, use of only one—which is slow—gives our vessel 70 round trips per year. If we use two cranes along side, we speed up loading so much that our vessel can make 80 round trips per year."

"What if fuel costs go up?" asked Charbonneau. "How will that affect us?"

"We need you to tell us that," was Kilpatrick's response.

Question One: What would the annual costs to Vancouver Pulpwood Co. be for operating its own vessel with a vessel-mounted crane?

Question Two: What would the annual costs to Vancouver Pulpwood Co. be for operating its own vessel but relying on one separate barge-mounted crane to load the vessel?

Question Three: Answer the same question as posed in Question Two but assume that two separate barge-mounted cranes are used.

Question Four: Which alternative do you think Charbonneau should recommend? Why?

Question Five: Assume that the price of fuel is expected to double. How, if at all, would this affect the answer you gave to Question Four?

Question Six: Kilpatrick, after leaving Charbonneau, receives a phone call from the owner of the barge-mounted cranes, who says he will need a long-term contract from Vancouver Pulpwood so that he can renegotiate his loan agreement with the Bank of Montreal.

Kilpatrick then tells Charbonneau to determine whether Vancouver Pulpwood Co. will need the services of the separate barge-mounted crane(s). If the answer is "yes," will it be one or two cranes? Kilpatrick says this decision should be made in conjunction with the decision whether to mount a crane on Vancouver Pulp's own vessel. Kilpatrick wants to know the long-term value to Vancouver Pulp of being able to depend upon one or upon two barge-mounted cranes. What are these values?

Case 13–2   Quaker State Airline Case

Headquartered in Pittsburgh, Pennsylvania, the Quaker State Airline served six cities: Pittsburgh, Philadelphia, Erie, and Scranton, Pennsylvania; Morgantown, West Virginia; and Dover, Delaware. Case Figure 13–2–1 is a map showing the location of these six cities plus the flying time for Quaker State's aircraft to fly one-way between them. The times shown include the minimum time the plane must spend on the ground to board, discharge, and allow for transfers of passengers, baggage, and air cargo.

Case Figure 13–2–2 shows the expected number of passengers who would fly daily between the various points in Quaker State's system at the existing fares if a high quality of service was offered. "High quality of service" is defined as a minimum of three non-stop flights per day from the passengers' origin to destination. Any level of service less than this will reduce the passengerloads shown in Case Figure 13–2–2.

Case Table 13–2–1 indicates the percentages of potential passengers (shown in Case Figure 13–2–2) that will be carried if one, two, or three direct flights are offered per day. The management of the Quaker State Airline is attempting to schedule three planes, each of which can carry 25 passengers. Because of competition, passengers will fly only on direct flights. That is, they will not transfer from one flight to another.

At the beginning of the 24-hour period being scheduled, all three planes are in Pittsburgh, and must start out at that point. For Questions One, Two, and Three, it is *not* necessary for the planes to be returned to Pittsburgh at the end of the 24-hour period, and they may end the 24-hour period at any airport. You can assume that on the following day, a different fleet of three will start out at Pittsburgh. Questions Four, Five, and Six are similar to the first three except that you *must* have the planes return to Pittsburgh at the end of (and within) the 24-hour period so that they will be ready to repeat their

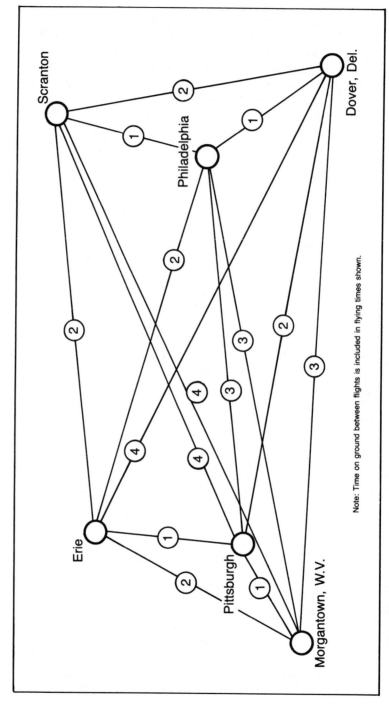

Case Figure 13–2–1 Non-Stop Flying Times in Hours Between Cities Served by Quaker State Airlines.

Note: Time on ground between flights is included in flying times shown.

Case Figure 13-2-2 Maximum Daily Passenger Demand in Quaker State's System.

schedules on the following day. For any schedule developed in answer to Questions One through Six, you may not schedule two identical flights at the same time.

The objective in developing these flight schedules is to maximize the number of passengers carried within a 24-hour period by the fleet of aircraft. Recall also that if you want to carry all of the passengers between any two cities (as shown in Case Figure 13–2–2), you must schedule *at least* three flights per day between those cities. With only one or two flights per day, passenger demand would decrease (see Case Table 13–2–1).

Question One: Schedule the fleet of three 25-passenger airplanes for a 24-hour period. All the planes must start in Pittsburgh but at the end of the 24-hour period may be at any airport in the system.

Question Two: Develop a flight schedule as in Question One, but with one additional constraint. For two hours during the 24-hour

CASE TABLE 13–2–1   Effect of Level of Service
on Passenger Demand

Level of Service	Percent of Maximum Demand
3 direct flights per day, non-stop, from origin to destination	100
2 direct flights per day, non-stop, from origin to destination	70
1 direct flight per day, non-stop, from origin to destination	40

Note: As an example of how this table works, assume that there are two direct flights daily from Morgantown to Erie; then a total of 17 passengers (70% × 25) would be carried on these flights. If there is just one direct flight from Morgantown to Erie, then it will carry 10 passengers (40% × 25).

period, each of the planes must be on the ground in Pittsburgh, undergoing maintenance. No two planes can be scheduled to receive maintenance at the same time.

Question Three: Ignore Question Two. Assume Quaker State Airline has a chance to trade its fleet of three 25-passenger planes for *four* 15-passenger planes. These smaller planes can complete trips with the same flying times as shown in Case Figure 13–2–1. Assume the same conditions as for Question One and also assume that the total costs per day of flying four 15-passenger planes are the same as flying three 25-passenger planes. Should Quaker State Airline make the trade? Why?

Question Four: Develop a flight schedule as in Question One except that at the end of the 24-hour period all three planes must be back in Pittsburgh.

Question Five: Develop a flight schedule as in Question Two except that at the end of the 24-hour period all three planes must be back at Pittsburgh.

Question Six: Answer the question posed in Question Three assuming that at the end of the 24-hour period all planes must be back at Pittsburgh.

Question Seven: In the real world, what other factors would be taken into account when developing the flight schedule for a small airline?

New Yorkers have a long history of coping with transit strikes. This picture shows how thousands improvised during a 1919 New York transit strike.

Photo courtesy Office of the Corporate Historian, Manufacturers Hanover Trust Company.

Trains used by the Washington Metropolitan Transit Authority.

Photo by Paul Myatt, courtesy WMATA.

14 Managing Carriers in the Public Sector

We at BART have lost over $4 million in federal funds in the last two years solely because we did not run up a large enough deficit. . . .

> FRANK C. HERRINGER
> former manager of the
> San Francisco Bay Area Rapid Transit
> 1979

. . . an event whose significance rises with the price of gasoline.

> MAYNARD JACKSON
> Mayor of Atlanta commenting on
> the opening of the Metropolitan
> Atlanta Rapid Transit Authority's
> rail service, June 1979

As Jim Wood, a Metropolitan Atlanta Rapid Transit Authority (MARTA) employee, leaves the new Hartsfield Airport terminal, he points toward an unfinished subway station. It was supposed to link the airport to downtown Atlanta with a nine-mile line by the start of 1986. But federal financing has dried up. . . . The Reagan administration's budget cuts have given Atlantans lots of company.

> The Wall Street Journal
> July 29, 1981

Introduction

This chapter covers management of transportation services provided by government bodies—at the federal, state, regional, and local levels. We learned why the various levels of government are involved in transportation back in chapter 2. There simply are many situations where private enterprise cannot be relied upon to meet transportation needs.

Government is involved in different forms of transportation in numerous ways. In the case of urban mass transit, a government body is likely to own and operate the vehicles. The U.S. Postal Service, a federal government agency, owns the vehicles used for local mail pickups and deliveries, but it often contracts with private firms to carry mail between cities.

With respect to water ports and airports, state, regional, or local government is the owner of the facilities, and makes them available to private carriers for a fee. Some public port authorities directly provide the service of transferring cargo between land and water carriers; other public port authorities lease out their cargo transfer facilities to private terminal operators.

In the case of Amtrak, the federal government owns the trains and contracts to use the tracks owned by private railroads. (It also owns some track.) Conrail is also owned mainly by the federal government; federal ownership is supposed to be only for a transitional period, during which the government will presumably prune away at its little-used lines, up-grade its necessary lines, and buy new rolling stock. In theory, Conrail is being returned to its "fighting trim."

Government employees also maintain and operate facilities that are vital to the functioning of the nation's transportation system. Examples are FAA flight controllers, lock tenders along the nation's waterways, and highway maintenance personnel.

The principal difference in managing a public carrier compared with managing a private carrier is the criterion used to judge performance. The private carrier must be profitable to survive, and profitability is the main criterion of success. The public carrier typically does not operate at a profit; it may substitute some indication of "performing public service" as the criterion by which its management wishes to be judged.

Public Service Goals Vs. Profitability Goals

Public opinion dictates that as a society, we should be striving for certain goals. Government responds by establishing programs aimed toward meeting these goals. Some goals are attainable, others are not. Setting programs aimed at unattainable goals or not recognizing that they are unattainable is a problem. We typically underestimate the costs necessary to achieve a desired end. "The Washington, D.C. Metro was constructed with cost overruns that seemed inspired by the Pentagon."[1]

The publicly-operated carrier is often expected to achieve more goals than is possible. Because the carrier must shoulder additional costs of pursuing these goals, carrier management feels that it should not be required to follow a profit-oriented decision-making process. For example, there are special-interest groups which benefit from the public carrier's program. These groups become "clients" of the carrier and are willing to speak on the carrier's behalf as the carrier

---

[1] Calvin Trillin, "U.S. Journal: San Diego: Thoughts While Riding a Trolley Toward Tijuana," *The New Yorker* (December 14, 1981), p. 129.

attempts to obtain even more subsidies to meet the needs of its existing and new client groups. When this happens, the public carrier's management often becomes confused and unable to distinguish between the legitimacy of claims for the carrier's limited service.

"From a profitable private business with a net income of more than $300 million in 1945, mass transit has become within 30 years a largely publicly owned or subsidized utility with a nationwide deficit exceeding $1.7 billion annually."[2] Today the mass transit industry is almost completely within the public sector. (Some examples of important goals which have been set for the mass transit industry follow.)

During the early days of Lyndon Johnson's administration, great interest was shown in protecting our natural environment from further encroachments by man and machine. The federal government was becoming involved in local mass transit, and this was justified, in part, by the argument that a single bus or transit car can transport as many people as several autos and creates less pollution.

It is also believed that if more travelers and commuters use mass transit, whether bus or rail, that would decrease the need for more and more freeway lanes leading between suburbs and cities. Reducing auto congestion within cities would improve the amenities of urban living. Some cities even adopted the concept of "auto-free" zones, areas from which autos are excluded and must park on the periphery; mass transit provides service between the auto parking area and points within the auto-free zone.[3] In the 1970's scarce and expensive fuel further promoted the idea of mass transit. Motorists gave up their autos to commute by public transportation.

All of these programs and concepts are aimed at making people less dependent on autos by providing convenient substitute forms of transportation.

Public subsidies of mass transit are also justified as a form of "income redistribution." Mass transit subsidies are considered a way of taxing the affluent to provide services for those who are less fortunate: the poor, the handicapped, those who can't drive, and those who lack access to automobiles. Motorists, even though they pay for mass transit subsidies, may favor them because mass transit is one way to reduce highway congestion.

The demands of the handicapped and the elderly for equal access to public transportation systems, however justified, make it difficult

---

[2] "New Initiatives for Financing," *Management Focus* (New York: Peat Marwick, Mitchell & Co., September/October, 1979), p. 30.

[3] See: Hays B. Gamble, "Automobile-Restricted Zones," *Transportation Research Record* 634, (Washington, D.C.: Transportation Research Board, 1977), pp. 7–13.

for mass transit operators to attract other riders, such as motorists, out of their autos. For example, to accommodate the handicapped on a bus route means that the bus run takes longer, making the bus less "time competitive." The costs of equipment for handling the disabled are not insignificant, and this further distorts any "profit-oriented" decisions on the part of transit management. In addition, as their costs per passenger climb, the public bodies funding the mass transit subsidy may become disenchanted and decide to reduce support for the entire program.

Relationships Among Carriers

A single government agency usually operates only one carrier, and it would be unlikely to have two or more competing carriers under its control. Government agencies may be involved with several modes of transportation, which sometimes compete. Examples are port agencies which operate both seaport and airport facilities since there is limited competition between ocean and international air cargo.

Government agencies also become involved with carriers, both public and private, because of the transportation terminals that the public agency provides and operates, leasing space to the various carriers which use it. Examples are airports, passenger and cargo terminals in ports, and a few bus terminals.

- *Terminal* implies termination or ending point. However, it is usually thought of as a transfer point between different routes of a single carrier, an interline connection between two carriers, or an intermodal connection between two modes, such as truck and air.

Why do government agencies provide terminals? Was this not once a function of private enterprise? Terminals were once privately owned, but the problem with that was that they were owned by carriers who would connect only with other carriers whose services complemented their own. Figure 14–1 is the cover of a booklet, issued at the time the Panama Canal was being built, containing arguments as to why the public should take over ownership of Seattle's port terminals. At that time they were owned by railroads who did not want to handle Panama Canal traffic since it was expected to be intercoastal (i.e., to or from East Coast ports) and competitive with the rail routes across the continent.

Public terminals are open to all carriers, usually without preference. Indeed, competing carriers often use the same facilities. Some-

PUBLIC OWNERSHIP OF DOCKS AND RAILWAY TERMINAL FACILITIES

Means the Industrial and Commercial Supremacy of the City of Seattle

Paper Prepared by ROBERT BRIDGES

SECRETARY OF THE

PORT COMMISSION OF THE PORT OF SEATTLE

DISTRIBUTED FROM THE OFFICE OF

McKENZIE, BRIDGES & McFARLANE

439-40 NEW YORK BLOCK
SEATTLE, WASH.

Figure 14–1 Cover of Booklet on Wharf Ownership. This booklet, dated about 1913, advocated public ownership of Seattle wharves. Courtesy: Port of Seattle *Reporter* (Fall, 1981).

times, through use of subsidies, some carriers are encouraged to serve specific terminals. New York State subsidizes the drayage of

- *Drayage*, originally applied to horse-drawn vehicles, now means local trucking.

containers between railheads in New Jersey and maritime terminals in Staten Island and Brooklyn.[4] Airports subsidize light rail transit connections to downtown areas.

Another reason why governments began constructing terminals was that local governments started competing with each other for trade and commerce. The more carriers serving a community, the more attractive a site it would be for industrial and commercial development. Carriers also encouraged governments to build public terminals because this would shift the financial costs of terminal construction from the carrier to the government. As tenants in terminals, the carriers pay only for the space they need and use and avoid the heavy capital outlays associated with construction.

A sensitive area of carrier relationships has been when publicly-subsidized carriers compete directly with carriers still operating in the private sector. Owners of both bus lines and airlines resent the heavy subsidies paid to Amtrak. In local areas, subsidized mass transit competes with Greyhound and other bus lines, taxicabs, and jitneys (small vans, privately owned, operating along regular routes and carrying passengers for a fee). Conrail competes directly with other freight carriers in the Northeast.

Relationships Among Government Transportation Agencies

While private carriers may complain about the number of overlapping government regulations to which they are subjected, public enterprise carriers are probably subjected to even more regulations. Public carriers are often subject to the same restrictions that apply to private carriers *plus* a host of additional regulations which cover the public carriers, simply because they are government agencies. The National Transportation Policy Study Commission identified approximately *1,000* federal transportation policies and programs, administered by 64 different federal agencies.[5] While state and local governments are somewhat less prolific when it comes to writing regulations, they also have regulations that govern the operation of

[4]"New York State Extends Drayage Subsidy," *Via Port* (December, 1981), p. 16.
[5]National Transportation Policy Study Commission, *A Compendium of Federal Transportation Policies and Programs* (Washington, D.C.: The Commission, 1979).

public carriers. Sometimes the programs of different agencies of the same level of government conflict with each other. In addition, the programs of agencies at different levels (state, federal, local) also conflict. The burden on the public operator is to comply with all the requirements. Even when possible, this is costly and difficult for the public transportation agency. It is also difficult for a public transportation agency to follow all of the rules set down by other government agencies and make decisions in the manner that would be followed by a profit-oriented firm. (A profit-oriented firm's management must make decisions—also profit-oriented—yielding desirable and efficient use of the resources at its disposal, such as equipment and personnel. Indeed, private management must make well-informed and profit-yielding decisions if the firm is to stay in business. A nonprofit-oriented manager need not make decisions that lead to efficient use of personnel or equipment.)

Public seaport authorities compete directly with each other by building expensive terminals to attract waterborne traffic. Since they are subsidized and can disguise their losses, the public and the taxpayer have little idea as to how well they are performing. Port directors measure their success in terms of tonnage or numbers of containers handled. But that may not mean anything when attempting to determine the costs and benefits to the community which provided the funds to build the port.

Public Transportation Cost and Revenue Structures

Government budgeting generally divides expenditures into two categories: capital outlays and operating expenses. Capital outlays are used to purchase or construct buildings, facilities, and equipment, all having a useful life longer than one year. Operating expenses include labor, fringe benefits, expendable supplies, rents or lease payments, and "short-term" contract services.

Prudent budgeting dictates that operating costs in a period of time should be covered by operating revenues or tax receipts in that same period of time (usually one year). Capital outlays could be funded through long-term borrowing, and the term of the debt should be about the same as the useful life of the facility purchased or built with the loaned funds.

Capital outlay and operating budgets must be coordinated through the planning process. For example, investment in capital equipment could reduce the number of workers needed to handle containers. Or, the opposite could occur, with an example being the construction of a fire station at an airport. Both building the station and buying a new fire engine to keep in it would be covered in a capital budget. However, staffing it with several shifts of firefighters after it was opened would become an item in the operating budget and would continue year after year.

Federal programs for transportation often provide grants to local communities to cover large shares of the total costs of building an airport, constructing a highway, or buying new buses. From the point of view of the federal government, these capital grants are highly visible, are positive, and produce almost immediate results.[6] Only later do communities realize the extent to which they were burdened with annual operating and maintenance costs. The *Urban Mass Transportation Act of 1964* started the massive infusions of federal money to communities so that they could buy up declining transit properties, convert them to public operations, and buy new fleets of buses and other transit equipment. The law provided that no mass transit employee would suffer a reduction in employment or status as the result of the federal grant. Local operating deficits grew and, 10 years later, in the *National Mass Transportation Assistance*

- Mass transit operations, whether public or private, are often referred to as *properties.*

Act of 1974, the federal government was forced to accept responsibility for subsidizing the operating expenses of local public transit operators as well. The Reagan administration is attempting to eliminate federal involvement in paying operating subsidies, with one reason being that they feel subsidies encourage local transit management to be too "generous" in wage negotiations.

Capital Outlays

Finding the right form of long-term financing is a time-consuming effort for inexperienced public transportation agency managers. A study dealing with the available sources of capital to fund barge harbor facilities in the St. Louis area listed four types of bonds, as well as loans from state and federal programs.

One type of borrowing is the *local general obligation* bond issued by the community; this type of borrowing contains a promise that the community will use its general powers to tax local property if

---

[6] From an auditing and program management standpoint, it is easier for federal agencies to make capital improvement grants since their responsibility for overseeing the use of federal funds ends when the project's construction or purchase is completed.

necessary to repay the debt. *Revenue* bonds could be issued by the port authority; the funds to repay the bond would come from lease and rental receipts collected from the port's tenants and those who use its facilities. *Consolidated* bonds can be issued by port authorities or similar public agencies which earn revenues from many sources; the port authority merely pledges its stream of revenues toward repaying their debts. *Industrial development* bonds would be used to build facilities for a specific industrial user of the port; and the specific user's lease agreement would serve as a "guarantee" of bond repayment. And, of course, there are also federal and state programs to help fund the development and construction of ports.

> Almost every public port in the United States receives some kind of public aid or subsidy from some level of government. These funds range from direct appropriations, direct taxes levied by the port district, and taxes levied by the local government on behalf of the port authority to exemptions from taxation or indirect subsidies incorporated in public community services provided to the port authority by the local, city, or county government.[7]

Operating Expenses

Operating expenses are usually budgeted annually. Expenses or commitments over longer periods than one year are handled as capital outlays. Table 14–1 lists the operating expense items for one year for a small public bus system. During that year, the company's receipts included $981,000 collected mainly at the fare box; $645,000 from state funds (collected as a part of a retail sales tax); and $525,000 in operating subsidies from the federal government. Receipts totalled $2,150,000 while expenses (exclusive of depreciation) were slightly less. During the year covered in the report, the bus system carried just under three million passengers, and it had 66 employees, and 28 buses.

In establishing an operating budget, a public transportation agency must project operating revenues plus receipts from various sources of subsidy. The funds from federal and state programs do not flow in a regular, steady stream; therefore, the public agency must have reserves on hand to pay day-to-day bills while waiting for the large federal and state checks. Unlike private business, *some* public transportation agencies cannot use their operating revenues to pay current expenses. Instead, receipts are deposited with the city or

---

[7] Robert G. Goodwin, Jr. "Port-Funding Dilemmas in a Regional Planning Context," *Transportation Research Record* 636, (Washington, D.C.: Transportation Research Board, 1977), pp. 22–23.

TABLE 14–1   A Bus Company's Operating Expenses:
Monterey Peninsula Transit Operating Expenses
for the Year Ended June 30, 1981

VEHICLE OPERATIONS		
Operators' Wages	$ 593,430	
Other Wages	88,144	
Fringe Benefits	244,480	
Supplies, Fuels, & Lubricants	304,479	
Tires and Tubes	23,180	
Other	23,448	
		$1,277,161
VEHICLE MAINTENANCE		
Wages	144,896	
Fringe Benefits	53,483	
Services	31,584	
Materials and Supplies	101,811	
Other	37,172	
		368,946
NON-VEHICLE MAINTENANCE		35,420
GENERAL ADMINISTRATION		350,226
DEPRECIATION		375,042
		$2,406,795

Source: *Monterey Peninsula Transit, Annual Report, Fiscal Year 1981* (Monterey, California, November, 1981).

county treasurer. Expenses are paid out of funds which have already been appropriated. These agencies operate under more traditional government budgetary approaches of collecting taxes and receipts in one year and then establishing a budget which spends them in the following year. Public agencies that are allowed to spend funds immediately after receiving them experience the same liquidity or cash flow adventures as do firms in the private sector.

Use of Surplus Funds

Unusual problems may occur when a public transportation agency unexpectedly earns surplus funds. First, a legitimate question may be raised as to why the operation is run by a public agency since, apparently, it is capable of earning a profit. This is difficult to answer. Sometimes, because the public agency is able to avoid many taxes and can borrow money at lower rates (because interest payments are exempt from federal taxation), it may be able to generate a surplus, where as a private firm could not.

The government body that reigns over the public transportation agency may covet this surplus for meeting its own needs. The senior government body and the transportation agency's directors may engage in a struggle to determine how the surplus will be spent. The transportation agency's directors will want the surplus used within their agency, while the senior government body will claim that it has been providing subsidies over the years and now is entitled to some of the surplus. Often the senior governmental body will insist that any surplus funds be turned over to it rather than be spent by the transportation agency.[8] One result of this is that the management of the public transportation agency has little incentive to operate in a manner that produces revenues in excess of costs.

The Golden Gate Bridge, Highway, and Transportation Agency, which was formed in the 1930's by the State of California to finance and construct the Golden Gate Bridge, was able to collect tolls far in excess of what was required to retire its bonds and maintain the bridge. As the last bonds were about to be retired, the District's directors asked the state legislature to expand their statutory powers to allow them to engage in mass transit operations. As a result, the District now uses toll receipts collected from motorists crossing the bridge to subsidize mass transit buses on routes crossing the bridge and to subsidize a ferry system connecting communities on both sides of the bridge. In 1981, the District's revenues and expenses were each approximatey $40 million. Receipts from bridge tolls were $19 million; receipts from bus fares were $11 million; receipts from ferry fares were $3 million; and transit subsidies from various levels of government were $7 million. Expenditures were $9 millon for the bridge; $22 million for the buses; $8 million for the ferries; and $1 million for subsidizing van-pool and ride-sharing programs.[9]

This is an example of "internal subsidies" with the bridge's surplus offsetting the bus and ferry deficits. While the motorists using the bridge are being "taxed" to support the mass transit passengers, it can be argued that they benefit since the mass transit riders would otherwise be in autos, further clogging the bridge during rush hours.

User Fees

Managers and designers of public transportation facilities must be able to devise methods to collect fees from *all* users. Some users think that because a facility is operated by a public agency, it is (or

[8]Recall from chapter 2 that Robert Moses expanded his power base by using toll receipts to finance new projects.

[9]*Golden Gate Bridge, Highway and Transportation District Annual Report, 1980–1981* (San Francisco: The District, 1982). In other years, financial assistance from the federal Urban Mass Transportation Administration had been used to help purchase the buses and ferries.

should be) "free." Airports and access roads to airports are often laid out in a manner that makes it almost impossible for anyone to enter the airport without paying some form of charge.

An example of charges levied by a seaport authority is this list of charges for the facilities by the Puerto Rico Ports Authority:

1. A port service charge on vessels entering the port; the charge is based on vessel size and number of days in port.
2. A dockage charge on vessels tied up alongside a dock; the charge is based on vessel size and time spent at dock.
3. Wharfage charge on cargo loaded onto or from a vessel. The rates vary by type of cargo. Charges on molasses are half a cent per hundred-weight; charges on petroleum are one cent per 42-gallon barrel; charges on empty containers are $4.09.
4. Passenger vessels (cruise ships) pay a fee of $3.75 per passenger carried on board.
5. Storage charges are assessed on cargo and containers which remain in the port area longer than a specified number of days.
6. Rent is charged for use of the port authority's land.
7. Vessels in port are also charged for fresh water, electric power, and telephone connections.[10]

The charges just listed deal mainly with use of individual shore-side facilities in a port. More recently, interest has developed in the idea of "port user fees" to recover the extensive costs paid by the U.S. government (operating through the Army Corps of Engineers) for dredging channels between open water and port facilities. At present, the government does not recover the costs, and many local ports are clamoring for additional federal dredging so that they can handle the larger sizes of ocean vessels. President Reagan's Director of the Office of Management and Budget, David Stockman, has "argued that 100 percent of the costs for port dredging should be assumed by local governments. According to Stockman, 100 percent local funding would 'lessen the distortions on the transportation system resulting from the federal subsidy for dredging.'"[11] The essence of Stockman's argument was that only at ports where users were willing to pay for the costs of dredging could one be certain that the dredging was worthwhile.

Public transportation agencies charge fees which they hope will cover many of their expenses. Since the public agency is subsidized,

[10] *Port Charges and Terminal Rates Applicable to the Marine Terminal Facilities Owned or Operated by the Puerto Rico Ports Authority, October 15, 1977—October 14, 1979* (San Juan: The Authority, 1978).

[11] "Concept of a Port User Charge Analysis Package," *Transport 2000* (November/December, 1981), pp. 42–44, 62.

it can usually charge lower fees than private firms, in case it happens to compete with them. In the San Francisco Bay area, private harbor tour boat operators complain that tourists and sight-seers use the heavily-subsidized ferries operated by the Golden Gate Bridge District, which reduces the private operators' revenues.

In theory, user fees charged by a public agency are supposed to approximate the prices a private operator would charge for providing the same service. If this happens, the user would make choices based on the approximate full costs for whatever type of transportation he chose to use. Unfortunately, federal income tax laws do not encourage local transportation agencies, especially public mass transit operators, to rely heavily on user fees to cover most, if not all, of the costs of providing service. The reason is that *taxes* paid to local government can be deducted from one's taxable income before computing income taxes which must be paid to the federal government. Hence, if you live in city A and $200 of the local property taxes you pay goes to subsidize a city-owned bus system, this $200 is subtracted from your taxable income for federal income tax purposes. If you're in the "25 percent" federal tax bracket, this means that you would save $50 on federal income taxes because of the $200 paid in local property taxes (in this instance to support the city-owned bus system).

Assume further that you are a regular bus rider and ride on the bus 200 days per year. If the city decided that it wanted to reduce its subsidies to the bus operation and made the riders pay more of the costs, it would raise fares collected as you boarded the bus. Assume that the city raised fares one dollar per day and eliminated most other subsidies to the bus system. How does this concern you? First, your local property taxes would be reduced by $200 per year. Second, the bus fares you pay for an entire year would increase by a total of $200 (one dollar per day times 200 days). It appears that you're breaking even. But you're not! Why? Because the $200 you pay in daily bus fares is *not* deductible from your income when calculating federal income taxes. However, your property taxes went down by $200 which you can no longer deduct from your income for federal tax purposes; hence your federal income tax just increased by $50 per year. So there is a real disincentive for you to want your city-owned bus system to cover its costs from fares collected at the fare box. "User fees tend to cost the individual more than other types of taxes, since they're not deductible on federal income-tax returns."[12]

[12]"Proposition 13: Who Really Won?" *Consumer Reports* (September, 1979), p. 548.

Marketing Public Transportation Services

Public carriers and private carriers have different marketing goals and marketing programs, although both are aimed at increasing patronage.

Service Mix

Public operators have less flexibility in developing a "mix" of services. Often, the laws creating the public agency are quite restrictive, specifying exactly what the public agency can and cannot do. In addition, private operators will cry "foul" if they feel the public operation is eating into their profit-making business; the best example of this is private taxicab and airport limousine operators who resist efforts of public transportation agencies to provide public transit service to the airport's passengers. A public port or airport authority can expect to be criticized whenever it competes directly with some operation that pays taxes to the community.

The mix of services may be dictated by public policy. Local public transit systems are expected to meet the needs of the following groups: school children, the elderly, the handicapped, the poor, white and blue collar workers, household cleaning help on their way to jobs in the suburbs, a few mid-day shoppers, Sunday churchgoers, and motorists whose autos are being repaired. (In addition, a local public transit system is expected to provide standby capacity to carry all of the rest of us who ordinarily drive cars in case we can no longer buy gasoline.) A public operator has much less discretion than a private operator (even one with a "common carrier obligation") when it comes to lopping off certain groups of unwanted customers.

Actual marketing goals are set by the public agency's governing body. These goals would tend to stress whatever was believed to be important to the community. In the hierarchy of public transportation, accomplishments are measured in terms such as passengers handled annually, number of new airline scheduled flights, or tonnage moving across the docks.

Pricing

There are usually two conflicting goals when policies are made regarding the pricing of public transportation services. User fees (or cost-based charges), which were discussed earlier, should minimize the amount of public subsidy required.

Some public transportation functions, particularly mass transit, offer service priced below costs so that low-income groups can afford to pay for it; if the full cost of service was charged, they could not afford it. User fees based on full costs discourage patronage. Even middle-class users of mass transit require subsidized fares if they are to be lured from their autos.

Those people who advocate that fees for transportation service should be based on paying for the full cost of that service maintain that this type of pricing results in minimal subsidies and is the most efficient use of equipment and labor; that is, the public transportation operator can assign equipment and personnel to routes where user-fee collections exceed costs. If the public operation does this, it would be minimizing its need for subsidies and would be following the same rules as a profit-oriented private enterprise operation.

On the other side of this issue are the advocates of subsidizing the costs. They maintain that the subsidies are a necessary and practical form of "income redistribution" and that many people who need transportation services cannot afford them.

Thus, when we consider the merits of the two conflicting goals, plus the federal "tax disadvantages" to the individual of user fees, we realize how difficult it is to determine what public transportation pricing policy is "best."

Advertising

Advertising by public transportation agencies differs little from that of private carrier firms. It is aimed primarily at increasing use of the public transportation facility. Figure 14–2 is informational advertising, an excerpt from a public bus operation brochure which clearly shows a route map and a time schedule.

Figures 14–3 and 14–4 are port authority ads. Figure 14–3 promotes Port Everglades and its greater available depths of water to handle large vessels. Figure 14–4 is an advertisement for the Port of Savannah aimed at potential port users who deal in heavy equipment requiring special "heavy lift" cranes for transfer of cargo between vessel and the shore.

Figure 14–5 shows a San Diego bus carrying advertising for the San Diego Zoo. In this instance, both the bus operation and the zoo are beneficiaries of the advertising.

2 LOVER'S POINT via Lighthouse

Franklin & Alvarado	Lighthouse & Hoffman	Lighthouse & Fountain	Lighthouse & 17 Mile Dr	Ocean View & Jewell	Lighthouse & Fountain	Lighthouse & Hoffman	Tyler & Franklin	
MONDAY - SATURDAY								
—	—	—	—	—	6.08*	6.12*	6.18*	7
6.30	6.34	6.40	6.44	6.50	6.57	7.01	7.07	@
7.30	7.34	7.40	7.44	7.50	7.57	8.01	8.07	@
8.30	8.34	8.40	8.44	8.50	8.57	9.01	9.07	8
9.30	9.34	9.40	9.44	9.50	9.57	10.01	10.07	8
10.30	10.34	10.40	10.44	10.50	10.57	11.01	11.07	8
11.30	11.34	11.40	11.44	11.50	11.57	**12.01**	**12.07**	8
12.30	**12.34**	**12.40**	**12.44**	**12.50**	**12.57**	**1.01**	**1.07**	8
1.30	**1.34**	**1.40**	**1.44**	**1.50**	**1.57**	**2.01**	**2.07**	8
2.30	**2.34**	**2.40**	**2.44**	**2.50**	**2.57**	**3.01**	**3.07**	8
3.30	**3.34**	**3.40**	**3.44**	**3.50**	**3.57**	**4.01**	**4.07**	8
4.30	**4.34**	**4.40**	**4.44**	**4.50**	**4.57**	**5.01**	**5.07**	8
5.30	**5.34**	**5.40**	**5.44**	**5.50**	**5.57**	**6.01**	**6.07**	8

Light face AM
Bold face PM

* — Except Saturday
7 — To line 7
8 — To line 8
@ — To line 8 Monday-Friday; to line 7 on Saturdays

SUNDAY & HOLIDAYS

No service on Sundays and Holidays

899-2555
OR
424-7695

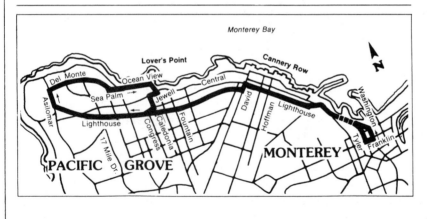

Figure 14–2 Excerpt from Bus Schedule. Courtesy: Monterey Peninsula Transit.

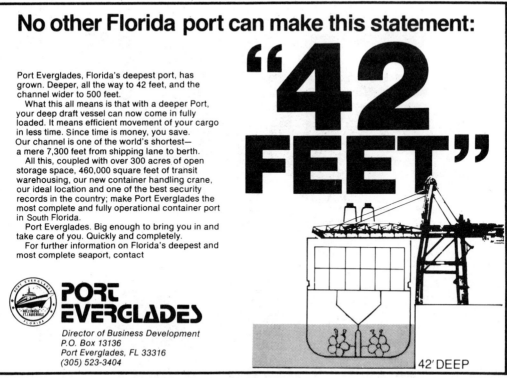

Figure 14–3   Ad for Port Everglades. Reproduced by permission of Ross Hancock Advertising, Hollywood, Florida, for Port Everglades Authority.

Public Relations

Public relations of public transportation agencies is aimed at creating and maintaining the "proper" image and awareness in the eyes of the public. Public relations also attempts to sway public opinion in certain directions. A study of ocean and Great Lakes ports found that over half of the larger ports had public relations staffs, ranging in size from one to five people. In explaining the growth in the ports' public relations function, the study said that in the mid-1960's:

> . . . there developed an overwhelming need for effective, on-going PR programs to address these newly-surfacing issues and developments: the vast technological changes such as containerization and new ship designs which placed heavy pressure on seaports to rapidly expand and modernize; the social considerations in the areas of environmentalism, consumerism, full public disclosure and energy conservation; more intense competition in attracting cargo; and increased federal government

Figure 14–4   Ad for Port of Savannah. Courtesy: Georgia Ports Authority.

Figure 14–5   Ad on Bus for San Diego Zoo. Courtesy: Winston Network, Inc.

involvement in areas such as dockworker safety, cargo security and environmental standards. The most critical area demanding effective PR, however, has been obtaining public support for financing expansion. . . .[13]

Note especially the last sentence. The public relations office of public transportation agencies spend public money to advocate the spending of even more public money.

Market Research: The Mass Transit Demonstration Projects

The federal Urban Mass Transportation Administration (UMTA) funded a highly successful program during the 1960's to test all possible combinations of equipment and service to determine which would be most attractive to riders. Local public transit agencies

[13]Dennis E. Deuschl, "Port PR Comes of Age," *American Seaport* (September, 1977), pp. 9–11 & p. 35. See also: Andrew Marshall Hamer, *The Selling of Rail Rapid Transit* (Lexington, Mass.: Lexington Books, 1976), p. 258.

could apply to the UMTA for federal funds to "test" various ideas they had for improving service and attracting riders.[14]

The experiments dealt with many problems, and the results of the experiments were many innovations in today's transit industry. Several examples of innovations in the bus industry resulting from these experiments are radio equipment on buses; standardized passenger shelters; expanded transit information (including brochures, timetables, signs at bus stops with schedules, etc.); and training courses for bus drivers. Other experiments resulted in things like improved flow of buses in traffic; bus-activated traffic signals; special ramps for buses entering and exiting freeways and busy intersections; and reserved lanes for buses on freeways. Some projects were designed to test the need for and success of expanded bus service, such as new routes to airports, to low-income areas, to job opportunities, to hospitals, and to parking lots. Demand-responsive systems (sometimes called "dial-a-ride"), which combine operating and service aspects of buses and cabs, were tried in several different settings (and with surprisingly little success). Computer programs for developing routes and schedules, programs for scheduling drivers and vehicles, and programs for scheduling vehicle maintenance were also developed. Experiments with varying fares were also conducted.

Rail transit service experiments tested the following: a system that would automatically determine the amount of a fare and collect it, parking lots at suburban commuter stations, and better coordination between rail and bus schedules. Funds were also used to help San Francisco's BART develop its car control technology, using space-age—rather than conventional railroad—technological approaches.

New transport technologies were also the subject of experiments. Studies examined the use of unmanned trains, similar to some that can be found at a few airports today. A hovercraft (a vehicle that travels on its own cushion of air) shuttle service between downtown San Francisco and two airports was also tried. A small study examined the use of Seattle's monorail, originally built to serve World's Fair traffic in 1962, to see whether monorails could serve mass transit needs.

In total, UMTA's demonstration project program would have to be considered a success. Every reasonable idea (and a few others) were tested. Today's transit manager can benefit from the accumu-

---

[14]George W. Hilton, *Federal Transit Subsidies* (Washington, D.C.: American Enterprise Institute for Public Policy Research, 1974), p. 13. The discussion here is based on Hilton's work. Reports were issued for each of the demonstration projects and copies of some of them are considered "collectors' items."

lated knowledge gathered from all of these undertakings. Even the projects that "failed" were helpful because they can enable others to avoid the same mistakes.

Organizational Structure of Public Transportation Agencies

Public transportation agencies are organized somewhat differently from private transportation agencies. The governing body of a public agency is either elected by the public or appointed by the governor, the mayor, or other elected official. In turn, the governing body chooses a full-time manager who is the "director" or "executive director" or "general manager" of the public transit operation. This manager is responsible for day-to-day operations.

There is no standard for organizing a public transportation function. A Michigan study, dealing with proposals to activate a public port agency for Detroit, said that the "most active" of the Great Lakes ports "have evolved from a municipal port commission (Toronto), a municipal port department (Milwaukee), a state regional port district (Chicago), and a county port authority (Toledo). The only feature in common was an outstanding professional port director." The report made some specific suggestions regarding a port authority for Detroit and Wayne County and then contained this paragraph which indicates the role of the director and a small staff:

> The Port Director will be the key figure in this . . . arrangement. He should be a top flight professional, creditable in the business and commercial communities and able to operate effectively and without undue turbulence through governmental channels and agencies. He should be appointed . . . after thorough examination and given a long enough work contract to permit evaluation of results (3 to 5 years). The Port Director's office should be supported by a staff of 10 to 12 professionals placed in administrative, planning and marketing divisions. The staff should be subject to Civil Service qualifications. . . . In recognition of the major promotional task to be done, the Marketing Division should be the largest and should incorporate elements for institutional promotion, tariff and trade, and at least two salesmen in the field. . . . The Planning Division will require at least three planners and engineers, not for the usual maintenance activities on brick and mortar, but to quickly arrive at a site specific plan for expanding into an intermodal port. The Administrative division should be a two-man operation with focus primarily upon financial and legal aspects of the port's operations. Clerical and staff assistance should be adequate. The new Port Director should be provided with some latitude in structuring the divisions according to his needs and style.[15]

[15] The Land and the River, Report of the Interagency Task Force for Detroit/Wayne County Riverfront Development (Lansing: Michigan Department of Commerce, 1976), pp. 9–10.

Public transit operations sometimes retain professional transit management firms which manage the operation from the top level. Several large transit management firms will bid for each available public transit management opportunity; they will expect to be paid a small percentage of the transit operation's gross receipts. Their managers have the advantage of exposure to transit operations in many cities and often can provide more detailed assistance in matters such as labor negotiations, purchasing, or use of computers for scheduling. The principal disadvantage of using these firms is that a transit operation's own employees see no "room at the top" because the top jobs regularly are filled by the professional management firm's personnel.[16]

It is not easy for public transportation agencies to restructure themselves organizationally; the state or municipal laws that created the agencies do not allow them much flexibility in reorganizing. Often the state or municipal laws may have to be amended in order for a reorganization to take place.

Planning

Public transportation agencies usually plan very far into the future, especially for fixed facilities, such as an airport or seaport.

Planning by public transportation agencies must be coordinated with the plans of other public agencies. States along the oceans and the Great Lakes are responsible for planning the use of the shoreline; their plans must take port uses into account. Airport plans must always be coordinated with the surrounding area's land-use plan because an airport and its approach zones not only take up large areas, they also have an effect on large areas beyond.

Planning by public agencies is subject to more scrutiny than planning by private transportation agencies. Opponents have more opportunities to delay or halt public transportation projects. In the late 1960's, environmental protection interests had successfully blocked airport developments at many major cities in the United States. The best known such project was a new airport to serve Miami. The planned airport complex was to be five times as large as Kennedy International Airport, and construction was started on the

[16]David B. Vellenga, "Can Professional Transit Management Improve Our Urban Transit Systems?" *Proceedings, 1973 Transportation Research Forum* (Oxford, Indiana: Richard B. Cross, 1973), pp. 345–350.

site in Big Cypress Swamp, six miles north of Everglades National Park, over the objections of "environmentalists." Further construction was blocked by the federal government after a Department of the Interior study concluded: "Development of the proposed jetport and its attendant facilities will lead to land drainage and development for agriculture, industry, housing, transportation and services in the Big Cypress Swamp which will inexorably destroy the south Florida ecosystem and thus Everglades National Park."[17]

The reason public ventures are more likely to be delayed is that the procedures that govern the operations of public agencies provide many more steps at which public opinion and comment must be solicited. Opponents of a project will seize each of these steps as an opportunity to delay, stall, and perhaps completely thwart the project.

Analyzing and justifying costs is often less critical at the point of establishing plans in public agencies than in private agencies. Some public plans are designed with only one objective—to provide service. Regard for cost seems to be a distant secondary objective. As an example, a study of Georgia's rural public transportation needs: (1) took population estimates of that state's rural elderly and handicapped residents who were without autos; (2) applied estimates of the number and distance of trips (mainly for shopping and to see doctors) each of the individuals should be able to take in order to be considered as "transportation sufficient"; and (3) looked at costs of various van fleets under a range of operating conditions and load factors in order to determine costs of meeting the need.[18]

Detailed financial projections and analysis are necessary in instances where revenue bonds are to be issued. This would be needed to show prospective investors that there would be a flow of revenue to cover interest payments.

The planning work is done by the public agency's own staff, or by other public planning agencies, or by private planning consultants. Determining how much planning work should be done "in house" and how much should be performed by others is difficult. One of the conclusions of a nationwide survey of community mass transit planning was: "Public accountability may be threatened when those

---

[17] *Our Nation's Wetlands* (Washington, D.C., a federal interagency task force report coordinated by the Council on Environmental Quality, 1978), pp. 41–43.

[18] Technically, what was described here would be more accurately described as a "needs" study, one of the early steps in the planning process. See: Hal S. Maggied, "Georgia's Critical Rural Transportation Needs," *Transportation Research Record 661* (Washington, D.C.: Transportation Research Board, 1978), pp. 40–42.

charged with transit planning cede their decision making authority to powerful consultants."[19]

Personnel Administration

Many employees of public transportation agencies are likely to be members of unions. Their rights as members of public employees unions differ from state to state. Many states, and the federal government, have laws prohibiting strikes or slowdowns by public employees, although it is clear that these laws are not always obeyed. Air traffic controllers in the United States who struck in 1981 were no doubt surprised (to say the least) at President Reagan's reaction.

The largest single group of public transportation employees who are unionized are those who work for municipal transit agencies; they are primarily drivers, although there are also mechanics. Transit drivers are locked into monotonous jobs with relatively little hope for advancement. However, they are important to the success of the transit system because they influence the decision of the public whether to ride transit. A survey conducted among bus riders in San Diego asked them to rate the importance of various characteristics of bus service. "Bus stops" ranked first, and "drivers" ranked second.[20] Another survey question specifically asked riders to rank bus drivers' individual characteristics in descending order of importance. The most important was "ability to handle bus smoothly," followed by "ability to run on time," "courtesy," "helpfulness," "traffic safety," "willingness to wait," and "personal appearance."[21] A challenge to transit managers is to maintain their drivers' interest in continually performing well in all these areas of importance.

Transit workers' unions are relatively strong because of their monopolylike position in providing a needed service. These unions have been very adept at capturing for their members many of the

[19] *An Assessment of Community Planning for Mass Transit* (Washington, D.C.: U.S. Congress, Office of Technology Assessment, 1976), p. 3. Readers interested in transit planning should read two papers appearing in the *Proceedings of the 1981 Transportation Research Forum* (Oxford, Indiana, Richard B. Cross, 1981). They are: Greg Mason, "Urban Transit: Myths of the Present, Realities of the Future and the Role of Technology," pp. 636–643; and Francis P. D. Nevin, "Urban Public Transit Subsidies in Canada," pp. 644–657.

[20] Dinoo J. Vanier, "On the Importance of the Bus Driver," *Mass Transit* (February, 1977), pp. 14–16. Other transit features, in descending order of importance, were: bus features, bus ride, schedule frequency, routes, transfers, and fares.

[21] *Ibid.*, p. 15.

benefits from the increased flow of federal subsidies for mass transit.[22]

Public agencies are expected to "lead the way" in minority hiring practices. As a goal, they often attempt to have the same ratio of minorities on their payroll as the ratio of the community's population. For example, the population of Oakland, California, consists of about 51 percent racial minorities; in 1978, 237 of its public port's 466 employees were from minority groups.[23] The port also participated in the federal CETA (Comprehensive Employment and Training Act) program which subsidizes the hiring and training of individuals who have been unemployed for over 30 days. The port actively seeks bids from minority firms to supply services or act as contractors. Construction contracts issued by the port require contractors to have and maintain their own minority employment programs, which the port monitors. Also, the port is attempting to have its tenants adopt minority hiring programs.

Public Transportation System Controls

Table 14–2 contains selected operating statistics for the same public bus operation whose budget was discussed earlier in this chapter. They can be used to measure changes in the overall effectiveness of the operation.

Many of the same controls used to manage private transportation carriers are also used to manage public service transportation operations. However, when dealing with public sector transportation undertakings, there are three additional concerns which relate to controls.

First, since there is little or no profit incentive for the public manager or supervisor, it is difficult to use "contribution to profitability" as a measure of the benefit derived from any expense. In private transportation, a manager may be able to justify unconventional decisions by showing how they contribute to the overall profitability. Furthermore, public managers are accustomed to dealing with losses, and we—as a society—are much poorer judges when it comes to determining how good a job the public manager is doing in

---

[22]Hilton, *op. cit.*, pp. 58–59, 109–113. Bargaining is described in: Jay A. Smith, Kenneth M. Jennings, and Earle C. Traynham, "Collective Bargaining in Mass Transit," *Proceedings, 1976 Transportation Research Forum* (Oxford, Indiana: Richard B. Cross, 1976), pp. 336–343.

[23]This, and the following discussion, are based on *Port Progress: Port of Oakland News* (1978, No. 3.).

TABLE 14–2 Selected Operating Statistics: Monterey Peninsula Transit 1974–1981

	FY 74	FY 75	FY 76	FY 77	FY 78	FY 79	FY 80	FY 81
Passengers	364,107	804,242	1,061,789	1,396,797	1,592,248	1,897,719	2,668,564	2,919,273
Miles of Service Operated	173,157	404,224	502,270	703,301	765,345	850,194	1,068,013	1,113,952
Passenger Boardings per Mile	2.10	1.99	2.11	1.99	2.08	2.23	2.50	2.62
Passenger Revenue	$ 86,243	$214,774	$ 220,389	$ 301,697	$ 361,332	$ 400,779	$ 594,127	$ 861,598
Revenue per Mile	$ .50	$ .53	$ .44	$ .43	$ .47	$ .47	$ .56	$ .77
Revenue per Passenger	$ .24	$ .27	$ .21	$ .22	$ .23	$ .21	$ .22	$ .30
Operating Expenses	$215,899	$511,249	$686,268	$801,107	$949,478	$1,192,631	$1,635,321	$2,019,358
Cost per Mile	$ 1.25	$ 1.26	$ 1.37	$ 1.14	$ 1.24	$ 1.40	$ 1.53	$ 1.81
Cost per Passenger	$ .59	$ .64	$ .65	$ .57	$ .60	$ .63	$ .61	$ .69
Farebox Recovery Ratio	40.0%	42.0%	32.1%	37.7%	38.1%	33.6%	36.3%	42.7%
Average Schedule Speed (mph)	16.0	14.3	14.0	14.8	15.4	14.5	15.5	15.8
Number of Routes	7	11	13	13	15	16	16	16
Number of Buses	9	14	21	21	21	23	28	28
Number of Employees	18	33	40	46	53	56	64	66

SOURCE: *Monterey Peninsula Transit, Annual Report, Fiscal Year 1981* (Monterey, California, November, 1981).

Note: Terms used in this table are as defined by California state law and administrative regulations.

controlling losses. We have more experience judging managers of enterprises that are earning profits.

Second, in the leasing out to private interests the land and terminal facilities in public airports and seaports, there is opportunity for graft. This is because the lessee is usually gaining limited monopoly rights in some transportation terminal or market and is often willing to spend a little extra money in hidden payments to public officials in order to obtain the lease. Many of these tenants are international carriers and quite accustomed to doing business this way in other lands. One of most important functions of a public manager is to devise leasing and bidding procedures that are relatively "cheat-proof." Constant surveillance is also required over the staff responsible for negotiating leases.

Third, safety of individuals and security of cargo is a matter of great concern to public transit operators and airport managers. There are cases where they operate their own police force. Crime in transit systems, both en route and at terminals and stations along the route, deters people from using mass transit.[24] Airport security is related to both security of passengers on flights departing from the airport and to the air cargo terminals at the airport where high-value merchandise is the target of thieves. Large airports and seaports in the U.S. have often been troubled by organized crime and labor racketeering.

Public Enterprise Leadership

As is the case for private carriers, selection of the individual to manage the public enterprise transportation undertaking is crucial. One example is the statement regarding the port director's post for Detroit and Wayne County indicating that the director be "creditable in the business and commercial communities and able to operate effectively and without undue turbulence through governmental channels and agencies." Management in the public sector requires a different set of skills than is necessary in the private sector. However, and as is the case for private enterprise management, there is no one "preferred" type of leadership. Successful leaders have their individual styles.

Managers of private transportation companies have more latitude since, in theory, they and their firms can do anything not prohibited

---

[24]Mass transit crime is discussed in: *Mass Transit* (March, 1978), entire issue; and by the "Safety and Security in Public Transportation" panel, whose reports appear in: *Proceedings, 1974 Transportation Research Forum*, (Oxford, Indiana: Richard B. Cross, 1974), pp. 214–245.

by the law, or in the case of regulated carriers, by the rules of the regulatory body. Public enterprise is often more restricted and can perform only those functions specifically permitted or assigned by law. Governing bodies of the public agency further refine these rules into statements of policy which their employees must follow.

An example of a comprehensive statement of policy was adopted by the Port of Seattle Commission which operates the Seattle-Tacoma (Sea-Tac) airport and seaport facilities along Seattle's shore line. The Port of Seattle Commission also promotes industrial development, and has the right to levy taxes on property within King County (the county of which Seattle is a part). Excerpts from the Commission's policy statements follow:

1. The primary purpose of the Port is to develop, maintain, and operate adequate transportation facilities for water and air transportation. . . . Wherever possible the Port will encourage the development of any portion of Port facilities as is feasible by private capital.
2. The Port has not accepted responsibility for providing surface transportation facilities . . . including highway and rail terminals, tunnels and toll bridges, but may . . . when a public purpose ancillary to the Port's primary responsibility is served and when private capital is unable to meet the need.
3. The Port has accepted a responsibility to provide some moorage . . . for fishing and pleasure boats, but endeavors to do so at rates which cover all expenses . . . , therefore diverting no funds from marine ocean-terminal and airport operations.
4. The total operations of the port are conducted . . . with the objective of earning sufficient net income to cover operating and administrative costs and depreciation. . . . For the forseeable future . . . the operating profit must be supplemented by investment of the general-purpose tax levy in marine-terminal facilities. . . . Revenue bonds will be used whenever feasible to supplement funds required for new facilities.
5. The Port shall maintain a plan of capital improvements and fund requirements projected at least five years into the future and a comprehensive plan of long-range development extending beyond that time. In planning . . . to meet its land-use needs, the Port will cooperate and coordinate fully with the development plans adopted by other government jurisdictions.

6. Properties required for Port development shall be acquired by negotiation or condemnation at fair market value, subject to statutory requirements on relocation assistance.

7. The Port will lease its land and facilities for a private operation whenever this can be done at a fair return without added cost or sacrifice of service to the public. . . .

8. All leases of Port property . . . are made with a view to the competitive value of the property compared to other ports, and to the customary return on investment in such class of property. The Port will attempt to earn amounts . . . adequate to amortize improvements over their useful life, and to earn a rate of return not less than the prevailing interest rate on long-term industrial real estate mortgages.

9. The Port will cooperate fully with other ports and labor, management and other public organizations in matters relating reducing impediments to trade, improving Port operations and establishing equitable and compensatory charges for services.

10. The Port is an equal-opportunity employer and maintains an affirmative-action plan to expand career opportunities for minorities and women.

11. In meeting requirements of the Shoreline Management Act and the Environmental Protection Act, the Port recognizes its reponsibility for developments which are . . . compatible with the environment and the community and will encourage citizen participation in planning projects affecting the public. In relation to the operation of Sea-Tac International Airport . . . the Port is implementing a significant noise abatement program.

12. The Port conducts its official actions in public meetings . . . , and its official records are open to the public for review. The Port encourages citizen participation in planning. . . .[25]

Additional policies dealt with internal organization of the Port, the responsibilities of its executive director, and the rights of its employees. A comprehensive policy statement, such as the one just summarized, guides the Port's manager and staff in their day-to-day activities. The public can also refer to this statement when scrutinizing the specific actions of the port.

[25] "Port of Seattle Purpose and Objectives," in *1980 Annual Report of the Port of Seattle*, pp. 18–20.

Summary

In some areas, the management of public transportation systems is different from managing a private transportation system. Governments at state and local levels manage transportation such as local mass transit, airports, and seaports. The principal difference between managing a public transportation system rather than a private transportation system is that there is little use of profitability guidelines as measures of success. Transportation systems managed, operated, and subsidized by government are expected to follow various "public service" goals; few of these goals seem capable of paying their own way.

Sometimes public enterprise carriers compete directly with carriers still operating within the private realm. Communities subsidize their seaport or airport in order to attract business away from similar facilities in other communities.

Public transportation budgets are broken into two categories: capital outlays and operating expenses. Capital outlays are financed with long-term borrowing; operating expenses must be covered out of receipts or current appropriations. Because public transportation system operations have little need to show a profit, their managers often "hide" any surplus funds which may accumulate. At other times, the surplus funds are used to "internally subsidize" some other operation which cannot cover its costs.

Public transportation operators "market" their services although their goals are to increase patronage or to meet some other "public service" goal, rather than to operate at a profit. However, some will attempt to minimize losses. Pricing in a situation where one is attempting to increase patronage has little relationship to costs and cost structures. "User fees" represent the concept that users should pay for use of the public service based on the costs of providing that service.

The organizational structure of a public transportation agency differs from a private transportation agency in that the governing board is elected or appointed by elected officials. The governing board then chooses an executive director to whom all other employees are subordinate. Some public transit agencies retain outside management firms to provide the "top level" management for the system.

Public transportation agencies engage in long-range planning, probably more so than do private transportation operations. Planning by public agencies is subject to more scrutiny than planning by private agencies, and a public project's opponents have many steps at which to block it. Detailed financial projections are needed in situations where debt must be paid off.

Most public transportation employees are subject to civil service rules which, in addition to "rights" they may have under union contracts, makes them somewhat insulated from meaningful discipline. Most public employees are forbidden by law to strike, although the law is sometimes ignored. Public agencies are expected to "take the lead" in minority hiring and training programs.

Questions for Discussion and Review

1. What are some of the differences between managing a public transportation undertaking and one which is in the private sector?

2. List some "public service" goals that public transportation ventures are supposed to pursue.

3. Does pursuit of "public service" goals make it more difficult to manage a public transportation enterprise? Why or why not?

4. Why do governments, rather than private carriers, often provide airport or seaport terminals?

5. How can a public transportation agency obtain funds to carry out its operations?

6. What different kinds of bonds can a public transportation agency issue? What do you think would be the most secure investment? Why?

7. What are user fees charged by public agencies? How high do you think they should be set? Why?

8. As noted in this chapter, interest has developed recently in the area of port user fees. Take a position on this issue and present your argument.

9. How do federal income tax laws influence a local property owner's preference for a local bus system that is highly subsidized with local, public funds or for one that collects high user fees at the fare box from all riders?

10. Assume you are the mayor of a medium-sized U.S. city that operates its own buses. You could set very high fares which might cover the costs of running a few buses. Or at the other extreme, you could operate your buses without fares, i.e., offering "free" rides for

everybody. Given those two extremes, what fare would you set? Why?

11. What duties are likely to be performed by a public transportation agency's public relations staff?

12. Do you think that a public port's public relations agency should promote the idea of additional public subsidies for the port? Why or why not?

13. Describe some of the ideas tested by demonstration projects funded by the Urban Mass Transportation Administration in the 1960's.

14. Describe how a governing board and general manager are typically selected for a public transportation undertaking. How does this differ from the private sector?

15. How do the skills required to be a manager of a public transportation operation differ from the management skills needed in the private sector?

16. What are the advantages and disadvantages to a local public transit operation of retaining an outside "professional" transit management firm?

17. Why is it important to a transit operator to have high morale among its drivers?

18. Why does the lack of a profit incentive make it more difficult for outsiders to judge the effectiveness of public transportation undertakings?

19. How would you measure the performance of a local public airport manager? What criteria would you use?

20. Review the policy statement governing the operation of the Port of Seattle and the Seattle-Tacoma airport in the section "Public Enterprise Leadership." Adapt these guidelines to some public transportation undertaking in your own area.

Additional Chapter References

Alpert, Mark, and Shane Davies, *The Marketing of Public Transportation: Method and Application* (Austin: University of Texas Council for Advanced Transportation Studies, research report 19, 1975).

Anderson, J. Edward, *Transit Systems Analysis and Design* (Lexington, Mass.: Lexington Books, 1978).

Anderson, Shirley Coffer, "The Michigan Transit Performance Evaluation Process: Application to a U.S. Sample," *Annual Proceedings of the Transportation Research Forum* (1980), pp. 94–104.

Baker, H. Scott, Oliver Scheftan, and Francis D. Routh, "Transit Operator Absenteeism: Extent, Costs, and Strategies for Reducing It," *Annual Proceedings of the Transportation Research Forum* (1980), pp. 105–115.

Biemiller, Andrew and Steve Munro, "Estimating Annual Operating Costs of Urban Transit Routes," *Annual Proceedings of the Transportation Research Forum* (1980), pp. 568–577.

Boske, Leigh B., and Mark J. Wolfgram, "A Social Decision-Making Framework for Analyzing Rail Service Abandonment Impacts," *Transportation Journal* (Summer, 1977), pp. 78–85.

Brandwein, Robert, Nancy W. Sheldon, Hiroko Sakai, and Frank J. Remley III, *The Economic and Social Impacts of Investment in Public Transit* (Lexington, Mass.: Lexington Books, 1973).

Due, John F., "The Experience with Municipal Operation of Railway Lines," *Transportation Journal* (Summer, 1975), pp. 5–17.

Falcocchio, John C., and Edmund J. Cantilli, *Transportation and the Disadvantaged: The Poor, the Aged, and the Handicapped* (Lexington, Mass.: Lexington Books, 1974).

Fiander, A. D., "Realities of Public Transport in Small Urban Areas," *Annual Proceedings of the Transportation Research Forum* (1981), pp. 553–562.

Fuller, John W., "Financing State Transit Subsidies," *Annual Proceedings of the Transportation Research Forum* (1973), pp. 359–370.

Giuliano, Genevieve, and Roger F. Teal, "Taxi-Based Community Transit: A Comparative Analysis of System Alternatives and Outcomes," *Annual Proceedings of the Transportation Research Forum* (1980), pp. 86–93.

Gray, George E., and Lester A. Hoel, eds., *Public Transportation: Planning, Operations, and Management* (Englewood Cliffs, N.J.: Prentice-Hall, 1979).

Heads, John, "Transport Subsidies: An Overview," *Annual Proceedings of the Transportation Research Forum* (1978), pp. 600–606.

Hovell, P., W. Jones, and A. Moran, *The Management of Urban Public Transportation: A Marketing Perspective* (Lexington, Mass.: Lexington Books, 1975).

Jennings, Kenneth J., Jay A. Smith, and Earle C. Traynham, Jr., "The Relationship Between Labor and Transit Performance," *Annual Proceedings of the Transportation Research Forum* (1981), pp. 164–165.

Johnson, Christine, Anthony M. Pagano, Claire McKnight, and Leonard Robins, "The Costs of Providing Paratransit Services," *Annual Proceedings of the Transportation Research Forum* (1980), pp. 79–85.

Lieb, Robert C., "Urban Transportation Labor Issues in the 1980's," *Transportation Journal* (Winter, 1980), pp. 50–56.

Mason, Greg, "Urban Transit: Myths of the Present, Realities of the Future and the Role of Technology," *Annual Proceedings of the Transportation Research Forum* (1981), pp. 636–643.

McDermott, Dennis R., "Mass Transit Issues from a Marketing Perspective," *Transportation Journal* (Fall, 1978), pp. 28–35.

McGean, Thomas, *Urban Transportation Technology* (Lexington, Mass.: Lexington Books, 1976).

Mohr, Eric, "Urban Transport Peaks and Work Schedule Innovations," *Annual Proceedings of the Transportation Research Forum* (1973), pp. 277–287.

Morlok, Edward K., and Philip A. Viton, "Self-Sustaining Public Transportation Services: Lessons From the C&NW Experience," *Annual Proceedings of the Transportation Research Forum* (1980), pp. 116–124.

Navin, Francis P. D., "Urban Public Transit Subsidies in Canada," *Annual Proceedings of the Transportation Research Forum* (1981), pp. 644–657.

Nelson, David O., and Marcia L. Spano, "An Evaluation of Fixed Route Accessible Bus Service in Connecticut," *Annual Proceedings of the Transportation Research Forum* (1981), pp. 265–273.

Pikarsky, Milton, and Daphne Christensen, *Urban Transportation Policy and Management* (Lexington, Mass.: Lexington Books, 1976).

Saltzman, Arthur, Marion Blair, Joyce Johnson, and Jon Burkhardt, "Predicting Rural Public Transportation System Effectiveness," *Annual Proceedings of the Transportation Research Forum* (1974), pp. 406–412.

Schwartz, Martin L., "Motivations and Barriers to Riders' Acceptance of Bus Transit," *Transportation Journal* (Summer, 1980), pp. 53–62.

Smerk, George M., "The Transit Act That Never Was: Public Transportation Legislation 1979–1980," *Transportation Journal* (Summer, 1981), pp. 29–53.

Steuart, G. N., R. G. Rice, R. M. Soberman, and E. J. Miller, "A Framework for Policy Development: The Federal Role in Urban Transportation," *Annual Proceedings of the Transportation Research Forum* (1981), pp. 563–577.

Thwaites, D. H. C., "Trolley Coaches—A Place in the 80's," *Annual Proceedings of the Transportation Research Forum* (1980), pp. 578–585.

United Nations, *Port Pricing* (Geneva: United Nations Conference on Trade and Development, 1975).

U.S. Department of Transportation and others, *The Report by the Federal Task Force on Motor Vehicle Goals Beyond 1980*, Volume 1, Executive Summary, Draft (Washington, D.C.: U.S. Government Printing Office, 1976).

Wilmot, Chester G., "Identifying the Optimum Features of an Urban Bus System," *Annual Proceedings of the Transportation Research Forum* (1981), pp. 274–284.

Case 14–1 Port of Short Beach Case

Eric Raff's small office on the fourth floor of the Port of Short Beach office building was in the rear, and its single window looked out over a Burlington Northern Railroad switching yard. Gathered with Raff on this February morning were Wyndham Young, who worked for Wyoming Minerals and who had flown in from Denver, and Loretta Brown, from the Short Beach City Attorney's office. Raff and Young were to work out more details of the contract referred to in Case Figure 14–1–1. Ms. Brown was there to provide legal advice

MEMO

FROM ___L. Langdon Langtree, Exec. Dir.___   DATE ___January 30, 1983___

TO ___Eric Raff, Terminals Div.___   SUBJECT ___Contract with Wyoming Minerals Co.___

I met yesterday, for the entire day, with F. Filbert Fulbright, the CEO of Wyoming Minerals, and with some of his top people. They have just about tied down a long-term contract to sell between two and three million tons of coal per year, for ten years, to Japan. Ours is one of several West Coast ports they could use. They need a tentative commitment from us, and from the Burlington Northern Railroad before they can finalize anything.

At my meeting with them, we agreed--subject to our board's approval and to their entering into contracts with the Japanese buyer and the Burlington Northern--to the following: they would pay us approximately 10-12 cents per ton per year for the first million tons they handled each year and 8-10 cents per ton for any additional tonnage each year. They would guarantee us a minimum of $200,000 per year for ten years. The reason for the range in the figures is that we have yet to work out all the other details of the contract to decide who will pay for what. That will be your job. Fulbright is sending his assistant, Wyndham Young, to meet with you.

We'll use the 42-acre Van Huntley dock site; I'll ask our law department to draw up its legal description.

Case Figure 14-1-1 Memo from Port of Short Beach Director.

since her office had to approve the legal format of any contract entered into by a city agency, such as the board of port commissioners.

Raff served coffee, and after a brief discussion of ski conditions throughout the Pacific Northwest, he suggested that they get down to business. "For starters," he said, "I don't think we're here to talk about money, but rather to decide about everything else the contract must include. Some of them will cost us, the Port; others will cost Wyoming Minerals, the tenant. Later, our higher-ups will have to decide who will be responsible for what and whether that should influence the rate of rental."

"How will the responsibilities be divided between the Port and the tenant?" asked Ms. Brown. "Who does what?"

"Ideally," responded Raff, "we provide the land and collect the rent checks. . . ."

"Ho-ho-ho," interjected Young, "most contracts entered into by West Coast ports are in the public record and most of them show that the ports do quite a bit more than that."

"Langtree's memo mentioned a legal description of the land involved," said Ms. Brown. "Will there be any problems there?"

"Negative," said Raff. "We have clear title and no property line or water rights disputes. Port policy only requires that it be used for 'navigationally-related' purposes, which this is. We've already sent maps and drawings to Wyoming's engineers who need them for their talks with the Burlington Northern."

"We appreciated your sending them promptly," said Young. "Also, let me mention something not in Mr. Langtree's memo, but agreed to, and that is that we will build the coal loading/unloading facility on your land. It will be able to handle incoming unit-trains of 100 cars each. Each car will be unloaded by being swivelled 170 degrees inside the unloading shed. Then it will be returned to the upright position, and the entire train will move ahead the length of one car. A new car will be in place, turned over and dumped, turned upright, and so on. The coal will be stockpiled outside. At times, there may be as much as several hundred thousand tons stockpiled. Along the water's edge, we'll have a vessel loader, which is fed from a conveyor system running below the stockpile. We'll be able to load vessels at a rate of 3,000 to 4,000 tons per hour."

"What kind of money will that cost?" asked Ms. Brown.

"Between seven and ten million," responded Young. "Since you're a public agency, we want you to borrow the money for building the loading/unloading facility since interest on your obligations is exempt from federal income taxation. You can borrow for less, and you can lease the facility back to us for ten years, effective the minute it's completed. We'll pay you 20 percent of your costs, the minute it goes into operation, and we'll pay the balance over six years at a rate of interest one percent higher than whatever you had to pay to borrow the money. That will be on top of the rent figures mentioned in Mr. Langtree's memo."

"Who owns the equipment after ten years?" asked Raff.

"You own it as soon as you pay the contractor," said Young. "We never own it. We just lease it from you for ten years—to coincide with our rental of the land."

Raff said, "That seems clear. Now, looking at other contracts we have, here are a few items we like to see in them. We want the tenant responsible for a private security system and for a fire sprinkler system inside any structures. You must maintain fire and related insurance on your structure and tenant liability insurance. You must agree to comply with all federal and state laws and local ordinances and building codes. The port engineer must approve plans for any structures placed on the property. You must agree to maintain all property. . . ."

"Hold on a minute, there," said Young, "I think you've just struck a nerve. The dock wall next to the water isn't in great shape right now. And, as you know, it will deteriorate naturally over ten years. I don't think we can blindly assume responsibility for maintaining the dock wall. It could cost several million to replace."

"Let's skip that for now," said Raff. "I'd better talk to our engineers before we pursue that issue further. Another 'standard' item I want to mention is that the tenant must collect and pass on to us the wharfage charges that all commercial vessels using our port facilities must pay. They're based on vessel length and run two dollars per foot of vessel length per 24-hour day. We don't worry about cheating on this item, since it's pretty hard to hide a vessel. The last item, almost 'boilerplate' in nature, is that we agree to an arbitrator in case disagreements arise under this contract."

"Aside from maintaining the dock wall, how do the other standard items sound to you?" asked Raff.

"Oh, all right, I guess," Young replied. "Of course, our legal staff will have to approve them but they're not obstacles."

"Well, that's good," said Raff. "Obviously, Langtree wants a contract you folks can live with."

"This meeting is going along more quickly than I anticipated," said Ms. Brown, as she accepted her second cup of coffee. "When are you going to mention the port director's favorite charity, Eric?" she said with a mischievous grin.

"Oh," exclaimed Raff, "I wish you hadn't mentioned that, Loretta!" Young looked up, surprised.

"Why not?" replied Ms. Brown. "He'll have to learn sooner or later."

"Well, what it is, is this," said Raff, speaking slowly. "It seems my boss, Mr. Langtree, thinks the city council and the board of port commissioners are both niggardly when it comes to funding his entertainment and travel budget. So, to overcome this deficiency, a number of port tenants show their appreciation for the good job he's doing by kicking into a 'special' port development fund that the director uses as he sees fit."

"That sounds accurate," said Ms. Brown, as Raff gave her a dirty look.

"I assume this is not in the written contract," said Young, dryly.

"You'd better believe it, kid," responded Ms. Brown.

"Is this the only 'special accommodation' expected of us?" asked Young, who realized that the discussion had moved away from routine matters.

"As a matter of fact," said Ms. Brown, "the party in power, people like my boss, also likes to know that port tenants appreciate them. . . ."

"Interesting as this is," said Young, "I don't think I'm authorized to make any commitments of this sort. We operate in a lot of foreign countries and, obviously, what you're saying to me isn't new. Tell you what, Eric," he continued, "the next time Mr. Langtree meets with my boss, he'd better lay all of this out in front of him."

"Oh, Mr. Langtree would never say anything directly," responded Raff. "He relies on his staff for help in matters such as this."

"Look, and I'm repeating myself," said Young. "This is a matter outside my authority. If Langtree won't discuss it with Mr. Fulbright, the best I can do is mention it to Fulbright or whomever I talk with when I call in later today to discuss items you and I can't resolve. Now, let's move on."

"One thing I'd like to raise now is whether Wyoming would object to a clause in the contract that restricted you to handling only the outbound movement of coal. We don't like our tenants subleasing their facilities to handle other cargos because they may then compete with our other tenants," said Raff.

"Well, then," responded Young, "would you agree not to lease any other lands for handling export coal during the period of our agreement?"

"I'd have to think about that," answered Raff.

"I think we'd like the right to handle other bulk materials, in case markets for them develop," said Young, "which leads me to think that some of them are denser than coal and—when loaded aboard a ship—would cause it to set deeper in the water. I understand that right now you've got 35 feet of water, below low tide, alongside the property. . . ."

"That's right," said Raff, "and that's deep enough to handle the vessels you're likely to use for coal."

"But what if we wanted it deeper?" probed Young.

"I see two problems there," answered Raff. "First of all, why do you need it? Secondly, there are limits to the dock wall's strength. If we dredge more alongside it, the whole thing may give way and collapse into the water. . . ."

"That may be," interjected Young, "but for our investment and with the potential of the Japanese market for coal, we don't want to be limited right off the bat as to the size of ship we can use. What if the charter rates for larger ships drop? We won't be able to take advantage while some of our competitors will."

"We can guarantee that you'll have 35 feet of water along side," offered Raff.

"We may insist on 40," was Young's reply.

There was a long discussion as to the delays that could be caused by environmental protection reviews and by possible protests from individuals along the coal trains' proposed routes. It was agreed that there would be two contracts. The first would be a somewhat binding "letter of intent" indicating that the final contract would not become effective until the entire project had been approved by all governmental review bodies.

Young said they would want some provision specifying that the port make available at least one mile of rail trackage for possible use by a waiting unit-train. While the parcel of land to be rented would accommodate the train being unloaded, there would be times when a second train would be waiting.

"Why can't you work this out with the Burlington Northern, in your contract with them?" asked Raff. "They've got lotsa tracks."

"In the East, where coal-loading ports are congested, everybody's blaming everybody else for the problem," was Young's response. "We think you are in a better position to guarantee us a mile of vacant track, just where we'll need it; we don't want our 100-car train 'somewhere' on the BN system. And, while we're on the subject, we want you to place electric crossing signals everywhere our tracks cross roads in the port area."

"Every road?" asked Ms. Brown. "You're talking about some that must handle five or ten cars and trucks a day at the most. Aren't you being a little elaborate?"

"You may be right," answered Young. "What we'll have to do in our contract is specify what kind of signals will be provided at each and every intersection. I assume that in this state the railroad also shares this responsibility. Maybe you and the BN should work this one out."

"One other thing," said Ms. Brown. "Will you have any heavy trucks moving in and out? In our other contracts, we need some provisions about that to protect our port's roads."

"Negative," was Young's answer. "It would only be in emergency situations."

"I'll look up how we've handled this in other contracts," said Raff. "We'll have to insert something about axle spacings and weights."

It was now noon time, and the trio went to a nearby waterfront seafood restaurant for lunch. Raff offered to "pick up the check," adding that it was being paid out of the port director's "special" fund. As they were studying the menu, Young noted that the prices of his two favorite West Coast seafoods, salmon and crab, climbed each time he came to the Coast.

"You're so right," said Raff. "We follow the economics of fishing since some of our land is leased to commercial fishermen. Their prices are going up, just like everybody else's. Which reminds me, our contract with you has to have in it some adjustments so that the rents keep up with the cost-of-living."

"Will that cover everything in the contract?" asked Young.

"Yes," answered Raff.

"I don't think it should cover the purchase/leaseback of the materials-handling equipment," said Young. "We're reimbursing you for the interest rate you have to pay (plus one percent) and I think that the interest rate the market sets already reflects the rate of inflation."

"I hear you," answered Raff. "I'll have to run that one by my boss."

The meal was served and the three engaged in small talk, and walked back to Raff's office quickly, because a rainstorm was threatening. As they sat down in Raff's office, the drops of rain started splashing on the window sill. Ms. Brown asked Young, "Will rainy weather affect your operation here?"

"Not really," was Young's answer. "We'll have a moat around our entire facility and the runoff from the coal piles will be collected, and the coal particles and dust removed, before the water is allowed to drain into the bay. Wet coal has slightly different handling characteristics but our equipment can take them into account. Of course, wet coal loads heavier into a ship."

"That raises a question," said Ms. Brown. "You're going to pay us by the ton. Is that a wet ton, a dry ton, or what? It seems to me that we should insist you drench your coal piles with thousands of gallons of water every day as a 'dust suppression' measure. Then we'll collect more money as you load those 'heavy' tons."

Young grinned and said, "Coal is sold on a BTU-content basis. Our loading facility will have a tiny conveyer belt feeding off of the main conveyer belt that loads the ship. The tiny conveyor leads into a testing lab where a 'third party' collects and analyzes the samples and then tells us the number of BTU's that were loaded on the ship."

"Who is the third party?" asked Ms. Brown.

"An independent testing lab that we and the Japanese coal buyer pay jointly," was Young's answer. "We'll use the lab figures to determine how much we owe you."

The next issue discussed was whether tugs were necessary to dock the coal vessels. Raff said the Port felt they were since if a vessel went aground because of mishandling, it might tie up vessel traffic and harm the business of other dock operators.

Young complained that the decision whether to use tugs should be left the ship's captain. Requiring tugs for all vessels would add to Wyoming Mineral's overall costs. He said that an international firm such as Wyoming Minerals had to avoid being saddled with "useless" local work practices, which other ports where they also operated might try to impose. "The only wording we've accepted elsewhere deals with requiring tugs for vessels above a certain size," said Young.

The last items the three discussed were allowing the Port of Short Beach to audit Wyoming Mineral's records, insofar as was necessary to determine volumes of coal the dock handled; options for Wyoming Minerals to have "first right" of renewal of the contract at its expiration; and definitions of "Acts of God," embargos, labor disputes, etc., to the extent that they would relieve one or both parties from fulfilling one or more parts of the contract.

One item the three could not resolve was who should pay for any additional environmental protection equipment that other government agencies might require during the ten-year contract period. "In the seventies," said Young, "we were sometimes forced to add expensive dust suppression equipment even though our contract with the port had only one or two years to go. We feel that since ports are also government agencies they should bear those costs which their sister or brother governmental agencies suddenly decide are necessary."

Questions One through Four require you to draft proposed paragraphs of the contract under consideration. For your purposes, assume that your language must be as unambiguous as possible.

Question One: Assume you are Raff. From his (the port's) standpoint, draft the paragraph dealing with maintenance of the dock wall and provision of 35 feet of water depth alongside. (Try to place the burden on the tenant.)

Question Two: Assume you are Young. From Wyoming Mineral's point of view, draft the paragraph that deals with maintenance of the dock wall and the provision of 40 feet of water depth alongside. (Try to place the burden on the port.)

Question Three: From the standpoint of either party, write a paragraph that incorporates use of the "cost of living" index into adjusting the dollar amounts of rental payments in future years.

Question Four: From the standpoint of either party, write a paragraph that covers the purchase by the port and lease back to Wyoming Minerals of the materials-handling equipment. Should this include additional language that takes into account the changing value of the dollar over time? Discuss.

Question Five: Wyoming Minerals and the Japanese buyer will jointly rely on a "third party" contractor to calculate the actual BTU value of the coal loaded aboard ships. Is this an adequate measure for the Port of Short Beach to rely upon to determine how much rent it should collect? Discuss.

Question Six: Assume you are Young's superior and he reports to you the conversation regarding contributions that tenants are apparently expected to make to the "special" funds of the port director and other elected officials in Short Beach. What should your (Wyoming Minerals') response be? Why?

Question Seven: Without regard to what the contract ultimately entered into may say, assume that—at some later date—an environmental protection agency insists that more expensive pollution control devices be installed at the coal dock. Who do you think should pay? Why?

Case 14–2 Brandon Bus Company Case

Bill McClure had been public relations director for the Brandon Bus Company for six months. Prior to that, he had worked in both the customer service and personnel departments. He had a friendly manner, and the bus company's management felt that he did a good job in both handling the complaints that came in daily from riders as well as planning for some programs that would help the company acquire new ridership. McClure was a part-time student at a local business college, studying for a degree in personnel management.

McClure was a bit disappointed in his new job since he spent more time listening to customer complaints than he cared to. In instances where the driver was obviously wrong, he could do little but report the incident to the driver's supervisor who might or might not decide to call the driver in for a discussion of the incident and perhaps to reprimand him (the driver). Recently, the bus company's top management had become a bit more concerned about drivers' attitudes toward customers. The reason for this new interest was that the city's mayor and council members had begun criticizing the bus company for its rude drivers and had suggested that this rudeness was discouraging additional bus ridership.

Johnny Czek, head of the drivers union, retorted that low ridership was caused by the rowdy teenagers who rode buses in the late afternoon. Several weeks ago they had terrorized a bus, snatched several purses, and escaped. In this episode, several elderly passengers had been hurt, two requiring overnight hospitalization. The matter received wide publicity in the local press, and Czek was saying that policemen should be assigned to ride buses during after-school hours. He had also hinted that matters such as this made his entire union membership "sick" and that he wouldn't be surprised if the next incident would result in *all* of the drivers being sufficiently sick that they would be unable to work for a while.

McClure wondered what to do. Because he had so recently worked in the personnel department, his thoughts tended to focus on the drivers and their relationships with the public. At the company's weekly staff meeting, he said, "I feel a real concern over the drivers' morale. When I was a job interviewer, I would see the new drivers' enthusiasm. But in only a few months, this enthusiasm had disappeared. They quit or seemed bored. Some told me that because of their minimal seniority, they drew the worst runs and got the wildest passengers. Luckily, they're still young enough physically that they can command some respect from the teenage hoods. They just hope to hang in there until they build enough seniority so they can draw some of the safer runs. We have drivers in their late twenties who appear to have 'middle-age burnout'."

LeRoy Jenkins, the bus company's general manager, looked bored when he said, "I don't want to sound crass, but that publicity about the old folks being jostled will fade away. They should know better than to be on a bus after school lets out. I don't think many people blame the bus company for juvenile delinquents."

"What about Czek's threatened 'sickness'? Do we want a strike?" asked McClure.

"A strike on this issue wouldn't bother me at all," retorted Jenkins. "If police on buses are needed, that's the police chief's problem. Let *him* go to the council and tell them why *he* needs more money. The magic words with this year's council are 'law and order' so he'd get twice as much as he needs. He'll probably ask for enough to put two cops on every bus." Jenkins started looking at his watch, a sure sign that he hoped the meeting was about to end.

McClure summoned all his courage, raised his hand, noted Jenkins' sudden frown, and said, assertively, "I don't think we are coming to grips with this issue at all. With all due respect, we aren't taking a single step ourselves and are merely tossing the hot potato to the police chief and council. I think we can do something to help our drivers be more satisfied and make them a bit less antagonistic toward our passengers!"

Others in the meeting looked up and started paying attention. They realized that the meeting was not over. Most of them probably were amused that the young McClure was challenging Jenkins' do-nothing attitude, and some were wondering how long it would take Jenkins to squelch another new idea. They displayed poker faces.

Jenkins looked at his watch again and said, "Make it quick, I've got another important meeting at lunch. What did you have in mind?"

McClure spoke eagerly, perhaps a bit too rushed. "I've heard that the Dauphin Transit District is running some trial 'human relations groups' for its drivers to see whether such groups can help reduce driver/rider problems. The District has contracted with an industrial psychologist who has had extensive experience with short-term groups."

"Groups? What kind of groups?" asked Jenkins.

"They're known as 'therapy groups'," responded McClure. "Under some professional guidance, the drivers hash over some of their experiences and gripes and see whether they can help each other find solutions. Sometimes a person with problems can be helped just by discussing them with others."

"This sounds kind of squirrelly to me," said Jenkins. "We pay our drivers to drive, not to sit around telling each other their problems. If they got problems, they can blow off steam at a union meeting. Let Johnny Czek hold their hands for a while. He's got nothing to do."

"But," started McClure, who stopped.

"You know, boy," continued Jenkins, "when you start telling men they have to mess around with psychologist types, you can be in a heap of trouble. When I was in the Navy, only two types of men got sent to shrinks: bedwetters and. . . ."

"But that was 30 years ago!" shot back McClure, throwing caution to the winds. "A lot has happened since then with respect to understanding human behavior. I think we could help some of our drivers."

"Help them?" asked Jenkins, sarcastically. "Our drivers get $7.42 per hour plus $1.11 fringe plus a free uniform each year, and you think we should help them. Let me tell you how it was when I started out driving." Jenkins stopped for a minute to glance at a note, written in longhand, which was given to him by Hedda Kabbage, his secretary, who had been taking the minutes of the staff meeting. Jenkins looked at the note, paled, and paused for a moment, gathering his thoughts. In a much calmer voice he said, "McClure, why don't you contact the Dauphin people, go visit their operation if you want, and come back here with a first-hand report? Now, I've got to adjourn this meeting."

Jenkins crumpled the note Ms. Kabbage had handed him, threw it on the table, and walked out. He was followed by everyone except McClure, who paused until the room was empty. He wanted to see what magic hold Ms. Kabbage had that she could exercise by sending notes. He picked up her crumpled note to Jenkins and read it. It said, "The blood vessels on your forehead are throbbing!"

It was several weeks later. McClure was in Dauphin at the main office of the Dauphin Transit District. He had made arrangements to visit them, and they were allowing him to observe a human relations group session through a one-way mirror. A hidden microphone allowed him to listen in on the session. Five drivers in dull-green uniforms were awkwardly sprawled in a semi-circle of chairs. A sixth man, wearing a corduroy jacket and smoking a pipe, entered.

"Hello, fellows. I'm Roger Carl. I have a list of your names. But why don't we all introduce ourselves since I haven't met any of you before? I'm not much of a bus rider myself, ha-ha," said the psychologist. "Don't get up," he added, while realizing that the statement was unnecessary.

"We all know each other, anyhow," said a grizzled white man.

"We meet at the carbarn when shifts change. Everyone knows that I'm Joe Japlonsky. I've got run number 22 and have had it since 1969. Here's Tom, who's been driving almost as long as me. And this is Roberto, and Al, and the young one is Chuck." The men nodded uncertainly toward Carl.

"I'm sincerely pleased to meet all of you today," offered Carl. "Do any of you have questions regarding this meeting?"

"Why do we have to come to these psycho, er, a, psychological-type groups, anyhow?" spoke Joe. "I've been driving since 1953, and this is the first time that I was told to do something like this. There haven't been that many complaints off of my run."

"You were selected at random," answered Carl, "which means all drivers had an equal probability of being selected. I suppose that some of you might resent having to come here in the first place."

"You said it," retorted Tom. "Today's bus driver could do better with lessons in karate." With a swift chop of his hands, inadvertently jolting Joe, Tom shouted, "Pow! Take that, you Spicksliver!"

Joe regained his calm and said, "Watch it, *meester*, or I'll slice up your seats." Then, noting Roberto's glare, he added, "Whoops, sorry, Roberto, nothing personal."

Carl tried to regain control by saying, "Sorry, but teaching karate isn't my field. Roberto, what did you think about Joe and Tom's remarks?"

"They're bigots," replied Roberto. "I didn't need to come here to learn that. They've always been angry at me and my type ever since their sons couldn't get driving jobs with the Transit District. They probably couldn't pass the tests."

"Tests had nothing to do with it!" shouted Joe. "It was those damn minority hiring quotas. All they would have needed was a suntan and a name like Santiago. Personally, I don't think the minority quotas have helped our system one bit. I don't think some of those colored types go to Mass every Sunday."

"I don't think that going to Mass means much about being a driver," said Al, the only black in the group. "I've known Japlonsky since I was a sweeper at the carbarn, and I'll never forget some of his insults when I became one of the first 'non-white' drivers for the district. Did you learn that in church, Joe?"

Joe chose not to reply. Only Chuck had not spoken, and Carl asked, "Chuck, do you ever get taunting like this?"

"Yeah," said Chuck. "I'm new and I get the worst runs. I hate it when those high school hoods get on my bus in gangs, glaring at me, daring me to say something if one or two walk by without paying. When the last one is aboard, I shout at them all to get to the rear of the bus, mainly 'cause I don't want them near me. If they don't move fast enough, I wait until I see a few aren't hanging on, then I goose the bus and hope to send a few of them sprawling. It feels good.''

"You mean, you think you are letting the kids know you're really mad. Does it do any good?" asked Carl.

Roberto spoke up. "I've got a blood pressure cuff at home, and my wife uses it on me. After some runs with teenagers I just about pop the gauge."

"Okay, Chuck and Roberto," said Carl, "you've both got problems with teenage rowdies. For the rest of us, why don't the two of you 'act out' a situation with Roberto being the driver and Chuck being the young white hood?"

"I—I can't do that right now," stammered Roberto, looking uneasily at the other men.

"Well, I've got a beef about my passengers," said Tom.

"What kind of beef can you have about passengers? All you've got on your run is nursing homes and hospitals," said Joe.

"That's my problem," replied Tom. "They're mostly cripples, and it takes most of them a month of Sundays to board the bus and get seated. If I wait for them I get way behind in my schedule and get chewed out. For a while I made believe that I didn't see them waiting for the bus, but then some of them started writing in letters of complaint. *Long* letters of complaint. I guess they've little else to do during the day. They've got sharp eyesight, though. They write down the number of whatever bus passes them by. It's pretty hard to argue my way out of that."

Chuck spoke up: "You've got a legitimate gripe. You should tell the dispatcher or Johnny Czek that you need more time on your run. Let old man Jenkins ride with his stop watch one day and see what he says. You know—once in a while they have to listen to us. Especially if we're going to get buses with wheelchair lifts. Hell, if we play it right, we can add five minutes on to every schedule in the city. Think what that means!"

The session continued with Al complaining that some older passengers would call him "boy."

"Tell them you prefer being called 'Al'," suggested Tom. "I can remember when you told me that, yourself, 15 to 20 years ago."

"That's right," answered Al. "I'll try that for a while."

"You bet," added Chuck. "Tell 'em politely, but quickly, and then your stomach won't churn all day."

The discussion returned to the problem of handling rowdy teenage passengers. Little was settled, although it was evident that drivers especially disliked riders who were of a racial background that differed from their own. However, the drivers were a bit more restrained in the comments concerning other races and religions. At four o'clock sharp, Carl announced the session was over and that they would meet again in two weeks. He said they would engage in "role-playing" in the next session, taking turns at being the driver and being disruptive passengers. He asked each driver to be ready to play the role of the most obnoxious passengers he had ever encountered.

The drivers left, and Carl was introduced to McClure. Carl had been aware that his session was being monitored. McClure asked him more about his program, and Carl responded that it consisted of five one-hour sessions for groups of five drivers each. He added that, contrary to what he had told the session participants, the groups were chosen to consist of older white drivers, minority members, and "new hires." This was to provide for some interaction between ages and races.

McClure asked him what the groups were supposed to accomplish.

"Only two things, in so short a time," answered Carl. "With 'Archie Bunker' types like Joe, the best we can hope for is that they may realize that minorities have a few gripes. Second, we're trying to get all drivers to learn to deal with conditions which cause anger and fear more directly. If a passenger insults them, they should handle the matter promptly—although tactfully. What Chuck said was right—they shouldn't let their stomach churn all the time. It's that continual tension that causes high blood pressure, heart attacks, and ulcers. In this area we're very close to having these afflictions declared as 'job-caused' for purposes of collecting worker disability compensation."

Carl excused himself to join a second group of bus drivers. McClure had no further questions of the Dauphin management, so he drove to the airport for his return flight to Brandon.

Question One: What do you think McClure should recommend? Why?

Question Two: How would you go about measuring the *cost-effectiveness* of the therapy group approach for the Brandon Bus Company drivers?

Question Three: If the Brandon Bus Company does decide to use therapy groups for its drivers, should the drivers be compelled to attend? Why?

Question Four: Assume that only a limited number of drivers can go through the program each year. How should they be selected?

Question Five: How effective do you think the session conducted by Roger Carl was? Discuss.

Question Six: Assume that the Brandon city council was debating whether to appropriate funds to pay policemen to ride on Brandon buses *or* to pay for group therapy sessions for Brandon bus drivers. List the comparative advantages and disadvantages of each alternative.

Export coal being loaded from barges onto an ocean ship in the lower Mississippi River. Loading away from the shore, as shown, allows larger vessels to be used.

Photo by Paul F. Steen, courtesy T. Smith & Son, Inc., New Orleans, La.

The Roadrailer idea is not new. This photo from the early 1960's shows trailers fitted with rail wheels at the rear and mounted on a special dolly at the front. The whole unit was then attached to a passenger train. They carried U.S. mail on the Chesapeake and Ohio Railway.

Photo courtesy Chessie System Railroads.

15 Future Issues and Prospects

The transportation system in this country is much like a Stradivarius violin—it's the finest in the world, but it's very fragile! Therefore, regulating our transportation system must be done with a great deal of care, because tightening the strings, either too little or too much, creates disharmony rather than music.

REESE H. TAYLOR, JR.
Chairman, Interstate Commerce Commission
Speech to Transportation Research Forum Annual Meeting
November 4, 1981

Introduction

Transportation is a dominant and pervasive factor in the American economy. The previous 14 chapters have presented an overview of the transportation industry, including its strengths and weaknesses, from three viewpoints: (a) the government, which provides some portions of our transportation systems and regulates a decreasing portion of all transportation activity; (b) the carriers; and (c) the users, especially the shippers.

This, the closing chapter, will examine six aspects of transportation that are expected to have a significant impact on the *future* of America's transportation system. We will examine the future impact of each of the following issues, although the order in which we present them in no way ranks their importance. They are all important to development of transportation between now and the year 2000. The six topics we will discuss are:

1. Federal government's role in transportation.
2. Intermodal "warfare."
3. Intermodal cooperation.
4. U.S. coal exports.
5. Effects of deregulation.
6. Future transportation technology.

The Federal Government's Role in Transportation

The federal government has historically provided facilities, services, and subsidies to all modes of transportation. This has varied from minor programs assisting oil pipelines (the granting of the right of

TABLE 15–1 Capital Investments by Governments
(Federal, State and Local) in Transportation Facilities
(in Millions of 1975 Dollars)

Mode	1976–1985	1986–2000	Total, 1976–2000
Highways	294,411	606,035	900,446
Local Public Transportation	58,055	108,669	166,724
School buses	1,612	2,419	4,031
Amtrak	1,900	3,000	4,900
Ports, Harbors, Channels, Facilities & Equipment	10,312	19,206	29,518
Airports	13,531	21,110	34,641
Air navigation aids	2,760	5,286	8,046
TOTAL	382,581	765,725	1,148,306

SOURCE: *National Transportation Policies Through the Year 2000* (Washington, D.C.: The National Transportation Policy Study Commission, 1979), pp. 171–174.

Note: Excluded from the estimates are any government investments in Conrail.

eminent domain) and railroads (aid in funding the Railroad Retirement System) to generous programs helping the truckers, airlines, and inland water carriers by providing their rights-of-way.

Future public expenditures for transportation are expected to be large. Table 15–1 shows projections made by the National Transportation Policy Study Commission of actual and projected public expenditures for transportation in the last quarter of this century. Federal, state, and local programs are combined on Table 15–1. Many programs combine funds from all three levels of government.

The federal government has not provided a consistent and logical procedure for funding and administering all of its federally-assisted transportation programs. Each program seems to have been based on whatever was politically the "right" thing to do when the program was enacted. It would have been better to have had each program carefully woven into the overall needs of the nation's transportation system. Often the federal government's "right hand" does not seem to know what its "left hand" is doing. The result is a patchwork of inconsistent legislation. Brock Adams, former U.S. Secretary of Transportation, observed that federal financial aid to transportation "has too often been conferred without logic."[1] The primary cause of this incongruity, according to Adams, is:

> The past Administration and the Congress, both, are fragmented in their dealings with transportation. The DOT building has one floor for policy

[1] Information Letter, Association of American Railroads, No. 2212 (February 16, 1977), p. 1.

makers and nine floors to house the semi-autonomous administrations that hand out money. The maritime industry has its own little enclave at the Department of Commerce, and the Corps of Engineers, whose actions and decisions have a major impact on our transportation network, seems answerable only to some mysterious voice which brings it dazzling cost-benefit ratios from on high. In fact, more than 32 different agencies in the Executive Branch have an important role in transportation, and, of these, only eight are in DOT.[2]

The Reagan Administration is committed to following a steady and predictable course when it comes to transportation policy and funding. Three broad policies have clearly emerged. First, President Reagan will veto non-military spending bills that exceed his budget. This policy precipitated the August, 1981, strike by PATCO (Professional Air Traffic Controllers Organization) members, because they demanded a larger salary increase than the Reagan Administration had budgeted. Because federal employees cannot legally strike, the PATCO personnel were fired. As a result of the strike, the Department of Transportation has determined that there were too many Federal Aviation Administration controllers prior to strike action. Therefore, Reagan has publically stated a goal of reducing the number of air controllers from 16,000 to 10,000 people, although this will require increased dependence on computers.[3]

A second principle of the Reagan Administration is that the federal government should not encroach upon states' rights. In other words, whenever possible, the federal government should allow governmental units that are closer to the population—i.e., state and local governments—to make decisions that directly affect these people. Illustrative of this concept is the Reagan Administration's decision *not* to support a bill calling for the federal right of eminent domain for coal slurry pipelines. Reagan stated:

> This administration will not support legislation which has been introduced in Congress to provide a federal right of eminent domain to override these difficulties [of obtaining coal slurry pipeline right-of-way authorization]. Our commitment to the vitality of state governments should not be abandoned simply because it may at times be inconvenient. The extension of federal powers of eminent domain should not be undertaken lightly.[4]

[2] Brock Adams, "Government, the Silent Partner for Private Enterprise," *Handling and Shipping* (January, 1977), pp. 49–50. (The Maritime Administration is now part of the Department of Transportation.)

[3] See: "Why PATCO Strikers Are Out of Luck," *Business Week* (November 16, 1981), pp. 51–52.

[4] "Administration Opposes Coal Slurry Pipelines," *Railnews* (November 18, 1981), p. 4. See also: "Still Battling Over Coal-Slurry Pipelines," *Business Week*, (November 23, 1981), p. 151.

Increased utilization of user charges is the third guiding principle of the Reagan Administration. Senator Nancy Kassebaum, a member of the Senate Commerce Committee, tersely stated Reagan's transport policy, "The user pays and if he doesn't, then we cut."[5] This policy is fully consistent with a major transportation policy statement recently issued by the National Chamber Foundation, which is the public policy research organization of the U.S. Chamber of Commerce. The report (*Transport Tomorrow: A National Priority*) stated, "User charges should be set so that the funding required to maintain, rehabilitate or expand the system can be provided."[6] Two modal rights-of-way will be directly affected in the future by this philosophy—highways and inland waterways. Regarding the former, the Highway Trust Fund since 1979 has been spending more than it has generated. In November, 1981, the Reagan Administration suggested raising the federal fuel tax from four cents per gallon to eight cents per gallon.[7]

While the fuel tax for highways may double, even greater user-charge increases are possible for users of the inland waterway system. At present, barge users pay six cents per gallon, and this tax is already scheduled to increase to ten cents per gallon in 1985. However, the Reagan Administration has proposed that this fuel tax should be in the neighborhood of thirty cents per gallon: at this rate it would cover most of the federal government's outlays for new construction, maintenance, and operation of the inland waterway system.[8] The management consulting firm of A. T. Kearney calculated the user tax would have to be thirty-eight cents per gallon just to recover the maintenance and operating costs of the inland waterway system.[9]

A final note regarding user charges is that the Reagan Administration also believes in helping a mode—the railroads—that has provided its own right-of-way. The Reagan sponsored *Economic Tax Recovery Act of 1981* allowed railroads to depreciate their right-of-way costs more rapidly. A *Wall Street Journal* article noted:

> The 1981 tax law permits the railroads to start writing off, this year, about $8 billion in rail track, some of which has been carried on the books since

[5]*Railnews* (March 25, 1981), p. 1.
[6]Paul O. Roberts, "A Prescription For Effective Transportation Policies," p. 21. This policy statement was issued in two volumes. The second is, "Transportation: Forces of Change." Together they form the report, *Transportation Tomorrow: A National Priority.*
[7]"A High-Powered Drive To Raise the Gas Tax," *Business Week* (November 23, 1981), p. 52.
[8]See: *Newsletter* of the National Waterways Conference (March 27, 1981), pp. 1–12.
[9]*Railnews* (March 11, 1981), p. 4.

1887. The write-offs will reduce or eliminate the railroads' federal tax bills. This year, in which the biggest part of the break occurs, few if any carriers will pay any federal income taxes at all.[10]

Intermodal "Warfare"

Railroads, inland water carriers, and truckers are involved in a heated "warfare" of words. No cessation of hostilities appears to be on the horizon. *Business Week* noted why this intermodal skirmish was started:

> In a gentleman's agreement over the past few years, railroads and truckers stayed clear of each other, while they fought their own congressional battles over deregulation. With that fight now ended, the gloves are off. And the Railroads' renewed war with their old enemies—the truckers and barge operators—is more intense than ever.[11]

Railroad Position

The railroad industry believes it has been at a serious competitive disadvantage vis-a-vis truckers and inland water carriers because the government provides the latter carriers with rights-of-way. To correct this situation, the railroads' trade association, the Association of American Railroads, launched a $2 million publicity campaign aimed at increasing the user charges of their competitors (see Figure 15–1). William H. Dempsey of the AAR stated unequivocally, "This issue is more important to us than deregulation."[12] Why? Because in the newly deregulated and highly competitive transportation environment, rates will often be near the costs of producing the transportation service. Railroads believe they cannot effectively compete when their rivals' costs are unreasonably low because their federal and state user charges do not reflect the governments' full costs of providing the rights-of-way.

This issue is emotional. Witness this statement by Frank N. Wilner of the Association of American Railroads:

> If there is a battle raging, it is a battle between society and the major trucking and barge corporations. A nation being asked to eliminate social programs for the hungry, sick, aged and otherwise needy is not about to permit a continuation of unnecessary subsidies to a handful of profitable truck and barge corporations.

[10]John D. Williams, "Tax Changes Give Railroads A Big Break," *The Wall Street Journal* (October 27, 1981), p. 25. See also: "A Tax Credit Bonanza For The Railroads," *Business Week* (November 23, 1981), p. 45.

[11]"A Collision Over Subsidies," *Business Week* (July 27, 1981), p. 64.

[12]*Ibid.*

Myth:
All freight carriers compete on an equal basis.

Fact:
Public subsidies for
trucks and barges throw
competition out of balance.

You, as an individual, pay part of the cost
for everything shipped by truck or barge—
whether you use it or not.

The public roads and highways—the
rights-of-way for heavy trucks—are built and
maintained primarily by money collected
from drivers of passenger cars and light
trucks. If a product travels by barge, it moves
through locks and dams and over waterways
built and maintained almost entirely with
your tax dollars.

Nearly all of America's freight railroads
build, maintain and pay taxes on their track
and rights-of-way, and these costs are paid
from dollars earned by the railroads. As a
result, it costs the railroads 34¢ for every
dollar of revenue for track and rights-of-way,
compared to the 5¢ paid by trucks and the
.003¢ paid by barges, neither of which
amounts to a fair share of costs.

All transportation has received government assistance at one time or another. The
freight railroads, however, have reimbursed
the government for most prior aid. Much of
the current aid to some railroads is in the
form of loans to be repaid with interest. On
the other hand, trucks and barges have long
received outright subsidies.

All forms of freight transportation
should pay their full costs of doing business.
When they do, the American people will
receive the most economical transportation
services—and a needless burden will be lifted
from the motorist and taxpayer.

For more information, write: Competi-
tion, Dept. 10, Association of American
Railroads, American Railroads
Building, Washington, DC 20036.

Surprise:
Rights-of-way costs are
heavy for America's freight
railroads; motorists and
taxpayers carry most of the
burden for highways and
waterways.

Figure 15–1   Railroad Ad Advocating Increased User Charges for Trucks
and Barges. Courtesy: Association of American Railroads.

Inflation has this nation in a stranglehold. The railroad industry supports a changed public policy that will end subsidies to all modes, including railroads, and force all modes to compete on the basis of market forces rather than subsidy. . . .

Our inland navigation locks are congested because they appear to be free goods. Our highways and highway bridges are crumbling beneath truckloads of freight. Meanwhile, our freight railroads, many with excess capacity, continue to post sub-standard earnings, making it increasingly difficult to attract new equity capital for motive power and freight car renewals and expansions, and rights-of-way improvements.[13]

Motor Carrier Industry Response to the Railroads

The trucking industry is not taking these allegations lying down! The president of the American Trucking Associations, Bennett C. Whitlock, Jr., asserted:

No transportation industry, has received or still receives the public largess the railroads have. The railroad industry to this day continues to be the beneficiary of what must be the biggest government giveaway program in history—the land grant program of 1850. The railroads nuzzled up to the public trough then and they are still there today.

The railroad industry has launched a massive lobbying, public relations and advertising campaign aimed at recovering their long-lost competitive advantage vis-a-vis the trucking industry. They are attempting to con the American public into supporting this effort by posing as righteous corporate citizens whose primary concern is the preservation of our nation's highway system.

Their thinly-disguised purpose is being pursued at both the state and federal levels and has two objectives: (1) The imposition of unreasonable taxes upon truck owners and operators and (2) artificially restricting the productivity of the trucking industry.

The railroads are relying upon the so-called big lie technique: You make a statement sufficiently outrageous, publicize it, repeat it often enough and people will come to believe it.[14]

Specifically, the trucking industry advocates three positions that are repugnant to the railroad industry. First, they propose a special tax on railroad fuel and equipment, which is supposed to at least partially recover some of the subsidies that the federal government makes available to the railroad industry.[15] (These subsidies to the railroads include funds to Conrail, Amtrak, the Federal Railroad Administration, and the Railroad Retirement Act.) Next, the trucking

---

[13] "Rail Spokesman Advocates Termination of Subsidies For All Transport Modes," *Traffic World* (October 26, 1981), p. 33.

[14] "Railroad-Trucker Battle Heats Up As ATA Proposes Special Rail Tax," *Traffic World* (June 22, 1981), pp. 18–19.

[15] *Ibid.*

industry advocates termination of all future Conrail funding by the federal government. The ATA declared, "It is time Congress recognized Conrail for what it is—a parasite that lives only through government largess."[16] Finally, the ATA decided to hit the rail industry where it really hurts—they have decided to lobby in favor of federal eminent domain for coal slurry pipelines.[17]

Inland Water Carrier Response to the Railroads

Similar to the truckers, the inland water carriers have not been timid with their response to the railroad industry's campaign to increase inland waterway user charges. Richard A. Wilson, president of a barge firm and a regional officer of the American Waterways Operators charged:

> What the rail industry fails to make public is a complete accounting, by mode, of federal subsidies received. Representative James J. Florio (D-N.J.) was quoted in the *Congressional Record* as saying the government has paid $11 billion in subsidies to the railroads over the past five years, while federal subsidies to barge lines do not exceed $4 billion since 1824. These subsidies include the rail retirement fund, current mineral revenues from the huge land grants extended to the rail industry, special tax breaks, Conrail and many others. In fact, the government has as recently as last week voted to appropriate between $15 million and $50 million to finance a major rail classification yard in St. Louis to improve rail efficiency.
>
> We must agree with Mr. Wilner and his association [Association of American Railroads] that all modes must be treated equally in order to preserve the competitive balance between the major modes. That is why the government cannot in good conscience seek cost-recovery user charges from river carriers without extending the same treatment to railroads, who have benefited to a much greater degree from federal dollars.[18]

Even more blunt in his counterattack against railroads was John W. Lambert, chief executive officer of Twin City Barge and Towing Company. He asserted:

> I would wish that those railroad moguls who call the shots for that entire mode would understand that this is 1980, not 1880.
>
> It is time for them to discard the old axiom that the only good water carrier is a dead one.

---

[16] "Truck-Railroad Battle Heats Up on Conrail's Government Funding," *Traffic World* (May 25, 1981), p. 43.

[17] "ATA To Counter Rails' Anti-Truck Campaign; Will Support Pipelines," *Traffic World* (May 4, 1981), p. 43.

[18] "Railroad Allegations Against Truck, River Industries Hit by AWO," *Traffic World* (November 16, 1981), p. 33.

It is time for them to recognize that they can't rape and loot the shipping public and then cry "foul" when that public goes to a competitive mode.[19]

Such bickering will not abate until intermodalism becomes more accepted. It is the subject of the next section.

Intermodal Cooperation

The previous section has examined various forms of intermodal animosity. While this feeling of hostility is real, it does not prevent significant cooperation from existing between transport modes. This cooperation can take two forms: (a) voluntary exchange of cargo between modes and (b) the formation of multimodal transportation companies that own and operate more than one mode of transportation. Each of these alternatives will be examined.

Advantages of Intermodal Transportation

The most prevalent form of intermodal cooperation involves piggyback—trailer-on-flatcar (TOFC) or container-on-flatcar (COFC)—transportation service. In 1980 American railroads loaded 1.7 million piggyback rail cars, second only to coal in rank of carloadings by traffic group. Piggyback accounted for about 7.5 percent of all rail carloadings. TOFC/COFC service is highly concentrated on two main corridors: New York-Chicago and Chicago-Los Angeles. These two city pairs account for about 40 percent of piggyback traffic.[20] The Santa Fe Railroad has been a leader in piggyback service, especially on its main-line trackage between Los Angeles and Chicago. When movement of fresh fruits and vegetables was deregulated for railroads in 1979, the Santa Fe started to aggressively price their service to attract this business away from highway carriers. Their first produce customer gave them 150 trailerloads (two or three trailers are transported on each rail flatcar) and by the end of 1979 the railroad had transported 4,900 trailers of produce. This figure grew to a little more than 12,000 in 1980 and to about 30,000 in 1981. Because of this type of growth, piggyback accounts for 17 percent of Santa Fe's carloading and more than 20 percent of

[19]John W. Lambert, "Wish List For The 1980's," speech to the Annual Meeting of the American Society of Traffic and Transportation (August 14, 1980), mimeographed, p. 5.

[20]Joan Feldman, "In Pursuit of the Multimodal Carrier," *Handling and Shipping Management* (March, 1981), p. 68.

total revenues.[21] Figure 15–2 shows the Santa Fe's new "10-Pack" cars used to carry TOFC traffic between Chicago and Los Angeles.

The U.S. General Accounting Office has recommended that piggyback (trailer-on-flatcar or container-on-flatcar) service be used whenever possible—especially on long trips—because of the inherent fuel economy of railroads versus individual trucks.[22] This allows the most efficient aspects of rail and motor carriage to be combined in a fuel-efficient manner. Truckers perform the pickup and delivery service while the more fuel-efficient railroads perform the line-haul transportation. Until the 1960's TOFC/COFC was not substantially utilized because railroads were *not* performing a reliable line-haul service. Today, however, railroads realize that consistent, on-time delivery is a key to successful TOFC/COFC business. The Chicago and North Western (C & NW) railroad runs a piggyback train—named "Falcon"—daily from Chicago to the Union Pacific connection point at Fremont, Nebraska. In 1977 it averaged greater than 95 percent "on-time" deliveries. One C & NW employee noted that there was no quicker way to get "separated" from the railroad than to "foul up" and cause "Falcon" to be late.[23] In 1981 the Burlington Northern Railroad designated piggyback service as one of its expected high-growth areas for the 1980's. *Railway Age* magazine noted:

> What BN is looking at is increased emphasis on shipments in trailerload lots as receivers try to balance their desire to keep inventory costs low against their fear of stock-outs. The key to meeting this sort of demand, BN believes, will be consistency of service. And the key to consistency of service? It's in the terminals—which is why BN is now evaluating its intermodal terminals in order to determine how much ought to be spent, and where to promote traffic growth and to enable BN to handle it.[24]

Another reason TOFC/COFC is growing in acceptance is that this service is often faster than all-motor carrier service—especially on trips of over 1,000 miles. The Santa Fe operates the "Chief" between Chicago and Los Angeles on a consistent 50-hour schedule for the 2,200-mile trip. (Faster piggyback service is possible. For several years the Santa Fe operated the "Super C" between Chicago and Los Angeles. It was an all TOFC/COFC train that consistently delivered freight between these cities in less than 40 hours. It was cancelled in

---

[21] Gus Welty, "TOFC/COFC: It's A Growth Market Again," *Railway Age* (November 30, 1981), p. 24.

[22] *Traffic World* (September 4, 1978), p. 11.

[23] "With Service Improved, C & NW's Falcons Are Bagging Bigger Game," *Railway Age* (October 31, 1977), p. 20.

[24] Gus Welty, *loc. cit.*, p. 24.

Figure 15–2 Santa Fe's "10-Pack" Cars. A single "10-Pack" car is on each track in this photo. Each car is articulated (meaning it can bend around curves) and carriers ten trailers. Ten cars are joined to form a unit-train carrying 100 trailers. A crane is used to lift trailers on and off the rail cars. The trailer's front is hitched to the raised platform (in foreground); the trailer's rear tires rest on the two lower platforms on each side of the center frame. The "10-Pack" cars are much lighter than conventional TOFC flatcars, and this weight-saving allows the Santa Fe to save 6,000 gallons of diesel fuel on a ten-car (100-trailer) train's round trip between Chicago and Los Angeles. Courtesy: Santa Fe Railway.

1976 because shippers were unwilling to pay the premium price it required.)[25]

Intermodal cooperation is not limited to domestic transportation. Standardized containers that can be transferred between ocean vessels, railroads, and trucks are commonly utilized. These containers significantly reduce labor costs because once the container is loaded, it does not have to be unpacked until it reaches its destination. Carriers only have to handle the large containers, not the individual contents.

An example of the labor saved by containerization is the time it takes to load and unload an ocean ship transporting manufactured products. In the 1950's a typical ship would require two to five days to unload and load. Each article would be handled separately, typically in wooden crates. Today the same size ship using standardized 8-feet by 8-feet by 40-feet containers can be unloaded and loaded in less than eight hours. Longshoremen—the workers who unload and load ships—have not liked containerization because it reduces the number of workers required to unload and load ships. Nevertheless, through employee protection agreements and by attrition and early retirement programs funded by the shipping industry, the containerization movement was not stymied by the longshoremen's union.

To make containerization more attractive, container "pools" have recently been established. These containers are owned by individual carriers or by the pool collectively, and they freely circulate between different shippers and carriers as they are needed. Monthly accounting and billing are provided to each member of the pool.[26]

Deterrents to Increased Intermodal Freight Transportation

There are four problem areas that have retarded intermodalism. First, intermodal shipments require packaging that is sufficient for the mode causing the roughest handling. For example, a shipment traveling by truck, then by rail, and then by truck would experience its roughest handling on the railroad. It would have to be packaged to withstand the rigors of the rail trip and these-additional packaging costs might offset some of the other advantages of intermodal service. The general traffic manager for PPG Industries, Inc., indicated that his firm does not use TOFC extensively. Why? "It requires too much blocking and bracing of loads as compared with over-the-

[25] Gus Welty, "Piggyback Loadings Race Ahead of '75," *Railway Age* (May 31, 1976), p. 18.
[26] *Traffic World* (April 17, 1978), p. 35.

highway shipments."[27] Another shipper declared, "Our shipping costs via piggyback are much higher due to the extensive blocking and bracing required when loading on a trailer for rail movement. This must be compared with loading on an over-the-road trailer, where, in most cases, a minimum of blocking is necessary and chains are tied down by the driver."[28]

A second problem inhibiting development of intermodal traffic deals with claim responsibility. From a loss and damage point of view, intermodal shipments complicate "pinning down" responsibility. Each mode claims the other caused the loss or damage, and the result is often a frustrated shipper or consignee because neither carrier is willing to pay the claim.

A third problem limiting the growth of TOFC/COFC is that it often costs the same as an all-motor carrier shipment. However, since the trucker service is superior in certain aspects, the shipper opts to not use intermodal transportation. Joseph A. Guard, director of traffic and transportation for the Celotex Corporation noted, "We expect to use piggyback on movements where it appears that service will be comparable to that of competing motor carriers and cost will be lower. Generally speaking, piggyback service is slower than motor-carrier service with rates usually on a par with trucks. The only circumstances that would produce a switch would be either drastically lower rates or very much improved service."[29]

Another factor limiting TOFC/COFC is restrictive railroad work rules. The Santa Fe "Chief" piggyback train from Chicago to Los Angeles takes 50 hours. With a crew of four people, this produces 200 man-hours or 25 man-days (200 hours divided by eight hours per day). In fact, the Santa Fe pays for 88 man-days. This discourages the railroads from offering shorter trains that depart more frequently. *Railway Age* notes that union work rules may be the *most serious* restraint to rail involvement in intermodal transportation.[30]

Multimodal Transportation Companies

A multimodal transportation company is a firm that offers transportation services using more than one mode. Historically, U.S. statutes and regulatory bodies have discouraged multimodal transportation companies because it was thought that if one mode could own a

[27] "Are the Railroads Really Pushing Piggyback?" *Railway Age* (October 25, 1976), p. 23.
[28] "TOFC/COFC in '77," *Railway Age* (October 31, 1977), p. 29.
[29] "Are the Railroads Really Pushing Piggyback," p. 24.
[30] "Can Piggyback Widen Its Markets?" *Railway Age* (April 24, 1978), p. 28.

potentially competitive mode, there would be the possibility of a decrease in total competition.

The recent deregulatory climate in transportaton promises to reduce the relatively few remaining regulatory restrictions on intermodal transportation.[31] Therefore, the 1980's will witness more announcements such as this December 3, 1981, headline in the *Wall Street Journal:* "Norfolk and Western Railroad To Acquire More Piedmont Aviation Shares." The N&W now owns 20 percent of the common stock of Piedmont Aviation. This stock purchase was subject to Civil Aeronautics Board (CAB) approval because current law specifies that CAB authorization is necessary when any company or individual "substantially engaged" in the business of being an airline, railroad, or trucking company purchases more than 10 percent of the stock of an airline. Does the Norfolk and Western and its new merger partner, the Southern Railway, have any other transportation merger plans? Harold H. Hall, currently president of the Southern, hinted that in the future the merged Norfolk Southern could become "a total transportation company, perhaps acquiring a piggyback trucking company, a barge line or two."[32]

Because multimodal transportation companies promise to become commonplace in the 1980's, they will be examined from four viewpoints: (a) their advantages, (b) their drawbacks, (c) the Canadian experience with them, and (d) a case study of one of the United States' most advanced multimodal companies, Tiger International.

Advantages of Multimodal Transportation Companies

Three advantages are commonly noted by advocates of multimodal transportation companies. First, this concept encourages transportation service to be performed by the mode of transport that is most economically efficient. Brock Adams, former U.S. Secretary of Transportation, speaking at a 1978 conference on multimodal transportation companies, noted: "In my opinion, there is little doubt that distribution and collection and relatively short-haul traffic is most efficiently done with a motor vehicle, and that long-haul traffic is best done by rail."[33] This position regarding modal efficien-

[31] See: Rodney E. Eyster, "Federal Rules on Intermodal Ownership of Common Carriers," in Clinton H. Whitehurst, Jr., ed., *Forming Multimodal Transportation Companies: Barriers, Benefits, and Problems,* a conference sponsored by American Enterprise Institute for Public Policy Research, Washington, D.C. (1978), pp. 11–22. See also the comments in the same proceedings by J. Robert Hard on page 81.

[32] "Connubial Bliss—Southern Style," *Forbes* (January 4, 1982), p. 201.

[33] Cited in Clinton H. Whitehurst, Jr., ed., *Forming Multimodal Transportation Companies,* p. 125.

cies is also supported by William G. Mahoney, an attorney who represents railroad labor organizations. At the above mentioned conference, he observed:

> I think we are quite a way from where we would be if we had multimodal ownership. If we were to cut back the railroads to, say, four or five east-west and north-south mainlines—which is what I see as the ultimate end of multimodal ownership—many of the lines that are profitable today would be abandoned. Branch lines that are at least marginally profitable, or that break even or lose very little, would be abandoned. The type of transportation system would be changed.[34]

A second advantage is that the shipper can have an intermodal shipment and still have the advantage of one carrier responsibility when it comes to loss and damage claims. The general traffic manager of Westvaco Company, Clifford L. Worth, stated:

> One nuisance in an industrial traffic manager's life is the problem of pinning down responsibility for transit damage in intermodal transportation. Carrier A will claim damage must have occurred while the shipment was in the possession of carrier B and vice versa. One real advantage of dealing with a single intermodal transportation company would be the ability to side-step the issue of where liability lies, thereby speeding the appropriate recovery.[35]

A third factor arguing in favor of multimodal transportation companies is that they will *not* stifle competition in the transportation industry. Some people believe—this point will be examined shortly—that railroads, once they are able to own trucking and barge companies, will raise rates for their new subsidiaries in order to encourage traffic on their railroad. James V. Springrose, vice-president–transportation, Cargill Incorporated, believes the above fear lacks merit. He noted:

> If the railroads tried to do it—and they are the ones that seem to be pointed to in this regard—and if a monopolistic situation developed and freight rates were too high, it would be easy for others to come back into the trucking and the barging business. To some extent shipping is capital intensive, but it is quite easy to get into private trucking. . . .
>
> The threat of the development of monopolies as a result of intermodal ownership has long since passed. The fledglings of the industry that were being protected when the current statutes were written have now matured, and I do not believe they need that protection any more.[36]

In summary, both the National Transportation Policy Study Commission and the U.S. Department of Transportation have recom-

[34] *Ibid.*, p. 116.
[35] *Ibid.*, p. 102.
[36] *Ibid.*, p. 100.

mended that multimodal transportation companies should be encouraged. The Department of Transportation maintains:

> A shipper could be served by a single company employing the best mode or combination of modes for each shipment. Such operations likely would encourage synchronization of the modes used and development of modal interfaces and common equipment, such as containers. The same carrier would be responsible for any loss and damage claims. The administrative work associated with shipments would be less. Differences in governmental treatment that now exist between competing modes would be mitigated since competing transportation companies would probably operate similar combinations of modes.[37]

Disadvantages of Multimodal Transportation Companies

Two primary problem areas are typically noted by opponents of multimodal transportation companies. First, larger transportation firms will absorb smaller firms for the sole purpose of "killing off" these acquired smaller firms. The long-term effects will be a greatly decreased number of total competitors in the transportation industry. This position is commonly held by members of the trucking industry. Witness this statement by Robert C. Dryden, vice-president–traffic, Georgia Highway Express, Inc.:

> I see no reason why they [railroads] should be permitted to enter into common ownership, which would create interfraternity cannibalism and provide opportunity for nefarious schemes ultimately leading to oligopolies.[38]

The stifling of managerial initiative is the second major potential problem of multimodal transportation companies. One large-volume shipper, Clifford L. Worth, noted:

> A considerable negative effect would be the possibility that the mere bigness of a multimodal company would stifle internal entrepreneurship and innovation . . . . In my opinion, the ability of a carrier to react to ideas and to implement change is inversely proportional to its size and the layers of management that must be penetrated.[39]

The Canadian Experience with Multimodal Transportation Companies

Since Canada has never restricted the utilization of multimodal transportation companies, the Canadian experience is instructive.

---

[37] *National Transportation Trends and Choices*, U.S. Department of Transportation (January, 1977), pp. 79, 81.

[38] Cited in Clinton H. Whitehurst, Jr., *Forming Multimodal Transportation Companies*, p. 80.

[39] *Ibid.*, p. 104.

The best example is Canadian Pacific Limited, which includes an international airline, transcontinental trucking and railroad service, a telecommunication system, and a fleet of ocean ships.[40]

What has been the overall effect of multimodal transportation companies in Canada? Most people who have studied this issue conclude multimodal companies have been a positive benefit to the Canadian economy for three reasons. First, the railroads have been able to expand their operations into newer forms of technology. Thus, management that is knowledgeable in the transportation sector of the economy can diversify its operations where it already possesses expertise. Second, the railroads can substitute high-cost services with more efficient ones. The Canadian Pacific has basically eliminated less-than-carload traffic, using instead its trucking subsidiary. Third, customers benefit from being able to select the exact service/cost combination they desire. Trevor D. Heaver of the University of British Columbia observed:

> The marketing of transportation by a multimodal company offers service advantages to the shipper. Through transport is more likely to be possible with advantages in documentation and clear responsibility in cases of loss and damage. "One stop shopping" is possible for rate quotations and advice concerning physical distribution design.[41]

Tiger International: A U.S. Case Study in Multimodal Transportation Companies

As previously noted, in the United States there are relatively few restrictions today, from a legal viewpoint, to stop a firm from becoming a multimodal transportation company. One firm that is very advanced in this area is Tiger International (TI), a holding company which owns a number of different transportation modal companies. Specifically, TI now owns: Flying Tiger Line (air freight), Seaboard World Airlines (air freight), Hall's Motor Transit (motor carrier), Warren Transportation (motor carrier), Dohrn Motor Express (motor carrier), North American Car Corporation (leases rail cars), and Bi-modal Corporation, developer of the Roadrailer (which is discussed later in this chapter). In 1982, TI was the largest U.S. air freight company and the tenth largest U.S. motor common carrier.

---

[40] Frank Malone, "CP Rail: The Marketing Approach to Railroading," *Railway Age* (March 26, 1979), pp. 22–32.

[41] Trevor D. Heaver, "Multi-Modal Ownership—The Canadian Experience," *Transportation Journal* (Fall 1971), p. 18. See also: Karl M. Ruppenthal, ed., *Issues in Transportation Economics* (Columbus: Charles E. Merrill, 1965), Chapter 5, entitled, "The Question of Common Ownership"; and H. L. Purdy, *Transport in Canada* (Vancouver: University of British Columbia Press, 1972), Chapter 7, entitled, "Intermodal Ownership and Transport Competition."

Tiger International is committed to providing a total transportation service to the shipping public (see Figure 15-3). An example of a new service available from TI is that Hall's Motor Transit picks up cargo from the area of Boston to Baltimore and then takes the cargo to Flying Tiger terminals on the East Coast. The freight is then shipped

TOTAL TRANSPORTATION.

The concept is becoming a reality at Tiger International.

In the 70's investors followed specific industries: airline, railroad, and trucking. Today, the transportation industry is changing.

The change began in 1978, when the U.S. Government began deregulating certain segments of the industry. What followed was an opportunity for a company to integrate various modes of transportation.

Tiger International was quick to recognize the opportunity and move toward an entirely new industry concept—total transportation. A concept which allows for greater efficiencies, economies and growth potential.

Today, we are Flying Tigers, the world's largest air cargo carrier; North American Car, one of the nation's most innovative railcar service companies; Hall's Motor Transit, a major U.S. trucking company; Warren Transport, the largest carrier of farm equipment in America; and TigerAir, a growing international aviation service and supply company.

Tiger International is a blend of companies that balances cash needs with cash flows and labor and capital intensities.

We are moving forward in the 80's. Follow our involvement toward total transportation and you will be following the leader.

To learn more about us, write or call: Rosanne O'Brien, Tiger International, 1888 Century Park East, Los Angeles, California 90067, (213) 552-6345.

TIGER INTERNATIONAL

FLYING TIGERS ■ NORTH AMERICAN CAR ■ HALL'S MOTOR TRANSIT ■ WARREN TRANSPORT ■ TIGERAIR

GROWING TOGETHER FOR TOTAL TRANSPORTATION

Figure 15–3 Tiger International Ad. Courtesy: Tiger International.

to the West Coast on a space-available basis. Although the service tends to be much faster than an all-truck service—two or three days versus five to nine days—the freight cost is equal to the-all truck rate.[42]

Wayne M. Hoffman, chairman of TI, is very bullish on the long-term prospects for this company. He notes:

> We're trying to build a company which is broadly based in transportation, which has a management that is skilled in transportation, broadly defined, and which, in the process, will do a better job of filling the true marketing needs of shippers.
>
> We feel our company has a very strong marketing position in the sense that we hope to understand the shippers' needs and to fill those needs in valid ways.[43]

Expanding U.S. Coal Exports

The United States has the potential to be a net *exporter* of energy by 1990.[44] Senator John W. Warner of Virginia exuberantly noted why this is feasible:

> Coal is America's most abundant energy resource. Moreover, America has more mineable coal reserves than any other country in the world, with roughly one-third of the world's reserves lying beneath its soil. If the studies are correct and coal does become the world's growth fuel, the United States, with the largest known reserves, would become the biggest exporter—the Saudi Arabia of coal.[45]

Another enthusiast is Eliot R. Cutler, an attorney who has specialized in energy issues. In a 1981 *Wall Street Journal* article he confidently declared:

> Time is short. In the world of major energy facilities and transportation systems, 15 to 20 years is an instant. The U.S. has the opportunity, once again, to be a net energy exporter. We have the opportunity to help build the energy bridge that can assure a stable, growing economy for ourselves and for other nations. It is important to us and to the world that we seize that opportunity.[46]

[42]"Tiger International: Is Its Grand Transportation Plan More Than A Dream," *Business Week* (April 27, 1981), p. 91.

[43]R. Stanley Chapman, "Full Transportation Service the Goal As Seaboard and Tigers Join Forces," *Traffic World* (October 13, 1980), p. 50.

[44]This section relies heavily upon: James C. Johnson, James P. Rakowski, and Kenneth C. Schneider, "U.S. Coal Exports: Problems and Prospects," *Colorado Business Review* (April, 1982), pp. 2–4.

[45]Letter to Senator Robert C. Byrd, May 27, 1980, located in *Coal Exports*, Hearings before the Committee on Energy and Natural Resources, U.S. Senate, 96th Congress, 2nd Session, September 16, 18, and 19, 1980, Publication No. 96–159, p. 36. Hereafter cited as *Coal Exports*.

[46]Eliot R. Cutler, "The U.S. Role in World Coal, *The Wall Street Journal* (March 18, 1981), p. 26.

The U.S. federal government has taken a strong position encouraging coal exports for three reasons. First, coal exports help our allies reduce their dependence on OPEC energy sources. Second, the U.S. trade balance is helped by export sales of coal and reductions in U.S. imports of natural gas and petroleum. Finally, coal exports increase U.S. employment and national income. The U.S. Department of Energy projects that coal exports by 1990 will produce 38,000 new mining jobs and an additional 190,000 new jobs in coal mining communities.[47]

Future Coal Exports

Historically, coal has been a dominant energy source for industrialized nations. In 1940 coal contributed 49 percent of the world's energy requirements. By 1973—the year OPEC started what eventually became by 1981 a ten-fold increase in oil prices—coal's position as an energy source had slumped to 29 percent of the world's requirements.[48] This decline in relative importance was caused by three major factors: (a) great quantities of low-cost oil were available from the Middle East and North Africa, (b) oil was more convenient than coal to handle, transport, and store, and (c) environmental concerns regarding coal burning and storage made oil the energy choice of preference.[49]

Increases in the prices of oil reversed these trends and worldwide demand for coal has been increasing recently. For many years, the United States had been a major supplier of metallurgical coal (used to make the coke needed for steelmaking) but, starting in about 1980, U.S. exports of "steam" coal (used mainly for generating electric power) began climbing—if not surging—upward. Several factors explain this phenomenon.

First, oil prices nearly doubled in the 1979–80 period while coal prices remained relatively stable. Second, earlier price increases in oil had led many European countries, such as France, Spain, Italy, and England, to convert their existing electric generating units from oil to coal. However, their domestic coal industry did not have the ability to expand coal production, and therefore steam coal had to be

---

[47] "Statement of the American Association of Port Authorities," in *Coal Exports*, p. 431.

[48] *Interim Report of the Interagency Coal Export Task Force*, U.S. Department of Energy, January, 1981, p. 1.

[49] "Coal Exports Study," U.S. Department of Energy, December, 1979, in *Coal Exports*, p. 139.

imported. The U.S. was the obvious choice, with by far the world's largest reserves and with 100 million tons of annual excess capacity.

Australia has historically been a major supplier of steam coal to Europe. However, this relationship has become strained recently, in part because of reliability problems. Jerry E. Gobrecht, vice-president—coal of The Chessie System, remarked, "The Australian situation is also difficult, with myriads of labor and political problems. Today, there are thirty-two separate labor unions involved in getting coal from the mine face to the ports in Australia. I was told recently by a reputable German coal importer that not one ship in the past two years, bound ultimately for Germany, had escaped some sort of serious delay because of labor problems in Australia."[50] A second factor, and one of more significance, is that the recent increases in bunker (fuel) for coal-carrying ships has made Australian coal significantly more expensive than U.S. coal in European markets. From Perth to Rotterdam is approximately 12,500 miles, while from Norfolk to Rotterdam it is 4,000 miles.

Another factor conducive to higher U.S. coal exports has been the recent political unrest in Poland. Poland has been a traditional large supplier of coal to western European countries. The Soviet Union has recently served notice that much of Poland's future coal production will be dedicated to Warsaw Pact nations. In fact, Poland has already reneged on a number of long-term contracts to European countries.[51]

For the above reasons, U.S. coal exports are expected to increase dramatically during the next twenty years. In 1980, coal exports were 70 million short tons (MST). A federal government interagency study group made the following coal export estimates: 1985, 75 MST; 1990, 110 MST; and 2000, 197 MST.[52] At present, metallurgical coal exports account for 50 MST and this figure is expected to stay approximately stable to the year 2000. Therefore, steam coal will be responsible for almost all of the growth in coal exports in the next twenty years.

[50] Speech by Mr. Jerry E. Gobrecht at Johns Hopkins University, World Trade Center, Baltimore, Maryland, October 15, 1980, mimeographed, p. 2.

[51] Speech by Carl E. Bagge, president of the National Coal Association, to the annual convention of the American Association of Port Authorities, Norfolk, Virginia, October 22, 1980, mimeographed, p. 5.

[52] Moving U.S. Coal To Export Markets, prepared by U.S. Army, Corps of Engineers, Maritime Administration, Department of Energy and Department of Transportation, June 10, 1980, p. S-1 and Interim Report of the Interagency Coal Export Task Force, p. 6.

Transportation Constraints on Coal Exports

The general consensus is that inland transportation facilities will be adequate to transport the expected increases in steam coal from mines to ports. The Interagency Coal Export Task Force stated:

> In spite of the very sizeable increases projected for coal exports, this traffic will still be but a small percentage of the total demand placed on the rail and barge systems, as well as a small percentage of rail and barge coal traffic. Consequently, major inland transportation improvements will usually be primarily oriented toward domestic coal traffic and secondary toward export coal traffic.
>
> The lead times for making improvements to the land transportation system are usually shorter than lead times for mine and port development, therefore, road and railroad improvements generally can be completed in time to serve new mines or port facilities.[53]

The major transportation constraints on increased coal exports are at ports. In February, 1981, over 175 colliers were waiting at East

- An ocean-going vessel that carriers coals is often called a *collier.*

Coast ports for a berth to a load coal. The average wait of these ships was 40 days; some have been delayed more than 60 days.[54] This situation was still serious a year later. In January, 1982, there were 124 colliers waiting at just two East Coast port cities, Newport News and Baltimore.[55] Each ship waiting at anchor costs its charter owner $15,000 to $20,000 per *day.*[56] Two problems primarily account for the delay colliers experience waiting for steam coal.

First, existing coal terminals at East Coast ports were designed for metallurgical coal. Since there are about 500 varieties of metallurgical coal, it is not feasible to store each type in a separate pile on the ground. Therefore, this type of coal is stored in the rail car in which it has been shipped to the port. (Figure 15–4 shows an accumulation of such rail cars.) Steam coal, on the other hand, is homogeneous enough that it can be stored on the ground at the port before being loaded. This allows rapid turnaround of rail coal cars, in contrast to the present "in car" storage of metallurgical coal. However, East Coast coal ports have relatively little additional room for ground storage of steam coal. John P. Fishwick, president of the Norfolk and Western Railway, commented on this issue:

> One million people are in the Norfolk area, and the problems inherent in finding suitable facilities there and complying with the ecological re-

[53] *Coal Exports: Inland Transportation,* report of the Inland Transportation Working Group, prepared for the Interagency Coal Export Task Force, December, 1980, p. iii.

[54] Jean A. Briggs, "Shaping Up To Ship Out," *Forbes* (February 16, 1981), p. 57.

[55] "CSX Net Sets High," *The Wall Street Journal* (January 5, 1982), p. 25.

[56] See: *Coal Exports,* p. 103.

Figure 15–4   Rail Cars of Coal Waiting To Be Unloaded at Norfolk. Courtesy: Norfolk and Western Railway.

quirements that undoubtedly should be made are enormous, and we have had numbers of people, numbers of coal operators and others searching out properties that can be served by rail and can be made into suitable facilities for handling export coal.[57]

The second problem area involves inadequate harbor depths that prevent modern supercolliers from using East Coast ports. William W. Mason, President of the U.S. Coal Exporters Association, observed, "The single most important constraint which could limit

[57]*Ibid.*, p. 394.

our participation in the growing international coal market is inadequate port and transportation facilities."[58] At present, Hampton Roads is dredged to 42 feet and Baltimore is at 40 feet. By way of comparison, Richards Bay, South Africa—one of the world's most modern coal ports—has a depth of 65 feet. Other ports have the following depths available: Antwerp, Belgium, 61 feet; Kashima, Japan, 72 feet; and Le Havre, France, 55 feet. U.S. ports can serve colliers that are no larger than 70,000 dwt (dead weight tons).[59] At present, about one-third of the colliers calling at East Coast ports can not fully load because of port depth limitations.

In 1970, only 3 percent of colliers could transport 100,000 dwt. By 1977, 25 percent of coal vessels were of this size. Today, many ships of 150,000 dwt are on the high seas. These vessels draw 55 feet of water.[60] It is estimated that a 150,000 dwt vessel can transport coal on a per-ton basis for about one-third less than a 72,500 dwt ship.

Solutions to Transportation Constraints

The inadequate port facilities responsible for long queues of colliers at East Coast ports have caused private enterprise to respond to the situation. New piers and associated coal-loading equipment are being planned and construction is rapidly taking place. It is estimated that these new facilities should be adequate to meet projected export requirements by mid-1983. In 1981, approximately 18 million tons of annual coal-handling capacity were under construction on the East Coast and an additional 81 million tons of capacity were being planned. At Gulf Coast ports, 5 million tons of annual capacity are currently under construction and another 33 million are being planned. West Coast ports presently have 47 million tons of additional capacity in the planning stage.[61]

The above new facilities may be an over-zealous reaction according to some observers.[62] William B. Bales, vice-president—coal and

[58]"Coal Export Boom Spurs New Port Projects," *Coal News* (September 29, 1980), p. 5.

[59]*Coal Exports*, pp. 103, 276.

[60]*Ibid.*, p. 276.

[61]*Interim Report of the Interagency Coal Export Task Force*, p. 7. For a description of specific projects that have been started or are in the planning stage, see: *Coal Exports*, pp. 180, 308, 322. See also: Richard P. Page and Paul R. Farragut, "Export Coal: Implications for U.S. Ports," *Annual Proceedings of the Transportation Research Forum* (1981), pp. 112–120; Gus Welty, "Coal Exports: Railroads, Ports Get Set for a Surge," *Railway Age* (December 14, 1981), pp. 24–29; David Fairbank White, "The Coal-Export Gamble," *Fortune* (December 14, 1981), pp. 122–136.

[62]See: *Coal Exports*, p. 403; and Thomas Petzinger, Jr., "Inadequacy of U.S. Coal-Export Terminals Sparks Oil-Money Push To Expand Capacity," *The Wall Street Journal* (February 27, 1981), p. 19. See also: David Fairbank White, *loc. cit.*

ore traffic for the Norfolk and Western Railway, noted:

> Right now, as I speak, there are probably a number of groups representing interests in all parts of the world, scouring the Atlantic and Gulf Coasts of the United States in search of locations suitable for the construction and operation of coal export terminals. This frenetic activity is illustrative of the euphoria that often accompanies new economic ventures. For example, in the nineteenth century during the great growth and expansion of American railroads, such euphoria led to a vast duplication of lines and great system overcapacity, problems from which the industry continues to suffer to some degree today. . . .
>
> Norfolk & Western has been widely criticized for not announcing plans for new or expanded export coal facilities, as many others . . . already have done. However, we continue to feel that we must complete our review of long-term market potential and to determine the most efficient system of handling existing and new business. The export coal market may soon, like other new economic ventures of the past, be characterized by over-capacity in the near term if all facilities now being planned are built. It may be a number of years before long-term international demand rises to the level of present spot market demand. When and if a shakeout comes and the present bubble bursts, we believe that those who have made investments and committed capital carefully and rationally, not in the emotion of the moment, will be those who survive.[63]

A second solution to transportation bottlenecks is to use the existing coal terminal facilities more efficiently. A leader in this approach is the Norfolk and Western Railway. By utilizing long-term contracts with both transshippers and foreign purchasers, the railroad is able to reduce port congestion by carefully planning and coordinating a more orderly flow of coal from mine to ship. John P. Fishwick, president of the N & W, estimated that long-term contracts allow existing port facilities to be 25 percent more efficient than at present. The N & W has recently negotiated two such contracts. One two-year agreement with transshippers states that the N & W will pay $20 per car per day if it does not meet specific loading dates. On the other hand, transshippers pay the N & W $20 per car per day when rail cars cannot be unloaded at specified times.[64] In January, 1981, the N & W announced it had negotiated a two-year contract with the Association Technique de l'Importation Charbonniere (ATIC), which is the only coal importer into France. The contract calls for the shipping of a minimum of 800,000 tons of coal per year.

[63] Speech by William B. Bales at Coal Outlook's third annual "Mine to Market: Coal Transportation Today and Tomorrow" Conference, November 10–11, 1980, mimeographed, pp. 8–9.

[64] Robert C. Dart, "Transportation Link Seen as Hurdle to Meeting Coal Export Projections," *Traffic World* (December 22, 1981), p. 11.

Mr. Fishwick declared:

> The contract N & W is offering to coal shippers establishes specific dates on which vessels will be loaded, and sets forth significant financial penalties that can apply to either the railroad or to the shipper if they are unable to meet their responsibilities for getting the coal and the ship to the port in time to meet the specified loading date. Ships loading under long-term contracts will be able to bypass the lengthy queue of vessels that has developed at Hampton Roads. . . .[65]

The utilization of coal slurry pipelines is another solution to the existing port congestion situation. One plan envisions the slurry to be pumped directly into the vessel and then dewatered by means of a second pipeline back to shore. Boeing Company and the Maritime Administration researched the feasibility of such a system and found the concept to be both economically and technically viable. Their study involved a coal pipeline from Wyoming and Colorado to the West Coast with the ultimate destination being the Far East.[66] The Continental Resources Company is studying a similar project for the southeastern portion of the United States, with a terminal at Charleston, Savannah, or Jackson.[67]

Transportation Deregulation: What to Expect

Previous chapters have examined the recent deregulation laws affecting the airlines, trucking, and railroad industries. This section will briefly discuss the future effects of deregulation on the transportation industry. It should be noted that the trend toward transportation deregulation is *not* restricted to the federal government. State governments are also freeing their intrastate carriers from economic regulation. Florida's trucking deregulation bill took effect on July 1, 1980.[68] In Arizona, a state-wide referendum was held to decide if the trucking industry should be deregulated on July 1, 1982. This measure was passed by greater than a two-to-one margin in November, 1980.[69]

---

[65]"N & W, French Importing Agency Arrange Contract," *Traffic World* (January 26, 1981), p. 7.

[66]*Moving U.S. Coal to Export Markets*, p. S-9.

[67]*Coal Exports*, p. 448.

[68]"Florida's Test of Truck Deregulation," *Business Week* (September 22, 1980), pp. 125, 129.

[69]"Arizona Voters Pass Deregulation Measure, *Transport Topics* (November 10, 1980), p. 3.

Deregulation and Rate Charges

In a deregulated environment, it can be expected that transportation rates will become closer to the carrier's actual cost of providing the service. Therefore, some transportation rates will decrease and others will increase. However, the preponderance of rate changes will be downward because the full forces of price competition have now been unleashed in the transportation industry.

Illustrative of rate decreases is this quote from the *Wall Street Journal:*

> Until mid-March, Anchor Hocking Corporation, maker of glass, tableware and containers, paid $530 to ship a truckload of bottle tops from Baltimore to Jersey City. Then a new carrier offered to haul each truckload for $457. Still another trucker dived into the fray with an offer to haul the freight for $361 a truckload—32% less than the first trucker charged.[70]

Notice that this significant rate reduction occurred for *truckload* (TL) traffic. This is because most of the new for-hire trucking companies that have entered the trucking industry since the 1980 *Motor Carrier Act* have been non-union, relatively small companies that are only interested in TL shipments. Why? Because less-than-truckload (LTL) truckers require terminals where the freight is consolidated for the line-haul portion of the transportation between origin and destination. At destination, LTL freight again is sorted at a terminal for delivery to the consignee. Notice that LTL service is much more capital intensive—because of the freight terminals—than TL service, which requires no terminals because the freight is picked up at the shipper's location and transported directly to the consignee's receiving dock. Rollins Maxwell, a trucking industry financial analyst for E. F. Hutton, Inc., observed in late 1981:

> In the past year and a half, LTL freight has been profitable and truckload freight has not been profitable. There's too much competition and overcapacity in truckload freight. This situation, over time, will certainly change. You're going to purge the system of overcapacity, over say, the next five years, maybe three, maybe seven years, and we'll have a profitable for-hire truckload freight system. But the transition period is going to take time. The LTL carriers, which are the publicly owned trucking companies that we all follow, are avoiding truckload freight, both because the freight isn't there, and also because they can't make any money on it. That's probably likely to remain the case for another year at least.[71]

[70]Michael L. King, "Deregulation by ICC Appears to Hold Down Truck-Rates Inflation," *The Wall Street Journal* (May 9, 1980), p. 1.

[71]"Trucking Industry," *The Wall Street Journal Transcript* (September 7, 1981), p. 7.

Because newer non-union trucking firms have been taking significant quantities of freight away from the established firms who have Teamster labor, the union agreed to an unprecedented reopening of the existing Teamster contract. The new contract was ratified by the Teamster membership in early 1982. Teamster president Roy Williams noted that trucking management needed wage/work-rule concessions from the union because over 120,000 Teamsters were presently unemployed, while 300,000 still retained their jobs. Mr. Williams declared, "We are confident we have produced a contract that will preserve the jobs of those now employed and will help regain the thousands of jobs lost through layoffs and business failures in the trucking industry."[72]

From the shipper's viewpoint, many trucking rates have dropped significantly. Charles S. Davis is transportation manager for General Electric's major-appliance facility in Louisville, Kentucky. He controls approximately $150 million that GE spends annually on freight transportation at the Louisville complex. The *Wall Street Journal* noted the following about this highly-paid executive: "His days are spent negotiating to reduce freight rates and improve service, devising transportation plans that enhance GE's marketing strategies and playing host to troops of freight haulers seeking GE's business."[73] Because of deregulation, TL rates have decreased greatly. The cost of shipping a truckload of washing machines from Louisville to Chicago has dropped from $780 to $359.

While shippers enjoy this highly competitive rate environment in the trucking industry, many truckers are less than exuberant! An article in *Handling and Shipping Management* noted:

> One angry trucking executive with a small carrier denounces the current situation as "the rape of the carriers." Shippers—particularly large companies—are driving the industry to the brink by whipsawing one carrier against the other to squeeze out rates they know can't be compensatory.[74]

Rail rates have also been volatile after deregulation. Some rates have significantly increased: for example, an eastern rail executive said, "We're going to raise our furniture rates double-digit. If this means we lose furniture business to trucks, so be it. If they stay with

---

[72] *Traffic World* (January 25, 1982), p. 41.

[73] Michael L. King, "Transportation Official at GE Finds His Role Rises With Fuel Prices," *The Wall Street Journal* (December 31, 1981), p. 1.

[74] Patrick Gallagher, "Stuck With Overcapacity, Truckers Await the Recovery," *Handling and Shipping Management* (January, 1982), p. 28.

us despite the higher rates, we'll finally make a profit on furniture."[75]

The above quote represents what many people believed would be typical of railroad actions after deregulation. However, the reverse situation has become more commonplace. From April to September, 1981, Western rail rate bureaus reported 544 rate increases and 10,027 rate decreases. In the East there were 510 rate increases and 3,037 decreases. Only in the southern region were there more increases (376) compared to decreases (359). Many of these rate decreases are designed to take business away from truckers. On one 200-mile movement, Conrail cut its TOFC rate from $1,368 to $585, a reduction of almost 60 percent.[76]

The Birth of New Carriers and the Death of Old Ones

A key aspect of deregulation in the airline and trucking industries has been a lessening of entry controls. Many new trucking companies are being formed monthly. From July, 1980, to January, 1982, about 5,000 new for-hire trucking companies have been approved by the ICC.[77] In addition, over 36,000 new for-hire certificates and permits for additional operating rights were issued to existing for-hire truckers[78] Very few applications for either expanding operating rights for existing carriers or for starting a totally new trucking company are denied by the ICC. Therefore, Commission Chairman Reese H. Taylor, Jr., has proposed that the only entry requirement in the trucking industry should be a "fitness" test. If the applicant has safe equipment and is financially fit, then the application will be automatically approved.[79]

In addition, new passenger airlines are being formed. In 1980 Midway Airlines started to serve Chicago's Midway Airport and other midwestern cities such as Minneapolis-St. Paul, Detroit, Cleveland, and Kansas City.[80] In late 1980 New York Air started a low-fare commuter service between LaGuardia Airport in New York City

[75] John D. Williams, "Rail-Rate Increases Due For Early Arrival Thanks To New Law," *The Wall Street Journal* (October 14, 1980), p. 1.

[76] Paul F. VanWicklen, "New Attitudes Shape Rail's Future," *Handling and Shipping Management* (January, 1982), p. 33.

[77] Patrick Gallagher, *loc. cit.*, p. 26.

[78] *Traffic World* (November 16, 1981), p. 33.

[79] *Traffic World* (December 21, 1981), pp. 16–19.

[80] See: Bernard F. Whalen, "Midway Airlines Takes Off Without Marketing Research," *Marketing News* (January 25, 1980), pp. 1–10; and James Ott, "New Carrier Gains Acceptance," *Aviation Week and Space Technology* (November 26, 1979), pp. 21–23.

and Washington, D.C.'s National Airport.[81] Finally, People Express commenced operation in April, 1981, serving the East Coast and Florida.[82]

Airline deregulation has also greatly increased the number of new commuter airlines, which have been formed to service smaller cities that had lost jet service. Three years after deregulation, the great majority of smaller cities are now receiving more frequent air service, on smaller, propeller-driven planes, from commuter airlines than previously was available under regulation.[83]

While new firms are being established, others are "sick" or dying, especially in the trucking industry. This is exactly what economic theory would have predicted. In a provocative article in *The Wall Street Journal*, Joel A. Bleeke and James W. Goodrich observed, "Performance variability among firms within the deregulated industry will increase, with weak firms becoming weaker more rapidly than strong firms get stronger."[84] The reason for this situation is that under regulation, the weaker firms are protected from the full forces of competition by the regulatory commission. As an indication of the ICC's former effectiveness, no major trucking company failed between 1960 and 1973.[85] This "security blanket" no longer exists for the trucking industry. *Forbes* magazine noted that some trucking company executives predicted that 20 percent of the 17,000 interstate for-hire trucking companies will go out of business during the 1980–82 period.[86]

The business failures that seem likely in the trucking industry would be caused by the double effects of deregulation and the economic recession. The great majority of these firms will be relatively small companies with gross annual revenues of less than $500,000. However, starting in 1980 a number of major common carrier trucking companies went bankrupt, including Chippewa Motor Freight, Wilson Freight, Johnson Motor Lines, and Cooper-Jarrett, Inc. This "shakeout" in the trucking industry is expected to continue throughout the 1980's.

[81] "New York Air To Compete Vigorously," *Marketing News* (November 28, 1980), p. 12.

[82] "Upstarts in the Sky: Here Comes a New King of Airline," *Business Week* (June 15, 1981), p. 80. See also: Peter Nulty, "People Express: A Champ of Cheap Airlines," *Fortune* (March 22, 1982), pp. 127–134.

[83] "Deregulated Airlines Give Small Towns A Lift," *Business Week* (January 11, 1982), p. 24.

[84] Joel A. Bleeke and James W. Goodrich, "Winners and Losers Under Deregulation," *The Wall Street Journal* (December 7, 1981), p. 24.

[85] Patrick Gallagher, *loc. cit.*, p. 27.

[86] Lisa Gross, "Down But Not Out in Lima," *Forbes* (November 10, 1980), p. 200.

A New Environment for Shippers

In the authors' opinion, transportation deregulation will have very important and beneficial effects on the career status of transportation and physical distribution/logistics executives. Why? Because the service and rate options now available to the PD/L manager have increased astronomically. Walter E. Morgan, manager of transportation policy for Union Carbide, prophetically stated, "We can't stick with just the green-eyeshade traffic clerk any longer. We'll all have to expand our traffic staffs and hire new transportation analysts."[87] An executive of the management consulting company A. T. Kearney expressed it this way: "The role of the traffic manager becomes more entrepreneurial. He must minimize the risks by being more sensitive to opportunities."[88] Richard Haupt, director of transportation and traffic for the Ford Motor Company, is extremely bullish on the new environment for traffic executives. He boldly declared:

> Because of deregulation, things will never be the same, and to that I say "great." It's time that we had some change in transportation, and while some of the experiences have been traumatic for those involved, there also have been many benefits. I think that today many more people will agree that, on balance, the results have been good and hold promise for the future.[89]

Shippers will find the new transportation environment highly challenging. Because of the new fluidity of rates, shippers will have to expand their computerized information systems, which can be rapidly updated and accessed from many locations. These rate bases will be a key element in shipment planning and carrier rate bill verification. In addition, carrier service levels will also have to be incorporated into the shipper's information system.

What specific changes can be expected? The experience from Florida, which deregulated intrastate trucking in July, 1980, has been beneficial to the shipping public. One study performed for the ICC by Industrial Traffic Consultants of Miami concluded:

> Shipper responses reveal that high quality trucking service has been maintained. Of the shippers reporting changes in service availability and quality, the vast majority said service has improved. Despite inflation, most Florida shippers have available to them rates that are the same or lower than prior to deregulation.[90]

[87] John D. Williams, *loc. cit.*, p. 1.

[88] "Changed Transportation Environment Elevates Status of Traffic Manager," *Traffic World* (December 14, 1981), p. 31.

[89] "Speakers Differ In Appraisals of Deregulation," *Traffic World* (November 30, 1981), p. 19.

[90] "Florida Consultants Report Good Results From Intrastate Deregulation," *Traffic World* (August 31, 1981), p. 20.

Similar findings are also being observed at the national level. With service levels increasing[91] and rates either decreasing—or at a minimum increasing *less* rapidly than inflation—many shippers are opting *out* of private transportation in favor of for-hire carriage. Kaiser Aluminum's Director of Domestic Transportation, James P. Falk, observed, "We found in many cases that we can no longer compete with the special commodities divisions of the truck companies. So we've been reducing our fleet. It's good management."[92]

Many transportation managers, in their quest to negotiate better freight rates, have chosen to minimize the total number of carriers utilized in any given market. Why? Because this increases the quantity of traffic given to each carrier that is used, and therefore the shipper becomes a larger and more important customer to the carrier.[93] Sears, Roebuck and Company used to utilize over 4,000 trucking companies and over 200 air freight forwarders in the United States. Today, in order to better monitor carrier service levels and to have more "clout" with those remaining carriers, Sears has drastically cut back the total number of carriers utilized. It now deals with only 200 trucking firms and 10 air freight forwarders.[94]

Another change in shipper-carrier relations that will become commonplace in the 1980's is an increase in contract carriage. Although this trend will also increase in the trucking industry,[95] its main thrust will be in the railroad industry. By the end of 1981, over 700 rail contracts had been filed with the ICC.[96] Once the advantages to both shipper and carrier are more fully recognized, it is expected that the utilization of rail contracts will significantly increase. Richard E. Briggs, a senior officer of the Association of American Railroads, believes that eventually one-third of all rail shipments will be covered by contract rates.[97] Even more optimistic is Harry J. Bruce, senior vice-president of the Illinois Central Gulf Railroad, who stated that in late 1981 his carrier received 4.5 percent of its

[91] See: Michael L. King, *loc. cit.;* and Lyman Coddington, "Air Cargo Industry Gives Deregulation Good Marks," WWS/World Ports (December/January, 1982), pp. 85–86.

[92] Patrick Gallagher, *loc. cit.,* p. 30.

[93] "What Deregulation Has Done To The Truckers," *Business Week* (November 9, 1981), pp. 70–79.

[94] "Transportation: Tiger International," *Business Week* (April 27, 1981), p. 92.

[95] See statement by Rollins Maxwell in *The Wall Street Transcript* (September 7, 1981), p. 4.

[96] Paul F. VanWicklen, *loc. cit.,* p. 35.

[97] Richard E. Briggs, "What Railroad Deregulation Can Mean To The Grain Industry," *Railway Age* (October 12, 1981), p. 34.

gross revenues from contract rates. He believes that sometime in the 1980's, this percentage will climb to 50 percent.[98]

Roger Kallock is a co-founder of the physical distribution/ logistics consulting firm Cleveland Consulting Associates. In the following statement, Kallock presents an excellent summary of the transportation manager's role in the 1980's:

> Desperately needed transportation productivity is now within reach of the thousands of transportation professionals throughout the country who are able to see their way through the new maze created by deregulation. The alert transportation manager will rapidly adjust to his increasingly important role by expanding carrier alternatives, negotiating preferential rates, reviewing carrier selection guidelines, and upgrading service and cost data bases for all locations and major traffic lanes.
>
> Recently in our consulting business we have seen two consumer product transportation managers get the jump on deregulation. Each generated savings estimated at $1 million annually. They are also attracting top management attention and increasing the visibility of the transportation department's organization, its capabilities, and its successes.
>
> Asleep-at-the-switch managers who continue to hope that it will be business as usual are in for an unpleasant awakening. Spending valuable time voicing their disapproval of deregulation, they may fail to examine the implications of the changes. In the end, they are likely to jeopardize themselves and their companies as external pressures from customers, carriers, and competition place their companies at a disadvantage.[99]

Future Technological Changes

This section will examine a number of changes in transportation technology that may become commonplace in the 1980's. Many of these changes will involve fuel savings. For example, the Burlington Northern Railroad has been successfully experimenting with a new technique to transport frozen goods. At present, food products are kept frozen in mechanically-refrigerated rail cars, each of which burns about 25 gallons of diesel fuel per day. The new procedure utilizes a heavily-insulated rail car that is loaded at the origin with liquid carbon dioxide which forms powdered dry ice once in the rail car holding tanks. One application of the carbon dioxide will keep a rail car's inside temperature below freezing for up to ten days. This

---

[98]Perry A. Trunick, "Contracting For Transportation," *Handling and Shipping Management* (November, 1981), p. 56.

[99]Roger W. Kallock, "Uncle Sam Deals Shippers A New Hand," *Handling and Shipping Management* (August, 1980), p. 28.

system promises to be significantly more cost efficient than the present system utilizing mechanical refrigeration units.[100]

Other proposed technological changes appear to be more appropriate for a Jules Verne novel. One such concept involves the utilization of giant submarines to transport liquid natural gas (LNG) from Alaska to West Germany. General Dynamics Corporation has proposed to build 28 such submarines at a total cost of $20 billon. Each submarine would be 1,470 feet long and would transport 37 million gallons of LNG at a minimum temperature of minus 260 degrees Fahrenheit, which is the required temperature to keep natural gas in a liquefied condition. The undersea ships would be necessary in order to utilize the direct route under the Arctic Icecap between Alaska and Germany. At present, General Dynamic Corporation has not been able to arrange financing for this revolutionary concept.[101]

The following discussion will examine four technological changes that will undoubtedly become operational in the 1980's.

Coal-Powered Railroads

With the rapid advances in the price of oil, the return of coal-powered locomotives is becoming feasible. In 1970, a million BTUs generated by oil cost 51¢ more than the equivalent amount of energy produced by coal. By 1974, the difference was $1.21 and in March, 1982 it was $4.46. Remember that fuel cost is the second largest railroad operating expense item.

Because of the potential for utilizing a significantly less costly fuel, the American Coal Enterprises (ACE) Corporation is designing a modern coal-powered locomotive (see Figure 15–5). Known as the

[100]"Carbon Dioxide Breathes New Life Into BN Reefers," *Railway Age* (August 10, 1981), p. 21.

[101]"Giant Subs To Haul LNG Under Arctic In Proposal," *The Wall Street Journal* (November 19, 1981), p. 3.

Figure 15–5   The Ace 3000: A Modern Coal-Burning Locomotive. The propulsion unit is on the right; the service module, on the left. Source: John A. Armstrong, "Solid-Fuel Railroading in the '80s," *Railway Age* (October 13, 1980), p. 36.

ACE 3000, it is designed to produce, at 1982 fuel costs, a minimum fuel savings of at least one-third compared to a comparable locomotive using diesel fuel.[102] If all locomotives in the U.S. were coal powered, the annual savings would have been $1.2 billion in 1980. The ACE 3000 weighs 650,000 pounds and produces 3,000 horsepower. It is a two-unit locomotive, comprised of a "service module" and the "power unit." The former will carry three 11-ton "coal packs" that are loaded at a coal mine and transported to where needed by rail flatcar. In addition, the service module transports the water that will be converted into steam. Coal is automatically fed, via conveyor belt, into the firebox in the power unit. This system allows the ACE 3000 to travel 500 miles between fuel stops and 1000 miles before water must be taken aboard.

To make the ACE 3000 environmentally compatible, it will collect almost all ash produced. The ash will be "scrubbed" from the exhaust gases and conveyed to a five-ton "ash pack" module which is removed during servicing. The ACE Corporation hopes to have two prototypes of the ACE 3000 in operation by the mid-1980's. It is estimated that the two prototypes will cost $25 million.[103]

Roadrailer

Another promising equipment innovation is the Roadrailer, which is illustrated in Figure 15–6. It involves a trailer that is 45 feet long and appears to be a standard highway freight trailer. However, it has a railroad axle and wheels which can be lowered into position to ride on railroad tracks. A series of Roadrailers can be connected to form a railroad train. This would eliminate the need for railroad flatcars and the time required to transfer the highway trailers on and off flatcars. Also, because the weight of the flatcar does not have to be transported, significant energy savings are possible. The Federal Railroad Administration tested the Roadrailer concept at its extensive facilities in Pueblo, Colorado, and found the Roadrailer was 51 percent more fuel efficient than traditional trailer-on-flatcar operations.[104]

The Roadrailer is a fully-tested concept. The Burlington Northern has run Roadrailer trains between Chicago and Seattle.[105] The Illi-

---

[102] Arthur H. Rotstein, "Man Bets Coal Power Can Derail Railroad Diesels," *Minneapolis Tribune* (March 15, 1981), p. 9D.

[103] John H. Armstrong, "Solid-Fuel Railroading in the '80's," *Railway Age* (October 13, 1980), pp. 36–37.

[104] Francis J. Quinn, "Energy-Efficient Equipment Spurs Intermodal Growth," *Traffic Management* (March, 1980), p. 59.

[105] "Bi-Modal Claims 19% Cost Savings," *Railway Age* (August 10, 1981), p. 10.

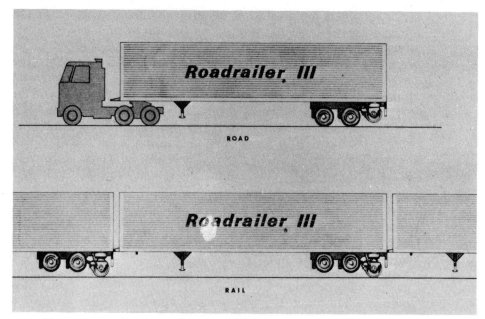

Figure 15–6 Roadrailer Intermodal Trailer. Source: "The Roadrailer: Return of an Idea," *Traffic World* (June 19, 1978), p. 23.

nois Central Gulf is currently running Roadrailer trains between Memphis and Louisville. These 50-car trains have proven highly successful, according to ICG and Roadrailer officials. Because flatcars are eliminated, total weight is reduced by 56 percent compared to the usage of TOFC equipment. This significant weight reduction allows total operating costs to be reduced 17 to 20 percent below traditional TOFC. In addition, the Roadrailer eliminates the need for trailer-loading cranes and ramps, and less land is therefore needed for intermodal terminals.[106] It should be noted that Roadrailers cannot be mixed with regular rail cars. The latter are much heavier and sturdier, and would damage Roadrailer equipment if the train made a sudden stop.

James H. Ozanne, president of North American Car Corporation (which owns Bi-Modal Corporation, the builder of Roadrailer equipment), is optimistic about the future of Roadrailers. "We project that by the end of 1984 there will be 17,000 Roadrailer units in service.

[106] See: "Roadrailer Runs Between Memphis and Louisville," *Traffic World* (June 1, 1981), p. 39 and "For Roadrailer A Different Kind of Test," *Railway Age* (May 25, 1981), p. 9.

We expect to receive revenues of well over $100 million from the program in 1983."[107] Equally enthusiastic is the Union Pacific Railroad after testing Roadrailers between Los Angeles and Chicago. Thomas B. Graves, Jr., UP's financial vice-president referred to Roadrailer's as "possibly the breakthrough which railroads need"[108] to cut intermodal fuel costs.

Lighter-Than-Air Cargo Vessels

Because of the high cost of fuel, a small British air cargo company has ordered four helium airships from Airship Industries Ltd. Each airship is 600 feet long and costs about $2.5 million. The four airships will be delivered to Redcoat Cargo Airlines by 1984. Each ship has the carrying capacity of one and a half wide-body aircraft. Fuel savings are estimated to be about 30 percent less per ton-mile compared to jet cargo planes. Why did Redcoat order these airships? Keven McPhillips, a director of Redcoat stated, "We're opting out of conventional aircraft. Redcoat decided a long time ago that fuel costs would be the main problem to be faced in the future and decided to go for alternatives."[109]

Each of the airships will have a maximum lift of 58 metric tons and will cruise at 85 miles per hour. Propulsion is provided by four 1,120-horsepower engines. Redcoat plans to use the new airships in service in West Africa, the Middle East, and in Central America. In addition, two-and-a-half-day Atlantic crossings between the United States and Europe are also contemplated.

Sailing Cargo Vessels

The previous technological example of a coal-powered locomotive indicates that technology can be recycled. The last change to be examined here also represents a situation where technology has evolved "full circle." Two hundred years ago all large ocean vessels used wind as the means of propulsion. Then mechanical techniques were discovered. Today, because of energy costs, sailing vessels are making a comeback. (See Figure 15–7.) The Japanese government has been a leader in testing ships that have both engines and sails. Notice that the sails in Figure 15–7 can be furled (closed by means of rolling into a compact roll) and opened by remote control from the

[107] "Roadrailers To Be In Use Next Fall," *Traffic World* (February 11, 1980), p. 36.
[108] "Transportation: Tiger International," *Business Week* (April 27, 1981), p. 94.
[109] "Redcoat Cargo Line Looks To Dirigibles To Cut Fuel Costs," *The Wall Street Journal* (July 14, 1980), p. 16.

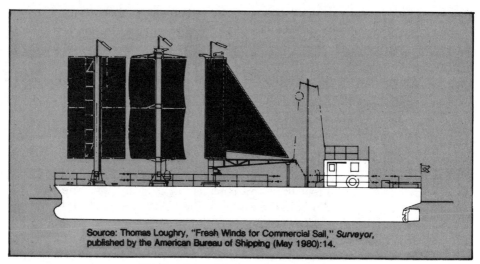

Source: Thomas Loughry, "Fresh Winds for Commercial Sail," *Surveyor*, published by the American Bureau of Shipping (May 1980):14.

Figure 15–7   Modern Sailing Vessel.

ship's bridge. In addition, each mast can be rotated from the bridge by means of large electric motors. This allows the sails to "catch" the wind most advantageously.

The test vessels operated by the Technical Research Center in Kawasaki, Japan, have been able to consistently save approximately 10 percent of fuel requirements, compared to a similar-sized ship without auxiliary sails. With winds at over 40 knots, the sails were not utilized for safety reasons. Under favorable wind conditions, the sails save over 20 percent of the fuel utilized by a ship without sails.[110] Lloyd Bergeson, a well-known naval architect, predicted that by the 1990's, 75 percent of all ocean vessels will be designed with auxiliary sails.[111]

Summary

Transportation represents one of the most dynamic aspects of the American economy. This chapter examined a number of transportation areas that will experience significant change in the 1980's.

[110] See: "New Age of Sail?" *American Shipper* (June, 1981), pp. 66–68; and Wesley Marx, "Seafarers Rethink Traditional Ways of Harnessing the Wind For Commerce," *Smithsonian* (December, 1981), pp. 51–58.

[111] Walter Sullivan, "Cargo Ships of Future May Sail Into Port," *Minneapolis Tribune* (May 6, 1979), p. 10.

The early 1980's have witnessed a significant increase in intermodal "warfare." The perpetrator of this aggression has been the railroad industry, which believes it has been at a serious competitive disadvantage vis-a-vis truckers and inland water carriers because the government provides the latter carriers with their rights-of-way. The trucking and barge carriers have counter-attacked the railroad industry.

While there is a significant amount of hostility between the transport modes, they do cooperate in the interchange of freight. The most prevalent form of intermodal cooperation involves TOFC/COFC transportation service. In 1981 the Burlington Northern Railroad designated piggyback service as one of its expected high growth areas for the 1980's. Multimodal transportation companies will become common in the present decade. The U.S. leader in this area is Tiger International.

One of the most promising growth areas for U.S. railroads and ocean shipping firms is the exportation of coal. Senator John W. Warner of Virginia suggested that the United States could become the biggest exporter of coal—"the Saudi Arabia of coal."

Transportation deregulation became a fact of life in the early 1980's. In a deregulated environment, it can be expected that transportation rates will become closer to the carrier's actual cost of providing the service. It appears that the preponderance of rate changes will be downward because the full forces of price competition have now been unleashed in the transportation industry. The authors believe that transportation deregulation will have significant and very beneficial effects on the career status of transportation and physical distribution/logistics executives.

The chapter concluded by examining several future technological changes, including (a) coal-powered railroads, (b) Roadrailer, (c) lighter-than-air cargo vessels, and (d) sailing cargo vessels.

Questions for Discussion and Review

1. The Reagan Administration is reorienting the role of the federal government vis-a-vis the transportation sector. What changes are taking place? Do you agree? Defend your answer.

2. One section of this chapter was entitled, "Intermodal 'Warfare'." What is the issue involved? Do you believe the railroad, motor carrier, or barge industry position is correct? Why?

3. Discuss the "counter-attack" launched by the trucking industry against railroads.

4. What are some recent examples of intermodal cooperation?

5. Discuss four problem areas that have retarded intermodalism.

6. What is a multimodal transportation company? Do you believe they would be beneficial to the shipping public? Why?

7. What has been the Canadian experience with multimodal transportation companies?

8. Why has the demand for U.S. coal recently increased in foreign markets?

9. Discuss transportation constraints that impede coal exports.

10. What solutions are available to correct existing transportation problems for coal exports?

11. What has been the effect on rate levels of transportation deregulation?

12. Deregulation has made it easier for new motor common carriers and airlines to begin operations. Do you believe this is a good time to establish a new carrier? Defend your answer.

13. Do you agree with the authors that "transportation deregulation will be one of the most important and beneficial events ever to take place regarding the career status of physical distribution/logistics executives." Why?

14. Discuss the role of contract carriage in the "new" transportation environment.

15. Look at the quote by Roger Kallock (at the end of the section "A New Environment for Shippers") regarding the effects of deregulation on shippers. Do you agree with it? Defend your position.

16. Do you believe labor unions in the transportation industry will be stronger or weaker in 1990 compared to today? Why?

17. Discuss coal-powered railroads. Do you think they will be greatly utilized in the 1980's? Why?

18. What are the advantages of the Roadrailer system?

19. Why are sailing cargo vessels making a comeback?

20. Which section in this chapter was (a) the most interesting to you? Why? and (b) the least interesting? Why?

Additional Chapter References

Constable, G. A. (Sandy), "Propane Carburetion—Future Potential," *Annual Proceedings of the Transportation Research Forum* (1981), pp. 536–541.

Garges, Rod, "Meeting the Distribution/Logistics Trends of the 80s," *Annual Proceedings of the National Council of Physical Distribution Management* (1981), pp. 872–886.

Harris, Ralph F., "Technological Change in Transport: Panacea or Limited Prospect?" *Annual Proceedings of the Transportation Research Forum* (1979), pp. 48–54.

Heads, John, "The Organization of the Transport Research in Government to Meet the Challenges of the 1980's," *Annual Proceedings of the Transportation Research Forum* (1981), pp. 658–665.

Page, Richard P., and Paul R. Farragut, "Export Coal: Implications for U.S. Ports," *Annual Proceedings of the Transportation Research Forum* (1981), pp. 112–120.

Seguin, V. C., "Freight Transport Technology to the Year 2000—A Forecast Update," *Annual Proceedings of the Transportation Research Forum* (1981), pp. 203–212.

Case 15–1   Farmers and Merchants' Trust Co. Case

Betsy Bertram worked in the commercial loan office of the Farmers and Merchants' Bank in Chicago. She supervised the section that handled loans to transport carriers and manufacturers of transportation equipment. Her new boss had just been transferred from the bank's computer department and asked Ms. Bertram to write—or have prepared—a series of brief papers that addressed some current transportation issues.

You are Ms. Bertram. Write a paper, 250 to 400 words in length, that responds to whichever of the following questions you are assigned.

Question One: How is deregulation affecting the economic health of various carriers?

Question Two: Are airlines earning enough money so that they will be able to pay for new planes?

Question Three: The bank's trust department thinks it should increase its holdings of stock in transportation equipment manufacturers. Manufacturers of what types of transportation equipment have the brightest future?

Question Four: What should the trust department do with its large holdings of stocks in domestic automobile manufacturers?

Question Five: What mode of transportation would have the "best" prospects in case petroleum prices increase as much in the 1980's as they did in the 1970's?

Question Six: The bank may want to increase its loans to and investments in international transportation undertakings. What do you recommend?

Case 15–2   The National Transportation Issues Case

United States Senator Thaddeous T. Thornblower was about to address a national meeting of a transportation organization. His talk was to deal in generalities about national transportation policy, but he wanted to be prepared to answer questions from the floor. One of his staff members (actually a summer intern from Memphis State University) wrote out the six questions, appearing below, which she thought the Senator should be prepared to answer. Using information in the book and, possibly, other sources, draft a suggested answer (200 to 300 words long) to whichever questions you are assigned.

Question One: Is it in the national interest to allow coal slurry pipelines the right of eminent domain so they can't be blocked by railroads?

Question Two: What did the 1982 hostilities in the Falkland Islands dispute demonstrate about the relationship between transportation and a nation's defense?

Question Three: How well is transportation deregulation working?

Question Four: Should the nationwide 55-miles-per-hour speed limit on highways be repealed?

Question Five: Did President Reagan wisely handle the air traffic controllers' strike?

Question Six: Should the U.S. government sell Conrail?

Name and Corporation Index

Subject Index